The Georgia Open History Library has been made possible in part by a major grant from the National Endowment for the Humanities: Democracy demands wisdom. Any views, findings, conclusions, or recommendations expressed in this collection, do not necessarily represent those of the National Endowment for the Humanities.

NATIONAL
ENDOWMENT
FOR THE
HUMANITIES

Colonial Records of the State of Georgia

Original Papers of Governors Reynolds, Ellis, Wright, and Others
1757-1763

VOLUME 28
PART I

Edited by
KENNETH COLEMAN
and
MILTON READY

Copies Made from Original Records in England and Compiled under Authority of Allen D. Candler, 1902

Sponsored by
The Georgia Commission
for the National Bicentennial Celebration

University of Georgia Press
Athens

Copyright © 1976 by the University of Georgia Press
Library of Congress Catalog Card Number: 74-30679
International Standard Book Number: 0-8203-0379-8
All rights reserved

Transcripts of Crown-copyright records in the
Public Record Office appear by permission of
the Controller of H.M. Stationery Office.

Most University of Georgia Press titles are
available from popular e-book vendors.

Printed digitally

Reissue published in 2021

ISBN 9780820359083 (Hardcover)
ISBN 9780820359076 (Paperback)
ISBN 9780820359069 (eBook)

CONTENTS

Foreword to the Reissue vii

Preface xiii

Introduction xv

Original Papers of Governors Reynolds, Ellis,
    Wright, and Others, 1757-1763   1

Index 469

These Volumes are for

Georgia's Archivists and Librarians

This Volume is for

MARY GIVENS BRYAN

FOREWORD TO THE REISSUE

Volume 27 and volume 28, parts 1 and 2, of the <u>Colonial Records of the State of Georgia</u> consist of original papers of the colony's royal governors John Reynolds, Henry Ellis, and James Wright (and several others). These papers are primarily reports written to the Board of Trade in London between 1754 and 1782—though only a few are from the tumultuous years between 1776 and 1782. They provide us with an exceptional view into the life of the frontier colony and the personalities of these men.

The governorship of Georgia was considered a dubious honor by London officials because the colony was renowned as a poor, hot, and unsophisticated place that required too great an effort to live in and oversee. Yet John Reynolds served between 1754 and 1757, Henry Ellis between 1757 and 1760, and James Wright between 1760 and 1782, with his service interrupted by the first years of the Revolutionary War. Once one begins reading their correspondence, it becomes readily apparent that they were all highly literate, possessed trained minds, and were keenly observant and adventuresome. Their letters conveyed many complex details to the Board, and these details help us gain a sense of their world, often one of urgency and tension.

They administered and were held accountable for the large subsidies provided by Parliament, and while these subsidies kept the colony afloat, there was never enough money to meet the many challenges they faced. They all regularly requested additional funds, primarily to establish stronger defense and to repair crumbling infrastructure. Written by hand, their correspondence was placed in boxes for transport by ship, and this slow and precarious exchange might take as long as six or seven months each way, if it arrived at all. The governors' letters reveal how they met the many challenges they faced while governing the colony, the most important of which was to keep peace with the neighboring Creek Indians.

Much is written by the three governors about the colony's ever-changing relationship with the Creeks, who were both their greatest military threat and greatest ally. During John Reynolds's and Henry Ellis's governorships (1754–60), the colony's relationship with the Creeks was complex because these Indigenous neighbors were trading partners and military allies not only with the British but also with the Spanish and French. After the end of the French and Indian War in 1763 and during the remaining years of James Wright's governorship (1760–82), the world of the Creeks and their neighbors to the east, the Cherokees, began to change dramatically. Often the governors expressed frustration about Indian problems in their letters, which at times convey a sense of their desperate need to find a way to defend the colony, to avert an Indian war, and to work with neighboring royal governors to create an enforceable Indian policy.

Much has been written about the Creek and Cherokee Indians during the colonial period, with the focus primarily on formal relations brought about by treaties and negotiations and the breaking of them, the benefits of these formal agreements to the colonists, and the resultant profound losses experienced by the Indians. While these are significant topics, it is important to recognize the emotional content in the governors' letters when they wrote about anything to do with Indians—Creeks in particular. Their words can convey a strong sense of fear for the colonists' and the colony's survival as well as their personal attitudes toward the Indians. These high emotions convey to us the shifting, dangerous, and traumatizing conditions the inhabitants of royal Georgia endured and help us to consider the long-term effects these conditions had on the population.

Each governor was concerned with maintaining and improving the infrastructure of the colony's few towns and ports, in part for defense and also for promoting colonization and everyday life. The governors focused their attention chiefly on the capital and principal port, Savannah. Johann Christoph Bornemann described it in the mid-1750s as a mid-size European village with all the houses looking no better than market booths. Two decades later, Ebenezer Hazard described Savannah as a small town situated on the top of a sand hill. Reynolds, Ellis, and Wright knew it well as they resided and governed there, and each suggested to the Board that the capital be moved to a healthier and more secure location down the coast. One wonders why all three governors wanted to leave Savannah.

Their letters, and the legislation included in them, detail what needed to be repaired, demolished, constructed, or cleared in the town and environs and the governors' efforts to arrange the work and the financing. These details give us information about the town's generally dilapidated condition over time and the need to improve it. A look back at the Trustee period might offer additional clues to the town's condition when the colony first became royal.[1] Although the colony slowly grew in prosperity, its capital never matched the orderly vision of its famous town plan and was heavily damaged in 1779 during the Revolutionary War. The governors' tireless efforts to improve the infrastructure of Savannah, hampered as it was by insufficient funds, can provide us with a broader understanding of the town itself, as well as the infrastructure conditions of the rest of the colony.

All three governors suffered from a profound lack of operating funds, which they never hesitated to mention to the Board and never overcame. The colony was not self-supporting and relied on the annual parliamentary appropriations in pounds sterling, which paid the salaries of Georgia's government officials but was insufficient to ever meet the colony's many infrastructure and defense needs. Due to the overwhelming poverty of the population—which dated back to the Trustee period—the governors could not raise any significant amount of local revenue through the collection of duties or taxes. Nor could they establish a quitrent tax law, which meant that no one had to pay tax on land. Most Georgians used their land and crops to barter and obtain credit, and Georgia's private debt structure rested on land. Each governor, along with asking for additional funds, had a scheme or two of their own to get the colony out of debt and raise money, and these are described in detail and offer insights into the colony's economic challenges in these volumes. This lack of money had a lasting effect not only on the colony's growth and the poverty-stricken colonists' ambiguous political stance but also on the future state of Georgia.

These three volumes, spanning nearly three decades, contain many new opportunities for research on topics both large and small. The many problems, places, and people that come alive through the original papers of the governors and others offer us the opportunity to better understand the colonists' world.

The documents contained in volume 28, part 1, are chiefly the papers of Henry Ellis, Georgia's second royal governor, and his successor, James Wright, along with some papers of Georgia's first royal governor, John Reynolds, and cover the time period from 1757 to 1763. Ellis arrived in Georgia prior to Reynolds's departure, and Wright arrived prior to Ellis's departure. It is thought provoking to imagine their possible conversations with each other. Savannah was a small town, and they would certainly have had much business to discuss and perhaps would have enjoyed becoming acquainted.

Henry Ellis (1721–1806) was truly a man of the Enlightenment, for he was an explorer, an author, and a member of the Royal Academy, as well as a slave trader—all prior to becoming Georgia's second governor. He appears to have been a natural leader and quickly gained the support of the council members and colonists. He also had a flair for finance while governor, and after his return to England, he helped develop a plan for taxing the colonies. Ellis's descriptive letters provide us with a sense of his lively mind and detail his concerns as governor as well as the many incidents of life he observed while in the colony.

Governor Ellis utilized his many talents for the betterment of Georgia, and nowhere more lastingly than in his efforts to achieve and sustain Creek Indian neutrality. Soon after becoming governor, he and the council formulated a cohesive Indian policy that led to a treaty with the Creeks that renewed their neutrality. This neutrality held throughout the French and Indian War (1754–63), keeping Georgia at peace. According to scholar Edward H. Cashin, a document attributed to Ellis advised the British ministry of the serious effect French propaganda had on Indian neutrality and suggested calling nearby tribes to Augusta to reassure them. The minister for the colonies, Lord Egremont, took this suggestion seriously, and the result was the 1763 Treaty of Augusta. Henry Ellis's contribution to Indian diplomacy warrants further research.

James Wright (1716–85) succeeded Henry Ellis as royal governor, and this volume contains his letters from 1760 to 1763.[2] Born in London and raised in South Carolina, he studied law at the Inns of Court and was a member of the Charlestown planter elite. Prior to becoming governor of Georgia, he served South Carolina as attorney general and then as its colonial agent in London. An extraordinarily able administrator, Wright's detailed letters describe his deep concerns for defense, infrastructure, and settlement. His strong response to South Carolina's land grab in 1763 is an incident worth noting. Governor Wright was a man familiar with the ways of both the southern frontier and the British ruling class, and this perspective was perhaps his greatest asset as governor of Georgia. he successfully ushered the colony through tumultuous years.

This volume also contains the final papers concerning the Bosomworth claims and John Reynolds's answers to the charges brought against him by Georgians.[3]

Leslie Hall

Notes

1. Volumes 20–26 and 29–31 in the series contain letters from the early colonists to the Trustees and the Trustees' responses to these letters, respectively.

2. Volume 28, part 2, in this series contains further letters from Governor Wright.

3. Volumes 26 and 27 in this series contain details on the Bosomworth claims, and volume 27 in this series contains the charges against John Reynolds.

PREFACE

The history of Georgia's colonial records has been a varied one. Her customs records were destroyed in early 1776 when the vessel upon which they had been stored for safekeeping was burned during the "Battle of the Rice Boats" at Savannah. During the Revolutionary War, Georgia sent many of her records as far north as Maryland to protect them, and some of these never found their way back to Georgia. Many old records were left at Milledgeville when the state's capital was moved to Atlanta in 1868. As late as the twentieth century colonial records were destroyed in Savannah to make room for current records. Normal loss and destruction through improper use and storage over the years have taken their toll as well.

With all this loss and destruction, it is not surprising that most of the colonial records which survive are the letters, reports, etc. sent to London by colonial officials and now deposited in the Public Record Office on London's Chancery Lane. Georgia first had these records copied in the 1830s and 1840s and they were used by several historians before being burned accidentally in the late nineteenth century. Early in the twentieth century the Georgia volumes (mainly P.R.O., C.O. 5/636-712) were copied a second time by the state.

Between 1904 and 1916 twenty-five volumes of these transcripts were published as The Colonial Records of the State of Georgia (Vols. I-XIX, XXI-XXVI). Allan D. Candler began compiling and printing these volumes, and Lucian Lamar Knight assumed the work after Candler's death in 1910. Essentially Candler and Knight arranged the transcripts and printed the volumes with no further editorial apparatus.

Immediately the published volumes had an influence upon the writing of Georgia's colonial history. The unpublished transcripts, arranged in fourteen volumes in the state archives have been used considerably less. Some of these unpublished volumes contain very valuable materials such as the letters of Georgia's three royal governors, the record of Georgia's hesitant entry into revolt from 1765 through 1775, and other topics.

Many scholars, including the present editors, have long hoped that the remaining volumes could be published. This project is now undertaken by the Georgia Commission for the National Bicentennial Celebration and is being published by the University of Georgia Press as a part of their contribution to the national bicentennial and making Georgia's historical sources more available to scholars and students.

Athens, Georgia   Kenneth Coleman

                                                            Milton Ready

INTRODUCTION

This volume spans the years from 1757 to 1763, a period dominated by the uncertainties caused by the French and Indian War. The volume begins with one of the most dazzling letters ever written in colonial Georgia, the initial letter of Governor Henry Ellis to the Board of Trade after his arrival in Georgia. Dated March 11, 1757, Ellis' letter summarized his view of the situation in the colony. As an incisive, detailed, highly literate account of Georgia in the critical year of 1757, Ellis' letter served to establish his reputation as a royal official and to discredit that of his predecessor, Captain John Reynolds.

The volume continues with Ellis' correspondence, tracing the vagaries of events from 1757 to 1760. Seldom venturing far from Savannah, Ellis concerned himself with the colony's fortunes, Indian affairs, the state of defenses, land grants, population increase, acquisition and distribution of Indian presents, relations with the Assembly and local Savannahans, wartime emergencies and dislocations, and finally the Bosomworth claims. Increasingly "the affair of the Bosomworths" became the cause celebre of Ellis' administration. Arising in conflicting land claims dating from the colony's first settlement, involving relations between London, Savannah, and the Creek Indians, and the personalities and ambitions of Mary and Thomas Bosomworth--the Bosomworth claims exasperated Georgia's second royal governor. Taking up much of this and the two preceding volumes, the accounts of the Bosomworth affair provide valuable insight into a complicated and inadequately explored aspect of Georgia's past. Fatigued by the rigors of a southern climate and the tedious detail of his office, Ellis asked for relief after less than three years in Georgia. On October 12, 1760, James Wright arrived in Savannah and soon replaced Ellis, who returned to London and resigned his governorship.

Based upon his long service in the provincial government of South Carolina, James Wright brought to Georgia a deeper understanding of the colony's role and needs in the expanding southern frontier. Anxious to secure land from the Creeks to allow Georgia's white population to increase and suspicious of greedy

Carolinians, Wright diligently worked to remove obstacles hindering the colony's growth. To that end he patiently but firmly courted favor with the Board of Trade in London, sending lengthy but pointed reports on Indian affairs, the colony's expenses and needs, illegal settlements south of the Altamaha, the state of the silk culture, and the necessity of expanding Georgia's frontiers by a cession from the Creeks. When South Carolina attempted to move into the lands south of the Altamaha after the Treaty of Paris of 1763, Governor Wright already had laid the groundwork for Georgia's assertion of its claim to the region. It took only a legal protest and caveat to South Carolina and an indignant letter to the Board of Trade to assert Georgia's natural right to this area. Appropriately this volume closes with an account of the Creek land cession of 1763 and with the customs records of Sunbury, opened in 1763 as the colony's second port--both clear signs of the progress Wright so ardently desired.
Thus 1763 ended on a hopeful note for Georgia, and James Wright confidently reported to London that the colony was in "a flourishing state."

There is more to this volume than this brief recital presents. The records contain information on almost every facet of Georgia's history from 1757 to 1763. Estimates of the colony's annual expenses, official treaties and facts sent to London, reports on wandering bands of Indians and whites, comments on the problems of overseeing a provincial government in an expanding British Empire, and asides on colorful figures and events. All this forms part of the outline of Georgia's history for these six years. The correspondence of Ellis and Wright stands out for its content and its clarity. Rich in detail and rare in candor, the letters provide essential historical material for further study of this important part of Georgia's history.

Editorial Guidelines

The original volume division and internal arrangement created by Allen D. Candler and Lucien Lamar Knight, the original editors of this series, are retained. This will facilitate references in works already published which used these volumes in manuscript.

Original spellings are retained unless the meaning is not clear. A single word may be explained in brackets immediately after its appearance in the text. More lengthy explanations will be given in footnotes. Punctuation, often absent in eighteenth-century manuscripts, has been supplied for the sake of clarity, though many sentences are long by modern standards. All raised letters have been lowered, abbreviations which are not clear have been expanded, and slips of the pen have been corrected silently. No attempt at uniform spelling, even of proper names, has been attempted; rather the original text has been followed. For proper names a single most common spelling has been used in the index.

Each document is given a short introduction which contains the name of the writer and recipient, place written, date written, date received and/or read where indicated, Public Record Office location if available, and the topic or topics treated in the document.

ORIGINAL PAPERS OF GOVERNORS REYNOLDS, ELLIS, WRIGHT, AND OTHERS, 1757-1763

Memorial of Benjamin Martyn, Agent for Georgia, to the Board of Trade, March 8, 1757, London, read March 10, 1757, C.O. 5/645, B. 37, praying the Board's warrant to enable him to pay several sums from remaining Trustees' balance.

Humbly Shewith

    That in Obedience to Your Lordships Orders he sent to Georgia in December last the Sum of £500 by the Lieut. Governor, Henry Ellis Esqr; to be by him applied upon Account to discharge Expences of the Silk Culture from the time of his Arrival in the said Colony; And that the Land Carriage of the said Money to Portsmouth amounted to £2.4.6, and the freight of the same to £10.

    That by Your Lordships Orders he procured Insurance on the said Sum of £500, Which, at eight Guineas per Cent, amounted, with the Policy, to £42.4.6.

    That he begs leave to represent also to Your Lordships, that out of the Sum of £1500, granted by his Majesty for Presents to the Indians bordering on the Province of Georgia, he has expended the Sum of £1201.16. in purchasing and shipping the same. That the Fees on receiving the said Sum of £1500 and for Orders for Shipping the Guns and Powder, Part of the said Presents, amounted to £8.3.10, And that the remaining Sum of £292 will be wanted to answer the necessary Drafts for Expences attending the Distribution of the said Presents, and therefore he humbly offers to Your Lordships Consideration, whether it may not be proper to pay the Sum of £55.10 for freight of the said Goods, and the Sum of £75.16.6 Insurance on the same at six Guineas per Cent, with the aforesaid Sum of £2.6.6, and £2 and £62.2.6 out of the Surplus Money lying in Your Memorialists hands, which he is authorized and required, by a Warrant from the late Lords Justice, to pay for such sums and Services as Your Lordships, by Your Warrant, shall direct and appoint.

Henry Ellis to the Board of Trade, March 11, 1757, Georgia, read April 5, 1758, C.O. 5/646, C. 25, giving his view of the situation in Georgia upon his arrival.

My Lords

 I embrace this early opportunity of transmitting to your Lordships the truest idea I can form of the situation of things here upon the best but still imperfect information I have had time to acquire.
 I arrived at Charles Town the 28th of January where I was received with the greatest Marks of respect by the principal Inhabitants who think themselves closely connected and deeply concerned in the fate of Georgia. The friendly & confidential reception I met with from Govr Lyttleton was no less agreeable as the advantage I reaped from his advice and information effectually answered the purpose of my touching there since it afforded me an opportunity of Settling a plan of good correspondence with him,[1] of removing some provincial prejudices & of concocting such designs as seemed best calculated to unite & reconcile as much as possible the variety of little views and interests that subsist here & are apt to influence & interfere with the public measures.
 On my arrival here Mr. Reynolds resigned his Commission & Instructions into my hands conformable to your Lordships Commands whereupon I immediately qualified & took upon me the administration of Government. The first instance of which I shewed in rejecting Mr Reid & Mr Patrick Mackay two Councillors lately admitted by Mr Reynolds in the room of two others that absented themselves, but were not suspended & who returned to their Seats on this change. But I did this with such apparent justice & impartiality that no umbrage was taken even by these Gentlemen.

---

 1. Ellis and Governor William Henry Lyttleton of South Carolina seem to have gotten along very well during Ellis' stay in Georgia. His letters to Lyttleton are in the Lyttleton Papers, Clements Library, University of Michigan, Ann Arbor, Michigan. See also Lewis M. Wiggin, The Faction of Cousins: A Political Account of the Grenvilles, 1733-1763 (New Haven, 1958), especially 163-166; and M. Eugene Sirmans, Colonial South Carolina: A Political History, 1663-1763 (Chapel Hill, N.C., 1966), 308-335.

I found the people here exceedingly dissatisfied with each other & an almost universal discontent arising from the late proceedings & persons in power. Few approached me that were not inflamed with resentment & liberal in invectives urging that I should take some immediate and very violent steps such as a total change of public Officers & the dissolution of the Assembly and notwithstanding their prepossessions offered some very cogent reasons for this procedure. Sensible of my own inexperience & of the violence of such Councils, fearful of being misled & aiming rather at healing the wounds & extinguishing the flame of Party than stirring it anew, I forebore making any material alteration until I should be qualified to Act from observation & experience in order that the changes I shall then make may rather be attributed to my own judgement than to the advice of designing and interested people. This suspense will give time for mens passions to subside & for truth to appear through the cloud of party prejudice that at present obscures it.

I believe it may be advanced as a fact that the present assembly was formed by dint of very irregular & improper means. Threatenings were used, promises made, offices created, new Commissions granted, old ones altered to facilitate the bringing in of such men as were to be the implicit tools of Mr Little who it was preconcerted should be their Speaker.[2] These Machinations

---

2. The reference is to William Little, private secretary to John Reynolds, Ellis' predecessor as Governor of Georgia, and to the political intrigues centering around Little's conduct. Relying upon Little for advice and support, Governor Reynolds appointed him to seven offices. Little's arrogant personality coupled with his many official functions served to alienate most of Savannah's leading figures and even many of Reynolds' own supporters. Ellis had been forewarned of the situation and he moved cautiously on his arrival in Georgia. Much of this story is told in other volumes of this series. See Allen D. Candler and Lucian L. Knight, eds., The Colonial Records of the State of Georgia, 26 vols. (Atlanta, 1904-1916). Vols. 20, 27-39, now being printed for the first time, are presently in manuscript at the Georgia Department of Archives and History, VII, 253; XIII, 111-126, 152; XXVIII, MS, 16-17, 46-48, 95, 187-213; South Carolina Gazette, Feb. 17, 1757; and W. W. Abbot, The Royal Governors of Georgia, 1754-1775 (Chapel Hill, N.C., 1959), 43-54, 56, 60-65.

succeeded; men at their devotion were chosen; flexible weak & ignorant, ready to join in anything they were put upon however destructive to the true intent of their Constituents.

Not dishonest in their private characters but easy, credulous, & equally disposed to good or evil. And it is to be wished that those who had acquired such a degree of influence had employed it to other purposes than those of a private & sinister nature. As the former Assembly was treated with remarkable haughtiness, a conduct quite the reverse has been shewn to this for very obvious reasons.

Those in power were early apprized of your Lordships intention to inquire into their conduct hence there was a necessity of taking some steps towards their justification. Such is the Address to His Majesty in favour of Mr Reynolds Administration, not to mention a variety of other designs that the activity & opposition of the contrary Party rendered abortive. For carrying these points it was not sufficient to have a Majority in the Assembly who had but little credit, it was necessary the Governor & his Minister should flatter the people even to the detriment of the Province. Hence that remarkable Speech at the opening the Assembly declaring that the former Taxes were sufficient & that no more would be asked, notwithstanding the sum arising from them the last year was one third short of the Service for which it was intended. It produced but £200 & the Service required £300 the deficiency was taken from the contingent money which was to be reimbursed out of that to be raised the present year altho they were sensible it would be inadequate to the ordinary expenses of Government exclusive of such a Debt.

Other concessions were made such as the Assemblys recommending persons for the Commissions of the peace at the request of the Governor. The Council too were desired to recommend Officers for the new raised Troops, precedents equally unjustifiable & impolitic, but which were to serve two purposes, to cajole the people & to embarrass a future Governor. From these considerations joined to an information I received that the Assembly intended to address me at the instance of Mr Little their Speaker in such a manner as would lay me under difficulties in case I found a dissolution requisite--which I had strong reason to believe would be the case from the dislike of the people which they were preparing to testify by addresses from the different districts--& finding a recess would be agreeable at this Season of the Year after so long a Sitting I thought it prudent to adjourn them for a Month, & do intend to adjourn them further as I find it expedient.

It behoves me to be very circumspect in what steps I take otherwise I shall soon find myself intangled in some very untoward transactions that neither quadrate with my own views nor those of Government. Such is the affair of Bosomworths claims,[3] which I suspect great pains have been insidously taken to establish from very selfish motives. At the conferences with the Indians they were present, & treated respectfully. Insnaring questions were asked that led to the desired answers. All possible countenance was given them in the inquiry made in consequence of your Lordships directions and it is even suggested, not without some appearance of reason, that a charge was made upon the Bench & Mr Little chosen to preside there with a view to facilitate the establishment of these peoples pretensions at the approaching Tryal. But I shall take care to defeat this design by appointing two honest men as Judges in the room of Mr Little, & another who were improperly commissioned by Mr. Reynolds. My Lords there are a hundred occasions that daily evince the urgent necessity of a Chief Justice from England sufficiently qualified for that important imployment. Nothing can be more irregular & unprescedented than the proceedings of our Courts owing to the ignorance & partiality of those who have hitherto presided. Everything is precarious in such a Situation. We find here a Councillor prosecuting a man for Scandalum Magnatum; the Speaker of the Assembly is presented

---

3. Henry Ellis inherited the "Bosomworth Claims" from former Governor John Reynolds. Stemming from the assertion of Thomas and Mary Bosomworth of title to the islands of Ossabaw, Sapelo, and St. Catherines and to compensation for Mary's services to the colony under James Oglethorpe, the affair had not been settled by 1757. Unlike his predecessor, Ellis did not sympathize with the Bosomworths in their claims against Georgia and he passively sought to prevent the pair from prosecuting their case in London. Never settled until 1760, the "Bosomworth Claims" clouded Ellis' administration, effectively preventing an Indian cession to the colony and alienating Savannah from Lower Creek leadership. See E. Merton Coulter, "Mary Musgrove: 'Queen of the Creeks': A Chapter of Early Georgia Troubles," Georgia Historical Quarterly, XI (March, 1927), 1-31; David Corkran, The Creek Frontier: 1540-1783 (Norman, Okla., 1967), 114-115, 131-161, 170-171, 188-191. A great deal of material is found in later pages of this volume.

by the Grand Jury among other Nuisances; & a person was actually hanged two days before the time fixed by the Judges as a specimen of the Governors superior power.

Whilst I am mentioning the inconveniences that abound here I think I ought not to omit the following very material one namely that many Lots of the best Land in the Province lie vacant in consequence of claims that are said to exist & were derived from a verbal Cession of Mr Oglethorpe. The Claimants themselves have not attempted to establish their pretensions nor complied with any one condition in the Royal instruction.[4] They do not reside here nor is it well known where they are but it is probable they are lying at lurch until contiguous lands [are] improved & the value of those they claim raised thereby. By this means the settling of the Province is retarded & a considerable part of the quit Rents lost. I therefore humbly beg leave to propose to your Lordships whether it would not be proper to summon these people in the London Gazette, in that of South Carolina & by advertisements here to put in their claims & prove their rights within a given time to prevent the lands being forfeited and regranted. I presume nothing can be more equitable, & certainly nothing more immediately necessary therefore I shall impatiently expect your Lordships opinion of, & instructions concerning it. For by the steps I intend taking which upon a future occasion I shall communicate to your Lordships. I make no doubt but we shall soon have a great influx of Inhabitants.

The alarms to the Northward & other circumstance, seem to favor such an expectation.

Upon this occasion I cannot help expressing my surprise that

---

4. As Georgia's first royal governor, John Reynolds was ordered to straighten out the confusion in land titles created by the Trustees' irregular and frequently conflicting land policy. After identifying holders of Trust grants, Reynolds was to see to it that new patents were issued. Accordingly Reynolds issued two proclamations to that effect, the first on January 1, 1754/5, and another in May, 1755. Both were ignored widely and Trust grants continued to trouble royal government. See Reynolds' Instructions, Aug. 6, 1754, CRG, MS, XXXIV, 57-59; reprinted in Albert Saye, ed., "Commission and Instructions of Governor John Reynolds, Aug. 6, 1754," Georgia Historical Quarterly, XXX (June, 1964), 149-152; and CRG, MS, XXVIII, 224-226, 228-231, 257.

the Acadians which were sent here were not better disposed of than to be suffered to leave the Province. Out of near 400 that arrived only about 100 remain some of which are dispersed among the Plantations & others have built themselves huts near this Town & are very useful to the Colony as they employ themselves in making Oars hand spikes & other implements for sea Craft that are immediately brought up & sent to the Islands where they meet with a good market.[5]

I am informed by Mr Reynolds that your Lordships have had transmitted you an Account of a encounter that happened on the River Ogechee between some of our Settlers & a party of the Creek Indians wherein two of the latter were killed. This untoward accident had near involved the Province in a Cruel war with them. All the Creek Nations were alarmed & on our side a general consternation prevailed. With advice of the Council Mr. Reynolds resolved to raise some Troops for the defence of the Province. In consequence of which Officers were commissioned & one Troop of Rangers begun to be lured but was not quite completed when a Conference with the Indians produced a temporary pacification. To this succeeded fresh causes of alarm for from several quarters advices were received of a design meditated by the French against these Provinces. This produced an Address from the General Assembly entreating the Governor to provide for their defence which is said to have occasioned orders to be issued to build another Scout Boat, & raising two more Troops of Rangers.

But no part of this was actually put into execution at the time it was known here that I had landed at Charles Town. Then every thing was precipitated. Officers were named & every other step taken that could deprive me of the means of obliging any person in the execution of this measure should it take place. Things were in this Situation when I arrived at Savannah, & I was reduced to the dilemma either of cancelling this proceeding, commenced

---

5. Four hundred Acadians from Nova Scotia were sent to the Savannah area by the British in December, 1755. Resented by the local populace, they settled a small village west of Savannah and were given only low-paying, menial jobs. The last Acadians, forty-four in all, left Savannah on Jan. 9, 1764, aboard the brig Polly and Betsy bound for Cape François. See E. Merton Coulter, "The Acadians in Georgia," Georgia Historical Quarterly, XLVII (March, 1963), 68-76; Georgia Gazette, Dec. 22, 1763, Jan. 12, 1764.

upon very substantial & pressing considerations, or risking the continuation of it upon my own Credit--notwithstanding an instruction that directs us to undertake no military operations without the Concurrence of the Commander in Chief.

But reflecting that this was an exigence wherein that could not be obtained, & that disbanding the men already raised might be attended with bad consequences, as well as being very unpopular, since the people here would have concluded that they were to be abandoned to the mercy of their Invaders. I judged it most eligible to let things remain as they were until His Majesty's pleasure, or the opinion of Lord Loudoun[6] upon this affair should be known. I was induced the more to this by a Letter I had from his Lordship, wherein he acknowledges the acceptance of some Bills drawn on him by Mr Reynolds for the raising & support of these Troops, without blaming or approving the measure itself by desiring that no more should be drawn upon him till the purposes for which they are drawn be signified whence I would infer that his Lordship has not been so fully informed upon this subject as he had a right to expect.

Before I received the honor of his letter I had wrote his Lordship one notifying my arrival & containing the best account I was able to give of the state of this Province together with the particulars relative to these Troops & begged a positive & precise instruction concerning them. But as the Men already raised being about 40 must be subsisted the Captain takes this upon himself depending upon the honor of the Government for his reimbursement requiring only Certificates of me of the Service. My Lords whatever motives of a foreign nature might induce Mr Reynolds to raise this force there are other very weighty considerations that prove the necessity of it at this juncture when danger threatens us from every quarter. The sources of all our embroils with the Indians are the irregularities committed by the Indian Traders and the out Settlers; & how can we prevent these disorders without some coercive means of bringing Offenders to justice? The Laws at present are insufficient for this purpose & will be so without a Military Force whilst we are so thinly peopled & whilst so many find their Account in disobeying them. To this weakness & insecurity may in a great measure be imputed the little progress

---

6. A reference to the fourth Earl of Loudoun, John Campbell (1705-1782), commander-in-chief of British Forces in America, 1756-1757.

this Colony has made, notwithstanding the great & frequent helps it has had from England, for in a Country that is exposed to every kind of outrage & injustice within & from without to every sort of depredation & attack how can we expect that people will trust themselves of their property? Incessantly uneasy, incessantly in alarm, no person that has anything to lose or is exempt from the terrors of a Jail will come among us. Besides, the Indians, excited by the French, allured by the prospect of advantage & having no reason to dread our resentment from a knowledge of our debility, will practise every species of enormity whilst it can be done with impunity.

 The Sum of all this will prove to your Lordship beyond dispute how indispensable necessary it is to have some kind of military force in this province not only to preserve its inward tranquillity but to defend itself & the other provinces to which it must be considered as a barrier against such powerful neighbours as the French, Spaniards, & two of the most formidable of the Indian Nations. At present we enjoy a sort of Calm. We hear of no settled plan among the Indians to attack us, altho' we are convinced they are not entirely satisfied with us. For some time past it is said they have been ill supplied by the French and this may be one of the causes, why the late quarrel was so easily accommodated & that they remain quiet. When I came here I found Acouthla one of the Chiefs of the Lower Creek Nation with several of his people who had been many days in Town without being taken any notice of by Mr Reynolds. I thought this was a time that could not justify such a neglect. They were in great want of provisions which induced me to order them an immediate supply, which was received with very singular marks of satisfaction. I then appointed a day to have a conference with them before the Council & upon that occasion urged every thing I was capable of to fix them in our interest & excite them to annoy our enemies & what I said made such an impression that Acouthla told me he had 100 Warriors at our Service; that he had given proof of his love to the English in the late War; and that he was glad of this occasion to renew them for which purpose he requested a Captains Commission. I readily gave him one together with a drum, flag, gun, hatchet, & a few other presents to himself and his followers & acquainted them that we would give 20 shillings for every scalp of our Enemies & 40 shillings for every prisoner. I did this with the advice of the Council whom I convinced of the expediency of it. All this was highly pleasing to the Indians & as they set out immediately for their own Country, I sent by them a Salutation to the Chiefs of the Creek Nation & signified my intention of seeing them so soon as some presents which I expected from England should arrive.

Thoroughly convinced of the importance of standing well with these people I shall exert every means & employ every art that contribute to that end. It were greatly to be wished that those little forts which were intended to secure our frontier such as Augusta upon this River & Argyle upon the Ogechee, as well as the fortifications on the Islands towards the Spaniards were put into a defensible condition. At present they are quite in ruins & are rather marks of our weakness than power. Was it practicable to raise a fund for this purpose here I would very gladly attempt it nor should I despair of effecting it but the poverty of this Province makes it impossible. Nevertheless poor as we are we are not without hands & I will endeavor to direct them to the execution of a plan that I have formed of raising a little fort here out of the wretched materials we have but which may enable us to make a short stand, & be some cover against any sudden attack by Sea or incursion of the Indians. For at this place where we are most liable to be hurt by the enemy no one Work has been constructed towards its defence save a little platform on which are 4 small Guns improperly called a Battery; as its situation is such that it neither covers the Town nor could obstruct any armed Vessels coming up the River should such an attempt be made. Yet however useless this is it has been sufficiently expensive.

The Representation of the defenceless state of this Province that has been transmitted to your Lordships by Mr Reynolds is true as far as I can judge, & the plan proposed by Mr Debrahme[7] of fortifying the Province is judiciously concerted but so expensive that I despair of seeing it suddenly carried into execution. All therefore we can reasonably expect is what is absolutely & immediately necessary such as the reparation of fort Augusta, Argyle and Frederica, with two or three Troops of Irregulars which

---

7. William John Gerar DeBrahm came to Savannah in March, 1751, as a surveyor for the British government. By 1763, he had become Surveyor-General for the Southern District. An excellent cartographer and engineer, DeBrahm designed several British fortifications, including the ill-fated Fort Loudoun. For DeBrahm's defense plans for Georgia, see Louis DeVorsey, ed., DeBrahm's Report of the General Survey in the Southern District of North America (Columbia, S. C., 1971).

I hope your Lordships will see the necessity of & I doubt not will use your instances to obtain.

As soon as that spirit of contention has subsided which has long disturbed the minds of the people here, & that I have taken the necessary precautions against any exigence that may happen in my absence, I intend making a tour of the Province. I have a double view in this journey--one to inspect those places that are judged most proper to be fortified; the other to examine a spot that is esteemed a very proper situation for the Capital. The former is very material for the safety of the Province, & the latter no less concerns its interior prosperity. The spot I mean is Hardwicke[8] in regard to which different interests operate & consequently produce different opinions though all agree in condemning our present situation which indeed is a healthy one & that is all that can be said for it. Being upon the extremity it is exceedingly ill supplied & very inconvenient for Trade & for the communication of the Inhabitants that are widely dispersed over the province. Besides the Lands contiguous to it are barren & the River shallow & intricate. These natural disadvantages joined to the uncertainty of continuing here have for some years past deterred any one from building new or repairing old houses. Its vicinity to Charles Town has prevented it from having any commerce of its own for from thence the people here are usually supplied. Hence it is that there has been so little encouragement for Merchants to come here. The few that are settled among us having but a small vent for their goods are obliged to sell at a high advance to the great detriment of the poorer sort of Inhabitants. Hence it is that Carolina drains us of all the little specie that comes here, & the real value of the Province is concealed by its Commodities being sent thither to discharge our Debts & going home as the produce of that Colony. For the exports from thence are annually increasing, & will encrease as the people seem to have got into a right tract. This Province has been strangely misrepresented; it is evidently capable of great

---

8. Governor John Reynolds first had advocated moving the capitol from Savannah to Hardwick, twelve miles to the south at the mouth of the Ogeechee River. Ellis subsequently adopted the idea but no move ever was made. Georgia's last colonial governor, James Wright, finally abandoned the plan altogether in 1760. See Wright's letter to the Board of Trade, Oct. 23, 1760, below in this volume.

improvement; it abounds with the finest Rivers imaginable; the Lands in general are good & have already afforded specimens--& those very large ones--of the best Indico made in North America. The raising of Silk seems to be no longer a matter of curiosity. It employs many poor people, & is approaching towards a Staple. Had there been a sufficient quantity of seed this year a great deal of silk would have been produced as numbers seem to engage in it eagerly from an experience of its benefit.

    I have visited the fillature here & found it much out of repair, & standing in need of several material alterations such as moving the pans & sinking a Well. Mr Otterlinghe[9] seems very capable and is zealous & active in his department. It is a pleasure to do business with such men. He convinced me how much these alterations were wanting & undertakes the inspection & management of the masons who are already begun to work. Mr. Boltzias the Minister of Ebenezer is very solicitous that the fillature there should be employed as he thinks it would conduce to extend a knowledge of the art at present too much confined. Mr. Otterlinghe admits this but insists that it is too soon to employ two fillatures before there is a sufficient quantity of Cocoons to supply one. Many Arguments are offered on both sides to support their opinions & induce me to take part in this matter; but not thinking myself well qualified to decide, & having no instruction about it I have thought proper to refer them to your Lordships. Your Lordships were pleased to direct me to report my opinion upon the Bill relative to the paper Currency that has been issued here. As it is a matter of great concernment to the Inhabitants of this Province, I am taking the most effectual method to obtain their judgments upon it by sending circular notes to the principal people desiring their sentiments which when they come to hand I shall transmit to your Lordships together with my own.

---

    9. Called by William Stephens, then President of the colony, "an obstinate little convert from Judaism," Joseph Ottolenghe came to Georgia in March, 1752. Sent by the Trustees to oversee the operation of the filiature and to teach the art of winding silk to young women, especially Salzburger girls, Ottolenghe remained in Georgia after interest in sericulture waned. Well regarded by his superiors in Savannah, he eventually was granted a yearly pension of £50 sterling. See CRG, XXIV, 319, 344; XXVII, MS, 307; E. Merton Coulter, ed., The Journal of William Stephens, 2 vols., (Athens, 1958-1959), II, 88.

In the multiplicity of business that necessarily crowds in upon me in the commencement of my Administration your Lordships will be so indulgent as to excuse any inaccuaracy you may meet with & my silence upon some things that I reserve for a future occasion. And if in the course of this long Letter where many characters are necessarily introduced there should appear any thing harsh or severe your Lordships will be pleased to ascribe it to that candour & regard for truth which I hope I shall always preserve & which your Lordships have the utmost right to expect from me. I have a variety of designs in my own mind which have for their object the utility & happiness of this Colony. But perhaps it would be premature to enter upon them before I am qualified to judge of their practicability & whether they are well or ill adapted to our circumstances. This knowledge can only be derived from experience & that requires time.

My Lords I was just going to put a period to this long Letter, when I was interrupted by a visit from Mr Little, who among other things had the insolence to insinuate to me that if I had any design of dissolving the Assembly the consequences I might expect from such a step would be defeated inasmuch as he had taken measures to have the same men rechosen. I do not think myself at liberty to act as a private man nor to gratify my indignation at the expense of the public tranquillity otherwise we should try titles. I am in hopes I shall be able to effect my designs by gentler methods. 'Tis yet a moot point with me whether in a political light the Members of this Assembly ought not to be considered as delinquents for I do not find that they have committed any Constitutional Offence. All that can be apprehended from them is an opposition to my measures in order to justify the conduct of their friends lately in power, & to whom they certainly owe some regard since 11 of the 19 Members have been distinguished by such places of honor & trusts as this Governement affords. However 'tis possible they may be more tractable than is imagined especially as whatever I shall propose, will be most apparently for their own good. But if they should be obstinate or fractiously inclined I think a way has to be found of getting rid of them without appearing to act from resentment.

In the Instructions it is recommended to divide as soon as possible into Counties this province, & to make a distribution of the Representatives conformable to that division. This a regulation that will at all times be popular & is now earnestly wished for & of which as may avail ourselves in case of need, for whenever it takes place a dissolution will naturally follow. Altho' the Kings instructions recommend this measure they do not point out by what method it is to be done whether at the will of the Governor solely or with the advice of Council. I should be glad your Lordships would explain this in the first letter you honor me with, & as I flatter myself I have proved clearly the necessity of removing the Seat of Government to a better situation, I am in great hopes your Lordships will enable me to do this as soon as possible Since it can be done with much less inconvenience or injury to any person at present than some time hence when greater improvements are made here. The only obstruction to our immediate removal is want of money for the construction of the public buildings. £2,000, I apprehend would be sufficient, as a Church, Court House & Jail are the only ones wanting. These that we have here are so ruinous as to be in a manner past repair so that this expense must take place either here or there forthwith.

And my Lords it is not possible that a fund for this purpose might be found out of the Savings of the Silk Money? Our Church is so decayed that were the props which surround it knocked away it must inevitably tumble to the Ground at once; & the public prison is shocking to humanity. It is scarce 15 feet Square & filled with Felons Debtors &c. promiscuously, & being quite exposed to the scorching Suns of this Climate & often much crowded, the filth and vermin that these occasion is intolerable.

P.S. The Allegations set forth in your Lordships Representation to the King in reference to Mr Reynolds conduct to wit that he has permitted Mr & Mrs Bosomworth to be present at the interview with the Indians at Augusta had appointed his own menial Servant to the place of Provost Marshal & Mr Littles to that of Searcher for this Port, I find upon enquiry are strictly true.

Henry Ellis to the Board of Trade, March 20, 1757, Georgia, read April 5, 1758, C.O. 5/646, C. 25, reporting on events since his conveyance of March 11, 1757.

My Lords

I have wrote by two Conveyance the most ample account I could collect of the present state of things in this province, & as nothing has occurred worth mentioning since I forwarded these dispatches I must beg leave to refer your Lordships to them & only say in general that after so violent a ferment as I found this province in on my arrival we are now perfectly quiet; faction loses ground daily and I hope will disappear with its authors.

We have had no late alarm from the Indians I even flatter myself that they will not be suddenly troublesome at least we are not yet informed of any settled plan for that purpose. But in times so precerious as these there can be no security but what arises from the utmost vigilance & attention to every object that can possibly occasion disturbance. This I shall bear constantly in mind, & I hope not unprofitably. From our exposed condition we have every thing to apprehend, & I doubt not but your Lordships are so thoroughly convinced of this & of the importance of this frontier Colony not only from the Representation of it but from the other lights that your Lordships have been long possessed of, that something will soon be undertaken for its security.

I find my Lords that people claim as a right 50 Acres of Land for every person in family, whites or blacks, by which means as their Stocks encrease their Lands will encrease also to an exorbitant extent which I presume never was the intention of his Majesty, especially as people do not think themselves obliged to cultivate any part of the additional Lands they take up but are contented with cultivating so much more of their Old Lands as they ought by their Grants to cultivate of the New; until it suits their own conveniency to enter upon the new Lands.

By this means particular people will not only soon get possession of immense Tracts of Lands but a great part of them will be suffered a long time to lye waste, directly contrary to the Interest of the Colony. And as this practice may in time become a great inconvenience I am humbly of opinion that some methods should immediately be taken to prevent. Suppose my Lords the family rights as they call it or pretensions more properly should end when it exceeds 50 or any other number or suppose that each person in family above the number prescribed should be entitled to 10, 20 &c. Acres only. This is a regulation of such moment that I dare not attempt anything towards it, without your Lordships express commands.

Herewith I send two Addresses [not received] from the principal Inhabitants of this Colony that will explain themselves, & will account for Mr Reynolds staying here so long after my arrival. The substance of them is; that whereas Mr Reynolds & Mr Little have been underhand collecting Affidavits & certificates to invalidate the charges against them. Your Lordships are requested to postpone the Tryal until their Accusers can have an opportunity of procuring wherewithal to support their allegations, which indeed might easily be done, as I find they are in general true; but my private opinion is that these people will think no further about it for they are extremely indolent & unconnected.

Henry Ellis to the Board of Trade, May 5, 1757, Savannah, read Nov. 8, 1757, C.O. 5/646, C. 3, his visit to the southern parts of the province.

My Lords

    The last letter I did myself the honour to write to your Lordships was dated the 20th of March, Since which many matters have occurred but none of great importance and yet too much so, not to be mentioned.
    In my last I acquainted your Lordships that I intended visiting the Southern parts of this Province which I have since done & was not a little gratified by the state of things there.
    I examined very minutely the principal rivers & found that called the Great Ogechee to have advantages much superior to any of the others. Its entrance is so deep as conveniently to admit of Fifty Gun Ships & would be a very proper station for our Men of War intended to intercept the french Vessels returning from the Mississipi. The spot that is thought proper to build the Capital upon is about 12 Miles up & very well adapted as your Lordships will see by the Carte[10] I transmit herewith. It is of a proper heighth, dry, & consequently healthy, an excellent soil for Gardens & the Lands contiguous are rich & well settled. Its Situation is very capable of being fortified, the Harbour is excellent, & the Ships by a circumstance peculiar may be preserved from the worm as on one side of the Peninsula the water is fresh & free from those destructive reptiles.
    There are many other convenient rivers or inlets such as Midway, Newport, Sappelo, & St Simons that must in time greatly facilitate the commerce & navigation of this Province.
    The Lands towards the Southern frontier are abundantly more fertile than those near Savannah. Many good Settlements are already made there by people of a very sober and industrious turn that came from Carolina but being greatly in debt are not yet

---

    10. "Cartes," or maps, long ago were detached from letters in the British Public Record Office and filed separately.

in a capacity of contributing much to the support of the Colony, though in such a likely way of extricating themselves from these difficulties as can hardly fail unless some publick calamity prevents it.

In my journey I met with many Parties of Indians that were hunting with whom I had much conservation. They seemed well disposed towards us, tho' they are apt to commit little disorders, such as killing of Cattle & frightening the Inhabitants, which it is next to impossible to prevent, so long as there appears no power amongst us capable of restraining them, & they claim the Lands that are above the flowing of the Tides,[11] which if they cannot be induced to relinquish, must greatly straiten us that way. I think it would be possible to bring this about if we were authorized to undertake it, had a sufficient quantity of presents, & watched a proper Season. And until it is effected it is much to be feared that our Back Settlers will always be harassed by them.

Whilst I was in those parts I accidently saw that odd character Gray, who occasioned so much disturbance here at Mr Reynold's arrival & whose Settlement since on the South of the Alatamaha excited some fears that he would embroil us with the Spaniards.[12] Your Lordships have heard that the Governor of St Augustine had sent a party of horse to threaten him with ill treatment if he continued there, which so terrified him that he removed to Cumberland's Island, whence after a short stay he returned, & has since

---

11. Oglethorpe's 1733 and 1739 treaties with the Creeks ceded to Georgia only the lands as far inland "as the tides flowed." See "Oglethorpe's Treaty With the Lower Creek Indians," Georgia Historical Quarterly, IV (March, 1920), 3-16.

12. A Quaker, Edmund Gray (Grey) came to Georgia in 1750, establishing a shadow government in the back country around Augusta. Expelled by the Assembly on January 27, 1755, for seditious activities, Gray and a group of his "Virginians" moved south across the Altamaha River where no government could reach them. Ellis tolerated Gray's settlement at New Hanover and further encouraged the dissidents to move to Cumberland Island, perhaps in the belief that his affiliation with Gray would prevent the outcasts from associating themselves with either the Spanish or Creek Indians. See Charles C. Jones, The History of Georgia, 2 vols.,(Boston, 1883), II, 27; Abbot, Royal Governors of Georgia, 38-43, 45-63, 72; CRG, VII, 94-97, 252; XIII, 18-39, 68; XXVII.

entered into a connection with one Alexander a very bold sensible fellow, who has long dwelt, & acquired a great influence among the Lower Creek Indians that reside towards the Bay of Apalachee.[13] By Grays management this fellow has prevailed upon some of the chiefs of these people to go to Augustine & threaten the Spaniards with a War, if for the future they presume to molest or disturb those Settlers. Intimidated by these menaces & alarmed by some of the indian irregularitys, the Governor has sent to invite Gray & Alexander to settle upon the River St Johns, & establish an indian trade under his protection, promising to furnish them amply with proper goods from New York.

This proposition Gray took an opportunity of communicating to me & of shewing me letters relative thereto from one Fish who resides at that fortress[14] & is Agent to a Company at New York that supplies the Garrison with provisions. He had conceived an opinion that this permission would tend to preserve our claim to the Lands on this side of that River provided he traded there with my License. But to me it seemed a dangerous experiment, as it would afford an opportunity to the Spaniards of practicing on these Savages, of removing their old prejudices & fixing a good correspondence with them, and from their natural fickleness, of bringing them even to change sides, an event that could not fail of pernicious consequences. Under these apprehensions, joined to my fear that Gray might turn Traitor, I have urged every sort of argument to dissuade him from this design & as his activity will prompt him to some other enterprize. I have proposed to him to fix upon the River St Mary's opposite to Fort William & assured him of all manner of countenance so long as he behaves well. To this he has agreed and I have granted him a License to trade with the Indians who inhabit thereabouts which must be very advantageous to him, as that place is nearer the center of the Creek Country than even Augusta & he now seems inclined to quit the character of Legislator, which he has long assumed, for that of a Merchant. He is a shrewd sensible fellow & affects an austerity of manners by which he has acquired a considerable influence among the

---

13. Probably a reference to Ephriam Alexander, "one of Gray's principal Adherents," who moved to Cumberland Island and established a small trade with the Lower Creek Indians. Alexander still lived on the Island at the end of the French and Indian War.

14. St. Augustine.

people of this Colony & made some impression upon the Indians
& if he can be managed may prove an useful instrument in many
respects. I cannot but admire the address of the Spanish Governor.[15] He seems to be a man of excellent understanding, and to
pursue a plan of sound policy. He has taken infinite pains to
gain the friendship of the Indians, by a conduct full of uprightness
& generosity. But their aversions are not easily conquered; he
has had recourse to every justifiable art, but hitherto unprofitably.

Had this taken effect it would have been a master stroke, as
indeed is another that he is actually putting into execution. I
mean that of drawing & settling about Augustine, in hopes they
will cover him from the Indians, many of our Back Settlers who fly
for crimes, and from the disturbances to the Northward.

But I do not despair of counteracting him by means of Gray &
his Partner who frequently go thither & are well received by the
Governor from a knowledge of their consequence. This is one of
the uses I intend to make of them. Another will be to furnish us
with early intelligence, which they may easily do as they will be
a kind of advanced party, not to say Barrier against the Spaniards
& their Indian Allies of Florida.

There has been another extraordinary fellow with me lately, one
Moor a Man of distinguished valour, who asks a Commission to
go up, no purchase no pay, with about fifty resolute fellows, good
marksmen, his Colleagues, to join the Chickassaws against the
French.[16] His intention is to intercept their boats, in which when
the floods have subsided, about the latter end of July, they carry
goods from their Settlements on the Bay of Mexico, to supply that
chain of Forts that extends behind our Colonys.

I do not know how far this Maurauder might facilitate Lord
Loudoun's designs, as hitherto I have not been acquainted with

---

15. Alonso Fernandez de Heredia.

16. The "Moor" mentioned here likely is the son of James Moore,
a famed South Carolina Indian fighter who, in 1704, with fifty
Carolinians, went to the Lower Towns and raised one thousand
Creek warriors to attack the Apalachee missions. The elder Moore
was known for his Indian diplomacy and his open hostility toward
the Spanish and French. See W. S. Jenkins, ed., "South Carolina
Journals of the Commons House of Assembly, 1692-1779," 20 reels,
microfilm, in South Carolina Department of Archives and History,
Columbia, S. C., VII, 422.

them sufficiently to judge; but my own opinion is, that his scheme can have no bad consequences. Nevertheless I suspect encouraging him until I have consulted Govr Lyttleton.

My Lords I have been fully employed of late in examining the interior state of this Province in regard to its Revenue & Debts, its Militia its Laws &c. & on a careful survey have found every thing in great disorder. Your Lordships are already acquainted with what passed here in 1755 when the conduct of Mr Little created such general disgust, that the Assembly attempted to inquire into it, but were prevented by their dissolution at the beginning of the Session; whereby no taxes were imposed for that year, while the expenses of the Government were going on; and when the next assembly met it was found impossible from the poverty of the people to provide for more than one years expenses at once.

By this means the Province was burdened with a heavy debt which occasioned great embarrassment. This Mr Little took advantage of by instigating the Assembly to usurp the power of auditing the accounts & issuing the publick money, a Measure that at one stroke put our Assembly on the footing of that of Carolina and subverted that check which ought to subsist for curbing the proceedings of that body. Not satisfied with this usurpation he betrayed extreme partiality in the execution of it. He allowed of (for this Assembly was led by him) the Accounts of his Creatures only, which he contrived to pay out of the contingent money, granted by Parliament, & rejected & tore those of his Opponents, tho examined & passed by the Governor in Council. By these & other unjustifiable steps he increased his interest with the Assembly, & procured the Address & Representation of the State of the Province, which he has carried with him for his Masters and his own vindication. I need not anticipate your Lordships reflections upon these proceedings, which were surely unauthorized by the Royal instruction, incompatible with our Constitution; and pregnant with numerous & great inconveniences, as we daily experience. However I believe I shall be able to extricate the Government from these difficulties & even prevent the like hereafter.

But ere I explain myself upon this point I must enter into a detail concerning the Paper Currency. Your Lordships were pleased to direct me to report my opinion of the expediency of establishing it here by Law. I have not been hasty in doing this lest I should mistake; & until I had made a tryal of what might be done without it. The sum of my Enquirys upon this subject convence me that such a Medium is absolutely necessary here owing to the great scarcity of Gold & Silver. If I am not mistaken your Lordships were acquainted that these people of their own accord & without the royal authority, did issue £2700 in paper Bills, by way of Loan upon the security of Lands & Negroes, which at present is almost the only money current amongst us. Yet tho' the issuing of this was thought necessary & connived at by the late Governor, he took so little care to support it or rather took so great pains to depreciate it, by refusing it in fees, & for Bills of Exchange &c that at my arrival it passed exceeding heavily, & bore a very large discount. But so soon as I was convinced that paper money was requisite, I resolved to try whether this might not be put on a good footing, & accordingly made a Declaration that I would receive all my Perquisites in currency, & would give the Bills of Exchange to be drawn for the Silk & contingent money in lieu of it alone & not in specie, which gave it an immediate activity. Now my Lords this will not only serve as a Medium to carry on traffick which was indispensable, but it will destroy the credit of a number of paper Bills issued by private people & what is more important will yield a considerable Revenue arising from the interest it produces, which being unappropriated will likewise afford a means of discharging our Debt. The Scheme I have formed is this.

To issue £350 more (the amount of it) with which I shall pay the public creditors & apply the interest of that already circulating to sink this sum, which it will do in three years, & a half as it yields about £100 per annum. The Taxes of the present year will answer the services of the same, or if there be any deficiency we shall lay on a small addition to answer it. And to prevent for the future our being ever reduced to a like dilemma, I propose to imitate the practise of England, by laying an Estimate of the necessary expenses every year before the Assembly that they may raise money & appropriate it accordingly. Whereby we shall avoid the inconveniences that are felt by the neighbouring Governments, the great evil of running in debt, & the publick Creditors will be paid without partiality or delay.

I cannot but lament my Lords that considering all the inconveniences that naturally result from the want of a proper frame of Government that the ablest men were not sent originally to these Countrys for its establishment. For my own part I tremble at every step I take lest the errors that may flow from my inexperience should be a sourse of future embarrassment and contention. These considerations make me more impatient for the arrival of our Chief Justice of whose abilities I might avail myself.

The Assembly have not met since my arrival, but have been

adjourned & prorogued from time to time that I might have leisure to settle my plan conformable to the disposition of the people which I have taken great pains to get acquainted with. I have now determined to call them together the 16th of June for a short Sitting, as it will be a busy time of the year. I propose the passing of three Acts only, the heads of which are already prepared, that is to say, One for the execution of my Scheme to pay off the provincial Debt, Another for employing the hands intended for opening the Roads, to the construction of some places of defence; and a Third for affording an Asylum for seven years against their Creditors to all persons in distressed circumstances, save such as come from that part of Carolina only that lies to the Northward of us. This exception is requisite to prevent the ill uses that might be made by the people residing there, who would have it in their power to contract Debts one day, & elude the Laws, & their Creditors the next by flying into Georgia. It will also prevent any provincial altercation, & hinder the people of that Colony from making an opposition to this Bill, as it will shew a disposition to be just to them, while we are endeavoring to serve ourselves & manifest an equal regard to Debtor & Creditor, since people from the more distant provinces will have sufficient time to pursue their Debtors, whom if they could not overtake in passing such a wide extent of Country as that of South Carolina, probably would not overtake them at all. But the main object of this Act is the Speedy peopling of the Colony, by drawing a number of Insolvents from the neutral islands of Santa Croix & Eustatia; where they have fled for shelter, & those also in the Northern provinces who are in like circumstances: And not to weaken our Neighbours which in effect would be gaining nothing, as it would divide the power without augmenting it.

    We already begin to apprehend that we shall have more people than we can furnish with good Lands, for the Indians, imagining that all above the flowing of the Tides are theirs, consider any Settlement thereupon, without their leave, as a trespass, which they have a right to punish by plundering so that we are considerably confined Westward, since the tides do not flow above 30 Miles up where the Lands are more fruitful, & tempt people to plans without liberty. These Savages would have had no idea of fixing our limits that way had it not been put into their heads by Bosomworth who laid claim to those lands that lie behind us, & I am assured encouraged them to destroy the Cattle they found there. He is a most mischievous, crafty, & obstinate fellow & his practices have so much intimidated people here, that although at the late Courts he was afraid to try his title, from the measures I took to render abortive the ill designs that had been concerted before my arrival it is doubtful with me whether our people would have dared to decide against him, thro' fear of the troubles he might create by means of the Indians, with whom he keeps up an influence by insinuating that he is the Guardian of their Interests, which however without more substantial means would avail little. But he frequently makes them presents, & treats them kindly at his House, where he encourages them to come, & this he is enabled to do by one Levi a Jew, who resides to the Northward & who has given him a thousand pounds for half of the Lands, he claims, and for half of the profits of the residue which are leased to him for fifteen years. This connection joined to the encouragement he had from the late Governor has been, I imagine, the principal cause of his persisting so obstinately in his pretensions. From the little countenance he has had from me & what has reached his ears that I have said concerning the precariousness of his Title, & the improbability of his ever reaping any advantage from it; it is likely if a Compromise was thought necessary we should find him sufficiently tractable. And my Lords it were earnestly to be wished that some expedient might be fallen upon, to put an end to this thorny affair, either by way of equivalent, by confirming to him a part of what he claims, or by any other method that your Lordships wisdom may suggest, as this Colony in my opinion can never be exempt from apprehensions while it subsists. In my tour Southwards I took a view of the Islands Ossebaw, St Catherines & Sappelo, which indeed are very fine & worth contending for as they are said to contain near 40,000 of the best land in the province which unfortunately must be waste till this contest be ended.

Whilst I am so anxious about extending our frontier, I am not less attentive in distributing to the best advantage the Lands we have already. The monopolizing large tracts has been the common misfortune of these provinces. The people here are aiming at the same thing. Many purchase considerable quantitys & then apply to me in Council for their family right as they call it. As some of the Councillors themselves have a passion for this practice, I find it difficult to restrain it, so that I humbly conceive that if your Lordships were pleased to give me a positive instruction to grant no lands to any person possessing above a certain quantity, say 1, 2 or 3,000 Acres whether obtained by grant or purchase, it would give no material umbrage & could not fail of the best effects, by multiplying the Plantations, & consequently affording maintenance to a greater number of people.

In a former letter I took the liberty to represent to your Lordships the grievance that this province labors under from the quantity of Lands reserved for Absentees, or others who have never qualified themselves to hold them by the performance of any one condition requisite, & whose names are only known by tradition, there being no Register of their Titles. I must now beg leave to remind your Lordships of it by a particular instance that affects the people of this Town very severely as well as others. Among the many visionary ideas that Mr Oglethorpe entertained this was not the least absurd. He imagined that people here might subsist & even become affluent upon such small parcels of Land, as the little farms in England, which is absolutely impossible. The Lands themselves are different, as well as the nature of the culture, the produce & the climate. But rivetted to this chimaera, he established many little Townships, and minced all the lands round them into whimsical figures of five, and forty five Acres which he put people in possession of by a written order directed to the Constable.

A proclamation was published by Mr Reynolds at his arrival, enjoyning Claimants to confirm their Titles, by new Grants from the Crown, which induced many people to do so; but numbers have omitted it. Hence it follows that for five Miles round, being the extent of this Township, it is checquered with Lots, that have & have not apparant Owners. The Lots themselves are too small for a Plantation, & cannot be enlarged by obtaining a Grant or even purchase of those adjoining, till their property be ascertained, so that this Tract which ought to supply the Town with Necessarys lies uncultivated & must continue so until your Lordships find out a remedy. Since my arrival here some people of property have come in, & many more are expected, from a belief that measures different from those hitherto pursued will take place.

Abundance of Grants have lately been taken out & probably will continue to be applied for so that good Lands & convenient situations must soon become scarce which makes me more earnest to have it in my power to grant such as are vacant. I mean those said to belong to absentees, which are now useless, and even detrimental to the province, as they separate the inhabitants & consequently weaken them, as well as encrease their labour upon the publick roads &c; an evil that ought to be attended to, whilst the people are so poor & so involved with their neighbours of Carolina; that their utmost industry affords them but a scanty subsistence & a small surplus that goes thither to pay their Debts. If we can forbear burdening them with publick services & taxes, a little time will free them from their incumbrances & accelerate the prosperity of the Province. This consideration makes me cautious of attempting many things highly necessary but which cannot be done without money. The publick Buildings are in a ruinous condition. The Light House at the Entrance of this River--an Edifice raised at a vast expense & become extremely necessary for the commerce of these two provinces--is upon the point of tumbling down. Many fruitless remonstrances were made upon this subject to the late Governor. It was intended that the Pilot residing there should have a house built at the public charge, without which it was scarce possible for him to continue. This has been resolved upon in Council, but like many other useful things neglected. These remonstrances were renewed to me & the facts sufficiently supported to convince me that there was an immediate necessity to take measures in consequence of them. I therefore advertised my intention of repairing the Light House & building a dwelling house for the Pilot & desired those that were willing to undertake them to send in their proposals sealed to me in Council. At the same time I signified that those whose proposals were most reasonable should be preferred. This had a good effect in convincing the publick that I will not proceed on partial & jobbing principles. And the work will be done cheap as we have been able to contract for £150 to defray which there is about £70 in the hands of the Treasurer produced by an impost upon Shipping appropriated for that service. The deficiency I shall be able to make up out of about £130, the remains of some money belonging to the Trustees, which I found in the hands of some of their old Servants; a very seasonable discovery in our circumstances. I cannot without indignation & surprise reflect upon the conduct of my Predecessor, in telling the Assembly in his Speech at their last Meeting that the taxes would be sufficient for the publick service when at the same time if he knew anything he could not be ignorant that the publick were indebted double the annual Revenue or how he could think of leaving this province to me in such embarrassed circumstances after having practised every kind of art to prevent my having any influence that might be directed towards its relief.

For every publick Office that either existed or were likely to be established, were filled with his Creatures, even when he knew of my arrival in America. Yet I am in hopes that if this was intended to answer any sinister purpose it will be defeated, & that I shall be able to furnish the people here with better reasons for assisting me than those of a private, partial, or mercenary nature.

I have just been Regimenting the Militia, which before consisted of independant Companys, without connection, without subordination & without discipline. This step has afforded me an opportunity of gratifying some worthy men, who are vain of Military Titles, of putting the Militia in a condition of being useful & I may add of establishing a right that Mr Reynolds intended giving up to the Assembly that of appointing the Officers.

I have made a few alterations in the Publick Offices by bringing in a pretty good man as Deputy Clerk of the Council, & a very good one, Mr Thomas Burrington, to act as Clerk of the Assembly in the room of wretched Tools. Mr John Graham who is known to some of your Lordships, I have named to the place of Clerk of the accounts & indian Commissary, in the room of Mr Little. I have made some other petty regulations, not worth your Lordships notice; but I hope the whole of these movements have been directed by a regard to integrity, & ability only & have therefore excited no jealousy or umbrage.

We have lately had Mr Stephens here to instruct us in his method of making Pot Ash which he exhibited before many of the principal Inhabitants & succeeded so far as to evince that it was practicable. Tis certain this Manufacture can be attempted no where with a greater prospect of advantage than in this Country, which has determined several of our Planters to make a tryal. I hear that Mr Atkin[17] is just arrived at Charlestown from the Northward. If it is not improper I should be glad your Lordships would condescend to explain to me the nature of his instructions, that I may be qualified to act properly in case I should have any correspondence with him.

Scarce a Week passes but we are visited by Gangs of Indians, led here by an expectation of receiving presents in consequence of the change of Government. We treat them in the best manner we are able, furnishing them with provisions some promises, a few presents & a great many fair words, & upon the whole have so managed that none have left us discontented. I hope the presents from England will soon arrive for tho' it is possible to retain these people in good humour for some little time by such methods yet

---

17. Edmund Atkin served as Indian Superintendent for the Southern District of North America from 1756 to 1761. Before his arrival in Charleston, Atkin had spent most of the previous year preoccupied with Indian concerns in Virginia. Henry Ellis thought that he understood the Creeks better than Atkin, and accordingly he resented the Superintendent's attempts to assert control over trade and Indian affairs in Georgia.

they cannot be practised long with success.

 I mention at the beginning of this letter that I send herewith a Carte of the Sea Coast, & some of the principal rivers of this province. But reflecting that if it should fall into the hands of the enemy it might have extreme bad consequences, I do not venture to send it, until I can have a safe conveyance by a Man of War which I expect will soon offer. In the meantime I hope that this will not prevent your Lordships from deciding as to the expediency of removing the Seat of Government, as things here will be in a great measure at a stand until that point be determined.

 Perhaps it may not be improper to repeat that if this alteration is to take place £2,000 at least will be wanting for the construction of the Publick Buildings. Could the saving from the Silk money be applied to this purpose they would go a great way & any deficiency might be made up, out of the produce of a Vessel lately condemned here to his Majesty by Mr Reynolds, said to amount to six or eight hundred pounds of which doubtless he can give your Lordships an exact account.

 I have wrote several letters to Lord Loudoun touching the situation of things here, to none of which I have yet received any answer, but which I am in daily expectation of, & not a little impatient about, as the credit of our Captain of the Rangers, is stretched to the utmost, to subsist the few men who were raised here in Mr Reynolds time. I shall not here repeat what I have already wrote concerning the condition this province is in of making a defence should it be attacked, but only add that I have no reason to contradict the substance of my former letters upon this subject.

 From this long letter your Lordships will see in what manner I have been occupied.

 Could I flatter myself that my endeavors would be productive of the smallest publick utility, or gain your Lordships approbation I should think myself extremely happy.

John Reynolds to Board of Trade, May 19, 1757, Bayonne, France, read June 7, 1757, C.O. 5/645, B. 40, explaining his capture by a French privateer and asking the Board to intercede on his behalf.

My Lords

 In obedience to Your Lordships Commands I Embarked for England on board the Charming Martha Capt. Thomson, and after a tedious Passage as far as the Soundings of the Channel, had the

Misfortune to be taken by a French Privateer of Thirty Six Guns, who sent me a Prisoner into this Port. I have no doubt but your Lordships Generosity and Compassion will induce you to make proper Application for my being speedily Exchanged or Released. And from the same Noble disposition I hope that You'll be pleased to inform me how far I may draw upon the Agent for my support in the Country, by directing Your Commands for me to Monsieur Dominique Sallenare, Negotiate at Bayonne.

The Departure of the Post will not permit me to say more.

Henry Ellis to William Pitt, May 25, 1757, Savannah, read Oct. 11, 1757, congratulating him on his appointment as Secretary of State.

Sir

I have just had the honour of your letter of the 7th December, signifying His Majesty's most gracious appointment of You to be one of his principal Secretarys of State, upon which Sir I humbly beg leave to congratulate You.

I shall for the future take particular care to address to you all Letters that may contain matters of such importance as are proper to be known to his Majesty. Nothing of that nature now occurrs, nor indeed any thing uncommon, things remaining here in a State of quiet, tho' from our weak & exposed condition, the activity of the French and the disposition of the neighbouring Indians, we are apprehensive that our tranquillity will not be of long duration.

I heartily thank you Sir for sending me the King's most gracious Speech, & the Addresses of both Houses, which convey to me a precise idea of the present posture of affairs in Europe.

Henry Ellis to the Board of Trade, May 25, 1757, Georgia, read Nov. 9, 1757, C.O. 5/646, C. 4, notifying the Board of the arrival of Indian presents, arms for the militia, and the state of sericulture within the colony.

My Lords,

I did myself the honor to write to your Lordships on the 5th instant.

On the 18th. arrived here the Juno Captn Leslie with the Indian

presents on board, & also the arms granted by His Majesty for
the use of the Militia of this Colony. We are now landing them
& so far as we have gone they appear to be in good order. But I
am sorry the arms are not of the kind I mentioned to Mr Martyn,
but such as from their weight & clumsiness will be managed with
difficulty in this warm Country. It must be in times of the greatest
danger when many inconveniences must be submitted to, that the
people will be persuaded to use them. Through want of a Magazine we are obliged to lay them & the Ammunition in a ruinous
wooden store, to which any ill disposed person might set fire,
did we not post the few Rangers that we are on foot to guard it.

As Govr Lyttleton has not yet seen any of the Chiefs of the
Creek Nation, I imagine he would be very desirous of such an opportunity. I have therefore wrote to him for his opinion, as to the
most proper place of assembling them, to distribute the Presents;
& intimated if his Excellency had any inclination to treat with
them, I would endeavor to bring them to Savannah, which is upon
the border of his own province, otherwise I should consult our own
convenience, & that of the Indians only. This supply is very seasonable for we had little or no ammunition left in the province, &
our Indian Presents were quite exhausted. And scarce a day passes that we are not visited by these Savages, whom it is necessary to entertain & dismiss contented. Hitherto we have been
fortunate enough to do so but with much difficulty & fatigue, for
which we are amply rewarded by the good demeanour of these
people, who since my arrival have been tolerably quiet. The bulk
of them are from home at present, & widely dispersed in partys
over the Country, this being their grand hunting season. They
generally return towards the middle of July. Before that time or
sooner if possible, I shall have my plans settled, & an Envoy in
their Country. And this is more immediately necessary, as a
Gentleman that arrived here a few days ago from the Bay of Honduras, a man of credit & property intending to settle among us,
informs me, that on the 14th instant, off of Cape Corientes (the
West End of Cuba) he fell in with three french men of War, one of
sixty four Guns, & two Frigates of thirty six each, convoying nine
Vessels that seemed to be Transports steering towards the Mississippi. They did not offer to pursue. The reason whereof he apprehends, was, there being two English Vessels in sight one of which
sailed very fast, & would certainly have escaped, & published
their arrival in those seas. They therefore kept their course &
attempted to disguise themselves, by hoisting English Colours,
but this Gentleman insists that he cannot have been deceived as

he is well acquainted with the mould & ornaments of the French
Ships, which he could discern and distinctly being within Gun
Shot. This small squadron I imagine comes out in consequence
of the Treaty concluded between the Cherokees, & the Governor
of New Orleans in November last. 'Tis to be feared there are a
considerable number of Troops on board, & what may operate
worse, probably a quantity of Indian Presents. I have notified
this intelligence with my conjectures thereupon to my Lord Loudoun,
& the other Governors upon the Continent, not to alarm but to turn
their thoughts this way. For my own part your Lordships may entirely depend that I will give the utmost attention, & use the
strongest endeavors to gain the friendship of the Indians which is
certainly an object of the last moment, at this conjecture, as, if
we succeed therein it will effectually disconcert the projects of
our enemies. I may perhaps be too importunate with your Lordships in renewing my solicitations for a small body of Troops to
be stationed at particular places in this province, but the necessity of the service prompts me to it & I hope will plead my excuse.
They would certainly add great weight to our negotiations with the
Indians, restrain their wantonness, secure the frontier, ease the
minds of the inhabitants, create respect to Government, & give
force & effect to our Laws, all of which are wanting in a great
degree.

 Our cocons are now pretty well wrought up.

 The quantity of the Silk they produce this Season will be upwards of 360 lb wtt which is far short of what might have been
expected had there been eggs enough saved from the destruction
of last year; of if those which Mr Martyn intended sending, could
have been sent early, & our Spring been more temparate & equal.
The warm weather is apt to hatch the eggs too soon, & the un-
equality of the climate is such that sharp frosts succeed the
warmest days, to the certain destruction of these tender Reptiles,
unless they are carefully treated. I therefore strongly recommend
to the people, the building proper houses, the use of Stoves, &
keeping the eggs in such cool places, as may retard their maturity,
which would greatly tend to lessen, the natural impediments to
their encrease, a practice that I expect will be followed up by a
few leading people which in time may influence the rest. I cannot
upon this occasion help expressing my uneasiness that proper
measures are not taken to instruct a Successor to Mr Otterlinghe.
He is but of a delicate & tender constitution probably will be but
a short liver, & I conceive is not over sollicitous of having any
person capable of supplying his place, from a peculiar jealousy &
a fear of being supplanted.

Whatever his motives may be in withholding his instructions, or not chusing a Colleague, I humbly conceive your Lordships will think that such a precaution is not unnecessary, & that if a proper person was appointed here with a small Salary to assist this Gentleman, & qualify himself for the direction hereafter it would be a prudent measure. For unprovided as we are I cannot see how this Culture could be supported if Mr Otterlinghe should drop off. It is a produce that is worth raising, a design that is worth encouraging & I have great reason to believe will succeed in the end, notwithstanding all the difficultys that have hitherto impeded its progress. If your Lordships think that my sollicitude in this matter is well founded, I shall be very glad to receive your commands thereupon.

Letter from Mr. Henshaw, master of a vessel recently sailed from Georgia, May 31, 1757, Cowes, received and read June 7, 1757, C.O. 5/645, B. 41, acquainting the Board of Trade that Lt. Gov. Ellis entrusted him with several letters and dispatches, but, that having been taken by a privateer, he had destroyed them.

My Lords

I thought it my Duty on my Arrival here, to acquaint your Lordships, that having received several Dispatches for your Lordships, from Governor Ellis in Georgia, which place I left the 15 April. But having the Misfortune to be taken by a French Privateer about 60 Leagues to the Westward of Scilly, on the 20 May, was obliged to destroy them, agreeable to my Instructions from Governor Ellis. Everything was quiet in that Country, & all Ranks of People highly satisfied with their present Governor when I left the Place.

Henry Ellis to Board of Trade, July 8, 1757, Georgia, received Oct. 11, 1757, read Nov. 7, 1757, C.O. 5/646, C. 5, an account of the present state of affairs with the Assembly.

My Lords

My last letter to your Lordships was dated the 28th. May & comprehended the material occurrences of this Government to that period. Our Assembly met the 16th ulto according to prorogation with appearances very unpromising, as they discovered a scheme had been laid by the late Administration in concert with a majority of the Members to disturb my Government. An incendiary letter which I send herewith to your Lordships, was wrote by Mr Little, directed to the Members of that House, & introduced by their Speaker. It will be unnecessary to expatiate upon the style & design of so extraordinary an epistle, as your Lordships will have the perusal of it yourselves. But it will be proper to explain the whole of this scheme. As it was apprehended it would dissolve the Assembly, most of the Members being the Creatures of my predecessor, measures were taken early to have the same chosen. So that at all events a Junto was to be kept up, whose business would be to impede & frustrate all my designs however salutary. The disorders this opposition would necessarily occasion was to be a foundation for addressing the King to restore Mr Reynolds to this Government. Mr Patrick Mackay, a very artful person, & of no good character, whom on my arrival I removed from the Council, was to be the chief actor in this plot.[18] With him the letter was left, & it was intended that he should get into the Assembly, then be chosen Speaker & head the faction. This & other reasons determined me to discountenance his being elected, & suspend him from the Bench where he sat as senior Justice, & one of the most partial ones imaginable. He it was that Mr Reynolds fixed upon to manage Bosomworths affair. These steps had all the effect I could wish & I presume gave the finishing stroke to party, he lost the election & is retired with disgust & disappointment to his plantation. So that by address, by bold, but honest arts, & by doing

---

18. A Lowland Scot, Patrick MacKay came to Georgia in 1735. Receiving a grant of five hundred acres at Joseph's Town on the Savannah River, MacKay abandoned it in 1738 when the Trustees refused to let him use slave labor and moved across the Savannah River to South Carolina. From that strategic location, MacKay engaged in the coasting trade, principally with the Montaiguts of Charleston, dealt illicit rum to the Indians for deerskins, purchased the two sloops owned by Bethesdea orphanage for his expanding trade, and accumulated rice plantations on both sides of the river. A wealthy man by 1756, he was appointed member of the King's Council by Reynolds and in 1757 a judge of the General Court. Ellis disapproved MacKay's "clandestine activities." See CRG, II, 112, 120-121, 124, 166; IV, 108, 115-116, 160; IV, Supplement, 74-75; V, 17, 40; VIII, 44; IX, 51; XXI, 272; XXII, Pt. I, 72; XXIII, 280.

my duty in a way unusual here, I have at length been able to change
the temper of my opponents to my wishes, for except this person I
dont know any other dissatisfied. That hydra faction who had long
preyed upon the happiness of the people seems at present expiring.

The utmost harmony has taken place, between the several
branches of the Legislature & the publick business goes on with
ease & expedition. The Bill I mentioned to your Lordships calculated for the speedy peopling of this Colony by affording protection
to Insolvents for seven years, has passed both Houses. 'Tis well
guarded & exceptions are made to such as are indebted to Great
Britain, Ireland & our neighbouring province South Carolina. The
former was necessary to the general credit of America, the latter
to prevent the ill uses that might be made of this indulgence by
those who reside so near us & to avoid the discontent & altercation
that their conduct might create between the two provinces. This
Act is especially necessary at this time, as the Governor of St
Augustine gives great encouragement & protection to such of our
people as are in those circumstances, who will go & settle there
& has actually seduced a good many with whom he hopes to form
a useful Colony. An Act has likewise passed for the construction
of a Log fort in five different districts, which is to be effected by
those hands that were to have wrought upon the Roads, & a general tax of one shilling a head on Negroes. Also a Bill for a general Patrole. One for the better discipline of the Militia, establishing more frequent musters. One to prevent the conveying
Cattle & provisions by Land to St Augustine (tho' this place is not
particularized in the Act) where great quantitys have lately been
sent from Carolina. One for regulating & licensing public houses,
& to prevent the Indians & negroes from being supplyd with spirit-
uous liquors whence great disorders have arisen. One is depending to oblige the Inhabitants to carry Arms to places of publick
worship to prevent any surprise from Negroes &c & one to discharge
the publick debt, & to restore its credit now at the lowest ebb.
In a former letter I took occasion to mention to your Lordships the
disordered situation in which I found things here. I took notice of
Mr Reynolds conduct in telling the Assembly in his Speech that an
increase of Taxes would be unnecessary, which I ascribed to a
design of gaining a temporary popularity. Indeed I was but im-
perfectly informed at that time, tho sufficiently to suspect, that
must have been his aim. If it was not he must have been unaccountably ignorant of the circumstances of his Government for we
now find the publick debt amounts to £850 & the ordinary Revenue
but to £260. We have £390 in hand to discharge part of it & the

rest is to be paid off, by the expedient I mentioned to your Lordships in my letter of the beginning of May. By this means I shall be able to accomplish, what I had so much at heart the raising of the money previous to the Services instead of doing it subsequent to them. A Method that had crept into this Government by the indiscretion of those who presided & must in the end have been attended with the worst consequences. Besides this the Assembly have enabled me to maintain people as Look Outs whom I have stationed upon the Sea islands, for alarming the Inhabitants at the approach of the Enemy's ships. And I have insisted upon the necessity of doubling the former Tax, to keep the Province out of debt, & have some little resourse for accidents, & I have good grounds to conclude this will be done. I am sorry there is a necessity for it, as I know the poverty & distress of the people which indeed is great. Could we spare them for a few years they would be able to do something without hurting themselves. But as we are now circumstanced I am afraid that cannot be done. For the safety of our Arms & Ammunition, (having no Magazine) & to enable the inhabitants to arm the trustiest of their slaves upon any sudden emergency, & make the best resistance possible I intend to distribute small quantitys in the hands of the principal Magistrates thro' the Country not to be made use of but in time of danger, & returned to the publick Store when our apprehensions are over. We continue to be visited by the Indians & exert ourselves to keep them in the disposition that they seem to be in at present, which is not bad if we may trust appearances.

 I have sent up Messages to the Chiefs of the Nations acquainting them with the arrival of our presents & my desire of seeing them here, when they return from Charlestown, where Governor Lyttleton it seems had previously engaged them to go, and that he thinks will be much better than their coming here first.

Copy of Mr. Little's Letter to the Assembly, May 25, 1757, Savannah, received Oct. 11, 1757, read Nov. 9, 1757, C.O. 5/646, C. 6, explaining his actions.

Gentlemen

 The late change in the administration of Government, and my own affairs having made it necessary for me to return to England. The Chair in which you did me honor to place me & my Seat in your Assembly are both vacant. I have endeavored to discharge the Trust you reposed in me with uprightness & impartiality & tho' many may be found superior to me in abilities yet no one can exceed me in an inviolable attachment to what appeared to me your true interest. Opposing to the most salutary measures must be expected in every popullar Meeting, but you will carefully guard against any attempt that may be made to induce you to censure your own conduct (1) & to condemn proceedings you went thro' with so much chearfulness, & in which so remarkable a Majority prevailed as to make them clearly the sense of the whole province. Such a design can arise only from men actuated by infatuation (2) who have been openly employed in the promulgation of falsehood, to exasperate & inflame the minds of the people whose sentiments & inclinations they for the sake of their private interests did first artfully misrepresent in order to betray into measures (3) which could have no other event than to render an Administration uneasy & alienate the affections of the inhabitants. Charity would lead one to hope that those men might in time alter their conduct but whoever will reflect that they have gone too far to return, & that they have all along steadily pursued schemes destructive to the general good of this province, & remained invariably fixed to their principles of self interest (the only principles to which they have ever been true) must suffer his own understanding to be greatly imposed upon before he can entertain any such hopes.

Arts of delusion will no doubt be practised upon the occasion but it is easy to distinguish betwixt those men who have in view lucrative employments & those who have no other motive in advancing the publick welfare, than the benefit they will thereby enjoy in common with every member of the community. Malevolence & resentment will endeavor to hide themselves under the Cloak of Patriotism & it will be insinuated (4) that nothing more is intended than to reconcile interests, that have for many years been incompatible, & to extinguish all heats & animosities. But when those who have long laboured under oppression are by those specious pretenses lulled asleep, then violence will take

---

(1) By reversing the Representation of the state of the Province, and the address to the Governor last Session.
(2) The Council two of whom Mr Reynolds suspended and the others lay under persecution.
(3) The Governor.
(4) by the New Governor.

place, & schemes now latent be executed with unrelenting vigor and subtle & wicked means they (5) have long used to support their power, will be, indeed, have been again exerted.

Their Dependents are encouraged to weaken your Constitutional credit, to asperse you as men desirous of confusion who have no real weight in the Country & who scarcely merit any attention. A private Society (6) have been put in competition with a provincial Assembly, & in some respects have the preference given to it. This conduct however contemptible in a private light, yet in a publick view may have very extensive very pernicious consequences. When Petitions are drawn up (7) & recommended by persons who may justly be supposed to speak by authority, & who meanly beg hands to them, insinuating that this is the most acceptable Service; when the discontent of the people is alleged (8) as a reason to take a most extraordinary measure (9) that discontent which (10) they have themselves laboured to stir up by exaggerations & false representations, tis highly probable, the people will upon other occasions, claim that priviledge, they are now for a particular purpose* complimented with, & except to be consulted on every emergency, not in their collective Body but as individuals (11) & thus will the Constitution be shaken to its very basis & foundation. These proceedings should animate you to redouble your efforts in proportion to the occasion, & to convince your Constituents, that it is incumbent upon them to despise the

---

(5) Some of the Councillors who were employed under the Trustees Government.
(6) The Georgia Society whom Mr. Ellis received an address from but adjourned the Assembly when he was acquainted they were upon the same business, & that it was intended to make use of that opportunity to compliment Mr. Reynolds on his Administration.
(7) To reinstate those removed from Office by Mr. Reynolds.
(8) By His Majesty's Ministers.
(9) A Change of Governors.
(10) The Complainants or the Ministers--'tis doubtful which is meant.
(11) By private letters. There is an obstinate incoherence and incoherence and obscurity here, well understood by the party.

*Your Lordships must know for what particular purpose I was sent here. H. Ellis.

gilded bait, & to oppose all innovations, which in the end must make Assemblys lose their importance, after which they must soon become useless & be no longer the resort of liberty, & the barrier against wanton power, which is more dangerous in the hands of a Junto, than in one man, for that an aristocratical form of Government is perhaps of all others the least eligible. You may call to witness the Decemvirate of old Rome, & the modern States of Genoa Venice & Holland. Steadiness & resolution in you who legally represent the people (12) may avert those evils, for nothing can elude the force of an Assembly, enlivened with zeal for the publick happiness, & this is so true, that you cannot long feel any internal hurt, but such as must arise from your own choice. The calumnies with which I have been loaded have made it necessary for me to offer fully to you my sentiments, & will I hope plead my excuse for having done it in so free a manner.

    I am well acquainted with your inclinations & desires & my behaviour in the execution of your Orders in England (13) shall be conformable thereto, & I flatter myself that with all candid men, heartiness & sincerity will allow for my imperfections.

---

(12) In contradistinction to the Council in their Capacity of an Upper House of Assembly
(13) To endeavour to remove Mr Martyn from the Agency, for having a friendly connection with some of the Council who were in power under the Trustees Government.

Henry Ellis to the Board of Trade, July 10, 1757, Savannah, received Oct. 11, 1757, read Nov. 9, 1757, C.O. 5/646, C. 7, cover letter for public papers transmitted to London.

My Lords

    Tho' I have repeatedly demanded the Papers I send herewith;[19] I was not able to obtain them before the reason alledged for this delay by the Secretary was the slowness & incapacity of the late Deputy Clerk of the Council whom I removed, & the accumulated business that has taken place since my arrival. They promise

---

19. Only a "Schedule of Publick Papers," and not the papers themselves, was sent. The "Schedule" was not found with this letter.

to avoid such neglects for the future. 'Tis but lately that I learned
that Mr Little, who was Clerk of the Assembly, omitted Copying,
and Mr Reynolds transmitting, the Minutes of that House the last
Session. Little being Speaker he employed a Deputy to officiate
as Clerk a person whom I have likewise removed for incapacity &
inapplication. The present Clerk of the Assembly will, so soon
as the Session is over redouble his diligence to complete the Minutes to that time, which shall be immediately transmitted to your
Lordships.

Henry Ellis to the Board of Trade, Aug. 1, 1757, Georgia, read
Nov. 9, 1757, C.O. 5/646, C. 8, his observations upon some
acts lately passed in that colony.

My Lords

    My last letter was dated the 6th. ulto since which little more
than the completion of the measures then in agitation has occurred.
    Our Assembly broke up the 28th ulto in very good temper. All
the Bills that in my former letter I mentioned to be depending have
been passed, but as in the Preamble of each, their respective intention will appear. I presume it is unnecessary for me to say
any thing particular about them; except that intended to establish
an Asylum here for Insolvents which being of an uncommon nature
may require a full recital of the motives that induced me to propose & pass it which are these
    1st. The speedy peopling of the Colony necessary on a double
account, for its own defence & to protect the other provinces to
which it is a frontier.
    2dly. Because many of His Majesty's Subjects who have taken
shelter from their Creditors in the Neutral Islands have lately
signified to me by persons come from thence their great desire
of settling here could they obtain the protection they now enjoy.
    3dly. Because the Governor of Augustine gives all manner of
encouragement to the King's American Subjects in the same circumstances, who will go & settle in that Neighbourhood under
the protection of His Catholic Majesty.
    4thly. Because an Asylum is already afforded by Gray, who
is settled to the Southward of the River Altamaha & has drawn a
number of such people around him, who being unrestrained by
Government, & out of the reach of Laws may in time give great
umbrage to the Spaniards, perhaps embroil us with the Indians.

Now the only motive that induces people to settle there, being that protection it is probable none hereafter would go thither if they could have the same advantage in this Colony not to mention that it will be a likely means of drawing from thence & from Augustine those who are already settled at those places.

5thly. It will be a means of regaining a number of subjects & their property, that otherwise would be absolutely lost to the Nation, & will deprive our Enemies or Rivals of the benefit of their strength and their industry. They will very probably in a little time take the heavy charge of supporting this Province off the Mother Country, & make it a real barrier to the Southern Provinces. It may cause the natural advantages that are peculiar to the Soil & Climate of Georgia to operate more speedily to the emolument of Great Britain. In fine it may serve to give this Colony a sudden strength & prosperity not obtainable by any other measure.

These My Lords are the principal considerations that induced me to pass this Bill which when compared with any inconveniences that may arise from it will I hope appear a very sufficient justification of me. If they are strong enough to influence your Lordships to approve of what I have done I shall think myself extremely happy & at the worst I hope you will indulge me in believing that my errors proceed from no other motive but an honest tho' mistaken zeal for what I take to be the good of my Country. The act itself is extremely popular here & your Lordships will find it is as well guarded, & as suitable as it is possible for such an Act to be to produce any effect at all. If it should be rejected by his Majesty it will produce no inconvenience. On the contrary it may be an advantage to particular people who may find their Debtors here, when they could not have reached them any where else. I intended at first not to have passed it 'till I had wrote to your Lordships & had your opinion & consent, but upon mature deliberation I found such a delay would be extremely prejudicial & in a manner defeat the end of the Bill, from which we expect an immediate benefit. This too hindered me from passing it with a suspending Clause as it is usually so long a time before his Majesty's pleasure is known concerning Bills passed in this manner. Nevertheless if your Lordships will be pleased to signify your opinion that it will not be approved by the King I can put an immediate stop to its operation.

By another Act the Assembly have ordered that £630 more Paper Currency be issued for discharging the debts of this Province which sum is to be called in & sunk in three or four years by a fund appointed for that purpose an account of which I gave your

Lordships in a former letter.[20] The Services of the Current Year are provided for by a renewal of the Taxes, which have been more than doubled this Session.

So that your Lordships will find that I have accomplished what I aimed at, the restoring of the right of auditing the accounts, & issuing the public money to the Governor and Council to whom it properly belongs. For as things stood before no money was to be issued but by a special Order from the Lower House of Assembly. As this point has been carried with much difficulty I hope no Governor hereafter will ever be so infatuated as to relinquish it.

By the Fort Act five are appointed to be erected in different parts of the province vizt; one at Darien, one at Augusta, another at Medway, a fourth at Ogeachy & the principal one at Savannah.[21] All the hands capable of Labour, black & white throughout the province, are to work twelve days upon them, which alone is equal to a Tax of £1000 Sterling not to mention 1 shilling a head that is to be Levied for completing the Fort at Savannah. As I have the superintendency of these Works, & have a considerable influence with the Commissioners & people in general I have advised, & indeed convinced them of the utility of fortifying this whole Town in a regular manner with five whole & 2 demi-Bastions joined by Curtains. The work itself to consist of a ditch 12 feet wide, a Breast work of earth 5 feet high within including the Banquette, & 10 without, face with pallisades to prevent its being easily scaled.

This indeed is a great undertaking, but it is resolved upon. It will certainly have vast advantages over a fort, since it will be spacious enough to contain most of the Inhabitants of the Province, & equally capable of being defended against any Indian Enemy whatever; or indeed any other who do not employ artillery. But it would be difficult to defend anything we could raise against that. Another advantage that will be gained is that the houses already built will serve for Barracks, Store Houses, Magazines &c & the constructing of Ovens & sinking of Wells, & many other

---

20. Henry Ellis to the Board of Trade, May 5, 1757, above, p. 16.

21. Located at the 1735 Highland Scot settlement on the Altamaha River, the Darien fort presumably would guard the southern part of the colony. In similar fashion, the Augusta, Midway, and the Ogeechee stockades were placed in strategic locations on Georgia's principal rivers.

expensive & necessary works will be avoided. Indeed it is a question whether the hands destined to work upon it will be able to finish it in the time allotted but it is pretty certain if they do not that the Assembly will take further measures for its completion.

I cannot procure to send by this opportunity more than 4 Acts, that passed this last Session & those have immediate reference to the subject of this letter.

The Minutes of neither the two last Sessions of the Lower House of Assembly, nor those of the late Sitting of the Upper House, are ready to go by this opportunity. The former proceeds from the neglect of Mr Little who was both Speaker & Clerk of that House & who I find has neither copied nor transmitted them to your Lordships, whether through design or otherwise is uncertain. But the Clerk whom I lately appointed promises to be more punctual. The Clerk of the Council engages the same, indeed his Business has been so considerable since I called him to that Office that it was almost impossible for him to keep pace with it especially as he found things there much behind hand. But I hope and conclude this will not be the case for the future as matters are now under a letter regulation.

Before our Assembly rose I received a letter from the Right Honourable William Pitt Esqr. one of His Majesty's principal Secretarys of State directing me to call them together & recommend the raising a considerable body of Troops to be maintained by this Province for its immediate defence, & the assistance of those to the Northward. A Copy of this letter I laid before both Houses, as I was instructed.

Herewith I send your Lordships an Address I received upon that occasion, which is a true picture of the state of this province. The above letter which I conclude was a circular one, however suitable to the circumstances of the other provinces, was certainly improper for us who are daily & with good reason solliciting for Assistance ourselves. This will plainly appear when it is remembered that 'till within these few years the whole people of this Province were maintained at the nations expense.

Provision was served to them out of the public Store & brought from other Countrys for little or none was raised here, nor any other produce, until the admission of Slaves. For the first Settlers were very unfit to establish a Colony, being such whose illness was the cause of their poverty & misfortunes. But since an alteration has been made in the original Constitution framed by the Trustees, many industrious but poor people have come here, constrained by the harshness of their Creditors to quit their former residence & have been labouring ever since under great hardships & difficultys to gain a subsistence & lessen their incumbrances. So that your Lordships will easily distinguish that the circumstances of this Colony are peculiar, both with respect to the smallness of our numbers and our poverty.

I daily have many Indian Guests & some of them of the first rank of the Creek Nation, & by all that I can learn from them, they do not seem disposed to break with us hastily, tho' they are far from being satisfied with what passed at Ogeachy towards the end of Mr Reynolds administration.[22] The Brother of one of those that were then killed, I am informed has lately been to Charlestown to demand further satisfaction, & behaved with uncommon insolence to Governor Lyttleton. Perhaps he will come here upon the same errand, if he does I shall not be over submissive to him, as these rascals are apt to take advantage of the least appearance of pusillanimity.

Besides the handsome fellow who is now with me the Little Warrior lately gone from hence, principal Rulers of the Oakfuschee Town one of the most considerable in the Upper Creek Country, have thrown out some hints that that Nation will not embroil themselves further about this Matter & that a proper talk & a few presents may reconcile every misunderstanding. The chief men among these Savages have not yet come formally & with a national character to treat with me, but I expect them in the beginning of winter, having sent invitations for that purpose.

In regard to the movements of the french I have heard nothing very lately. The Supplies sent a few Months ago to the Mississipi, have not yet had any visiable operation, tho 'tis to be feared they will soon but where or how is uncertain. For some weeks past there have been some french privateers cruizing upon our Coast, who tho' unable to do us much damage have nevertheless given great uneasiness, & kept the Inhabitants of the Southern parts of the Colony constantly under arms.

---

22. On September 3, 1756, Tuckabatchee Creeks stole several horses from a group of English settlers illegally invading the Creek country on the Ogeechee River. In retaliation, settlers pursued the Creeks and killed three of them. Known as "the Ogeechee incident," the affair almost caused an open Creek break with the English. As it was, Creek resentment against the British smoldered for years. See W. S. Jenkins, ed., "South Carolina Book of Indian Affairs, 1710-1760," microfilm, South Carolina Archives Department, Columbia, S.C., V, 176, 207.

My Lords I cannot help again expressing my surprise that one of the Kings Ships is not stationed here as the Enemies Vessels generally make this Coast, being obliged to put into Augustine for intelligence refreshment &c and indeed all their Vessels from their Settlements on the Bay of Mexico, which necessarily come thro' the Gulph of Florida, which of late those from their Islands have done also to avoid our Cruizers cannot well pass above 50 Leagues from our Coast, so that no Station is more proper for annoying the Enemy, if the protection of this Colony was to be no consideration.

The Vessels usually stationed at South Carolina are of no use in this respect. The Harbour of Charlestown has a bar & is beside so shallow & intricate that Ships of burden cannot go out & in with that facility & dispatch which is necessary upon those occasions.

A Schooner of about sixty Tons lately put in here from that place on board whereof I had information there were contraband Goods upon which I ordered the Officers of the Customs to examine her when they found sixty six Barrels of Rice destined for Augustine which being contrary to Law she has been seized and condemned, & I believe will yield about £200 her Owner is here but has made no defence. A few of these Strokes will put a stop to such practices.

I have not yet had the pleasure of one line from your Lordships but I flatter myself I shall soon.

I am very unwilling to apologize to your Lordships for the incorrectness that my present hurry occasions, but the interruption I meet with from these Indian Gentry, a multiplicity of other Business & the sudden departure of the Vessel by whom I send these dispatches, greatly abridges me in point of time, & prevents me from saying many things that the points I touch upon would naturally give rise to.

Henry Ellis to William Pitt, Aug. 1, 1757, Georgia, received Oct. 21, 1757, giving a state of the colony's defenses.

Sir

I had the honour of your letter of the 4th february, & in obedience to it I immediately called our Assembly together & laid the principal matter of it before them & in consequence of which I received a few days after the Address that I have the honour to transmit herewith.

It contains a very true Representation of the State of this Province, & so full a one that I do not know what to add & can only say in general that there is every disposition that could be wished in the people to answer the most sanguine expectations, but they really are incapable of doing more than they have done which tho it may appear inconsiderable is a great deal in their circumstances. They have laid a Tax of 3/ a head upon their Negroes & 2/ upon every 100 Acres of land they are possessed of, the whole of which from the small number of the people will amount to little more than £500. They have also resolved to build five Log Forts in different parts of the province, upon which Themselves & their Negroes are to work Twelve days, which alone is a considerable Tax upon them, & when it is considered Sir that the Poverty of the Colony is such that the Mother Country defrays the expences of this Government, our inability of contributing any thing to the common Cause, will strongly appear.

This Colony has been settled but Twenty five years, & was originally intended to be a receptacle for the poor & our parishes, & Jails, & till within these eight or ten years, the bulk of the people had their provisions served to them out of the publick Store, which expence was annually provided for by Parliament. For by the exclusion of Slaves very little provision, or any other produce was raised here.

Within these few years that Regulation has been broke thro' & several people have come in, but they were such as could live no where else. The greatest part of their Substance they were obliged to sell to pay off part of their Debts, & the remainder they have been labouring under great hardships & difficultys ever since to discharge. Our whole people are only between 4 & 5000 whites, (out of which 700 are capable of bearing arms) & 2000 Negroes. The former in general are so very poor that they but barely subsist themselves. I am confident there are not Ten men in the province that are worth £500 each. So that you will see Sir there is something very peculiar in our case, & that however inclinable our few people might be to give proofs of their zeal & affection, & assistance to the common Cause, it is totally out of their poor [sic].

A few french Privateers have been on our Coast these several days, & have caused great uneasiness to the Inhabitants, who have been constantly under Arms since their appearance, & indeed with good reason as there is nothing to prevent their Landing & plundering those plantations that are situated near the rivers.

It were greatly to be wished that the importance of this Province was more generally attended to for it has certainly all the conveniences & advantages of any of the rest, in respect of Situation & the goodness of its ports greatly exceeds them all. A Ship of War could no where be better stationed for annoying the Enemy, whose Ships from the Islands of late go thro' the Gulph of Florida to avoid our Cruizers, & all their Vessels from their Settlements on the Bay of Mexico, must take the same Track, our vicinity to which would therefore be of great convenience. The ships that are usually stationed at Charlestown are not so well calculated for this Service, as that place is more distant, & the harbour more intricate & shallow than ours.[23] I need not insist here upon the expediency & even necessity of some measures being immediately concerted at home for putting this province in a posture of defence. I think all this will fully appear from the facts set forth, in the Address of our Assembly. But when or how this is to be undertaken we must humbly submit to his Majesty.

We have had no late Accounts here of the Movements of the Enemy, but it is certain they are with much industry practising upon the Savages in our Neighbourhood. It will be a great evil if they can make those impressions upon them that they desire; as they are so warlike & numerous, that they would easily overwhelm this province in its present weak & defenceless condition.

I have several of the principal men of the Creek Nation now with me, & find them pretty well inclined to us, a disposition that I shall strenuously cultivate, as indeed the very being of this Government depends upon it. Not to mention the influence it might have upon our other designs and operations.

The present occasion affords me nothing further.

I have just had the honour of your letter of the 19th february, to which I shall pay all manner of regard, & obedience.

Address of the Upper House and Commons House of Assembly to Henry Ellis, July 28, 1757, Savannah, read Nov. 9, 1757, C.O. 5/646, C. 9, explaining Georgia's defenseless state and its position as a southern barrier to the French, Spanish, and Indians.[24]

---

23. In truth, Savannah's harbor was "more intricate and shallow" than Charleston's, a fact earlier admitted by Ellis.

24. The address is given in CRG, XVI, 236-238.

An Abstract of Grants of Lands Registered in Georgia, Jan. 27 to July 27, 1757, Savannah, received Nov. 9, 1757, C.O. 5/646, C. 10.

Grant dated 9th. Decemr 1756,
To George Golphin [Galphin] for 400 Acres of Land in the District of Augusta, Registered 4th Feby 1757.
Allotted to him by the late President and Assistants.

Grant dated 16th. Decemr 1756,
To Ralph Kilgore for 250 Acres of Land in the District of Augusta, Registered 4th. Febry 1757.
Allotted to him by the late President & assistants.

Grant dated 8th. Septr 1756,
To Christian Robenhorst [Rabenhorst] for 500 Acres of Land in the District of Ebenezer, Registered 4th. Febry 1757.
Allotted to him by the late President and Assistants.

Grant dated 8th. Septr 1757,
To the Heirs of David Kraft deceased for 500 Acres of Land in the District of Ebenezer, Registered 4th. Febry 1757.
Allotted by the late President and Assistants.

Grant dated 8th Septr 1756,
To James Deveaux Esqr: for 1000 Acres of Land being Warsaw Island, Registered 8th. Febry 1757.

Grant dated 8th. Septr 1756,
To James Deveaux Esqr for 500 Acres of Land on Scidoway Island, Registered 8th. Febry 1756.
Allotted him by the Late President & Assistants.

Grant dated 8th. Septr 1756,
To James Deveaux Esqr for 500 Acres of Land on Argyle Island, Registered 8th. Febry 1757.
Allotted by the late President and Assistants.

Grant dated 8th Septr 1756,
To James Deveaux Esqr. for a Lot in the Town of Savannah No 9 in Sloper Tything Percival Ward and 50 Acres of Land in said Tything and Ward, Registered 9th. Febry 1757.

Colonial Records   47

Grant dated 8th. Septr 1756,
To James Deveaux Esqr for 45 Acres of Land in the Township of
Savannah, Registered 10th Febry 1757.

Grant dated 8th. Septr. 1756,
To James Deveaux Esqr for a Town lot in Hardwicke No 28, Registered 10th. Febry 1757.

Grant dated 8th. Septr 1756,
To Samuel Mercer for a Lot in the Town of Hardwicke No 31, Registered 12th. Febry 1757.

Grant dated 8th. Septr 1756,
To Samuel Mercer for a Lot in the Town of Savannah No 9 in Hucks Tything Percival Ward & 50 Acres of Land in said Tything and Ward, Registered 12th. Febry 1757.

Grant dated 8th. Septr 1756,
To Samuel Mercer for 500 Acres of Land in the District of Savannah, Registered 12th. Febry 1757.
Alloted to him by the late President and Assistants.

Grant dated 8th. Septr 1756,
To Elizabeth Mercer for a Lot in the Town of Savannah No 5 in the Third Tything Reynolds Ward and 50 Acres of Land in said Tything and Ward, Registered 12th. Febry 1757.

Grant dated 8th. Septr 1756,
To Elizabeth Mercer for life Remaindr to John Teasdale in fee for a lot in the Town of Savannah No 1 in Wilmington Tything Derby Ward and 50 Acres of Land in said Tything and Ward, Registered 12th. Febry 1757.
Allotted by the late President & Assistants.

Grant dated 9th. Decemr 1756,
To John Teasdale for a Lot in the Town of Savannah No 5 in Carpenter Tything Deckers Ward and 50 Acres of land in said Tything & Ward, Registered 14th. Febry 1757.
Allotted him by the late President & Assistants.

Grant dated 9th. Decemr 1756,
To Benjamin Brownjohn for a Lot in the Town of Savannah No 10 in Hucks Tything Percival Ward and 50 Acres of Land in said

Tything & Ward, Registered 14th. Febry 1757.
Allotted by the late President and Assistants.

Grant dated 8th. Septr 1756,
To the Heirs of William Cross deceased for a Lot in the Town of
Savannah No 7 in the second Tything Anson Ward and 50 Acres
of Land in said Tything and Ward, Registered 14th. Febry 1757.
Allotted by the late President and Assistants.

Grant dated 8th. Septr 1756,
To Elizabeth Evans for a Lot in the Town of Savannah No 3 in Carpenters Tything Deckers Ward and 50 Acres of Land in said
Tything and Ward, Registered 14th. Febry 1757.
Allotted by the late President and Assistants.

Grant dated 9th. Decemr 1756,
To Elizabeth and Jane Evans for a Lot in the Town of Savannah
No 7 in the Third Tything Anson Ward and 50 Acres of Land in
said Tything and Ward, Registered 14th. Febry 1757.
Allotted by the President and Assistants.

Grant dated 5th. Febry 1757,
To Samuel Mercer for 300 Acres of Land in the District of Savannah, Registered 15th. Febry 1757.

Grant dated 9th. Decemr 1756,
To Patrick Mackay for 600 Acres of Land in the District of Savannah, Registered 22d. Febry 1757.
Allotted to him by the late President and Assistants.

Grant dated 9th. Decer 1756,
To Patrick Mackay for 600 Acres of Land in the District of Savannah, Registered 22d Febry 1757.
Allotted by the late President and Assistants to John Mackay.

Grant dated 9th. Decemr 1756,
To Patrick Mackay for a Lot in the Town of Savannah No 5 in
Digby Tything Deckers Ward and 50 Acres of Land in said
Tything and Ward, Registered 22nd. Febry 1757.
Allotted to him by the late President and Assistants.

Grant dated 5th. Febry 1757,
To John Graves for 500 Acres of Land at the head of Newport
River, Registered 24th. Febry 1757.

Colonial Records 49

Grant dated 5th. Febry 1757,
To Mathias Brandner for Town Lot Garden Lot & 100 Acres of
Land in the Township & district of Ebenezer, Registered 24th.
Febry 1757.
Allotted to him by the late President and Assistants.

Grant dated 5th. Febry 1757,
To Thomas Bailey for 300 Acres of Land in the District of Savannah, Registered 24th Feby 1757.

Grant dated 11th. Febry 1757,
To Benjamin Farley for 350 Acres of Land in the District of Newport, Registered 24th Febry 1757.

Grant dated 9th. Decemr 1756,
To James Read for 500 Acres of Land on Great Ogechee River,
Registered 25th Febry 1757.
Allotted by the late President & Assistants to Richard Ion's.

Grant dated 11th. Febry 1757,
To James Read for 275 Acres of Land in the District of Newport,
Registered 25th. Febry 1757.

Grant dated 5th Febry 1757,
To James Habersham Esqr for 300 Acres of Land in the District
of Ogechee, Registered 25th. Febry 1757.

Grant dated 9th. Decemr 1756,
To Francis Harris Esqr. for 500 Acres of Land in the District of
Savannah, Registered 26th Febry 1757.

Grant dated 9th. Decemr 1756,
To John Bailey for 500 Acres of Land in the District of Ogechee,
Registered 26th. Febry 1757.
Allotted by the late President and Assistants.

Grant dated 9th Decemr 1756,
To John Bailey for a Water Lot on the Bay of Savannah No 2,
Registered 26th. Febry 1757.
Allotted by the late President and Assistants.

Grant dated 11th. Febry 1757,
To Hugh Clark for 500 Acres of Land in the District of Sappola,

Registered 26th. Febry 1757.
Allotted to him by the late President & Assistants.

Grant dated 11th. Febry 1757,
To William Clark for 500 Acres of Land in the District of Sappola, Registered 26th. Febry 1757.
Allotted to him by the late President and Assistants.

Grant dated 11th. Febry 1757,
To Donald Mackay for 250 Acres of Land in the District of Newport, Registered 28th Febry. 1757.
Allotted to him by the late President and Assistants.

Grant dated 11th. Febry 1757,
To John Mackintosh M for 150 Acres of Land in the District of Darian, Registered 28th. Febry 1757.
Allotted to him by the late President & Assistants.

Grant dated 11th. Febry 1757,
To William Mackintosh for 500 Acres of Land in the District of Newport, Registered 28th. Febry 1757.
Allotted to him by the late President and Assistants.

Grant dated 11th. Febry 1757,
To Lauchlan Mackintosh for 500 Acres of Land in the District of Newport, Registered 28th. Febry 1757.
Allotted to him by the late President and Assistants.

Grant dated 11th. Febry 1757,
To John Mackintosh D for 434 Acres of Land in the District of Sappola, Registered 28th. Febry 1757.
Allotted to him by the late President and Assistants.

Grant dated 11th. Febry 1757,
To George Mackintosh for 500 Acres of Land in the District of Darian, Registered 28th. Febry 1757.
Allotted to him by the late President and Assistants.

Grant dated 8th. September 1756,
To James Mackay Esqr for 650 Acres of Land at the head of Newport River, Registered 1st March 1757.

Grant dated 8th. Septr: 1756,
To James Mackay Esqr for 500 Acres of Land on the South side of
Great Ogechee River, Registred 1st March 1757.
Allotted to him by the late President and Assistants.

Grant dated 8th. Sepr. 1756,
To James Mackay Esqr for 50 Acres of Land being part of an Island
in St Catherine River, Registered 1st March 1757.

Grant dated 8th. Septr 1756,
To Hugh Mackay for 500 Acres of Land in the District of Great
Ogechee, Registered 1st March 1757.
Allotted to him by the late President and Assistants.

Grant dated Sepr 8th. 1756,
To David Stephens for a Lot in the Town of Hardwicke, No 55,
Registered 1st March 1757.

Grant dated 8th. Septr 1756,
To John Savage in Trust for Ann the Wife of James Mackay 500
Acres of Land in the District of Great Ogechee, Registered
2nd. March 1757.
Allotted by the late President and Assistants.

Grant dated 8th. Septr 1756,
To William Elliott for 500 Acres of Land in the District of Newport, Registered 2d March 1757.

Grant dated 8th. Septr 1756,
To William Elliott for 500 Acres of Land in the Forks of the Rivers
Ogechee and Coonoche, Registered 2nd. March 1757.

Grant dated 8th. Septr 1756,
To William Elliott for 500 Acres of Land in the District of Great
Ogechee, Registered 2d March 1757.
Allotted to him by the late President and Assistants.

Grant datod 8th. Scptr 1756,
To William Elliott for a Lot in the Town of Hardwicke No 1,
Registered 2d March 1757.
Allotted to him by the late President & Assistants.

Grant dated 8th. Sepr 1756,
To David Truan for 135 Acres of Land in the Township of Savannah, Registered 4th. March 1757.
Allotted by the late President and Assistants.

Grant dated 8th. Septr 1756,
To Edward Chapman and Jane his Wife in Trust for the Heirs of William Grigson deceased a lot in The Town of Savannah No 7 in Holland Tything Percival Ward & 50 Acres of Land in said Tything and Ward, Registered 4th. March 1757.
Allotted by the late President and Assistants.

Grant dated 8th. Septr 1756,
To Davis T. Bear for 50 Acres of Land in the Township of Vernonburgh, Registered 4th. March 1757.
Allotted to him by the late President and Assistants.

Grant dated 8th. Septr 1756,
To Parmenus Way for 300 Acres of Land in the district of Midway, Registered 7th. March 1757.

Grant dated 8th. Septr 1756,
To Nathaniel Wey [Way] for 500 Acres of Land in the District of Midway, Registered 7th March 1757.
Allotted to him by the late President and Assistants.

Grant dated 8th. Septr 1756,
To John Osgood John Stevens &c for 300 Acres of Land in the District of Midway, Registered 7th. March 1757.
Allotted to him by the late President and Assistants.

Grant dated 8th. Septr 1756,
To James Edward Powell Esqr for 470 Acres of Land in the District of Savannah, Registered 7th. March 1757.
Allotted by the late President and Assistants.

Grant dated 8th. Septr 1756,
To Christian Reidelsperger for 200 Acres of Land between Abercorn & Ebenezer, Registered 7th. March 1757.
Allotted to him by the late President and Assistants.

Grant dated 5th. Febry 1757,
To Mathew Mauve for a lot in the Town of Savannah No 8 in the

1st Tything Anson Ward and 50 Acres of Land in said Tything
and Ward, Registered 14th March 1757.
Allotted to him by the late President and Assistants.

Grant dated 5th. Febry 1757,
To Robert Bolton for a lot in the Town of Savannah No 3 in the
Third Tything Anson Ward and 50 Acres of Land in said Tything
and Ward, Registered 14th. March 1757.
Allotted to him by the late President and Assistants.

Grant dated 9th. Decemr 1756,
To Joseph Gibbons for 600 Acres of Land in the District of Newport, Registered 22d March 1757.

Grant dated 9th. Decemr 1756,
To Joseph Gibbons for 500 Acres of Land in the District of Newport, Registered 22d March 1757.

Grant dated 9th. Decemr 1756,
To Andrew Way for 500 Acres of Land in the District of Newport, Registered 22nd March 1757.

Grant dated 5th April 1757,
To Joseph Minis for a Lot in the Town of Hardwicke No 99, Registered 8th. April 1757.

Grant dated 5th. Febry 1757,
To John McClellan for 750 Acres of Land in the District of Ogechee, Registered 11th. April 1757.

Grant dated 11th. Febry. 1757,
To John Smith for 500 Acres of Land in the District of Savannah, Registered 11th. April 1757.

Grant dated 5th. Febry 1757,
To John Burton for a lot in the Town of Savannah No 3 in the first
Tything Anson Ward & 50 Acres of Land in said Tything and
Ward, Registred 11th. April 1757.
Allotted to him by the late President and Assistants.

Grant dated 5th. April 1757,
To William Burton for a Lot in the Town of Savannah No 5 in the
first Tything Anson Ward & 50 Acres of Land in said Tything

& Ward, Registered 11th. April 1757.
Allotted to him by the late President and Assistants.

Grant dated 5th. April 1757,
To Christian Rabenhorst, Ludwig Meyer &c for 100 Acres of Land in the District of Ebenezer, Registred 14th. April 1757.
Allotted to him by the late President and Assistants.

Grant dated 5th. April 1757,
To Michael Weber for 50 Acres of Land in the District of Abercorn & Goshen, Registred 14th. April 1757.
Allotted to him by the late President and Assistants.

Grant dated 5th. April 1757,
To Christian Birk for a Garden Lot & 50 Acres of Land in the Township & District of Ebenezer, Registred 14th. April 1757.
Allotted to him by the late President and Assistants.

Grant dated 5th. April 1757,
To Thomas Goswandel for Town Lot Garden Lot & 50 Acres of Land in the Township & District of Ebenezer, Registered 14th. April 1757.
Allotted to him by the late President and Assistants.

Grant dated 5th. April 1757,
To Simon Reutter for Town Lot Garden Lot and 50 Acres of Land in the Township & District of Ebenezer, Registered 15th. April 1757.
Allotted to him by the late President and Assistants.

Grant dated 5th. Feby 1757,
To Ludwig Weidman for 50 Acres of Land in the District of Ebenezer, Registered 16th. April 1757.
Allotted to him by the late President & Assistants.

Grant dated 5th. April 1757,
To Hannah Elizth. Gronou & Mary Frederica Gronou for a Town Lot & 6 Garden Lots in the Township and District of Ebenezer, Registered 16th. April 1757.
Allotted by the late President and Assistants.

Grant dated 5th. April 1757,
To John Cornberger for a Town Lot & 100 Acres of Land in the Town

Colonial Records 55

and District of Ebenezer, Registered 18th. April 1757.
Allotted to him by the late President and Assistants.

Grant dated 5th. April 1757,
To Christian Leimberger for a Town Lot & 100 Acres of Land in the Town & District of Ebenezer, Registred 18th. April 1757.
Allotted to him by the late President and Assistants.

Grant dated 5th. April 1757,
To Christian Stainer for a Town Lot Garden Lot & 100 Acres of Land in the Town & District of Ebenezer, Registred 18th. April 1757.
Allotted to him by the late President and Assistants.

Grant dated 5th. April 1757,
To James Gallache for a Lot in the Town of Savannah No 10 in the fourth Tything Anson Ward and 95 Acres of Land in said Tything and Ward, Registred 20th. April 1757.
Allotted to him by the late President and Assistants.

Grant dated 5th. Febry 1757,
To the Reverend Bartholomew Zouberbuhler for 300 Acres of Land in the District of Savannah, Registred 22nd April 1757.

Grant dated 9th. Decemr 1756,
To Mary Bateman for 300 Acres of Land in the District of Newport, Registered 22d April 1757.

Grant dated 5th. April 1757,
To Nathan Levi for a Lot in the Town of Hardwicke No 18, Registred 25th. April 1757.

Grant dated 5th. April 1757,
To Grey Elliott for a Lot in the Town of Hardwicke No 157, Registered 25th. April 1757.

Grant dated 11th. Feby 1757,
To Christian Vanmunch for 500 Acres of Land on Savannah River, Registred 25th. April 1757.
Allotted to him by the late President and Assistants.

Grant dated 11th. Febry 1757,
To Christian Vanmunch for 50 Acres of Land at the head of

Augustine Creek, Registred 28th. April 1757.
Allotted to him by the late President and Assistants.

Grant dated 11th. Febry 1757,
To Thomas Vanmunch for 500 Acres of Land on Augustine Creek,
Registred 28th April 1757.
Allotted to him by the late President and Assistants.

Grant dated 11th. Febry 1757,
To Charles Vanmunch for 500 Acres of Land on an Island in the
River Savannah, Registred 28th April 1757.
Allotted to him by the late President and Assistants.

Grant dated 5th. April 1757,
To George Heckall for a Town Lot and 50 Acres of Land in the Town
and District of Ebenezer, Registred 29th April 1757.
Allotted to him by the late President and Assistants.

Grant dated 5th. April 1757,
To Michael Snyder for 50 Acres of Land in the District of Ebenezer,
Registered 29th April 1757.
Allotted to him by the late President and Assistants.

Grant dated 5th. April 1757,
To John Michael Herse for 50 Acres of Land in the District of
Ebenezer, Registered 29th. April 1757.
Allotted to him by the late President and Assistants.

Grant dated 9th. Decr 1756,
To Samuel Burnley for 300 Acres of Land in the District of Newport, Registered 4th. May 1757.

Grant dated 5th. April 1757,
To Henry Younge for 300 Acres of Land in the District of Midway,
Registred 4th. May 1757.
Allotted to him by the late President and Assistants.

Grant Dated 5th. April 1757,
To John McIntosh M for 350 Acres of Land in the District of Sap-
pola, Registred 4th. May 1757.
Allotted to him by the late President and Assistants.

Colonial Records 57

Grant dated 5th. April 1757,
To John MacBean for 100 Acres of Land in the District of Darian,
Registred 5th. May 1757.
Allotted to him by the late President and Assistants.

Grant dated 5th. April 1757,
To Thomas Carter for 100 Acres of Land in the District of Newport,
Registred 5th. May 1757.

Grant dated 5th. April 1757,
To Anne Graham for a Lot in the Town of Hardwicke No 44, Registred 23rd May 1757.
Allotted by the late President and Assistants.

Grant dated 5th. April 1757,
To Anne Graham for a Lot in the Town of Savannah No 9 in the third Tything Reynolds Ward and 50 Acres of Land in said Tything and Ward, Registered 23rd May 1757.
Allotted by the late President and Assistants.

Grant dated 5th. April 1757,
To Anne Graham for a Lot in the Town of Savannah No 5 in Wilmington Tything Derby Ward and 50 Acres of Land in said Tything and Ward, Registered 23rd May 1757.
Allotted by the said President and Assistants.

Grant dated 5th. April 1757,
To Anne Graham for 600 Acres of Land in the District of Savannah, Registred 25th. May 1757.
Allotted by the late President and Assistants.

Grant dated 5th. April 1757,
To Veit Leckner for a Town Lot and 150 Acres of Land in the Town and District of Ebenezer, Registred 25th May 1757.
Allotted to him by the late President and Assistants.

Grant dated 5th. April 1757,
To John George Snyder for a Town Lot and 50 Acres of Land in the Town and District of Ebenezer, Registered 25th. May 1757.
Allotted to him by the late President and Assistants.

Grant dated 9th. Decemr 1756,
To James Whitefield for 300 Acres of Land in the District of Ogechee, Registred 26th. May 1757.

Grant dated 9th. Decemr 1756,
To George Love for 500 Acres of Land in the District of Newport, Registered 30th. May 1757.

Grant dated 9th. Decemr 1756,
To George Love for a Lot in the Town of Hardwicke No 145, Registred 30th. May 1757.

Grant dated 5th. April 1757,
To Christopher Cramer for Town Lot Garden Lot and 100 Acres of Land in the Township of Ebenezer, Registered 2d June 1757. Allotted to him by the late President and Assistants.

Grant dated 5th. April 1757,
To Frederick Bruckner for Town Lot Garden Lot and 100 Acres of Land in the Town and District of Ebenezer, Registred 2d June 1757.
Allotted to him by the late President and Assistants.

Grant dated 5th. April 1757,
To Daniel Shubdrien for Town Lot Garden Lot and 100 Acres of Land in the Town and District of Ebenezer, Registred 4th. June 1757.
Allotted by the late President and Assistants.

Grant dated 5th. April 1757,
To Veit Landferder for Town Lot Garden Lot and 50 Acres of Land in the Town and district of Ebenezer, Registered 4th. June 1757. Allotted by the late President and Assistants.

Grant dated 9th. Decemr 1757,
To John Spencer for 500 Acres of Land in the District of Newport, Registred 6th. June 1757.

Grant dated 9th. Decemr 1756,
To Maurice Dullea for 200 Acres of Land in the District of Midway, Registered 6th. June 1757.

Grant dated 5th. April 1757,
To James Mackay Esqr for 500 Acres of Land in the District of Newport, Registered 8th. June 1757.

Grant dated 5th. April 1757,
To James Mackay Esqr for 200 Acres of Land in the District of Ogechee, Registred 8th. June 1757.

Grant dated 5th. April 1757,
To White Outerbridge for 500 Acres of Land in the District of Newport, Registered 10th. June 1757.

Grant dated 5th. April 1757,
To White Outerbridge for a Lot in the Town of Hardwicke No 20, Registered 10th. June 1757.

Grant dated 5th. April 1757,
To George Cuthbert for 100 Acres of Land in the District of Savannah, Registred 11th. June 1757.

Grant dated 7th. June 1757,
To Kenneth Bailey for 500 Acres of Land in the District of Midway, Registred 13th. June 1757.
Allotted to him by the late President and Assistants.

Grant dated 5th. Feby 1757,
To Kenneth Bailey for 350 Acres of Land in the District of Midway, Registred 13th. June 1757.

Grant dated 5th. April 1757,
To Philip Fenny for 500 Acres of Land in the District of Newport, Registred 13th. June 1757.

Grant dated 7th. June 1757,
To Charles Weste for 300 Acres of Land in the District of Newport, Registred 15th. June 1757.

Grant dated 7th. June 1757,
To Charles Weste for a Lot in the Town of Hardwicke No 7, Registered 15th. June 1757.

Grant dated 16th. Decemr 1756,
To Alexander Wylly for a Town Lot and 50 Acres of Land in the Town and District of Savannah, Registred 15th. June 1757.

Grant dated 5th. April 1757,
To Joseph Masey for 500 Acres of Land in the District of Newport, Registred 28th June 1757.

Grant dated 5th. April 1757,
To Anne Hopkins for 500 Acres of Land in the District of Hallifax,
Registred 28th. June 1757.
Allotted by the late President and Assistants.

Grant dated 5th. April 1757,
To Joseph Butler Senr for 500 Acres of Land in the District of
Ogechee, Registred 14th July 1757.
Allotted by the late President and Assistants.

Grant dated 5th. April 1757,
To Joseph Butler Senr for 500 Acres of Land in the District of
Ogechee, Registred 14th. July 1757.
Allotted by the late President and Assistants.

Grant dated 5th. April 1757,
To Joseph Butler Senr for 500 Acres of Land in the District of
Ogechee, Registred 16th July 1757.
Allotted by the late President and Assistants.

Grant dated 5th. April 1757,
To Joseph Butler Senr for 300 Acres of Land in the District of
Ogechee, Registred 16th. July 1757.
Allotted by the late President and Assistants.

Grant dated 5th. April 1757,
To Joseph Butler Senr for 300 Acres of Land in the District of
Ogechee, Registred 16th. July 1757.

Grant dated 5th. April 1757,
To Joseph Butler Senr for 140 Acres of Land in the District of
Ogechee, Registred 16th. July 1757.

Grant dated 5th. April 1757,
To Joseph Butler Senr for a Lot in the Town of Hardwicke No 96,
Registred 18th. July 1757.
Allotted to him by the late President and Assistants.

Grant dated 5th. April 1757,
To Joseph Butler Junr for 500 Acres of Land in the District of
Ogechee, Registred 18th. July 1757.

Grant dated 5th. April 1757,
To Joseph Butler Junr for 500 Acres of Land in the District of
Ogechee, Registred 18th July 1757.

Grant dated 5th. April 1757,
To Joseph Butler Junr for a Lot in the Town of Hardwicke No 115,
Registred 18th. July 1757.

Grant dated 5th. April 1757,
To Shem Butler for 500 Acres of Land in the District of Ogechee,
Registred 18th. July 1757.

Grant dated 5th. April 1757,
To Charles Zigmund Ott for a Garden Lot and 50 Acres of Land in
the District of Ebenezer, Registred 20th. July 1757.
Allotted by the late President and Assistants.

Grant dated 5th. April 1757,
To Daniel Burgstainer for a Town Lot and 50 Acres of Land in the
Township of Ebenezer, Registred 20th. July 1757.
Allotted to him by the late President & Assistants.

Grant dated 5th. April 1757,
To George Swijger [Swyger] for Town Lot Garden Lot and 50 Acres
of Land in the Township of Ebenezer, Registred 20th. July
1757.
Allotted to him by the late President & Assistants.

Grant dated 7th. June 1757,
To Christian Rabenhorst for 3 Town Lots in the Town of Ebenezer,
Registred 22nd July 1757.
Allotted to him by the late President & Assistants.

Grant dated 7th. June 1757,
To Kenneth Bailey for 500 Acres of Land in the District of Midway,
Registred 22d July 1757.
Allotted by the late President and Assistants.

Grant dated 7th. June 1757,
To Joseph Atkinson for 200 Acres of Land in the District of
Augusta, Registred 22nd July 1757.

Grant dated 5th. April 1757,
To John Petitcrew for 200 Acres of Land in the District of Augusta, Registred 22d July 1757.

Grant dated 5th. Feby 1757,
To William Newberry for 500 Acres of Land in the District of Augusta, Registred 22d July 1757.

Grant dated 7th. July 1757,
To Elizabeth Hunold for life and to the Heirs of John Hunold at her decease 50 Acres of Land in the District of Ebenezer, Registred 22d July 1757.

Grant dated 7th. June 1757,
To John Davis Senr for 450 Acres of Land in the District of Newport, Registred 25th. July 1757.

Grant dated 7th. June 1757,
To John Davis Junr for 500 Acres of Land on the Island of Skidoway, Registred 25th. July 1757.
Allotted by the late President and Assistants.

Grant dated 7th. June 1757,
To John Davis Senr for a Lot in the Town of Hardwicke No 100, Registred 25th. July 1757.

Grant dated 7th. June 1757,
To John Davis for 500 Acres of Land in the District of Midway, Registred 25th. July 1757.
Allotted to him by the late President & Assistants.

Grant dated 7th. June 1757,
To William Davis for 200 Acres of Land in the District of Newport, Registred 25th. July 1757.

Grant dated 7th. June 1757,
To John Todd Junr for 100 Acres of Land in the District of Newport, Registred 25th. July 1757.
Allotted to him by the late President and Assistants.

Grant dated 7th. June 1757,
To John Martin Bolzius for 2 Town Lots and 100 Acres of Land in the Town and District of Ebenezer, Registred 25th. July 1757.
Allotted by the late President and Assistants.

AN ABSTRACT of all the Grants Registred in the Province of Georgia from 27th. January to 27 July 1757. Examined and compared with the original Register at Savannah this 29th. day of July 1757.

> PAT: HOUSTOUN, Register.

A True Copy of a Form for Granting Land in Georgia, July 29, 1757, received Nov. 9, 1757, enclosed with abstract of grants, C.O. 5/646, C. 10.

George the Second by the Grace of God of Great Britain France and Ireland King Defender of the Faith and so forth; To all to whom these presents shall come greeting. Know ye that we of our special grace certain knowledge and mere motion have given and granted and by these presents for us our heirs and successors Do give and grant unto   his heirs or Assigns all that Tract of Land containing   Acres situate and being in the District of   in our Province of Georgia bounded   having such shape form and marks as appears by a Plat thereof hereunto annexed together with all woods under woods Timber and Timber Trees Lakes Ponds Fishings waters Water courses profits commodities Hereditaments and appurtenances whatsoever thereunto belonging or in any wise appertaining together also with privilege of hunting hawking and fowling in and upon the same and all mines and minerals whatsoever saving and reserving nevertheless to us our heirs and successors all White Pine Trees if any should be found growing thereon and also saving and reserving unto us our heirs and successors One tenth part of Mines of Silver and Gold only To have and to hold the said Tract of   Acres of Land and all and singular other the premises hereby granted with the appurtenances unto the said   his heirs and assigns for ever in fee and common Soccage he the said   his heirs or assigns yielding and paying therefore unto us our heirs and successors or to our Receiver General for the time being or to his deputy or deputies for the time being yearly and every year on the twenty fifth day of March at the rate of Two shillings Sterling for every hundred Acres and so in proportion according to the quantity of Acres contained herein the same to commence at the end and expiration of two years from the date hereof Provided always and this present Grant is upon condition nevertheless that he the said   his

heirs or assigns shall and do within three years after the date
hereof for every 50 Acres of Plantable Land hereby granted clear
and work three Acres at least in that part thereof as he or they
shall judge most convenient and advantageous or else do clear
and drain three Acres of Swamp or sunken grounds or drain three
Acres of Marsh if any such contained herein and shall and do
within the time aforesaid put and keep upon every fifty Acres
thereof accounted barren three Neat Cattle or six sheep or goats
and continue the same thereon until three Acres for every fifty
Acres be fully cleared and improved or otherwise if any part of
the said Tract shall be stony or rocky ground and not fit for
planting or pasture shall and do within three years as aforesaid
begin to employ thereon and so continue to work for three years
then next ensuing in digging any stone quarry or Coal or other
Mine one good and able hand for every hundred Acres it shall be
accounted a sufficient cultivation and improvement Provided also
that every three Acres which shall be cleared and worked or
cleared and drained as aforesaid shall be accounted a sufficient
Seating Planting Cultaivation and improvement to save for ever
from forfeiture fifty Acres of Land in any part of the Tract hereby
granted and the said   his heirs and assigns shall be at
liberty to withdraw his or their stock or to forbear working in
any quarry or mine in proportion to such cultivation and improvement as shall be made upon the plantable Lands Swamps sunken
grounds or marshes herein contained and if the said RENT hereby
reserved shall happen to be in arrear and unpaid for the space of
one year from the time it shall become due and no distress can
be found on the said lands Tenements and hereditaments hereby
granted that then and in such case the said lands tenements and
hereditaments hereby granted and every part and parcel thereof
shall revert to us our heirs and Successors as fully and absolutely as if the same had never been granted Provided also if this
Grant shall not be duly registered in the Registers Office of our
said Province within six Months from the date hereof and a Docquet thereof also entered in the Auditors Office of the same (in
case such Establishment shall hereafter take place) that then
this Grant shall be void anything herein contained to the contrary
notwithstanding Given under the Broad Seal of our Province of
Georgia Witness our trusty and well beloved Henry Ellis Esquire
our Lieutenant Governor and Commander in chief in and over our
said Province the   day of   in the year of our Lord
       and in the   year of our Reign.

PAT: HOUSTOUN, Register.

Colonial Records 65

A True Copy of a Form for Granting Land in the Township of Savannah, July 29, 1757, received Nov. 9, 1757, enclosed with abstract of grants, C.O. 5/646, C. 10.

George the Second by the Grace of God of Great Britain France and Ireland King Defender of the Faith and so forth; To all to whom these Presents shall come Greeting. Know ye that we of our Special Grace certain knowledge and mere Motion have given and Granted and by these Presents for us our heirs and Successors do give and grant unto   his heirs and assigns all that Town Lot known by the Number   in the first Tything Anson Ward in the Town of Savannah in our Province of Georgia containing sixty feet in front and ninety feet in depth and all that Garden Lot thereto belonging containing five Acres situate East of the said Town and known by the number   and also all that farm Lot to the said Town Lot and Garden Lot laid out and belonging containing forty five Acres and known by the Number   having such shape form and marks as appears by a Plat thereof hereunto annexed together with all woods underwoods Timber and Timber Trees Lakes Ponds Fishings waters Watercourses Profits Commodities Hereditaments and appurtenances whatsoever thereunto belonging or in anywise appertaining together also with Privilege of hunting hawking and fowling in and upon the same and all mines and minerals whatsoever saving and reserving nevertheless to us our heirs and Successors all white Pine Trees if any should be found growing thereon and also saving and reserving unto us our heirs and successors one tenth part of Mines of Silver and Gold only To have and to hold the said Town Lot Garden Lot and Farm Lot and all and singular other the premises hereby granted with the appurtenances unto the said   his heirs and assigns for ever in free and common soccage he the said   his heirs or assigns Yielding and paying therefore unto us our heirs and successors or to our Receiver General for the time being or to his deputy or deputies for the time being yearly and every year on the twenty fifth day of March at the rate of two shillings sterling for an hundred Acres and so in proportion according to the quantity of Acres contained herein the same to commence at the end and expiration of two years from the date hereof Provided always and this present grant is upon condition nevertheless that he the said   his heirs or assigns shall and do within three years after the date of these presents erect and build or cause to be erected and built on the said Town Lot hereby granted one good dwelling house after the usual manner

of building in our said Province containing at least 20 feet in
length and sixteen feet in breadth and also shall and do put and
keep upon the land hereby granted three Neat Cattle or six Sheep
or Goats or otherwise to clear and work three Acres in that part
thereof as he or they shall judge most convenient and advantageous and if the said Rent hereby reserved shall happen to be in
arrear and unpaid for the space of one year from the time it shall
become due and no distress can be found on the said Lands Tenements and hereditaments hereby granted that then and in such case
the said Lands Tenements and hereditaments hereby granted and
every part and parcel thereof shall revert to us our heirs and successors as fully and absolutely as if the same had never been
granted Provided also if this Grant shall not be duly registered
in the Register's Office of our said Province within six Months
from the date hereof and a Docquet thereof also entered in the
Auditors Office of the same (in case such establishment shall
hereafter take place) that then this Grant shall be void any thing
herein contained to the contrary notwithstanding Given under the
Broad Seal of our Province of Georgia Witness our Trusty and well
beloved Henry Ellis Esqr our Lieutenant Governor and Commander
in Chief in and over our said Province the   day of
in the year of our Lord   and in the year of our Reign

           PAT HOUSTOUN, Register.

A True Copy of a Form for Granting Land in the Town of Hardwick,
July 29, 1757, received Nov. 9, 1757, enclosed with abstract
of grants, C.O. 5/646, C. 10.

 George the Second by the Grace of God of Great Britain France
and Ireland King Defender of the Faith and so forth; To all to
whom these Presents shall come greeting. Know ye that we of
our special grace certain knowledge and meer Motion have given
and granted and by these presents for us our heirs and Successors
Do give and grant unto   his heirs and assigns all that
Town Lot in the Town of Hardwicke in our Province of Georgia
known by the number   bounded as in and by the Certificate hereunto annexed under the hands of our Surveyors General
of Lands in our said Province may more fully appear and contains
in width Seventy Six feet and an half and an hundred thirteen feet
and an half in depth To have and to hold the said Town lot hereby

granted with the appurtenances together with all Trees thereon growing or being ways waters passages privileges and appurtenances whatsoever to the said lot belonging or in any wise appertaining unto the said   his heirs and assigns for ever in free and common Soccage he the said   his heirs or assigns Yielding and paying for the said Town Lot unto us our heirs and successors Yearly and every Year one peppercorn if demanded Provided always and this present Grant is upon condition nevertheless that the said   his heirs or assigns shall within two years next after the date of these presents erect and build upon the said lot hereby granted one good sufficient tennantable house with one Brick Chimney at least and if it shall happen that the said   his heirs or assigns shall neglect to build a house as aforesaid upon the Lot hereby granted then and in that case the said   his heirs and assigns shall forfeit and pay unto us our heirs and successors the sum of one pound sterling money yearly and every year for not building upon the said Lot as aforesaid until such house shall be completely finished and also if the said   his heirs or assigns shall not within the space of ten years from the date hereof erect and build an house upon the said Lot according to the dimensions aforesaid that then the said Lot hereby granted not being build upon as aforesaid shall revert to us our heirs and successors as fully and absolutely to all intents and purposes as if the same had never been granted Provided also if this Grant shall not be duly registered in the Register's Office of our said Province within six Months from the date hereof and a Docquet thereof also entered in the Auditors Office of the same (in case such establishment shall hereafter take place) that then this Grant shall be void anything herein contained to the contrary notwithstanding Given under the Broad Seal of our Province of Georgia Witness our trusty and well beloved Henry Ellis Esquire our Lieutenant Governor and Commander in Chief in and over our said Province the   day of   in the Year of our Lord   and in the   year of our Reign.

PAT: HOUSTOUN, Register.

Henry Ellis to the Earl of Holderness, Sept. 20, 1757, Georgia, received March 27, 1758, acknowledging new instructions to be given to captains of privateers not to attack Spanish ships and giving some comments on English-Creek relations in wartime.

My Lord

By Your Lordship's Letter of the 20th May inclosing an Extract of a Letter from Vice Admiral Townsend, & some Affidavits thereunto annexed, I am made acquainted with the pyratical Proceedings of the Commanders of some of our Privateers towards the King of Spains Subjects. His Majesty's Commands in consequence of them, I shall shew the utmost regard to by doing everything in my power to bring such notorious Offenders to justice, should they put into any port of this Province. The additional printed Instructions for the direction of the Captains of Privateers, I shall distribute as occasion offers, & strongly insist upon the rigour with which the breach of them will be punished.

I have nothing to add My Lord but that this Colony at present enjoys perfect tranquillity. The Creek Indians have been dissatisfied with us, but I flatter myself that some steps which we have taken, & others that we intend to take at a Congress that I expect soon to hold with them, will reconcile every misunderstanding, tho' it may be proper to observe to Your Lordship that the french have acquired such ascendency over those Savages owing to our negligence in times of peace, that it will scarce be possible to effect more than to keep them quiet during the War. There is a necessity for giving constant attention to these people, the uniform conduct of the french in this respect deserves our imitation. Some of the Indians have told me that the English are kind to them only in time of War, in which there may be some truth. Your Lordship may be assured that I am thoroughly sensible how necessary it is to stand well with these people at this juncture, and that I will strenuously exert myself in every measure conducive to that end.

Henry Ellis to the Board of Trade, Sept. 20, 1757, Savannah, read Feb. 22, 1758, C.O. 5/646, C. 12, giving an account of Indian affairs since his last letter.

My Lords

The last letter I did myself the honor to write to your Lordships was of the 1st of August accompanied by several other dispatches. I now transmit all the public papers that are ready together with a list of them and of those above.

Since my last I had an interview at Port Royal with Governor Lyttleton and Colonel Bouquet, the Commander of the forces in the Southern provinces where the plan of our future proceedings with the Indians and many other matters of less moment were settled, Besides concerting the best measures we could devise for our common safety. Mr Lyttleton is solicitous that his Government should have the Lead in all Indian Negotiations, a point that I very willingly yield to him, for I shall be sufficiently happy if the object of them is obtained without concerning myself about preeminence. It is therefore fixed that the Indian Chiefs of the Creek Nation visit them before they come here & this is not improper considering the superior ability of that Colony to provide amply for them, & the number of troops that are now there which will impress a stronger idea of our power than anything that could be seen here, tho' this Province is in a better condition at present, than it has been at any time since the reduction of General Oglethorpe's Regiment. Four of Five forts of earth and Wood are built and building in different Districts, & this Town is now inclosed in the manner I described in my last letter. Several small cannon that were buried in the Sand I have raised and mounted the greatest part on Carriages as I intend to do the rest.

Lord Loudoun has authorized me to keep the Troop of Rangers on foot that Mr Reynolds began to levy until His Majesty's pleasure concerning them shall be known. Besides Colonel Bouquet on my application has spared us 100 of the Provincial Troops of Virginia who are Quartered in this Town. The Rangers have posted near the Great Indian Pass upon the Ogechee River, with orders to make themselves perfectly acquainted with the Country, and to raise a strong intrenchment round their Camp. These are all the Military dispositions our circumstances will allow us to make. The last accounts we had from the Indian Countrys contain nothing unusual. Some of those people are inclined to the French, others to us, whence I am willing to conclude that as long as that different sentiments subsist we shall not be in much danger of an attack from that quarter, tho' the french employ every art to bring it about. Scarce a week passes but I have indian visitants who, not coming under a national character, I can only talk with them upon general topics. The substance of our conversation your Lordships will find in the Minutes of Council. There are many that we use no formalities to, and with whom I have often conferences at my own house where I always entertain them in the best manner I can as they are very sensible of respect, I observe this kind of treatment is very grateful to them. But these hospitalities are very expensive, and draw an unusual number about us, yet surely no pains or charges are lost that have a tendency to retain these people in our interest, for it is terrible to think of the devastation and destruction that a breach with them would produce. I therefore beg leave to entreat your Lordships that endeavors may be used to enable us to support and maintain this good Correspondence which I apprehend cannot be done, but by means of annual presents and a competent fund to entertain them and supply their accidental necessitys. I grant that this will occasion considerable expense but when that is put in competition with the great evils, & much greater expense it may prevent, the Nation must be reconciled to it. If my Lord I speak ignorantly or too freely upon this subject being unacquainted with the powers & Commission Mr Atkins may have I hope I shall experience your usual indulgence and I must further use the freedom to observe that let the nature of that Gentlemans employment be what it will it may probably take some years before the Indians will be brought to treat with them separately, and upon national matters, regardless of the Governors of His Majestys Provinces, as they cannot suddenly comprehend the design or expediency of such appointments nor forsake at once a course they have been long accustomed to. The Agent I sent up to the Creek Nation some Months ago I have yet received no accounts from; but am informed by some straggling Indians, that he arrived there discharged his Commission and that the Head Men are preparing to come down. In regard to our people they are quiet and as far as I can judge content. They begin to think I have their interest sincerely at heart and shew all manner of disposition to second my endeavors and contribute to my case & happiness.

John Reynolds to the Board of Trade, Oct. 14, 1757, London, C.O. 5/646, C. 1, notifying them of his return to England.

My Lords

In obedience to your Lordship's Letter to me of the 5th of August 1756 I am returned to this Kingdom from my Government of Georgia & desire to know when I may have the Honour to wait upon your Lordships to receive your further commands.

William Pitt to the Board of Trade, Oct. 20, 1757, Whitehall, C.O. 5/646, C. 2, asking that the Board inquire into Reynold's conduct as Governor of Georgia.

My Lords

Having laid before the King your Lordships letter of the 13th July last acquainting me for His Majesty's information that Mr Reynolds Governor of Georgia who had been directed to return to England in consequence of your Lordships Representation of the 29th July 1756 is arrived. I am commanded to signify the King's pleasure to your Lordships that you do proceed to an enquiry into the conduct of Mr Reynolds and the state of the Province of Georgia during his residence there as Governor and that you do report your opinion what it may be proper for His Majesty to do thereupon.

Henry Ellis to the Board of Trade, Oct. 22 1757, Georgia, read Feb. 22, 1758, C.O. 5/646, C. 13, relating a settlement intended to be made by the Spaniards between St. Augustine and Pensacola and other affairs of the province.

My Lords,

The occurrences from the 1st of August to the 20th of September were comprised in a Letter I wrote your Lordships of the latter date; those that happened since shall be the subject of the present.
I have received certain advice from St Augustine that the Governor there is by order from his Court is intent on settling the lands between Augustine & Pencacola, the Appalachee fields and those bordering upon us but how far this way I cannot learn. For this purpose 500 families are appointed 70 whereof are just arrived. His Catholic Majesty allows a Piaster a day to each person for the first year besides a certain quantity of provisions, and Utensils of Husbandry to the head of every family. How such a Settlement will affect us is not very clear, but were our boundaries so actually defined that no altercation could thence arise, 'tis possible it might be beneficial to us by opening a new Vent for our Manufactures & other commodities in times of peace. Nor would it upon the whole be disadvantageous in case of a war.

The Spaniards in Florida are formidable at present from their being shut up in Forts & consequently cannot easily be annoyed by us, who on the contrary from our dispersion are liable to be injured in many places. But were they scattered in small Settlements they would be equally vincible and have the same inclination to maintain a good correspondence with our Neighbours. That Province can never arrive at a dangerous pitch of power, being so detached from the rest of the Spanish Dominions & hemmed in by the French & us. Besides they have other almost insuperable difficulties to contend with--the barrenness of the Soil, the natural indolence of the Spaniards, the jealousy of the Creek Indians-- are impediments that will retard its progress a hundred different ways.

The apparent motive which induces the Spaniards to attempt establishing this new Colony is to have subsistence in their own power for the Garrisons of Augustine & Pencacola, who often experience the greatest hardships for want of provisions as all that is consumed in those place is furnished by us, & the French; Augustine from New York & Pencacola at an exorbitant rate from the Settlements on the Mississippi. These circumstances joined to the consideration of the declining state of our Commerce with the Spaniards, naturally suggest the expediency & even necessity of a discretionary power being given to the Governors of the Southern Provinces of admitting Spanish Vessels into our Ports, to supply themselves with certain Articles which we can spare without prejudice to ourselves. Were they allowed to introduce their Bullion, Log Wood, Cochineal, and such other produces, as are of national benefit, & to carry away none but British Manufactures of a certain species, doubtless great advantages would accrue to the Mother Country. In fact such a traffick would be between Great Britain and the Spanish Colonies by the Channel of our Provinces as all the commodities supplied the latter must come from home & whatever we get in exchange go thither. This trade is not prohibited by the English Laws where our own shipping are employed. On the contrary it has been the constant policy of the Nation to encourage it; but the great risk to our Adventurers from the vigilance of the Spanish Officers & Guarda Costas & the frequent differences it has occasioned between the two Nations has put an almost effectual stop to it; and bereft us of a very lucrative branch of Commerce. But none of these difficulties will occur in alloeing the Spaniards to take such risks upon themselves which they are sufficiently inclined to. 'Tis true such indulgence seems not to square with the letter of the Navigation Act, but I presume it not repugnant to its spirit, since it would have a tendency to encrease our heights and Shipping instead of diminishing them.

Vast quantities of french manufactures are introduced by that people among the Spanish Settlements in the Bay of Mexico which would not find so ready a vent there if the Spaniards were permitted to furnish themselves at an easier rate from our Plantations. They even attempt to force this for scarce a Month passes that some of their Vessels are not to be found in our Harbours or hovering upon our Coasts, & our utmost vigilance can hardly prevent them in a Country abounding with excellent Ports, where there are but few Officers, & no Cruizers to guard them. These observations shew the advantageous situation of this Colony which improves daily. 'Tis expected that the years produce will be double the last & by the best calculation I have been able to form with the assistance of the most intelligent people here there is not less than the value of £40,000 of British Manufactures annually imported for the consumption of the Inhabitants and the Indian Trade. Besides other articles from the West India Islands, & Northern Colonies. The Southern part of this Province is thicker settled & better improved than near Savannah particularly on the River Medway, where a Town called Sundbury is building. The Inhabitants thereabouts have entreated me to move your Lordships that it may be made a Port of Entry.[25] Their Address for this purpose I transmit herewith.

As to other affairs of the Province they do not much differ from what I described in my last letter. Every body seems satisfied and at ease. No new alarms have arisen. Could we depend that our present Situation would be lasting, we might reckon ourselves the happiest people at this time in America. But our weakness renders this quiet extremely precarious exposing us to the attacks of the enemy & the caprice & insolence of the Creek Indians. 'Tis true they have not given us any recent grounds for apprehension, but on the contrary have been more orderly than usual & as far as I can penetrate they are inclinable to observe a neutrality between us and the French, tho' they are incessantly teized by them, & their Emissaries, some Vagrant Shawanese settled near the Albamas who breath nothing but revenge for the loss of three of their Clan, lately cut off by a party of our men & a few

---

25. Sunbury officially was declared Georgia's second port of entry in 1763.

Cherokees near Fort Loudoun.[26] Still I am willing to flatter myself that neither their endeavors nor those of the French, will be capable of detaching the Creeks from our Alliance. It may not be amiss to observe to your Lordships that these Savages are very attentive of late to the encroachments of the Europeans, & have already taken the alarm at the Spanish New Settlement. One of their Tribes a few days ago attacked a plantation near Augustine, destroyed the Cattle, set fire to the Houses & carried off the people. Previous to this they had seized two Spaniards on the Borders of this Province, whom they would have put to death immediately had not some of our people interposed. These by my mediation were released. The same Indians were soon afterwards with me at Savannah when I used many arguments to dissuade them from persisting in such outrages. Whatever impressions I made upon them did not prevent others from even committing greater enormities. I was early apprised of their dissatisfaction & designs, & immediately wrote the Spanish Governor all I knew at the same time declared my disapprobation of such proceedings & tendered my good offices for a reconcileation in which I was very sincere, as the preservation of a general tranquility in these parts is what I have much at heart. But tho' my professions & conduct seem to acquit me in the Governor's opinion of secretly kindling this flame yet he harbours other sentiments of Gray & his followers whom he impeaches as Incendiaries, & in a letter he sent me desires that the English settled on the Catholic Kings Territories may for these reasons be commanded to withdraw, a requisition that I shall answer in vague & general terms but so as to render a further correspondence upon these points unnecessary.

This misunderstanding between the Spaniards & Indians will probably keep the latter more steadily in our interests, & be productive of other good effects. We must be attentive to this incident, & tho' there appears danger in intermeddling yet I conceive advantages may be reaped from it. It would be rash to point them out, since they depend upon a discreet and very delicate conduct, always adapted to the circumstances of the conjecture. To attempt diminishing the deep rooted aversion these Savages have to the Spaniards would certainly be bad policy and it is evident

---

26. Lower Creeks from the town of Swaglaw who, upset by the movement of white settlers into their area, displaced to the Tuckabatchees near the French-held Fort Toulouse in 1756. The Swaglices reputedly were nativist, anti-English in their sentiments.

that while they are thus embroiled there is less danger of their breaking with us. On the other hand I am entirely sensible that at this juncture the giving umbrage to the Court of Spain might be attended with the worse consequences; but this I shall scrupulouly avoid. I am well aware that this is a ticklish business & must be managed with the utmost caution & prudence for which reason I shall take no steps without consulting my friend Governor Lyttleton. Your Lordships shall have Copies of all letters upon this subject in due time, to the end that if any explanation at home becomes necessary the means may be in your possession.

There remains to mention to your Lordships that the affair of the Bosomworths is still depending. I confess I have used some art to put off the tryal as the peoples notion of their power with the Indians is such that it is doubtful with me whether that alone on a hearing would not influence them to decide in their favor. Indeed it is not only mine but the wishes of the whole Colony, that this troublesome Affair was finished, for Mrs Bosomworth has questionless great ascendancy over some of the Indian tribes, which upon this occasion might be of service to us instead of being employed to our prejudice. I will therefore hope that your Lordships will think of some expedient of bringing it speedily to an issue either by sending out a Chief Justice capable of asserting the rights of the Crown, & such other means as will enable us to baffle the efforts of these people with the Indians, should matters go against them, or authorise some person to adjust it in any other way that your Lordships wisdom will suggest for in this case a delay alone is in many respects exceedingly injurious to the prosperity of the Colony.

Receipt from John Graham to William Little, Agent for Indian Affairs, Feb. 16, 1757, received March 2, 1758, read same day, C.O. 5/646, C. 14, for Indian presents.

Received of William Little Esqr the following Indian Presents		Received also an Order upon David Douglass
Calicos	1 Piece	3 pieces & 10 yards Calico
Vermilion	1/2 pound	18 pound vermilion
Striped Duffils	2 Pieces	1 piece 3 yards striped duffils
Strouds	5 pieces	5 pieces 8 yards Strouds
Blue Plains	0	4 pieces blue plains

Embroidered Serge	17 Yards	50 Yards embroidered Serge
Saddle	1	1 Saddle
Stone Rings	0	11 doz Stone Rings
Horn Combs	3	5 doz & 1/2 horn Combs
Ivory Combs	0	2 doz Ivory Combs
Claspt Knives	4 doz	11 doz Claspt Knives
Razors	1 doz & 2	4 doz & 5 Razors
Scissars	1 doz	5 doz & 1/2 Scissars
Looking Glasses	6	2 doz & 8 Glasses
Gilt Trunks	2 Nests	2 nests Trunks
Shirts	3 doz & 10	7 doz & 7 Shirts
Coats	5	5 Coats
Waistcoats	1	1 Waistcoat
Hats	3	5 Hats
Brass Wire	3 small hanks	0
Hawks Bells	a few	0
Hatchets	0	3 doz & 10 hatchets
Tin Kettles	0	3 Nests Tin Kettles
Potts	2	2 doz & 10 Potts
Pipes	some	some
Tobacco	0	Some
Cadis	2 Gross	2 Gross & 8 pieces Cadis
Gartering	1 Gross	1 Gross Gartering
Trading Guns	5	9 Trading Guns
Fowling Pieces	4	3 Fowling Pieces
Bullets	51 Cags & 1/2	5 Cags of Bullets
Gun Powder	15 Barrels & 1/2	1 Barrel

also an order upon Capt John Barnard two Barrels of Gunpowder and two Cags of Bullets which Goods being Indian Presents when delivered to me I will be accountable for

                                   John Graham

Bond given by Martin Campbell, et al, Indian Traders, to William Little, June 15, 1756, Augusta, received and read, March 2, 1758, C. O. 5/646, C. 15, for the safe carrying up of presents to the Chickasaw Indians.

GEORGIA

KNOW ALL MEN by these presents that we Martin Campbell of Augusta in the Province aforesaid merchants Jerome Courtone John Brown and John Pettigrove Indian Traders are holden & firmly bound unto William Little Esquire Agent for Indian affairs in the sum of five hundred pounds sterling lawful money of Great Britain to be paid unto the said William Little his certain Attorney heirs executors administrators And Assigns or to the [Agent] of Indian affairs for the time being to which payment well and truly to be made we bind ourselves our heirs executors and administrators firmly by these presents Signed and sealed with our Seals and dated the 15th. day of June An Dom 1756 and in the twenty ninth year of His Majesty's Reign.

The condition of the above obligation is such that if the above named Jerome Courtone John Brown & John Pettigrove or either of them do immediately and safely carry up to the Checkesaw Nation the presents designed for the Indians of that Nation now delivered to them by David Douglass as by a List or Schedule is hereunto annexed and there distribute them to the head men and others of the Checkesaws residing there in the name of His Excellency John Reynolds Esqr. Governor of the Province of Georgia (inevitable and unavoidable accidents only and always excepted) and bring a receipt or testimony of such delivery & distribution from the said head men of the Indians & from what white people may be in the Checkesaw Nation at that time then this obligation to be void and of non effect or else to remain in full force and virtue.

Signed and sealed in   MARTIN CAMPBELL (L.S.)
the presence of   JEROME COURTONE (L.S.)
     JOHN BROWN   (L.S.)
DA DOUGLASS
JAS GRAY

A List of Indian Presents to the Chickasaws delivered to Augusta, June 15, 1756, received and read March 2, 1758, enclosed with C.O. 5/646, C. 15.

One Nest Tin Kettles
One dozen quart one dozen pint
     one dozen half pint Tin Pots
One dozen and a half of Looking
     Glasses

Two pieces of Calico
One dozen check shirts
One dozen striped cotton ditto
One dozen and a half of Garter
     ditto

One dozen and a half of ruffled ditto
Six pieces strouds
Three pieces striped duffels
Two Nests gilt Trunks
One piece of blue plains
Twenty yards embroidered serge
Two Gross Gartering
Two Gross Cadis
Eight dozen knives
Five laced hats
Five Coats
One gross bell buttons
Two dozen Razors
One dozen Scissors
Four dozen stone Rings
One dozen Ivory Combs
One dozen Hatchets
Four pound and a half of brass wire
One dozen horn Combs
Forty eight trading Guns
Ten fowling pieces
Three hundred best flints
Two thousand Common ditto
Two Saddles and Bridles
One ditto with a blue fringed housing
Twenty five yards white plains
Eight pounds of Paint
Five hundred weight of Gunpowder
One thousand pound weight of Bullets
Tobacco 1 Bag

Received the above Articles from Mr Douglass in good order and well conditioned.

JEROME COURTOUNE.

Certificate of David Douglass and Edward Barnard, Esquires, Augusta, received and read March 2, 1758, C.O. 5/646, C. 16, respecting the distribution of the Indian presents at Augusta.

WE David Douglass and Edward Barnard Esqrs. two of His Majesty's Justices of the Peace for the District of Augusta being informed that several evil minded people have been industrious to spread abroad a false Report that the Presents sent by his Majesty for the Indians in Amity with this Province of Georgia were distributed at Augusta in such a manner that the Indians went away disgusted and the presents thereby rendered useless to his Majesty's Service & the Benefit of the Province. We therefore declare that we were present at the distribution of the Presents and that it appeared to us to be made with the strictest justice discretion and frugality; and tho' one of the Head Men demurred a little about his coming in yet when he came he was fully satisfied, and they all in general went away perfectly well pleased and as well satisfied as could be wished.

> DA: DOUGLASS
> EDWD. BARNARD.

Certificate upon Oath of Four Indian Traders, Nov. 20, 1756, Augusta, received and read March 2, 1758, C.O. 5/646, C. 17, respecting the distribution of the present to the Indians.

GEORGIA

WHEREAS we have been informed that several evil minded people have been industrious to spread about a false Report that the presents sent by his Majesty to the Indians in Amity with this Province of Georgia were distributed at Augusta in such a manner that the Indians were disgusted and the presents thereby rendered useless to His Majesty's Service and the benefit of the Province WE the several Indian Trades whose names are hereunto subscribed do upon our Oath declare that we were present at the distribution of the Presents and that it appeared to us to be made with the strictest justice discretion and frugality and tho' one of the Chiefs seemed at first displeased at the Governors return to Savannah yet being soon convinced of the necessity of it he was satisfied and the Head Men in general went home perfectly pleased with the friendly Reception they met with and the Event has proved they were sincere.

Sworn to at Savannah
the twentieth day of
November 1756 before me

    JAS. CAMPBELL

LACHLAN MC: GILLIVRAY
GEORGE GALPHIN
GEORGE JOHNSTON
JAMES GERMANY

[Enclosure 6]

A General Account of Indian Presents Distributed by Order of His Excellency John Reynolds Esqr. Governor of Georgia from the 16th day of December 1755 to the 15th day of February 1757 inclusive by William Little Agent. C.O. 5/646, C. 18.

[Legend for the following chart; letters to the right represent entries.]

16   To Micho Lacho or the Gun Merchant and the people of the Upper Creek Towns met by invitation at Augusta----------A

To Ehula Micho or the Priest and the people of the Lower Creek Towns met at the same place----------------------B

To Minga Mastobey & the Chickesaws settled at New Savannah, met at the same place-------------------------C

Total given at Augusta-------- D

31st Sent to Malatchi Head King of the Coweties------------- E

To Old Oakley of the Oak fuskees old Braket of the Cutabatchees and the War King of the Cusatews---------- F

To the Captain of the Eufalies with eight men and four women---G

9th To the Holland King and three other Indians-------------H

20   To Cussitusco and thirty one Cherokees------------------I

15th To Paifamingo and five Chickesaws from the Nation-------J

16   To Mingo Push Cush and nine Attendants-----------------K

17   To Abraham a beloved Man in the lower Creek Nation----- L

15th To sent up to be distributed in the Chickesaw Nation-----M

21   To Suckabatchy and McCletaby and some Cherokees who came to declare they would live and die with the English- N

29th	To a party of Creek Indians during the time of the alarm	O
30	To sundry white persons during the alarm	P
22	To the handsome fellow and his Attendants at Savannah	Q
12th	To ditto and his party on their return from Savannah (at Augusta)	R
	To several different parties of Indians that came down to Savannah in the time above mentioned	S

Savannah in Georgia
Feby 15.th 1757

WILLM LITTLE--Agent

Total Issued to the 15th February 1757----------T

remaining unissued to be accounted for-----------U

Total received-----V

As to the deficiency of Six Barrl of Powder there was given to Lieutenant Outerbridge of the Fort at Augusta

Decemr 11.th 1755	For Salutes to the Indians	One Barrel
Sept 12 1756	To ditto in the time of the alarm	One Ditto
1756 & 1757	To the Governor at Savannah for Salutes on Rejoicing days and for Returns to Merchants Ships	Four Ditto

And as to the deficiency of one piece of Strouds it was expended in making a Tent for the Governor to lie under in the Woods.

	Callicoes	Vermillion	Tobacco	Striped Duffils	Blue Strouds	Red Strouds	Blue Plains	Embroidered Serge	Saddles 1st sort	Saddles 2d sort	Stone Rings	Horn Kombs
	yds	lb	lb	yds	yds	yds	yds	yds	No	No	doz	doz
A.	3	3		4	6	2½	1	33	1	2	2½	2
B.	3	3		4	6	2½	1	33	1	2	2½	2
C.	1	1		1	1	0	0	10	0	1	0	0
D.	7	7		9	13	5	2	76	2	5	5	4
	yds	lb		Blankts.	yds	yds	yds	yds	No	No	No	No
E.	2	1		2	6	0	3	3	1	0	0	0
F.	0	0		8	6	0	10	10	0	0	0	0
G.	0	0½		4	6	0	10	10	0	0	0	0
H.	0	0 1/16		0	0	2	0	0	0	0	0	0
I.	0	3		12	22½	0	12	0	0	0	4	0
J.	0	0½		1	0	0	0	0	0	0	0	0
K.	0	0½		5	0	0	0	0	0	0	0	0
L.	0	0 2/16		0	0	0	0	0	0	0	0	12
M.	36	8		40	66	44	32	20	1	0	4	12
N.	0	0½		6	6	6	0	10	0	0	0	0
O.	8	0½		12	16	0	0	0	1	0	0	0
P.	0	0		0	0	0	0	0	0	0	0	0
Q.	18	0 14/16		0	11	14	13	13	0	0	0	0
R.	0	0		0	0	0	0	0	0	4	0	0
S.	34	9		20	36½	44	64	21	2	2	0	0
	yds	lb		yds	yds	yds	yds	yds	No	No	doz	doz
T.	12½	31½		16 10/15	21	10	6	163	7	11	13	6
U.	4½	18½		3 5/15	6	4	4	67	1	1	11	6
V.	17	50		20	27	14	10	230	8	12	24	12

	Clasp'd Knives	Razors	Scissors	Looking Glasses	Gilt Trunks	Check Shirts	Garlix Shirts	Coats 1st Sort	Laced Waistcoats	Coats 2d Sort	Hats 1st Sort	Hats 2d Sort	Brass Wire	Hawk's Bells
	doz	doz	doz	doz	Nest	doz	doz	No	No	No	No	No	lb	gr
A.	12	2	2	1	2	5	7	2	2	7	1	7	8	
B.	12	2	2	1	2	5	7	2	2	7	1	7	8	
C.	0	0	0	0	0	1	0	0	0	2	1	1	2	
D.	24	4	4	2	4	11	14	4	4	16	3	15	18	
	No	No	No	No	No	No	No	No	No	No	No	No	lb	N
E.	3	0	0	0	0	0	4	1	1	0	1	0	2	
F.	0	0	0	0	0	2	2	0	0	0	0	0	0	
G.	10	0	0	0	0	0	10	0	0	0	0	1	1	
H.	4	0	1	1	0	1	0	0	0	0	0	1	0	
I.	24	6	6	6	5	2	9	0	0	1	0	4	1	
J.	0	0	0	0	0	0	6	0	0	1	0	0	0	
K.	4	0	0	0	0	0	0	0	0	0	0	0	0	
L.	2	10	0	0	1	0	1	0	0	0	0	1	0	
M.	72	24	12	18	10	12	24	0	0	5	0	5	5	
N.	1	0	0	12	5	0	8	0	0	1	1	0	0	
O.	0	0	0	12	0	0	10	0	0	0	0	0	0	
P.	0	0	0	0	0	0	0	0	0	0	0	0	0	
Q.	0	0	0	12	0	0	0	1	1	1	0	1	0	
R.	0	0	0	0	0	0	0	0	0	0	0	0	0	
S.	0	0	0	21	0	0	0	0	0	1	0	1	0	
	doz	doz	doz	doz	Nest	doz	doz	No	No	No	No	No	lb	gr
T.	34	$7\,5/12$	$5\,6/12$	$8\,10/12$	8	$12\,3/12$	$20\,2/12$	6	6	26	5	29	27	
U.	14	$4\,7/12$	$6\,1/2$	$3\,2/12$	4	$6\,9/12$	$4\,10/12$	2	2	8	1	7	15	
V.	48	12	12	12	12	19	25	8	8	34	6	36	42	

	Hatchets	Tin Kettles	Tin Pots	Pipes	Cadis	Gartering	Trading Guns	Fowling Pieces	Flints	Balls [Kegs]	Gun Powder
	doz	nest	doz	gro	gro	gro	No	No	No	Caggs	lb
A.	3	2	0 ½		2	2	32	8	1500	12	6
B.	2	2	0 ½		2	2	32	8	1500	12	6
C.	0	0	0	0	0	0	10	1	200	2	1
D.	5	4	1		4	4	74	17	3200	26	13
	No	No	No	No	yds	yds	No	No	No	lb	lb
E.	0	0	0	0	0	0	1	0	0	0	0
F.	0	0	0	0	0	6	0	0	0	0	0
G.	0	0	2	0	3	3	0	0	0	50	25
H.	4	1	1	0	0	0	1	0	0	8	4
I.	10	5	6	0	12	24	5	0	200	100	50
J.	2	0	0	0	0	0	1	0	200	24	12
K.	0	0	0	0	0	0	0	0	200	48	24
L.	0	0	0	0	1	1	1	0	0	6	3
M.	12	5	12	0	12	12	48	10	2000	1000	500
N.	0	0	0	0	12	12	0	2	0	0	200
O.	0	2	0	0	0	0	0	0	0	66	38
P.	0	0	0	0	0	0	0	0	0	24	21
Q.	0	0	0	0	0	6	0	0	0	50	50
R.	10	2	3	0	0	0	9	1	0	0	0
S.	0	0	0	0	0	0	6	3	200	400	200
	doz	nest	doz	gro	gro	gro	No	No	No	Caggs	lb
T.	8 $2/12$	7	3		7 $4/12$	9 $4/12$	146	33	6000	61½	35
U.	3 $10/12$	3	3		4 $8/12$	2 $8/12$	14	7	0	58½	18
V.	12	10	6		12	12	160	40	6000	120	54

The Address and Remonstrance of the Assembly of Georgia to the Board of Trade, Feb. 2, 1757, Savannah, received and read March 2, 1757, C.O. 5/646, C. 19, on certain points relative to the state of that province and the government thereof.[27]

Two Resolutions of the Assembly of Georgia appointing William Little Agent to the Board of Trade, Feb. 2, 1757, Savannah, received and read, March 2, 1758, C.O. 5/646, C. 20.[28]

Henry Ellis to the Board of Trade, Nov. 25, 1757, Savannah, read March 10, 1758, C.O. 5/646, C. 22, relating Indian affairs in the province.

My Lords

I did myself the honor to write to your Lordships on the 22d October a material transaction has since happened which I shall now relate. In my former letters I mentioned that I had sent an Agent to the Creek Country to invite the Chiefs to Savannah to receive his Majesty's presents & to renew our friendships and alliance with them. At the same time I acquainted your Lordships that I had lately had a Meeting with Governor Lyttleton at Port Royal when it was agreed that these Indians should first go to Charlestown where his Excellency had received intelligence they were preengaged to go by Mr Pepper his Agent who had been dispatched for that purpose to the Creek Nation from an apprehension that our interest was declining fast there. But Mr Littleton was misinformed, his Envoy tho sent up at a great expense and esteemed, well qualified, did not succeed in his Commission for the headmen could not be prevailed upon to return with him, although our Agent was instructed not to attempt bringing them here until they had been at Charlestown unless it appeared they had no immediate intention of going there. Mr Peppers miscarriage proceeded I believe from his being invested with, & exciting a power that gave offence to the Traders in the Nation, who to lessen his consequence

---

27. Given in CRG, XIII, 146-151.

28. Ibid., 152.

& gratify their resentment counteracting his measures tho' at the risk of their own safety.[29]

To prevent any obstruction of this sort & even avail myself of these peoples influence I wrote a particular & complaisant letter to each requesting their assistance at this juncture in behalf of their Country.

The consequence was that they all to show their importance, exerted themselves to oblige me. The principal Indians of 21 Towns to the number of 150 were induced to accept my invitation, set out accordingly with my Agent & arrived at this place the 29th. October as your Lordships will see by the Minutes of Council that accompany this.[30] These Minutes contain a distinct and ample account of their reception and our transactions with them. I shall therefore only touch upon the principal parts. A treaty was concluded confirming all our former ones & by a new Article therein it was declared that the Indians never sold nor alienated the Lands & Islands in dispute to Mrs Bosomworth or to any other private person whatever but that they now gave the said Lands & Islands to me In trust as Representative of his Majesty.[31] Your Lordships will readily see the importance of this concession which paves the way for obtaining an entire grant of these Lands, greatly invalidates the Bosomworth's Pretensions, & leaves them in a manner at the mercy of the Crown. The Indians of their own accord made this proposal in Council to which however they were induced by the impressions that I had been making on them for several days before the Talk during which time I constantly entertained select

---

29. Captain Dan Pepper, former commander of Fort Moore, was sent by Governor Lyttleton to reside among the Creeks for an extended period of time in order to push the English point of view and to counter a growing Creek-Cherokee nativist coalition. Using Lyttleton's peace message and trade concessions as tact, Pepper successfully calmed the restive Creeks, urging them to forget the "Ogeechee incident." Only the traders, especially the ones at Augusta, objected to Pepper's mission, and they expressed their strong disapproval to Governor Ellis. See Jenkins, "Book of Indian Affairs," V, 176, 207, 215-218, 229, 284-285, 336-337; VI, 12, 36, 29, 30, 45-47, 56, 228-229.

30. See CRG, VII, 643-644, 657.

31. Ibid., 665.

parties of the leading men at my own house. The letter inserted in the minutes was from his Majesty to the Indians & was formed in consequence of the Agents telling them I had one as a stronger inducement for them to come down. It will perhaps seem strange to your Lordships that during the whole negotiation I never instigated the Indians to make war upon our Enemies. But I hope to demonstrate that in this I acted prudently. 'Tis certain that the French by means of the Albama fort whence the Indians are daily supplied with presents have acquired a numerous party among those Savages wherefore if we should endeavor to make a breach between them it could only cause a civil war in the Nation which would immediately destroy our Indian Trade & considering our defenceless state might greatly endanger the safety of this Province. Hence 'tis my firm opinion that it would be rash to attempt causing the Indians to break thro' their Neutrality & that all I ought to endeavor is the maintaining our interest with them and this will be a great deal in our circumstances. The french, who are also sensible of their weakness on the Mississippi, observe the same conduct, but they disguise their real motive under the mask of friendship & regard for the Indians boasting in all public Talks of their disinterestedness & moderation.

"Whereas the English say they are restless and fond of spilling "human blood their ambition prompts them to it why else should they "be incessantly teazing you to murder us? & what is the object of "this ambition but to extirpate us whom they consider as your "friends & protectors in order the more easily to enslave & destroy "you & then possess themselves of your Lands." These insinuations must have done us much prejudice but my late and future conduct will perhaps render them less effectual.

The Indians stayed with us near three Weeks & the charge of maintaining and accomodating such a Number has been very considerable. I think about £270 exclusive of the Agents expense & wages which amount to £70 more & yet I can truly say there was not sixpence spent unnecessarily. I gave them about 3/8th of the presents, which I distributed with my own hands knowing that would make them go much further & be better received. Besides they had their Guns Saddles & other Utensils repaired, a job as chargeable as buying new ones but this being customary in Carolina they expect it here & I thought that at such a time nothing in reason should be denied them lest a refusal in one instance should destroy the merit of all we had been doing. On the whole I am convinced there never was in this Country so large a number of principal Indians that departed better satisfied with their treatment & if I know anything of their disposition I may safely affirm that they will not easily be gained from us unless there be some neglect or mismanagement on our part. At the same time I must take the liberty to observe that in order to avoid such a misfortune the Governors of these Provinces or whoever has the charge of Indian affairs, should be effectually supported. That your Lordships may have a clear idea of what consequence it is to keep well with the Creek Indians, I send herewith an authentick List of the Number of Men fit to bear arms in each Town of that Country. These Indians are peculiarly connected with this Province they are constantly hunting in some part of it & perpetually in want of necessaries & they come regularly here for supplies. These must be furnished from home, the people here being in no condition to be at such an expense. £1,000 a year will scarce be sufficient for this service while our Enemies are so industrious & successful & surely this expense cannot be put in competition with the advantages that may accrue from it. I have ordered Mr Graham the Clerk of the Accounts to transmit to Mr Martyn an exact account along with the Vouchers of the particular charges attending this transaction. I have likewise wrote to Mr Martyn myself, & given him my opinion at large of the properest assortment of Goods for Indian presents hereafter & as no relaxation or neglect must be suffered in this critical time I hope your Lordships will employ your good offices to obtain an immediate supply for what remains of the last must soon be exhausted.

A List of the Number of Gun men in the Different Towns of the Upper and Lower Creek Nations, Georgia, read March 10, 1758, enclosed with Ellis to the Board of Trade, Nov. 25, 1757, C.O. 5/646, C. 22, taken from the best accounts to be got from Indian Traders and the Indians themselves.

In the Upper Creeks		In the Lower Creeks	
In the Tuckabachees	65	In the Cowetas	130
Tellasees	45	Cussetas	125
Nosabees	20	Uchees	60
Ottoses	30	Ousuchees	40
Weekes	65	Chehaws	70
Pulknatalahasse	55	Oakmulgees	50
Coosas	40	Etchelas	65
Breed Camp	40	Palacuckulas	35
Abbacochees	50	Ocoonees	65
Savannas	100	Coosatown	28

Hellabees	60	Swagalas	37
Wahahokees	40	Little Ocoonees	28
Suckapogas	35	Old Swagalas	42
Oakchoas & Oakfusches	175	Ussalas	125
Kealyias & Ussalas	105	Forks	55
Oheclomkes & Albamas	65		
In different small villages from the Ottoses to the Mucklasses	176	Lower Creeks	955
Small village at the Great Falls	25	Upper Creeks	1191
	1191	in all	2146

Henry Ellis to the Board of Trade, Dec. 7, 1757, Georgia, received March 30, read April 5, 1758, C.O. 5/646, C. 27, giving an account of the practices of Bosomworth with the chiefs of the Creek Indians and proposing a compromise with Bosomworth.

My Lords

Your Lordships I hope will receive a letter I did myself the honor to write to you the 25th of last Month wherein was a full & circumstantial account of our proceedings with the Head Men of the Creek Nation lately here together with the Minutes of Council during our negociations and a Copy of the Treaty concluded at that time. I shall now relate to your Lordships an incident that deserves particular notice.

Among the Chiefs who signed that Treaty was a Son of the late Malachi who was stiled Emperor of the Creeks; he was the great friend of the Bosomworths & the person who took upon him to sell them the Lands they claim. Part of the consideration given for them consisted in Cattle which were left to breed on the Island St Catherines for the benefit of Malachi; they are now multiplied to 100 head & may be worth £200 Stirling. Whilst the Young Man was here the Bosomworths sent some of their Indian Emissaries to acquaint him with this circumstance & engage him to visit them on his return from me. These Savages are all mercenary. The prospect of so considerable an advantage tempted him to go thither where so many false & artful insinuations were employed as prevailed on him to return here in order to disavow the cession of those Lands which the Indians by treaty made over to me in Trust. Mrs. Bosomworth accompanied him & he demanded a hearing before the Council at which she should be present. But this I peremptorily refused & pointed out the absurdity of his attempting singly to cancel what had been done by the unanimous consent of the Head Men of this Country. I convinced him how injurious such a step would be to his own reputation & future interest refuted all the idle & false stories he had heard & dismissed him to all appearance entirely satisfied. Yet Mrs Bosomworth had influence enough to carry him home with her again & what new impressions she may make on him I cannot say. The current report now is that she intends going with him to the Nation in order to solicit a New Grant of the Lands. But this may prove a difficult task as I have instructed our Agent who returns thither forthwith to take proper measures for traversing her intrigues. Your Lordships must behold with indignation this insolent attempt to obstruct the public measures, & render fruitless all the expense & endeavors that have been employed for the general good. An attempt that under no other Government could be suffered with impugnity but which our want of power & the circumstances of the Times impel us to overlook. However to put it out of the power of any persons embroiling us hereafter in this way I shall endeavor when the Assembly meets to have a Law passed to prohibit & invalidate all purchases of Land from the Indians.

In my former letters I took the liberty to give it as my opinion that it would be highly conducive to the prosperity of this Colony were the disputes with these people amicably decided. I still retain the same sentiments & before the Indian Congress, I had sounded Bosomworth by means of some of my friends on this head. He seemed tractable & soon after sent me proposals for a Compromise, a Copy of which I now transmit to your Lordships, to which I must add that he engages to obtain an absolute Cession of those Lands to the Crown provided his terms are accepted. Indeed they are much beyond what he ought to expect & perhaps what he would submit to. Yet should your Lordships think it proper to comply with them I believe two thirds of the sum he requires might be raised by the Sale of the Islands Ossabaw and Sappalo.

Perhaps my Lords it would be superflous for me to urge further the expediency of finishing this troublesome affair which for several years has been a sourse of variance with the Indians, kept the people of this Colony under constant apprehensions & a large quantity of the best lands on our Sea Coast waste. And though the lands in question are now given in Trust to me as Representative of his Majesty I see no way at present whereby they may be effectually gained to the Crown and settled but by some such expedient as is now proposed. The expectations of this kind that the Bosomworths entertain prevent their taking any very violent steps which I am persuaded they would not stop at were they drove to despair. Nothing that I have hitherto done in this matter is conclusive my intention being only to amuse and procrastinate till a more favorable season; for until I should be furnished with fuller powers & instructions from your Lordships concerning it.

I have now the pleasure to acquaint your Lordships that the kindness we lately shewed the Creek Indians is like to produce very good effects upon the Chactaws, a numerous nation bordering upon the Creeks & hitherto in alliance with the French. For I had yesterday information from those parts that many of them have been in the Creek Nation purchasing English Goods, & making Overtures to our Traders of entering upon a friendly & commercial correspondence with these provinces. I shall exert myself to improve this incident which may be productive of the best consequences.

This with the greatest concern & regret My Lords that I just learn by a letter from Mr Martyn dated in August that your Lordships had then received no letters from me though I have wrote every Month since I came here in the most circumstantial manner & always sent four Copies of each Letter. I now send a fifth copy of my whole Correspondence by way of New York.

Proposal of Thomas Bosomworth's to Lt. Gov. Henry Ellis, Oct. 31, 1757, Savannah, received March 30, read April 5, 1758, C.O. 5/646, C. 28, enclosed with Ellis to the Board of Trade, Dec. 7, 1757, for surrendering his pretensions to certain lands and islands in Georgia.

WHEREAS the Revd Thomas Bosomworth & Mary his Wife in the year 1754 took a Voyage to England as well to complain of the great grievances they had then suffered from the then President & Court of Assistants as to solicit payment for services performed & money advanced for his Majesty's service in that province & did accordingly present sundry Memorials & Petitions to & also lay their Accounts & Vouchers before the proper Boards in England praying relief & the only opposition to their then obtaining it arose from the President & Assistants having in their letters & journals (called the Records of the Province) from time to time represented the said

Bosomworth & his Wife as the Authors of great disorders & having done very ill Offices to the prejudice of the Colony; And as their Lordships (The Lords Commissioners for Trade and plantations) were of opinion that they could not enter properly into a consideration of the merits of the said Bosomworth's Services & claims & allegations without first giving the late President & Court of Assistants an opportunity of making good their charges against them, their Lordships sent over a Commission to the then Governor of Georgia with directions to call before him the parties concerned & examine into the truth of the charge and allegations of each part & to report upon the whole. So that after a tedious voyage & solicitation that cost them near £1000 Sterling driven to the necessity of parting with the reversion of a paternal Estate in England to enable them to return; & labouring under every sense of injury & circumstance of distress by the long delay of payment of their just claims & demands; They came back to Georgia to attend the execution of the said Commission which in its Consequences proved the charges & allegations exhibited against the said Bosomworth & Wife to be false groundless & malicious & no attempt was made to disprove or controvert any of the facts set forth in the aforesaid Memorials &c or to support any of the former charges against them; Two Copies of which proceedings have already been sent for England but 'tis feared neither of them has arrived which greatly adds to the said Bosomworth's misfortunes.

And whereas the said Thomas Bosomworth & Mary his Wife also presented a Memorial to the Right Honorable the Lords Commissioners for Trade and plantations setting forth their right & title to certain Islands in the Colony of Georgia known by the name of St Catherines Sapala & Ossabaw & a certain Tract of Main Land upon Savannah River known by the name of the Indian Land; withal complaining of injuries by them sustained in encroachments made upon the main land some of which about the year 1750 had been run out in virtue of Warrants for that purpose from the late president & Court of Assistants, Altho it [is] well known that the said Mary Bosomworth was in possession of the said Land in her own right before Georgia was settled & the same moreover was ratified & confirmed to her by the Creek Nation in 1737 at a General Meeting at the Town House in Savannah in the presence of James Oglethorpe Esqr & by her peaceably & uninterruptedly enjoyed to the time of the aforesaid Encroachments made; & the Title Deeds of the said Thomas & Mary Bosomworth to the aforesaid Islands & also the Treaties &c upon which they were founded were with the said Memorial produced & examined at their Lordships Board & their

Lordships were pleased to give for Answer "That it was a matter which their Lordships could not possibly take cognizance of not being a prudential consideration but a question of property which must be heard & determined by a legal process in the Courts of Common Law or equity in the Colony from which if any of the said parties should not rest satisfied with the Judgment or Decree they would have the liberty of Appeal to His Majesty in Council."

And altho' the said Thomas & Mary Bosomworth are well assured by the opinions of as able Council as any in England of the legality of their Titles; have seen the Decree at the Court at Kensington of the 10th August 1732 in a case of similar nature respecting Lands in the province of Massachusetts Bay purchased from Indians by Sir Bibye Lake & others in favor of the purchasers & have already been at considerable expense in bringing Ejectments against the Tenants in possession of some of the said Lands yet as the final determination of the causes may be very expensive & tedious & must consequently in the interim retard the cultivation & improvement of the lands for the benefit of the Colony & the Crown: In proof of their zeal & loyalty & of their good wishes for the more speedy establishment of the province the said Thomas Bosomworth & Mary his Wife are willing to make a Resignation to the Crown of all their Claim Right and Title in & to certain portions of the said Islands & Main Land & all other pretensions of that kind whatever; (except as hereafter excepted) & also to give a full discharge of all debts claims & Demands upon the Government for moneys advanced or services performed in Georgia for his Majestys service since the first settlement of the Colony upon the following terms & conditions namely:

That they will by good & effectual conveyances in the Law release all their right title & interest whatsoever in & to the said two Islands Ossabaw & Sapala, & the Tract of Main Land upon Savannah River from the Out lines of the Town Common to a place called Pipe Makers Creek.

That in consideration thereof & in full of their demands for Money advanced for His Majesty's Service & Mary Bosomworths personal service since the first settlement of the Colony (as by the several Accounts now lying before the Lords Commissioners for trade & plantations & vouchers in the hands of their Agent fully appear) the sum of £3,000 sterling shall be paid the said Thomas Bosomworth in the space of twelve Months from this date clear of all deductions.

That the said Thomas Bosomworth shall also be sufficiently indemnified & saved harmless against Isaac Levy late of Broad Street London Esqr in respect to certain Articles of Agreement entered into between them the said Bosomworth & Levy in the penal sum of £1,000, a true copy of which said Articles are hereunto annexed.

That the Island St Catherines shall be ratified & confirmed by the Crown to the said Thomas Bosomworth & his heirs upon the terms that other Lands are held in the province; & also that the said Thomas Bosomworth shall have a reasonable time allowed him to withdraw any Stock or Interest of his that may be upon the Islands of Sapala or Ossabaw at the time these proposals shall be accepted.

That the above proposals not being approved of, or not duly carried into execution, according to the Intent & true meaning thereof the said Thomas Bosomworth & his Wife do hereby save & reserve to themselves all right title claim interest & benefit in the premises with full liberty to prosecute in such manner as they shall think expedient without suffering prejudice by the construction of any matter or thing herein contained.

Given under my hand & seal at
Savannah this the 31st October
1757

THOS BOSOMWORTH

This Instrument was executed
in the presence of

Copy of Articles of Agreement between Thomas Bosomworth and Issac Levi, Oct. 14, 1754, Georgia, received March 30, read April 5, 1758, C.O. 5/646, C. 29, enclosed with Ellis to Board of Trade, Dec. 15, 1757.

Articles of Agreement indented had made concluded & fully agreed upon this 14th. October in the 28th year of the Reign of our Soverign Lord George the Second by the Grace of God of great Britain France & Ireland King defender of the Faith, & so forth, & in the Year of our Lord 1754 Between Thomas Bosomworth of Fetter Lane, London, Clerk, & Mary his Wife (late named Coosaponakeesa rightfull & natural Princess of the Upper & Lower Creek Nations in America) of the one part & Isaac Levy of Broad Street London Esqr. of the other part as follows that is to say:

First it is covenanted & agreed by & between the said Parties hereto & the said Thomas Bosomworth & Mary his Wife for the

Consideration herein after mentioned have agreed to sell & convey
unto the said Isaac Levy & his heirs and the said Thomas Bosomworth for himself & the said Mary his Wife their heirs Executors &
Administrators doth covenant promise & agree to & with the said
Isaac Levy his heirs Executors Administrators & Assigns by these
presents that they the said Thomas Bosomworth & Mary his Wife &
their heirs shall & will on or before the 18th. October instant by
such Conveyances Assurances Ways & Means in the Law as the
said Isaac Levy his heirs or Assigns or his or their Council shall
advise fully & absolutely grant bargain sell release convey & assure unto him the said Isaac Levy & his heirs Executors & Administrators mutually covenant & agree with each other that from &
immediately after such Grants & Confirmations from the Crown of
the said three Islands or such part thereof as shall be applied for
shall be procured as aforesaid. And in Case the same Grants &
Confirmations shall be refused from & immediately after the present Title which the said Thomas Bosomworth & Mary his Wife have
to the said three Islands shall be found to be good valid & effectual
in the Law without such Grants & Confirmations being obtained
and from & immediately after the said Isaac Levy shall be in the
full quiet & peaceable Possession of the said one undivided Moiety
of the said three Islands to the Use of him & his heirs That then a
joint & equal Copartnership shall be entered into by Articles in
Writing by & between them the said Thomas Bosomworth & Isaac
Levy with proper Covenants for the term of 14 years for the better
stocking cultivating & improving the said three Islands & for the
trading & trafficking to & from the same which is to be done by the
said Isaac Levy in such Manner as he shall think proper & reasonable at his sole Expence One Moiety or half part of all which Expenses with Carolina & Georgia forever or to whom he or they shall
direct & appoint One undivided Moiety or half part the same into
two equal parts to be divided of all that Tract or Tracts of Land,
Island, or Islands known or distinguished by the names of hussoope
or hussaba Islands Coleygee or Saint Catherines Islands & Sappala
Islands bounded on the North East by Hussaba Sound on the South
West by doebay Sound & divided by the Sound of Saint Catherines
& Sappala, on the South East by the Sea, & on the North West by
several Rivers & Creeks having no particular Names which divide
the several Islands from the Continent & thro' which Boats & other
small Vessels are navigated to & from the Town of Frederica & to
& from the Northern Parts of Georgia aforesaid & South Carolina
which are the Right of the said Mary by descent or purchase To
hold from henceforth to him the said Isaac Levy his heirs & Assigns

for evermore And also that they the said Thomas Bosomworth & Mary
his Wife shall & will by the like Conveyances & Assurances in the
Law grant bargain sell ratify & confirm the said undivided Moiety
of all & singular the said Premisses unto him the said Isaac Levy
his heirs & Assigns for ever To the Use & Behoof of him the said
Isaac Levy his heirs & Assigns for evermore from & immediatly after
such Time as Grants & Confirmations may or can be obtained from
the Crown of Great Britain effectually to establish the Right of the
said Mary & her heirs to the said Premisses or of such part of the
said premisses as the Crown shall think fit to make Grants of to the
said Thomas Bosomworth & Mary his Wife or either of them; their
or either of their heirs or to any Person or Persons in Trust for them
or either of them or their Heirs.

Secondly it is further covenanted & agreed by & between the
said Parties & the said Isaac Levy for himself his heirs Executors
& Administrators in Consideration of the Premisses doth covenant
promise & agree to & with the said Thomas Bosomworth & Mary his
Wife & their heirs that he the said Isaac Levy shall & will as soon
as conveniently may be after the said 18 October instant on such
Conveyances being made to him as are first above mentioned at the
proper costs & Charges of the said Isaac Levy (if the Council of
the said Thomas Bosomworth & Isaac Levy shall think it fit & proper
to be done) apply to & sollicit his Majesty in Council (or otherwise
as shall be advised) & use his utmost endeavours to obtain such
Grants & Confirmations from the Crown of all & singular the said
Premisses unto the said Thomas Bosomworth & Mary his Wife &
their heirs or to one of them & his or her heirs And also shall &
will from time to time as there shall be Occasion pay & supply unto
the said Thomas Bosomworth & Mary his Wife or either of them
during their Stay in England any Sum or Sums of Money which the
Exigency of their Affairs shall or may require not exceeding the Sum
of £300 of lawfull Money of Great Britain (over & above the Expence & trouble that the said Isaac Levy is to be at towards the
obtaining of the said Grants & Confirmations as foresaid) upon the
Terms & Conditions herein after mentioned & expressed & also
shall & will by & out of the first Rents profits & produce which
shall be made or arise to the said Isaac Levy his heirs Executors
& Administrators out of the said Isaac Levy's Moiety of the said
three Islands & Premisses will & truly pay or cause to be paid unto the said Thomas Bosomworth & Mary his Wife their Executors
Administrators & Assigns the full Sum of £200 of lawfull Money of
Great Britain for their own Use.

Thirdly it is covenanted & agreed by & between the said Parties
hereto & the said Thomas Bosomworth for himself & for the said

Mary his Wife & their heirs Executors Administrators & Assigns
doth covenant promise & agree to & with the said Isaac Levy his
heirs Executors & Administrators by these Presents that in case
the said Applications to his Majesty in Council shall not be succeeded in & the said Grants & Confirmations shall not be obtained
that then the said Thomas Bosomworth & Mary his Wife & their
heirs shall on refusal thereof by proper deeds & Writings in the
Law mortgage & assign the other Moiety of the said three Islands
hereby reserved to themselves & such reserved Moiety of the said
Islands shall Stand & be a Security to the said Isaac Levy his
heirs Executors Administrators & Assigns for the Moneys so to
be paid & supplied by him to the said Thomas Bosomworth & Mary
his Wife as aforesaid until the Money together with lawfull Interest shall be fully satisfied & repaid. But in Case such Grants &
Confirmations shall be obtained & procured from the Crown of the
said three Islands & premisses or such part thereof as shall be
applied for & such Conveyances shall be immediatly thereupon
made & executed to the said Isaac Levy & his heirs of one undivided Moiety thereof as aforesaid that then the said Sum of £300
shall not be repaid to the said Isaac Levy but such belong to the
said Thomas Bosomworth & Mary his Wife their heirs Executors &
Administrators.

  Fourthly it is hereby mutually covenanted & agreed by & between the parties to these presents & the said Thomas Bosomworth
& Isaac Levy do for themselves severally & for their several heirs
Executors & Administrators mutually covenant & agree with each
other that from & immediately after such Grants & Confirmations
from the Crown of the said three Islands such part thereof as shall
be applied for shall be procured as aforesaid and in case the same
Grants & Confirmations shall be refused for & immediately after
the present Title which the said Thomas Bosomworth & Mary his
Wife have to the said three Islands shall be found to be good valid
& effectual in the Law without such Grants & Confirmations being
obtained and from & immediately after the said Isaac Levy shall
be in full quiet & peaceful possession of the said one undivided
Moiety of the said three Islands to the use of him & his heirs.
That then a joint & legal Copartnership shall be entered into by
articles in writing by & between them the said Thomas Bosomworth
& Isaac Levy with proper Covenants for the term of 14 years for the
better stocking cultivating & improving the said three Islands &
for the trading & trafficking to from the same which is to be done
by the said Isaac Levy in such Manner as he shall think proper &
reasonable at his sole Expense One Moiety or half part of all which

Expenses with Carolina. Interest for the same is in the first place to be deducted by & repaid to the said Isaac Levy by & out of the Rents Issues & Profits & Produce of the said Thomas Bosomworth & Mary his Wife's Moiety of the said three Islands arising from the mutual Cultivation of the said Islands, Stock thereon & Stock in Trade.

And for the true performance of all & every the Covenants & Agreements herein contained which on the part & behalf of the said Thomas Bosomworth & Mary his Wife & their heirs Executors & Administrators are or ought to be paid done performed & kept, he the said Thomas Bosomworth doth hereby bind & oblige himself his heirs Executors & Administrators to the said Isaac Levy his heirs Executors & Administrators in the penal Sum of £1000 firmly by these Presents & for the true performance of all & every the Covenants & Agreements in these Presents contained which is the part & behalf of the said Isaac Levy his heirs Executors & Administrators are or ought to be paid done performed & kept. He the said Isaac Levy doth bind & oblige himself his heirs Executors & Administrators to the said Thomas Bosomworth & Mary his Wife their Heirs Executors & Administrators in the penal Sum of £1000 firmly by these Presents. In Witness whereof the said Parties to these Present Articles have hereunto interchangeably set their hands & Seals the day & year first above written.

Tho. Bosomworth   Mary Bosomworth
                           Isaac Levy

    Sealed & Delivered (being first duly Stampt) in the Presence of Us-

                              A. Bosomworth
                              James Barnard
                              John Morton

J. Clevland, Secretary to the Lords of the Admiralty, to the Board of Trade, Feb. 14, 1757, London, read Feb. 17, 1757, C.O. 5/645, B. 36, desiring the ship Juno to be conveyed into the Savannah River.

Sir:

    I have laid before my Lords Commissioners of the Admiralty

your Letter of the 5th. Instant, signifying the Desire of the Lords of Trade and Plantations, that one of the Ships of War bound to North America, may be appointed to convoy the Juno, bound to Georgia with Presents for the Indians, & Military Stores for that Settlement, safe into the Savannah River; And in return I am to acquaint you, for their Lordship's Information, that the Ships of War will, it is hoped, be at Spithead by the 20th. Instant, and that Directions will be given for one of them to see the Juno safe off of the Savanna River, as their Lordships desire.

Henry Ellis to William Pitt, Dec. 10, 1757, Georgia, received March 30, 1758, assuring the Privy Council that the rule of neutrality will be observed and informing him of a recent treaty with the Indians bearing on the Bosomworth Claims.

Sir

'Tis but within these few days that I have had the honour to receive your Letter of the 11th. of January from the Council Office; annexed to an Instruction from his Majesty relative to the Neutrality to be observed by our Ships in the Gulph of Naples. I shall take particular care to communicate these Instructions to the Commanders of any private Ships of War that may put into the ports of this Colony, & insist upon an exact obedience being shewn to them. It gives me a great deal of concern Sir that my Letters from Ministry are so long on their way hither, & I am at a loss what to attribute this to.

I did myself the honour to write to you in August last, in answer to a letter I had then from you, in which I gave a short description of our situation.

Since that time no material occurrence has happened, except that I have had a Great Meeting with the Head Men of the Creek Nation of Indians, renewed our Friendship & Alliance with them & settled some other matters that hitherto had been productive of a good deal of uneasiness & altercation between us.

This Sir is all I have been able to accomplish, for the french have acquired so strong a party in their Nation, that to propose to the Indians to act offensively against them, would have given great umbrage, & been employed to our disadvantage by the Enemy, who being yet weak on the Mississippi, make a virtue of necessity, in affecting the greatest moderation, & aversion to spilling human blood, which has made impressions in their favour upon the minds of the Savages. I have distributed his Majesty's Presents to these Indians in as judicious & frugal a manner as I was capable, & dismissed them perfectly satisfied with their treatment. It will be necessary however to continue our attention & kindness, whilst the french are so active & assiduous to corrupt them. The more effectually to counteract their measures it would be highly requisite to have annual Supplies of Presents. This, tho' a considerable expence, may prevent a much greater one in maintaining an armed force here, which must be done should our Enemies gain their point. Herewith I send a Copy of our Treaty: the Article respecting Lands Islands was inserted at the desire of the Indians themselves, & regards certain claims that a man trumped up here by virtue of a Marriage with an indian Woman, & a Purchase he pretends to have made from some of the principal people of that Nation. This Affair which has caused many disputes with the Indians, strong apprehensions in the minds of our people, & a quantity of the best Lands on the frontier.

I have wrote pretty fully on this subject to the Lords of Trade, & the Agent for this Province.

I shall not here mention the defenceless condition of this Country, as the Representation of it by our Assembly, which I have already transmitted to you, contains every thing that need be said on this points.

It may not be improper to acquaint you Sir, that the Spaniards are intent on settling a Colony of 500 Families in Florida, & that some misunderstandings have lately fallen out between them, & the Indians, owing to some indiscretions of the former, & a jealousy entertained of their encroachments by the latter. I have wrote all I have been able to learn upon this matter to the Board of Trade.

Copy of a Treaty of Peace and Friendship between Gov. Ellis with the Upper Creek Indians, Savannah, Nov. 3, 1757, enclosed with Ellis to Pitt, Dec. 10, 1757.[32]

Henry Ellis to the Board of Trade, Dec. 15, 1757, Georgia, received March 30, read April 5, 1758, C.O. 5/646, C. 30, answering the Board's June 9 letter requiring an account of iron made in Georgia.

---

32. The treaty is given in ibid., 665-667.

My Lords

The only Letter I have received from your Lordships since I arrived here was one of the 9th. of June that came to my hands the 10th. instant wherein agreeable to His Majesty's Commands your Lordships desire I would immediately transmit an account of the quantity of Iron that has been made in this Colony between the years 1749 & 1756 distinguishing year.

In answer to which I must acquaint your Lordships that hitherto there has been no Iron Work erected in this Province nor any Essay made of the Ore with which it abounds.

Henry Ellis to the Board of Trade, Jan. 1, 1758, Georgia, received March 30, read April 5, 1758, C.O. 5/646, C. 31, giving an account of the state of the province, urging the expediency of a compromise with the Bosomworths and the necessity of a military force in the colony.

My Lords

I have received but within these few days two Letters from Mr Secretary Pownall one of the 7th March the other of the 3d June. The first inclosed an Act relative to the exportation of Corn from his Majesty's Plantations &ca which has been publisht here & all manner of regard will be shown to it. The other Letter conveyed to me the Resolutions of the house of Commons of the 23d May last upon certain pretensions of the Jamaica Assembly which I have communicated to the principal people here not to their disatisfaction & I shall endeavor having them inserted in the Journals of our Assembly at their next Meeting. This Body was industriously attempting to usurp the same power influenced by the example of South Carolina & had indeed made a considerable progress therein during the Administration of my Predecessor. The reducing things to their proper bounds has been a great object with me & not the least difficulty I have had to combat, tho' tis a satisfaction that my endeavors have not been altogether fruitless. 'Tis a great mortification to me that so many of my letters have miscarried as I flatter myself they would have furnished your Lordships with as true & circumstantial an account of the posture of affairs in this province as have hitherto come to your hands. In a former letter I touched upon the Misunderstanding that had fallen out between the Spaniards in this Neighbourhood & the Creek Indians as also the Correspondence it produced between the Governor of Augustine & myself. I have since learnt the whole truth of that affair which has enabled me to clear our people from the unjust suspicions the Spanish Governor harboured of their being instrumental to that disturbance. I now enclose to your Lordships a Letter he sent me & two that I wrote him which will fully explain our proceedings. I have not yet had an answer to the second Letter but have seen a Gentleman from Augustine who assures me the Governor is convinced of his mistake & has taken some measures for restoring the quiet of those parts.

My Lords I cannot help resuming the subject of the Bosomworths disputes. I am every day the more convinced of the expediency of terminating them in a satisfactory manner. My situation in respect to this Affair is very disagreeable. All the pains I take to detach the Indians from the Interest of the Bosomworths serve to excite their activity & increase their efforts to embroil us by poisoning the minds of the Savages by wicked & false suggestions. If on the other hand I should temporise & shew them any degree of countenance I might subject myself to suspicions of betraying the Interests of the Crown. These people would gladly take advantage of our national distress to accomplish their ends yet I believe nothing further is to be apprehended from them at present than retarding the Settlement of the Colony which indeed is a great evil.

I am persuaded they would accept of conditions much inferior to those I transmitted to your Lordships & I presume it would not be difficult to shew that it is the interest of the public in many respects as well as of the Bosomworths that an accomidation should speedily take place. In my former letter I represented the necessity of having a small Military force here & mentioned what had been done by Mr Reynolds towards raising three Troops of Rangers. The Officers were commissioned & about 40 of the first Troops levied. These for some time were subsisted by means of negotiable Certificates that acquired credit for a notion that the Crown would discharge them as it had done those Mr Oglethorpe issued in the last War.[33] That expedient soon failing I have since

---

33. Oglethorpe's expenses, incurred from 1738 to 1743 and amounting to £34,749.10. sterling, are included in Records of the British Public Records Office, Treasury Papers, T.1/306 to T.1/312. Additionally, in 1752, the Trustees paid Oglethorpe £583.0.4 ½ sterling for his military services to the colony.

been enabled to maintain them by a Credit the Earl of Loudoun gave me upon the deputy Pay Master at New York until he should hear from home. This is their present state & except these few Irregulars there are no forces in the Province. 'Tis greatly to be wished a Troop or two of these Rangers were kept on foot during the present War being well calculated for this Country service especially in case of Indian disturbances as they can shoot on horseback & ride full speed thro' the Woods. I have wrote pretty fully to Mr Martyn concerning them in order that he may solicit their establishment. We had lately a Company of the Virginia Regiment but they are just recalled for the defence of their own province. I continue to be visited by parties of Indians from the Creek Country whom I am obliged to entertain & give presents to, but this I do in a less degree than formerly as we have no fund to support it. I apprehend the whole expense attending these transactions will exceed the sum reserved for them near £1,000 which 'tis possible we may be able to discharge with part of the money annually allowed for contingencies provided no extraordinary demands are made upon it which however cannot be foreseen. Notwithstanding the very large sum drawn by Mr Reynolds to defray the expenses of the last Indian Congress at Augusta there are demands outstanding for upwards of £140 but I must confess the utmost prodigality & indiscretion was shewn upon that occasion. I must now mention to your Lordships an affair that deserves some regard. The present Manager of our Silk Fillature Mr Otterlinghe is in an indifferent state of health, & cannot be expected to live many years. No step has been taken to provide a Successor to him the consequence of which should he drop off would be that this culture so valuable, practicable; & nursed for many years at a considerable expense to the nation must immediately fall to the ground. Being upon no Establishment & naturally jealous I cannot prevail on him to instruct any body in this Art & he does not scruple to assign the precariousness of his Situation for a reason.[34]

See ibid., T.1/350, and Amos Aschbach Ettinger, James Edward Oglethorpe: Imperial Idealist (1936, Clarendon Press, reprinted 1968), 273-274, for a description of Oglethorpe's finances in 1750 and in 1752. He did not begin to collect meaningful sums from the Crown until after 1752.

34. Writing in 1743, William Stephens thought he had discovered the reason skilled instructors such as Mary Camuse refused

I humbly presume my Lords that as your justice & humanity can never permit you to put a hardship upon this poor man it would not be improper to ascertain his Annual Allowance & authorize me to appoint him an Assistant with a small Salary who might soon be qualified to seccced him. We have lately received two Boxes of Silk Worm Eggs forwarded from England by Mr Martyn, & are not without hopes that this important undertaking will at length compensate for the pains & expense that has attended it. The Society for the Encouragement of Arts & Manufactures have generously extended their regard to us by allowing a premium of 3 pence a pound on our Cocoons of the best quality which will induce more people to employ themselves that way.

There remains but to inform your Lordships that the people of this Colony are in general contented, & enjoy a great share of happiness & tranquillity in these calamitous times; that there is a visible spirit of industry & improvement among them & that numbers come daily into us drove from their habitations on the frontiers of the northern Colonies.

Henry Ellis to the Governor at St. Augustine, Aug. 22, 1757, Savannah, received March 30, read April 6, 1758, C.O. 5/646, C. 32, enclosed with Ellis to Board of Trade, Jan. 1, 1758, assuring him that Georgians did not provoke Indians in the southward to attack Spaniards.

Sir

I take this occasion of acquainting your Excellency with the honor the King has done me in appointing me to preside over this Province.

Indeed I ought to have notified this to you before but no

---

to teach others the art of winding silk. "If I am rightly informed," Stephens maintained, " 'tis Death for any Piedmontors. . .who shall divulge the Art (of winding silk) in another country." Like Mary Camuse, a Piedmontose from northwestern Italy, Ottolenghe also was a covetous and zealous guardian of his expertise, teaching only enough to maintain his position as a sericulturist. See Coulter, ed., The Journal of William Stephens, II, 83, 88; and CRG, XXIII, 227, 344, 468.

opportunity offered for that purpose.

I am no sooner made acquainted with your Excellency's Abilities & great personal merit but I learn that we are soon to have the misfortune of losing you from these parts which upon my own Account I cannot but lament as I flattered myself with having great satisfaction in holding a friendly Correspondence with you which might possibly contribute to our mutual advantage, & that of our Royal Masters.

I cannot omit informing your Excellency that a Report prevails here that the Savages are meditating some mischief against you & by a letter I had from the Southern parts of this Province I find that they have already seized four Spaniards. Upon which occasion I have wrote to the Magistrates & other persons in power to endeavor to recover them if no other means will prevail even to purchase them from the Indians. I have also desired our people to use their best efforts to accomodate any difference that may subsist between your Government & the Indians. And I assure your Excellency upon my honor that I have constantly & strenuously inculcated to those Savages who live in amity with us to shew the same regard to your Nation with whom we are in peace & friendship as to ourselves & I will upon all occasions discountenance every thing that may tend to the commission of such barbarities as are proscribed amongst men of religion & humanity. These are the Sentiments which I hope your Excellency will entertain of me & which I do not despair to justify by my conduct.

If there is any way wherein I can be of use to your Excellency here you may with great freedom command.

Alonso Fernandez de Heredia, Governor of Florida, to Henry Ellis, Sept. 19, 1757, St. Augustine, received March 30, read April 6, 1758, C.O. 5/646, C. 33, enclosed with Ellis to Board of Trade, Jan. 1, 1758.

Mui Señor Mio.

He rizevudo la de Va. de 27 del prossimo pasado Mes de Agosto con la estimacion que se merezen las atentas expresiones que en ella me haze, y satisfaziendo por mi parte, a las que debo a su generosidad, Digo que celebro que S. M. B. aiga confidado a Va. el Govierno de esa Provincia, y que se halle con ordones de su Soberano para mantener todo genero de buena correspondencia con este Govierno, en el que mientras quo Yo me mantenga observare con la major puntualidad las demonstraciones que piden la buena armonia, y neutralidad establecida entre neustras Cortes, y por lo que espero merezen a Va. para que no se interrumpa esta perfecta disposicion se sirva mandar ritirar de los Dominios de S. M. C. mi Soberano los establesimientos que trubiere en ellos de Ingleses, que mobiendo a los Indios, y subministrando les armas y municiones, vienana a inquietar estos Contornos y a trazer dano a los Hazendades que descuidades, y en la buena fee que se delic conservar en la tranquillidad en que nos hallamos padezen muchos persuicios como succedio la vez pasada de que Va. haze mencion, y antes de aier nuevamente cometieron iguales extorciones; este desorden Juede causar fatales consequencias, y el que hazen las embaraciones Inglesas con las Espanolas, a las que robando, sa que ando, y deteniendo en su navegacion como a contecio dias pasador una Balandra que venia a este Puerto darian motibos de sentimiento a la misma Carte de Inglaterra, la que deseando como Va. me dice una sincera inteligencia entre estos dos Goviernos no desaprobaráque Va. me facilitélos Vineras por mano del Asentista Dn. Jesse Fish que le judiere para este presidio que tiene hecha contrata con la casa de los Waltones vezinos de la Neuba York, pero sinque se mezele efectos de ropas niotras ad herentes que son prohibidos por Leyes establescidas de nuestro Soberano.

Va. vea si yo le puedo servir en este pais en alguna cosa que le executarécon la atencion debida procurandome a honor de complacerle on quanto penda de mi arbitrio.

Dios Güe a Va. Mr. A como desea &cc.

Dn. MONSO FERNZ de HEREDIR. [sic]

Translation[35]

I have received your letter dated the 27th of August with the esteem your polite expressions deserve, and also to satisfy those expressions I owe you because of your generosity. Let me say that I rejoice that his Majesty has entrusted you with the government of that province, and that you find yourself with orders from

---

35. The editors are grateful to Professor Marcel Andrade of the Department of Spanish at the University of North Carolina at Asheville for this translation. The incorrect Spanish is undoubtedly due to the copy available being made by a clerk in Savannah who knew no Spanish.

your Sovereign to maintain good correspondence with this government in which, while I serve, I will observe, with great punctuality, the Demonstrations required by the good harmony and neutrality established between our courts, and for what I believe it merits. So that this perfect arrangement is not interrupted, I ask you to please withdraw from the domains of his Majesty, my Sovereign, the settlements you may have among them of Englishmen. By subverting the Indians and supplying them arms and ammunition, they come to disturb these surroundings. They bring harm to the homesteads which are not cared for and damage the good faith that must be preserved for the tranquility in which we now find ourselves. They suffer many damages, as it happened the last time you mentioned. The day before yesterday they committed similar exploitations. This disorder can have fatal consequences, as can that damage which is done by English ships to Spanish, which they rob, plunder, and stop their sailing, as happened a few days ago to a Bilander[36] which was coming to this port.

These things would distress the English court, which, as you say, desires a sincere understanding between these two governments. It [the English government] would not disapprove your furnishing us supplies through the hands of the contractor, Jesse Fish, a factor for this garrison, which he has in the form of a contract with the house of the Waltons of New York, but without mixing clothing or other things forbidden by the laws established by our Sovereign.

Your Excellency should call upon me if I could be of service in this region in some way. I carefully will do whatever I can, always considering it an honor to please you in all that is within my power. May God guide your Mercy.

D. Monso Fernz. de Heridir

Henry Ellis to the Governor at St. Augustine, Nov. 28, 1757, Georgia, received March 30, read April 6, 1758, C.O. 5/646, C. 34, enclosed with Ellis to Board of Trade, Jan. 1, 1758, giving an account of the Creek raid against St. Marks.

---

36. A bilander was a small, two-masted ship used on the canals and along the coast of the Netherlands and Europe. In America, bilanders were of the same genre as periaguas, small boats of all sorts plying the coasting trade.

Sir

I have the honor of your Excellency's letter of the 19th. of September & have very seriously considered the Contents of it.

I am not a little surprised that your Excellency should harbour any suspicions of his Britannick Majestys Subjects encouraging the Indians to give disturbance to your Government. I have made the strictest enquiry I was able into this matter & cannot learn that any one step has been taken by our people of this tendency. I have made the same enquiry among the chiefs of the Creek Indians who were lately with me & have collected from their joint information that the difference subsisting between your Government & these Savages had its rise from several irregularities committed by the Garrison of St Marks whom the Indians impeach of having used some indecencies with their women. Tho' at the same time the Indians declare that when they attacked the Spaniards at that place it was unpremeditated; for a party had set out from their Country with an intention to hunt the florida Indians, but having altered their opinion & resolved to return home they thought it would be shameful to do so without carrying a Scalp with them & this consideration induced them to take that opportunity of resenting the indignity they conceived had been offered them by the Spaniards; That in the rencounter which thereupon ensued one of their head Men was killed & his friends thinking it incumbent on them to revenge his death committed the subsequent outrages. This is the best state of the case I can obtain & I have reason to believe that the information your Excellency has received by this time will confirm it & give you different sentiments of the English than you entertained when you wrote me.

Your Excellency has been pleased to request that I would order his Majesty's Subjects to retire from the Territories of the Catholic King.

I do not find that any such are settled in pacts that come under that description otherwise I would use my endeavors to remove them & indeed every other just cause of misunderstanding between the two Governments. And I cannot but repeat the Assurances I have already given that I have nothing more at heart than the Maintenance of that friendship & harmony that happily exists between the two Nations.

Your excellencys recommendation of Mr Fish has great weight with me and he may depend upon receiving every good office & indulgence from me that is consistent with the fundamental Laws of my Country and further I am sure your Excellency or he cannot expect as a breach of them would subject me to a severe censure.

An Abstract of Grants of Lands Registered in Georgia from 27 July 1757 to 27 Jan. 1758, received April 24, read June 1, 1758, C.O. 5/646, C. 40.

Grant dated 7th. June 1757
To James Hartley for 100 Acres of Land in the District of Medway, Registred 1st August 1757

Grant dated 5th. Febry 1757
To Edward Barnard for 500 Acres of Land in the District of Augusta, Registred 4th. August 1757
Allotted to him by the late President and Assistants

Grant dated 5th. Febry 1757
To John Stewart Junr for 500 Acres of Land in the District of Newport, Registred 4th. August 1757

Grant dated 7th. June 1757
To John Adam Trittlen for 100 Acres of land in the District of Goshen, Registred 8th. August 1757

Grant dated 5th. April 1757
To Michael Stutz for 100 Acres of Land in the District of Ogechee, Registered 8th. August 1757

Grant dated 7th. June 1757
To James Macfrary for 150 Acres of Land in the District of Ebenezer, Registred 8th. August 1757

Grant dated 7th. June 1757
To Michael Switzer for a Lot in the Town of Savannah No 8 in the Second Tything Anson Ward & 50 Acres of Land in said Tything & Ward, Registred 15th. Augt 1757
Allotted to him by the late President & Assistants

Grant dated 7th. June 1757
To Michael Switzer for a Lot in the Town of Savannah No 10 in the second Tything Reynolds Ward & 50 Acres of Land in said Tything & ward, Registred 15th. Augt 1757
Allotted by the late President & Assistants

Grant dated 7th. June 1757
To Balthaser Backer for 100 Acres of Land in the District of Ebenezer, Registred 27th. Augt 1757
Allotted to him by the late President & Assistants

Grant dated 7th. June 1757
To John Reutter for Town Lot & 50 Acres of Land in the Town & District of Ebenezer, Registred 27th. Augt 1757
Allotted to him by the late President & Assistants

Grant dated 7th. June 1757
To Ezekiel Backler for 200 Acres of Land in the District of Ebenezer, Registred 15h Septr 1757

Grant dated 5th April 1757
To John Deaveaux for 950 Acres of Land in the District of Ogechee, Registred 4th. October 1757

Grant dated 5th. April 1757
To John Deveaux for 500 Acres of Land in the District of little Ogechee, Registred 4th. October 1757
Allotted to him by the late President & Assistants

Grant dated 5th April 1757
To Mark Carr for 500 Acres of Land in the District of Medway, Registred 4th Octr 1757
Allotted to him by the late President & Assistants

Grant Dated 5th. April 1757
To Mark Carr for 200 Acres of Land being an Island in the District of Medway, Registred 4th. Octr 1757
Allotted by the late President & Assistants

Grant dated 5th. April 1757
To Thomas Carr for 500 Acres of Land in the District of Medway, Registred 4th Octr 1757
Allotted to him by the late President & Assistants

Grant dated 5th April 1757
To Daniel Donnam for 550 Acres of Land in the District of Newport, Registred 4th. Octr 1757

Colonial Records

Grant dated 5th. April 1757
To Donald McDonald for 200 Acres of Land at the head of the Branches of Newport River, Registred 5th. Octr 1757

Grant dated 5th. April 1757
To Solomon Shad for 250 Acres of Land in the District of Ogechee, Registred 5th. Octr 1757

Grant dated 5th. April 1757
To Henry Snider for 150 Acres of Land in the District of Ogechee, Registred 5th. October 1757

Grant dated 5th. April 1757
To George Peters for a lot in the Town of Savannah No 8 in Belitha Tything Heathcote Ward & 50 Acres of Land in said Tything & Ward, Registred 5th. Octr 1757
Allotted to him by the late President & Assistants

Grant dated 30th Septr 1757
To William Dunham for 500 Acres of Land in the District of Newport, Registred 14th. Octr 1757

Grant dated 30th. Septr 1757
To Nathan Taylor for 500 Acres of Land in the District of Medway, Registred 14th. Octr 1757
Allotted to him by the late President & Assistants

Grant dated 30th. Septr 1757
To John Smith for Town Lot Garden Lot & 50 Acres of Land in the Town & District of Ebenezer, Registred 15th. Octr 1757
Allotted to him by the late President & Assistants

Grant dated 30th. Septr 1757
To Gotleb Stayley for 150 Acres of Land in the District of Goshen, Registred 15th. Octr 1757
Allotted to him by the late President & Assistants

Grant dated 30th. Septr 1757
To Valentine Depp for Town Lot & 50 Acres of Land in the Town & District of Ebenezer, Registred 15th. Octr 1757
Allotted to him by the late President & Assistants

Grant dated 7th. June 1757
To William Elliott for 500 Acres of Land in the District of Newport, Registred 18th Octr 1757

Grant dated 30th. Septr 1757
To Audley Maxwell for 150 Acres of Land in the District of Midway, Registred 18th. Octr 1757

Grant dated 30th. Octr 1757
To Jacob Ports for 50 Acres of Land in the District of Goshen, Registred 22d Octr 1757
Allotted to him by the late President & Assistants

Grant dated 30th. Septr 1757
To John Pletter for Garden Lot & 50 Acres of Land in the District of Ebenezer, Registred 22d Octr 1757
Allotted to him by the late President & Assistants

Grant dated 30th. Septr 1757
To John Hangleter for 100 Acres of Land in the District of Ebenezer, Registred 24th. Octr 1757
Allotted to him by the late President & Assistants

Grant dated 30th. Septr 1757
To Ruprick Ershberger for Town Lot Garden Lot & 50 Acres of Land in the Town & District of Ebenezer, Registred 24th. October 1757
Allotted to him by the late President & Assistants

Grant dated 30th. Septr 1757
To Ludwig Ernst for Town Lot Garden Lot & 50 Acres of Land in the Town & District of Ebenezer, Registred 26th. Octr 1757
Allotted to him by the late President & Assistants

Grant dated 30th. Septr 1757
To Gabriel Maurer for Town Lot & 50 Acres of Land in the Town & District of Ebenezer, Registred 26th Octr 1757
Allotted to him by the late President & Assistants

Grant dated 30th Septr 1757
To John Maurer for Town Lot Garden Lot & 50 Acres of Land in the Town & District of Ebenezer, Registred 28th. Octr 1757
Allotted to him by the late President & Assistants

Grant dated 30th. Septr 1757
To Nicholas Cronenberger for Town Lot & 200 Acres of Land in the Town & District of Ebenezer, Registred 28th. Octr 1757
Allotted to him by the late President & Assistants

Grant dated 30th. Septr 1757
To George Fowl for 100 Acres of Land in the District of Ebenezer, Registred 28th. Octr 1757

Grant dated 30th. Septr 1757
To William Graves for 200 Acres of Land in the District of Newport, Registred 28th. Octr 1757

Grant dated 30th. Septr 1757
To Middleton Evans for 500 Acres of Land in the District of Medway, Registred 1st Novr 1757
Allotted to him by the late President & Assistants

Grant dated 7th. June 1757
To William Moore for 250 Acres of Land in the District of Ebenezer, Registred 1st Novr 1757

Grant dated 7th. June 1757
To Aaron Ward for 150 Acres of Land in the District of Hallifax, Registred 1st Novr 1757

Grant dated 30th. Septr 1757
To David Cunningham for a Lot in the Town of Savannah No 7 in the second Tything Reynolds Ward and 50 Acres of Land in the said Tything & Ward, Registred 2d Novemr 1757
Allotted to him by the late President & Assistants

Grant dated 30th. Septr 1757
To James Brooks for a Lot in the Town of Savannah No 4 in the second Tything Reynolds Ward & 50 Acres of Land in the said Tything & Ward, Registred 2d Novr 1757
Allotted by the late President & Assistants

Grant dated 30th. Septr 1757
To Robert Baillie for 500 Acres of Land in the District of Newport, Registred 2d Novr 1757
Allotted to him by the late President & Assistants

Grant dated 30th. Septr 1757
To John Prethero for 300 Acres of Land in the District of Hallifax, Registred 2d Novr 1757

Grant dated 7th. June 1757
To John Emanuel for 100 Acres of Land in the District of Augusta, Registred 8th. Novr 1757

Grant dated 30th. Septr 1757
To Daniel Nunez Rivers for 300 Acres of Land in the District of Great Ogechee, Registred 9th. Novr 1757

Grant dated 30th. Septr 1757
To Abraham Sarzedas for a Lot No 87 in the Town of Hardwicke, Registred 9th. Novr 1757

Grant dated 30th Septr 1757
To John Spencer for a Lot No 9 in the Town of Hardwicke, Registred 11th. Novr 1757

Grant dated 30th. Septr 1757
To John Sheraus for 100 Acres of Land in the District of Goshen, Registred 12th Novr 1757
Allotted to him by the late President & Assistants

Grant dated 7th. June 1757
To Sir Patrick Houstoun for 1000 Acres of Land in the District of Darian, Registred 12th. Novr 1757

Grant dated 30th. Septr 1757
To John Jacob Metzger for 2 Town Lots & 50 Acres of Land in the Town & District of Ebenezer, Registred 16th Novr 1757
Allotted to him by the late President & Assistants

Grant dated 30th. Septr 1757
To David Ashperger for a Town Lot & 50 Acres of Land in the District of Ebenezer, Registred 16th. Novr 1757
Allotted to him by the late President and Assistants

Grant dated 30th Septr 1757
To Hugh Kennedy for 150 Acres of Land in the District of Ebenezer, Registred 16th. Novr 1757

Colonial Records 115

Grant dated 30th. Septr 1757
To Henry Bourquin for 500 Acres of Land in the District of Savannah, Registred 18th. Novr 1757

Grant dated 30th. Septr 1757
To Henry Bourquin for 500 Acres of Land in the District of Little Ogechee, Registred 18th. Novr 1757
Allotted to him by the late President & Assistants

Grant dated 30th Septr 1757
To Henry Bourquin for 500 Acres of Land in the District of Little Ogechee, Registred 19th. Novr 1757
Allotted by the late President and Assistants

Grant dated 30th. Septr 1757
To Henry Bourquin for 500 Acres of Land in the District of Little Ogechee, Registred 19th. Novr 1757
Allotted by the late President & Assistants

Grant dated 30th Septr 1757
To Donald Mackintosh for 200 Acres of Land in the District of Newport, Registed 26th. Novr 1757

Grant dated 30th Septr 1757
To Donald Kennedy for 150 Acres of Land in the District of Sappelo, Registred 28th. Novr 1757
Allotted to him by the late President & Assistants

Grant dated 30th. Septr 1757
To William Kennedy for 50 Acres of Land in the District of Ebenezer, Registred 29th. Novr 1757

Grant dated 30th. Septr 1757
To Simon Reitter for 150 Acres of Land in the District of Ebenezer, Registred 29th. Novr 1757

Grant dated 30th. Septr 1757
To John Farley for 250 Acres of Land in the District of Ogechee, Registred 1st. December 1757

Grant dated 7th. June 1757
To Frederick Tradling for 150 Acres of Land in the District of Goshen, Registred 1st Decemr 1757
Allotted to him by the late President & Assistants

Grant dated 30th. Septr 1757
To George Dressler for a Lot in the Town of Savannah No 10 at Vernon Tything Heathcote Ward & 50 Acres of Land in said Tything & Ward, Registred 2d Decemr 1757
Allotted by the late President & Assistants

Grant dated 30th. Septr 1757
To Thomas Smith for 150 Acres of Land in the District of Newport, Registred 2d Decemr 1757

Grant dated 30th Septr 1757
To John Gaspar Walthour for 145 Acres of Land in the District of Little Ogechee, Registred 5th Decr 1757
Allotted to him by the late President and Assistants

Grant dated 30th. Septr 1757
To David Montagut for a Lot No 46 in the Town of Hardwicke, Registred 5th. Decr 1757

Grant dated 30th Septr 1757
To David Montaigut for 500 Acres of Land in the District of Savannah, Registred 5th. Decemr 1757
Allotted to him by the late President & Assistants

Grant dated 30th. Septr. 1757
To David Montaigut for a Lot in the Town of Savannah No 5 in the first Tything Reynolds Ward & 50 Acres of Land in said Tything & Ward, Registered 5th. Decr 1757
Allotted to him by the late President and Assistants

Grant dated 7th. June 1757
To John George Henry for 50 Acres of Land in the District of Goshen, Registred 6th. Decemr 1757
Allotted to him by the late President & Assistants

Grant dated 7th. June 1757
To John McCollum for 200 Acres of Land in the District of Hallifax, Registred 6th. Decemr 1757

Grant dated 7th. June 1757
To William Alexander for 150 Acres of Land in the District of Augusta, Registred 6th. Decemr 1757

Grant dated 7th. June 1757
To John Perkins for a Lot No 103 in the Town of Hardwicke, Registred 6th Decemr 1757

Grant dated 30th Septr 1757
To Joseph Alther for 117 Acres of Land on the Branches of Augustine Creek, Registred 5th. Decr 1757
Allotted to him by the late President & Assistants

Grant dated 30th Septr 1757
To Anne Parker Widow for 500 Acres of Land in the District of Savannah, Registred 10th. Decemr 1757

Grant dated 30th Septr 1757
To Anne Parker Widow for 500 Acres of Land in the District of Little Ogechee in Trust for the Heirs of Henry Parker Esqr deceas'd, Registred 20th Decr 1757
Allotted by the late President & Assistants

Grant dated 30th. Septr 1757
To Henry William Parker for 500 Acres of Land in the District of Little Ogechee, Registred 20th. Decr 1757
Allotted by the late President & Assistants

Grant dated 30th. Septr 1757
To Henry William Parker for 500 Acres of Land in the District of Little Ogechee in for Joseph Parker, Registered 20th Decemr 1757
Allotted by the late President & Assistants

Grant dated 6th. Decemr 1757
To Edward Goodale for 300 Acres of Land in the District of Little Ogechee, Registred 22d Decemr 1757
Allotted to him by the late President & Assistants

Grant dated 6th. Decr 1757
To James Baillou for a lot in the Town of Savannah No 1 at Belitha Tything Heathcote Ward & 50 Acres of Land in said Tything & Ward, Registred 26th. Decr 1757
Allotted to him by the late President & Assistants

Grant dated 6th Decr 1757
To Isaac Baillou for a Lot in the Town of Savannah No 5 in Sloper

Tything Percival Ward & 5 Acres of Land in said Tything & Ward, Registred 26th Decr 1757
Allotted by the late President & Assistants

Grant dated 6th Decr 1757
To Robert Stewart for 300 Acres of Land in the District of Darian, Registred 27th. Decr 1757

Grant dated 6th. Decr 1757
To Joseph Winn for 200 Acres of Land in the District of Newport, Registred 27th Decr 1757
Allotted to him by the late President & Assistants

Grant dated 6th. Decr 1757
To Jacob Keibler for 100 Acres of Land in the District of Abercorn, Registred 27th Decemr 1757

Grant dated 6th. Decr 1757.
To John Barns for 100 Acres of Land in the District of Great Ogechee, Registed 27th. Decemr 1757

Grant dated 6th. Decemr 1757
To Peter Torquintz for 100 Acres of Land in the District of Hallifax, Registred 28th. Decr 1757

Grant dated 6th. Decr 1757
To Philip Box for a Lot in the Town of Savannah No 10 in the first Tything Anson Ward and 50 Acres of Land in said Tything & Ward, Registred 28th. Decr 1757
Allotted to him by the late President & Assistants

Grant dated 6th. Decr 1757
To Angus McKay for 150 Acres of Land in the District of Newport, Registred 29th. Decemr 1757

Grant dated 6th. Decr 1757
To James Pritchard for 150 Acres of Land in the District of Newport, Registred 29th Decr 1757

Grant dated 6th Decr 1757
To William Norton for 200 Acres of Land in the District of Newport, Registred 29th. Decr 1757

Colonial Records 119

Grant dated 6th. Decr 1757
To John Stailey Senr for 50 Acres of Land in the District of Goshen,
Registred 31st Decr 1757
Allotted to him by the late President & Assistants

Grant dated 6th. Decr 1757
To John Stailey Junr for 50 Acres of Land in the District of Goshen,
Registred 31st Decr 1757
Allotted to him by the late President & Assistants

Grant dated 6th Decr 1757
To Samuel Hastings for 750 Acres of Land in the District of Newport, Registred 31st Decr 1757

Grant dated 30th Septr 1757
To Michael Boarman for 50 Acres of Land in the District of Goshen,
Registred 4th. Jany 1758
Allotted to him by the late President & Assistants

Grant dated 30th Septr 1757
To Michael Boarman for 100 Acres of Land in the District of Goshen,
Registred 4th. Jany 1758
Allotted to him by the late President & Assistants

Grant dated 30th. Septr 1758
To Michael Boarman for 100 Acres of Land in the District of Goshen,
Registred 4th Jany 1758

Grant dated 6th Decr 1757
To Paynter Dickinson for 250 Acres of Land in the District of Medway, Registred 6th. Jany 1758

Grant dated 6th. Decr 1757
To Stephen Dickinson for 200 Acres of Land in the District of
Darien, Registred 6th Jany 1758

Grant dated 30th Septr 1757
To Mattias West for 100 Acres of Land in the District of Goshen,
Registred 7th Jany 1758
Allotted to him by the late President & Assistants

Grant dated 30th Sepr 1757
To Peda Clara Stroub for Town Lot & 50 Acres of Land in the Town

& District of Ebenezer, Registred 7th. Jany 1758
Allotted to her by the late President & Assistants

Grant dated 6th Decemr 1757
To Conrade Rahn for 50 Acres of Land in the District of Ebenezer, Registred 16th Janry 1758

Grant dated 6th. December 1757
To Jasper Rahn for 100 Acres of Land in the District of Augusta, Registred 16th. Janry 1758
Allotted to him by the late President & Assistants

Grant dated 6th Decemr 1757
To Theobald Keiffer for 130 Acres of Land in the District of Ebenezer, Registred 16th Jany 1758

Grant dated 6th. December 1757
To Joseph Butler Senr for 460 Acres of Land in the District of Newport, Registred 16th Jany 1758

Grant dated 6th. Decr 1757
To Louis Mettear for 200 Acres of Land in the District of Great Ogechee, Registred 16th Jany 1758
Allotted to him by the late President & Assistants

Grant dated 6th. Decr 1757
To Paul Fuick for 50 Acres of Land in the District of Ebenezer, Registred 18th. Janry 1758
Allotted to him by the late President & Assistants

Grant dated 6th. Decemr 1757
To John Gugell for 50 Acres of Land in the District of Ebenezer, Registred 18th. Janry 1758
Allotted to him by the late President & Assistants

Grant dated 6th. Decr 1757
To Martin Lackner Senr for a Town Lot Garden Lot & 100 Acres of Land in the Town & District of Ebenezer, Registred 18th Jany 1758
Allotted to him by the late President & Assistants

Grant dated 6th Decr 1757
To Martin Lackner Junr for Town Lot & 100 Acres of Land in the

Town & District of Ebenezer, Registred 18th Jany 1758
Allotted to him by the late President & Assistants

Grant dated 30th Septr 1757
To Mattias Zettler for Town Lot Garden Lot & 100 Acres of Land in the Town & District of Ebenezer, Registred 19th Janry 1758
Allotted to him by the late President & Assistants

Grant dated 30th Septr 1757
To Peter Arnsdorff for Town Lot Garden Lot & 50 Acres of Land in the Town & District of Ebenezer, Registred 19th Jany 1758
Allotted to him by the late President & Assistants

Grant dated 30 Septr 1757
To Christopher Peters for 250 Acres of Land in the District of Savannah, Registred 19th. Jany 1758

Grant dated 6th. Decr 1757
To William Spencer for a Lot No 50 in the Town of Hardwicke, Registred 23rd Jany 1758
Allotted to him by the late President & Assistants

Grant Dated 6th. Decr 1757
To William Spencer for a Lot in the Town of Savannah No 6 in the third Tything Anson Ward & 50 Acres of Land in said Tything & Ward, Registed 23rd Jany 1758
Allotted to him by the late President & Assistants

Grant dated 6th. Decr 1757
To William Spencer for 500 Acres of Land in the District of Little Ogechee, Registred 23 Jany 1758
Allotted to him by the late President & Assistants

Grant dated 6th. Decr 1757
To Joseph Shubdrien for 100 Acres of Land in the District of Ebenezer, Registred 24th. Jany 1758
Allotted to him by the late President & Assistants

Grant dated 6th. Decemr 1757
To Nicholas Shubdrien for 50 Acres of Land in the District of Ebenezer, Registred 24th Jany 1758
Allotted to him by the late President & Assistants

Grant dated 30th. Septr 1757
To Elisha Butler for 200 Acres of Land in the District of Great
Ogechee, Registred 25th Jany 1758

Grant dated 30th. Septr 1757
To Elisha Butler for 500 Acres of Land in the District of Newport,
Registred 25th. Jany 1758

Grant dated 30th Septr 1757
To James Weston for 200 Acres of Land in the District of Ebenezer,
Registred 26th. Janry 1758

Grant dated 6th. Decemr 1757
To Jacob Walthour for 50 Acres of Land in the District of Goshen,
Registred 26th. Jany 1758
Allotted to him by the late President & Assistants

Grant dated 6th. Decemr 1757
To Maria Catherine Cranwetter for a Town Lot & 50 Acres of Land
in the Town & District of Ebenezer, Registred 26th. Janry 1758
Allotted to her by the late President & Assistants

An Abstract of all the Grants Registered in the province of Georgia from 27th. July 1757 to 27th. January 1758. Examined and compared with the Original Register at Savannah this 1st day of Febry 1758.

Pat Houstoun, Register

J. West, Secretary to the Chancellor of the Exchequer, to John Pownall, Secretary to the Board of Trade, Feb. 15, 1758, London, informing the Board that the Treasury will prepare and lay before the House of Commons a 1757-1758 estimate of the expenses for Georgia.

Sir

I desire you will acquaint the Lords Commissioners of Trade and Plantations that the Chancellor of the Exchequer hath received his Majesty's commands that their Lordships should prepare and lay before the House of Commons an Estimate of the Expense attending this Colony of Georgia from the 24th day of June 1757 to Midsummer 1758.

Henry Ellis to the Board of Trade, Feb. 18, 1758, Georgia received April 10, read April 12, 1758, C.O. 5/646, C. 35, giving an account of the colony, its new laws just passed, and his own deplorable state.

My Lords

The last letter I did myself the honor to write to your Lordships was of the 23d of December acknowledging the receipt of Mr Secretary Pownal's Letter inclosing Resolutions of the House of Commons.

These Resolutions I have shewn to every body of consequence here with good effect.

I called our Assembly together the 11th. ultimate & communicated the same to them to the end that they may be entered in their Journals to be referred to upon future Occasions which I have reason to think will be done without opposition.

The principal design of convening the Assembly now was to enforce a Law passed in the time of the Trustees to prevent an unlicensed intercourse with the Indians in the Neighbourhood of this Province. This Law was become obsolete & impracticable by reason of certain powers vested thereby in Officers that since the Change of Government no longer exist. This was discovered by the Out Settlers who thereupon set up a number of little Stores which drew multitudes of the Indians into the Settlements & produced great disorders. That & the purchasing of Land from them were evils that threatened the most fatal consequences to this Province if a speedy remedy should not be applied. I had therefore a Bill brought into the Assembly which is since passed subjecting any person or persons to a penalty of £100 sterling & confiscation of Goods, who shall hereafter presume to have any traffic or intercourse with the Savages bordering upon this Province without License from the Commander in Chief. I chose that the Bill should have this form free from other restrictions & regulations common to such Bills in order that it might be permanent as well from its unlimited duration as from the power that the Governor of this Province is invested with thereby to vary & accommodate it to whatever change or circumstance may hereafter arise. The method to be pursued is this as no person can trade without license upon application for one the person enters into Bond with Securitys for £2,000 Sterling the obligation of which is that the strictest obedience shall be shewn to the Instructions he receives with that permission.

These instructions contain a regulation of the Trade & the particular conduct the Trader is to observe both in respect to the Indians & this Government.

The other part of this Act which respects purchasing of Lands from the Indians by private people makes all such Purchases void & subjects the purchaser to a penalty of £1000 one half to his Majesty & the other to the person who shall sue for the same. This will effectually disable such people as Bosomworth from embroiling us & prevent him from attempting to acquire a further Title to the lands he claims to which at the last Congress the Indians declared he had no right whatsoever.

In a former letter to your Lordships I mentioned the inconveniences this province suffers from the quantity of lands that lie unoccupied said to belong to absent people whose names are scarce remembered whose titles are no where upon Record & whose services neither to the Public or in the performance of the conditions of their tenure entitle them to any regard. At the same time that the Inhabitants are by their means doubly burdened with Taxes & public labor, the Colony weakened by that separation of the Settlements that these vacant Tracts occasion, its population retarded & his Majestys quit Rents left unpaid. A Bill has therefore been brought into the Assembly & has already passed both Houses whereby all persons who shall neglect to ascertain their claims & take out proper Grants in the time therein prescribed are to forfeit & the lands to revert to the Crown to be regranted as his Majesty shall think proper. I encouraged this Bill because I conceive it will be productive of immediate & very beneficial conseuquences to the Colony & because a step of this nature from the Crown might be interpreted as harsh & unpopular but cannot appear in that light when it comes from the people themselves. At the same time this measure does not preclude the Kings indulgence to such who may be in danger of suffering innocently. There are some other Acts depending which may be attended with public utility such as a parish bill or to encourage the introduction of white Handercraftsmen by prohibiting Negroes being bred to Trades, one to renew & amend the Militia Act which is near expiring with some others of less consequence which may not pass at this Sitting As the Season of the Year will soon oblige me to adjourn the Assembly. As to the other matters people are perfectly easy & at rest there are no fresh alarms from any quarter. All our Accounts from the Indian Countries are favorable & though we discourage them as much as is prudent yet we continue to be visited by numbers of the Creeks, 40 of whom are now coming here & are but a few miles distant. I should not at all be displeased with such Guests provided I had a sufficiency to entertain them & dismiss them with content but we shall soon be much straitened in this respect & indeed have been as sparing of late in our Hospitality & Gifts as was possible considering the number of our Visitants. In regard to myself my Lords I shall soon be reduced to the necessity of requesting your good offices to obtain my recall especially if things continue long in their present situation.

The unavoidable expenses that my Station imposes on me I cannot long support with my present means. I am already upwards of £1200 Sterling out of pocket exclusive of the reimbursement of my Salary & perquesites & yet I have been as frugal as I could with decency, but coming out in a private Ship on my own expense by way of Carolina the necessaries I have been obliged to provide here & the excessive price that every thing bears with us is such that I daily spend nearly twice my income. I would freely devote my time, my quiet, & my labour to the public service & even a large share of my private fortune was I sure that this would not in the end reduce me to a state of necessity & dependance which it becomes every prudent man to guard against. Such my Lords is my situation which I hope your goodness will lead you to consider & to take such measures thereupon as your justice & wisdom may suggest.

Memorial of William Little to the Board of Trade, n.d., London, read April 12, 1758, C.O. 5/646, C. 36, containing observations on the silk culture in Georgia.

May it please your Lordships,

The Culture of Silk in Georgia having engaged the attention & encouragement of the British Parliament & being capable of becoming by proper management an Affair of importance but as it is now conducted by the Manager must prove abortive & frustrate all expectation, I have agreeably to your Lordship's permission set down some observations that occurr'd to me during my abode in that Colony.

In the year 1756 there was raised at Savannah 1024 lb. 14 oz of Cocoons at Ebenezer 1232 lb. 11 oz amounting in the whole to 2257 lb. 9 oz in Georgia. In Carolina there were raised the same year for the Filature at Savannah 1525 lb. 4 oz - for the Georgia

Cocoons were paid at 3 shillings per pound £328.12.9 for the Carolina at 1 shilling 6 pence per pound £114.5.5, so that there was more than half the quantity of Silk made in the single Town of Purghburgh [Purrysburg] in Carolina as in the whole Colony of Georgia & that too for half price & under the discouraging circumstances of being obliged to carry their Cocoons near thirty miles by water so that being under the necessity of waiting for a proper number many were lost by not being baked in due time, the Worm eating through & spoiling the Ball, from this short detail it is plain that a premium upon the Cocoons only, tho' so very great as to be more than double their value (for the Carolina people find their account in raising them for half what is given in Georgia) is not sufficient to answer the purpose and some other method is necessary to be taken. The most obvious is a reward for planting Trees but this has been constantly opposed by the Managers for no other possible reason than that it would render the culture more extensive, diffuse the art of reeling among the people & thereby lessen their own importance. It is indeed objected that such a Reward would open a door to many frauds & abuses which could not without great difficulty be prevented but be the difficulties ever so great they are far from being insuperable & unless they are overcome the culture can never be extended so as to become a provincial Concern much less a national Advantage, for tho' it is artfully suggested that there is no Want of Leaves yet that must be understood to mean for the subsistence of the Worms where they are at present hatched not for such an increased number as must be made to render this Business of any real importance as there is a space of some years from the planting the trees to the time of their yielding Leaves fit for the Nourishment of the Worms and they must be fenced round to preserve them from the Cattle.

    The distant prospect of a premium upon Cocoons will never induce poor people to undergo this trouble for their necessities require immediate payment for their labour & they are moreover not without apprehensions that the Parliament may be unwilling to grant future sums of money for encouraging a Work on which no progress is made & if that should be the case all their labour would be lost. To the Conduct of the Manager it must be ascribed that the Filature at Ebenezer has been un-employed nay so fearful was he lest it should interfere with his self interested views that it was concealed from the Governor that there ever was such a things in the Province until he himself discover'd it in his way up to Augusta and found it better constructed than that at Savannah particularly in having the Chimnies built on the Out Side a Circumstance very material in a hot Climate; there is also a well with plenty of the clearest water near it & wood to be had in abundance at a small expense; the people at Ebenezer are most remarkably assiduous in raising Cocoons & they are no less so in reeling them off & it is not only a great Hardship upon them to be denied the liberty of reeling at home, but as it has hitherto much retarded the Culture must in the end prove the utter Destruction of it for as they observe the circumstances of the Women alter almost very year so that their going down to Savannah is much hinder'd as some have small Children others are sickly. Others have Cattle to look after & all these could easily attend the Silk Business at their own Filature, tho' they can not go down to Savannah so that by not exercising themselves they lose their required dexterity & forget what they have learned & other Young Women who are exceedingly desirous to learn are deprived of an opportunity of doing it. The Women can live much cheaper at home than at Savannah for there they can scarcely find Lodgings & are under many other inconveniences which greatly diminish the reward of their labour. There are also many old Widows and other weakly persons who would be very glad to be employed in picking & sorting the Cocoons and other services for a small reward. By sending down their Cocoons they suffer great loss since they must pay boat hire can not send them in small quantities but must wait till a Boat full is brought together, and in the mean time the Aurelia bites through the Silk & makes it unfit to be sold. The Silk is exposed in a Boat to bad Weather & loses much of its fine colour beauty hardness etc. all which might be prevented by its being reeled off at Ebenezer.

 These Reasons are so Cogent that the Governor permitted them to make specimens of their skill in both sorts of silk & I believe when they appear as they will do if they are not secreted by the Manager they will prove to be as good as any made at Savannah, but if they should prove to be of any inferior kind it is humbly submitted to your Lordships whether it is not more eligible to have large quantities of Silk made in many Filatures of a some thing less value at first than to confine the Culture to the prime sort only at Savannah in one Filature since the practice of any Art is the most likely means of attaining perfection, nor can any inconvenience attend the employing many distinct Filatures in different parts of the province except the Trouble the Manager may in the beginning have in going from home at proper seasons to superintend & inspect the Work & even this trouble may be spared at Ebenezer the people there being as well versed in the Art as himself.

I have in compliance with my duty humbly presumed to lay these
things before your Lordships and cannot forbear deploring my Unhappiness in being precluded by your Lordships Minutes of the
14th. of March from offering many Tracts to your Lordships Consideration that might fully illustrate & explain several other parts
of the address & Remonstrance of the Assembly of Georgia to your
Lordships.

Henry Ellis to William Pitt, Georgia, Feb. 20, 1758, received
May 30, 1758, giving an account of a Spanish ship captured by
a Bermudan privateer and brought to Savannah.

Sir

    The 25th Instant I had the honour to receive your letter of the
16th of September relative to Monsr. Dabreu's complaints, of
divers Violences and depredations committed by his Majestys Subjects in America against those of Spain. The Kings Additional Instructions of the 5th of October upon that subject, I was honoured
with before; and have not failed to give Copys of them to the Commanders of all Privateers that have since touched at the Ports of
this Province, and at the same time, strenuously exhorted them to
a strict obedience thereof. I shall redouble my efforts upon every
future occasion that may offer, effectually to suppress such infamous proceedings which certainly have a direct tendency to embroil us with all the Neutral Powers. There has been but one
Spanish Vessel brought into any Port of this Province since I have
presided here viz the Aurora commanded by Don Ilario D'Aranda
from Pensacola, who, upon an examination of the Circumstances
which induced the Captain of a Bermudas Privateer to bring him
in, I immediately set at Liberty, with an offer of full reparation
for any Loss or Damages he might have sustained thereby, which
however he did not insist upon, the Bermudian Captain I severely
threatened and reprimanded, which may probably deter him from
doing the like hereafter.
    No Alteration has taken place in the Circumstances of this
Province since my last Letter of the 3rd of January, which contained every thing material that then occurred. We continue to
be Visited by great Numbers of the Creek Indians, who appear to
be well satisfyed with us; but expect entertainment and a few
presents when they come here which if they are refused, may disgust them, and give our Enemies an advantage. And as at present
we have not sufficient means to do this I must beg Leave Sir to

repeat my wishes that a Sum may be annually Allowed for this Service. £1500 at least, would be necessary, and no money could be better laid out, as the Creeks are the most formidable Tribe of Indians we have any Correspondence with upon this Continent. While they are at peace with us, they are a good Barrier against the French and Spaniards who, sensible of their importance spare no pains or expence to break their Connections with us, which however they may find a difficult task, if we are properly supported.

William Pitt to the Lords of Trade, March 7, 1758, Whitehall, read April 26, 1758, C.O. 5/646, C. 38, respecting a settlement made by some of his Majesty's subjects to the south of the river Altamaha.

My Lords

Having laid before the King your Lordships Letter of the 1st inst giving an account that certain of His Majestys subjects had without any license or authority made a settlement to the South of the River Alatamaha the reputed Southern Boundary of Georgia & of the conduct of the Spanish Governor of Augustine thereupon and your Lordships apprehending that this Transaction may be of dangerous consequence to the Provinces of South Carolina & Georgia from the influence those Settlers are represented to have with the neighbouring Indians & also that it may disturb the peace & friendship subsisting with the King of Spain; I am commanded to signify to your Lordships the Kings pleasure that you do forthwith acquaint me for his Majesty's information at what distance this Settlement may be from any of those which his Majestys subjects are possessed of in those parts & also what is the supposed number of the said Settlers; And it is the Kings further pleasure that your Lordships do report your opinion what Orders it may be most advisable to give for effectually preventing the bad consequences which your Lordships apprehend from so irregular a proceeding.

John Reynolds to the Board of Trade, March 7, 1758, London, asking for copies of his commission, instructions, and public papers to reply to the articles against his conduct.

My Lords

In perusing the Articles against my conduct in the Government of Georgia, which your Lordships have been so good as to allow me a Copy of and which I received this Morning I find it will be necessary for me to have recourse to my Comission and instructions the Copies of which and of most of my public papers I sunk when I was taken by the French and therefore beg that your Lordships will be pleased to order that I may have a Copy of the said Commission and instructions and likewise of such paragraphs of other papers either received or transmitted by me to your Lordships during my administration of that Government as I may find necessary for my inspection, in order to the justification of my conduct in the same in which I hope to give perfect satisfaction.

Henry Ellis to the Board of Trade, March 31, 1758, Georgia, read Nov. 21, 1758, C.O. 5/646, C. 43, giving an account of the present state of the Colony together with several acts lately passed by the Assembly.

My Lords

My last letter was dated the 18th. of Feby I then mentioned whatever occurred to me deserving your Lordships attention particularly that an Act had just received my Assent respecting our intercourse with the Indians which I now send for your Lordships inspection together with three others that were afterwards passed.

I have nothing to observe upon the object of these Bills as the design of them will fully appear in the Contents.

The planting Season advancing apace & no very material matter occurring I was induced to adjourn the Assembly the 15th. Inst. to the 15th. of June next.

The same good correspondence as formerly still subsist between the several Branches of the Legislature & the people in general continue quiet & contented.

Since my last upwards of an hundred of the Creek Indians have been with me upon the old errand in expectation of presents. They very chearfully acceded to the late treaty & tho' we were unable to treat with them the same munificence that those experienced who preceded them, Yet they departed well satisfied with their reception. Such numbers of them have late resorted here as have occasioned a great deal of employment & fatigue to me & not a little expense to the public. It is in vain to plead that the presents are exhausted for were they even convinced of this they would still come & expect to have their Guns Saddles etc. repaired & themselves subsisted in the meantime which alone would amount annually to a very considerable sum.

However irksome & inconvenient all these circumstances are I am afraid they must at this juncture be submitted to in order to preserve the friendship of such formidable & Capricious Neighbours & I may add that even a further supply is indispensably necessary to defeat the extraordinary efforts of the French who persist with unabating assiduity in their design of currupting & gaining them from us. I have about a third of the last presents that were sent us still left but no fund to defray the expense that will necessarily attend their distribution much less to support the charges that are continually growing from the frequency of Indian visits & I am persuaded your Lordships will not be surprised at this when it shall be known that no less than 1280 of these savages have been entertained at Savannah since my arrival. An inconvenience that proceeds from their attachment to & good understanding with us & how this is to be avoided without involving ourselves in much greater ones is difficult to comprehend.

This province still enjoys perfect tranquillity & we hear of nothing that is likely to interrupt it suddenly but however promising our prospect may seem it shall not prevent our taking proper precautions against the worst that may happen.

I am in hopes that long before this time the many dispatches I sent from hence are in your Lordships hands. The want of a direct Conveyance to England is at this time a great misfortune but I see no remedy for it until our exports are sufficient to encourage a number of Ships to come here. In the mean time the intelligence we receive from or transmit to Europe must be very much out of time as indeed we here & I find many of our friends at home experience. I generally send Copies of my dispatches by way of New York which must needs subject them to many unavoidable accidents & delays.

P.S. The Acts which accompany the first & second copies of this Letter & go by way of South Carolina & New York are the following vizt.

An Act for dividing the Province into Parishes & establishing the Church of England Worship.

One for regulating Indian Affairs

One to prohibit Slaves from being taught handicrafts

One to limit the time for Absentees to make good their claims to lands & take out Kings Grants

One to amend the Militia Act

One to enforce the fortification Bill &

One to amend the Market Act.

John Reynolds to the Board of Trade, April 17, 1758, London, read April 18, 1758, C.O. 5/646, C. 37, giving his answers to charges brought his administration as governor of Georgia.[37]

> THE ANSWER OF JOHN REYNOLDS Esqr Governor of his Majestys Colony of Georgia in America to a certain Paper entitled "State of the facts "respecting the Conduct of John Reynolds Esqr "& the state of the Colony of Georgia during "his residence there as Governor thereof" Received from John Pownall Esqr your Lordships Secretary by order of your Lordships on 6th. March 1758.

THIS RESPONDENT saith that his Majesty having been graciously pleased to appoint this Respondent Captain General & Governor in chief of the said Colony of Georgia in America by his Royal Commission bearing date the 6th. day of Aug 1754, This Respondent did in a few days after the date of the said Commission embark for the said Colony & on the 29th of Octr following Landed at Savannah where this Respondent immediately proceeded to take upon himself the Exercise of the Government of the said Colony & continued in the Administration thereof till the 16 day of Feby 1757 when this Respondent received your Lordships Letter of the 5th of Augst 1756 Signifying his Majesty's pleasure that this Respt should return to this Kingdom "To the end that an account of the present Situation "& circumstances of the Province & of this Respondents Conduct

---

37. Worried over the "Declining State" of Georgia under Reynolds' administration, the Board of Trade sought reasons for the colony's lack of progress. In the spring of 1756, Alexander Kellett, provost marshal and councilor, left for England at the request of "most of the Councillors, Representatives, Public Officers, Planters of Substance and Character" in Georgia to present a memorial to the Board. Extremely detailed, the memorial constituted a severe indictment of Reynold's activities as governor. It was to these charges that Reynold's replied in his April 17, 1758, letter to the Board of Trade. See CRG, XXVII.

"in the Administration of Government these might be laid before "his Majesty for his further directions thereupon" & at the same time directing this Respondent to resign the Government of the said Colony into the hands of Henry Ellis Esqr his Majesty's Governor thereof. And this Respondent saith that in obedience to his Majesty's Commands he immediately upon the receipt of your Lordships Letter resigned the Government to Mr Ellis accordingly & in a few days afterwards proceeded upon his return to England by the first opportunity which offered on Board a Merchant Man named the Charming Martha Wm Thomson Master bound from Georgia to the Port of London having previously furnished himself such necessary decuments & papers (so far as the time would permit) as he apprehended would best enable him to obey his Majesty's Commands agreeable to your Lordships letter. This Respondent not being at that time apprized of any particular charge exhibited against him nor informed of Mr Kelletts Memorial (which this Respondent now finds was exhibited to your Lordships on the 7th. of July 1756) nor having so much as heard of the names of any other of his Accusers whose letters your Lordships were pleased to refer to in your letter of the 5th. of August (& to wch Letters as well as the Authors of them this Respondent still remains a Stranger) And this Respondent saith that in his return to England the Vessel on which he was embarked was on the 9th day of May 1757 unfortunately taken by a french privateer M. Garralon Commander & carried into the Port of Bayonne from whence this Respondent procured a passage home having been stripped by the Enemy of this Journal & all his other papers & every thing else of value belonging to him & on the 7th. day of July 1757 this Respondent arrived in London from which time this Respondent hath yielded his constant attendance at your Lordships Board till the 6th. of March last when your Lordships were pleased to favor him with a Copy of the said State of Facts, to which this Respondent now proceeds to return his answer in the best manner his present circumstances will admit of under the disadvantage of the loss of his papers the interval of time elapsed since several parts of his conduct now enquired into were administered his ignorance till very lately of the particular Transactions objected to him Save by your Lordships letter of the 5th of Augt 1756 & the great distance at which he finds himself removed from the scene of those transactions from whence his Vindication as well as his charge must proceed; But this Respondent at the same time he laments the difficulties of his present situation must acknowledge your Lordships goodness in indulging him with the use of the Office Copys of his Commission & instructions & with access to the papers transmitted to the Board of recd from them by him during his administration.

Answer to the 1st Article. In answer to the 1st Article of the said State of Facts whereby it is imputed to this Respondent that many Articles of his Majestys Instructions upon points whereon he is directed to act with the advice & consent of the Council have not been entered upon the Council Books as usual in other Colonys. This Respondent cannot help expressing his wishes that the Articles here pointed at had been particularly specified that his Answer might have been more immediately adapted thereto. But this Respondent having upon this General Charge reviewed his Instructions Finds the fourth Instruction to run in the following words vizt "You are forthwith to communicate unto our said Coun-"cil such & so many of these our Instructions where in their ad-"vice & consent are required as likewise all such others from time "to time as you shall find convenient for our Service to be imparted "to them." By which Instruction as this Respondent conceives there is a general liberty reserved to him of communicating or withholding his instructions from the Council at his own discretion except as to such only where their advice & consent is required & even those instructions are not required to be entered upon the Council Books; But upon a further perusal of his instructions he does not find himself directed to enter any of them upon the Council Books except the 11th. Instruction relative to the power vested in him of suspending the Councellors for non attendance upon their duty; And ten other instructions from 40 to 49 both inclusive relating to the habeas corpus Act. And this Respondent saith It appears by the Council Books transmitted by this Respondent That he did on the 1st of Novr 1754 being in two days after his arrival cause his first instruction containing his Majestys appointment of Councellors for the said Colony to be read & entered in the Council Books & on the 4th of the same Month caused his said 11th. instruction to be read & entered in like manner & on the 7th of the same Month also communicated to them his Majesty's instructions in regard to the calling of a General Assembly & on the next day likewise communicated to them his instructions relating to the erecting of Courts of Judicature & on the same day also directed his ten instructions relating to the habeas corpus Act to be read to the Council & entered upon their Books & this Respondent does not recollect that he was required to enter any other of his Instructions upon the Council Books.

And as to such of his instructions which he was directed to communicate to the Council where their advice & consent was required tho' not to enter the same upon their Books; This Respondent saith he did communicate the same accordingly by frequently & distinctly reading the same over to them when in Council assembled nor can a single instance be produced wherein this Respondent has ever acted without their concurrence where his instructions required it. But this Respondent did not think it incumbent upon him or consistent with his Majesty's service (which was always his principal object) to give them Copys of all the Instructions he had received from his Majesty to which they seemed to think themselves entitled as apprehending themselves invested in an equal share of the Administration of the Colony with this Respondent & so he acquainted them in his Speech delivered to them in Council on 30th Septr 1755 which was transmitted to your Lordships with this Respondents letter of the 15th. Jany following. And this Respondent submits to your Lordships the inconveniencies which must have resulted from a General Communication by entry upon the Council Books of all his Instructions & whether the same would not have been a breach rather than a compliance with his Majesty's orders. And as to the usage of other Colonies in this respect this Respondent owns himself a stranger thereto nor can such usage whatever it may have been be considered as the rule and measure of his conduct to which he was never required to pay the least conformity.

Answer to the 2d Article. To the 2d and 3rd Articles this Respondent saith That his instructions as he apprehends no where direct him to advise with the Council as to the time manner or place of delivering this Majesty's presents to the Indians or to communicate to them afterwards what should pass at such conference with the Indians or to acquaint them with the disposition of the money allowed to answer the contingent expenses of this Service notwithstanding which this Respondent well remembers that he did consult them as to the delivery of the presents & that they approved of his proposals upon that occasion And that no particular minute or entry was made of such their approbation in the Council Books was owing with many other like neglects & omissions to the Neglect or Incapacity of the Clerk of the Council who was likewise one of the Members of the Council. But this Respondent saith that in the Minutes of the proceedings of the Council on the 7th. of Novr 1755 there is the following entry vizt "His Excellency acquainted the Board that he thought it was

"necessary that a Committee of the Council should be present
"with him at Augusta where he was shortly going to meet the In-
"dians to distribute his Majestys presents to them And therefore
"desired that three Gentlemen of the Council would go with him
"Accordingly Sir Patrick Houstoun Bart James Habersham & James
"Edward Powell Esqrs were nominated to attend his Excellency"
By which entry it appears as this Respondent apprehends that the
Council neither were nor were intended to be kept in Ignorance as
to the time manner or place of delivering these presents & that
this Respondent requested & they consented to give their attendance & assistance upon that occasion nor have they ever since
as this Respondent knows in their collective capacity signified
the least dislike as to the delivery of the said presents.

And this Respondent further Saith That not contented with consulting the Council this Respondent did also advise on that Occasion with many of the principal Indian Traders who were much
better acquainted with Indian affairs than were any of the Members of the Council (who this Respondent apprehends understood
very little of Indian Affairs) & agreeable to their advice this Respondent governed himself therein & this Respondent saith that
apprehending himself to be at full liberty for any thing to the contrary contained in his instructions to act in all affairs relating
to the Indians without the concurrence of the Council he this Respondent did not acquaint them in form with what passed at the
conference with the Indians the rather for that the proceedings at
such conference were of the most trivial & common nature & were
public & notorious neither did this Respondent particularly acquaint them with the disposition of the money allowed to answer
the contingent expenses of this Service nor did the same appear
necessary to this Respondent as he transmitted regular accounts
of such expenses to your Lordships to which no objections have
as he apprehends been at any time made & which now remain to
be passed with the Auditor of the Impress & this Respondent saith
that having communicated to the Council the Intent of his progress
to Augusta (vizt to meet the Indians to distribute his Majestys
presents to them) & having therefore desired them to accompany
him he this Respondent fully intended & would have consulted &
advised with them in their Capacity of Members of the Council
had any opportunity offered for that purpose. But this Respondent
saith that as the Indians did not meet him according to their appointment He had no occasion to hold a Council upon that subject
& consequently no entry could be made thereof in the Journals of
the Council nor could this Respondent transmit to your Lordships

regular minutes of any such proceedings had with the Indians. But this Respondent saith that in a letter he had the honor of transmitting to your Lordships of the 8th of Octr 1755 after acknowledging the receipt of the Indian presents this Respondent further acquainted your Lordships that he had already dispatched letters to all their chiefs acquainting them with the arrival of the presents & inviting them to an interview at Augusta & in a subsequent letter of the 5th. of Janry 1756 this Respondent further acquainted your Lordships that he had sent the Indian presents to Augusta to be distributed & appointed all the Indian Chiefs to meet him there in the first week of Decemr. That this Respondent went thither accordingly but the Indians neglecting the time of appointment this Respondent stayed there 10 days & then returned to Savannah leaving Mr Wm Little Commissioner & Agent for Indian affairs to deliver this Respondents speeches & the presents to them which he did to above 300 Indians who arrived there a Week after this Respondent came away & peace & friendship were renewed between them as fully appears from the Affidavit & Certificate of the gentlement & Indian Traders present at the Meeting hereinafter stated.

ANSWER TO THE 4th ARTICLE. To the 4th Article this Respondent saith That he did in his said letter of the 5th. of Jany 1756 acquaint your Lordships That whilst he was absent at Augusta (& which was one reason for his returning to Savannah so soon) two Transports arrived there from Nova Scotia with 400 French papists & Letters to this Respondent from Lieutenant Governor Laurence acquainting him that for the better security of that province he had sent those people to Georgia & did not doubt of this Respondents concurrence. That the Season of the year would not admit of their going back again & therefore this Respondent was obliged to receive them etc. & this Respondent further saith that he did according to the best advice invite the Indians to meet him at Augusta on a fixed day in the first week of Decr 1755 & they agreed to meet him accordingly in order to receive his Majestys presents & to renew & confirm the peace & friendship which subsisted between the Kings Subjects & them as usual upon the arrival of a new Governor in any of his Majestys Colonies upon which occasion they always expect handsome presents. And this Respondent further saith That after having waited 10 days at Augusta in expectation of seeing the Indians according to their own appointment but to no purpose this Respondent was advised by persons who perfectly understood the temper of the Indians to return to Savannah for that it would give the Indians a very mean opinion of the new Governor if he should suffer himself to be trifled with by waiting for them at Augusta any longer than he did after the time of their appointment was expired. And indeed this Respondent had been previously informed in his passage to Augusta That their meeting him at that Season of the year was very uncertain notwithstanding their promise & which information this Respondent received by several letters from some of those Traders whose interest it was to keep the Indians to their winters hunting advising this Respondent to go back again & defer the interview until the Month of April for that they were sure the Indians would not come as they had appointed. But which advice this Respondent then disregarded as considering it was his duty to be steady & keep his appointment with them whether they did or did not regard their appointment with him & therefore this Respondent proceeded to Augusta. But whilst this Respondent stayed there different expresses from the Indians arrived every day with accounts some times that they would come & at other times that they would not according as they were instigated by the Substitutes of the Indian Traders who have great influence with the Indians among whom they reside.

Their Meeting being thus uncertain & the extraordinary occurrence of the arrival of no less than 400 french Papists at Savannah happening at the same Juncture (by which this Respondents presence was become absolutely necessary there) did at length determine this Respondent to return to Savannah. But this Respondent before his departure from Augusta drew up in writing such speeches to the Indians & such instructions for Mr Little as he thought proper for him to observe in case the Indians should afterwards arrive in the course of that Month, leaving Mr Little at Augusta where he was directed to consult with the principal Indian Traders (who all reside there) in regard to the best means of delivering this Respondents Speeches & a part of the presents as his Majestys free Gifts whilst this Respondent proceeded to Savannah where he consulted the Council & took such steps as were proper in regard to the 400 french who were then lying before the Town in Two Transports & this Respondent saith that such being his motives for his return to Savannah.

So he doth not recollect to have made any mention in his said letter of 5th. Jany 1756 that there were a great number of material points in reference to disputes with the Indians concerning lands granted by them to private persons in prejudice to his Majestys Rights & other matters of great consequence to the Colony necessary to be attended to & settled with the Indians at that Interview

(However this Respondent must herein refer himself to the said Letter when produced) on the contrary this Respondent saith The presents to be then distributed to the Indians were considered as his Majestys free gift to them & the Customary Gratuity upon the Arrival of a new Governor & according to the best intelligence this Respondent could procure of the disposition of the Indians at that time. It would have been very impolitic to have given them these presents in consideration of any Cession of their Lands in return or even at that ime to have seemed at all desirous of their Lands. And the french being then very industrious in using every Art to gain the Indians over to their Interest one of their chief arguments was that the English wanted nothing but their lands & then to make slaves of them of which your Lordships will find early mention made in this Respondents Letter of the 5th. of Decr 1754. To obviate which Insinuations of the French, These presents were intended as a free Gift entirely without any material Negotiation being then settled with the Indians more than the Renewal & confirmation of the peace & friendship before subsisting.

As to Mr Little's qualification for this Trust this Respondent was then assured & is now convinced that he could not have found a more proper person in the Colony & he being at the same time Agent for Indians Affairs the discharge of this Trust fell more immediately within the province & no objection as this Respondent has heard was ever made to his conduct therein. As to the personal charges against him in his private character This Respondent begs leave to defer giving a more particular Answer thereto till he comes to some of the following Articles where the same are more particularly pointed out. But this Respondent saith It appears by an Affidavit of several Indian Traders Sworn the 20th. of Novr 1756 & by the Certificate of David Douglass & Edward Barnard Esqrs two of his Majestys Justices of the Peace for the District of Augusta (& Mr Douglass then Speaker of the Assembly & Representative for Augusta) the said several persons having been all present at the distribution of the Indian presents, That the same appeared to them to be made with the strictest justice discretion & frugality & that tho' one of the Chiefs seemed at first displeased with this Respondents return to Savannah yet being soon convinced of the necessity of it he was fully satisfied & all the head men went home perfectly well pleased & as well satisfied as could be wished & that the event has proved they were sincere. To which Affidavit & certificate now in your Lordships Office this Respondent begs leave to refer.

ANSWER TO THE 5th. ARTICLE. To the 5th Article this Respondent saith That he did previous to the interview with the Indians advise Mrs Bosomworth & her husband not to be present thereat. But as these Meetings are always held in the most public manner where every person may be present that pleases It was not in the Respondents power to prevent their presence. Neither if it had been practicable would it have been prudent to prevent their presence. Neither if it had been practicable would it have been prudent to have forcibly kept them from the Conference Since her Interest with the Lower Creek Indians (being Indian & nearly allied to Malatchy their then Emperor) was such that she might have raised a disturbance on that Account. Since this State of Facts delivered to this Respondent some questions upon this head In answer to which this Respondent then alledged to your Lordships that nothing was transacted at this Meeting relative to Lands & this Respondent again begs leave to repeat his former assertion; For tho Mrs Bosomworth in private conversation with the Indians prevailed upon them to bring the matter of her Grant from Malatchi in question during the confernece Yet in public she was not permitted to have any discourse with them & they were particularly cautioned to regard nothing but what they heard from such as were duly Authorized to confer with them & the discussion of that Grant at that time was waived for several reasons. Because the Agent declared to them he had no authority to do any thing with regard to Lands as it was entirely foreign to the Intention of the Meeting & principally because the Upper & Lower Creeks were divided amongst themselves as to the power of making such Grants. So that the matter was preferred to a future General Meeting of the Upper & Lower Towns not the validity of Mrs Bosomworth's Grant in particular but the power of making any Grants at all which method was taken as well to avoid the ill consequences which the Entring into a Contest with the Indians might occasion as also because her greatest if not sole influence with the Indians depended on Malatchi who was then dangerously ill & whose approaching death was foreseen & soon after followed & because Mrs. Bosomworth herself could not in the course of nature Live long & whenever she dyes all disputes upon that head will be at an end her husband having no more interest with the Indians than the greatest stranger to them.

Your Lordships were pleased upon this Respondents late attendance at the Board to produce a paper which had been transmitted under the public Seal amongst other papers the Bosomworths thought necessary for the support of their cause in regard to which this Respondent apprehends that the truth of such paper is no more Authenticated by being put under the Seal than that of many other papers (many of which are contradictory to each other) & this Respondent did not at that time recollect that any such paper had been sent for it had not the least reference to the matter than under enquiry which was the usage the Bosomworths had received from the Court of President & assistants & therfore this Respondent might easily pass it over as an useless paper for it appears from the Report which this Respondent had the honor to make to your Lordships that no notice is taken of this paper which is false in every essential point & when it was frequently offered to the agent it was as often rejected by him as fictitious nor would he make any alteration in it tho frequently importuned so to do but declared the whole to be a false Representation of every thing material. And this Respondent further begs leave to observe that it is impossible this pretended Abstract cou'd have any consequences Since it is the constant & invariable Rule never to Regard any thing as the Sense of the Indians but what is delivered by the Mouths of Sworn Interpreters. And here this Respondent cannot forbear again lamenting his difficult Situation. For had this Article been transmitted to him in Georgia he could have proved the whole to be true as above related by the Testimony of all the Interpreters & great numbers of other Persons who were present at the conference.

ANSWER TO THE 6th. ARTICLE. To the 6th. Article this Respondent Admits that Mr Little whom he had appointed to be the Agent for Indian Affairs was allowed to charge 6 Per Cent upon the original cost of the Presents as a Commission to himself; Because this Respondent was informed by letters from Carolina That such was the usual allowance in that Colony upon the like occasion & because the same Commission had been allowed to Mr Patrick Graham the former Agent for the delivery of Indian Presents And this Respondent presumes it will not appear that this charge was extravagant if it be considered that there is a great trouble & fatigue in attending the delivery of these presents to the Indians for 16 Months together & keeping the accounts during that time (for they were not half of them delivered at Augusta but kept in store to be issued as occasion should require And some of them were yet when this Respondent came away from Georgia) & the whole Commission claimed by Mr Little amounted to no more than £45 being 5 Per Cent on £900 the prime cost of the Goods. As to the variety of other charges for entertainments etc. This Respondent is well assured there was no more money expended on this occasion than was absolutely necessary & the best Oeconomy was observed therein. Nor did the charges exceed the money allowed to answer the contingent expenses of this service. Nor did Mr Little furnish any materials for those entertainments but the Bills for the several particulars were attested by those people who furnished them which this Respondent saw before he would pass the Accounts.

ANSWER TO THE 7th. ARTICLE. In answer to the 7th. Article this Respondent agreable to his former letter to your Lordships of the 5th of January 1756 already here stated begs leave once more to assure your Lordships That neither of the two Transports mentioned in this Article & that letter were arrived at Savannah before this Respondent set out for Augusta but just as this Respondent was going into the Boat to proceed thither he was informed that one of those Transports with 120 French was then at Tybee at the distance of 16 Miles from Savannah & would arrive the next Tide. Whereupon this Respondent wrote an order to the chief Pilot forbidding him at his peril to bring any more such people into the province & directing him to give orders accordingly to the other Pilots which would effectually have prevented the Second Transport from coming into the Province (as there was no danger apprehended from the first Since she brought but 120 People mostly women & children Whereas the second had 280 mostly Men) had not Mr Jones (who was one of the Council & Senior Justice of the General Court & first Officer of the Militia) and to whom this Respondent Gave it in especial charge to send his said order down immediately to the Pilot at Tybee Neglected to do so till the Ships were actually arrived. And this Respondent has since had strong reason to believe This Neglect was designed. Had this Respondent upon the sudden intimation given him of the expected arrival of one of the Transports stayed at Savannah a day longer (as he must have done to have called a Council) he would not have been able to prosecute his Voyage to Augusta (being then unable to Ride 150 Miles) for the River then began to fall & had actually fallen many feet So that there would not have been Water enough for the Boat to pass up the River & the Indians would have been highly affronted. If this Respondent had disappointed them which this Respondent considered might have the worst consequences as the French would gladly have availed themselves of such a circumstance. When the Respondent arrived at Augusta He received an Account from one of the Members of the Council of the arrival of these Transports with 400 French at Savannah together with the Minutes of the Proceedings of the Council which he had held thereupon in this Respondents absence wherein it appeared that a supply

of provisions was sent on board the Ships which this Respondent
approved of & this Respondent says he apprehends it would have
been irregular for him to have concerned himself in sending home
the minits of the proceedings of a Council held without his being
present & who sat without any authority from him & not being able
to assemble of their own authority what they then did could not be
considered as the proceedings of a Council & this Respondent further saith that the Business thus transacted by the Council might
as well have been done by Mr Russell the Commissary alone as it
would have been according to the orders this Respondent had sent
him if no Council had been held.

And this Respondent further says he does not believe that any
of those French Inhabitants perished for want since those who
were sick or otherwise unable to work for their living were supplied out of the contingent money. And it appears by the Minutes
of the Council of 14th. Decr 1755 at which Mr Kellett himself was
present That orders were then given for leave to the French passengers on board the Prince Frederick to land & that they should
be allowed for 10 days a pound of rice to each person & that Boats
should be provided to carry them to different parts of the Colony
& letters to be wrote by the Clerk of the Council to the Magistrates recommending them to their care & it was further ordered
that Mr Russell the Commissary should furnish them with provisions & boats. That many others of them built boats for themselves & left the Colony this Respondent knows to be true for
having no orders to receive or detain them or fund for their support
this Respondent judged it best to let them go as they were all Papists & consequently enemies to our Religion & Government &
unfit to be suffered to remain in such a very weak & defenceless
Colony as Georgia then was. And many of them were gone out of
it before this Respondent came from thence. As to the authentic
papers produced by Mr Kellett or any other persons relative to
this or any other of the Articles in the State of Facts this Respondent having had no opportunity of seeing the same cannot give a
more particular Answer thereto but in General this Respondent
begs leave to assure your Lordships that there is nothing advanced in this his Answer which he shall not be able with your
Lordships permission to clear up & support in the most satisfactory & most unexceptionable manner.

ANSWER TO THE 8th. ARTICLE. To the 8th Article this Respondent saith that he did very truly allege to your Lordships in his
letter of 29th. of March 1756 That the three Members who had
been chosen & returned upon this Respondents Writs to compleat

the number which his Majesty had been pleased to direct that the Assembly should consist of were none of them admitted to sit. And in case it should not appear to your Lordships from the Journals of the Assembly that they refused to admit these Members or that these Members ever applied or produced any qualification of their having taken the oaths this Respondent humbly Apprehends the Silence of the Assembly in Journals of their own framing in respect to their own irregular proceedings cannot be changed into proof that no such irregular proceedings were had or be alone sufficient to destroy this Respondents Assertion That the three Members were neither admitted nor sworn is not only evident from the silence of the Journals in that respect but from this Respondents Message to the House entred in the Journals of the 13th. in answer to their Message of that day wherein this Respondent acquaints them that he will receive no Message nor book upon any thing valid that may be done by them till his former message be complied with & the elected Members therein mentioned be admitted into the House. So that the non admission of those Members appears to this Respondent to stand confessed upon the face of their own Journals & that the Misunderstandings between the Assembly & this Respondent were occasioned solely by that incident & that they had it in their power from this Respondents own overture to them to remove this understanding by their bare compliance in the admission of those Members which Concession their Journals Show they were not willing to make. If further proofs were necessary as to the non admission of those Members This Respondent begs leave to say It is of public notoriety in the Colony & that if he was now upon the spot he could produce a hundred people to give their testimony both of the refusal of the Assembly & that the Members did attend to be admitted & for that purpose came from distant parts of the province.

As to these Members producing their qualification of having taken the Oaths at the time they applied to be admitted which is mentioned as an essential circumstance necessarily previous to their taking their Seats This Respondent saith It appears from the Journals to have been the custom after the introduction & admission of a Member for the House to send two of their own Members with the Person to be Admitted to take the state oaths before the Governor. The irregularity of this proceeding has been already pointed out to your Lordships by this Respondents Letter of the 29th. of March & by his Message to the Assembly of the 12th. of Febry 1756 transmitted to your Lordships in their Journals & therefore this Respondent will enlarge no further upon it But

submits it to your Lordships that had it been such an irregularity
& misbehaviour as would have allowed of a discussion by way of
address That yet the Address of the Assembly in Answer to this
Respondents Speech upon that occasion so far as it respected the
Admission of the Members was wholly evasive & uncandid nor did
this Respondent otherwise decline the discussion of an address
than by Insisting upon the admission of the excluded Members
as a preliminary thereto, till which time no Address could be considered as the Act of that branch of the Legislature but of a few
Individuals only. Having thus dismissed them with a second Message in answer to their Address This Respondent thought it proper
as he had done before to give them time to cool by adjourning them
for a few days & reasoning with the most dispassionate Members.
Nor did this Respondent entertain the least thoughts of dissolving
the Assembly till he found that the Moderation of his Measures
only served to encourage them to a more violent & outrageous procedure. For the motives to this dissolution this Respondent must
beg leave to refer your Lordships to his Speech upon that occasion
to the Assembly upon the 19th. of Feby 1756 as entered upon their
Journals to the Speakers protest of the 16th. of the same Month
accompanying the same to this Respondents Letter to your Lordships of the 29th. of March 1756. And this Respondent submits
it to your Lordships whether (after the violent proceedings of the
Assembly) on the 13th. of Febry upon the Receipt of this Respondents Message of Adjournment inforcing the same by violence from
the hands of the Speaker in confining him (who was paying due
regard to this Respondents adjournment of them) in his chair &
compelling him to sign a paper of address to this Respondent
against which proceedings the Speaker drew up his declaration
and protest in writing (this Respondent could consistent with his
duty to his Royal Master & the honor & dignity of the character
with which he stood invested so far countenance these irregular
& violent proceedings of only eight or nine persons) (for there
were not above 12 Members that attended the House at this Session) as to permit their further continuance together & whether
this Respondent was not therefore under an indispensible necessity of resorting to the only means in his power to put a stop to
this ferment by dissolving such an Assembly who had excluded
the three Members above mentioned & had reduced themselves to
so small a number that their opinion was far from being the sense
of the province (which nineteen persons had a right to represent).

ANSWER TO THE 9th. ARTICLE. In answer to the 9th. Article
This Respondent saith That his Majesty in his 13th. Instruction

to this Respondent was pleased to declare his Will & pleasure
that the General Assembly should consist of 19 Representatives
to be chosen in manner therein mentioned & by the 17th. Instruction this Respondent is restrained from giving his assent to any
Law for enlarging or deminishing the number of the Assembly.
Agreeable to which instructions (both entered on the Journals of
the Council) & the obvious sense & meaning thereof as the same
appeared to this Respondent He did in his Message to the Assembly of the 12th. Febry 1756 Expostulate with them for their refusal
to admit the excluded Members (tho' without complaint from the
district for which they were returned or Petition from any other
Candidate) as a very unjustifiable proceeding not only as it was
irregular in point of form & a violation of the privileges of the
subject but as it was a contempt of the authority his Majesty had
been pleased to invest him with to take care that the Assembly
consisted of 19 Members & that this number should not be enlarged or diminished. That it was apparent to this Respondent
that it was not compleat by the promotion of 2 Members & the removal of one to serve who had never qualified (which was signified to this Respondent in Council under the hand of the said Member) & therefore this Respondent caused the proper Writ to be issued
in the Kings name to compleat the number of the Assembly as he
was authorized & commanded by his Majesty so to do. That to
proceed upon public business without admitting all the Members
would be robbing their Constituents of their undoubted right of
being consulted in their Representatives & consequently an infringement of their privileges. By which Message this Respondent never intended nor does the same as he apprehends import that
the Assembly should understand that no less than 19 could make a
House but only that 19 Members had a right to represent the province. If such a number were desirous of being admitted & willing
to give their attendance and this Respondent humbly apprehends
it was his duty to take care that the whole number if duly elected
should be admitted if they desired the same, otherwise ten Members might take upon them to represent the Assembly & exclude
the other nine. As to this Respondents issuing Writs for filling
up the vacant seats during the interval of the Session it arose
from the general discontent there was in the Province in regard to
the Laws past in the preceding Session on account of the small
number of Members of which the assembly was composed & the
difficulty of attending the execution of some of the Laws. And
the Members being otherwise duly elected This Respondent submits whether the Writs not being issued in consequence of an

application from the House to the Governor (which could not be made during a recess) will be considered as a circumstance of sufficient weight in a Country so newly established as to vitiate such Election & make them void leaving the Assembly at liberty to consider those Elections as void without any enquiry into the merits or providing for new Elections upon a supposition of their being void & at the same time to proceed in the ordinary course of Business as if the House was compleat.

ANSWER TO THE 10th. ARTICLE. In answer to the 10th. Article this Respondent says it appears from the Journals of the Assembly That on the 3rd of Feby 1756 a Message was sent from the Council to the Assembly desiring that House to inform them what was become of two Bills One for "establishing & regulating patrolles in this province" and the other "To prevent the illegal "settling of Lands in the Province of Georgia." Both of which were returned to that House after the Council had agreed to their Amendments & passed the same the last Session & neither of which were ever presented to the Governor for his assent. And that on the next day the 4th. of Feby upon a Motion made to take the Message at that time in to their consideration the same passed in the negative & the consideration thereof was ordered to be postponed but that the same was not afterwards resumed on that day & that on the next day (the 5th.) after having previously proceeded upon other Business upon a second Message from the Council to the House Resolved to take the same into consideration at 3 o clock that afternoon on which last mentioned day this Respondent admits he did adjourn the Assembly till that day sennight. But this Respondent denys that the Council charged Mr Little or any other person with having secreted these Bills otherwise than as in their Message Nor did he make this short Adjournment in order to skreen Mr Little from any inquiry into his conduct but for the reasons already given by this Respondent in answer to the 8th. Article & as to the charge made upon Mr Little by this Article & supposed to be insinuated by the Message of the Council about his having secreted two Bills, It had appeared upon enquiry to the house during the preceding Session & after they had sent the same up to the Council that the Patrole Bill as it was framed gave great offence to the Inhabitants of Savannah & therefore the same day took those amendments into consideration & they referred the further consideration thereof to the 27th. of March before which time they knew they should be prorogued & they were accordingly prorogued on the 7th. of March by which that Bill miscarried for that Session. As to the other Bill for preventing illegal Settlements of Land The House

being of opinion upon further consideration thereof after the same
had been returned with Amendments from the Council on the 21st
of Febry 1755 That the inconvenience proposed to be remedied by
that Act were already sufficiently provided for Did therefore agreeable to their Method of proceeding the same day upon the Patrolle
Bill adjourn the further consideration thereof 'till the 28th. of the
same March. So that both these Bills (if it may be allowed to
reason from the usage of Parliament) were at an end without ever
receiving the Assent of the Assembly in their amended state or
being brought to a Maturity for the Governors Assent & consequently the Message of the Council in a subsequent Session relative to those Bills was irregular & inconsistent with the usage of
Parliament. All which is apparent from the Journal of the Assembly
transmitted to your Lordships in the year 1755.

ANSWER TO THE 11th. ARTICLE. In answer to the 11th. Article
This Respondent Saith That this Respondent having represented to
your Lordships the extraordinary proceedings & resolutions of the
Assembly upon a former occasion your Lordships were thereupon
pleased to write to this Respondent That you were concerned to
find that this Assembly had laid in such early claims to privileges
& powers which tho' of long usage enjoyed by some other Assemblys were inconsistent with all Colony constitution whatever, contrary to the practice of the Mother Country in like cases & the express directions of his Majestys Commission by which alone that
Assembly was constituted & that this Respondent should do well
therefore to use such Arguments with the most cool & dispassionate Members upon this point as this Respondent should think would
be the most likely to prevail upon them to recede from those unjustifiable claims & pretensions. This Letter the Respondent considered
not as written merely upon the occasion then existing which had
subsided before this Respondent could receive the Letter but as a
general Rule & direction for his future conduct in case of any subsequent Irregularities in the Assembly. Accordingly when this Assembly began again their unjustifiable proceedings in refusing
admittance to three Members whose Election was never in the least
questioned This Respondent did use such arguments with the most
diapassionate Members as he thought most likely to prevail in
their private Capacities as Individuals but finding the same ineffectual this Respondent was then obliged to speak out to them in
their Collective Body as he did by his Message of 12th. Febry
1756 in the language of your Lordships Letter tho' not as part of
any such Letter but as the General sense of His Majestys Ministers
communicated to this Respondent in respect of their irregular

proceedings. And it is with the utmost concern this Respondent finds your Lordships considering this as an improper use of your confidence in him by reminding the Assembly of their duty in the most critical conjuncture as this Respondent apprehended in Terms the most significant & expressive for that purpose.

ANSWER TO THE 12th. ARTICLE. In answer to the 12th. Article This Respondent saith It is very truly mentioned in the Memorial of the Council to this Respondent as entred on their Journals on the 12th. of Septr 1755 That Mr Little was this Respondents Private Secretary. But it is not otherwise mentioned therein as this Respondent apprehends that he was appointed by this Respondent to the Office of Secretary Since he never was appointed nor acted in any other Capacity than as Private Secretary to this Respondent for which he received no Salary from the Public. This Respondent admits he did also appoint him Clerk of the Assembly because no other person in the Colony was so well qualified to that Station & this Respondent did also appoint him to the several Offices of Clerk of the Crown & Peace & of the General Court as well on account of his Abilities as for that no other person capable of the Business would accept of this united Clerkship when the profit of those three places together did not amount to £10 a year. This Respondent did likewise for the same reasons appoint him Agent & Commissioner (but not Secretary or Commissary as he is styled in this Article) for Indian Affairs & did also appoint him this Respondents Aid de Camp & justice of the Peace in which Station he did more service to his Majesty & the Province than any other person there. And this Respondent begs leave to observe to your Lordships that there was no Salary annexed to any of these Offices (except £20 a year for being Clerk of the Assembly) & the whole profits of all the places together as this Respondent is very credibly informed did not amount to £80 Sterling per Annum & as the whole of this profit accrued from some few only of the Offices he exercised this Respondent thought it necessary to oblige him to exercise some others which were attended with much trouble & no profit at all.

As to Mr Little being charged by the Council with Malversation in every one of those Offices in a remonstrance said to be printed by them this Respondent answers that he knows nothing of the printing of that Remonstrance & apprehends that the printing & publishing the same was a very indecent & improper proceeding in the Council but admits that Mr Little put in an answer thereto & that the remonstrance which had been delivered to this Respondent on the 2d Septr 1755 was entered upon the Journals of the Council together with Mr Little's Answer thereto upon the 12th of the same

Month being the day when this Respondent received the answer & before which time as the Council were themselves the Accusers there did not appear to this Respondent any necessity for entering the Remonstrance upon the Journals & this Respondent admits it appears by the Journals that on the same day the consideration of the Memorial was deferred till the return of Mr Habersham one of the Councellors & also Clerk of the Council who was then absent in South Carolina. The Article is silent & therefore this Respondent cannot conjecture by whom or in what manner it could be alleged that notwithstanding this the Respondent had a hearing before himself before that Councellor Returned the contrary thereof being true. But this Respondent saith that the Memorial being addressed to himself as Governor & as an application to him in that Capacity he this Respondent did afterwards proceed to hear the same upon Evidence when this Respondent from the Evidence given was clearly of opinion to acquit Mr Little of every charge brought against him Except that he had taken a Dollar from such as offered so much to him instead of s2:d4 for administring the State Oaths in Court as the Act directs. But though it appeared that Mr Little had taken this dollar in some few instances instead of s2:d4, Yet it appeared that he had in no case demanded it but only as it was offered accepted it. Yet in order to satisfy his Accusers & the whole Country of this Respondents impartiality This Respondent dismissed him from those Offices wherein this Transaction happened. The Memorial & Answer together with a second Memorial & this Respondents speech upon the same occasion are all entered upon the Journals of the Council & therefore this Respondent did not apprehend it necessary to transmit to your Lordships any further account of this affair the further proceedings whereon were had before this Respondent only & not before the Council & the rather as the transmission thereof could only tend to reflect discredit upon the Council who had exhibited so heavy a charge which they were so ill able to support. Nor could such Trial as this Respondent conceives appear upon the Minutes of the Council as they were themselves the Accusers and Witnesses & therefore could not with any consistency be the Judges.

ANSWER TO THE 13th. ARTICLE. In answer to the 13th Article This Respondent saith that the person he appointed to be Provost Marshal in the Room of Mr Kellett & whom this Respondent recommended to your Lordships in his letter of the 29th. of March 1756 as a person this Respondent had known many years to be a man of very good character & capacity (tho this Respondent admits him to have acted as his Steward but not as his menial Servant as here alleged) was much better qualified for that Office than any person in the Province being a sober diligent & alert person & in good circumstances in regard to fortune & for the 12 Months he acted did his duty to the universal satisfaction of the people. As to the person appointed to be Searcher of the Customs this Respondent is informed he is the Son of a reputable Tradesman in London & that he never wore a Livery but served Mr Little in copying papers & he was appointed by this Respondent in consequence of a blank Commission being left by Mr Cleland the Surveyor General of the Customs.

ANSWER TO THE 14th. ARTICLE. In answer to the 14th Article This Respondent humbly submits to your Lordships that no other leave of the Crown was necessary to the passing Grants to this Respondent of the 3810 Acres of Land & the three town Lots (containing less than half an Acre each) mentioned in this Article as this Respondent had the advice & consent of the Council thereto. For that this Respondent was authorized by his Commission & instructions with their advice & consent to order Grants of Land to be made out to any of His Majesty's Subjects desiring the same (in proportion to their ability to cultivate & improve the Lands to be so granted). And this Respondent saith that before the obtaining of these grants he had wrote to Messrs Bell & Harrison (his Agents in London) to contract with proper persons in the African Trade for 50 Negroes to be sent him in Georgia which with the 6 persons in this Respondents family would according to the Rule of his instructions intitle him to take up 2850 Acres And this Respondent was allowed by his Instructions to take up or Grant 1000 Acres to any person that should be desirous of taking up a larger quantity of Land than the number of persons in family would intitle them to provided they were in condition to cultivate the same & that they paid to the Receiver of the quit Rents 5 shillings for every 50 Acres so granted on the day of the date of the Grant & tho' it so happened that this Respondents Agents in London did not make the Contract for the Negroes as this Respondent had ordered them on account of the War's breaking out. Yet as this Respondent was in expectation of their arrival this Respondent took up the said Lands for them to occupy on their arrival that they might not be idle & at an expense upon his hands when they came. And this Respondent further saith that as to the 2000 Acres of these lands this Respondent found (after he had taken them up) that they were barren Land & therefore this Respondent took up the extraordinary 1000 Acres & the whole are of so little value that this Respondent would gladly accept of six pence an Acre for his 3810 Acres or less than £100 sterling for the whole tho' the fees upon the Grants & surveys of the same have cost him near £20 Sterling. But this Respondent admits that he did not pay the £5 which was payable for his extraordinary 1000 Acres to the Receiver of the Quit Rents as in the multiplicity of his Business not being reminded of it the same slipt his Memory & this Respondent further begs leave to observe that several of the Planters in Georgia had more land in the Country than he & several of the Council (& amongst the rest Mr Kellett) petitioned him to Grant them 6000 Acres each Alledging it was the custom throughout America & the West Indies for Members of the Council to have so much granted to them on account of their being Members of the Council. Which Petition of Mr Kellett if the Clerk of the Council had done his duty would have been inserted in the Journal. And this quantity of Lands for the whole of which this Respondent would gladly accept of £100 or less are the whole which this Respondent has to show for £1000 which his equipment for Georgia cost him in the year 1754.

This Respondent having thus in compliance with your Lordships Commands submitted such Answers to the Articles delivered to him in writing by your Lordships order as he is at present enabled to make under the several disadvantages already taken notice of further entreats your Lordships permission for a few words more in respect to some matters mentioned at a late personal attendance at your Lordships Boards relating to the paper Bills current in the Colony.

That this Respondent did not direct the commissioners of the Loan Office (who were the President of the Council another Member of the Council the Surveyor General & two other Members of the Assembly) to be prosecuted for issuing out paper Bills was in compliance with the earnest & repeated solicitations of many of the principal Inhabitants, Members of the Council & Assembly who represented in the strongest terms the necessity the Colony was under of having some thing for want of Cash to serve as a Medium of Trade there being scarce any currency in the Province but promissory Notes of Haris & Habersham & because there was no possibility any other way for the Country to defray the expenses of the Courts of Oyer & Terminer & this Respondent took care that those Bills should never be regarded as a legal tender or be of any other force than mutual Credit might give them & that they never should be accepted for quit Rents or customs or any thing due to the King. If the Secretary of the Province was permitted by this Respondent to receive them for fees due to this Respondent such permission was given at the hazard of the loss purely out of compassion to the circumstances of the Colony. The Clerk of the Accounts did also as this Respondent is informed give Bills of Exchange for them but with this precaution that they should be first accepted in payment by such as had demands upon the Government & notes were likewise taken to make good any deficiency if any should happen from their being refused. This Respondent had also first advertized in the Public Papers at Carolina to get money for Bills of Exchange but without success nor did this Respondent receive more uneasiness in any part of his Administration than from the constant clamor that was raised about those Bills not having a stronger sanction given to them by being accepted in all payments. The necessity this Respondent was under of acting as he did may appear further from this consideration, That the Lieutenant Governor as this Respondent is informed by letters from Georgia has during this Respondents Absence given his Assent to the stamping & emitting more of those Bills to the amount of £638.7.1 1/2 for the payment of the public Debts & the method of giving Bills of Exchange for them has likewise since been constantly followed.

In the course of this defence this Respondent has endeavored & trusts he has kept clear of every wilfull misrepresentation. For any imperfections it may contain his present circumstances must be his excuse. The foundation upon which the charge has been framed he must submit to your Lordships. The Journals either of Council or assembly as they were not of his composing nor the Clerk of the Council of his Appointment he humbly hopes will not be received with all their defects & imperfections of which your Lordships are so well apprised at least as conclusive proofs against him. Much less will he trust the allegations or even letters of anonymous persons (for complaint this Respondent as yet knows of none except from Mr Kellett only), have the least weight with your Lordships to this Respondents prejudice without evidence to Corroborate the same & an opportunity to this Respondent of knowing his Accuser & making his defence to such particular accusation. If Mr Kellett is to stand forth as this Respondents Accuser this Respondent is most ready & willing upon the least intimation from your Lordships to answer every imputation He has already has brought or may hereafter Attempt to bring upon him. But your Lordships will permit this Respondent at the same time to produce some proofs even now in this Respondents hands of that Gentlemans personal misbehaviour in the execution of his Office of Provost Marshall & in his General deportment during his residence in the Colony of which your Lordships must have observed some mention in the Journal of the Council & Assembly.

This Respondent may have been guilty of mistakes but not of any thing criminal or of wilful disobedience of orders. And as for the former this Respondent is persuaded he need not entreat your Lordships Indulgence when you reflect upon the circumstances in which Respondent found this Colony upon his arrival amongst them as the first Kings Governor they had ever received. When your Lordships consider the Arduous task a Governor has to perform who is to frame the first Laws which regulate the police & constitution of Government & that in a Country so poorly inhabited where very few people are to be found oapable of executing even the most inferior public Offices & above all when the only persons most capable of contributing their Assistance & who are appointed for that purpose of this Respondent's Council Instead of contributing the assistance justly expected from them either because they did not owe their appointment to this Respondent or because so many of them having been formerly in the Administration before the Arrival of a Governor were unwilling to part with that power they had so long arbitrarily exercised & to accept a less degree of authority or that they hoped to extort compliances from this Respondent in Breach of his duty became the Authors & promoters of every disorder which crept into the Government & then at last were the first to complain of that confusion themselves had created in order to throw imputations upon this Respondent which he trusts he shall be found not to have Merited since it is as well known that long before the Lieutenant Governor left England there was the most perfect harmony between this Respondent & the people of the Colony in general (except a very few Individuals only who hoped to escape with impunity for their bad conduct by keeping up a misunderstanding) for the new Assembly elected after the dissolution of the former Assembly instead of wasting their time in laying claims to unwarrantable privileges applied themselves during a Session of 3 Months preceding this Respondents departure from the Colony with the most remarkable Assiduity to frame & pass many Bills of great public utility to which this Respondent gave assent & their address of thanks to his Majesty for his gracious appointment of this Respondent to be their Governor transmitted to your Lordships as also to the Secretary of State fully shews their sense of the rectitude of this Respondents administration.

 The importance of the charge is so great & the Respondents character so involved in it that he entertains not the least doubt but your Lordships will indulge him with every opportunity & method of making his defence which the law and usage in like cases will admit of more particularly a permission to procure all necessary proofs in support of his vindication together with the Assistance of Council to explain support & enforce them.

Order in Council, May 8, 1758, Kensington, C.O. 5/646, C. 39, directing the Board of Trade to draft a commission and warrant for Henry Ellis to be Governor in Chief of Georgia in the room of John Reynolds.

Upon reading this day at the Board a Representation from the Lords Commissioners of Trade and Plantations dated the 21st of last Month proposing that Henry Ellis Esqr the present Lieutenant Governor of his Majestys Colony of Georgia may be appointed Governor of his Majestys Colony of Georgia may be appointed Governor in Chief of the said Colony in the room of John Reynolds Esqr His Majesty in Council approving thereof is pleased to order, as it is hereby ordered, that the said Henry Ellis Esqr be constituted & appointed Governor in Chief of his Majestys said Colony of Georgia in the room of the said John Reynolds Esqr & that the said Lords Commissioners for Trade & Plantation do prepare a draught of a Commission & Warrant for passing the same under the Great Seal & also draughts of instructions for the said Henry Ellis & lay the same before his Majesty at the Board for his Royal approbation.

W. BLAIR

Henry Ellis to the Board of Trade, May 20, 1758, Georgia, read Nov. 21, 1758, C.O. 5/696, C. 43, giving the state of the colony's defenses on his recent southern journey.

My Lords

I did myself the honor to write to your Lordships the 31st of March when I forwarded the principal Acts that passed here the last Session.

Immediately after our Assembly arose I took a Journey to the South in order to examine the state of things in that quarter. On my way I touched at the River Ogechee & saw the Fort that had lately been raised there in consequence of the Resolutions of Assembly the last year. It is of a quadrangular figure each side measuring 100 yards constructed with thick Logs set upright 14 feet long 5 whereof are sunk in the earth & has 4 little Bastions pierced for small & great Guns which would make it very defencible. From thence I proceeded to Midway where I found the Inhabitants had inclosed their Church in the same manner & erected a Battery of 8 Guns at Sunbury in a very proper situation for defending the River. I reached Frederica 2 days afterward; the ruinous condition of which I could not view without concern. A dreadful fire that lately happened there has destroyed the greatest part of the Town. Time has done almost as much for the fortifications; Never was there a spot better calculated for a place of Arms or more capable of being fortified to advantage. It lies on the West side of the Island St Simon & on the Chief & most Southern Branch of the Great River Altamaha. The Military works were never very large but compact & extremely defensable. The sound will conveniently admit of 40 Gun Ships & those of 500 Tons burthen may come abreast of the Town but for 3 Miles below it the River winds in such a manner that an enemy must in that space be exposed to our Fire without being able to return it. In short it is of the last importance that that place should be kept in constant repair & properly Garrisoned as it is apparently & really the key of this & the rest of the Kings Provinces to the South but the wretched condition in which it now is makes it easy to conjecture what would be its fate should a Spanish War suddenly break out.

From hence I went to the Island of Cumberland in the South point whereof stands fort William; A post of no less consequence as is evident from the defence it made against 28 Spanish Vessels & considerable land force that attacked it unsuccessfully in the Year 1742.

General Oglethorpe has in my humble opinion displayed a great deal of skill in his choice of such Situations. This Fort commands a noble inlet from the Sea the entrance of the River St Mary which runs deep into the Country & the inland passage thro' which the runaway Negroes & other Deserters are obliged to go in their way to St Augustine. The works are of no great extent but admirably contrived to be maintained by a small Garrison & might be repaired with no very great expense £3000 sterling would be sufficient & Frederica might be rebuilt with solid & lasting materials as well as be rendered very strong for about £10,000 & until these things are done I apprehend this province & I believe I may add the next will be very insecure.

While I was at Cumberland I saw & had much discourse with Mr Gray. He is a very unintelligible character shrewd sagacious & capable of affording the best advice to others but ridiculously absurd in every part of his own conduct.

He is now settled upon that Island with his family & engaged in a small traffick with the Spaniards & Creek Indians. With him I found a person lately come from St Augustine who informed me that a new Governor & 200 fresh Troops from the Havannah were just arrived there & that the Spaniards persisted in their design of settling a new Colony in the environs of that Castle; & that they were preparing to build two or three other Forts on the River St Juan.

This information has a little alarmed our people which is not much to be wondered at considering their defenceless condition. Another circumstance which augments their fears in an account we have received that 3 french privateers are now cruising upon our Coast whilst we have no vessel of war stationed here to molest them & but a very incompetent force to prevent their Crews doing much mischief should they attempt a descent. It is more than a year & a half since a troop of Rangers were begun to be raised here. The Late Governor drew Bills upon the Earl of Loudoun for their subsistence which were protested. Upon the most urgent & repeated remonstrances his Lordship 10 Months ago furnished me with a Credit upon the Pay Master at New York for £850 Sterling to maintain them till further orders. That sum is expended but those Orders are not yet arrived notwithstanding his Lordship has embarked for England. I am now supporting them upon my own credit which that I may be the longer able to do, I have been compelled to disband half their number & if General Abercromby[38] to whom I have repeatedly & pressingly wrote upon this Subject does not speedily authorize me to keep them on foot & appropriate a proper fund for that purpose I shall be constrained to dismiss the rest.

There remains but to acquaint your Lordships that every thing is quiet here & that the Colony improves apparently.

There is a probability that the raising of Silk will engage the attention of our people more than heretofore & that that important undertaking will one day or other compensate for the trouble & expense which has attended its infancy. This Season promises fair in its behalf 6000 weight of Cocoons of a good quality are already brought to the Filature & more are yet expected.

Order in Council, June 16, 1758, Kensington, received May 21, read July 8, 1760, C.O. 5/647, D. 10, approving Henry Ellis' commission & warrants as governor of Georgia and forwarding them to the King for his signature.[39]

Whereas the Lords Commissioners for Trade and Plantations, have this day laid before His Majesty at this Board (pursuant to His Majestys Order for that purpose) a Draught of a Commission, prepared by them, for Henry Ellis Esqr to be Captain General and

---

38. James Abercromby commanded British forces in America at the attack on the French at Fort Ticonderoga in 1758. Defeated in that battle, Abercromby was recalled to England that same year.

39. These Orders are placed in the original volume according to the date read; in this case, July 8, 1760.

Governor in Chief of His Majestys Province of Georgia, together with a Warrant for His Majestys Royal Signature, for passing the said Commission under the Great Seal of Great Britain. Which Draught of a Commission and Warrant being in the usual Form His Majesty was pleased with the Advice of His Privy Council to Approve thereof, and to Order, as it is hereby Ordered, that the Right Honourable William Pitt Esqr One of His Majesty's Principal Secretarys of State, do lay the said Draught of a Commission and Warrant (which are hereunto annexed) before His Majesty for His Royal Signature.

W. Sharpe.

Henry Ellis to the Board of Trade, June 28, 1758, Georgia, read Nov. 21, 1758, C.O. 5/646, C. 44, proposing a compromise for the Bosomworth claims and troubles.

My Lords

    My last letter to your Lordships Board was dated the 20th of May & contained every thing that then occurred to me worthy of remark. The incidents that have fallen out since & my observations upon them are intended to be comprised in this.
    Soon after I had finished my Journey to the Southward (mentioned in my last) I was visited by several Gangs of the Creek Indians with no other view however than to obtain what they could. I gave them a few presents and sent them away contented.
    These have been succeeded by about 50 of their Country men now with me among whom are some principal men deputed by their nation to resign in a formal manner to the King for ever the Islands St Catharines, Ossaba & Sappelo & the Indian Land adjacent to the Town which has so long been an object of contention in the Colony. This my Lords is a matter of great consequence to us in as much as it disengages the Indians & leaves this dispute to be decided with the Bosomworths in whatever way may be thought most eligible. Yet still my Lords as I am clearly of opinion that a compromise with these troublesome people will be the most prudent speedy & effectual method of terminating it with advantage both to the Crown & the Colony. I presume it cannot be of much moment who possesses the Lands in question provided they are peaceably & actually annexed to this province & that the possessors of them comply with the terms prescribed by his Majesty to other Settlers. It is not sufficient that nothing is done on the part of the Government towards

dispossessing these people since they look upon this as a forbearance which is to last no longer than is convenient & think it incumbent on them in the meantime to employ every means to keep the Indians on their side. The way in which they attempt this is at once the most prevalent & injurious to our Interests.

 I mean by inspiring them with Jealousies of our dispositions & designs by disclosing the secrets of our policy which has a tendency to discredit our professions & frustrate our endeavors for the public Service by instigating them to plunder the out settlers which having been repeatedly done with impunity discovers our weakness & encourages them to persist in such profitable outrages & by numerous other flagitious practices that interrupt the quiet of the Colony, weaken our influence, alienate the affections of these Savages & equally favor our Enemies views & their own. These my Lords appear to me as so many reasons; yet how can we punish the authors of them upon Indian Evidence? And no other can be obtained & how is it possible to endure such enormities with patience or suffer them to continue without exposing the imbecility of this Government in the most glaring colours? The little subordination subsisting among the Indians is an unhappy circumstance As the disagreement of a small number of leading men greatly impedes & in some degree invalidates their public Resolutions & it must be allowed that a few of these are still firmly attached to the Bosomworths. Moreover Mr Bosomworth himself is cunning industrious & desperate, his Wife is sensible, speaks the language of the Indians perfectly, & is related to them besides. They are supported by many people here in Carolina & to the Northward to whom they are indebted & who have no other way of reimbursing themselves but by establishing their Title to the Lands in dispute. It is therefore manifest that they are capable of doing a great deal of mischief; yet the steps I have taken to traverse their measure & the ascendency they perceive I have acquired over the Indians has made them tractable. We should avail ourself of this disposition. Delays are highly dangerous & can answer no good purpose for tho' it is probable I may for some time be able to prevent any disturbance from happening yet this engrosses too much of our time & attention, creates infinite trouble to Government, keeps the Inhabitants under continual apprehensions & occasions an extraordinary expense to the public. And I humbly conceive My Lords that temporary expedients should never be employed but in cases of unavoidable necessity; 'tis doing nothing to patch up a sore today in such a manner as to be liable to break out tomorrow & grows more malignant by being tampered with & who

knows what alterations the incessant importunities & artifices
of Bosomworth may produce in the minds of a people so fickle
& mercenary as the bulk of these Savages are? My Lords I cannot help being sanguine in this affair. My zeal for the public
prompts me to it as I can plainly forsee a multitude of good or
bad effects that may flow from the manner in which it is settled.
Should the Spaniards come to a rupture with us we might expect
powerful assistance from the Creeks & no one would be better
qualified to negociate such succours than Mrs Bosomworth who
was constantly employed by General Oglethorpe upon such occasions.

Were these people once made satisfied & embarked in one
common interest with the other Inhabitants of this province they
would be as zealous for its welfare & I am convinced that many
advantages of a different nature from what I have mentioned might
be gained to the Colony by the additional influence that their Interest would give us for if we have been able to effect so much
notwithstanding a steady & violent opposition from them what
might we not accomplish if their weight was in the other scale.
From these considerations I have reason to expect that your
Lordships will enable me as soon as possible to reclaim these
enemies of the safety & prosperity of the province & put a period
to a dangerous & growing evil.

Copy of an Order in Council, July 8, 1758, Kensington, received
May 21, read July 8, 1760, C.O. 5/647, D. 11, approving
drafts of general instruction and trade for Henry Ellis, Governor
of Georgia.

The Kings most Excellent Majesty in Council

Upon reading this day at the Board a Report from the Right
Honorable the Lords of the Committee of Council for plantation
Affairs dated the 7th of this Instant, upon considering the
Draughts of General Instructions, as also of those relating to
the Acts of Trade and Navigation prepared by the Lords Commissioners for Trade and Plantations, pursuant to His Majestys
Order in Council of the 8th of May last, for Henry Ellis Esqr
Captain General and Govr. in Chief of His Majestys Province
of Georgia in America. By which Report it appears, That in the
said Draughts, the said Lords Commissioners have made no Alterations from the Instructions given to John Reynolds Esqr the

late Governor of the said Colony, except only in the following particulars. That in the present Draught of General Instructions, they have amended the 58th Article, relative to the supplying of Vacancys, occasioned by the Death or Suspension of Patentees or their Deputies, so as to make it conformable to the Instructions approved by His Majesty, and given for the like purposes, to the Governor of the Massachusets Bay, New Jersey, and such others, as have been lately appointed; That in the 67th Article relative to Grants of Land; they have inserted such Terms of Cultivation and Improvement as were prescribed by His Majestys Additional Instruction to Mr. Reynolds in August 1755, That they have omitted the 95th Article directing the Governor to enforce the Observance of the 5th and 6th Articles of the Treaty of Neutrality, such Direction being useless and improper in Time of War; And that the Draught of Instructions relative to the Acts of Trade and Navigation, is exactly the same as that approved by His Majesty for the late Governor of Georgia, and all other His Majestys Governors on the Continent of North America. And the Lords of the Committee being of Opinion, that the said Alterations were proper to be made in the said Draught of General Instructions. His Majesty was thereupon pleased, with the Advice of His Privy Council, to approve of both the said Draughts of Instructions, together with the Alterations made in the said Draught of General Instructions, and to Order as it is hereby Ordered, That the Right Honourable William Pitt Esqr, One of His Majestys Principle Scorotarys of State, do lay the same before His Majesty for His Royal Signature.

W. Sharpe.

Henry Ellis to the Board of Trade, July 20, 1758, Georgia, read Nov. 21, 1758, C.O. 5/646, C. 45, informing them of the filature's burning, of Indian affairs, and of a troublesome French privateer.

My Lords

I have wrote your Lordships several letters of late which an Embargo on the Shipping in these parts have prevented me sending away. My last was dated the 28th of June which I judged would close my packet by this Conveyance; but with the unexpected detention of the Convoy new incidents have fallen out to convince

me of my mistake. On the 4th. instant a dreadful fire broke out
in the public filature & raged at once through the whole building
with such irresistable fury that it was impossible to save more
out of it than about 340 lb of wound Silk & the Eggs of the worms
reserved for the next season. Between 2 & 3000 Wt of Cocoons
were consumed upon that occasion together with all the utensils
of the house near £40 in money & many other things of value belonging to Mr Otterlonghe. Had there been the least breath of
wind our Council House the provincial Records Arms & ammunition
which were lodged therein must inevitably have perished. For
tho' that Building was at the distance of an hundred feet yet the
heat was so intense as to set it many times on fire & had it not
been for the extraordinary efforts of some Sailors (as the case
was) it could not have been saved, the Towns people being intimidated by the dangerous situation of the powder which mirac-
ulously escaped. Tho' this unlucky accident is not to be filed
with the List of impediments to the raising of Silk yet I cannot
help being very much concerned even on that account as the
generality of Men are but too apt to ascribe things to wrong
causes, besides I am extremely mortified by the destruction of
the Cocoons as I had flattered myself we should have been able
to send home a much larger quantity of Silk this year than ever
had been raised here in one Season; however I must endeavor
to forget what cannot be remedied & only think of guarding a-
gainst such misfortunes hereafter. The late Filature was dangerously constructed the Basement & floor which should have been
brick or Stone were of Fir teeming with turpentine & of course
very liable to kindle in a house where seven or eight fires were
constantly burning. This disaster seems to have been merely
accidental & it is supposed was occasioned by some embers
falling between the Boards of the floor where they long lay concealed without making any considerable progress, for the fire
did not break out until 4 o'clock next Morning. I propose that
the new Building shall be upon a different plan to the end that
it may be more convenient as well as secure. Whereon I shall
immediately consult the Council as we shall have no more than
time to finish it before it may be wanted, a circumstance which
puts it out of our power to obtain your Lordships approbation of
our design or directions concerning it. Nevertheless every thing
shall be done according to the best of our Judgment & with the
greatest regard to economy & the public Service.

    This Colony still enjoys a state of uninterrupted repose the
generality of our accounts from the Indian Country are favorable.

All the Towns of the Upper & Lower Creeks are well affected to
us except the Cowetas where the Interest of the Bosomworths
chiefly centers. The Son of the late Emperor Malatchi who was
so well treated here last Winter & departed with the most evident marks of an entire satisfaction is by the insinuations & intrigues of these restless people become extremely discontented
& jealous of the English which he has manifested by a late visit
to the French Fort at Mobile, but I am not very apprehensive of
any immediate effects from what may have happened there notwithstanding. I am of opinion that the smallest disaffection should
not pass unattended to. The Wolf King Superior of the Upper Creeks
is of a different disposition. He has sent a courier with a letter
to acquaint me that he has in concert with the head men of the
neighbouring Towns to the number of 200 projected an expedition
against the new French Fort upon the Cherokee River. At the same
time he has for this purpose sent for ammunition & vermilion & desires I will not be impatient as to the event since he expects to be
absent three Months & concludes with strong assurances of his
fond attachment to the English & resentment to their Enemies which
he hopes upon his return to produce the most convincing proofs of
it.

While I am upon such Topics I cannot avoid remarking upon the
conduct of the Captains of the Kings Ships stationed at Charles
Town during these two Summers. We have been infested with privateers from the Mississippi who have insulted with impunity the
Coasts of these provinces & carried off every vessel to be met
with. 'Tis true the Men of War have sometimes gone out stood
off & on before Charles Town Bar for two or three days & then returned to port again instead of stretching towards St Augustine,
the usual Rendevoz of those privateers and their prizes. 5 English vessels have lately been sent thither by a privateer of 10 &
another of 6 carriage Guns, the Captain of whom had the insolence
to threaten dismantling Fort William & Frederica.

In order to punish this presumption I have fitted out a vessel
for a six Weeks cruise with 14 Carriage 14 Swivel Guns and 90
Men commanded by tried Officers whom I cannot doubt will give
a good account of these Gentlemen if they are so fortunate to meet
with them.

In a former letter I have observed to your Lordships how ill
calculated the Harbour of Charles Town is for Cruising Ships the
shallowness of the Water the difficulty of Pilotage the attractives
to men of pleasure which that Town affords & the remote situation
of the Port from the Tract of the Enemy's Vessels excepting those

that cruise for their Trade are circumstances that will always interfere with the service if the Admiralty should think proper to station a Sloop of War either at Frederica Green Island Harbour at the entrance of Ogechee or at the Mouth of this River merely to cruise upon the Enemy. I think such a Vessel could not fail annoying them extremely as all their Trade from the Mississipi as well as that from their Sugar Islands which of late have come through the Gulph of Florida to avoid our Men of War in the West Indies would be very apt to be intercepted. 'Tis a strange circumstance that the two privateers above mentioned should have cruised 10 Weeks upon these Coasts without interruption notwithstanding there being in that time generally three of the Kings Ships at Charles Town.

Extracts from two letters of Henry Ellis to the Georgia Agent, April 18 & June 27, 1758, Georgia, read Nov. 28, 1758, C.O. 5/646, C. 47, concerning his proposal for arming a coasting vessel, enclosed with Ellis, July 20, 1758, to the Board of Trade.

Extract of Henry Ellis to the Agent April 18th. 1758

The proposal I made for a Stout sailing Boat to go occasionally to the different Coasts of this & the neighbouring province by sea I still think a good one & I am confident a crew particularly for her consisting of a patroom of Coxswain & 8 hands upon the same Establishment with the Scout Boat & at the same Wages with her people would be extremely proper & necessary at this juncture. Such a Boat might cost about £120 Sterling.

Extract of a Letter from Ditto 27th June 1758

Sure I am that the Saling Boat would be of great service in the present conjuncture of affairs. I have sent you an Estimate of the expense that would attend the maintaining her but I see I have there ommitted a sum for repairs etc. which doubtless would amount to £50 per Annum & provisions to the Soldiers stationed at Frederica in the Southern part of the Province. The Crew consist of a Coxwain & 10 Men. It is maintained by the Government & the estimate for the same (settled by the Lords of the Treasury in 1752) is £426.7.6 per Ann. The pay Bills certified by the Governor are returned to Merchants in England & paid by the pay Master General by a Warrant from the War Office countersigned by the Lords of the Treasury.

Henry Ellis to the Board of Trade, Aug. 30, 1758, Georgia, read Jan. 16, 1759, C.O. 5/646, C. 49, informing them that he has received no royal letters or instructions since his stay in Georgia.

My Lords

I have just received a letter from Mr Martyn dated the 26th April wherein he acquaints me he had by that conveyance forwarded a packet for me with another to Governor Lyttleton from your Lordships Board. But by a Letter I had from his Excellency to day I learn that the Captain who had the care of these dispatches threw them over board upon being hailed in french by a Bristol Privateer which he took to be an enemy so that I am yet totally uninformed of your Lordships pleasure or what number of my letters etc. have come to hand not having received one line relative to either since I have been in Georgia. I must beg leave to observe to your Lordships upon this occasion that if duplicates of the dispatches you intend to honor me with are not sent also I may remain here without any instructions. I have just perused my last letters. I find I can add nothing material to 'em; every thing continuing peaceable & I may say precisely in the same state as when they were wrote so that this will only serve to notify the Miscarriage of your Lordships letters & afford me an opportunity of subscribing myself.

Henry Ellis to the Board of Trade, Oct. 25, 1758, Georgia, read Feb. 7, 1759, C.O. 5/646, C. 52, lamenting the defenseless state of his frontier province.

My Lords

My last letter dated the 30th of Augt only served to notify the Miscarriage of the dispatches your Lordships intended for me by Capt Fairweather & though nothing very material hath since occurred I cannot suffer any opportunity to slip without transmitting an idea of the present state of things here since I am persuaded nothing can be more satisfactory in times of danger than frequent intelligence from the places exposed to it.

Your Lordships are too well acquainted with the real circumstances of this frontier province to blame my solicitude for its safety or my entertaining some apprehensions of what may happen in consequence of its neglected condition. I have perhaps

been too frequent & importunate in my representation upon this
head to your Lordships whose zeal for the public I am well convinced of. Nevertheless I cannot avoid being so whilst my remonstrances to other Branches of Ministry seem to be disregarded.
I have repeatedly urged these matters in the strongest terms to
the Right Honorable The Secretary of State & to the Commanders
in Chief of the Kings forces in these parts but hitherto with less
effect than I could wish; one point in particular concerns me so
much that I cannot now be silent upon it notwithstanding I have
so often mentioned it, I mean what relates to the Rangers raised
here by my predecessor who are not yet upon any Establishment
but have for many Months past been maintained upon my own
Credit & risque. They are highly necessary to be kept on foot
& have been more than tacitly allowed of by the Earl of Loudoun.
I am therefore afraid I cannot answer to disband them although I
am not able to support them much longer.

His Lordship gave me a credit last year for £850 to subsist
them until further orders but those have never arrived & that sum
has been expended long ago.

Since General Abercromby assumed the chief command I have
wrote no less than 4 times successively to him upon this very subject but I cannot be favored with one Line to answer. In short this
affair has created me a great of uneasiness & embarrassment especially as I have not been able to procure the smallest instruction
altho' no method to gain it has been left untryed. Indeed I am
equally in the dark in regard to some other points of moment & notwithstanding my best endeavors I find myself in a very unpleasant
& hazardous situation much exposed to censure & mischance.

Surely my Lords if the present times were less perturbed &
dangerous there would be sufficient reason for keeping up a
small body of Troops here the want of means to inforce the Laws
necessarily brings the Government into contempt & constrains
me to wink at many enormities committed by our own people &
the Savages. It is not uncommon for the former to set their civil
power at defiance & Gangs of the latter have more than once
lived at discretion upon the Out settlers & drove away numbers
of their Cattle. A few Months ago some stragling Indians from
the Northward (who are now settled in the Creek Country) robbed
& murdered a whole family not 40 Miles from this Town. I immediately insisted upon satisfaction from the Creeks who with
some difficulty & reluctance in part gave it to me for one of the
Murderers they put publicly to death the others made their escape but partys are sent in quest of them & I have strong

assurances that they shall suffer the same fate when they can be taken. It is very happy this affair ended thus for had those Savages been more averse to do justice we could not have compelled them. Our weakness then must have been most apparent & crimes of this Nature would probably have been perpetrated daily. It would be endless to relate to your Lordships the various shifts & expedients I have been induced to conceal our mobility. This sort of management may do for a season but mankind are too penetrating to be long imposed upon even by the most refined policy. As to the rest we remain very peaceable & considering the discouragements of the times the Colony grows & thrives apace. Our savage neighbours in general appear extremely well affected to us & the influence we have acquired with them adds greatly to our Security but it cannot be denied that these people are unaccountably fickle & capricious & that that Security which depends upon their humours must be extremely precarious.

I ought to inform your Lordship that Mr Atkin his Majesty's Agent for Indian Affairs has been with me these 10 days past. He is just now setting out for the Creek Nation. I have very honestly endeavoured to serve him & render his employment easy to himself & beneficial to the public by furnishing him with all the lights & assistance in my power & by giving him my sentiments on Indian matters with the utmost plainness & candour. In the mean time I must confess I am not entirely convinced of the expediency of his visiting that Nation where every thing at <u>present</u> is perfectly quiet & whilst affairs of an alarming nature are left unsettled behind him. For by my last accounts to the Northward the Cherokees & Virginians were upon the verge of a quarrel with each other & it said that many of the former have deserted General Forbes's Army; However Mr Atkin assures me he has taken some measures in consequence thereof which I hope will be effectual.

Henry Ellis to William Pitt, Oct. 31, 1758, Georgia, received Feb. 14, 1759, asking for instructions to maintain and keep a troop of Rangers to secure the province's frontiers.

Sir

I was honoured with your Letters of the 30th of December and 7th of January last, which I immediately acknowledged, but as I have not been favoured with any information relative to the points touched upon in my last Letters, I must now beg leave to resume them and lay before you some further particulars of consequence.

In some former Letters I had the honour to receive from your self, and the Earl of Holderness, I was directed to apply to the Commanders in Chief of the Kings forces in North America, for any assistance that might be thought necessary to the safety of this frontier Province. Convinced of its exposed and defenceless condition, and urged by the solicitations of our Assembly, and the principal Inhabitants here, I applyed to the Earl of Loudoun near two years ago, for a few Troops to remove the apprehensions of the People and protect them from the growing insolence of the Savages, who seemed sensible of our Weakness and inclined to take advantage of it by committing daily outrages and irregularities, at the same time that we were threatened with insults from the Enemys Privateers, who for three months together, infested our Coasts without molestation; there being no Naval force here to interrupt them. This I likewise unsuccessfully represented to Admiral Holbourn.

In consequence of some very Alarming appearances amongst our Indian Neighbours, the late Governor in December 1756 began to raise some Rangers for the defense of the Colony. The Officers for three Troops were Commission'd and forty men for the first one levyed which to this day are unestablished.

When I entered upon this Government I did not fail to write frequently to My Lord Loudoun concerning them, and pressed him in the strongest manner to instruct me how to proceed, whether I should compleat the Troop which was half raised or disband them. His Lordship saw the expediency of keeping them on foot, but gave me no positive, or direct instruction about them further than to authorize my drawing upon the deputy Pay Master at New York for a certain Sum to maintain what were raised untill further orders; but I heard no more from his Lordship.

Upon the change in the chief Command of the Kings Forces I wrote four times successively to General Abercomby upon the same subject, but I have never been able to obtain one Line for answer. So that after soliciting and remonstrating near two years upon this and other material points relative to the Security of this Colony, I find myself precisely where I set out; The Forts on the frontier in the most decayed condition, and except these few Rangers which for eight or Nine Months past have been subsisted upon my own Credit and risque and a small detachment from one of the Independant Companies of South Carolina stationed upon the Ruins of Frederica, no other force is near us. As the above Rangers are highly necessary to be kept up, and were more than tacitly allowed of by the Earl of Loudoun as being well calculated for the Service, I am loth and even afraid I cannot answer to dismiss them, which however I shall soon be obliged to do, if I receive no orders to the contrary. I am therefore to entreat you Sir, that I may be honoured with the Kings Commands upon this Head, for no situation in Life can be more uneasy and embarrassing than that in which I have been for these twenty months past. I have indeed been very fortunate in accommodating most of the differences that subsisted between this Colony and the Creek Indians; and the influence I have acquired amongst them, adds greatly to our security. But it is generally known how unaccountably capricious these people are, and how precarious that Security must be, that depends upon their humours. In the mean time the Colony thrives apace, the people are pretty easy in their minds, and a general tranquility prevails.

Order in Council, Nov. 6, 1758, Kensington, received May 21, 1760, read July 8, 1760, C.O. 5/647, D. 12, ordering William Pitt to lay a warrant for William Grover to be Chief Justice in Georgia for His Majesty's signature.

The Kings most Excellent Majesty in Council

Whereas the Lords Commissioners for Trade and Plantations have this day laid before His Majesty at this Board (pursuant to His Majestys Order for that purpose) a Warrant to authorize and require the Governor or Commander in Chief of His Majestys Province of Georgia in America, to cause Letters Patent to be passed under the Seal of the said Province, for Constituting and appointing William Grover Esqr. to be Chief Justice of that province, to hold and execute the said Office during His Majestys Pleasure and the residence of the said William Grover within the said Province And His Majesty in Council having been pleased to approve of the said Warrant (which is hereunto annexed) Doth hereby Order, That the Right Honourable William Pitt Esqr One of His Majestys Principal Secretarys of State, do lay the same before His Majesty for His Royal Signature.

Order in Council Nov. 6, 1758, Kensington, received & read Nov. 7, 1758, C.O. 5/646, C. 41 approving William Grover as Chief Justice in Georgia and ordering the Board of Trade to prepare a warrant for the King.

The Kings most Excellent Majesty in Council

Upon reading this day at the Board a Representation from the Lords Commissioners of Trade & Plantations dated the 25th of last Month setting forth that it is expedient for his Majestys Service that a Chief Justice should be appointed for his Majesty's Colony of Georgia & that William Grovor Esqr hath been recommended to them as a person every way qualified to serve his Majesty in that Station they therefore propose that he may be appointed Chief Justice of His Majestys said Province of Georgia. His Majesty in Council approving thereof is pleased to order as it is hereby ordered that the said William Grover Esqr be constituted & appointed Chief Justice of His Majestys said Province of Georgia And that the said Lords Commissioners for Trade & Plantations do cause a Warrant to be prepared for that purpose & lay the same before his Majesty at this Board.

Henry Ellis to the Board of Trade, Nov. 9, 1758, Georgia, read Feb. 7, 1759, C.O. 5/646, C. 53, thanking the Board for his appointment as Governor and forwarding a letter from an Indian trader.

My Lords

Although I have yet had no Letter from your Lordships Board I have accidently heard that His Majesty has been graciously pleased to appoint me Governor in Chief of this province an honour which I am well convinced is owing more to your Lordships goodness in representing my conduct favorably to the King than to any pretensions of mine. I must therefore beg leave to return your Lordships my most grateful & hearty thanks & to assure you that I will very strenuously endeavor not to forfeit the favorable opinion your Lordships are pleased to conceive of me nor disgrace his Majestys Commission.

In my last letter to your Lordships of the 25th. of October I took notice of some dangerous appearances which were arising among the Cherokees but I have since received accounts from several hands acquainting me that affairs there were likely to take a different turn. The following is an extract of a letter to me from a very sensible Indian Trader, which as it contains the best account of this matter that has reached my hands, I beg leave to transcribe for your Lordships perusal.

"Of late our affairs among the Cherokees seem'd to be on a tottering foundation owing to the unlucky management in Virginia. They attempted to form a confederacy of all the Indian Nations against the English particularly the Virginians. Their Embassadors however met with no encouragement from the Creeks who declared that they would take no part in any quarrel between them & the English nor were they more successful with the Chicesaws at New Savannah who gave them a very cold reception & immediately acquainted me with their proceedings."

"In the interim there happened to be some of the Upper Creeks of the Oakfushee Town in the Cherokees who were beat & abused by the latter at a rum frolick. The Creeks resented this treatment for next day they took their departure & killed 2 Cherokees & scalp'd them. This unexpected blow threw the latter Nation into so great a consternation that it gave an immediate turn to all their designs & seemed at most entirely to quash their resentment against Virginia for now they court their Traders as their only support in time of distress who before were upon the point of being murdered. Should this affair not extend to a rupture between the two Nations it will at least keep them shy & at a distance from each other for some time which will be conducive to the safety of the English provinces in the present critical juncture of affairs."

As to any thing else my Lords no alteration has taken place since my last.

William Grover to the Secretary of the Board of Trade Nov. 28, 1758, London, received & read Nov. 28, 1758, C.O. 5/646, C. 46, asking the Board's pleasure with respect to the Offices of the court and the commencement of his salary.

Sir

Your favor is come to hand for which I am much obliged to you & shall obey the commands of their Lordships. I must beg to know their Lordships pleasure with respect to the Offices of the Court & as to the commencement of my Salary for which purpose I am desirous of attending their Lordships Board or Lord Hallifax will receive their Lordships Resolutions from you as to them shall be agreeable.

Order in Council, Dec. 4, 1758, St. James, received May 21, read July 8, 1760, C.O. 5/647, D. 13, giving Henry Ellis permission to repair to a northward colony during Georgia's hot months to recover his health.

The Kings most Excellent Majesty in Council

Whereas there was this day read at the Board a Representation from the Lords Commissioners for Trade and Plantations dated the 29th of last Month, Setting forth, That Henry Ellis Esqr His Majestys Governor of the Province of Georgia, hath represented to them, That his Health has been much impaired by the extraordinary Heat of the last Summer, and requested that he may have His Majesty's Permission, in case he shall find it necessary, to repair to some of His Majestys Northern Provinces during the Hot Months of the ensuing Summer; The said Lords Commissioners Therefore propose That His Majesty would be graciously pleased to grant the said Governor The same permission as is constantly given to the Governors of His Majestys Islands in the West Indies, of quitting their Government, and repairing to any Northern Colony on the Continent of America, whenever it is necessary for the Recovery or Preservation of their Health. His Majesty having taken the same into Consideration, and approving of what is above proposed, is hereby pleased, with the Advice of His Privy Council to permit and allow the said Henry Ellis Esqr Governor of the Province of Georgia, in all times of Sickness to repair to the province of New York, or any of His Majestys Northern Plantations, and there stay for such a Space of time, as the Recovery of his Health may absolutely require.

Memorial of Benjamin Martyn, Agent for Georgia to the Board of Trade, Dec. 18, 1758, London, read Dec. 19, 1759, C.O. 5/646, C. 48, asking permission to pay £155.5.10 for the listed services to the colony.

Sheweth

That your Memorialist was authorized by a Warrant from the

Lords Justices July 29th 1755 to pay a surplus of an Account amounting to £1,400 then lying in your Memorialists hands for such uses & sources as your Lordships should appoint & there being at this time the sum of £790.7.4 3/4 remaining of the said sum of £1,400 your Memorialist humbly desires your Lordships Warrant for his paying the sum of £155.5.10 for the following services, vizt.

For the purchase of 18 Copper Basons one pair of Copper Scales with a Beam & proper weights, 12 Brass Scummers & 12 pounds of large brass wire for the use of the Filature	26	13	2
For a pewter Standis for Ditto	0	8	0
For 2 volumes of the Statutes at large sent to Georgia under the care of Mr Clifton	4	10	0
For freight of the Indian presents sent to the Harrietta Capt Rames	58	18	6
For Insurance on the said presents at the London Assurance office	64	16	2
	155	5	10

Order in Council, Jan. 11, 1759, Whitehall, read Jan. 18, 1759 C.O. 5/646, C. 50, instructing the Board of Trade to present its proposed settlement of the Bosomworth claims.

WHEREAS there was this day laid before the Lords of the Committee a Report made by the Lords Commissioners for Trade & plantations dated the 6th. of last Month upon considering the Memorial & Representation of Cousaponakeesa Rightful & natural born Princess of the Upper & Lower Creek Nations in behalf of herself her Chieftans subjects & Vassals praying a reimbursement of what she has expended for the British interest & such recompense for 20 years personal services as His Majesty shall think fit. The Lords of the Committee taking their said Report into their consideration & agreeing in opinion with what is proposed by the said Lords Commissioners for Trade & Plantations Do therefore hereby order that the said Lords Commissioners do prepare a draught of an instruction for the Governor of Georgia conformable to what is proposed by the said Report & lay the same before this Committee.

Henry Ellis to the Board of Trade, Jan. 28, 1759, Georgia, received April 25, read May 8, 1759, C.O. 5/646, C. 54, giving an account of the new Hanover settlement and of the current state of the province's affairs.

My Lords

My last letter to your Lordships Board was dated the 9th of Novr since which nothing very material has occurred in this Government. Yet I cannot allow myself to neglect any safe opportunity of conveying to your Lordships an account of every incident that happens here.

I have lately received a letter from the Right Honorable Mr Secretary Pitt directing me to give immediate orders in his Majestys Name to those people who have settled Southward of the River Altamaha without his Majestys license & authority to remove from thence forthwith.[40] In the execution of the said Commands Governor Lyttleton is instructed to act in concert with me. We have accordingly consulted together upon the best method of proceedings herein & the course we determined upon was to send from each province Commissioners properly authorized who are to follow the Inclos'd Instructions which are exactly conformable to the orders we have receiv'd. Those Commissioners set out upon that service with the Scout Boat of each province last Week but it is too soon to learn what reception they met with or the time they have given the said Inhabitants to depart with their effects. These points I shall mention here after. In the mean time I am to acquaint your Lordships that this just measure gives great uneasiness to the Inhabitants of our Southern districts who considered these Settlers as a sort of Security to the Colony & to say the truth they were become unfit in diverting the Indians from the thicker settled parts & in intercepting Negroe Slaves who frequently attempt to desert that way to the Spaniards. Yet I am

---

40. By this time, Edmund Gray's settlement at New Hanover had become a pawn in the diplomatic game between England and Spain. Ellis' official correspondence reflects a stronger position than he actually took. With a lingering claim to the region, South Carolina also objected to Gray's presence and, together with Georgia and in compliance with Pitt's instructions, sent a commissioner to New Hanover to deliver official instructions to evacuate the settlement.

far from thinking these advantages equivalent to the Mischiefs
that might justly be apprehended from an association of so li-
centious a Crew unawed as they were by Government. Nevertheless I humbly conceive My Lords that if it were the Kings pleasure to extend the jurisdiction of this Government indefinately as
far as his Majestys rights upon this Continent reached to the
South these mischiefs might easily be prevented without giving
umbrage or even a handle to the Spaniards to commence any contest about the limits.

If I recollect right by the last Treaty with Spain each power
was to keep whatever Lands they were then possessed of in America save such as were therein excepted.[41] For many years past
the River St Juan has in these parts been considered as the line
of partition between us & the Spaniards & it may be needless to
remind your Lordships that when General Oglethorpe commanded
here we had a fort upon an Island at the Mouth of that River which
he afterwards demolished & that we still have one upon the South
point of the Island of Cumberland where a small Garrison is now
maintained altho' this lies 60 Miles Southward of the River Altamaha.
So that I presume there can be no question of our rights extending
at least so far & possibly no great inconvenience would arise from
those parts being settled. 'Tis true in consequence of some outrages committed by the Indians on the Spaniards at the supposed
instigation of Grey, The Governor of Florida addressed himself to
me in October 1757 requesting I would give Orders that such people
as had settled upon what he loosely called his Catholic Majestys
Territories should remove there from, but the answer I made to this
requisition prevented any further application.

These people have continued there ever since cultivating the
Lands & trading with the Spaniards by virtue of secret encouragement given them from the Government of Florida itself. There may
nevertheless be good reasons why they should not longer remain
there. A very good one indeed it is that they have dared to settle
the Kings Lands without license from his Majesty or those acting
under his authority. But this objection may not lie against others
who might be properly authorized & who would be responsible to

---

41. Ellis' reference is to the 1748 Treaty of Aix-la-Chapelle
which ended the War of Jenkins' Ear and preserved the status quo
in the region. The story is best told in Herbert E. Bolton and
Mary Ross, The Debatable Land (Berkeley, Calif., 1925), 77-
97.

Government for their conduct. This is not the case of the present Settlers who have fled from their Creditors in this & other provinces & who without some peculiar indulgences must abandon this Country altogether. Hence there is danger of their going to the Spaniards to whom they may be very useful in promoting their design of Settling a Colony in Florida & should they afterwards attempt & succeed in opening an intercourse & establishing a friendly correspondence between that people & the Creek Indians; such an event might prove highly prejudicial to us. I could therefore have wished it had been in our power to have prevented this by giving them liberty to settle upon the Island of Cumberland. They would then have been serviceable to this Country in general & to our Garrison there in particular which would have kept them in order & I cannot help thinking such a liberty might still be expedient & even necessary altho' our present Institutions do not authorize it. I hope your Lordship will excuse the freedom with which I perhaps too often presume to offer my sentiments upon such subjects. When our Commissioners set out upon this Business I detached the few Rangers we have on foot to the Southward & have posted parties of them at the principal passes upon the River Altamaha which gives much satisfaction to the people thereabouts since they will be some Security against the desertion of their Slaves. They will also be useful in taking up deserters from his Majestys & the provincial Troops; many of whom fly to the Spaniards & are received & incorporated with the Troops of that Nation. They will likewise contribute to the supressing a practice carried on by some people here & in South Carolina of furnishing the Spaniards at St Augustine with abundance of Cattle & other provisions by Land & thro' the Island passages by water whereby the object of Embargoes has in some measure been defeated. For by such means Magazines have been formed there to supply the Settlements of the French whose privateers are admitted & encouraged to resort to that Port where they occasionally refit are provided with necessarys & intelligence & from whence they have for 2 years together greatly interrupted the commerce of these parts. And here My Lords it may not be improper to observe that notwithstanding the goodness & advantageous situation of the ports in this province for his Majestys Ships to be stationed at for the protection of the British Trade & annoying that of the enemy yet we are still without a single vessel. And on the other hand altho this is a very dangerous frontier from its vicinity to the French Settlements & some numerous Tribes of Indians yet it is still suffered to continue in a condition too alarming to be described.

The Rangers which I have so often troubled your Lordships about are yet unestablished. I dare not disband them & I have no fund for their support. Upon the expiration of the Earl of Loudouns credit to me upon the Pay Master at New York for this Service I continued to draw Bills as usual until I should receive orders to the contrary but those Bills to the amount of £600 Sterling are now come back upon me protested but no orders. The only alternative now left me is to pay them out of my own pocket or draw Bills upon the Pay Master General at home; the latter I shall venture to do in hopes they will be honor'd for otherwise my situation will be truly hazardous and perplexing nor shall I know how to act upon any future emergency. I am therefore humbly to intreat that your Lordships will be pleased to assist in relieving me from this dilemma by enforcing the representations I now make to the Right Honorable the Secretarys of State & War, The objects of which are that these Troops may be established & their arrears paid.

By this Conveyance I transmit what public papers are ready & a List of what were sent by the last Carolina Fleet which I very much fear have not got to hand as we are just now alarmed by an Account that the greatest part of those Ships were met by a Squadron of french Men of War who took & destroyed many of them. Your Lordships will therefore be pleased to direct that I may be inform'd whether those papers have miscarried to the end that if they have I may forward other Copies.

Our Assembly is now sitting upon the usual Business of this Season. The Members are very solicitous that the duration of their Service in that capacity should be fixed. They lately prepared a Bill for this purpose which I caused to be suppressed in the Upper House after the former had threatened to do no business unless I would pass it but I convinced the Majority of them separately of the absurdity of such conduct & the impossibility of their forcing a compliance which has so far wrought upon them that they proceed as usual relying however that I will represent to your Lordships the great hardship it is upon the people in their circumstances to be obliged to serve the public at a great expense & without the least prospect of being at any time relieved from it.

Might I be permitted to give my sentiments upon this matter they would be that the duration of the Assembly might without any considerable inconvenience be limited to 5 or 7 years and I conceive if something of this sort is not soon done the discontent of the people hereupon will probably increase & be productive of some disagreeable consequences. But I cannot think it should have any power to nominate returning officers, ascertain the qualifications of the Electors or Elected, or to fix or alter the distribution or number of Representatives.

In respect to other matters there are no complaints, for the province under all the discouragements of insecurity improves very fast. Our numbers are augmented from less than 500 Whites to upwards of 7,000 & the Negroes from about 1800 to more than 2,100. When I arrived here the Militia amounted to but 745 & now 1264 are enrolled, other things are increasing in proportion. The produce of the Country is more than doubled but the sum of it cannot be gathered from the Entrys at the Custom House since the greatest part of it is conveyed into Carolina in small Boats the Owners of which neglect those forms which the Laws of Trade prescribe & this is impossible to be prevented in a Country where there are so many inlets, so few Officers, & where every one may export his goods from his own landing place unobserved. Nevertheless the accounts I have collected from the Merchants & planters may be near the truth & they suppose that there was exported from hence last Year 25000 wt of Indico & about 5500 Barrels of Rice besides a very large quantity of Corn & Lumber to the West Indies.

By this Conveyance Mr Martyn will receive a state of the public Accounts which I suppose he will lay before your Lordships.

Henry Ellis to James Edward Powell, Jan. 22, 1759, Savannah, received April 25, read May 8, 1759, C.O. 5/646, C. 55, instructing him to go south of the Altamaha and order the settlers of New Hanover to move.

WHEREAS by a Commission under the Seal of this Province bearing date the 22d day of Jany 1759 which will herewith be delivered unto you I have commissionated constituted & appointed you the said James Edward Powell to do & perform all such matters & things for the due & faithful execution of His Majesty's pleasure concerning the Inhabitants of a certain Settlement to the Southward of the River Alatamaha (made without His Majesty's License or authority & called by themselves New Hanover) as you shall by these Instructions be required & directed. You will therefore (with the Commissioner constituted & appointed by His Majestys Governor of South Carolina on his part to act in concert with you in the execution of His Majestys pleasure signified to us concerning the said Inhabitants) proceed from hence with all convenient speed to the Settlement above mentioned & being arrived there you will cause your Commission to be read & published with all due solemnity & after publication thereof you will immediately give orders in his Majesty's name to the Inhabitants of a certain Settlement made without his Majestys license or authority & called by themselves New Hanover to remove forthwith from thence. And if any other Settlement or Settlements shall have been made without His Majestys License or authority you are in like manner to order the Inhabitants thereof to remove immediately from thence.

But for as much as a certain time will be indispensably necessary for the removal of the said Inhabitants with their effects you are to name a day on or before which the said Inhabitants are to remove & when you have so done you are with all convenient speed to return to Savannah. And you will not fail to act in concert in all your proceedings with the Commissioner appointed to act with you by & on the part of the Governor of His Majestys Province of South Carolina & to keep exact minutes & to transmit an account thereof to me by all proper and safe opportunities.

Samuel Martin, Secretary to the Chancellor of the Exchequer, to the Board of Trade, Jan. 31, 1759, read Jan. 31, 1759, C.O. 5/646, C. 51, desiring the Board to lay before the Chancellor an estimate of Georgia's expenses from June 24, 1758, to midsummer, 1759.

I desire you will acquaint the Lords Commissioners of Trade & plantations that the Chancellor of the Exchequer hath received his Majestys commands that their Lordships should prepare & lay before the House of Commons an Estimate of expense attending the Colony of Georgia from the 24th day of June 1758 to Midsummer 1759.

Order in Council, Feb. 2, 1759, St. James, received May 21, read July 8, 1760, C.O. 5/647, D. 14, approving the draft of an instruction for Henry Ellis to dispose of lands the Creeks lately ceded to His Majesty.

The Kings most Excellent Majesty in Council

Upon reading at the Board a Report from the Right Honourable the Lords of the Committee of Council for Plantation Affairs dated

the 1st of this Instant, humbly Offering to His Majesty for His
Royal Approbation, a Draught of an Instruction prepared by the
Lords Commissioners for Trade and Plantations, for Henry Ellis
Esquire His Majestys Governor of the Province of Georgia, Authorizing and directing him, to dispose of the Lands which the
Nations of Creek Indians have lately surrendered to His Majesty,
in the manner and for the purposes proposed by the said Instruction.
His Majesty this day took the said Report and Draught of Instruction into Consideration, and was pleased with the Advice of His
Privy Council to approve of the said Draught of Instruction (which
is hereunto annexed) And to Order as it is hereby Ordered, That
the Right Honourable William Pitt Esqr One of His Majestys Principal Secretarys of State, do lay the same before His Majesty for
His Royal Signature.

Henry Ellis to the Board of Trade, Feb. 10, 1759, Georgia, received April 25, read May 8, 1759, C.O. 5/646, C. 56, objecting to the Appointment of Patrick Mackay and James Reid to
the Council.

My Lords

The 5th instant I received the Kings Commission appointing
me Governor in Chief of this Colony with which I think myself
highly honored. The same Conveyance brought for my direction
& guidance the Royal Instructions.

I was not a little surprised & concerned to find in the first
Article Mr Patrick Mackey & Mr James Reid nominated of His Majesty's Council for this province whether I am to impute this nomination to the powerful solicitation of their friends at London or
to the Miscarriage of those dispatches of mine wherein I had given
their Character I cannot determine but I am inclined to think the
latter for I can hardly admit that your Lordships would disregard
any circumstance whereon the peace of the Colony depends.
These Gentlemen were introduced when there were already 7 Members in the province & for the support of the most indefensible
measures. The latter is a person of no consequence of small
fortune moderate abilities & no interest in the Country. Yet these
objections are trivial in comparison to those which lie against
the other.

I acquainted your Lordships in my first letter that when I qualified as Lieut Governor I had not summoned these two Gentlemen
to Council nor of course ever since they were then so well

satisfied that I acted without prejudice & agreeable to the Kings Instructions that they seemed not to take the least umbrage.

Mr Mackay had been appointed by Mr Reynolds Senr Justice in the Kings Courts in the Room of Mr Jones one of the Council removed from that Board & the Bench to gratify Mr Little & it is positively affirmed to promote the establishment of Bosomworths Titles to the Indian Lands with a view to share the spoil. Though I was apprised of this intention I took no other step to defeat it than that of encreasing the number of Judges by the addition of 2 Gentlemen of unexceptionable character. Notwithstanding this alteration the Chief Judge conceived he had the sole power upon the Bench & exerted it accordingly in the most arbitrary & partial manner. I will relate one instance to your Lordships as a specimen of his conduct.

The Owner of a Vessel & Cargo which was seized & condemned here (in a very irregular manner by the late Governor) being heated with liquor & exasperated by the severity & unfairness of the preceedings threw out some indiscreet expressions to this effect that if he was deprived of his property the French would be in possession of the province in a twelve month. This being reported to the Governor the man was immediately seized imprisoned & at length sent to England under a charge of treason. Soon after his confinement his Attorney demanded from the Marshal of the Admiralty a Copy of his commitment which was refused. The Attorney prosecuted the Marshal upon the Statute of 31 of Charles 2d which subjected him to a penalty of £100 Sterlg. The Judges unanimously declared he had incurred it but he being an Active & servile tool to the late Governor the Senior Justice exerted himself in his behalf, adjourned the Court in spite of the remonstrance of his colleagues to evade signing the Judgment & contrary to his Oath, became his private Councellor & with his own hand wrote a Memorial & Petition for the delinquent addressed to me setting forth the iniquity of the Judgment & praying for a rehearing. This & several other of his transactions equally inconsistent & unjustifiable proved him most unworthy to preside in a Court of Judicature.

In the mean time he kept up the fairest correspondence with me visiting me by day & plying me with the warmest professions of friendship & attachment whilst at Night he associated with a Cabal of Mr Reynolds partizans composed of no less than 14 Members of the Assembly & 4 or 5 of the Council who solemnly engaged to unite in supporting the late measures & maintaining a strenuous oppositon to mine. Moreover he was privately exerting himself to get into the Assembly where it was agreed he should

be chosen Speaker & head the Faction. Being told by one of the
party that I had got intimation of his practices & would certainly
suspend him from the Bench if he persisted in them he publickly
replied "there was no danger for he knew I had neither the power
nor spirit to do it." The temper & moderation I had hitherto preserved in all my proceedings might possibly have deluded in
that imagination & encouraged him to go on; accordingly the next
thing I heard was his introducing to the Assembly an inflammatory
Letter left with him by the late Speaker, many Copies of which I
transmitted for your Lordships perusal. He likewise offered himself a Candidate to represent the Town of Savannah in Assembly
in the room of that Gentleman. It now became highly incumbent
on me to check his career by exposing him & publishing my disapprobation of his behavior which I accordingly did & suspended
him from the Bench. The consequences were that he lost his
Election & retired highly chagrined. This Miscarriage dissolved
the Cabal; & gave me an opportunity of undeceaving the people
& reconciling their jarring humours. From that period the Government has been easier administered & the Colony has throve in a
remarkable manner. It would be a great evil were those unhappy
times revived; & this my Lords would certainly be the Case should
that Gentleman be again called upon the Theatre & invested with
any degree of power or influence. For all the acrimony & rancour
of his party is collected & exalted in him by the remembrance of
the mortifications his conduct brought upon him. And should not
such irregular & audacious proceedings be discountenanced &
publickly stigmatized but on the contrary overlooked & even
tacitly approved, there will seem to be no discrimination no reward to distinguish the worthy from the unworthy every restraint
upon indecency & insolence will be removed all the petulent &
restless spirits among us will be in motion; His Majesty's Government will fall into contempt & I shall entirely loose my authority
& the power of defending the rights of the Crown & promoting the
prosperity of the Colony.

The facility with which I have been able to establish several
capital points here may in a great measure be ascribed to the
influence I have had in the Council for the Assembly are already
a Match for the other branches of the Legislature united. But
should I loose my weight there by the introduction of violent &
disaffected Members every thing must fall into confusion And
such a situation of things would have infinitely more pernicious
consequences at this time than at any other for now every point
is contested as the first steps in the introduction of a constitution
became a part of it.

I am therefore persuaded that when your Lordships consider these matters attentively you will be convinced that to reinstate Mr Mackay would be highly impolitic & I have good reason to believe that had he not been an Offender in a public Capacity his private character alone would be a sufficient objection to your Lordships allowing him any I have in the Administration of this Government. For he is universally disliked was disdainfully rejected by the people at several Elections where he offered himself a Candidate & is esteemed an artful implacable & disingenuous Man. He does not even reside in the Colony nor has he ever rendered it any service.

I shall beg leave to detain your Lordships but a moment longer whilst I make a few remarks with respect to the situation of the other Members.

Mr Robinson has been absent from this Province upwards of three years. Mr Russell would never act as Counsellor. Mr Clifton the Kings Attorney declined that honor at first because of the attention the erecting the Courts & forming their constitutions required, but he afterwards qualified & admitted as your Lordships will see in the Minutes of Council & has been extremely useful especially as a Member of the Upper House especially in defending the prerogative against the attempts of the Lower House which is ever ready to invade it as well as in complying & drawing up the public Acts. Indeed this Gentleman & Mr Knox are the only persons there possessed of any talents that way & among the rest if we except Sir Patrick Houstoun & Mr Powell there is not the least zeal for his Majestys Service to be found.

Mr Jones was suspended by Mr Reynolds, Mr Martyn likewise but whether his Majesty has been pleased to confirm or reverse those Suspensions I have not been informed. 'Tis true Mr Jones' Name is again in the Instructions but whether of course or in consequence of an approbation does not appear.

Mr Martyn is left out tho he has a mandamus which indeed is of a prior date to these instructions yet I am at a loss to know what regard I ought to pay to it; To admit Mr Jones & reject Mr Martyn without sufficient authority would be subjecting my self to censure at home & give great offence as well as occasion disagreeable animadversions here; These several considerations have prevailed upon me to let things remain as they were to qualify upon & continue to act by the former instructions (which differ from the last only in the first Article) until I can learn by your Lordships means the Kings pleasure hereupon; and if I have acted imprudently in this affair I hope your Lordships will attribute it to want of information & judgment; for I can truly affirm I have done for the best, being persuaded that very mischievous consequences might result from my proceeding which cannot happen from any delaying to carry that particular instruction into execution since every thing is perfectly quiet here & this matter not divulged.

'Tis possible some regard may be paid to this representation, if there should it may not be improper for me to mention such Gentlemen as are best qualified to supply future vacancies in the Council.

Mr Clifton the Kings Attorney is known to your Lordships; A very good Man. Charles Pryce Esqr a Man of Good dispositions independent fortune & bred to the Law. William Butler Esqr a considerable planter of good parts & universally esteemed. Captn William Mackenzie a Settler from North Carolina of sufficient fortune & understanding & strongly recommended to me by Govr Dobbs as an honest and worthy man.

Henry Ellis to William Pitt, Feb. 12, 1759, Georgia, giving an account of the New Hanover settlement and ideas about the southern frontier.

Sir

Last month I had the honour to receive your letter of the 10th of June, I immediately consulted with Governor Lyttelton upon the subject matter of it; and the best manner of carrying the Kings Commands into execution, in respect to the people settled to the Southward of the River Altamaha, the reputed Boundary of Georgia.

The Course we at length agreed upon, was to send Commissioners properly authorized from each Province, a Copy of the Instructions given them is enclosed herewith. Those Gentlemen set out upon that Service but last Week; it is too soon therefore to know what reception they met with, or the time they have allowed those people to depart with their effects; these particulars I shall mention hereafter. At present Sir, I have only to observe that as these Setlers have fled from their creditors in the different Provinces to the North; whither they cannot return, there is danger of their putting themselves under the protection of the Spaniards at St Augustine, to whom they may be very useful in promoting their intention of setling a Colony in Florida; and if they should afterwards attempt opening an intercourse, and establishing a friendly correspondence between that Government and the Creek Indians which they will probably do with success such an event will prove highly prejudicial to his Majestys Interest in these parts. I could therefore have wished it had been in our power to have prevented this, by allowing them to settle upon the Island of Cumberland, where we have a Fort and Garrison that would have kept them in order; and to which they would have been useful.

At present the Lands between Georgia and Florida are said to constitute a part of South Carolina, but I am persuaded Sir you will readily see the impropriety of this State of things, the many inconvencies attending it, and may possibly affix some remedy.

I humbly apprehend that to settle those Lands as far as the River St Mary (at the entrance of which stands Fort William) could give Umbrage to our Neighbors as the River St Juan which in these parts is considered as the common Boundary of the Territory of his Majesty and the King of Spain lies Sixty Miles Southward of St Marys.

When General Oglethorpe Commanded here we had a Fort upon an Island at the Mouth of the River St. Juan, from whence the Garrison was withdrawn in 1736, to quiet the minds of the Spaniards at St Augustine and in consequence of a Treaty between the Governor of that Fortress and Mr Oglethorpe, which act it was stipulated should not prejudice his Majestys Rights in those parts, but no objection has been made to Fort William which is still kept up and Garrisoned. And give me leave Sir to suggest upon this occasion that if it were the Kings pleasure to annex these Southern Lands to this Province either expressly, or in general terms, by extending the jurisdiction of this Government as far as his majestys Territorys extended to the South, the Irregularities of Setlers there would be prevented by the operation of our Laws.

Everything remains quiet here and the Colony is in a thriving condition under many circumstances of insecurity.

Henry Ellis to William Pitt, Feb. 12, 1759, Georgia, acknowledging notification of Major General Amherst's appointment as Commander of the King's forces in America.

Sir

A few days ago, I was honoured with your Letter of the 18th of September, notifying his Majestys appointment of Major General Amherst to the Chief Command of the Kings Forces in America, and signifying his Majestys pleasure that I should apply to and correspond with that General upon every matter, that may concern, or promote his Majestys Service. As also to obey such Orders, as he may think proper to honour me with, relative to the said Service.

All and every particular of these Commands I shall pay the strictest regard and obedience to, upon every necessary occasion.

Nothing material occurs at present.

Henry Ellis to William Pitt, March 1, 1759, Georgia, transmitting report of Commissioner sent to expel settlers south of the Altamaha.[42]

Sir

The 12th of February last I did my self the honour to acknowledge your Letter of the 10th of June, relative to the people settled South of the River Altamaha, the reputed Boundary of this Province. At the same time, I took the liberty to give my sentiments upon the situation of things there; (to which I beg leave to refer) and related the steps I had taken preparatory to the carrying the Kings Commands into execution, in reference to the said Setlers.

I now transmit the Report of the Commissioner who was employed on my part in that Service; and also that, of the Commanding Officer of a detachment of the Kings Troops stationed at Frederica, whom I directed to inform me in what manner these people should act after the departure of the Commissioner and the time Limitted for their removal. And tho' according to the accounts I have received they have done everything which was required of them, yet, I am not without suspicions that they will soon steal back to their habitations; and this I am afraid, it will be impossible for me effectually to prevent; however, I shall exert myself by every means in my power, to divert them from it.

Henry Ellis to the Board of Trade, March 1, 1759, Georgia, read July 11, 1759, C.O. 5/646, C. 58, transmitting a copy of the report of the commissioner sent to displace the settlement south of the Altamaha together with his comments.

My Lords

Since the sailing of the last Convoy from Charles Town there has happened no opportunity of conveying to your Lordships an

---

42. The report follows the next letter.

account that our Commissioner effected with the people South of
the Altamaha. I now enclose a Copy of his Report to me which
comprehends a detail of his proceedings & the state in which he
found things in that quarter.

I should have mentioned before that this Gentleman carried a
Letter from me to the Commanding Officer at Frederica directing
him to repair to the Settlements of these people (after the time
fixed by the Commissioners for their departure) in order to see in
what manner the Kings Commands should be obeyed & his Report
accompanies that of the Commissioners.

Your Lordships will perceive by these papers that the number
of people settled South of our Boundary is about 300 as most of
those whose names are in the inclosed Lists are heads of families; & upwards of two thirds of them had left New Hanover some
time ago & sat down with Gray upon the Island of Cumberland.
I should have been glad our Instructions had authorized us to
suffer their continuing there upon which point I have already taken
the liberty to give my sentiments at large in my letter of the 28th
of January. I do not think there is a great deal of regard to be
had to the steps reported to have been taken by Gray & his adherents as I know him to be a fellow of infinite Art & Finesse; &
therefore I am inclined to think these people will steal back to
their habitations very soon & it will not be in my power to prevent
it having no directions to use rigourous measures for that purpose.

Report of James Edward Powell, Commissioner from Georgia to the
inhabitants of settlements southward of the Altamaha Jan. 23, 1759,
Georgia, read July 11, 1759, C.O. 5/646, C. 59, enclosed with
Ellis' letters to William Pitt and the Board of Trade, March 1, 1759,
on the success of his mission.

Thursday the 1st of February We arrived at the place proposed
for their principal Town by the Settlers South of the River Altamaha.
The spot they have chosen for this purpose lyes 30 Miles from the
Entrance of the Noble River Sitility & upon its Banks. The extent
& depth whereof is such as ranks it amongst the most considerable
Rivers in the Southern Provinces being navigable for large Vessels
upwards of 70 Miles & much farther with small ones. There we
were kindly received by the Principal Settlers & very much pleased
to find their dispositions better than had been represented; for
altho' they had made valuable improvements in one of the finest
parts of North America they very submissively agreed to abandon

them conformably to His Majestys Commands by us signified to them in the annexed Notification which we put up in the most public places after having read & published our Commissions. This being done we immediately proceeded for the Island of Cumberland where we arrived the next day Summoned the Inhabitants together & repeated the same steps we had taken at Sitilly. The Majority of these people attended but many of the most profligate & refractory stayed away & are suspected of having received encouragement from the Governor of Florida to go & settle there in conjunction with a number of Spanish Families lately sent from their Islands purposely to establish a Colony in those parts & as Edmund Gray the Leader of our people was apprehensive many bad consequences might result from the desertion of so many of his followers which he seemed desirous to prevent he with our approbation drew up the following Instrument & prevailed on the Majority of his Associates to sign it vizt:

Whereas the Inhabitants of New Hanover having been duly required to assemble this day to consider of proper places to remove to in obedience to His Majesty's commands published here by Commissioners from Georgia & South Carolina And many failing to attend gives us too much reason to believe what we have heard with regret vizt: That some rash persons are resolved to remove into the Spanish Territorys & are seducing many unthinking people to follow their example or connive at a project so contrary to their allegiance & the national Weal. We therefore intreat them to decline a step so undutiful to his Majestys, injurious to the public, destructive to themselves, reproachful to us their fellow Adventurers & contrary to the plain meaning of our Mutual Compact.

But lest any should persist in a design so weak & wicked We do hereby appoint John Cubbage to go to their respective places of abode & assure them that we knowing our duty are determined to adhere to it & will not suffer them or any of them to retire to any place without His Majesty's Dominions & that we have enjoined him to watch their conduct & take effectual means to prevent whatever may be disrespectful to his Majesty's Orders or prejudicial to the British Interest & do promise to hold ourselves in readiness to aid & assist him in such manner as he may think most eligible. The first immediately inviting all those that may be well disposed to sign this writing & jointly with us enter into measures so indispensibly necessary.

Signed

1 Edmund Gray   2 Andrew Maxton

Colonial Records 189

3 James Mathews
4 Marmaduke Perry
5 Joseph Blythe
6 John Copland
7 Edmund Gillman
8 Saml Richardson
9 Edward Bristoe
10 William Hester
11 John Hester
12 Oliver Shaw
13 Joseph Fortner
14 Samuel Mills
15 Edmond Pierce
16 Nathl Wilson
17 Joshua Latman
18 Henry Bedford
19 John Kerrol
20 John Cubbage
21 William McGregor

We then collected the following Names of persons Mostly heads of families who were settled there abouts but we Learned that there were a considerable number of Straglers besides who subsist chiefly by Hunting.

John Williams
Willm Hester
Saml Mills
Andw Palmer
William Ross
Wm Steadman
Thos Carr
John Loney
John Lofter
John Evans
Jas Bryant
Ephm Alexander
Saml Richardson
Doctor Brisko
William Chadows
Joseph Blythe
Joseph Gray
Richard Hazard
Wm McGregor
Joseph Wilson
Marmad Perry
John Pemberton

Giles Moore
Thoms Clemons
Andw Maxton
Anty Fernands
Joseph Goodby
John Cubbage
John Cane Junr
Andw Collins
Joseph Goodson
John Duncan
John Hester
Saml Mills Junr
Henry Bedford
John Copland
James Mathews
Edmund Pierce
Oliver Shaw
Joseph Faulkner
Patrick O'Neal
Wm Carpenter
Edmund Gray
John Cane

Saml Piles
Wm McKintosh
James Westly
Danl Mackay
Philip Sutton
John Bryant
Jacob Whitman
William Gray
Jno Chumby
Jacob Helvenstine
John Percival
Francis Cane
James Jones
John Bennet
Joshua Lipman
Jeremh Helvenstine
Edward Gillman
John Carrol
James Green
Richard Ogilbie
Robert Lucas
Nathl Watson

NOTIFICATION

Whereas His Majesty has been pleased to signify his Royal Will and pleasure to their Excellencys William Henry Lyttleton

Esqr Captain General & Governor in chief of His Majesty's Province of South Carolina & Henry Ellis Esqr Captain General & Governor in Chief of his Majesty's Province of Georgia That the Inhabitants of a certain Settlement to the Southward of the River Altamaha made without His Majesty's License & authority & called by themselves New Hanover shall immediately remove from thence & if any other Settlement or Settlements shall have been made to the Southward of the said River Altamaha without such License & authority that they the Inhabitants of any such Settlements shall likewise immediately remove. And whereas their said Excellencys have commissionated constituted & appointed Major Henry Hyme on the part of the Province of South Carolina & James Edward Powell Esqr on the part of the province of Georgia to make known to the Inhabitants of the said Settlement or Settlements His Majesty's will & pleasure concerning them & pursuant thereto to order them immediately to remove from thence. We the said Commissioners do therefore in His Majesty's name order all & singular the Inhabitants of the said Settlement to the Southward of the River Altamaha made without His Majestys License & authority & called by themselves New Hanover & all & singular the Inhabitants of any other Settlement or Settlements which shall have been made to the Southward of the said River without such License & authority to remove from thence. But whereas it may greatly distress the said Inhabitants to be obliged to remove from their said Settlements without some time given them to procure others & to carry off their Stock provisions &c We also in consideration thereof allow them 28 days that is to say till the 1st day of March next ensuing the date hereof for that purpose.

> Given under our hands & seals this 1st day of February in the 32nd year of His Majestys Reign & in the Year of our Lord 1759.
>
> JAMES EDWD POWELL
>
> HENRY HYME

Order in Council March 3, 1759, St. James, received May 21, read July 8, 1760, C.O. 5/647, D. 15, disallowing six Georgia laws passed in 1755, 1756, and 1757.

The Kings most Excellent Majesty in Council

Whereas by Commission under the Great Seal of Great Britain the Governor Council and Assembly of His Majestys Province of Georgia are Authorized and empowered to make constitute and Ordain Laws Statutes and Ordinances for the Publick Peace, Welfare and good Government of the said Province, Which Laws Statutes and Ordinances are to be, as near as conveniently may be, agreable to the Laws and Statutes of this Kingdom, and to be transmitted for His Majestys Royal Approbation or Disallowance. And Whereas in pursuance of the said Powers Six Acts have been passed in the said Province in the years 1755, 1756, and 1757, and transmitted, entituled as follow vizt:

An Act to prevent fraudulent Deeds and Conveyances.
   Passed in March 1755.
An Act for the ease of Dissenting Protestants within this
  Province who may be scrupulous of taking an Oath
  in respect to the manner and Form of Administring the
  same
   Passed in December 1756.
An Act for the better regulation of Courts of Request
   Passed in December 1756.
An Act for declaring and Establishing the Method of Drawing
  and Summoning Jurors in the Province of Georgia
   Passed in December 1756.
An Act to explain and amend an Act entitled An Act tor
  declaring and Establishing the method of drawing and
  Summoning Jurors in the Province of Georgia.
   Passed in February 1757.
An Act for the better settling the province of Georgia.
   Passed July 1757.

Which Acts, together with a Representation from the Lords Commissioners for Trade and Plantations proposing the Repeal thereof having been referred to the Consideration of a Committee of the Lords of His Majestys most Honourable Privy Council for Plantations Affairs. The said Lords of the Committee did this day Report to His Majesty as their Opinion that the said Acts ought to be repealed His Majesty taking the same into Consideration, was pleased, with the Advice of His Privy Council, to declare His Disallowance of the said Acts and pursuant to His Majestys Royal pleasure thereupon expressed, The said Acts are hereby repealed, declared Void, and of none effect. Whereof the Governor or Commander in Chief of His Majestys Province of Georgia, for the time being and all others whom it may concern are to take Notice and Govern themselves accordingly.

Report of Thomas Goldsmith, Commanding Officer at Frederica, to Governor Ellis, March 6, 1759, saying that the settlements at New Hanover and Cumberland Island had been abandoned.

Sir

In consequence of your Excellencys Commands & agreeable to what I had the honor to write to you the 5th. of February I arrived at the intended Town of New Hanover & found that the people inhabiting there had quitted the place. I also fell down the River to the Island of Cumberland where the Major part of these people did formerly reside & found that they likewise had left their habitations save one Man only to take care of the effects they had not time to carry off & the fields of Rye which grow there in great plenty.

Henry Ellis to the Board of Trade, March 15, 1759, Georgia, read July 11, 1759, C.O. 5/646, C. 60, giving an account of his recent troubles with the Assembly.

My Lords

In my Letter of the 28th of January I took notice of the growing discontents among the Representatives in our Assembly owing to the expense they were put to, the injury they suffered in neglecting their private affairs during their attendance on the public Business & to the unlimited duration of their service in that capacity which entailed those hardships upon them. I also mentioned their having prepared a Bill to remedy those inconveniences which with some difficulty I caused to be suppressed in the Upper House. But finding afterwards that the stopping its progress there was like to excite much clamour against the Gentlemen of the Council & apprehending that a diminution of their Credit might be attended with bad consequences hereafter I suffered them to revise the consideration of it which made all smooth again. After some alterations therein it passed both Houses, was presented to me, & laid aside by the Parliamentary Phrase "that I would consider of it." This disappointment occasioned the enclosed Address which was presented to me before the Assembly rose & in consequence thereof I now transmit to your Lordships a Copy of the Bill;[43] my thoughts upon the subject of it are contained in my Letter of the 28th of January.

At present I shall only observe in general that exceptionable as it is in some parts perhaps there never was a more moderate & innocent one framed by an American Assembly. And really my Lords I do not perceive considerable objection to it except that the term proposed for the duration of Assemblys seems too short. And persuaded I am that the people here will never rest until they can obtain some indulgence in these matters; but particularly in respect to this last point which affects them most. I am likewise clear that if any future Assembly should form a Bill with the same views it would be infinitively more objectionable than the present one. For these reasons I should be extremely glad your Lordships would condescend to bestow some consideration upon it soon as it is really a point deserving attention, and in order that the inconvenience complained of for want of such limitation as is sought for may be felt as little as possible & to the end that the discontent of the Members may not increase & infect the people in general I shall in all probability be under a necessity of dissolving the Assembly before long & indeed I intend to suggest as much at the opening of the next Session in November. This step may prevent any immediate complaints & give me time to procure your Lordships advice as to my future conduct herein which I shall impatiently wait for. It would be happy for us if South Carolina was at a greater distance as our people are incessantly urging & aiming at the priviledges enjoyed there. And all those arguments have but a momentary effect which are employed to prove that those privilidges are so many encroachments which in their operation & effects are not so favorable to liberty & the subject as they imagine.

It would fatigue your Lordships were I to recite the many instances wherein these Carolina notions have prevailed with our people over every other consideration. And I am afraid so long as our present intercourse with & dependence upon that Province subsists they will not alter their ideas.

During the late Sitting of the Assembly many Laws were passed but none of so singular & important a nature as to merit particular notice. Some of them have already & the rest will be transmitted by the first safe Conveyance.

---

43. Given in CRG, XIII, 408-410.

Our usual tranquillity continues All the Accounts from the Country of the Indians are favorable but not uncommon. I have frequent visits from small parties of them which serve to keep up an intimacy & are less expensive than formal Meetings. I have not yet had the honor of a Line in answer to the many Letters I have wrote to your Lordships Board; but I flatter myself this will not be the case long.

Bill to ascertain the manner of electing members to the Commons House of Assembly and for limiting the time of their sitting, read July 11, 1759, C.O. 5/642, C. 61. Enclosed in Ellis to Board of Trade March 15, 1759.[44]

WHEREAS the choosing of Members of the Commons House of Assembly for this His Majesty's Province of Georgia by Parishes & Districts is thought to be the most just and least expensive method and approaches nearest to the form and method of choosing or electing Members in other His Majestys Provinces therefore We humbly pray your most sacred Majesty that it may be enacted, AND BE IT ENACTED by his Excellency Henry Ellis Esquire Captain General and Governor in Chief of the province of Georgia by and with the advice and consent of His Majesty's Honorable Council and Commons House of Assembly of the said province in General Assembly Met & by the authority of the same that the persons who shall be chosen to serve as Members of Assembly after the passing of this Act shall be elected and chosen in the manner herein after directed.

AND BE IT FURTHER ENACTED by the authority aforesaid that all Writs for the future Elections of Members of Assembly shall be issued out by the Governor or Commander in Chief for the time being forty days before the day appointed for the Meeting of the said Members, and shall be directed to the provost Marshall requiring him to make out Warrants of Election for the several Districts of this Province. And the said Provost Marshall is hereby impowered and required to execute or cause to be executed every such Writ faithfully according to the true intent and meaning of this Act. And each and every returning Officer by him appointed shall some time before the day of Election take an Oath before any

---

44. No such bill was passed in Georgia until June 9, 1761. See CRG, XVIII, 464-472.

Justice of the Peace for the due and faithful execution of his Office agreeable to the directions of this Act; which person so qualified shall ten days before the day of Election post up a Notice in writing on the door of the Parish Church or other public places in the District setting forth the day and place when and where the said Election shall be held to the intent that the time and place of Election may be the better and more fully known. Which Elections respectively shall be executed upon the same days and at the same places as in the Warrants are directed, Provided always that the Elections for the several Districts shall be appointed to be held on different days.

AND BE IT FURTHER ENACTED by the Authority aforesaid that every Freeman (those that were Slaves and their Offspring only excepted) who has attained to the age of twenty one years And is in actual possession of and hath a legal title to a Freehold of at least fifty Acres of Land or a Town Lot with improvements thereon to the value of Ten pounds sterling in the District where he offers his Vote shall be deemed a person qualified to Vote for a Representative.

It is HEREBY FURTHER ENACTED that the Names of the Electors shall be fairly entered in a Book or Roll for that purpose provided by the Returning Officer to prevent any person's Voting twice at the same Election and the manner of their Voting shall be as follows: that is to say, each person qualified to vote shall put into a Box or Sheet of paper prepared for that purpose by the person as aforesaid a piece of paper roll'd up wherein shall be written the names of the person or persons he votes for to which paper the Elector shall not be obliged to subscribe his own Name. And if upon a Scrutiny two or more papers be found roll'd up together or more persons names be found written in any paper than ought to be voted for all and every such paper or papers shall be invalid and of no effect and those persons who after all the Votes are delivered in as aforesaid that shall be found to have the Majority of Votes he or they is and are hereby declared duly elected Members of the Commons House of Assembly if they be found qualified as is hereinafter directed.

AND BE IT FURTHER ENACTED by the Authority aforesaid that no Election for any District shall continue longer than one day beginning at Nine in the Morning and ending at four in the Evening. And that at adjourning the Poll at convenient hours in the time of an Election the Returning Officer shall seal up the said Box or Sheet of paper wherein are put all the Ballots roll'd up and delivered in by the Electors as aforesaid with his own Seal and the

Seals of any two or more of the Electors that are there present and upon Opening the Poll shall unseal the said Box or Sheet of Paper in the presence of the said Electors in order to proceed in the said Election.

AND BE IT FURTHER ENACTED that the Returning Officer shall within three days after the Scrutiny is made give public notice in writing at the Church door or in places where there is no Church at some other public place in the Parish or District where the Elections was made to the person or persons so elected that the inhabitants have made choice of him or them to serve as their Representative or Representatives in the Commons House of Assembly under the penalty of ten pounds sterling for his neglect or default therein to be recovered and applyed as is hereinafter directed.

AND BE IT FURTHER ENACTED that the Inhabitants of the several Districts in this Province qualified to vote for Members of Assembly as in this Act before directed shall upon the day of Election according to the precept aforesaid meet at the respective places therein appointed and there proceed to choose their Representatives according to the numbers following (that is to say): For that part of the Parish of Christ Church called the Town and District of Savannah four Members, for that part called the District of Little Ogechee one Member, for that part called Acton one Member, for that part called Vernonburgh one Member, and for the Sea Islands in the said Parish one Member, for that part of the Parish of Saint Matthew called the Town and District of Ebenezer three Members, and for that part called the District of Abercorn and Goshen one Member, for the parish of Saint George and District of Hallifax two Members, for the Parish of Saint Paul and Town and District of Augusta three Members, for the Town of Hardwick and Parish of Saint Philip two Members, for the Parish of Saint John three Members, for the Parish of Saint Andrew Two Members, for the Town of Frederica and Parish of Saint James one Member; and the said several Candidates who upon the Scrutiny are found to have the Majority of Votes they being qualified as is herein after directed shall be and they are hereby declared to be the true Representatives for the said Parishes and Districts.

AND BE IT FURTHER ENACTED by the Authority aforesaid that every person who shall be elected and returned as is before directed by this Act to serve as a Member of the Commons House of Assembly shall be qualified as follows, vizt: He shall be a free born subject of the Kingdom of Great Britain or of the Dominions thereunto belonging or a foreign person naturalized by Act of Parliament in Great Britain or Ireland that hath attained to the age of 21 years and hath been resident in this Province for twelve Months before the date of the said Writs and having in this Province a Freehold in his own right of at least 500 Acres of Land or has in his own proper right to the value of one hundred and fifty pounds Sterling in Houses Buildings Town Lots or other Lands in any part of this Province.

AND BE IT FURTHER ENACTED by the authority aforesaid that the Returning Officer shall and is hereby authorized and impowered to tender and administer an Oath to any Elector at the time of his coming to vote if required so to do by any Freeholder then present which Oath shall be to the effect following (that is to say) I A. B. do swear that I am duly qualified to Vote for a Representative in the Commons House of Assembly of this Province for the District or Parish of _____ _____ agreeable to the directions of an Act of this Province intituled An Act to ascertain the manner and form of electing Members to represent the Inhabitants of this province in the Commons House of Assembly and to direct who shall be capable of chosing or being chose Members of the said House and for limiting the time of their Sitting. So help me God.

AND BE IT FURTHER ENACTED by the authority aforesaid that if any Member or Members hereafter chosen to serve in the Commons House of Assembly should die, depart the province, or refuse to qualify him or themselves as in this Act is directed or be expelled by the said House then and in such cases the said House shall by Message to the Governor for the time being desire him to issue a new Writ or Writs in manner as herein before is directed for choosing another person or persons to act in the place of such Member or Members so dead departed this Province or who shall refuse to qualify him or themselves or be expelled as aforesaid which person or persons so chosen and returned shall attend the Commons House of Assembly as by the precept shall be directed.

AND BE IT FURTHER ENACTED by the authority aforesaid that all and every Member and Members of the Commons House of Assembly of this Province chosen by virtue of this Act shall have as much power and priviledge to all intents and purposes as any Member heretofore of right had might could or ought to have in the said province.

AND BE IT FURTHER ENACTED by the authority aforesaid that if any returning Officer shall willingly or knowingly admit or take the Vote of any person not qualified according to the purport of this Act or after any Vote is delivered in at such Election shall open or suffer any person whatsoever to open any such Vote before the Scrutiny is begun to be made or shall make an undue return if any person for a Member of the Commons House of Assembly each person so offending shall forfeit for every such offence the sum of fifteen pounds sterling to be recovered and applied in such manner as is hereinafter directed.

AND BE IT FURTHER ENACTED by the authority aforesaid that all and every person and persons appointed to take votes as aforesaid shall for that purpose attend at the time and place of Election accordingly as he or they are directed by the said Warrants and attend likewise on the said House of Assembly two days if thereunto required and being paid his reasonable charges to inform them of all such matters as may be necessary to be known concerning any Election for which they were appointed Returning Officers as aforesaid and shall produce to the said House a List of the Votes for every person that was voted for at such Election (if required) and every person appointed to take Votes as aforesaid who shall omit or refuse to attend at either of the times and places as aforesaid shall forfeit the sum of forty shillings sterling to be recover'd and disposed of as is herein after directed.

AND BE IT FURTHER ENACTED by the authority aforesaid that if any person or persons whatsoever shall on any day appointed for the Election of a Member or Members of the Commons House of Assembly as aforesaid presume to violate the freedom of the said Election by an Arrest menaces or threats or endeavor or attempt to over awe fright or force any Elector to vote against his inclination or otherwise by bribery obtain any Vote or who after such Election is over shall menace, despitefully use, or abuse any person because he hath not voted as he would have had him, every such person so offending upon due and sufficient proof made of such his violence or abuse before any two Justices of the Peace shall be bound over to the next Court of Oyer and Terminer himself in six pounds sterling with two Securities in three pounds like money each and to be of good behaviour and abide the sentence of the said Court where if the Offender be found guilty of such Offence and is convicted thereof then he or they shall each of them forfeit the sum of six pounds Sterling and to be committed to Goal without bail or mainprize 'till the same be paid which fine so imposed shall be paid to one of the Church Wardens of the parish where the offence was committed for the use of the Poor thereof.

AND BE IT FURTHER ENACTED by the authority aforesaid that who ever is elected a Member to serve in the Commons House of Assembly before he be permitted to take his Seat and Vote in the said House shall qualify himself by taking the following Oath in the House to be administered by any Justice of the Peace then present or before any other Justice that may be required to administer the same vizt I A. B. do sincerely swear that I am duly qualified to serve and be chosen as a Member of the Commons House of Assembly of this Province for the Parish of _____ or District of _____ agreeable to the directions of an Act of this Province intituled an Act to ascertain the manner and form of electing Members to represent the Inhabitants of this province in the Commons House of Assembly and to direct who shall be capable of choosing or being chose Members of the said House and for limiting the time of their sitting and shall qualify himself for the same by taking the usual Oaths and make and sign the declaration appointed by the several Acts of Parliament of Great Britain.

AND BE IT FURTHER ENACTED by the authority aforesaid that all fines and forfeitures mentioned in this Act and not before particularly disposed of shall be one half for the use of the poor of the Parish where it is incurred to be paid to the Church Wardens of such Parish and the other half to him or them who shall sue for the same by Action of Debt suit bill plaint or information in any Court in this Province.

AND WHEREAS it is extremely inconvenient in this new Settled Province for Members of the Commons House of Assembly to continue to serve any long term of time be it therefore ENACTED by the authority aforesaid that this present general Assembly shall determine and be dissolved at the expiration of three years next after the date of the Writs issued out for calling the same and that every General Assembly hereafter called by virtue of any Writs as aforesaid shall determine and be dissolved every three years next after the date of the respective Writs by which they were called. AND BE IT FURTHER ENACTED by the authority aforesaid that the holding of General Assemblies shall not be discontinued or intermitted above twelve Months.

A true Copy taken from the
Original 7th May 1759

THOS BURRINGTON

Clerk of the Commons House of Assembly

Henry Ellis to the Board of Trade, April 24, 1759, Georgia, read July 11, 1759, C.O. 5/646, C. 63, commenting upon the acts recently suspended and various other subjects.

My Lords

The 5th instant and not before I had the honor of receiving the 3rd Copy of your Lordships Letter of the 21st of April and with it that wrote the 24th of November last.

The Approbation which your Lordships are pleased in so obliging a manner to express therein of several transactions of mine & the justice & honor you do me in ascribing even my errors to honest and upright motives have the strongest title to my most grateful and hearty acknowledgments.

My Lords I am satisfied that the measures which you object to are not right and therefore I shall not attempt to Justify them. I shall only beg the favor that your Lordships will be so indulgent as to permit me to describe those measures and their causes in the light they appeared here as that may to some degree account for their taking place.

In your first letter your Lordships are pleased to give your opinion on the Asylum Act. I must candidly own the reasons for repealing it appear stronger than those on the other side, And also that it has not been attended with the advantages which were expected as very few hitherto have taken the benefit of it. It was indeed calculated for such as were considered as lost to the state, I mean those who had put themselves under foreign protection. But the present troubles have put it out of their power to avail themselves of it; so that I do not think its repeal would affect us or be attended with any ill consequences even to the very few that it may have induced to come here.

The next point I shall take the liberty to touch upon is the paper currency. I must entirely agree with your Lordships that the issuing of it was illegal and not to be justified as in the act on which it was founded. There was a Clause suspending its operation until the Royal pleasure could be known. What has been issued in my time in the same way I have not failed to remonstrate against but I have been answered by the commissioners that the Bills so emitted were to be considered as their proper Notes of hand for which their private fortunes were answerable. And as every body knew this was the case they might accept or refuse them at their choice, that the public had been in suspense for the fate of the original Bill near three years and that the services to be provided for were urgent and admitted of no longer delay.

It may be proper to observe upon this occasion that the Act passed by Mr Reynolds authorizing Commissioners to issue a paper Currency differs very essentially from the Laws passed for

the same purpose in any other Colony for as much as it restrains
the Commissioners from issuing any but by way of Loan and that
in such small sums & upon such real Securities as exposes the
Acceptor to no kind of risque whereas the paper Bills made current
in our neighbouring province by a Law which I presume obtained
the Royal Assent were issued in payment of the Public Debts and
have for any thing I know to the contrary no better basis than that
Act which compels the people to take them.

The Act of Parliament quoted by your Lordships passed in 1750
I have not been able to get a sight of but I apprehend the object
of it was to prevent any paper Bills being issued for the sinking
whereof there was not a proper fund provided and appropriated.
Wherefore as no paper Bills have been issued here without such
provision having been previously made, it was apprehended no
evil could arise from them. As to the Currency emitted since the
Loan such Revenues have been appropriated for the calling in and
sinking of it as will infallibly do it before the year 1762 which is
the period fixed by the original Act for calling in the whole Currency.

The practice of issuing Certificates signed by Commissioners
appointed by Provincial Laws and giving these Certificates credit
for a certain number of years by virtue of a Clause recited in the
body of them obliging the Treasurer to receive them in all payments
of the Revenue appropriated for sinking them until the time limited
for their circulation expires is I believe an expedient which every
Colony in America has in some instances employed with great utility and convenience because it enables the Government to go to a
much larger expense in one year than the circumstances of the
people would bear to be raised in that time: And my Lords it was
imagined that as this method was frequently practiced by the Parliament of England it might be imitated here for the like purposes
and on a similar foundation. And it must be confessed that our
Currency upon its present basis is less exceptionable than the
above Certificates because no person is compelled to receive any
payment therein & there is a visible and unexceptionable Security
for its being made good when the possessors of it may think proper
to require it.

The advantages attending the several emissions of it are manifestly great as will appear by what follows:

As the Money lent to the planters was at a low interest they
found their advantage in investing it in Negroes the labour of
whom not only served to improve the lands but added also to the
export of the province and thereby diminished the Balance of Trade

against it. And the Revenue arising from the Interest paid for the use of that money enabled the Government to undertake several important and necessary services without any additional burthen to the people. A burthen that they would have been still less able to bear had they been deprived of the profit arising from the money lent them in consequence of the aforementioned Act. The sum of this Loan was about £2700 which at 6 per cent yielded £162 per Annum one fourth of which or £40.10. -- was by that law appropriated to defray the expenses of the Issue. The other 3/4ths remained unappropriated when Mr Reynolds was recalled. Then the debt of the Province amounted to near £700 and the ordinary civil expense to about £600. The Taxes did not produce £300 so that it became necessary to double them in order to defray the current expense. And as justice required that those who had lain longest out of their money should be first paid even that extraordinary tax must have been solely applied to discharge the Arrears so that the current service would never have been provided for until it was performed. Consequently every Officer would in a great measure have become dependant on the caprice and good pleasure of the Assembly for his maintenance the pernicious consequences whereof are notorious in South Carolina. It appeared therefore of high importance that the arrears should be paid off in order that the then present tax might be applied to the then present service. And as it was impossible to raise so large a sum at once as would discharge the debt & provide for the current services without exceedingly distressing & I may say ruining the Colony it was supposed that there could not be a more inoffensive way of proceeding than that of emitting paper Bills to the amount of the debt & appropriating the Interest of the Loan aforementioned for calling in & sinking them. This was the ground & object of the Bill passed in 1757.

In respect to that passed this last Session all that can be said upon it is this. The Taxes of the preceding year were so far from producing any surplus that they actually fell short of the ordinary expense about £100 in six. In order to keep things in their right track this arrear seemed indispensibly necessary to be provided for with the current service as well as an extra ordinary charge of £113 which was incurred by the measures taken here for the protection of our Coast when we were threatened with descents from the privateers of the enemy so that those two sums added to the ordinary expense amounted to as much as the increase of Taxable property in the province could be supposed to yield.

Your Lordships have been informed of the great danger to which this Town and I may add the Colony is exposed for want of a public Magazine & this danger was thought too alarming to be long overlooked especially when it was considered that any Negro or other ill disposed person had it in his power (with a fire brand) not only to destroy all the Records but disarm the Province at one blast since there is no other place to lodge the Military stores but in the Building where these papers are kept & this is of fir liable to catch fire with the first spark. Another service which could not be postponed was to secure the foundation of the light house at the entrance of this River. An Edifice of general use built at a large expense & which the inroads of the Sea threatened with immediate destruction. This by all means should have been prevented as its fall might be fatal not only to the lives & properties of His Majestys trading subjects in this part of the world but extremely prejudicial to the commercial Interest of this Colony.

The ruinous condition of the Church at Savannah was another object deserving attention it being such as was not only scandalous to Religion highly disreputable to the Colony but dangerous to the lives of those who frequented it.

The produce of the several funds allotted for these Services was insufficient to undertake them immediately; a further Issue of paper Bills was therefore thought requisite and the several funds before appropriated to those Services were now appropriated to the sinking of the Bills so issued.

And this My Lords is a true account of these proceedings which tho' irregular and illegal I humbly conceive neither has had nor probably will have any bad consequence.

Nothing in my humble opinion is more certain than that a currency of some kind or other is absolutely necessary here. Neither public nor private business can be carried on without it. We have had no trade that brings in any specie & if we had it would not remain here a moment so much is the Balance of Trade at present against us! Had we no paper currency our produce must be carried to and sold in Carolina or the Carolinians would send their Currency to purchase it and then I apprehend our circumstances would not be mended for the major part of that currency was issued without any real basis or even provision for the calling in & sinking of it and passes here only because it serves to pay our Debts in that province.

Upon the whole my Lords the enquirys I have made and the attention I have given to this subject incline me to think that our people in general are so well satisfied with the present state of our paper Bills that even the confirmation of the Act on which they are founded would scarce mend their credit. However in obedience to your Lordships commands I will take those steps in regard to it which you are pleased to recommend so soon as I can have it in my power to peruse the Resolutions of the British Parliament and the Act which I am referred to.

I am now my Lords to say something upon that part of my conduct which relates to Mr Gray. It is well known he had been settled to the Southward of the River Alatamaha with several of his Adherents many Months before I arrived here or took any notice of him and when I did he was on the best terms and kept up a frequent & friendly correspondence with the Governor of Florida who was very desirous he should become a subject of Spain and settle on the River St John in order to open an intercourse with the Creek Indians whom the Governor apprehended would obstruct the settling a New Spanish Colony in these parts; a design which he had very much at heart & had already engaged his Court in. But as Gray was afraid to put himself in the power of the Spanish Governor & could not effectually be wrought upon he was promised the protection of that Government & was assured that he should not be interrupted by the Spaniards or their Indians altho' he should prefer settling on the Northern side of that River.

I had the most unquestionable proofs of the reality of this Negociation & of the truth of the above circumstances wherefore I concluded that if Grays settling so near the Spanish Territory was agreeable to the Governor of Augustine his fixing at a greater distance could not be umbrageous. Besides the permission I gave that fellow was not to cultivate & plant the lands but to traffick with our Indian allies, the Creeks, similar permissions having been given those who presided in this Colony ever since its first Settlement. From this view of things I am not without hopes that the steps I took in an affair so full of embarrassment and so big with mischief may appear to your Lordships in a more favorable light than heretofore especially when your Lordships recollect that my correspondence with the Spanish Governor occasioned by the hostilities of the Savages commenced many Months after I had given Gray a trading license and not before as your Lordships seem to suppose.

My Lords I have perused Mr Littles Memorial in reference to the silk culture a Copy whereof I have sent to Mr Ottolenghe for him to answer & I shall now give my own thoughts upon it as your Lordships are pleased to desire it.

It is universally suspected here and I believe upon good grounds that it was more to gratify his private resentments to discharge his engagements with those of his party and to procure them an advantage by employing another Filature which would necessarily be under their direction than to promote the welfare of the Colony by extending the silk culture that Mr Little composed his Memorial and I am sure I do not speak with the least prejudice when I say that altho it is wrote very plausibly yet it is far from being either just or solid. It is there asserted that the single Town of Purysburgh produces half as many Cocoons as the whole province of Georgia. This is not strictly true for the Cocoons which come annually from thence to our filature are I am informed raised in the three Southern Counties of Carolina where this Commodity had been long cultivated under the countenance and with considerable encouragement from that Government.

The employing a filature in Ebenezer would doubtless be a great convenience to those who raise Cocoons there & about Purysburgh, but I very much question that it would be attended with any advantage to the public.

First Because the Cocoons produced in this & the neighbouring Colony are not at present near sufficient to employ the Filature at Savannah.

Secondly Because this would open a door to very great frauds & impositions as the Manager would not be able to controul & inspect two filatures at once.

Thirdly--Because another Filature would require more people in direction and management who must be paid considerable Salaries which would absorb much of the bounty given by Parliament to promote the increase of this Article; And

Fourthly Because the Germans the only people settled thereabouts are already too much separated from the rest of the Colony insomuch that after 20 Years residence many of them scarce understand a word of English & the taking away the occasion of mixing and conversing with the other inhabitants would confirm this evil instead of removing it and be so far from diffusing that knowledge which is proposed that it would really confine it to those of them that are even now sufficiently versed in it. Besides the hardships that those are said to labour under who bring Cocoons from Purysburgh and Ebenezer to Savannah are far from being so great in themselves or injurious to the public as is represented because opportunitys of conveying the Cocoons generally happen two to three times a Week and if that were not the case they have been instructed how to prevent the Worm from piercing them. Indeed if there were a filature erected at Augusta or Sunbury it might have very good consequences as it would be a probable means to engage people there in the raising Silk which hitherto has not been attempted.

But I really think my Lords it is too soon to set the Ebenezer filature a working.

Mr Littles Assertion that to bestow a Bounty on the raising of Mulberry Trees instead of giving it upon Cocoons would have a greater tendency to advance the culture of Silk is I dare say contrary to his own judgment. Every body here knows that what was formerly given in that way was an entire misapplication of the public money for none of those who received the premiums had any other object in view & the Trees they planted for that purpose never came to any thing. The many flagrant instances of this kind determined Mr Reynolds to declare that to prevent such notorious impositions the premium would no longer be given on Trees but Cocoons & indeed this seems the properest way of bestowing it & the surest means of encouraging this Culture in all its states & gradations until it comes to the filature. There are at present great abundance of Mulberry Trees. Many people plant them as well for ornament as use since their fruit are excellent for raising poultry & the cattle are extremely fond of their leaves.

Those who plant with these views take care to fence & preserve the trees which was not the case when a temporary advantage only was aimed at. Nor is it the fact that these Trees must be several years old before they are fit for use the tenderest & best leaves are those from the youngest plants. In all the Counties of the East where a vast quantity of Silk is raised they cut down the Trees or sow Beds of Mulberrys to raise young ones every three years & perhaps if this example was followed here our Worms would be healthier and the Silk prove of a finer quality than it is. In fine My Lords I must think that Mr Littles Memorial contains many gross misrepresentations which must either have proceeded from ignorance or disingenuity. And tho' it cannot be denied that Mr Ottolenghe has been actuated by very narrow motives & extremely jealous of a competitor in his department, yet to do him justice he seems to have great knowledge in his Business & to have employed it in carrying this valuable commodity to perfection except when he apprehended his importance and subsistence were struck out by the late Rulers. Mean while I shall use my best endeavors to procure that Gentleman a proper Coadjutor & Successor agreeable to your Lordships Commands & I have signified to Mr Ottolenghe that your Lordships future favours will depend on his care to instruct the person whom I shall appoint & on a proper behaviour in other respects. Your Lordships are pleased to express some concern that the raising of Silk makes so inconsiderable a progress notwithstanding the great encouragement afforded for that purpose and desire I would point out the impediments to it which I will endeavor to do and My Lords I imagine they are chiefly these.

First, The aversion & backwardness wherewith all new projects are received when there can be any doubt of the success of them.

Secondly, To the scarcity of poor white people who seem peculiarly calculated for this undertaking as they find it an easier employment than working in the field and;

Thirdly and chiefly because the Planters who have many slaves think it more profitable to employ them in making rice and Indico and until they have a demonstration of the contrary they probably will not alter their opinions, but what many of them have lately attempted the silk with success & their example we may reasonably suppose will have an influence upon others. I cannot think this Country less favorable to this produce than those where great abundance is raised. On the contrary I believe it is well adapted to it for I have now by me several Cocoons spun upon the Trees in out Woods by a wild species of Silk Worm And tho' this Culture succeeds some years better than others yet this uncertainty is not peculiar to it; many Seasons are fatal to the rice and indico, nay I think these latter as precarious a produce as the silk which for my own part I cannot help thinking is making considerable strides towards perfection.

I am very glad your Lordships approve of the Law for vacating the Lands of absentees & this leads me to resume the subject of granting large tracts upon Family Rights. I have just perused his Majesty's Instructions upon that head and must crave leave to observe that tho the ability of the Petitioner for Land is recommended to our consideration therein yet the instruction that follows seems a little imcompatible with it: for there the quantity to which each person is entitled seems particularly specified. However this may be a misapprehension of mine & 'tis possible what I am going to say may be so too. Yet your Lordships will be good enough to excuse me when with the greatest deference I differ in opinion with you. Your Lordships are pleased to say that no mischief can be apprehended from the quantity of land granted provided it is properly improved. This my Lords may be true in respect to the Northern Provinces where the lands are cultivated by white people & where great improvement supposes numbers of such Inhabitants, but I humbly conceive where cultivation is performed by Negroes it makes a material difference for then the number of free & valuable subjects is to be computed from the number of settlements and not from the extent & quantity of the cultivation. I believe it will be allowed that with an hundred Negroes one planter will cultivate more than ten poor families of whites can do. Nevertheless I presume the latter will give more strength & be thought a more valuable acquisition than the former. Laws have been passed in several of our Colonies to oblige planters to augment their Whites in proportion to the increase of their Negroes but these Laws have not produced their effect, and the only measure I can think of that would is that of limiting the extent of plantations; and tho' this might be considered as an exclusion or at least an hardship upon the wealthy settlers yet it would not affect the middling people who are the most peaceable and useful members of Society. I am also of opinion that these restraints might & should be made up to the people in exemptions and indulgences of another nature. And may I add further my Lords that I conceive that system of policy which may be proper for the middle provinces upon this Continent is not so for those upon the frontier. The first object with the former is the increase of produce and extension of Commerce. In the latter it should be security & defence. The former are secured from danger by their situation the latter exposed to it from the same circumstance. The first might have more indulgencies of one kind, the last more of another. But to return. The regulation I would with submission suggest is this:

When any person is possessed of not more than sixty negroes he should be entitled to his family rights upon the present regulation; for each Negro in family above that number to only 20 Acres until they amounted to 100 & then to 10 Acres a head for any increased number.

This would not effectually prevent the evil of too large plantations and the danger from a multitude of Slaves it would nevertheless retard it and might make people improve lands in another manner; that is they would manure them which no body hath hitherto done the practice at present being to wear one spot entirely out and then clear another.

It gives me the greatest satisfaction that your Lordships have bestowed so much attention to the affairs of the Bosomworths & that there is now a prospect of there being speedily terminated. An event that will have many good consequences and be highly pleasing to the people here who already think themselves under the greatest obligations to your Lordships to whose powerful interposition they owe every thing they have of late obtained.

Mr Chief Justice Grover seems well calculated to please and I have great hopes will do so. Such a Magistrate was very much wanted.

The indian presents arrived safe from Charles Town a few days ago. The Ship on board of which they were appeared off our Bar on the evening of a stormy day, the Pilot being then not able to get off she proceeded thither & has sent us the goods in a sloop. Their arrival is apropos as our store was almost cleared by about four score Creek Indians who lately made me a friendly visit. All the accounts from their Country are uncommonly favorable. That great Nation of French Indians the Choctaws are very desirous to enter into a friendly connection with the English; for this purpose they have made piece with our old friends & their Enemies the Chickesaws & sent 30 of their head men into the Creek Nation. The Wolf King writes me he has detained them there until Mr Atkin, the Kings Agent arrives. The Mauanese a villainous tribe of Indians from the Northward attached to our Enemies & for some time past settled among the Creeks are alarmed at these appearances and have removed for their greater safety to a French Fort upon the Cherokee River as the Creeks have long been meditating their destruction. An hundred & forty of the Chicesaws their inveterate enemies are in pursuit & will certainly cut them off if they over take them before they arrive at their place of destination. These circumstances are favorable to the British Interest & if Mr Aikin makes a right use of them the french may be greatly harrassed & the commerce of the English vastly extended in these parts.

I can add nothing more to this long Letter but that every thing is perfectly quiet within the province & that this season promises fair for a large quantity of Silk.

There remains however to return your Lordships my most humble & hearty thanks for procuring me his Majesty's leave to go to the Northern provinces when the bad state of my health may make it necessary. Should the heats of the approaching summer prove more moderate than those of the last which were almost intolerable I would hope there will be no occasion for me to leave this Province.

Order in Council, May 31, 1759, Whitehall, received June 2, read June 19, 1759, C.O. 5/646, C. 57, revoking and annulling the first article of Ellis' instructions thus allowing him to change the composition of his council.

His Majesty having pleased by his Order in Council of the 21st of this instant to refer unto this Committee a representation from the Lords Commissioners for Trade & plantations proposing

that an additional Instruction should be forthwith sent to Henry
Ellis Esqre His Majestys Governor of the province of Georgia to
revoke & annul the first Article of His Majestys General Instructions to the said Governor wherein the Members of the Council
for the said Province are named & to nominate & appoint the following persons to be of His Majestys Council in the said Province,
Vizt: Sir Patrick Houston, James Habersham, Nobel Jones, Francis
Harris, Jonathan Brian, James Mackay, James Edward Powell,
William Knox, William Grover, William Clifton & Charles Pryce
Esqrs And also further proposing that in case it shall not be thought
proper to restore Mr Clement Martin who was suspended by the
late Governor that then William Butler Esqr, may be added to the
11 persons above mentioned. The Lords of the Committee this day
took the said representation into their consideration & being of
opinion that the said Mr Clement Martyn ought not to be restored
to his said Seat in the said Council Do therefore hereby order that
the said Lords Commissioners do prepare & lay before this Committee a Draught of an Instruction for the Governor of Georgia
agreeable to what is proposed by the said Representation & that
they do add the name of the said William Butler Esqr. to the afore
mentioned eleven persons in order to compleat the number of the
Council of the said Province.

Henry Ellis to the Board of Trade July 26, 1759, Georgia, received
Nov. 26, read Dec. 14, 1759, C.O. 5/646, C. 65, proposing a
settlement to the Bosomworth claims agreeable to all parties,
giving the current state of affairs with the Indians, and other subjects.

My Lords

The last letter I had the honor to receive from your Lordships
was acknowledged in mine of the 25th of April by the last Carolina
fleet. I have since received an instruction from His Majestys
authorizing me to settle the long depending dispute with the
Bosomworths in the manner recommended in your Lordships Report.
Accordingly I appointed a Meeting with those people & after a
great deal of discussion of the Merits of their service their disbursements on the public account & their Title to the Indian Lands
we fixed upon the following preliminaries each party reserving a
liberty of receding from them provided they should prove disagreeable to the friends of the Bosomworths on the one side or to the

sentiments of his Majesty's Council of this Province of the other.

The points premised were the following: First that Mr. and Mrs. Bosomworth should have a Royal Grant in the usual form for the whole Island of St. Catherines.

Secondly that he should have 2000 guineas paid him by the Crown provided that the Islands of Ossaba and Sappelo produced so much in the manner we agreed to sell them. And Thirdly That upon our performing these conditions Mr. & Mrs. Bosomworth should give the most satisfactory & ample discharges & securities against all future claims in regard to the Lands in question or an account of other demands upon the Crown of what nature or kind so ever. At a subsequent Meeting of both parties in the Council Chamber the consideration of these terms were resumed & debated and at length agreed to & an instrument framed thereupon which has been signed and sealed by Mr. and Mrs. Bosomworth on the one part and by myself & the Council on the other. And now these people declare themselves not only contented but entirely devoted to his Majesty's service & that they will upon all occasions be ready to exert their utmost influence with the Indians to promote the same & preserve the good correspondence which happily subsists at present & I am induced to believe they will endeavor to realize those professions when any occasion may require it. No event has happened here of late that has given such general satisfaction & indeed with some reason as these people were very capable & not a little disposed to do mischief & any wrong step of ours in respect to the Indians would have put it still more in their power.

This much I thought proper to relate to your Lordships upon this occasion but a more distinct account of our proceedings will be transmitted in the Minutes of Council when this matter is entirely finished, Which cannot be done for some time as the Islands are to be advertized for Sale during four Months in the Carolina Gazette.

By reviewing the proposals made by Mr. Bosomworth last year which are in your Lordships hands I flatter myself it will be thought that our present Agreement is full as advantageous as could have been expected from the obstinate temper of our opponents and the critical situation of things which they were well qualified to improve to their advantage.

For some time past the Spaniards & Creek Indians have been at variance a few of each have been slain in their rencounters & there is scarce a probability of their being on more friendly terms whilst the present Governor of St. Augustine continues to act as he has done; for it is to his imprudent conduct & morose deportment that not only the Indians but his own people ascribe the present defection & resentment of the Savages. I am very careful of intermedling in these disputes & keep up an amicable or rather ceremonious Correspondence with the Governor which I find answers some useful purposes.

Our last Accounts from the Creek Nation were not very unfavorable; those Indians appeared pretty well disposed. There were several principal men from the Chactaws amongst them waiting the arrival of his Majesty's Agent & extremely solicitous to open a Trade with the English. Mr. Atkin's dilatoriness in going to the Creeks tis said has been attended with two bad circumstances; one, that as it forewarned the French so it gave them time to provide presents to counteract him, & another that it so much disgusted the Chactaws that many of them went back to their Country before his Arrival but since then tis reported they have returned in consequence of his Messages & we have vague accounts (for I have no direct one) that a treaty of friendship and commerce is concluded with them but the manner of bringing it about we are told has not been very pleasing to the Creeks who think themselves somewhat slighted & our new friends too respectfully treated. As this intelligence comes to me from various hands it may be true tho' I will not answer it is strictly so in every particular since the Indian Traders who transmit it have not the most favorable sentiments of Mr. Atkin. Nevertheless I thought your Lordships had a right to be acquanited with everything I was in possession of in reference to these matters indeed I sincerely wish the Officers of the Crown in general would be more attentive to the national service than to the gratifying of pride vanity or any other narrow ridiculous passion or humour.

I am now to consult your Lordships upon a point highly necessary for me rightly to understand, I mean the manner of constituting a Court of Chancery whether his Majesty's Governor should preside as sole Chancellor as is customary in some of the Islands or that the Gentlemen of the Council should assist as they do in South Carolina &c. Tho God knows how little desirous I am of engrossing power who feel the anxiety & am sensible of the danger attending the exercise of it yet I cannot but think it absurd that the Decrees of Chancery should be formed upon the opinions of the Majority of Council which may happen not to quadrate with that of the Governor who is nevertheless to issue them as the result of his own Judgment. I know your Lordships are not ignorant that the present form of Government in South Carolina is far from being consonant to that of the Mother Country indeed this is no inconsiderable instance of the difference & if it should be thought improper for us to imitate that Colony in other Branches of Administration there can be no good reason for establishing a Court of Chancery upon the plan adopted there. If I am rightly informed the Governor of Barbadoes presides as Chancellor unassisted but by the Register & Master & if it be true that he has a power occasionally to authorise one of the Council to Officiate in his stead I humbly conceive it is a wise regulation as well as a great convenience on many accounts. I am therefore to request that your Lordships will be pleased to give me your opinion on these matters as such a Court becomes daily more necessary none yet having been established as also whether a provincial Law will not be necessary to give a sanction to its proceedings.

Whilst I am upon this subject I cannot avoid mentioning to your Lordships a great inconvenience the people here labour under by reason of the unseasonable times appointed for holding the other Courts. Mr. Chief Justice Grover having given me his sentiments hereupon in writing I beg leave to transmit them for your Lordships consideration apprehending I cannot make the alteration he requires without an instruction from the Crown since the days for holding the Courts of Oyer & Terminer are already fixed by His Majesty's General Instructions.

I should also think it highly expedient to appoint a Clerk of the Crown by Warrant with a competent Salary for otherwise no man of character or skill in the Law will accept of that employment the perquisites at present being trifling & it your Lordships should be at a loss for a proper person I would beg leave to mention Mr. Chas Pryce a Gentleman professing the Law here of good repute & sufficient abilities for that Office.

Mr. Martyn will doubtless acquaint your Lordships of the great demands made upon him this year for building the filature & purchasing Cocoons; and tho' the former has cost a large sum yet it has been done upon the very best terms. We thought indeed that we had made it sufficiently capacious for the present state of the Silk Culture but the great increase of Cocoons this Season has convinced me as it is necessary even to enlarge that Building. I am persuaded your Lordships will not be displeased at this circumstance seeing it affords good grounds to hope that this Undertaking will one day answer the public expectation to evince which we need but observe the progress it has made these three last years.

The year 1757 produced little more than 5000 wt of Cocoons,

1758 upwards of 7000, and 1759 near 12,000. When we are in possession of such facts further argument upon the point are needless.

As the ill state of my health can be of very little consequence in any other light than as it disqualifies me from doing my duty as I ought, this consideration alone induces me to mention to your Lordships that the heats of this Summer have caused a return of my former indisposition with some aggravation. I was indeed preparing to take the benefit of His Majesty's Leave of absence during the hot season which your Lordships had been so good to procure for me when I received the Royal Instruction to accomodate Mr. Bosomworths affair. This being a matter in my Judgment of very great consequence to the welfare of this Colony I could not with any satisfaction of mind defer the execution of it upon any account whatsoever. I was therefore obliged entirely to wave my design of going to the northward tho' with great inconvenience & hazard to myself; however I will do the best I can & then I will hope to engage your Lordships good Offices in obtaining my recal for I cannot in justice to the Public to your Lordships recommendation or my own character attempt continuing here a moment longer than I may be of service.

Some late accounts from the back parts of Carolina inform us that the Cherokees had committed several murders there and that they are greatly provoked with the treatment they met with to the Northward. It is certain General Forbes must have been ill advised or he could not have disarmed & dismissed those Savages in so ignominious a manner as we are told he did. I hope the Creeks will continue firm in our Interests since their neutrality has hitherto been the greatest check upon the Cherokees.

Chief Justice William Grover to Henry Ellis, May 5, 1759, Savannah, received Nov. 26, read Dec. 14, 1759, C.O. 5/646, C. 66, proposing changes in the judicial system. Enclosed in Ellis to Board of Trade, July 26, 1759.

May it please your Excellency.

I take the liberty of representing to you that I have received complaints from some of the principal persons here that the Jurors in this Province are summoned to attend the General & also the Courts of Oyer & Terminer at the distance of 150 Miles from Savannah & that they are, as these Courts are constituted, obliged to attend six times in a year & that two of these attendances are fixed at times of the year when the heat of the weather & the time of the Harvest render such attendances particularly inconvenient.

As I am not clear that it is in my power to lighten this Burthen by an alteration of the fixed days for holding these Courts I presume to suggest to your Excellency a method of doing it, vizt: by fixing the Courts of Oyer and Terminer for the future on the second Tuesday in October. As two of the general Courts are fixed on these days this Method would make the attendances only 4 times instead of six and would in a great measure remove the inconvenience of their travelling in excessive heats as the July Courts would be abolished. I doubt not but that your Excellency will give attention to this matter which seems of real concern to the Province.

I beg leave to represent one thing more relative to the Courts that there is only one Ministerial Officer the Clerk or prothonotary and that the person who occupies that employment a Merchant & planter and wholly unacquainted with Law or the forms thereof and it is absolutely necessary that such Officer should be a person well versed in both to preserve order in the proceedings and to prevent the Courts from being in the utmost contempt. The Office of prothonotary is now worth about £12 a year which prevents any Gentleman qualified for the business from accepting it, particularly as the prothonotary is disqualified from acting as an Attorney. I apprehend that if a Salary of £50 a year was established for this Officer a proper person might be found who would accept it.

Order in Council, Aug. 10, 1759, Kensington, received May 29, read July 8, 1760, C.O. 5/647, D. 16, approving two Georgia laws, one preventing private persons purchasing Indian lands, the other limiting the time to claim lands.

WHEREAS by Commission under the Great Seal of Great Britain the Governor Council and Assembly of His Majesty's Province of Georgia are authorized and empowered to make constitute and ordain Laws Statutes and Ordinances for the public peace welfare and good government of the said Province which Laws Statutes and ordinances are to be as near as conveniently may be agreeable to the Laws and Statutes of this Kingdom and to be transmitted for His Majesty's Royal approbation or disallowance. And whereas in pursuance of the said Powers Two Acts were passed in the said Province in February and March 1758 and transmitted entituled as follows:

An Act to prevent private persons from purchasing Lands from the Indians and for preventing persons trading without License:

An Act for limiting the time for Persons claiming Lands by virtue of Warrants of Survey, Allotments, nominal Titles or possession derived from and under the late honorable Trustees for establishing the Colony of Georgia their President or Assistants or any others acting by and under their authority:

Which Acts having been perused and considered by the Lords Commissioners for Trade & plantations and by then presented to his Majesty at this Board as fit to be confirmed. His Majesty was this day pleased with the advice of His Privy Council to declare his approbation thereof. And pursuant to His Majesty's Royal Pleasure thereupon expressed the said Acts are hereby confirmed finally enacted and ratified accordingly; Whereof the Governor or Commander in Chief of His Majesty's said Province of Georgia for the time being and all others whom it may concern are to take notice and govern themselves accordingly.

Henry Ellis to the Board of Trade, Sept. 6, 1759, Georgia, received Jan. 2, 1760, C.O. 5/646, C. 69, divulging a Cherokee plot to fall upon the back settlers of the province.

My Lords

In my last letter of the 26th of July I slightly hinted at the fluctuating & dubious state in which our Indian affairs then stood. Soon afterwards we were alarmed by some fresh Murders committed by the Cherokees & a discovery that they in conjunction with a few discontented frenchified Creeks had projected a design of cutting off the Traders in both Nations & falling upon our back Settlers. This Conspiracy (whether real or imaginary) was accidently detected a few days ago & that discovery we are told prevented its execution. An alarm was immediately spread and proper Measures taken for the public Security. An express was likewise dispatched to the Creek Nation to put the Traders on their guard and to acquaint the head men there that the Cherokees had disclosed the plot & laid the blame upon them. The Creeks were extremely provoked at this supposed treachery and absolutely denied having been concerned with the Cherokees, but their is reason to doubt their sincerity for the French have been excessively

Busy with & uncommonly liberal to them since the Agents intention of visiting those Savages has been known. In the meantime I have the satisfaction to acquaint your Lordships that the danger of their breaking with us is no longer apprehended. Nevertheless I have thought it necessary to send for some of the leading men in order to make them perfectly easy as to our doubts of their fidelity which might disturb them.

In respect to the Cherokees no sooner was their Councils divulged & the conduct of the Creek Nation known to them than they dispatched a Talk to me requesting that I would undertake to settle their difference with the neighbouring Governments. This was a most fortunate incident & has paved the way for recomposing matters & freeing the Inhabitants of these provinces from apprehensions which were growing daily more serious. To avoid any altercation with the Government of South Carolina which would have been excessively jealous of our intermeddling in an affair that seemed more particularly in its department and known the address & superior abilities of my friend Governor Lyttleton in the management of such transactions, I immediately sent the Cherokee talk to him & urged the necessity of availing ourselves of their overture at the same time offering either to act as mediator or leave the negociation altogether to him. The last was most agreeable whereupon his Excellency dispatched a proper talk to the Cherokees inviting them to a conference at Charles Town. This I seconded by another talk to the same people exhorting them to accept of that invitation & giving them hopes that upon proper submissions & a promise of behaving better for the future they would be restored to favour.

Thus are our Indian Affairs circumstanced at present I think in a very fair way of being reestablished upon as good a footing as ever. As to all other matters they remain in the same situation as when I last described them.

Your Lordships will be so good as to over look the defects of this Letter as the sudden departure of my Conveyance has scarce afforded me time to write much less to correct.

The Memorial of Benjamin Martyn to the Board of Trade, Nov. 12, 1759, London, read Nov. 13, 1759, C.O. 5/646, C. 64, asking a warrant to pay for rebuilding the filature in Savannah.

HUMBLY SHEWETH

That he has received a letter from the Governor of Georgia

with advice of his having drawn Bills of Exchange on your Memorialist to the amount of £483.1.4 for rebuilding the filature & that the said Building and its appurtenances have cost £500.

That there is no other provision for paying the said Bills but the surplus sum which he was authorized and directed by a Warrant from the late Lords Justices dated July 29th 1755 to pay to such uses & services for the Colony of Georgia as your Lordships by your Warrants should direct & appoint.

That the remainder of the said surplus sum in his hands (including what must be paid for passing the account of the same through the several Offices) is £671.6.6 1/4.

Your Memorialist therefore prays your Lordships Warrant for his paying the aforesaid sum of £483.1.4 And such further sums as may be drawn for rebuilding the filature & its appurtenances & also for the sum of £5.11.6 which he has paid for a silk Reel with a large case for the same and the sum of £6.1.6 for freight of the same to Georgia.

Henry Ellis to the Board of Trade, Nov. 25, 1759, Georgia, received Feb. 18, read March 11, 1760, C.O. 5/647, D. 1, offering his resignation because of continual suffering in Georgia's heat and suggesting a Lieutenant-Governor as a replacement until he returned to London.

My Lords

As my health continues in a very bad State, and there appears no prospect of recovering it here, I am at length reduced to the necessity of humbly Petitioning your Lordships that you will be pleased to obtain his Majestys Permission for me to return to Europe. The leave of going to one of the Northern Colony during our violent heats, which your Lordships were so good to procure for me last Year, I could not possibly avail myself of, without manifest prejudice to the Kings service. And as affairs are still in an unsettled poisture in these parts, and the Gentleman on whom this Government would devolve in case of my absence, is not at all qualified to administer it, nor capable of preserving that order and Authority which ought to be maintained.[45] My

---

45. Sir Patrick Houstoun, Bart., was the senior councillor and the man referred to by Ellis.

quiting the Colony under such circumstances would inevitably occasion much mischief and confusion. And as my remaining longer here under the pressure of an indisposition that almost incapacitates me from acting as I ought, can be of no service to the Publick; Yet my going home posibly may, having many things to lay before your Lordships in reference to the Affairs of this Quarter highly deserving attention. And I beg your Lordships will allow me to express an only wish upon this occasion; it is, that I might be relieved by a Lieut Governor, as Mr. Reynolds was, and retain my Rank, &c. until I got home, when I would chearfully resign it. I persuade myself your Lordships would pardon this seemingly presumptuous intimation did you know how much I am a Sufferer by this Government. But if my wish should be thought too unreasonable to be indulged, I must then earnestly intreat, that by your Lordships means, I may obtain his Majestys leave to resign this Government altogether; in order that I may be able to remove from hence before the intense heats of the next Summer begin; which is usually about the latter end of June. For I dread the consequence of continuing here much longer, with a constitution so greatly injured, that I have at present very little enjoyment of Life.

J. West to John Pownall, Secretary of the Board of Trade, Dec. 13, 1759, Treasury Chambers, received & read Dec. 14, 1759, C.O. 5/646, C. 68, informing the Board that the Chancellor of the Exchequer received his Majesty's command to prepare an estimate of Georgia's expense for 1759-1760 for the Board.

Sir

I desire you will acquaint the Lords Commissioners of Trade & plantations that the Chancellor of the Exchequer hath received His Majesty's Commands That your Lordships should prepare and lay before the House of Commons an Estimate of the expense attending the Colony of Georgia from the 24th day of June 1759 to Midsummer 1760.

Order in Council, Dec. 20, 1759, Whitehall, received Jan. 4, read Jan. 24, 1760, C.O. 5/646, C. 70, directing the Board of Trade to consider Issac Levy's petitions in the Bosomworth Affair and report to the Council.

HIS MAJESTY having been pleased by his order in Council of the 15th of this instant to refer unto this Committee Two Petitions, The one in the name of John Whiteside and Thomas le Breton of Sun Court Cornhill London, Gentlemen, Agents for and on the behalf of Isaac Levy formerly of Broad Street London Esqr but now resident at Philadelphia in America; And the other in the name of the said Isaac Levy both of which Petitions represent the right of the said Isaac Levy to a Moiety of some Lands in the Colony of Georgia which have been lately advertized to be sold at the Town of Savannah in Georgia agreeable to His Majesty's order in Council for the Benefit of Thomas Bosomworth & Mary his Wife, otherwise the Princess Couseponakeesa. And therefore pray that the said Isaac Levy may be restored to his share of the said Lands or to have a recompense for the same. The Lords of the Committee this day took the said Petitions into their consideration and are hereby pleased to refer the same (Copys whereof are hereunto annexed) to the Lords Commissioners for Trade & plantations to consider thereof and report to this Committee what they conceive adviseable to be done thereupon.

Petition of agents for Isaac Levy, enclosed with Order in Council of Dec. 20, 1759, London, received Jan. 4, read Jan. 24, 1760, C.O. 5/646, C. 70, asking that the sale of the three islands in Georgia be stopped until Isaac Levy's claim is satisfied.

> THE HUMBLE PETITION of John Whiteside and
> Thomas Le Breton of Sun Court Cornhill London
> Gentlemen Agents for and on the Behalf of Isaac
> Levy formerly of Broad Street London Esqr but
> now resident at Philadelphia in America

SHEWETH

THAT the Revd Thomas Bosomworth & Mary his Wife otherwise called Couseponakeesa the Princess and natural and lawful heiress of the Upper & Lower Creek indian Countrys in America being in England in the year 1754 entered into a Treaty with the said Isaac Levy for the sale of one Moiety of the Islands St. Catherines, Usseba, and Sappola which had been duly conveyed and granted to Opiya Mico Emperor of the Upper and Lower Creek Nations in behalf of himself his subjects and Vassals unto the said Thomas Bosomworth and Mary his Wife, otherwise the Princess Cousaponakeesa, and which grant had been duly ratified by the Seven

Kings of the Creek Nations in their general Assembly and the original Treaties entered into by Lieut. Genl. Oglethorpe by virtue of your Majestys Authority on behalf of the Trustees for establishing Your Majestys Colony of Georgia in America having been produced together with such Grants and Conveyances with other authentic evidences of the said Thomas Bosomworth and Mary his Wife the said Isaac Levy agreed to their proposals and advanced them several sums of Money thereupon:

That by Articles of Agreement of the 14th Oct. 1754 the said Thomas Bosomworth and Mary his Wife covenanted and agreed to convey a Moiety of the said Islands to the said Isaac Levy his heirs and assignes for ever on or before the 18th of the same October;

That in pursuance of such Articles of Agreement the said Thomas Bosomworth and his Wife by Indentures of Lease and release of the 17th & 18th days of October 1754 and bargain and sale inrolled conveyed a Moiety of the said three Islands to the said Isaac Levy his heirs and assignes for ever;

That the said Isaac Levy on obtaining this conveyance settled all his affairs in England and went to live and reside in America & hath been at great expenses in improving his aforesaid Acquisitions;

That the said Isaac Levy hath lately discovered that the said Thomas Bosomworth some time since unknown to the said Isaac Levy entered into a treaty for the surrendering up the said Two Islands of Usseba and Sappola to your Majesty and laid proposals for that purpose before his Excellency the Governor of your Majesty's Colony of Georgia in which he claimed to be indemnified and saved harmless against the said Isaac Levy with respect to the articles of Agreement entered into between them on the said 14th of October 1754 and annexed a Copy of such Articles to his proposals and also claimed to have the sum of £3000 sterling paid him and the said Island of St. Catherine ratified & confirmed to him and his heirs upon the Terms that other Lands are held in the province which proposals he executed under his hand & seal and delivered to the Secretary of the said Province;

That without any notice given to the said Isaac Levy or any consent obtained from him an Agreement was made with the said Thomas Bosomworth and an Advertizement published in the South Carolina Gazette giving Notice that on the 10th December would be exposed to sale agreeable to your Majesty's Order in Council in the Town of Savannah the valuable Islands of Osseba and Sappelo lying on the Coast of that province.

This Advertisement very much surprised the said Isaac Levy and he immediately thereupon procured an Advertizement to be printed and put up in all the public Places in Georgia and in the South Carolina Gazette reciting the Advertizement for the sales of Osseba and Sappelo and that he had a valid and legal title to a Moiety of the same Islands by virtue of a good & sufficient Deed of Bargain and Sale from Thomas Bosomworth and Mary his Wife who were the original Purchasers under Mico the Prince and Chief of all the assembled States of the Lower Creek Indians to whom the same formerly of right belonged which said Purchase has been ratified and confirmed in public Treaty with the said Indians & reciting that he was determined immediately in all humble manner to present a Petition to your Majesty setting forth his right & title to the same Moiety of the said Islands in humble hopes and assurance of having the same restored and secured to him agreable to his right and the rules of law and Justice.

Therefore he did thereby give notice and advertize the public and all such Persons as should become purchasers of the same Islands of his said Claim right and pretensions & of his intention and resolution of making such Application to your Majesty that such purchasers might purchase under the Incumbrance of his Title and might not take the advantages usually allowed to Bona fide purchasers without notice and at the same time the said Isaac Levy wrote to his Excellency the Governor of Georgia intreating him to put off the Sale to a further time till your Majestys pleasure might be known thereupon for that he would Petition your Majesty to be restored to his Moiety of the said Islands and the said Isaac Levy hath accordingly transmitted the Petition annexed and herewith laid before your Majesty;

That the said Isaac Levy is ready and willing to submit to any thing which your Majesty will please to order for the good and security of the said Province or your Majestys service and is willing if the same shall be required to surrender up his Title to the said three Islands to the Governor of Georgia or any other persons to be appointed by your Majesty and to release the said Thomas Bosomworth and his Wife from the said articles of the 14th October 1754 for which the said Thomas Bosomworth is to be indemnified upon the said Isaac Levy's receiving a proper recompense for the same either by Grants of Lands equivalent with those he shall give up or by a satisfaction in money.

>YOUR PETITIONERS therefore most humbly pray your Majesty that your Majesty will please to take the case of the said Isaac Levy into your Majesty's

consideration and give your Majesty's instructions to
the said Governor of Georgia or whomsoever else your
Majesty will be pleased to appoint to receive the proposals of and agree with the said Isaac Levy for the
recompense to be made him in lieu of His Moiety of
the said Islands and that in case any part of the said
Lands or any other Lands shall be agreed to be granted
him in discharge of his claim. That proper directions
may be given by your Majesty for passing Grants thereof to him in a proper form Or that your Majesty will
please to make such other Order in the premises for
the said Isaac Levys relief as to your Majesty in your
great wisdom shall seem meet And your Petitioner as
in duty bound shall ever pray.

Petition of Issac Levy, enclosed with Order in Council of Dec.
20, 1759, London, received Jan 14, read Jan. 24, 1760, C. O.
5/646, C. 70, seeking to demonstrate his right and title to the
islands of Ossabaw and Sapelo before they are sold to satisfy the
Bosomworth claims.

Most humbly Sheweth

THAT for many ages before the Settlement of any of His Majesty's Subjects upon the Continent of America different Nations
and Tribes of Indians who inhabited that vast Tract of Land were
the true and lawful Owners and proprietors thereof and have always been so held and esteemed by the English Nation as may
appear from many Treaties of peace and commerce entered into
with the said Nations by persons from time to time duly authorized by your most gracious Majesty's Predecessors Kings and
Queens of Great Britain: &ca

That on the 9th of June in the year of our Lord 1732 your most
gracious Majesty was pleased to grant your Letters Patent constituting a Corporation by the name of the Trustees for establishing
the Colony of Georgia in America with Capacity to purchase and
take up Lands from the natural born heirs the Indians for the enlarging your Majesty's dominions;

That in the year 1733 Lieut. General Oglethorpe entered into
a conditional Treaty with the Creek Nations in behalf of your
Majesty which was afterwards renewed and extended by a subsequent Treaty in the year 1739 concluded by the said General

Oglethorpe in behalf of the said Trustees by virtue of full power and authority from your Majesty with the assembled States of the Creek Nations. In which Treaty it is declared "That all the do-"minions territories and Lands from the River Savannah to the "River St. Johns and all the Islands between the said Rivers and "from the River St. Johns to the Bay of Appalache within which is "the Appalache Old Fields and from the said Bay of Appalache to "the Mountains do by ancient right belong to the Creek Nations "who have maintained Possession of their said Right against all "opposers by war and can shew the heaps of Bones of their Ene-"mies slain by them in defence of said Land." And the said Creek Nations did further acknowledge thereby the Grant they had before made to the said Trustees of all the Lands upon the Savannah River as far as the River Ogechee and all the Lands along the Sea Coast as far as the River St. Johns and as high as the tide flows and all the Islands as far as the said River particularly the Islands of Frederica, Cumberland and Amelia. But they further declare by the said Treaty "That they did and do reserve to themselves the "Lands from Pipe Makers Bluff to Savannah and the Islands of St. "Catherine, Useba and Sappala."

That Malatchi Miya Mico Emperor of the Upper and Lower Creek Nations in belief of himself his Subjects and Vassals did by his Deed of Feoffment under his hand and seal for a valuable consideration therein expressed and to him truly paid grant bargain sell enfeoff and confirm unto Thomas Bosomworth and Mary his Wife otherwise called Cousaponakeesa the Princess and natural and lawful heiress of the Upper and Lower Creek Indian Countries and to their Heirs and Assignes for ever all that Tract or Tracts of Land Island or Islands known or distinguished by the names of St. Catherines, Sappela and Useba Islands bounded on the North East by Useba Sound on the South West by Doeboy Sound and divided by the Sounds of St. Catherines and Sappela on the South by the Sea and on the North West by the said several Islands from the Continent together with their Priviledges and appurtenances; To hold to them the said Thomas Bosomworth and Mary his Wife their heirs and assigns as long as the Sun shall shine or the Waters run in the River for ever;

That the same day Livery Possession and Seizin of the Premises was had and taken by the said Thomas Bosomworth and Mary his Wife; To hold to them their heirs and assigns for ever according to the true Intent and Meaning of the above mentioned Deed of Feoffment in a due and legal manner;

That afterwards the 2nd day of August in the year 1750 the aforesaid Islands and premises by a Deed of Confirmation duly and legally executed were ratified and confirmed by the seven Kings of the Creek Indian Nations unto the said Thos Bosomworth and Mary his Wife their heirs and Assignes for ever according to the true Intent and Meaning of the said Deed of Feoffment;

That at a Conference or Treaty held by the Commissioners for and in behalf of your Majesty with the said Upper and Lower Creek Nations on the 15th, 16th, 17th, and 18th days of December 1755 the said Islands and Premises were again confirmed to the said Thomas Bosomworth and Mary his Wife and their Heirs. The Indians did then declare that they might give sell or dispose of them as they pleased;

That the said Thomas Bosomworth and Mary his Wife being seized of the Premises as aforesaid in fee by their Indenture duly executed bearing date the 18th day of October in the year 1754 did grant and convey unto your Petitioner his heirs and assignes One undivided Moiety or equal half part into two equal parts to be divided of and in the said Islands Premises and their appurtenances To hold to your Petitioner his heirs and assignes for ever;

That your Petitioner hath observed an advertisement in the South Carolina Gazette giving notice that on the 10th day of December next will be exposed to Sale in the Town of Savannah in Georgia agreable to your Majestys Order in Council the said Islands of Useba and Sappala.

> Your Petitioner therefore in all humble manner begs leave to show and remonstrate to your most Gracious Majesty his Right and Title aforesaid to one Moiety of the same Islands and to pray that he may be restored to the same.

Henry Ellis to the Board of Trade, Jan. 6, 1760, Georgia, read March 11, 1760, C.O. 5/647, D. 2, containing observation on several acts lately passed and on the conduct of Mr. Atkins, the Indian agent.

My Lords,

The last Letter I did myself the honour to write to your Lordships was of the 12th of November. It contained an account of the Cherokee disturbances, and our proceedings with the Creeks in consequence of them, and as I then foresaw that the former must submit, in case the latter did not join them, so it has come to pass. For Governor Lyttelton has advised me that on the 26th Ultimate he concluded a Treaty with the Cherokees,[46] whereby they have agreed to give satisfaction for their late Outrages; by which event the tranquility of these parts is again established. Considering the many difficulties Governor Lyttelton had to contend with, in the Prosecution of his Enterprize he has been extremely fortunate, tho it must be acknowledged, not more so than he deserves, for he has great Merit.

As to the Affairs of this Colony, they remain in their usual prosperous and quiet state. Our Assembly have sate for sometime, but without finishing any other business than the passing an Act for quitting possessions. This became very necessary, as many of the Inhabitants were frequently disturbed and Alarmed by the threats of Alderman Baker's Attorneys, and by many obsolete Claims which were daily trumping up against them. The Act I shall transmit by the first good opportunity, and I hope it will meet with your Lordships approbation. We have also found it necessary to strengthen the Law for preventing a clandestine traffick with the Neighbouring Indians, by adding a new Clause thereto, obliging Delinquents to give security to answer such Suits as their transgressions may involve them in.

His Majestys Agent Mr. Atkin is returned from the Creek Nation; and, as that Philosopher who first concealed truth in a Well, boasted of having brought it out, so this Gentleman piques himself on having left Matters there in a settled state, after he had greatly disturbed and embarrassed them. I can without any prejudice to Mr. Atkin assure your Lordships, that he appears very ill calculated for the employment he is in; and that in my humble opinion the Scheme for managing the powerful Indian Nations in this quarter, as to the Northward, by a general Agent, is liable to many

---

46. The treaty is given in South Carolina Gazette, Jan. 12, 1760. A thorough disaster, the agreement humiliated and angered the Middle Settlements of the Cherokees and strengthened the anti-English faction; by the time Ellis penned this letter, resentful Cherokees had begun to move against the South Carolina-Georgia back settlements.

considerable objections and inconveniencies. And nothing can
more strongly evince this observation than the Measures lately
pursued here in consequence of the Cherokee disputes, which I
presume could not easily have been composed by such an Agent.
I may possibly trouble your Lordships with some remarks upon this
Subject hereafter, but as I know of no certain Conveyance for what
I now write, I shall not enlarge further.

Henry Ellis to the Board of Trade, Feb. 15, 1760, Georgia, read
April 22, 1760, C.O. 5/647, D. 3, informing the Board of the
measures he has taken in relation to the Cherokees' violations of
the recent treaty signed with Gov. Lyttelton.

My Lords,

My last Letter to your Lordships was of the 6th Ultimate notifying Governor Lytteltons Treaty with the Cherokees. We were in hopes it would have re-established the tranquility of these parts, but the event has proved us mistaken. That Treaty was indeed a better one than I should have attempted to make. It was too mortifying to be observed by the Cherokees, and, they have broke it accordingly. We have received many Accounts of their hostile proceedings. The Inhabitants on the Frontiers of South Carolina have already suffered greatly. Many of them have been cut off, and numbers are daily flying to places of more safety. Those Savages have also attacked some of our setlers, but were repulsed by them. They did however kill one person his Wife and Child before the Neighbours could be got together. To prevent further mischief I have sent all the force I could collect to the back parts which I hope will enable the people there, to make a stand, untill succour arrives from the Northward. In the meantime, I have importunately demanded from the Creeks that assistance, which they promised to afford us, in case we should be Molested by the Cherokees. And as nothing would contribute more to our safety than the setting those two Savage Nations at variance, I am using my utmost endeavours for that purpose, and the better to effect it, my Agents have a Credit upon me for Goods to the Value of £1000 Sterling. I had made this reserve out of the Kings Presents, apprehensive that it might be wanted for such an occasion. I have likewise offered £5 Sterling a head for every Cherokee scalp brought in by an Indian. And as the Assembly is sitting I have proposed to them the Amending, reviving and carrying into execution, the Act for erecting places of defence throughout the

Province; and to provide Subsistence for 200 Militia, in case I shall be obliged to call them out upon actual Service. These points they have agreed to; and also engaged to second my other Measures to the utmost of their power.[47]

As these Expensive transactions, and the frequent intercourse I must keep up with the Creeks at this Juncture, will soon absorb the Kings Presents remaining in my hands, I must not neglect this opportunity of intreating your Lordships to employ your influence towards our speedily obtaining a further supply, which will be the surest means to preserve our Interest with these Indians, and avert those Calamities which their defection would inevitably bring on the People of these Provinces.

In the great hurry of business occasion'd by these disturbances, I have only time to assure your Lordships, that nothing shall be left undone for the Public Service.

Henry Ellis to William Pitt, Feb. 16, 1760, Georgia, read May 22, 1760, giving an account of the Cherokee uprising and the Colony's measures to combat the outbreak.

Sir:

---

47. The Cherokee assault on the Georgia frontier failed to materialize. On Jan. 29, 1760, John Downing, Bernard Hughes, and other escaping Middle Settlement traders passed through John Vann's place on the Broad River, warning the settlers of the impending attack. Alerting the militia, Vann successfully withstood the oncoming Cherokees. Checked at Vann's place, the Cherokees also faced large and hostile Creek hunting parties in the Georgia forests. Afraid of disrupting their lucrative trade with Augusta and Savannah and unwilling to ally themselves with whites, the Creeks instead screened the Cherokee attack on Georgia's frontier. Thus, only half a dozen Georgians were killed by the marauding Indians and the colony was spared the long war which followed.

In this instance, Ellis' policy of bribes, threats, and setting the two nations against one another worked, and it is largely to its successful outcome in 1760 that Ellis' considerable reputation as an Indian diplomatist rests. See South Carolina Gazette, Feb. 9, March 22, 1760; Maryland Gazette, March 13, March 20, 1760; Abbot, The Royal Governors of Georgia, 79-82.

In my last I had the honour to acknowledge the receipt of your Letter of the 5th of February and several others, which I received from Mr. Wood, notifying the Successes of his Majestys Arms in different parts. Things at that time being in a tranquil state here, I had no other subject of any Consequence to touch upon. But our quiet was soon afterwards interrupted by some discontented Cherokees, who apprehending they had receivd ill treatment, while they were attending the Expedition against Fort Duquesne, were determined to gratify their resentment nearer home. They accordingly committed several outrages and even Murders in the back parts of the neighbouring Provinces. Their insolence and cruelty increased to such a degree, that the Government of South Carolina judged it expedient to chastise them, and obtain satisfaction for their enormities. For this purpose Governor Lyttelton with the Regulars and a Body of the Militia of his Province marched into their country. On the appearance of this Force the Savages desired a Conference, and declared their inclination to settle matters in an amicable way. These overtures being agreed to after some days discussion a Treaty of Peace was concluded and hostages taken from the Cherokees as a Security for their performance of certain conditions stipulated therein. Matters being thus accommodated, the Army was disbanded and the Governor set out for Charles Town. But no sooner had he turned his back than these faithless barbarians broke out into an open War, massacred the English trading in their Country, and fell upon the Out Setlers of the Adjacent Provinces, many of whom they cut off by surprize, and have since spread terror and desolation throughout the frontiers. Their fury has not as yet been directed this way, altho they border close upon us. But how long we are to be spared is uncertain.

In the meantime, as our Assembly is sitting, I have represented to them the dangers with which the Country is threatned, and the necessity of taking the most speedy and efficacious measures to guard against them. In consequence thereof, they have enabled me to erect Log forts in the parts most exposed, wherein the helpless people may take shelter in case of any sudden Emergency. And they have also provided subsistence for 200 of the Militia whom I intend to draft and keep on constant duty until assistance can arrive. Inconsiderable as these efforts may seem, when compared to those of the other Provinces, they do nevertheless greatly exceed my expectations. And are indeed, the utmost in the power of this young Colony, as well as the strongest marks it has exhibited since its Establishment, of its growing strength and ability. As a further Security I have stationed the Rangers lately augmented, still more backward, so that the Enemy cannot easily approach undiscovered. And as the Creek and Chickesaw Indians continue our friends, I have sent for some of the head men of each nation, with a view, if possible, to engage their assistance. But as all these precautions may be insufficient to the end proposed, I have thought it necessary to acquaint General Amherst with our situation and circumstances and desired such succour as they may require. For should the Cherokees fall upon us it would be almost impossible, in our weak condition, long to resist, much less repel them, since their Number is double that of our Militia, which being dispersd over a large extent of country, is the less capable of Uniting to oppose any sudden erruption of so active and fierce an Enemy.

Henry Ellis to the Board of Trade, March 5, 1760, Georgia, read June 13, 1760, C.O. 5/647, D. 6, respecting the further measures he has taken for preventing the troubles that threaten the colony from the hostilities of the Cherokees.

My Lords

    The last Letter I had the honour to write to your Lordships was of the 17th Ultimate giving an account of the troubles broke out with the Cherokees, and our Measures in consequence of them. These Savages continue to annoy and desolate the back parts of South Carolina. Many of the Inhabitants are fled from thence and taking shelter amongst us. This Colony has been greatly alarmed of late, but as yet very little hurt by the Cherokees; and we owe this indulgence partly to our not having offended them, but chiefly, I apprehend, to our engagements with the Creeks, and their menacing to revenge any hostilities that may be committed on the Inhabitants of Georgia.

    The Chickesaws scout with our parties, and some of the Creeks have done the same. The former declare they will live and die with the English; but the latter dare not act openly, until they learn what part their Nation will take, which I am endeavouring by every Means in my power to involve in a War with the Cherokees.

    It would be endless to relate to your Lordships the variety of steps we have taken for this purpose. It may perhaps be sufficient to observe, that they were such, as are the most likely to succeed. Numbers of the Creeks visit me daily, who seem to have very good dispositions which I strive to improve to the utmost. This intercourse is expensive, and will probably be more so; whether these

Indians declare in our favour, or Adhere to their Neutrality, a further supply of Presents will therefore be very much wanted soon.

In respect to the interior concerns of the Colony no material alteration has fallen out since the date of my last.

Henry Ellis to the Board of Trade, March 15, 1760, Georgia, read June 13, 1760, C.O. 5/647, D. 7 acknowledging the receipt of two letters from the Board, containing an account of the present state of Indian affairs, and enclosing an abstract of lands granted from January 27, 1758, to July 27, 1758.

My Lords

I had the honour to receive your Lordships Letter of the 24th of July last, with an Instruction from his Majesty, repealing a former one, and nominating anew, the Members of the Council for this Province. They have taken their Seats accordingly, except Mr. Charles Pryce, and Mr. William Butler, who are at present obliged by much business and ill health to decline that honour. Your Lordships are very full and satisfactory in respect to the other points you were pleased to touch upon in the course of that Letter.

The 25th of last Month I had also your Letter of the 14th of November signifying the Kings Commands, that a day of public thanksgiving might be appointed here, in acknowledgment of the signal successes with which the Almighty had been pleased to bless his Majestys Arms. The same was accordingly appointed, and celebrated in the most solemn manner throughout the Province.

In my Letter of the 5th Instant I gave your Lordships an account of the situation of things here, and must beg Leave to refer to that Letter at present, as since that time no material alteration has taken place.

We do not hear of any fresh hostilities committed by the Cherokees in this Province; and our Accounts from the Creeks and Chickesaws are far from being unfavourable. The apprehensions of the people in general begin to abate, but our Measures to prevent any Mischief happening to them, will be continued. The Bosomworths are very active in promoting my design of seting the Creeks upon the Enemy, and have even prevailed on a party to go out against them and bloody the path, on certain conditions of reward, which I have agreed to. If these Savages perform this business, it will have excellent consequences.

I ought to acquaint your Lordships that these Indian troubles have discouraged people so much, that we could not sell for anything like their value, the Islands and Indian Lands lately claimed by the Bosomworths; and this has hitherto prevented our putting a finishing hand to that affair. But no ill effects can ensue from this delay, as they know it has been unavoidable and for their advantage. It was very fortunate that we accomodated our disputes with them at the very time we did.

Your Lordships will receive herewith all the Public papers that could be got ready.

An Abstract of Grants of Lands Registered in the Province of Georgia from Jan. 27 to July 27, 1758, enclosed with Governor Henry Ellis' letter to the Board of Trade, March 15, 1760, received June 5, 1760, C.O. 5/647, D. 8.

Grant Dated 30th September 1757.
To Edward Way for 450 Acres of Land in the District of Newport, Registred 2d February 1758.

Grant Dated 30th September 1757.
To Joseph Summers for 300 Acres of Land in the District of Little Ogechee, Registred 2d February 1758.
Allotted to him by the Late President and Assistants.

Grant Dated 30th September 1757.
To Joseph Summers for 270 Acres of Land in the District of Little Ogechee, Registred 2d February 1758.
Allotted by the Late President and Assistants.

Grant Dated 30th September 1757.
To Edmund Tannatt for a Lot in the Town of Savannah No.1 in the fourth Tything Reynolds Ward and 50 Acres of Land in said Tything and Ward, Registred 6th February 1758.
Allotted by the Late President and Assistants.

Grant Dated 30th September 1757.
To Edmund Tannatt for a Lot in the Town of Hardwicke No. 43, Registred 6th February 1758.

Grant Dated 30th Septemebr 1757.
To James Read for 500 Acres of Land in the District of Ogechee, Registred 8th February 1758.

Colonial Records

Grant Dated 6th December 1757.
To John Osgood for 100 Acres of Land in the District of Medway, Registred 8th February 1758.

Grant Dated 30th September 1757.
To Thomas Red for a Lot in Augusta No. 2, Registred 10th February 1758.
Allotted to him by the Late President and Assistants.

Grant Dated 30th Septemeber 1757.
To Thomas Red for 500 Acres of Land in the District of Augusta, Registred 10th February 1758.
Allotted to him by the Late President and Assistants.

Grant Dated 6th December 1757.
To Mungo Graham for a Lot in the Town of Hardwicke No. 83, Registred 10th February 1758.

Grant Dated 7th February 1758.
To John Elliott for 50 Acres of Land in the District of Medway, Registred 10th February 1758.

Grant Dated 7th February 1758.
To Benjamin Williamson for 203 Acres of Land in the District of Augusta, Registred 10th February 1758.

Grant Dated 7th February 1758.
To Henry Ellis Esqr. for 576 1/2 Acres of Land in the District of Great Ogechee, Registred 11th February 1758.

Grant Dated 7th February 1758.
To Henry Ellis Esqr. for Two Lots in the Town of Savannah, Registred 11th February 1758.

Grant Dated 6th December 1757.
To Adrian Loyer for a Lot in the Town of Hardwicke No. 243, Registred 14th February 1758.

Grant Dated 7th February 1758.
To Thomas Lee for 90 Acres of Land in the District of Savannah, Registred 14th February 1758.
Allotted to him by the Late President and Assistants.

Grant Dated 7th February 1758.
To Thomas Lee for a Lot in the Town of Savannah No. 1 in Holland Tything Percival Ward and 50 Acres of Land in said Tything and Ward, Registred 15th February 1758.
Allotted to him by the Late President and Assistants.

Grant Dated 7th February 1758.
To Thomas Lee for a Lot in the Town of Savannah No. 8 in More Tything Percival Ward and 50 Acres of Land in said Tything and Ward, Registred 15th February 1758.
Allotted by the Late President and Assistants.

Grant Dated 7th February 1758.
To Lachlan McGillivray & John Spencer for 500 Acres of Land in the District of Augusta, Registred 18th February 1758.
Allotted by the Late President and Assistants.

Grant Dated 6th December 1757.
To John Paul Miller for two Lots and 50 Acres of Land in the Town and District of Ebenezer, Registred 22d February 1758.
Allotted to him by the Late President and Assistants.

Grant Dated 30th September 1757.
To John Fitch for 300 Acres of Land in the District of Augusta, Registred 22d February 1758.

Grant Dated 30th September 1757.
To Jacob Kubler for 50 Acres of Land in the District of Goshin, Registred 22d February 1758.

Grant Dated 7th February 1758.
To John MacDonald for 100 Acres of Land in the District of Darien, Registred 24th February 1758.

Grant Dated 7th February 1758.
To Murdock MacLoud for 100 Acres of Land in the District of Darien, Registred 24th February 1758.

Grant Dated 7th February 1758.
To Daniel Mackay for 150 Acres of Land in the District of Darien, Registred 25th February 1758.

Colonial Records 235

Grant Dated 7th February 1758.
To John Humphrys for 400 Acres of Land in the District of Newport, Registred 25th February 1758.

Grant Dated 7th February 1758.
To Peter Manley for a Lot in the Town of Savannah No. 4 in Holland Tything Percival Ward and 50 Acres of Land in said Tything and Ward, Registred 28th February 1758.

Grant Dated 7th February 1758.
To Daniel Dunham for a Lot in the Town of Hardwicke No. 11, Registred 28th February 1758.

Grant Dated 30th September 1757.
To James Dunham and William Dunham for 500 Acres of Land in the District of Medway, Registred 1st March 1758.

Grant Dated 30th September 1757.
To Benjamin Andrews for 200 Acres of Land in the District of Newport, Registred 1st March 1758.

Grant Dated 7th February 1758.
To David Lewis for 200 Acres of Land in the District of Augusta, Registred 1st March 1758.

Grant Dated 30th September 1757.
To Thomas Burrington Esqr. for a Lot in the Town of Hardwicke No. 184, Registred 1st March 1758.

Grant Dated 30th September 1757.
To Thomas Burrington Esqr. for 400 Acres of Land in the District of Ogechee, Registred 3d March 1758.

Grant Dated 30th September 1757.
To Thomas Burrington Esqr. for 400 Acres of Land in the District of Ogechee, Registred 3d March 1758.

Grant Dated 6th December 1757.
To Abigal Minis for 500 Acres of Land in the District of Sapola, Registred 4th March 1758.

Grant Dated 7th February 1758.
To William Clifton for a Lot in the Town of Hardwicke No. 106, Registred 4th March 1758.

Grant Dated 7th February 1758.
To Thomas Bruce for a Lot in the Town of Hardwicke No. 107, Registred 6th March 1758.

Grant Dated 7th February 1758.
To Thomas Bruce for 200 Acres of Land in the District of Great Ogechee, Registred 6th March 1758.

Grant Dated 7th February 1758.
To Henry Yonge Esqr. in trust for his Son Henry 100 Acres of Land in the District of Savannah, Registred 6th March 1758.

Grant Dated 6th December 1757.
To John Martin Paulitsch for 50 Acres of Land in the District of Ebenezer, Registred 6th March 1758.
Allotted to him by the Late President and Assistants.

Grant Dated 6th December 1757.
To Jacob Cusmal for 200 Acres of Land in the District of Savannah, Registred 8th March 1758.

Grant Dated 30th September 1757.
To Conrade Hover for 179 Acres of Land in the District of Ogechee, Registred 8th March 1758.

Grant Dated 6th December 1757.
To James Miller for a Lot in the Town of Savannah No. 6 in the fourth Tything Reynold Ward and 5 Acres of Land in said Tything and Ward, Registred 14th March 1758.
Allotted by the Late President and Assistants.

Grant Dated 7th February 1758.
To William Bell for a Lot in the Town of Savannah No. 9 in the first Tything Reynold Ward and 50 Acres of Land in said Tything and Ward, Registred 14th March 1758.
Allotted by the Late President and Assistants.

Grant Dated 6th December 1757.
To Sarah Boddie for 500 Acres of Land in the District of Great Ogechee, Registred 22d March 1758.

Grant Dated 6th December 1757.
To Sarah Boddie for a Lot in the Town of Hardwicke No. 95, Registred 22d March 1758.

Grant Dated 6th December 1757.
To Alexander Rose for 250 Acres of Land in the District of Newport, Registred 24th March 1758.

Grant Dated 7th February 1758.
To Jeremiah Sliterman for a Lot in the Town of Savannah No. 1 in Laroche Tything Heathcote Ward and 50 Acres of Land in said Tything and Ward, Registred 6th April 1758.

Grant Dated 28th March 1758.
To Peter Elliott for 100 Acres of Land in the District of Augusta, Registred 6th April 1758.

Grant Dated 28th March 1758.
To William Russell for 45 Acres of Land in the District of Savannah, Registred 6th April 1758.

Grant Dated 28th March 1758.
To Donald Clarke for 500 Acres of Land in the District of Darien, Registred 8th April 1758.

Grant Dated 28th March 1758.
To William Ewen for a Moiety of a Publick Lot in the Town of Savannah Letter P, Registred 12th April 1758.

Grant Dated 28th March 1758.
To William Ewen for 200 Acres of Land in the District of Little Ogechee, Registred 12th April 1758.

Grant Dated 28th March 1758.
To James Burnsides for 400 Acres of Land in the District of Savannah, Registred 12th April 1758.

Grant Dated 28th March 1758.
To James Burnsides for a Lot in the Town of Savannah No. 3 in Tyrconnel Tything Derby Ward and 50 Acres of land in said Tything and Ward, Registred 13th April 1758.
Allotted to him by the Late President and Assistants.

Grant Dated 7th February 1758.
To William Kennedy for 50 Acres of Land in the District of Ebenzer, Registred 13th April 1758.
Allotted to him by the Late President and Assistants.

Grant Dated 28th March 1758.
To Philip Delegal for 500 Acres of Land in the District of Little Ogechee, Registred 14th April 1758.
Allotted to him by the Late President and Assistants.

Grant Dated 28th March 1758.
To Philip Delegal for 300 Acres of Land in the District of Little Ogechee, Registred 14th April 1758.

Grant Dated 28th March 1758.
To Philip Delegal for 150 Acres of Land in the District of Little Ogechee, Registred 14th April 1758.

Grant Dated 28th March 1758.
To Philip Delegal for 100 Acres of Land in the District of Little Ogechee, Registred 14th April 1758.

Grant Dated 28th March 1758.
To Jonathan Bryan for 140 Acres of Land in the Township & District of Savannah, Registred 20th April 1758.

Grant Dated 28th March 1758.
To Jonathan Bryan for 600 Acres of Land in the District of Savannah, Registred 20th April 1758.

Grant Dated 6th December 1757.
To Jonathan Bryan for a Lot in the Town of Savannah No. 8 in the second Tything Reynolds Ward & 50 Acres of Land in said Tything and Ward, Registred 20th April 1758.

Grant Dated 7th February 1758.
To John Graham for 700 Acres of Land in the District of Newport, Registred 20th April 1758.

Grant Dated 7th February 1758.
To John Graham for a Lot in the Town of Savannah Letter A, Registred 22d April 1758.

Grant Dated 7th February 1758.
To John Graham for a Lot in the Town of Hardwicke No. 68, Registred 22d April 1758.

Grant Dated 7th February 1758.
To Harriotte Crooke for 500 Acres of Land in Bermuda Island between Midway & Newport Rivers, Registred 22d April 1758.

Grant Dated 7th February 1758.
To Harriotte Crooke for a Lot in the Town of Hardwicke No. 137, Registred 22d April 1758.

Grant Dated 7th February 1758.
To Hugh Ross for 250 Acres of Land in the District of Darien, Registred 24th April 1758.

Grant Dated 6th December 1757.
To Hugh Ross for 100 Acres of Land in the District of Abercorn, Registred 24th April 1758.
Allotted to him by the Late President and Assistants.

Grant Dated 6th December 1757.
To Hugh Ross for 100 Acres of Land in the District of Abercorn, Registred 24th April 1758.
Allotted to him by the Late President and Assistants.

Grant Dated 6th December 1757.
To Hugh Ross for a Lot in the Town of Savannah No. 1 in the third Tything Reynolds Ward and 50 Acres of Land in said Tything and Ward, Registred 24th April 1758.
Allotted to him by the Late President and Assistants.

Grant Dated 28th March 1758.
To Joseph Wood for a Lot in the Town of Hardwicke No. 56, Registred 25th April 1758.

Grant Dated 7th February 1758.
To Jno. George Ziegler for 50 Acres of Land in the District of Ebenezer, Registred 26th April 1758.

Grant Dated 6th December 1757.
To William Gibbons for 90 Acres of Land in the District of Savannah, Registred 4th May 1758.

Grant Dated 6th December 1757.
To Isaac Tripp for 100 Acres of Land in the District of Newport, Registred 6th May 1758.

Grant Dated 28th March 1758.
To George Philip Bortz for 50 Acres of land in the District of Abercorn, Registred 6th May 1758.

Grant Dated 6th December 1757.
To Mathew Mauve for a Lot in the Town of Hardwick No. 152, Registred 10th May 1758.

Grant Dated 16th January 1756.
To Mary Jones for a Lot in the Town of Savannah No. 1 in Carpenters Tything Deckers Ward and 50 Acres of Land in said Tything and Ward, Registred 12th May 1758.

Grant Dated 16th January 1756.
To Noble Wimberly Jones for a Lot in the Town of Savannah No. 7 in Wilmington Tything Darby Ward and 50 Acres of Land in said Tything and Ward, Registred 12th May 1758.

Grant Dated 16th January 1756.
To Noble Jones for a Lot in the Town of Savannah No. 2 in the first Tything Reynolds Ward and 50 Acres of Land in said Tything and Ward, Registred 12th May 1758.

Grant Dated 16th January 1756.
To Noble Jones in Trust for Mary Pember her heirs & for a Lot in the Town of Savannah No. 2 in the fourth Tything Anson Ward and 50 Acres of Land in said Tything and Ward, Registred 12th May 1758.

Grant Dated 16th January 1756.
To Joseph Stanly for 100 Acres of Land in the District of Savannah, Registred 16th May 1758.

Grant Dated 16th January 1756.
To Joseph Stanly for 100 Acres of Land in the District of Little Ogechee, Registred 16th May 1758.

Grant Dated 30th September 1757.
To John Todd Senr. for 100 Acres of Land in the District of Newport, Registred 20th May 1758.

Grant Dated 28th March 1758.
To John Feaster for 100 Acres of Land in the District of Ogechee, Registred 20th May 1758.

Colonial Records 241

Grant Dated 7th February 1758.
To William Steadman for 70 Acres of Land on Skidoway Island, Registred 26th May 1758.

Grant Dated 7th February 1758.
To Benedict Bourquin for 500 Acres of Land in the District of Little Ogechee, Registred 1st June 1758.

Grant Dated 7th February 1758.
To Benedict Bourquin for 400 Acres of Land in the District of Great Ogechee, Registred 1st June 1758.

Grant Dated 28th March 1758.
To Benedict Bourquin for a Lot in the Town of Hardwicke No. 113, Registred 1st June 1758.

Grant Dated 28th March 1758.
To John Cain for 200 Acres of Land in the District of Medway, Registred 2d June 1758.

Grant Dated 15th May 1756.
To William Little for 500 Acres of Land in the District of Great Ogechee, Registred 2d June 1758.

Grant Dated 15th May 1756.
To William Little for a Lot in the Town of Hardwicke No. 52, Registred 2d June 1758.

Grant Dated 15th May 1756.
To William Little for Moiety of a Publick Lot in the Town of Savannah Letter O, Registred 2d June 1758.

Grant Dated 6th December 1757.
To Thomas Vincent for 300 Acres of Land on Wilmington Island, Registred 5th June 1758.

Grant Dated 6th December 1757.
To Thomas Vincent for a Lot in the Town of Hardwicke No. 48, Registred 5th June 1758.

Grant Dated 6th December 1757.
To Thomas Vincent for Moiety of a Publick Lot in the Town of Savannah Letter Y, Registred 5th June 1758.

Grant Dated 7th February 1758.
To John Stewart Senr. for 500 Acres of Land in the District of Newport, Registred 16th June 1758.

Grant Dated 7th February 1758.
To Nathaniel Clark for 200 Acres of Land in the District of Sapola, Registred 16th June 1758.

Grant Dated 4th October 1757.
To John Jagger for 400 Acres of Land in the District of Sapola, Registred 17th June 1758.

Grant Dated 4th October 1757.
To John Jagger for a Lot in the Town of Hardwicke No. 2, Registred 17th June 1758.

Grant Dated 28th March 1758.
To Robert Humphrys for 300 Acres of Land in the District of Ebenezer, Registred 20th June 1758.

Grant Dated 30th September 1757.
To Henry Curtis for 200 Acres of Land being Little Warsaw Island, Registred 28th June 1758.

Grant Dated 7th February 1758.
To Daniel Demetre for 200 Acres of Land in the District of Sapola, Registred 29th June 1758.

Grant Dated 7th February 1758.
To Daniel Demetre for 50 Acres of Land in the District of Sapola, Registred 29th June 1758.

Grant Dated 7th February 1758.
To Daniel Demetre for a Lot in the Town of Savannah No. 8 in Heathcote Tything Deckers Ward & 50 Acres of Land in said Tything & Ward, Registred 29th June 1758.

Grant Dated 7th February 1758.
To William Thomas Harris for 350 Acres of Land in the District of Sapola, Registred 1st July 1758.

Grant Dated 7th February 1758.
To William Thomas Harris for 136 Acres of Land in the District of Savannah, Registred 1st July 1758.

Grant Dated 7th February 1758.
To William Thomas Harris for a Lot in the Town of Savannah No. 7 in Frederick Tything Derby Ward & 50 Acres of Land in said Tything & Ward, Registred 3d July 1758.
Allotted by the Late President and Assistants.

Grant Dated 7th February 1758.
To William Thomas Harris for a Lot in the Town of Savannah No. 6 in Laroche Tything Heathcote Ward & 50 Acres of Land in said Tything and Ward, Registred 3d July 1758.
Allotted by the Late President and Assistants.

Grant Dated 6th December 1757.
To George Philip Bortz for 50 Acres of Land in the District of Abercorn, Registred 5th July 1758.

Grant Dated 30th September 1757.
To William Clement for 300 Acres of Land in the District of Augusta, Registred 5th July 1758.

Grant Dated 4th July 1758.
To Jonathan Bryan for 900 Acres of Land being Broughton Island on the River Alatamaha, Registred 5th July 1758.

Grant Dated 4th July 1758.
To Lachlan McIntosh for 500 Acres of Land being an Island on the River Alatamaha, Registred 5th July 1758.

Grant Dated 28th March 1758.
To Thomas Collins for 100 Acres of Land in the District of Ogechee, Registred 7th July 1758.

Grant Dated 7th February 1758.
To William Carr for 500 Acres of Land in the District of Medway, Registred 7th July 1758.

Grant Dated 4th July 1758.
To Samuel Gandy for 200 Acres of Land in the Parish of St. George, Registred 7th July 1758.

Grant Dated 7th February 1758.
To Richard Dowdee for a Lot in the Town of Hardwicke No. 84, Registred 8th July 1758.

Grant Dated 28th March 1758.
To William Booth for 300 Acres of Land in the District of Augusta, Registed 8th July 1758.

Grant Dated 4th July 1758.
To White Outerbridge for a Lot in the Town of Augusta No. 35, Registred 10th July 1758.

Grant Dated 6th December 1757.
To Jacob Lockerman for 350 Acres of Land in the District of Medway, Registred 11th July 1758.

Grant Dated 4th July 1758.
To Henry Ellis Esqr. for 700 Acres of Land on St. Simons Island in the Parish of St. James, Registred 11th July 1758.

Grant Dated 4th July 1758.
To Alexander Rose for 100 Acres of Land in the Parish of St. Philip, Registred 20th July 1758.

Grant Dated 4th July 1758.
To Nicholas Lawrence for 50 Acres of Land in the Parish of St. John, Registred 22d July 1758.

Grant Dated 4th July 1758.
To Nicholas Lawrence for 200 Acres of Land in the Parish of St. Philip, Registred 22d July 1758.

Grant Dated 4th July 1758.
To Nicholas Lawrence for 300 Acres of Land in the Parish of St. John, Registred 22d July 1758.

Grant Dated 4th July 1758.
To Robert Bolton for a Lot in the Town of Hardwicke No. 81, Registred 24th July 1758.

Grant dated 4th July 1758.
To Robert Bolton for 450 Acres of Land in the Parish of St. Philip, Registred 24th July 1758.

Grant Dated 4th July 1758.
To Matthias Kougle for a Lot in the Town of Hardwicke No. 128, Registred 26th July 1758.

Colonial Records 245

Grant Dated 4th July 1758.
To Thomas Young for a Lot in the Town of Savannah No. 10 in the fourth Tything Reynold Ward and 50 Acres of Land in said Tything and Ward, Registred 26th July 1758.

Examined and Compared with the Original Register at Savannah this 3d of August 1758 by
         Pat Houstoun, Register

Henry Ellis to William Pitt, March 5, 1760, Georgia, received May 22, 1760, giving an account of troubles with the Indians and measures he has taken to insure the colony's safety.

Sir

 The last letter I had the honour to write to you was of the 16th Ultimo, giving an account of the troubles broke out with the Cherokees, and our measures in consequence of them. These Savages continue to annoy and desolate the back parts of South Carolina. Many of the Inhabitants are fled from thence, and taking shelter amongst us. This Colony has been greatly Alarmed of late, but as yet, very little hurt by the Cherokees; and we owe this indulgence partly to our not having offended them, but chiefly, I apprehend, to our engagements with the Creeks, and their menacing to revenge any hostilities that may be committed on the Inhabitants of Georgia.
 The Chickesaws scout with our parties, and some of the Creeks have done the same; the former declare they will live and die with the English; but the latter, dare not act openly until they learn what part their Nation will take; which I am endeavoring by every means in my power to involve in a War with the Cherokees.
 It would be endless to relate to you Sir, the variety of steps we have taken for this purpose. It may perhaps be sufficient to observe, that they were such as are the most likely to succeed. Numbers of the Creeks visit me daily who seem to have very good dispositions which I strive to improve to the utmost. The intercourse is expensive and will probably be more so whether these Indians declare in our favour or continue in their Neutrality. A further supply of Presents will therefore be very much wanted soon. Thus I have directed the Agent for the Colony to Soliicit not doubting but the necessity of the Service will insure his Success.
 In respect to the other Concerns of this Government no material

alteration has fallen out since the date of my last except that I
have prevailed on the Inhabitants to erect Log-Forts in different
parts, and I shall omit nothing that prudence can suggest, or our
ability accomplish for the further security of the Colony.

Henry Ellis to the Board of Trade, April 16, 1760, Georgia, received July 1, 1760, read Nov. 12, 1760, C.O. 5/648, E. 1, urging the necessity of more presents to set the Creeks against the Cherokees.

My Lords

The 16th Ultimate I had the honour to write to your Lordships an account of the situation of Affairs in these parts, and our proceedings in Consequence of them. I mentiond that I was using my utmost endeavours to engage the Creek Indians in a War with the Cherokees, which I am still employed in, tho' it proves a work of much difficulty, as the french and Cherokees have great influence in that Nation. But whilst I am negotiating publickly I am working in private with the stragling parties of Creeks that occasionally visit me in hopes by their means to embroil their Nation insensibly, and as it were against their inclination. We have already prevailed on different gangs to go against the Cherokees, and I have this day had the satisfaction of seeing one party return with the Scalps of three of them. I shall to the utmost of my power endeavour to improve this earnest of success, but as nothing is to be effected with the Savages without distributing of Considerable Presents and treating the head Men and Warriors as well as subsisting their Wives and Children in their absence when they go to War, there is a necessity that I should be amply supplyd with Goods and Money for such purposes.

It is of the last importance that the Creeks should be induced to assist us, for otherwise the War with the Cherokees may prove a very tedious & Expensive one. £5000 laid out in this way may save ten times that Sum in another. I have already set the Chickesaws upon the Enemy who will be serviceable but Expensive Auxiliaries, and should I not have wherewithal to support our Interest and perform such promises as the Circumstances of affairs may oblige me to make to the Indians it may have very pernicious effects at this Juncture.

I have urged this matter to his Majestys Secretary of State, and I hope it will be considered with that attention its importance requires.

There has been no mischief done by the Cherokees in this Province since I wrote last, but it is not improbable that the parties fitted out from hence, and the endeavours we are using to set the Creek Nation upon them will provoke and iritate them so far as to bring them upon us, which if it is not to be avoided, we must make the best of.

As to other Matters they remain in their Usual situation, which makes it unnecessary for me to say more upon this occasion.

Henry Ellis to William Pitt, April 16, 1760, Georgia, received June 20, 1760, urging the necessity of more presents to set the Creeks against the Cherokees and proposing an expedition against the French fort at Mobile.

Sir:

The 5th Ultimate I had the honour to transmit to you a state of the affairs of these parts, and our proceedings in consequence of them. I mentioned that I was using my utmost endeavours to engage the Creek Indians in a War with the Cherokees which I am still employed in, tho' it proves a work of much dificulty as the French and Cherokees have great influence in that Nation. But whilst I am negotiating Publickly I am working in private with the stragling parties of Creeks that occasionally visit me in hopes by their means to embroil their Nation insensibly and as it were against its inclination. We have already prevaild on different gangs to go against the Cherokees, and I have this day had the satisfaction of seeing one party return with the Scalps of three of them. I shall to the utmost of my power improve this earnest of success, but as nothing is to be effected with the Savages without distributing of considerable Presents, and treating the head Men and Warriors as well as subsisting their Wives and Children in their absence when they go to War there is a necessity that I should be amply supplyed with Goods and Money for such purposes. It is of the last importance that the Creeks should be induced to assist us for otherwise the War with the Cherokees may be a very tedious and Expensive one. £5000 laid out in this way may save ten times that Sum in another.

I have already set the Chickesaws upon the Enemy who will be very serviceable but Expensive Auxiliaries and should I not have wherewithal to support our Interest and perform such promises as the Circumstances of affairs may oblige me to make to the Indians it may have very pernicious effects at this Juncture.

Whilst I am upon this Subject I cannot but express my Wishes that an Expedition were provided against the French Fort at Mobille which I am persuaded might be attempted with Success. Two or three thousand Troops and half a dozen flat bottom Vessels carrying four or Six large Cannon each would be a sufficient force. The Joint fire from those Vessels would carry every thing before it, especially if they were assisted by a Bombardment. The Fort at Mobille I am informed is very weak, constructed of Brick, mounts but fourteen Cannon, and is Garrisond by about 600 Men. Pilots for the River on which it stands might be procured at Charles Town, and the Winter is said to be a favourable Season for such an Enterprize which must not be attempted otherwise than by Water, whereas the natural difficulties and obstructions attendant to a long march by Land thro' such a country as this, the Indians would be apt to oppose it, as the french might easily persuade them they were to be attacked and not the French who we might only come at by Water. It would be of infinite Consequence to the Nation could we at this time possess our selves of that important post for the Fort of Tombegbi amongst the Chactaws, and that of Toulouse in the Country of the Albamas or Creeks would fall of course. It is by means of those Forts that the French maintain an Interest with those powerful Nations, and in a great Measure exclude us from a Correspondence with them as well as with the numerous tribes of Savages inhabiting the borders of the Mississippi. Hence the loss of Mobille would be followed by that of their Trade & influence in those parts which would augment and extend ours in proportion. Our present Indian Neighbours would become more Submissive and Manageable as more dependent, and the Cherokee War might be soon terminated. Was it only to raise our Military Character amongst the Savages of this quarter such an undertaking would be necessary for the fame of our Exploits to the Northward, so that the Artifices of the french made but slight impressions upon them.

It may be objected that such a Conquest amongst the Spanish Settlements would give Umbrage to Spain, which might happen. Yet I am persuaded it would be our Interest to make it, even were we to yield it to the Spaniards afterwards, who are less dangerous, and in every view more eligible Neighbours than the french.

Copy of an Order in Council, May 13, 1760, Kensington, received and read the same day by the Board of Trade, C.O. 5/647, D. 4, approving a representation to allow Gov. Henry Ellis permission to return to England for the recovery of his health.

Upon reading this day at the Board, a Representation from the Lords Commissioners for Trade and Plantations, setting forth, that Henry Ellis Esquire, His Majestys Governor of the Province of Georgia, hath represented to them, that the excessive heat of the Climate has reduced his health to so bad a State, as renders him almost incapable of discharging properly, the Dutys of his Station, and that he has no prospect of recovering in America; The said Lords Commissioners therefore propose, that His Majesty will be graciously pleased to grant the said Governor His Royal permission to return to this Kingdom. His Majesty in Council approving thereof, is pleased to Order, as it is hereby Ordered, that the said Henry Ellis Esquire be accordingly permitted to return to this Kingdom for the recovery of his health. And that the said Lords Commissioners for Trade and Plantations do cause a Warrant to be prepared for that purpose, and lay the same before His Majesty at this Board.

Copy of an Order in Council, May 13, 1760, Kensington, received and read the same day by the Board of Trade, C.O. 5/647, D. 5, approving a representation proposing James Wright to be Lieutenant Governor of Georgia and directing a commission to be prepared.

Upon reading this day at the Board, a Representation from the Lords Commissioners for Trade and Plantations, proposing that James Wright Esquire may be appointed Lieutenant Governor of His Majestys Province of Georgia, in America, His Majesty in Council approving thereof, is pleased to Order, as it is hereby ordered, that the said James Wright Esquire be constituted and appointed Lieutenant Governor of His Majestys said Provence of Georgia. And that the said Lords Commissioners for Trade and Plantations, do Cause a Commission to be prepared for that purpose, and lay the same before His Majesty at this Board.

Henry Ellis to the Board of Trade, May 15, 1760, Georgia, read Nov. 12, 1760, C.O. 5/648, E. 2, relating to the Chickasaw and Creek Indians.

My Lords,

   I wrote your Lordships the 16th Ultimate, an account of such matters as this place afforded. So little alteration has taken place since, that I am at a loss what to offer at present, and only write because there is an opportunity of doing so.

   Though the Cherokees continue to do much mischief in the Neighbouring Provinces yet the parties of Rangers and Indians that we keep constantly Scouting in the back parts, have prevented any late outrages being Committed upon the Inhabitants of this Colony. The Chickesaws and some gangs of Creeks which I prevaild on to go against the Enemy have brought in several Scalps, and United in burning Estatoe & Keowee, two of their Frontier Towns on this side. The Cherokees do not resent these hostilities of the Creeks, for fear of drawing that Nation upon them, which still adheres to its Neutrality; and disavows its authorizing the Violences of such of its People as are influenced by us. I am in hopes however, that in some of these Excursions the Enemy will kill some of the Creeks, whose death their friends must revenge, and so the Nation may be at length compelled to make the Cause its own. An Event that would be more advantageous than if our Solicitations prevaild on them to Join us; but the bringing this about will create an Expence that we have no way of defraying, for our Presents and funds are near Exhausted.

   In respect to other Matters, I have nothing new at present to mention. Our internal quiet continues, but the dangers with which the Colony is surrounded, must of course retard and check that prosperity which it had a fair prospect of attaining.

   As to myself My Lords, my health is in so poor a state, as renders it impossible for me long to support my self under the accumulated load of business and fatigue that these troubles occasion. I shall therefore humbly hope, and impatiently expect, that by your Lordships influence and good offices, I may be speedily relieved.

Henry Ellis to the Board of Trade, June 7, 1760, Georgia, read Nov. 12, 1760, C.O. 5/648, E. 3, acquainting the Board that, by the instigation of the French and Cherokees, several traders have been murdered in the Upper Creek towns.

My Lords

The last Letter I had the honour of writing to your Lordships was of the 15th Ultimate, and contained the then state of Affairs here, which was rather favourable than otherwise. But it is with very great Concern I must now acquaint your Lordships, that the Endeavours of our Enemies, the French and Cherokees, seem to have been more prevalent with the Creeks, than those we have been employing. For on the 4th Instant, I was by an Express from the Creek Nation informed, that several of our Traders in the Upper Towns were on the 16th Ultimate Murdered, and their effects Seized, and divided amongst some of those Savages. This step, is always looked upon as a declaration of War. But notwithstanding so alarming a Circumstance, considering the Number of our Indian friends, I cannot be persuaded the defection of that Nation in general, or that a War with us is determined, especially as several of their principal people are now with me, and many of them are dispersd thro' our Settlements, who would certainly have been early apprized of it, had there been such a design, and withdrawn themselves out of our power. For these reasons, I have not suffered any of them to be molested.[48]

I am very Sensible, My Lords, how exceedingly prejudicial it would be to his Majestys Service at this Juncture, should the Number of our Enemies be increased by so formidable a Tribe as the Creek Indians, I am therefore exerting my most strenuous efforts to prevent it, and frustrate the Views of the French, who spare neither pains nor Expense to embroil us with our Savage Neighbours. That I may the better succeed herein, I have thought it absolutely necessary to impute the Murder of our Traders to the deceiving

---

48. On May 16, 1760, in the Upper Creek town of Sugatspoges, young Abeika warriors under Handsome Fellow attacked John Ross' trading post and murdered him and his two Negro servants. Before the day ended, eleven traders at Sugatspoges, Okfuskee, Okchai, and Calailegies had been killed and their stores sacked. Led by Handsome Fellow and Red-Coat King, the Indians hoped to force the Creeks from their traditional neutrality into a conspiracy with the French against the English. Still, the scheme failed. Coupled with reassurances from responsible Creek headmen, Ellis responded with restraint, as his letter indicated. Once again, Ellis made the right moves and peace was preserved on the Georgia frontier. See CRG, VIII, 310, 316, 327, 349, 421; South Carolina Gazette, April 7, May 10, 17, 24, June 21, 1760; James Adair, The History of the American Indians (London, 1775), 278-283.

Arts, and false Suggestions of our Enemies, excusing the Creeks thereby, and giving that, an Affection for them, and a regard to our Treaties, as reasons for our not insisting upon the Murderers being immediately delivered to us.

By these temperate Measures, I am hopeful that if we shall not be able to establish the peace of this Colony on a lasting foundation, we may at least keep the Creeks quiet for some time; which in our present Circumstances would answer some very important purposes. For if the War with the Cherokees, and our Conquests to the North can be soon finished, I cannot doubt but that due attention will then be shown to the defence of this important frontier Colony; through which should the Creeks desert us, the French and their Indians will have an opportunity of greatly annoying the Southern Provinces. In the mean time, I have the satisfaction to find, that the Government of South Carolina entertains Sentiments conformable to mine, which encourages me to hope that we may yet elude the Storm which now threatens us.

My Lords I have often urged the insecure state of this Colony, the weakest in itself, and opposed to the most powerful Indian Neighbours of any Province upon this Continent; but I am sorry to say my remonstrances have not had sufficient effect. It is inconceivable the pains I have taken these three Years past, to preserve the repose of these parts, and keep the Creeks in good temper. For Carolina has in this period, too much Neglected them. Untill the Cherokees Joind their influence with the French, my labours were attended with Success and the Colony increased very much, even on this account, but now people start as from a dream finding themselves encompassed with, and threatned by, such formidable Tribes of Merciless barbarians, whose friendship appears so little to be depended upon.

And their apprehensions naturally increase when they observe this Government unable either from its own resources, or the assistance afforded it by the Mother Country, effectually to protect them. Hence hundreds of families have quitted their habitations, and are moving to the other Provinces, and we may expect many more will follow, if a War with the Creeks should prove unavoidable.

Your Lordships will be good enough to excuse my not touching on other matters untill I have a little more leisure, for these new troubles occupy me very much at present.

Memorial of Benjamin Martyn, Agent for Georgia, to the Board of
Trade, June 20, 1760, London, read the same day, C.O. 5/647,
D. 9, asking a warrant to apply £48.1.6 for the freight of goods
sent for Indian presents out of balance of contingency funds remaining
in his hands.

Sheweth,

That he has in his hands the Sum of £144.15.7-3/4, the remainder
of the Money, which he was authorised by the Lords Justices
to pay for such Services, as Your Lordships by Your Warrants
should direct and appoint.

That the Goods for Indian Presents, to the Value of about
£1250, are shipp'd on board the Union, Capt. James Strachan,
and the freight for the same amounts to £48.1.6.

That £250, the remaining Part of £1500 granted by his Majesty
for the Presents, is barely sufficient to defray the Expences attending
the Distribution of them.

Your Memorialist therefore begs leave to offer to your Lordships
Consideration, whether it may not be proper to pay £48.1.6
for the freight out of the aforesaid Sum of £144.15.7-3/4.

Henry Ellis to the Board of Trade, June 27, 1760, Georgia, received
and read Jan. 7, 1761, C.O. 5/648, E. 10, containing
a full account of the sale of Sapelo and Ossabau Islands and
other Indian lands to satisfy the Bosomworth claims against the
Crown, with four enclosures.

My Lords

Having at Length fully satisfied the Bosomworths, not only in
respect to their Demands on Account of Services done the Government
in the last Spanish War; but also, in reference to their Pretensions
to certain Lands which the Creek Indians had reserved
to themselves by Treaty with General Oglethorpe, I take this Opportunity
of laying before your Lordships the Grounds whereon,
and Manner in which we proceeded in this Transaction. As your
Lordships were pleased to represent to his Majesty the necessity
of Adjusting these Affairs, which in their unsettled State, threatned
very mischevious Consequences to the Colony, the King was
graciously pleased to honour me with his Royal Instructions for
that purpose, dated the 9th February 1759, whereby I was

Authorized to dispose of the Islands Ossaba and Sappalo and other Indian Lands near Savannah at Public Auction the same having been ceded to his Majesty by a Deed from the Head Men of the Creek Nation the 22d April 1758 and out of the Money arising therefrom to discharge the aforesaid Demands of the Bosomworths and to Grant to them the Island of St. Catharine in Consideration of their having settled & improved the same.

Your Lordships may remember that the Indian Lands near Savannah consisting of about 4000 Acres were by the President and Assistants allotted to several Persons who settled thereon and have continued to cultivate & improve them ever since 1752. These Settlers applied for his Majestys Grants, when the Royal Government was established here; but were prevented from obtaining them partly by Mr. Bosomworths entering Caveats against Grants being issued but chiefly by a Letter from your Lordships Board recommending an Examination into the Grounds of his Pretensions. As soon as I received the Kings Instruction impowering me to proceed in these Matters, I summoned Thomas Bosomworth and Mary his Wife to appear before me in Council to show Cause why those Caveats should not be rejected. At the Day appointed for this Purpose the Bosomworths attended, and after a fair hearing it appeared, that all they could alledge in support of their Claim to the said Lands was insufficient to establish it upon any legal or equitable Foundation. The Board therefore Ordered the Caveats to be dismissed. I was then presented with the Account (A) and Case (B) transmitted herewith specifying their other Demands upon the Government, which the Board having likewise examined and duely considered were of Opinion that Mrs. Bosomworth ought to be disbursed the Sum of £450 for and on Account of that value in Goods which She had expended for his Majesty's Service in the Years 1747 and 1748 by Order of Lieutenant Colonel Heron. And also that She should be allowed at the rate of one hundred Pounds per Annum for sixteen Years & a half during which Time she acted in this Government as Agent and Interpretess to the Creek Indians, and that the same should be paid to her agreable to his Majesty's Instructions out of the Monies arising from the Sale of the Islands Ossaba and Sappalo provided they produced so much. These Resolutions being signified to Mr. and Mrs. Bosomworth they after some Deliberation acquiesed therein & declared themselves perfectly satisfied therewith. Whereupon the Attorney General was directed (with the Assistance of the Chief Justice) to draw up the heads of this Agreement which was accordingly done and signed the next Day by the Bosomworths on the one Part, and myself and the Members of the Council on the other. This Affair being so far compleated Mr. and Mrs. Bosomworth withdrew, I then advised with his Majesty's Council as to the properest Method of disposing of the Islands Osseba and Sappalo whether in small Tracts or otherwise.

The Board upon due Consideration thereof was of Opinion that it might be best to sell them in parcels each Tract not exceeding a thousand Acres on Condition however that if the Sum arising from such Sale should not exceed what might be Offered in a private way for the whole of both Islands such Sale should be Void. After these Islands were Advertized in the Carolina Gazettes during four Months they were on the 10th December last put up at Auction in 500 Acre Tracts conditioned to go to the highest bidder in Case that the aggregate Sum bid for the whole should amount to two thousand Guineas and not otherwise that being deemed the lowest value of these Islands. But the Cherokee Troubles breaking out about that Time so discouraged People here that no more was bid for them than £1500 which Circumstances, altho' no private Offer had been made for either of them, induced me to declare the Sale invalid.

They were again advertized to be peremptorily disposed of on the 14th April last at Auction seperately and without dividing them in Tracts as before. In which Manner they were put up and the Island of Ossaba was Sold at £1350 and that of Sappalo for £700 which Sums respectively I paid to Mr. Bosomworth and made out a Grant to Mrs. Bosomworth of the Island of St. Catharine each of them having first executed a General Renunciation and Discharge of all Claims and Pretensions upon his Majesty of what Nature or kind soever, Copies of these Papers mark'd C & D accompany this and are Registered in the Secretary's Office of this Province.

In Respect to the Remainder of the said Indian Lands, Vizt., what lays between the Town of Savannah and Pipe Makers Creek, they being already as I have observed in the Possession of several Persons who settled and improved them on the Faith of the Trustees Government. I presume it is not his Majesty's Intention that they should be Sold notwithstanding these Lands are not excepted in the Royal Instruction, and therefore I have not given the present Possessors any uneasiness on that Account, being humbly of Opinion that, when his Majesty is made acquainted with their particular Circumstances, leave will be given to make out their respective Grants, or at least that they may be permitted to purchase them on the same Terms that vacant Lands

are purchased here from the Crown. It would be a great piece of
Justice, as well as an Act of Humanity should your Lordships
condescend to make these Peoples Case known to his Majesty
and procure for them the Indulgence I mention. I must not however neglect informing your Lordships upon this Occasion that I
discovered there were about 130 Acres, Part of those Indian Lands
bordering upon this Town Vacant, which had hitherto been deemed
Common. This I have sold in small Lots from whence after de-
ducting all Expences attending the different Sales there has been
produced and remains in my Hands the Sum of £606.10.3 as appears by the Account E which is to be applied hereafter to such
Service as his Majesty shall think proper to direct, & of which
I have in Obedience to the Kings Commands informed the Right
Honorable Lords Commissioners of his Majesty's Treasury. Thus
have I given your Lordships as clear and distinct an Account of
these Transactions as I am able.

A Statement of Mrs. Bosomworth's Case with respect to her services, losses, expenses, and demands of the colony of Georgia,
received and read Jan. 7, 1761, C.O. 5/648, E. 11, enclosure
A in Governor Ellis' June 27, 1760, letter to the Board of Trade.

That before the Charter for Establishing the Colony of Georgia
Mrs. Bosomworth with her Family was settled on the river Savannah, a small space above where the Town of Savannah now stands,
had large Credits from Merchants in Charles Town, South Carolina,
and Carried on a Considerable Trafic with the Indians whereby
she had already made very large Remittances in Skins, and was
moreover Possess'd of a very Good Cowpen & Plantation upon the
same River.

That Mr. Oglethorpe's Arrival with the first Adventures to settle a Colony under the aforesaid Charter gave great uneasiness
to the Indians then upon the spot, who threatne'd to take up arms
against them. Nor would they have permitted Mr. Oglethorpe &
his people a Quiet Possession (as they look'd upon the white
People's settling to the Southward of Savannah River contrary to
the Treaty of Peace, enter'd into between the Indians & the
Government of South Carolina after the Indian War in the year
1716) had not the Governor & Council wrote to Mrs. Bosomworth
(by Mr. Oglethorpe) to use the utmost of her Interest with the
Indians for that Purpose and to give the new settlers all the Aid
& Assistance their Necessities might require. In Compliance

with the request contain'd in that Letter, and from Motives of regard to the British Interest, Mrs. Bosomworth by her Influence, Quieted the Indians; allay'd all Animosity, obtain'd a present Asylum for the Adventures, and in about the space of twelve months, by her steady Adherence and good Offices settled & procur'd to be ratified a Treaty between the Indians & Mr. Oglethorpe in behalf of the Trustees for Establishing that Colony.[49]

That by the Trafic she then carried on with the Indians there was no Impediment to her soon raising a Considerable Intrest. Yet Mrs. Bosomworth could not unmov'd see a Colony (scarce begun) expos'd to the Incursions of the Spaniards & their Indians (the frequent & then late ravages of the frontiers of Carolina) and whose Protection she well knew in their defenceless situation, could only be secur'd by the Friendship and Alliance with the Creek Indians she therefore upon Promises of adequate rewards from the Government Induc'd the Indians who were her Hunters and supplied her with Skins, most Generally to Employ themselves in Expeditions for the Public Service.

That in the Years 1736 & 1737 when Mr. Oglethorpe thought it Expedient to Improve the southern Part of the Province, first by a settlement on the Island of St. Simon's, and by another settlement (of Scotch People) at Darian on the Altamaha River, the Assistance of the Creek Indians then became of so much greater Importance, as there were advices at that time that Spaniards were making Preparations to Dislonge the Inhabitants of this new Colony & the more still effectually to further the Preservation & Growth of the frontier settlements. Mrs. Bosomworth at the

---

49. This portion of Mary Bosomworth's narrative historically is well-founded. In 1717, Brims, Creek emperor of Coweta, gave his niece, Coosaponakessa, in marriage to Johnny Musgrove, the half-breed son of Colonel John Musgrove of South Carolina. Rumored to be the daughter of the explorer Henry Woodward by Brims' sister, Coosaponakessa had been educated as a Christian at Pon Pon in South Carolina. Thus Mary early became a regal pledge between Brims and the English to cement peace after the disastrous Yamasee War. The Musgroves then moved into the debatable land across the Savannah River to Pipemaker's Creek a mile west of present-day Yamacraw Bluff. By January, 1733, the Musgroves ran one of Carolina's most prosperous trading establishments. When Oglethorpe landed at Yamacraw, Mary was almost forty-six years old.

Earnest request of General Oglethorpe (buoy'd up by Extensive
Promises, & the Large Rewards so signal a Service for the public
Welfare would Merit) settled a Trading House on the south side
of the said River Altamaha about 150 miles up the same river by
water at a Place call'd Mount Venture, the Intention of which
settlement was that the Creek Indians, who would be constantly
with her there might be an advanc'd Guard to prevent any Incursions of the Spaniards, or Indians in friendship with them, and
be always more ready at hand when his Majesty's Service requir'd their Assistance which throughly Answer'd the Intentions
of the Public.

That after the Declaration of war against Spain the service of
the Indians were so frequently requir'd that no Benefit could possibly arise from any Trade with them that might induce Mrs.
Bosomworth's stay there, nevertheless so great was her zeal that
without the least Prospect of Interest to herself she was daily
expos'd at that Settlement, for the public Service, in keeping the
Indians upon Excursions, and sending for her Friends & Relations
from the nation to go to war whenever his Majesty's Service requir'd.

That at the time of Mr. Oglethorpe's first Arrival there being
no House or Settlement on the Place except Mrs. Bosomworth's,
She at the request of Mr. Oglethorpe, supplied the new Settlers
and other Persons Employ'd on Public Services in their Greatest
Wants not only with every thing her Plantation & store afforded
but also with Liquor & other Necessari's, purchas'd on her own
Credit from Merchants in Charles Town whereby she Loss'd in
bad Debts so Contracted and acumalated the sum of £826 sterling
as can be Evidently prov'd from a state of her Books, and has
been before amongst other Complaints, set forth & humbly represented to the Government.

That by Mrs. Bosomworth's Employing in his Majsty's service
those Indians who used by Hunting, to supply her with Skins (the
Chief support of herself & Family) her Trade naturally Decreas'd,
and went nearly to ruin, a large Party of them who she prevail'd
on assisted his Majesty's Arms & went to the siege of St. Augustine where many of them were kill'd, particularly her own Brother
& other near Relations. By this Incident she greatly suffer'd in
the Loss of Indian Debts amounting to several Thousand Weight
of Leather for which she never yet receiv'd any satisfaction altho
promiss'd it from time to time by Mr. Oglethorpe.

That from the time of settling the Southern Frontier aforemen-
tiond Mr. Oglethorpe was continually sending for Mrs. Bosomworth

on all Affairs of Consequence with the Indians which expos'd her
to many Dangers and Hardships the distance being Great & the
Convenience for Passage being only in an open Boat, her own
Affairs and Improvements on her Land neglected & running to ruin,
being left Intirely to the Management of Servants for Months at a
Time. That in the Spring 1739/40 Mrs. Bosomworth had a Large
Stock of Cattle at her Cowpen on Savannah River, but General
Oglethorpe hearing that her Cowpen Keeper was a very Good Woodsman, in the absence of Mrs. Bosomworth at the Alatamaha Settlement, without her Consent or Knowledge, sent orders to the said
Cowpen keeper to go directly as a Guide to a Troop of Rangers
who were sent by Land to the Siege of St. Augustine which Orders
he durst not to disobey, though sensible of the Loss would be to
Mrs. Bosomworth's Interest, and, as it happen'd the Loss of his
own Life; he being kill'd in that Expedition, by which means all
Mrs. Bosomworth's Affairs at Savannah, Stock of Cattle, Improvements etc., which were very Considerable, went intirely to ruin,
for which Losses no Satisfaction ever was made, although Constantly & solemnly Promissed her.

In the year 1742 Mrs. Bosomworth's then Husband, Captain
Matthews, being taken sick at her settlement on the Alatamaha
she was obliged to bring him from thence (On occasion of proper
sustenance and Advice) to Savannah where he soon after died.
Her Affairs on account of his Death demanding her stay in Savannah for some Time, The Indians at the Alatamaha were very uneasy
and Disgusted that she did not return, and on that Account left
the place. The small Garrison that were there being in great want
of Provisions & ammunition, a Party of Yamasee, or Spanish Indians came upon them, and after Committing several Barbarous
Murthers, totally burnt and destroy'd the settlement and all Mrs.
Bosomworth's Effects became a prey to the Enemy. Which great
Loss General Oglethorpe promiss'd her should be made up to her
by the Government; he well knowing in Truth that that Settlement
was Calculated and made for the sole Benefit of his Majestys
Service and the Protection of the Southern Frontier.

That in the Year 1745 Mr. Bosomworth was at the Expence of
a Voyage to England in order to Claim the Performance of the various Promises from time to time for a series of years made, or
otherwise to apply to the Government in behalf of his Wife but the
public Confusion at that Time in England rendering any Private
Application to the Government, unseasonable,[50] he was Obliged

---

50. This refers to the 1745 invasion of Scotland by Charles

to return to America, only with Assurances from General Oglethorpe, that as soon as the then Disturbances were settled, Mrs. Bosomworth might depend upon his Honour for full satisfaction for all her services, and that in the Interim Mr. Bosomworth might draw upon him for any sum not Exceeding £1000 as the Exigency of Affairs might require. This is all the satisfaction Mr. Bosomworth obtain'd in Consequence of that Voyage excepting a Letter to the Commanding Officer then in Georgia; a Copy whereof is annex'd.

In the year 1746 upon the Faith of General Oglethorps Promise, Mr. Bosomworth was induc'd to draw several Bills of Exchange upon him; but the Cloud he was at that time under in respect to his Conduct in the North,[51] render'd him incapable of paying any of them as appears by his Letter dated Whitehall July 16th, 1746 so that the Bills were all return'd upon Mr. Bosomworth with the heavy Charges of Protest etc., amounting to £600 or £700 sterling most of which remains at this Day unpaid.

That Mr. Bosomworth at his own great Expence in the year 1746 made another Settlement on the Alatamaha at a place call'd the Forks about 300 Miles by water up the same river; built a very good Dwelling House, outhouses, a large store and Fortify'd the whole round, against any Attempts of Enemy Indians, with an intent to carry on a Considerable Indian Trade, withal knowing of what Consequence a former Settlement on that river had been to the public welfare of Georgia and upon the Credit of his Bills drawn on General Oglethorpe had receiv'd for that Purpose a Large Cargoe of Indian Goods.

That upon the Arrival of Colonel Alexander Heron in the year 1747 to take the Command of his Majestys Forces in Georgia a General rupture with the Indians was thought unavoidable. He in his Letter the 8th July of that year applied to Mrs. Bosomworth then settled at the Forks to use her Endeavours & Influence to reconcile matters amongst the Indians; & in another Letter so soon after as the 20th of the same Month he informs her that he thought it Expedient to send an Agent to the Creek Nation and earnestly

---

Stuart, son of the Old Pretender. See Ettinger, Oglethorpe: Imperial Idealist, 275-276, for Oglethorpe's part in the rebellion.

51. In 1746 Oglethorpe was courtmartialed "for having disobeyed or neglected his orders and suffered the Rear of the Rebells near Shap to escape" in the northern campaign against the Jacobites. See Ettinger, Oglethorpe: Imperial Idealist, 264-270.

desires her to supply that Agent with such requisites as the Service demanded and also to give the Indians with her then at the Forks (then lately arriv'd there from the nation) such Presents as might Possibly appease them & secure their Friendship.

Accordingly at this Critical Juncture on the earnest solicitation of the said Colonel Heron, Mrs. Bosomworth advanc'd for his Majestys Service sundry Goods out of her own private Store to the amount of £650.15.7-1/2 as appears by a particular Account thereof laid before the proper Boards in England when for Reasons the Commanding Officer himself in the aforemention'd Letter of the 20th July; and in others to Andrew Stone Esquire, deputy secretary of State, it would not have been in his Power otherwise to prevent the dangerous Consequences of a Rupture with the Indians.

That no Consideration whatever would have induced Mrs. Bosomworth at that Time to strip her store of her Indian Goods (upon which the Fate of her Trade absolutely depended) but a firm Attachment to the Welfare of the Colony & the strongest Assurances from Colonel Heron that those Goods should be immediately replaced in her Store at the Forks as soon as ever Conveniencies could be got ready for sending them up the River; and that she might also depend on an Adequate Reward for all the Services done His Majesty.

That Colonel Heron failing to perform his Promise, when the service was perform'd on Pretense there was no Indian Goods in the public store, nor had he Credit to purchase any, obliged Mrs. Bosomworth entirely to abandon that Valuable Settlement, & forego a most Beneficial Traffic with the Indians. Thus her store being Exhausted of Goods, and no skins taken to make remittances for a fresh supply, the Loss she hereby sustain'd was not only in the Goods advanced for his Majestys Service, but for the Buildings, Improvements etc. made at that settlement, and in the great Advantages that must have arose from a Trade there.

That upon the reduction of General Oglethorpe Regiment in the year 1749 the most pressing Application was repeatedly made to Colonel Heron to discharge Mrs. Bosomworth's Account of Disbursements (By his Order) for his Majesty's service, by the Detension of which she had most Grievously suffer'd, but all the satisfaction that could be obtain'd was that he had advanced Considerable sums on his own Credit for the public services, had no fund to pay Mrs. Bosomworth, and that he knew of no redress for her sufferings, but by her going to England and applying to the Government for the payment of all Demands & Services.

That Mrs. Bosomworth & her Husband having no Hopes of

obtaining satisfaction, otherwise than by going to England and there soliciting Redress, had determin'd to embrace the Opportunity of a Passage in the Transport Vessell sent to Carry home the Disbanded Officers & Soldiers of the Regiment. But their Affairs being unhapily involv'd by having thus sacrific'd their private Interests to the public welfare the Malice and Instigation of some particular Persons who look'd upon themselves concern'd to prevent Mr. & Mrs. Bosomworth's Voyage to England.[52] Occasion'd Actions to be so fast brought against them by their Creditors that they Continued Prisoners as it were in the Province. Labouring under every Circumstance of Distress, till May, 1752 at which Time they arriv'd in Charles Town South Carolina with Intent immediately to proceed for England. On there [sic] arrival in Charles Town Mr. Bosomworth & his Wife were prevail'd upon by the Government of South Carolina to undertake a agency to the Creek Nation of Indians which Agency was not Compleated till the Year 1754, at which Time they went for England.

That upon Application in England for the services of Mrs. Bosomworth's services and Demands were found to be misrepresented by the then late Presidents and Assistants of Georgia so that all the satisfaction obtain'd by this Expensive Voyage (in Cost near £1000 Sterling) was a Commission from the Right Honourable the Lords Commissioners for Trade & Plantations directed to the Governor of Georgia, commanding him strictly to examine into the Truth of the Charge & Allegations of each Party and to Report to their Lordships Board his Opinion upon the whole; which Commission has long since been Executed.

That when General Oglethorpe was call'd home in the year 1743, He sent for Mrs. Bosomworth and then paid her £180 in sola Bills[53] which with a £20 Bill before receiv'd made £200 on delivering her these Bills. He Gave her a Diamond Ring from his finger with

---

52. An allusion to the President and Assistants in Savannah and to the Bosomworth's Charleston creditors.

53. From 1735 to 1740 the Georgia Trustees sent sola bills to the colony to circulate as money. By the end of 1755 all sola bills had been recalled and paid. See Eric P. Newman, The Early Paper Money of America (Racine, Wis., 1967), 88; and Harley L. Freeman, "Bills of Credit of Georgia, 1732-1786," Numismatist (July, 1931), 3-12.

Acknowledgement that he would never forget the service she had done him and the Public, and that the sum he then paid her was not intended for more than a years service, and he hop'd she would be pleas'd kindly to accept of it as all then in his Power to pay her (the Credit of his Bills being stop't in England) repeatedly Assuring her at Parting, that as soon as his Accounts were audited and paid by the Government she might draw upon him for £2000 Sterling and he would Honour these Bills. This £200 above mention'd is the sum total Mrs. Bosomworth ever receiv'd or Mr. Oglethorpe or any other Commanding Officer in the Province ever paid Her for all personal Services, her Interest with the Indians so frequently and with unabating ardour manifested, Salary as Interpretess (In which Capacity she was always Imploy'd by every Kings Commanding Officer in the Province) and all the various Losses sustain'd in her own private Affairs, and by neglect thereof on his Majesty's Service, which Losses, Expences, & Damages, in the Premises, moderately Computed have Annually, from the first Settlement of this Colony amounted to the Sum of two hundred Pounds sterling besides the Large Expences of two Voyages to England.

 For Demonstration of the Truth of the Facts herein set forth the merit of Mrs. Bosomworths past Services rendered the Crown; the Losses thereby sustain'd, & the Consequence of her present Interest, She humbly refers to the annex'd Letters & Testimonials under the hand of every Gentleman who has had the Command of his Majesty's Forces in Georgia since the first Settlement of the Colony and if higher Proof is demanded Mr. Bosomworth (on Time given him) has it in his Power to support some of the material Parts of the Case by Living Evidence.

 That it was ever his Majestys most Gracious Intention fully to reward his most Faithfull Servants; a Contrary Supposition must be highly Criminal. What a Reward such a number of Years of Mrs. Bosomworths past Life, and Advance of her Fortune in his Majestys Service; at the frequent Hazzard of her Life and manifest Neglect of her own Affairs, even to ruin, may Justly intitle her to, is in Appeal to your Candid Disquisition, and the whole humbly Submitted to your most serious Consideration

            Thomas Bosomworth

Savannah
23 July 1759.

A statement of Mrs. Bosomworth's account of her services performed, sums disbursed, and sums received, while serving Georgia, received and read Jan. 7, 1761, C.O. 5/648, E. 12, enclosure B in Governor Ellis' June 27, 1760, letter to the Board of Trade.

Dr. His Majesty's Service in the Province of Georgia with Mary Bosomworth p Contra

    To her personal Services and Influence in continuing the Creek Indians in the british Interest, employing them on his Majestys Service against his Enemies; and for Salary as Interpretess to the said Indians from the first Settlement of the Colony in 1732 to the middle of the Year 1749 inclusive being sixteen Years & a half at £200 p Annum £3400

1740 To Losses sustained in Indian Debts due from her hunters who were by her prevailed upon to assist General Oglethorpe at the Seige of Augustine, either killed in that Expedition or rendered incapable of paying their Debts by Reason of their being so frequently afterward employed on the Public Service 483.6.8

1742 To Losses sustained at her Settlement at Mount Venture on the Alatamaha River made as an Outguard and Protection for the Southern Inhabitants; all her Improvements and Effects there being destroyed by Spanish Indians 336.11.3

1747 To sundry disbursements made for his Majesty's Service during the Command of Lieutenant Colonel Heron by his Order from 10th July 1747 to 4th December 1748 as per particular Account laid before the proper Boards in England 650

1749 To Losses sustained in Buildings Improvements and Advantages that might be by Trade with the Indians at his Store at the Forks of the Alatamaha Mrs. Bosomworth being obliged to abandon that valuable Settlement on Account of her not being

reimbursed the sundry Species of Indian
Trading Goods supplied for his Majesty's
Service, and mostly at a Juncture when a
War was thought unavoidable 550

N. B. There is no Charge made of the Losses sustained in her Trade by employing her Hunters in the Infant and defenceless State of the Colony on his Majesty's Service. The great Losses sustained by accumulated Debts of the first Inhabitants, Nor the losses sustained in the Improvements of her Lands etc. Loss of her Stock of Cattle by her Cowpen keeper being ordered to the Seige of Augustine without her Consent or Knowledge, all which is submitted to your Excellency's Consideration.

1743 By Cash received by General Oglethorpe
     when he went for England £200

1747 By Sundries received from the Magazine
     at Frederica by Order of Lieutenant Colonel
     Heron commanding Officer of his Maj-
     esty's Forces from 25th June 1747 to the
     24th February following an Account of
     Issues and Supplies made to different
     Parties of Indians as Per Receipt given
     Mr. Griffith Williams 173.13.10-1/4

     By Debits from February 1748/9 to 29th
     May 1749 . . . .   70.0.1-1/2

It is to be observed that the Sundries received out of the Public Magazine were not for Mrs. Bosomworths private Use but to be distributed to the Indians for his Majesty's Service. And though she stands charged with the same in the public Books She had no other advantage therein but the Labour Fatigue and Trouble of Distribution.

Agreement between Chiefs of Upper and Lower Creek Nations deeding Ossabau, St. Catherines, and Sapelo Islands to Georgia, along with Indian land at Savannah, April 22, 1758, received and read Jan. 7, 1761, enclosed with Governor Ellis' June 27, 1760, letter to the Board of Trade.

PROVINCE OF GEORGIA

We the Micos, Chieftains, Captains, Warriors, the Assembled States of the Upper and Lower Creek Nations, Sole Owners and Proprietors of the Islands Ussabaw, St. Catherine & Sapala, and of a certain Tract of Main Land from a place called Pipe Makers Creek to the Boundaries of the Town of Savannah in Front, and all other Lands on the River Savannah commonly known by the name of the Indian Land; Do hereby declare, and make known to all Manner of People, that in Consideration of the great Love and Esteem we bear the English Nation, and of the many Presents and other Favours we have from Time to Time received from them. We the said assembled Estates have granted and for ever quitted and resigned, And hereby Do for ourselves, our Subjects, and Vassals grant, and hence forth for Ever quit, and resign unto the Great King George, All those the aforementioned three Islands called Ussabaw, St. Catherine, & Sappala, and Tracts of Main Land lying as before described, together with all the Timber and other the Appurtenances any way belonging to all or any Part or Parts of the said Islands and Main Lands. To hold those our aforesaid Lands, and Territories with all the Priviledges and Dignities to the same in any Manner appertaining unto the said King George, his Heirs, and Successors. And We the said Assembled Estates do hereby for ourselves, our Subjects and Vassals release resign and for ever give up unto the said King George all Claim whatsoever to the aforesaid Islands and Main Lands hereby granted, and to all other Lands and Territories by Us or our Ancestors heretofore granted and made over to the said King George, or any of his beloved Men, or by them treated for, at or since the first Settlement of the Colony of Georgia. And we do in like manner revoke, and disclaim all former Gifts, Grants, or Sales made of all or any Part of the Lands and Territories herein mentioned under any pretended Right or Title whatsoever. In Confirmation whereof We the said Micos, Chieftains, Captains & Warriors have hereunto set our Hands, and Affixed our Seals at the Macklasses the 22d April 1758.

Witness

John McGillivray
John Spencer
Theos. Perriman
William Rae

The Wolf King
Tamatla King
Spicogio Mico
Ockgoy Captain

Richard Hughes
Lauchlan McKintosh
Lewis Fryer (for the
    lower Creeks)
George Galphin
Samuel Alshenar
James Cussings
John Saller
Peter Randon
    his
Alexr. S. McGuen
    mark
    his
Stephen F. Forest
    mark
John Miller

Puckintallahasse Captain
Miccoyahula
The Lieutenant
Uphai Mico
Tutanagee Matla
The Captain
Estabeeg the little Ocgoys
Tuska Leiga of the Coossaws
The Second Man of the little Tellassees
The Captain of the New Town
The long second Man of Wiocas
Upaihitkla Mico of the Cullamees
The Wolf Warrior of the Tusatchees
The King of the Clewalies
Coweta Mico of the White Ground
King of the little Coossaus
Wilumkee
Tuskegies
Caileigies
Eupahlees
Tallassees

Pallachocola May the 1st 1758.

Long King
Oackmulga King
Stump Finger
Oakonne King
Hitchete King
Pallachocola King
The Head Warrior
The Head Warrior of Hitcheatas

Tomeacha
Hoyanne
Cussela King
Usehche King
Micco Togo
Hobog Micco Oakonees
Munchoy of Swaglows

Witness
    Joseph Wright

    Georgia

Register of the Records Office. Recorded in Book C folio 504 the 29th September 1760 & Examined per

    James Whitefield D., Registrar of the Records

Deed executed between Governor Henry Ellis of Georgia and
Thomas and Mary Bosomworth to settle all disputed matters between them, July 24, 1759, received and read Jan. 7, 1761,
C.O. 5/648, E. 13, enclosure C in Governor Ellis' June 27, 1760,
letter to the Board of Trade.

> Articles of Agreement indented concluded and agreed
> upon this twenty fourth day of July one thousand seven
> hundred and fifty nine and in the Thirty third year of
> the Reign of his Majesty King George the second Between Thomas Bosomworth of the Island of St. Catharine in the Province of Georgia, Clerk, and Mary
> his Wife of the one Part and his Excellency Henry
> Ellis Esquire Governor and Commander in Chief of the
> said Province of Georgia and the Members of his Majesty's Council of the said Province of the other Part.

Whereas the said Thomas Bosomworth having long since made
and Sollicited certain Claims and Demands on the Crown, as well
on Account of certain Services done and performèd by the said
Mary his Wife for the said Province of Georgia relative to Indian
Affairs during the Government of the late Trustees for establishing the Colony of Georgia as also respecting certain Islands
known by the Names of Usseba, St. Catharine, and Sappalo, alledged by the said Thomas Bosomworth to have been granted to
him and his said Wife by the Indians, which Islands have lately
been ceded to the Crown by Solemn Treaty made with the Creek
Indians. And Whereas for satisfying and discharging the Demands
of the said Thomas Bosomworth for the Services of the said Mary
his Wife and also for all Claims and Demands whatsoever by them
made on the Crown, it hath been proposed by his said Excellency
Henry Ellis Esquire the Governor by and with the Advice of his
said Majesty's Council to pay and allow unto the said Thomas
Bosomworth the Sum of two thousand one hundred Pounds as herein after mentioned in full payment and satisfaction for the said
Services and all Claims and Demands whatsoever.

And also in Consideration of his having settled and improved
the said Island of St. Catharine to make out his Majesty's Grant
to him of the same. And whereas the said Thomas Bosomworth
being willing to accept of the said Sum of two thousand one hundred Pounds in full payment and satisfaction as aforesaid and in
Consideration thereof to grant and convey all Right and Title by
him or the said Mary his Wife claimed to the said Islands as also to certain other Land called Indian Land near the Town of

Savannah and also to Release and Discharge the Crown of all Claims and Demands whatsoever for the said Services or otherwise howsoever. Now therefore for carrying the Premisses into Execution, It is agreed by these Presents and by and between the said Parties thereto That the said Thomas Bosomworth and Mary his Wife, shall in the first Place, as soon after the signing of these Presents as conveyances shall be tendered to them execute in due form of Law proper and Sufficient Conveyances of all and singular their Right and Title of any they have in and to the said Islands and all other the Lands by them claimed from the Indians unto or to the Use of his Majesty his Heirs and Successors, and also a Release and Discharge of all Claims and Demands whatsoever for the said Service of the said Mary Bosomworth or otherwise howsoever. And that thereupon the said Governor and Council for themselves and their Successors Do hereby agree to pay or cause to be paid unto the said Thomas Bosomworth the Sum of two thousand one hundred Pounds as soon as the same shall be raised by the Sale of the said Islands Usseba and Sappalo provided they shall produce that Sum, if not then such part of the said Sum of two thousand one hundred Pounds as the Purchase Money for the said Islands shall amount to. In Witness whereof as well the said Thomas Bosomworth and Mary his Wife as the said Governor and Council have hereunto set their Hands and Seals the Day and year above written.

Henry Ellis
Pat Houstoun
James Habersham
Francis Harris
Jonathan Bryan
James Edward Powell
William Clifton
William Knox

Thomas Bosomworth
Mary Bosomworth

Sealed and Delivered in Council in Presence of

Henry Yonge
Charles Watson

Deed for St. Catherine's Island executed between Governor Henry Ellis of Georgia and Thomas and Mary Bosomworth to settle all disputed matters between them, April 19, 1760, received and read Jan. 7, 1761, C.O. 5/648, E. 13, enclosure D in Governor Ellis' June 27, 1760, letter to the Board of Trade.

This Indenture made the nineteenth day of April in the thirty third Year of the Reign of his Sovereign Majesty King George the

Second and in the Year of our Lord one thousand seven hundred and sixty Between Thomas Bosomworth of the Island of St. Catharine in the Parish of St. John in the Province of Georgia, Clerk, and Mary his Wife of the one Part and his Excellency Henry Ellis Esquire Captain General and Governour in Chief of the said Province of the other Part. Whereas by certain Articles of Agreement bearing date the twenty fourth Day of July one thousand seven hundred and fifty nine and made between the said Thomas Bosomworth and Mary his Wife of the one Part and the said Henry Ellis Esquire Governor in Chief and the Members of his Majesty's Council of the said Province of the other Part reciting therein.

That Whereas the said Thomas Bosomworth had long since made and Sollicited certain Claims and Demands on the Crown, as well on Account of certain Services done and performed by the said Mary his Wife for the said Province relating to Indian Affairs during the Government of the late Trustees for establishing the Colony of Georgia, as also respecting certain Islands known by the Names of Osseba, St. Catharine and Sappalo alledged by the said Thomas Bosomworth to have been granted to him and his said Wife by the Creek Indians, which Islands had then lately been ceded to the Crown by Solemn Treaty with the said Creek Indians. And that whereas for satisfying and discharging the Demands of the said Thomas Bosomworth for the Services of the said Mary his Wife, and also for all Claims and Demands whatsoever by them made on the Crown it had been proposed by his said Excellency Henry Ellis Esquire the Governor, by and with the Advice of his Majesty's said Council to pay and allow unto the said Thomas Bosomworth the Sum of two thousand one hundred Pounds as therein after mentioned in full Payment and satisfaction for the said Services and all Claims and Demands whatsoever. And also in Consideration of his having setled and improved the said Island of St. Catharine to make out his Majesty's Grant to him of the same. And that Whereas the said Thomas Bosomworth being willing to accept of the said Sum of two thousand one hundred Pounds and his Majesty's Grant of the said Island of St. Catharine in full Payment and satisfaction as aforesaid and in Consideration thereof to grant and Convey all Right and Title by him or the said Mary his Wife claimed to the said Islands, as also to certain other Land called Indian Land near the Town of Savannah. And Also to Release and discharge the Crown of all Claims and Demands whatsoever for the said Services or otherwise howsoever.

And it was by the said Articles further agreed by & between the said Parties thereto That the said Thomas Bosomworth and

Mary his Wife should in the first Place, and as soon after the
signing the said Articles as Conveyances should be tendered to
them; execute in due form of Law proper and sufficient Conveyances of all and singular, their Right and Title in and to the said
Islands and all other the Lands by them claimed from the Indians
unto, or to the Use of his Majesty his Heirs and Successors and
also a Release and discharge of all Claims and Demands whatsoever for the said Services of the said Mary Bosomworth or otherwise howsoever.

And that thereupon the said Governor and Council for themselves and Successors did agree to pay unto the said Thomas
Bosomworth the Sum of two thousand and one hundred Pounds so
soon as the same should be raised by the Sale of the said Islands
of Osseba and Sappalo provided they should produce that Sum.
If not, then such Part thereof as the purchase Money for the said
Islands should amount to, As by the said Articles reference being
thereunto had will more fully and at large appear. And Whereas
the said Islands of Osseba and Sappalo have since been sold at
Public Vendue to the best bidder for the Sum of two thousand and
fifty Pounds only; Now this Indenture Witnesseth that in Pursu-
ance of the said Articles and for finally determining putting an
End to, and extinguishing all Right and Title and all Colour and
Pretence of Right of the said Thomas Bosomworth and Mary his
Wife in and to the said Islands and a certain Tract of Land called
Indian Land.

And also in Consideration of the Sum of two thousand and fifty
Pounds Sterling Money of Great Britain being the Sum for which
the said Islands of Osseba and Sappalo have been sold as aforesaid to them the said Thomas Bosomworth and Mary his Wife or
one of them in hand paid by the said Henry Ellis at or before the
Sealing and Delivery of these Presents in full Payment and Satisfaction of the said Services of the said Mary Bosomworth and of
all Claims Pretensions and Demands whatsoever of them the said
Thomas Bosomworth and Mary his Wife and which they or either
of them hath, or pretend to have on the Crown in any manner
whatsoever or howsoever, the Receipt of which said Sum of two
thousand and fifty Pounds the said Thomas Bosomworth and Mary
his Wife do hereby acknowledge and thereof and therefrom do
hereby acquit and discharge the said Henry Ellis his Heirs Executors & Administrators. They the said Thomas Bosomworth and
Mary his Wife Have granted, Bargained, Sold, aliened, released
and confirmed and by these Presents Do and each of them doth
grant, bargain, Sell, alien, release and confirm unto the said

Henry Ellis (in his actual Possession now being by Virtue of a Bargain and Sale to him thereof made by the said Thomas Bosomworth and Mary his Wife by Indenture bearing Date the Day next before the Day of the Date of these Presents for one whole Year commencing from the Day next before the Day of the Date of the same Indenture for the Consideration of ten shillings therein mentioned and by force of the Statute for transferring Uses into possession) and to his Heirs and Assigns All those the aforesaid Islands of Osseba and Sappalo situate, lying, and being on the Sea Coast within the Limits of the said Province And also All That Tract of Land extending Westward from the Town of Savannah to Pipe Makers Creek in the Province aforesaid commonly called and known by the Name of the Indian Land, together with all Woods, Underwoods, Timber and Timber Trees, Lakes, Ponds, Tithings, Water Courses, Profits, Commodities, Hereditaments and Appurtenances whatsoever to the said Islands and Land called Indian Land belonging or in any wise appertaining, and the Reversion and Reversions Remainder and Remainders thereof. And all the Estate Right, Title, Interest, Property Claim, and Demand whatsoever of him the said Thomas Bosomworth and Mary his Wife or either of them of in and to the said Islands and Land called Indian Land and all and Singular other the Premisses hereby granted and Released or hereby intended so to be with their and every of their of their Appurtenances unto the said Henry Ellis his Heirs and Assigns To and for the only proper Use and Behoof of his Majesty King George the second his Heirs and Successors for Ever, and to and for no other Use Intent, Trust, or Purpose whatsoever.

And this Indenture further Witnesseth that for the Considerations aforesaid and also in Consideration of his Majesty's Grant of the said Island of St. Catharine unto the said Mary Bosomworth and her Heirs to be made out and passed immediately after the Sealing and Delivery of these Presents. They the said Thomas Bosomworth and Mary his Wife for themselves their Heirs Executors Administrators and Assigns Do and each of them Doth hereby release, acquit, and for ever discharge his said Majesty King George the second his Heirs and Successors of and from all Claims, Pretensions, and Demands whatsoever on Account of the Services heretofore done and performed for the Crown by the said Mary Bosomworth or by the said Thomas Bosomworth and Mary his Wife or either of them in any manner however or of any other Matter or thing of what kind or nature so ever. And the said Thomas Bosomworth for himself and for the said Mary his Wife their Heirs Executors and Administrators and for every of them doth hereby Covenant promise and agree to and with the said Henry Ellis his Heirs and Assigns by these Presents in manner following that is to say that it shall and may be lawfull to and for his said Majesty his Heirs and Successors and all and every Person and Persons claiming under him or them from henceforth for ever peaceably and quietly to have hold and enjoy all and singular the Islands Lands and Premisses hereby granted and Released or intended so to be with their and every of their Appurtenances without any Let Suit Trouble or Interruption whatsoever of or by the said Thomas Bosomworth and Mary his Wife their Heirs or Assigns or of or by any other Person or Persons whatsoever lawfully claiming by from under or in Trust for him or them.

And Also that he the said Thomas Bosomworth and Mary his Wife and their Heirs and all and every other Person and Persons lawfully claiming any Estate Right Title or Interest of in or to the said herein before granted and Released Premisses by from, under or in Trust for him or them shall and will at any Time or Times hereafter within the space of five Years next ensuing upon the reasonable request and the proper Costs and Charges in the Law of his said Majesty his Heirs or Successors make, do, and Execute all and every such further and other lawfull and reasonable Act and Acts Thing and Things Conveyances Releases and Assurances in the Law whatsoever for the further better and more perfect and absolute granting conveying and Assuring all and singular the said hereby granted and Released Hereditaments and Premisses with their Appurtenances unto the said Henry Ellis his Heirs and Assigns To the Use of his Majesty his Heirs and Successors as aforesaid as by the said Henry Ellis his Heirs and Assigns or his or their Council learned in the Law shall in that Behalf be reasonably advised or required. In Witness whereof the said Parties to these Presents have Interchangeably set their Hands and Seals the Day and year first above Written.

Thomas Bosomworth	Sealed and Delivered
Mary Bosomworth	In the Presence of

James Habersham
William Clifton
Chas. Watson

I, Mary the Wife of the within named Thomas Bosomworth, do declare that I have freely and without any Complusion signed

Sealed and delivered the within Instrument in Writing passed between the said Thomas Bosomworth and the said Mary of the one Part, and his Excellency Henry Ellis Esquire of the other Part. And I do declare renounce all Title or Claim of Dower that I might claim or be intitled to after the Death of sd Husband to or out of the Lands or Hereditements hereby conveyed. In Witness whereof I have hereunto set my Hand and Seal the Day and year first within written.

            Mary Bosomworth

Acknowledged before me

    Chas. Watson, J.P.

Received the Day and year first within written of the within named Henry Ellis the sum of two thousand and fifty Pounds being the Consideration money within mentioned to be paid.

            Thomas Bosomworth

Witnesses

  James Habersham
  Willm Clifton
  Chas Watson

Georgia

  Register of the Record Office

Recorded in Book C Folio 501 the 29 Day of Septermber 1760 and Examined.

  Per Jas Whitefield, D. Regist of ye Records.

Copy of Indenture between Governor Henry Ellis of Georgia and Thomas and Mary Bosomworth to settle disputed matters between them, April 18, 1760, received and read Jan. 7, 1761, enclosed in Governor Ellis' June 27, 1760, letter to the Board of Trade.

This Indenture made the eighteenth Day of April in the thirty third Year of the Reign of our Sovereign Lord George the second King of Great Britain, France and Ireland and etc. And in the Year of our Lord one thousand seven hundred and sixty Between Thomas Bosomworth of the Island of St. Catharine in the Parish of St. John in the Province of Georgia, Clerk, and Mary his Wife of the one Part and his Excellency Henry Ellis Esquire Captain General and Governor in Chief of the said Province of the other Part.

Witnesseth that for and in Consideration of ten Shillings of lawfull Money of Great Britain to the said Thomas Bosomworth in hand paid by the said Henry Ellis before the Sealing and Delivery thereof the Receipt whereof is hereby acknowledged They the said Thomas Bosomworth and Mary his Wife Have granted bargained and Sold and by these Presents Do and each of them Doth grant bargain and sell unto the said Henry Ellis his Executors Administrators and Assigns All those the Islands of Osseba and Sappalo situate lying and being on the Sea Coast within the Limits of the said Province of Georgia And Also All that Tract of Land extending Westward from the Town of Savannah to Pipe Makers Creek in the Province aforesaid commonly called and known by the Name of the Indian Land together with all Woods Underwoods Timber and Timber Trees, Lakes, Ponds, Fishings, Waters, Water Courses, Profits, Commodities, Hereditaments and Appurtenances whatsoever to the said Island and Land called Indian Land belonging or in any wise appertaining and the Reversion and Reversions Remainder and Remainders thereof To have and to hold the said several Islands of Osseba and Sappalo and the said Land called Indian Land and all and singular other the Premisses herein before mentioned or intended to be hereby granted bargained and Sold with their Appurtenances unto the said Henry Ellis his Executors Administrators and Assigns from the Day next before the Day of the Date of these Presents for and during and unto the full End and Term of one whole Year from thence next ensuing and fully to be compleat and Ended.

Yielding and Paying therefore unto the said Thomas Bosomworth and Mary his Wife their Heirs or Assigns the Rent of one Pepper Corn only To the Intent that by Vertue of these Presents and of the Statute for transferring Uses into Possession the said Henry Ellis may be in the Actual Possession of the hereby bargained and sold Premisses and all and singular other the Premisses herein before mentioned or intended to be hereby bargained and Sold with their and every of their Appurtenances and every

Part and Parcel thereof and may be enabled to accept and take a Grant and Release of the Reversion and Inheritance thereof to him and his Heirs To the only proper Use and Behoof of his Majesty his Heirs and Successors for ever.

In Witness whereof the said Parties have to these Presents interchangeably set their Hands and Seals the Day and Year first above Written.

Sealed and Delivered
in the Presence of   Thomas Bosomworth (Seal)
                                    Mary Bosomworth   (Seal)
    James Habersham
    William Clifton
    Charles Watson

Account of money received by the sale of certain Indian lands and islands, received and read January 7, 1761, C.O. 5/648, E. 14, enclosure E in Governor Ellis' June 27, 1760, letter to the Board of Trade.

1760   SALES OF THE ISLANDS OSSABA & SAPELO.. £ S D

April 14th Paid William Ewen Vendue Master for
           selling the said Islands at Auction   10.10.--

          Paid for advertizing the Sale in the
            Carolina Gazette 4.15.--

                           Ballance . . . 2034.15.--
                                  £2050 -----

April 18th Received from Gray Elliott Esquire   £ S D
           the highest Bidder for the Island
           Ossaba. 1350.--.--

          Recd. from Gray Elliott Esquire the
            highest Bidder for the Island
            Sapelo 700.--.--

                                  £2050.--.--

Colonial Records

1760   SALES OF 146 ACRES OF LAND LYING NEAR   £ S D
THE TOWN OF SAVANNAH

October 20th   Paid Mr. William Ewen Vendue Master
for selling the several Lots at
Auction 16.14.9

                     Ballance 621.15.3

                                £638.10.0

May 14th   By John Gordon & several other   £ S D
Persons for the above Lands
divided in Lots agreeable to a
Plan in the Surveyors Office in
Georgia 638.10.--

ABSTRACT OF RECEIPTS AND PAYMENTS ON
ACCOUNT OF THE ISLANDS OSSABA &
SAPELO & THE 146 ACRES OF LAND LYING
NEAR SAVANNAH.

      Paid Thomas & Mary Bosomworth in   £ S D
discharge of all Claims and demands
on the Crown 2050.--.--

      Ballance remaining in the hands of
Henry Ellis Esquire 606.10.3

                                 £2656.10.3

      Ballance of the Sales of the
Islands Ossaba & Sapelo 2034.15.--

      Ballance of the Sales of the lands
near Savannah 621.15.3

                                 £2656.10.3

Memorial of Pickering Robinson[54] to the Board of Trade July 7, 1760, Savannah, received and read Jan. 7, 1761, C.O. 5/648, E. 15, setting forth his claim to certain lands in Georgia which are included in the tract sold for making satisfaction to the Bosomworths.

Humbly Sheweth

That whereas, in or about the Month of April 1755, your Petitioner, in Pursuance of his Claim before the Governor and Council of the said Province, did obtain Fiats for his Majesties Grants of three several Tracts of Land, containing Five hundred Acres Each, near the Town of Savannah, being part of a Tract called Indian Land which your Petitioner had begun to cultivate.

That, before the making out of said Grants, Caveats were entered in behalf of Thomas Bosomworth, Clerk, and Mary his Wife, who claimed Title to the said Indian Land against any Grant being made out thereof. That your Petitioner nevertheless continued to cultivate the said Tracts, and soon after, having Occasion to leave the Province, did committ the Care of his Plantation to Overseers, who, under your Petitioners Direction did proceed in the Cultivation thereof, and large Improvements have since been made thereon.

That your Petitioner in May last past did return to the said Province where understanding that said Bosomworth, had withdrawn the said Caveats, all matters having been adjusted between him and the Crown. Your Petitioner did thereupon apply to the Governor and Council for making out his Majesty's Grants for the said Tracts, agreable to the Fiats before issued. When your

---

54. Pickering Robinson came to Georgia in 1750 as an expert in sericulture to replace Mary Camuse, the quarrelsome "Worm Woman" of Savannah. The most popular of the instructors sent by the Trustees, Robinson quickly confessed that he did not understand the art of winding silk, and in 1752 Joseph Ottolenghe was sent to aid him. By 1758 Robinson had returned to England. See Amy C. Chambliss, "Silk Days in Georgia," Georgia Magazine, April-May, 1959, 20; Pauline Tyson Williams, "The Silk Industry in Georgia," Georgia Review, VII (1953), 39-49; and Marguerite Hamer, "The Foundation and the Failure of the Silk Industry in Provincial Georgia." North Carolina History Review, XII, (1935), 125-148.

Petitioner was informed that the said Indian Land was by his Majesties Instruction to the Governor directed to be sold, together with certain Islands, Ossaba and Sapella, for the Satisfying the said Thomas Bosomworth for certain Services done and performed for the Crown by the said Mary his Wife, and that the said Islands had accordingly been Sold for Two thousand Pounds of Lawfull Money of Great Brittain, which had been paid him in full for those Services and the said Thomas Bosomworth and Mary his Wife had thereupon released the Crown from all Claims and demands whatsoever.

And Your Petioner was likewise informed that there being no Exception or Reservation made in the said Instructions of such part of the said Indian Land as had been settled and Improved, no Grant therefore could be made to your Petitioner of his said Tracts untill his Majesties Pleasure was known therein.

Your Petitioner therefore most humbly prays Your Lordships to take into Consideration the Promisses, and, in as much as your Petitioner has with great Labour and Expence improved the said Tracts, it would be a very great hardship to him if obliged to purchase his own Improvements.

That Your Lordships would vouchsafe to procure His Majesties Instruction to the Governor or Commander in Chief of the said Province directing him to cause his Majesties free Grants of the said Tracts to be made out to your Petitioner.

Copy of an Order in Council, Aug. 10, 1759, Kensington, received May 21, 1760, by the Board of Trade and read July 8, 1760, C.O. 5/647, D. 16, confirming two acts passed in Georgia in Feb. and March, 1758.

Whereas by Commission under the Great Seal of Great Britain, the Governor Council and Assembly of His Majestys Province of Georgia are Authorized and empowered to make constitute and Ordain Laws Statutes and Ordinances for the Publick Peace Welfare and Good Government of the said Province; Which Laws Statutes and, Ordinances are to be as near as conveniently may be agreable to the Laws and Statutes of this Kingdom and to be transmitted for His Majestys Royal Approbation or Disallowance. And Whereas in pursuance of the said Powers, Two Acts were passed in the said Province in February and March 1758, and transmitted, Entitled as follows. Vizt:

An Act to prevent Private Persons from purchasing

Lands from the Indians, and for preventing persons Trading with them without Licence;

An Act for limiting the time for Persons claiming Lands by Virtue of Warrants of Survey, Allotments, nominal Titles, or Possession derived from and under the late Honourable Trustees for Establishing the Colony of Georgia, their President or Assistants or any others acting by and under their Authority.

Which Acts, having been perused and Considered by the Lords Commissioners for Trade and Plantations, and by them presented to His Majesty at this Board as fit to be confirmed; His Majesty was this day pleased, with the Advice of His Privy Council to declare His Approbation thereof. And pursuant to His Majestys Royal Pleasure thereupon expressed; The said Acts are hereby confirmed, finally enacted and ratified accordingly. Whereof the Governor or Commander in Chief of His Majestys said Province of Georgia, for the time being, and all others, whom it may concern, are to take Notice, and Govern themselves accordingly.

Henry Ellis to the Board of Trade, July 10, 1760, Georgia, received Aug. 27, read Nov. 17, 1760, C.O. 5/648, E. 4, giving an account of the success of his endeavors to prevent the Creeks from joining the Cherokees.

My Lords

In my last of the 7th Ultimate I mentioned to your Lordships, the Murders which had been recently committed in the Creek Country, and the steps we then took in consequence of them, which have happily succeeded so far, as to put a stop to further Violences; but considerable Mischief has arisen from the apprehensions of the people, who upon that occasion, abandoned their Plantations to seek for places of more safety, and thereby Neglected their Crops. But even those are daily returning to their Settlements as their fears Subside.

I have had a great deal of Correspondence with the head Men of the Creek Nation upon the Subject of those Murders. They still insist that it was a Mad affair, in which very few were Concerned, intreat us not to blame a whole people for the Crimes of a few; profess the same regard for us as heretofore; and suggest, that it might be prudent at this time, not to insist on the Murderers being delivered up, lest those rash fellows should be drove to greater lengths.

In answer to which, I have declared my belief of their sincerity and friendship for us; my disinclination to shed the Blood of the Indians, or have any quarrel with them, insisted however, upon the necessity of punishing those Vilains, who had endeavoured by so cruel an outrage, to dissolve our Ancient friendship; but I leave the punishment due, to be inflicted by the Creeks themselves and I have intimated that upon their behaving properly, and affording proofs of their disapprobation of what is past, they would entirely recover our Confidence and Esteem. I reminded them of their Engagements with us, and endeavoured to Convince them, that our Moderation is the effect of our regard to our Treaties, especially that, which I made with them; wherein it is stipulated, that the two Nations should not go to War with each other, for what the Mad People of either might Do, untill no hopes were left, of obtaining redress in a friendly way.

This My Lords is the only course we could take with prudence; for it is certain, that, had we specifyed the Nature and Extent of the satisfaction we expected, and they refused to give it, we must either have retracted, and exposed our inability, or insisted on those terms, which must inevitably have plunged us into a Cruel War; from whence, every bad Consequence might be apprehended. Whereas upon the present plan, we may either allow, or object to the sufficiency of the satisfaction they offer, according as Justice, and our Circumstances may require. After all, whether we shall be able in spite of the efforts of the French, and the Inclinations of the Creeks, to hinder them from assisting the Cherokees, is very uncertain; and may greatly depend upon the Success of Colonel Montgomerys Army, which is now in the Cherokee Country.[55] In the mean time there are some favourable appearances, which encourage us to hope, things will not grow worse, at least, for

---

55. On February 24, 1760, Lord Jeffrey Amherst, Commander-in-chief of the British forces in North America, assigned Colonel Archibald Montgomery of the Seventy-seventh Regiment together with twelve companies of Highlanders, nearly 1,320 officers and men in all, to undertake a punitive expedition against the Cherokees. Joined by South Carolina rangers, provincials, and guides at Ninety-Six in late May, Montgomery's force numbered 1,670 men when he entered Cherokee country in June, 1760.

some time. The Traders who escaped the Massacre are daily arriving here, and at Augusta with Peltry, a considerable share of the Effects of the deceased, has been collected, and some white people still remain in the Creek Country unmolested.

It is now a question difficult to be decided, which is most eligible, the stopping, or permitting Supplys to go again into the Nation. In my own Judgment, both Courses may be dangerous; but I think the former the most so; as the advantages accruing to the Indians from their Traffick with us, is one principal Cause of their adhering to us at any time. And should we deprive them of that, now, I think they would not hesitate, to Join our Enemies. On the other hand, if the Trade is renewd, it may furnish them with the Means of Annoying us more effectually, should their professions of Attachment be insincere. However, in order to gain time, and avoid as much as possible the Evils that threaten in either Case, I have sent an Agent to the Nation, who is to represent to the Creeks, that the Traders are afraid to venture their persons, or the Merchants their Goods amongst them, And to lessen their fears, I have thought of an Expedient which I hope the Nation will embrace, which is this; that a head Man, shall (by National Consent) be chose out of every Town to take charge of the Traders, and their Effects and who shall hereafter, be answerable to the English Governors for them and in Consideration of the faithful discharge of this Trust, Promise a Reward to such head Men respectively every Year and that we will receive all Talks from their Mouths, and distribute the Kings Presents through their hands. Should this regulation take place, and we think proper to avail ourselves of it, it may prove a real Security to the Traders; and, in time, Establish such an Authority, and Subordination among the Indians, as may render the Management of them less difficult than heretofore. At all events, it may divert those Savages from taking any sudden resolution to our prejudice, and we will hope that, as the danger increases in this quarter some effectual measures will speedily be taken for our Security, especially as I have made General Amherst fully acquainted with the defenceless State of this Colony, and the footing we are upon with our Neighbours.

There remains but to assure your Lordships that I have with great diligence and zeal done, and shall continue to do, everything in my power for the Kings Service and the good of my Country.

P.S. 15th July.

I have just received Advices of the 28th Ultimate from the Creek Nation, informing me, that the Indian Embassadors which

I sent there at the breaking out of the present troubles were well received and listend to. The French Captain at the Albama Fort assembled the Creek head Men immediately thereupon, and used every Argument to persuade them to break with the English and Join the Cherokees, but with no effect. The Creeks said it was wrong to press them upon this subject, and endeavour to plunge them into New Troubles, at a time, when they were in a fair way of accommodating those, which they were already involved in.

Henry Ellis to William Pitt, July 10, 1760, Georgia, received Aug. 29, 1760, giving an account of the success of his endeavors to keep the peace with the Creeks and to punish the renegades for murdering traders in the nation.[56]

P.S. I must observe to you Sir, that as the real weakness of this Colony is now generally known, and experiences, which by great Management had been Concealed; it is not probable that it will ever be properly settled, or indeed, that any Persons of real Property will come, or continue in it, unless some effectual Measures are taken for putting the Province in such a state of defence, as not to be at the mercy of its Savage Neighbours.

Henry Ellis to the Board of Trade, Aug. 25, 1760, Georgia, received Nov. 24, 1760, C.O. 5/648, E. 5, transmitting a schedule of laws recently passed and other public papers with observations upon two of the said laws.

My Lords,

My last Letter to your Lordships was dated the 10th Ultimo, and comprehended an Account of the then Situation of Things here, which in respect to the Indians, have since undergone little or no Change.

By the Friendship, Captain Ball, your Lordships will receive the several public Papers and copies of Laws, specified in the Schedule inclosed herewith: The reasons for framing the generality of those Laws, are recited in their respective Preambles,

---

56. This is the same as Ellis' preceding letter of July 10, 1760, to the Board of Trade but with a postscript.

which renders my repeating them unnecessary. There are however, two amongst them, that may require some Remarks of mine; as their Objects are partly the same with two Laws passed heretofore in this Province, which have been repealed. I mean the Jury Act, and an Act for the more easy recovery of small Debts.

The Objections of Sir Matthew Lamb,[57] to the former of these, as set forth in your Lordships Representation to his Majesty of the 21st February 1759, are, I apprehend, in a great measure obviated, in the present Jury Law. The 1st by making Housekeepers and Traders of Property eligible to serve on Petty Jurys, altho' they should not be possessed of the quantity of Land required as a Qualification, in the former Act. The 2d by shortning the Time between the ballotting for Jurors, and holding of the Courts. The 3d By fixing the Qualification of a Grand Juror, greatly above that of a Petty Jury Man. And as to the fourth Objection, it is entirely removed.

In respect to the second of these Acts, That has likewise undergone so considerable an Alteration, as renders it hardly the same Thing. The Sum triable in the Courts of Request has been lessened; the Number of Freeholders who are to assist the Justices in the trial of such Causes, are increased, so as to be equal to a Jury. An Appeal to the General Court is admitted, when the Matter in Litigation exceeds the Value of three Pounds Sterling; And these Courts are to be held but four times in a Year.

I must with submission, beg leave to observe to your Lordships upon this Act; That it is extremely necessary for the Relief of the poor Inhabitants of this Province, who can very ill afford to pay the exorbitant Charges with which the ordinary Proceedings of the Law are attended; no more than the Expences of Travelling from the Distant parts of the Country to Savannah & supporting themselves while they are detained here, which usually amounts to twice the Value in Dispute; to which may be added, the Loss and Inconveniencies these People suffer upon such Occasions by being so long Absent at such a distance from their Affairs and their Families. And really My Lords, I humbly conceive, that the

---

57. Sir Matthew Lamb, an adviser to Georgia Trustee Lord Egmont and legal counsel to the Board of Trade, deemed himself the caretaker of the colony's fortunes before the Board of Trade during the royal period. Lamb usually reviewed Georgia laws sent to the Board. See DNB, XVI, 432.

Settlers in new Countrys, especially, upon so dangerous a Frontier as this, ought to have all manner of encouragement and Indulgence given them, as an equivalent for the Risks they run, and the many hardships they labour under. And I persuade myself Your Lordships will not think that a regard to the Emoluments of the Officers of the General Court, should be put in competition, with the case, and prosperity of a whole Colony.

As soon as the Business of the last Session of Assembly was finished, finding it would be very agreable to the Members, and the People in general that a Period should be put to it, I dissolved the general Assembly, and issued Writs for the calling of another, returnable the 18th Instant. When the new Elected Members met accordingly; were qualified, and the House was adjourned to the 25th November next, as no Affair of Moment required their Sitting at present.

In Regard to other Matters, I do not recollect any thing worth mentioning on this Occasion, save, that while we continue unmolested by the Enemy, We are doing our utmost to put the Country in the best State of Defence our Circumstances will allow. A very good Logg Fort is built at Sunbury; another is constructing at Barrington; two are building on the River Ogechee, and at the North East Angle of this Town one is built at the Public Charge, of two hundred feet square, regularly laid out with four Bastions; in each of which, is a Tower mounting four Cannon; the whole Work is as defencible and substantial, as our Materials of Wood and Earth can make it. At the North West Angle, I have, at my own Expence (the Colony being at present unable to do it) built another Fort, which has cost me upwards of four hundred Pounds Sterling. This, is 120 feet square, flanked with four Bastions also, and a Tower is raised in the Center, mounted with four Cannon. Upon the two other Angles of the Town, We have Erected Block-Houses, each capable of bearing three Cannon, picquetted round; Which are likewise very tenable. Whether We shall have Occasion to avail ourselves of these Works cannot be foreseen. Certain it is, however, that they render us more Respectable in the Eyes of the Indians than we were; and have served to abate considerably the Apprehensions of our Own People.

Henry Ellis to the Board of Trade, Sept. 5, 1760, Georgia, read Nov. 26, 1760, C.O. 5/648, E. 6, respecting the present state of Indian affairs in reference to the conduct of the Creeks and Cherokees.

My Lords

The last Letter I had the Honour to Write to your Lordships was of the 25th past, it contained an Account of the Posture in which our Affairs stood at that Time, and tho' very considerable Alterations have since taken Place in the neighbouring Province by the Retreat of the Army under Colonel Montgomery, and the Surrender of Fort Loudon and its Garrison to the Cherokees, Yet I do not observe that these Events have had any Influence upon our Affairs hitherto.[58] The Creeks still remain quiet, not withstanding the French and the Cherokees cease not earnestly to Sollicit those Indians to enter into the War against Us. The last Advices which I received from their Country were of the 7th Ultimate and appeared rather favourable than otherwise.

The Cause of our Traders being Murdered there in May last, is now pretty well known; and is said to be this: The Efforts We had made to engage the Creeks in a War with the Cherokees were attended with such Effects as afforded Us the greatest hopes of succeeding therein; and alarmed the French to that degree, that they found there was a necessity of exerting themselves in an extraordinary Manner to prevent it. The best Expedient that occurred to them for this Purpose, was it seems, to induce some of their particular Creek Friends, to Massacre our Traders in the Towns

---

58. On Aug. 9, 1760, the British garrison at Fort Loudoun surrendered to the Cherokee Chief Oconostota and, as part of the capitulation agreement, prepared to march to Fort Prince George in South Carolina or to Virginia. Captain Raymond Demeré, a former officer in Oglethorpe's regiment then commander of the Fort Loudoun garrison, dispatched a renegade named McLamore to Governor Bull of South Carolina with the news. The next day, Aug. 10, the departing troops were ambushed and captured by angry Cherokees. Thus it is likely that when Ellis wrote this letter he knew of the surrender but not the ultimate fate of the garrison. Coupled with Montgomery's retreat from Etchoe on June 28, the Fort Loudoun tragedy checked British policy toward the Indians. See R. S. Cotterrill, The Southern Indians: The Story of the Civilized Tribes before Removal (Norman, Okla., 1966), 31-32; David Corkran, The Cherokee Frontier: Conflict and Survival, 1740-1762 (Norman, Okla., 1966); Governor William Bull of South Carolina to Lord Amherst, Oct. 19, 1760, Amherst Papers; B.P.R.O., W.O. 34/35; South Carolina Gazette, Aug. 23, Oct. 18, 1760.

near the Albahma Fort, in full Expectation, that a Proceeding so
atrocious, Could not fail of producing a Rupture between those
Indians and Us. They had Interest enough to carry the first part
of their Plan into Execution; but by the Assistance of our Friends
in the Nation, and the Moderate Conduct We pursued here; the
fatal Consequences which might naturally have been expected
from so cruel an Outrage, at so Critical a Time, have been thus
far prevented, and our Enemies disappointed.

The Agent which I sent to the Creek Country last Month with a
View to recompose Matters there, to Urge the Justice & Necessity
of punishing the Murderers, and endeavour to obtain some Security
for the Persons and Effects of the Traders who might hereafter
go thither, has been well received by the head Men; And is to
have a Meeting the 10th Instant with the Deputies of that Nation,
whereat my Talk will be delivered, and the Resolution of that People thereon declared. Tis a great Pity that we cannot at this Juncture invite those Deputys down here, where every thing could be
settled at once, and much better, than by Means of any Agent;
Which however, our Want of Goods to bestow, and Funds to Maintain those Indians while here, renders impossible. In the Mean
Time, those Savages seem concerned for what has past, and take
a good deal of Pains to collect from the different Towns the Effects
of the deceased; the greatest part whereof is already recovered
and sent down. And a Principal Indian who was Charged with
having abetted the late Murders, in Order to vindicate himself,
went out against the Cherokees lately and returned to Augusta
with one of their Scalps the 20th Ultimate. We likewise learn,
that the generality of the Chactaws, are disposed to live in
Friendship, and keep up a Correspondence with Us. The Traders
who went last to their Nation are arrived in the Creek Country
with profitable Returns, escorted by many Chactaws; but the
French have been endeavouring to Play the same Game in that Nation, as amongst the Creeks; for they prevailed on some of their
Adherents to cut off a Pack Horse Man belonging to the Chactaw
Traders.

This Circumstance, and the unsettled State of Things with the
Creeks, may discourage our People from Venturing that Way again
suddenly. All these Mischiefs have proceeded from our War with
the Cherokees; and as long as it continues, I shall not think the
Professions of Attachment, made to Us by the other Tribes of Indians, much to be depended on; for the French have made them
surprizingly Jealous of the Power, and Ambitious Views of the English, insomuch, that there seems to be a secret Combination of

all the different Nations of Savages upon this part of the Continent, to prevent any further encrease of our Power, and to protect themselves against what we already possess; for they are made to believe We intend exterpating the whole Race, Tribe, after Tribe.

This and many other weighty Considerations, make me very Sollicitous that an Accommodation should be brought about speedily between the Cherokees and Carolina, but the high Spirit of that Government, will not, I imagine, condescend to avail itself of an Expedient which I think might be devised for that Purpose, through the Channel of some of our Creek Friends. Governour Bull seems very capable, and well disposed to restore the Peace of these Parts was he at Liberty to follow his own Judgement, which I suspect he is not, however Your Lordships will be better informed from him, than me, of the true State of these Matters.

Henry Ellis to the Board of Trade, Oct. 20, 1760, Georgia, read Jan. 7, 1761, C.O. 5/648, E. 8, containing an account of Indian affairs, the arrival of Lt.-Gov. James Wright, and his intention to sail to Europe via New York.

My Lords,

The 5th of last month I did myself the honour to write to your Lordships the occurrences of this Place, and my thoughts upon them. Since then, I have rece'd accounts from our Agent and other white People in the Creek Country, importing, that those Indians still behaved with much civility towards them; and repeatedly declared their desire to live in Peace & friendship with us: They Acknowlege satisfaction is due for their past murders; but, our best Friends continue to advise us, not to be peremtory in demanding it at present. Not the guilty should repeat their attempts to involve the two nations in a War, in order to screen themselves from punishment. This seems to us good council, and such as the weak and defenceless state of the Province will compell us to follow.

In a former letter I acquainted your Lordship's that the French had instigated some Chactaws to murder a Pack Horseman belonging to the Traders, who went to that Country last Summer. They flattered themselves that this outrage would effectually interrupt our Corrispondence with those Indians; but it has had a contrary effect, for some of our Chactaw Friends, joined by many Creeks, lately attacked those murderers, near Tombegbie Fort, &

slew two of them, but were prevented Scalping more than one, by the French firing upon them.[59] This Scalp was brought to me a few days agoe by a principal Chactaw Chief, accompanied by several head men of his nation. At a conference I had with them upon that occasion, they presented the scalp and a white wing to me, intreated that I would accept them as an atonement for the Man we lost in their Country, and receive the Chactaws again into our Friendship, that the Trade with the English might be open to them as heretofore. They strongly urged the expediency, and practicability of dispossesing the French of Louisiana, and declared, that when our Troops should attempt it, the Majority of their Nation would rise & join them.

To all which, I gave very satisfactory answers, tho' couched in general terms; I promised that our People should have full liberty to carry plenty of Goods to the Chactaws, but I particularly remarked, that as the Creeks lay between them and us, and might when they pleased stop the Path, & destroy our Traders, so it greatly behoved the Chactaw Nation to guard against such a proceeding, by signifying in a formal manner to the Creeks, (as those Indians did to the Cherokees at the commencement of the present troubles) that if they molested or interrupted our Traders, the Chactaws would resent in a hostile way. This advice they greatly approved of, and promised to communicate faithfully to the head Men of their Country, to whom they were of opinion it would be mighty agreeable. When this discourse was ended, I entertained them with much kindness and respect; made them handsome Presents, and engaged them to visit Governor Bull, to whom they are now going, and who, I doubt not, will make good uses of them.

I am now to acquaint your Lordships that Lieutenant Governor Wright arrived the 3d Ultimate at Charles Town, and the 12 Instant at this Place. I am much pleased with him, for he seems to be a very capable & worthy man, and I dare say, will conduct the Affairs of this Government in the best manner. I have very honestly done him all the Service in my power, as well from inclination as duty. I imagine he will find the interior concerns of the Province, in full as good a situation, as could reasonably be expected. And tho' I think the Colony still on a very ticklish footing with regard to the neighbouring Indians, yet I conceive they may by

---

59. Fort Tombigbee lay on the river of the same name some two hundred miles north of Mobile. It was the principal French fort in Choctaw country in 1760.

prudent management be kept quiet, at least for some time.

Mean while, I cannot help expressing my surprize that his Majestys Southern Provinces should be suffered so long to continue exposed as they are, considering the vicinity, dispositions & power of the French, and the Savage Nations connected with them, in this Quarter. Surely my Lords 'tis disgraceful to us, that whilst our Arms are every where prevailing over the Forces of the most formidable state in Europe, a few Tribes of barbarians, are murdering the Kings Subjects, and ravaging his Provinces in America, with impunity. From my soul I wish such inattention may not be productive of the most mischievious consequences. In hopes to convince General Amherst that my apprehensions are not ill-founded, and if posible to engage some Assistance for this Province before it is too late, I purpose going home by and seeing him at New York. The Voyage is not what I would chuse to make at this season of the year, as it must necessarily be attended with some danger, expence, and great inconvenience to me. But these I shall disregard, as our People desire it, and I think it may be for his Majestys Service.

Since I began this Letter about 50 Creek Indians arrived here with a National Talk (as 'tis call'd) conceived in the same favourable strain with my other Advices from their Country. As I intend leaving the Province in a few days I judged it best not to enter upon any business with them, expecially as some days after these Indians left their Country, I had sent to invite the head-men of their Nation down to Savanah. I have therefore only Introduced the Lieutenant Governor to them and said, what I thought would give them the most favourable impressions of him, and reconcile them to my departure, which they pretended to be concerned for. Should the Creek head-men come down, as I imagine they will, it will for a time interrupt their intercourse with the Cherokees, excite the jealousy of these Indians and in the opinion of the best judges here, answer many other very useful purposes. Thus my Lords have I related every thing material, relative to the Affairs of this Province, that now occurs to me; those of the next, which continue pretty nearly in the same state as when I last touched upon them, I conclude Governor Bull has made your Lordships particularly acquainted with. There remains therefore upon this occasion, only to return your Lordships my most sincere and hearty Acknowlegements for procuring me his Majestys royal Licence to return to Europe, an indulgence which I stood in great need of.

James Wright to the Board of Trade, Oct. 23, 1760, Savannah, read Jan. 7, 1761, C.O. 5/648, E. 9, acquainting the Board of his arrival, of the apparent danger the colony is in, and the necessity of speedy succor.

My Lords

I have the Honour to Acquaint your Lordships that I Arrived here the 11th instant. Governor Ellis to whom this Province is much Indebted, and Who has undoubtedly great Merit, has with great Candour given me the fullest Information he Could with respect to the State and Condition of the Country, Which I take Liberty to assure your Lordships almost Literally Corresponds with the Memorial I had the Honour to Lay before your Lordships Soon after my Appointment, and the more I See, and the more I hear, the More am I Convinced of the Necessity of Immediate Succour, and of the Continuance of Some Troops, even after the Present Difficulties are Surmounted, and dangers over. Your Lordships must be already so fully Apprized of the Situation, Numbers and Power of the Creek Indians, and of the Exposed Condition, and Real Force of this Colony that it is totally Unnecessary, and Would be intruding on your Lordships time to Say more. The Success with which it has Pleased God to Crown His Majesties Arms in the North Part of this Continent, I am very hopefull will Soon Leave them at Liberty, at Least to Put this Southern Frontier in a State of Security, Without which, in Spite of every Effort it must Decline.

Governor Ellis talks of Leaving this in a few days, when I shall begin my Administration, and as Soon as time will Permit make a Report to your Lordships of Matters as they now Stand. It only Remains to Assure your Lordships, that every Measure Shall with Vigilance and Activity to the Utmost Extent of my Poor Abilities, be Exerted, for the Protection and defence of this Province, the Support of His Majesties Interests and Authority, and the good and Prosperity of the Inhabitants.

Sir Mathew Lamb's Report to the Board of Trade, Dec. 2, 1760, Lincoln's Inn, received Dec. 2, 1760, read Jan. 8, 1761, C.O. 5/648, E. 16, on acts passed in Georgia in 1759 and 1760.

My Lords

In Pursuance of Your Lordships Commands Signified to me by

Mr. Pownall's Letter wherein you are pleased to Desire my Opinion in Point of Law upon the following Acts Passed in Georgia in 1759 and in 1760 I have Perused and Considered the same (vizt.)
1. An Act for Appointing Commissioners to Repair and Secure the Foundation of the Lighthouse on Tyber [Tybee] Island
2. An Act to Amend an Act Passed in the third Session of this present General Assembly, Intituled An Act to Prevent private Persons from Purchasing Lands from the Indians And for preventing Persons trading with them without Licence
3. An Act for Establishing and Confirming the Titles of the Several Inhabitants of this Province to their respective Lands and Tenements
4. An Act for holding Special or Extraordinary Courts of Common Pleas for the Trial of Causes arising between Merchants, Strangers and Mariners

Upon Perusal and Consideration of the before mentioned Acts I have no Objections thereto in Point of Law.

James Wright to the Board of Trade, Dec. 23, 1760, Savannah, read Feb. 20, 1761, C.O. 5/648, E. 17, giving an accounting of the Creek Indians, the number of the colony's troops, the great want of other troops to assist them, and presents for the Indians.

My Lords

On the 23d of October last I had the Honour to Acquaint Your Lordships with my Arrival here, the 11th of that Month. Mr. Ellis left this Town the 2d of Nov.; Immediately After Which my Commission was Published. The General Assembly met the 3d of November Agreeable to an Adjournment of Mr. Ellis's, and Proceeded on Business untill the 2d of this Month when they were Adjourned to the 12th of January. It gave me great Satisfaction to find by Addresses, and Congratulatory Messages from all Quarters of the Province, that my Appointment to this Government was Extremely Agreeable & Pleasing to the whole Province, and doubt not but I shall Continue in the Same degree of Esteem & Respect Shewn me at the beginning, If a diligent Pursuit of every Measure that Occurs to me as Conducive to his Majesties Service & the Welfare of the Province in general will Effect it.

In my last I mentioned that as soon as time would Permit, I Should make a Report to Your Lordships on the affairs of this Province as they now Stand, but I'm afraid it will not be in my Power

My Lords to be so full & Clear as I ought, not having had Sufficent Leisure to See, Consider & determine, in the Manner I Could Wish to do, having had down with me since Mr. Ellis went away upwards of 140 Creek Indians, two Parties of 60 odd & a Smaller and Many of them being Head Men & Warriours of Considerable Weight & Consequence in the Nation, they took up much of my time & attention, in order to come at the Clearest & best knowledge of their designs & Intrigues with the French & Cherokees & to Convince them as far as Possible how much it is their Real Interest to Continue in Peace & Friendship with the English and in giving them Proper Written Talks to Carry up with them into their Nation. But they are so Poisoned & Corrupted by the French at Mobile & the Albama Fort That altho' they Acknowledged they were Clearly Convinced that they Could not Subsist without our assistance, and the whole in general gave the Strongest Assurances of their Friendship & good disposition & went Away Perfectly well Pleased and Satisfied. Yet while the French are Suffered to remain so near them, all that can be done at this distance is Soon Counteracted & rendered of little use or Weight in the Nation.

My Lords not to take up your time unnecessarily, The True State of the Creeks is Briefly and Clearly this. The French & Cherokees have used every Art Possible to Prevail on them to Join in the War against us, and there is 2 or 3 very leading Men of the Creeks who have Cherokee Women for their Wives, and who are Avowedly & Professedly in the French & Cherokee Interest, and have Raised a Pretty Considerable Party, by which Means the Creek Nation is divided, Part for Joining against us, and Part for Continuing at Peace. Some of the Elderly & more Cool & Sensible are for Peace, but others of them who are Corrupted by the French with the above Party & a great Many of the young Warriours are for Joining against us, and to which the young People are Strongly excited that they may have an Opportunity of Acquiring the only kind of Reputation Valuable amongst Indians, I mean that of Scalping, and things are at this Moment in the most Critical Situation. If the Cherokees Should have any further Success in Carolina, or if they are even Suffered to Continue as they are, much longer, without being Attack't & Chastised for what they have done, I am Pretty Clear that our Enemies Amongst the Creeks will Prevail, The Consequence of which to this Province in Particular, I need not Trouble Your Lordships to Repeat.

Our whole Strength at this day is as Follows, & no more: Two Troops of Rangers of 70 Men & 5 Officers Each; Three Regiments

of Militia; one at & about Savanah and on the Neck between
Savanah & Ogechee Rivers, Containing 582 Including Officers,
Alarm men, & Superannuated; one at Augusta & Parts Adjacent
now Containing at most 120, & one about Medway & the Southward Containing 193, so that there is 896 Militia, & Officers &
all Included & 150 Rangers, and this my Lords is the whole Present Strength of the Country. Let it formerly have been as it Might,
there is no more now, having Just received the most Exact & Correct returns in the Power of the Colonels to make, and Perhaps
not half, or, I may rather Say, a Quarter Part of these to be in
any Sort depended on in time of Real Danger, but would run away
into the next Province out of Danger. I have indeed Omitted to
Mention the detachment from the Carolina & Independent Company's amounting to 50 Effectives, and this leads me My Lords
to Mention the Absurd Footing this Handfull of Independants are
upon, most of them are doing duty on St. Simons in the Extreme
South Part of this Province, and yet are under the Immediate Order
& Command of the Governor of So. Carolina, at least Claimed to
be so. There is Something so inconsistent & so very Improper &
inconvenient to his Majesties Service in this, that Certainly it
can only Want to be known to your Lordships, to be rectified and
with great Submission my Lords it Seems most requisite that these
three Companys Should be Stationed in the Frontier Country, and
under the direction of the Governor of this Province, & not of Another. And what Troops may be necessary for South Carolina might
be Part of a Regiment. I humbly hope that if Your Lordships think
it Expedient that we Should have Some Troops or assistance here,
you will be Pleased to Represent the same, and that the gross absurdity with respect to the Command Will be rectified.

 I shall my Lords as Soon as I have time & the Season of the
year will Permit to Cross the Swamps & Rivers, take a View of the
Country across from Savannah River, our North Boundary, to Fort
Barrington on the Alatamaha River, the Present South Boundary,
and shall then trouble your Lordships with Such observations as
may Occur. But [I] begg leave now my Lords to Mention the Narrow Extent & Confined South Limits of this Province, and I must
observe that as the Indians Claim to Hold all the Lands above the
Flowing of the Tides which Lyes on our backs Westward, on all
the Rivers Except Savanah, we are hemmed in to very Small Bounds,
as I believe they do not Flow above 30 Miles, and the greatest
Part of which is already taken up, so that no great Encrease of
Inhabitants of any Consideration can be Expected, unless His
Majesty shall be Pleased to declare that all his Territories &

Dominions to the Southward of the River Alatamaha shall be a Part of this Province, and to give Instructions for granting Lands there to his Majesties Subjects.

In General Oglethorpe's time Notwithstanding, the Province was Bounded & Circumscribed as at Present, yet he always Claimed & held the Lands as far as St. Juans, & a Fort was Built & garrisoned at the South End of Cumberland Island, Which is the Inlet that go's up to the River St. Maries [Mary's]. And he then Claimed & held Marks of Possession on Amelia Island & as far as St. Juans. And With great deference, I Presume my Lords That only declaring as above and Authorizing the Governor to grant those Lands Would answer all Ends; & His Majesties Subjects Would Extend their Settlements gradually to the Southward, and in Such manner as would give no Umbrage to Spain, Which Probably an Express Settling of Limits or Bounds Might at Present do. Possibly this may be Premature, but my Zeal to Promote his Majesties Service & the better Settling of this Province, will not Suffer me to omit making Some Mention of this, as it Evidently Appears to me to be the most Effectual Method of drawing Inhabitants to this Frontier Country, because all or very near all the Land between the River Savanah & the Alatamaha on the Sea Coast, that is good for anything or worth Settling, is already taken up untill you go a Considerable Way back into the Country, as far as where the Indians Claim and further. As things are Circumstanced at Present we cannot Attempt to go, unless his Majesty Shall be Pleased to Order a Purchase to be made from them, & then by granting Such Lands, Settlers Would be Encouraged to come. But unless the Province is Extended further South beyond the Alatamaha, or to the West by Purchase from the Indians, I see no great Probability of any Considerable Acquisition of Inhabitants.

My Lords I shall conclude this Part of my letter by assuring your Lordships that you have here a very Just Sketch of the **Present** State & Condition of this Province. How it may have been in Fact heretofore, or how it may have Appeared to Other gentlemen, & have been Represented to your Lordships, I know not, but if there be any Material difference between this & former Accounts given your Lordships, I can only Say, that on the best Information Possible to Come at, thus things Appear to me at **Present**. And my Lords pray give me Leave once more to Repeat that Nothing can Effectually Strengthen & Secure this Province against the Creeks & Chactaw Indians, & give us Peace here, but the Reduction of the French Settlements at the Southward Especially

Mobile & the Albama Fort and without which we shall ever be disturbed & in danger.

The having Such a Number of Indians with me, who came down with high Expectations on an Invitation from Governor Ellis to receive Presents Sent them by His Majesty & those Expectations Raised by my being a New Governor on which Occasion it is always Customary to give them Something more than usual. These Circumstances together with the very Troublesome & Ticklish Situation the Indian affairs are in, Just now, Obliged me to make them more Considerable Presents than I Would Otherwise have done, and which has Sunk deep in those I brought out.

The Expence of Maintaining them, Mending their Guns, &c, as usual, Amounts to a Large Sum. I find the Province greatly Indebted on the Article of Indian Expences, which alone to the 24th of this Month without any one Article of Other Contingent Expences of the Government greatly Exceeds the Same in Mr. Martyns hands Granted by Parliament for the Contingent Services till June next. So that that Sum is Exhausted already, and Governor Ellis was under a Necessity of drawing on Mr. Martyn for the £250, reserved by him for defraying the Expence of distributing the Present I brought out before he went Away, so that my Lords I have not a Shilling to defray the Necessary Contingent Expences of the Government from June 1760 to June 1761, that Sume being Part drawn for & the Ballance not Sufficient to Pay the Account of Indian Expences already incurred by at least an £100 nor a Shilling to pay the above Balance of £100 on the Indian Account already due, nor a Shilling to Defray the further Expence of the Indians that may Come down from this day forward, & which must be very Considerable if they Continue to Come this Winter, & which Nothing can Prevent, but their declaring War against us. So that my Lords you See in what a State this Part of our Finances are at Present.

Governor Ellis left in the Store Presents of the Value of from £250 to £300; great Part of which & Many of those I brought out are already disposed of and as I Expect a great Number of Creeks here, and which as I have Said Nothing can Prevent but a War. Those Presents I have will be Soon gone. And I shall be reduced to the greatest Straights & difficulty for as they have been long told Presents were Coming from the great King. Therefore every one that comes down, will Expect Something, Especially on the first Visit. So that I must Entreat your Lordships that a Supply may be very Speedily Sent out, as there never was more Necessity for keeping the Creeks in Temper than now, as we have not

Sufficient Force to Oppose them and they are not to be reasoned With or Satisfied like Other People. But if they have not Presents & are not Well Entertained when they come hither, they Will go Away disgusted, and its difficult to Say what may be the Consequence. I hope your Lordships Will See this matter as I do, and be of Opinion that an Immediate Supply is absolutely Necesary. I have with the Commissary Stated a Memorandum by Way of direction to Mr. Martyn what things to send out, and what Part to reserve for defraying the Expence already incurred & to be incurred.

It has been Intended that the Seat of Government Should be removed from hence to Ogechee. But my Lords, with Submission, I do not See the great Utility of Such a Measure, for this Place is the most Convenient Situation for the Indian Trade, and there are now Some Considerable Improvements in the Town, and Many People so well Settled that even if Such a Measure was to take Place by far the greatest Part of the Inhabitants would Continue here where we now draw no inconsiderable Trade & Supplies from Carolina, which I Conceive would be lost to this Province, if the Seat of Government was to be removed. The few People there is would be too much divided & Scatter'd about, and if your Lordships should be of opinion that the Tract of Land to the Southward of the Alatamaha Ought to be declared a Part of this Province, then I humbly Conceive Some Spot or Place much further South than Ogechee (Which is but 14 Miles in a direct line from hence) will be more Central & Proper for a Seat of Government than the Place Called Hardwicke, and Which may take Effect Sometime hence when the Country is better Peopled. Your Lordships will Pardon my Throwing this out, as it is a thought amongst Others, on a general Consideration of what may be most for his Majesties Interest & the Welfare of this Province.

Inclosed your Lordship Will receive a Copy of an address Sent to me by the assembly the 20th of last Month. This money meant in that Address is a Balance in Governor Ellis's Hands Amounting to I think near £600 Sterling and my Lords if this Sume might be Applied to the Purchase of Negroes for his Majesties Service, as desired by the Assembly, I really think it Would be a very good thing. By that Means all or most of the Fortifications & Public Works would be kept in constant repair, which Otherwise will be always going to Ruin & decay, or be a Continual Charge to the Province, which they Cannot bear. The Materials of which all the Present Works are made being of no duration, and nothing but

Posts, Plank, Fascines[60] & Sand, Continually Rotting, decaying & falling down. Whereas if there was a Number of Negroes Purchased, they might in time make all the Forts etc. on any River with Tabby (a Composition of Lime, Sand, & Oyster shells, which in a very Short time Cements & becomes like a Solid Natural Rock) which would last for ages & be really defensible, & they Would also keep the Other Forts where these Materials are not to be had in good repair.

    I am under a Necessity of Laying this matter before your Lordships, agreeable to the Address, and begg leave to add that if it may be granted, it will undoubtedly be of great Utility to the Province in doing many very Necessary Works & things, which the Poverty of the People will not allow them to do, and it would also Encourage them to Contribute more Liberally Towards the Other necessary Expences of Government, and Extricating the Province from their debts and Incumbrances. I have not yet had time to Examine the different Laws for Raising & Issuing Money & to make an Exact inquiry into the State of our Finances which I find in very bad Order & every Fund or Means of raising Money Mortgaged & incumbered for Some time to Come and this Governor Ellis found it necessary to do, and I See I shall be Obliged to Continue the Same Method much against my Opinion & Inclination. But what can be done where there is in general such Wretched Poverty & an absolute Necessity of raising money on the most urgent Occasions, even for Immediate defence & Preservation. I shall in my next Endeavour to Lay before your Lordships as Clear a State of our Finances as I am able to Form, which the Constant Hurry & Fatigue I have hitherto been in, renders it Impossible for me to do by this opportunity.

    I Cannot Conclude my Lords without requesting your Lordships interposition for 150 Swivel guns with a Proper Quantity of Shot, I suppose 20 rounds might do as we can also use Musket Bullets in them. These would be Extremely usefull in our Little Forts & Block Houses here, & make them very defensible against Indians. I believe my Lords great Numbers of these Guns Lye useless & almost thrown Away from the Ships in the Kings yards and if a

---

    60. Fascines were bundles of sticks bound together and used to fill ditches and to strengthen the sides of trenches. For a discussion of this type of fortification used in eighteenth-century Georgia, see William A. Hunter, <u>Forts</u> <u>on</u> <u>the</u> <u>Pennsylvania</u> <u>Frontier</u>, <u>1753-1758</u>, (Harrisburg, Pa., 1960).

Number of them Could be sent over here, they would be of infinite Service & no Expence or Loss to the Crown, as I really believe on inquiry t'will be found they are of no use at home & Lye spoiling in the Kings yards. With respect to the Silk Culture, that is over for this year, it being all sent home & the Accounts Settled before I came here, and I Suppose Governor Ellis wrote your Lordships relative thereto. I will Endeavour in my next to Send your Lordships an Exact account of all the White Inhabitants in this Province and also of the Blacks.

Address of the Assembly to Lieutenant Governor James Wright, Nov. 20, 1760, Savannah, received with Wright's letter of Dec. 23, 1760, read Feb. 20, 1761, C.O. 5/648, E. 18, asking that Wright intercede with the Board of Trade to use the money from the sale of the Yamacraw Indian land to purchase Negroes to maintain the colony's defenses.[61]

May it Please your Honor,

The Commons House of Assembly, having Taken into Consideration the incapacity of their Constituents to raise such Large Sumes as will be wanted for Erecting & keeping in Constant repair the Fortifications necessary for the defence of this Province, with a view to relieve them from a Part of this Burthen, Humbly begg that your Honor will be Pleased to use your Interest with the Honorable Board of Trade, that they may intercede with his most gracious Majesty that the Money which hath arisen from the Sales of the Lands to the Westward of the Town of Savanah Commonly known by the Name of the Yammacraw Bluff, may be Appropriated to the use of this Province and Vested in Negroes to be Employed in Carrying on & keeping in repair the Fortifications & Other Public Works.

Signed Grey Elliott, Speaker.

J. West, Treasury Chambers, to John Pownall, Board of Trade, Jan. 7, 1761, London, received and read Jan. 7, 1761, C.O.

---

61. The minutes of the House, Nov. 20, 1760, given in CRG, XIII, 453, do not print this address but refer to its passage.

5/648, E. 7, asking that the Board prepare and lay before the House of Commons an estimate of the civil establishment of Georgia from midsummer 1760 to midsummer 1761.

Sir

I desire You will acquaint the Lords Commissioners of Trade and plantations, That the Chancellor of the Exchequer hath received his Majesty's Commands That their Lordships should prepare and lay before the House of Commons, an Estimate of the Expence attending the Colony of Georgia from the 24th day of June 1760 to Midsummer 1761.

Order in Council, Jan. 16, 1761, Court at St. James, read March 10, 1761, C.O. 5/648, E. 19, instructing Georgia's governor to reissue royal grants to possessors of land between Pipemakers Creek and Savannah originally issued by the Trustee.

Whereas there was this day read at the Board, a Representation from the Lords Commissioners for Trade and plantations dated the 13th of this Instant, Setting forth that Henry Ellis Esquire Governor of His Majesty's province of Georgia hath transmitted to them an Account of his proceedings in the Execution of His late Majesty's Instruction dated the 9th of February 1759, by which he was Authoriz'd for the Reasons and purposes therein set forth, to make Sale of the two Islands of Ossata and Sappalo, and of a Tract of Land lying between the Town of Savannah and Pipemaker's Creek, containing about Four thousand Acres which the Creek Indians ceded to His said Majesty in April 1758.

And that it appears by that Account, That the said Governor found almost the whole of the said four Thousand Acres to be in the actual possession of several Persons who by Virtue of Allotments made by the late Trustees of Georgia, settled there in 1752, and have continued to Cultivate and improve the said Lands ever since; That conceiving that it could not be the Royal Intention that Lands so occupied (tho' not excepted in the said Instruction) should be sold, he therefore forbore giving any Disturbance to the present Possessors; On the contrary he thought it his Duty to recommend them as fit Objects of the Royal Favour and protection, humbly hoping that His Majesty upon consideration of particular Circumstances will be graciously inclined to confirm to them severally their respective possessions.

And as the said Lords Commissioners entirely agree in Opinion with Mr. Ellis as to the Reason and Equity of the Indulgence which he recommends, They therefore propose that His Majesty would be graciously pleased by His Royal Instruction to Authorize the said Governor to give and grant, by Patent, in the usual Form, under the publick Seal of the Colony to each and every Person possessing any Lands between the Town of Savannah and Pipemakers Creek by virtue of any Allotment or Grant from the late Trustees the Quantity of Land whereof he is so possessed, subject to the payment of such Annual Quit Rent as is prescribed by His late Majesty's Instructions to the said Governor.

His Majesty taking the said Representations into Consideration was pleased with the Advice of His Privy Council to approve of what is therein proposed, and to order, as it is hereby ordered, that the said Lords Commissioners for Trade and plantations do prepare a Draught of an Additional Instruction proper to be sent hereupon to the Governor or Commander in Chief of His Majesty's said Province of Georgia, and lay the same before His Majesty at this Board for His Royal Approbation.

James Wright to the Board of Trade, Feb. 20, 1761, Savannah, read April 22, 1761, C.O. 5/648, E. 23, acquainting them of ceremonials used to mourn the passing of late King George II and of his reprieve of a person under sentence of death until his new majesty's pleasure is known.

My Lords,

On the 5th instant I had the Honour to receive your Lordships letter of the 31st October Inclosing an order from the Lords of His Majesties most Honorable Privy Council, Notifying the Death of our late most gracious Sovereign, and directing me to Proclaim the high and Mighty Prince George, Prince of Wales, King of Great Britain, France & Ireland, defender of the Faith, Supreme Lord of the Province of Georgia, and all Other his late Majesties Territories & Dominions in America. Also his Majesties Warrant Authorising me to make use of the old Seal untill a new one is Prepared, also four Printed Copys of his Majesties Proclamation Continuing all officers in the Plantations Civil & Military, untill his Majesties Pleasure Shall be further Signified, also his Majesties Instruction, Containing his Royal directions for an alteration in the Prayers for the Royal Family, and by which letter your Lordships are Pleased to direct me to return a Speedy Account of my Proceedings thereon.

In Obedience to which I have the Honour to Acquaint your Lordships that I immediately gave Orders for assembling as many of the Men belonging to his Majesties Troops of Rangers as could be Spared from their Posts near Savanah, also the Savanah Regiment of Militia, and the Inhabitants in general within a Reasonable distance. I also ordered Minute Guns to be fired from nine to Twelve OClock on Monday, and on Tuesday the 10th Instant.[62] His Most Sacred Majesty King George the Third was in the most Solemn Public and Respectfull manner Proclaimed in Savanah at the Council Chamber, at the Market Place, and in Fort Halifax, under a Triple discharge of Canon & Musketry, and in Presence of a Considerable Number of the Inhabitants, and I Sent Orders with Proper directions for Proclaiming his Majesty at Sunbury, at Frederica, and at Augusta.

His Majesties Proclamation for Continuing all Officers was Published, and sent to be Published at the above Places, an Order likewise Issued for Enforcing his Majesties Instruction for Altering the Prayers for the Royal Family, and Which will be duely Observed in all Parish Churches & other Places of divine worship throughout the Province. I have with the Council Taken the Oaths to his Present Majesty, and shall take care that all others do so in due time. By the Returns made to me His Majesty was in due form Proclaimed at Sunbury and at Frederica on the 14th Instant and at Augusta on the Seventeenth Instant.

There is no Material alteration with Respect to the Sate of Affairs here, Since I had the Honour to write to your Lordships of the 23rd of december, which I have just read over, and beg leave to Confirm & refer to, in every respect. Since that I have had upwards of an 100 more Creek Indians with me, many of them of very great Note, the Wolfe King a very Considerable Man in the Creek Nation, & some others I Prevailed on to go from hence to Charles Town, where seeing the Troops that are come from the Northward, & some Mohawk Indians I hope will make a good Impression.[63]

---

62. As part of the funeral ceremony for George II, in Savannah guns were fired at an interval of one a minute.

63. The "Wolfe King" was the Wolf of the Muccolassus, an Upper Creek town near Fort Toulouse on the Coosa River and a strong supporter of English policies. In Charleston, the Wolf King was entertained by Lieutenant Governor William Bull and duly

More are daily Coming, which Exhausts the Presents very much, & is Attended with a Vast Expence in Entertaining them, Mending their guns, Saddles etc., which they Expect, have always been used to, & will not be Satisfied without. And Therefore my Lords I humbly hope your Lordships Will be Pleased to Recommend a Speedy Supply of Presents etc. as they Will really be much wanted before they can Possibly Reach my Hands. Our Situation is Extremely Critical. I know Numbers of the Creeks have Meetings with the Cherokees in the woods between the two Countries and enter into Engagements & Promises to Join & assist them. I know also that many are Actually Amongst the Cherokees, and Join in the Massacres. 2 Soldiers were lately killed & Scalp't in sight of Fort Prince George, by Fellows who spoke the Creek Language. My Lords the Nation as I have said is greatly divided we have Some Friends amongst them, but many more Enemies, yet as I am well Acquainted & know how to deal with those sort of Creatures I hope I shall be able to keep things quiet till his Majesties arms shall have Leisure to Operate at the Southward, which will give us Effectual Peace & Security, but no Man can Promise or Engage with intire Certainty in the Situation I am, who have such Perfidious wretches to deal with, but My Lords it is in my Power to Engage and assure your Lordships that every Possible Measure Shall be Pursued by me for the Safety and Prosperity of this Province, and which your Lordships may rely upon.

 The State of our Finances & Number of Inhabitants and Negroes I have in Part Prepared, but not Sufficiently Clear to Transmit to your Lordships, but shall very Soon with the Journals. Since my Arrival, on the 29th of last month Mr. William Butler one of his Majesties Council in this Province dyed and Mr. Charles Pryce who was some time ago Appointed, has by letter declined Accepting of that Honour, so that there is now two Vacancies in the Council, of which Agreeable to my Instructions I take the Liberty to Acquaint your lordships and to Recommend Grey Elliott, Clement Martyn, James Read, James deveaux, Elesha Butler & Edmund Tannatt Esquires who I Esteem the best Qualified for that

---

impressed by a review of regular troops and Mohawk Indians preparing to march against the Cherokees in the spring. Returning to the nation, Wolf King vigorously supported the English position and, as a result, Ishenpoaphe and Escochahen, both Upper Creek supporters of the Cherokees, sent firm talks of friendship to Wright. See <u>CRG</u>, VIII, 470, 512, 514.

Trust. With respect to Mr. Martyn my Lords I understand he was formerly in the Council, and Suspended by Mr. Reynolds. How that matter Stands & the Reasons for that Suspension your Lordships best know. Mr. Read was also formerly Named of the Council but I believe not Summoned to Attend, and as I have mentioned those two Gentlemen again, I think it incumbent on me to declare to your Lordships that they appear to me as far as I can Judge, to be Sensible, discreet, well bred Men, and their Characters Extremely good & fair.

My Lords at the Court of Oyer & Terminer held in december last one Richard Swan was found guilty of Murder & a Sentence of Death Passed on him; but the Jury Recommended him to the Court, and desired the Court to Recommend him to me as an object of Mercy, upon which & hearing & Considering the Circumstances of this Case, I thought fit to Reprieve him untill his Majesties Pleasure be known therein, and of which with all Submission I now Acquaint your Lordships, and have the Honour to be with the Utmost respect My Lords.

James Wright to the Board of Trade, Feb., 1761, Savannah, read May 19, 1761, C.O. 5/648, E. 24, transmitting an address from Wright and the Council to His Majesty on his accession to the throne.[64]

My Lords

Having wrote your Lordships very lately with a return of my Proceedings on the Order for Proclaiming his Present Majesty, I have nothing Material to Offer, but beg leave to refer your lordships to those letters.

With this I take the Liberty to inclose to your Lordships an humble Address from myself & the Council to his Majesty, which in all humility & Duty we Could Wish to have Presented, if your Lordships think it Proper. If this should have been Transmitted to one of his Majesties Principal Secretaries of State, I humbly Beg Pardon for Troubling your Lordships, and hope you will be Pleased to order it in the right Course.

Order in Council, March 7, 1761, Court at St. James, received

---

64. This address is given in CRG, VIII, 495.

and read April 1, 1761, C.O. 5/648, E. 21, approving the Board of Trade's representation for Wm. Grover, Chief Justice, William Clifton, Attorney General, and James Habersham, Secretary of the Colony of Georgia and directing warrants to be prepared.

Upon reading this day at the Board a Representation from the Lords Commissioners for Trade and Plantations dated the 11th of this Instant, proposing that William Grover, Esquire, Chief Justice of the Colony of Georgia, William Clifton, Esquire, Attorney General, and James Habersham, Esquire, Secretary of the said Colony, all of whom His late Majesty was pleased to appoint to those Offices, may be continued in the said Offices respectively by His present Majesty's Royal Appointment. His Majesty in Council approving thereof, is pleased to Order, as it is hereby Ordered, that the said William Grover, William Clifton, and James Habersham Esquires be continued in their said Offices respectively. And that the said Lords Commissioners for Trade and Plantations do cause the usual Warrants to be prepared for that purpose and lay the same before His Majesty at this Board, for His Royal Approbation.

Order in Council, March 20, 1761, Court at St. James, received and read April 1, 1761, C.O. 5/648, E. 20, approving the Board of Trade's representation that James Wright be appointed Governor of Georgia and directing a commission and instructions to be prepared.

Upon reading this day at the Board a Representation from the Lords Commissioners for Trade and Plantations dated the 17th of this Instant proposing that James Wright Esquire the present Lieutenant Governor of His Majestys Province of Georgia may be appointed Captain General and Governor in Chief of that Province in the room of Henry Ellis Esquire. His Majesty in Council approving thereof, is pleased to order as it is hereby ordered, that the said James Wright be constituted and appointed Captain General and Governor in Chief of His Majestys said Province of Georgia, in the room of the said Henry Ellis. And that the said Lords Commissioners do prepare a draught of a Commission, and likewise a Warrant for passing such Commission under the Great Seal; and that they do also prepare Draughts of Instructions for the said James Wright, and lay the same before His Majesty at this Board for His Royal Approbation.

Order in Council, March 20, 1761, Court at St. James, received and read April 1, 1761, C.O. 5/648, E. 22, approving the Board of Trade's representation that Gray Elliot be appointed a councillor in Georgia and directing a warrant to be prepared.

Upon reading this day at the Board a Representation from the Lords Commissioners for Trade and Plantations dated the 17th of this Instant Setting forth that Gray Elliot Esquire hath been recommended to them as a Person well qualified to serve His Majesty as a Member of the Council in the Province of Georgia, and therefore proposing that he may be appointed of His Majestys Council in the said Province. His Majesty in Council approving thereof, is pleased to order as it is hereby ordered, that the said Gray Elliot Esquire be constituted and appointed a Member of His Majestys said Council in the Province of Georgia. And that the said Lords Commissioners for Trade and Plantations do cause a Warrant to be prepared for that purpose, and lay the same before His Majesty at this Board for His Royal Approbation.

James Wright to the Board of Trade, April 15, 1761, Savannah, received July 23, 1761, read Sept. 3, 1761, C.O. 5/648, E. 27, containing the present state of the colony's paper currency, Indian affairs, and other matters.

My Lords,

 In the last I had the Honour to write to your Lordship I Proposed to Transmit a State of our Finances here. The Several Emissions of Paper Money made in this Province, and now Passing Current appears to me as Follows, Vizt. Governor Reynolds on the 17 of February 1755, Passed an Act for Establishing a General Loan to the Amount of £7000 Sterling to be lent out to the Inhabitants on Good Security, for a Term not Exceeding Seven years on Interest at 6 per Cent per annum, the Interest to be Paid Annually, and one fourth to become Principal and be let again, and Appropriated at the end of Seven years towards sinking the Principal, and the other 3/4th to be Reserved to his Majesty for the use and defence of the Colony, and in Consequence of this Act, but before it had his Majesties Approbation in Governor Reynold's time was Issued the Sume of £2785.0.0
and on the 28th day of July 1757 Governor Ellis
finding the Province was Indebted £766.14.11-3/4,
Passed a Law Empowering the Commissioners of the

Loan office to Issue under the former Act a
further Sume of 638.7.1-1/2
Which with £128.7.10-1/2 Interest money
in the Treasurers hands, Paid the debt of
£766.14.11-3/4, and by the same Law was
Issued for Exchanging Defaced & Obliter-
ated Bills a further Sume of 200.0.0
And the Other 3/4ths of the interest on the
whole money Issued is appropriated towards
sinking these Sumes. And on the 29th of
March 1759, Another Law was Passed for
Issuing in like manner £799.8.11 more for
the following Purposes Vizt. £300 for Repairing the Church at Savannah, £100 for
Building a Public Magazine, £288.18.11 to
Repair the Light House at Tybee, £59 to make
good the deficiency of the last Tax, £7.10.0
to make good a deficiency that happened by
Fire, and £44 to defray the Expence of Stamping
& Issuing etc.
in all 799.8.11

                                                4422.16.0-1/2

And the Same Law Provides for Sinking this Money[65] in the Following manner vizt, to sink the £300. for repairing the Church,
the moncy Arising on Tavern Licences is Applied. This Sume may
be Annually about £60 and to Sink the £100. for Building the Magazine, the Powder Money is Applied. This Amounts to about £50
per Annum and is Mortgaged or incumbered till Towards the End
of the year 1762. And for Sinking the £288.18.11 for Repairing
the Light House they Appropriate the Fund or Money Arising by

---

65. "Sinking money" from the general appropriations meant
to pay up the amount, thus reducing it, in this case by a tax on
tavern licenses. See William E. Heath, "The Early Colonial
Money System of Georgia," Georgia Historical Quarterly, XIX
(June, 1935), 145-160; M. L. Burstein, "Colonial Currency and
Contemporary Monetary Theory: A Review Article," Explorations
in Entrepreneurial History, III (1966), 220-233; and E. James
Ferguson, "Currency Finance: An Interpretation of Colonial Monetary Practices," William and Mary Quarterly, X (1953), 153-180.

the Impost on Shipping which amounts to from £35. to 40 per Annum so that there is £4422.16.0-1/2 Issued under the general Loan Act, which is to be sunk Partly by Calling in the money let out at Interest, and Partly in the manner herein mentioned and from which it Appears how far our Revenue is Mortgaged & incumbered.

There is also a Law Passed the 24th of April 1760, for Raising £1100. for putting the Town of Savanah in a better state of defence, which is to be sunk in 5 years by a General Tax on Lands & Negroes, £220 each year, so that besides the general Annual Tax for the Support of the Province, there is a debt of £220 per Annum for 5 years and also an Annuity of £50 per Annum to Governor Ellis for a Purchase made of him and I much fear I shall be under a Necessity of going on in the same way, I mean by Raising Money for Purposes of defence etc. and to be Sunk annually by Future Taxes, and that the debt or incumbrance will rather be increased, but this I will avoid if it be Possible. And from this State of our Currency your Lordships See that the whole Sume for the Medium of Trade & all other Purposes whatever only amounts to £5522.16.0-1/2 Sterling, Part of which is Called in & sunk every year, and the whole if Continued is by no means a sufficient Sume, as our Trade increases, and whenever our Indian Affairs, & some other matters formerly mentioned are settled I am clear that both Trade & Inhabitants will increase very Considerably. And this My Lords leads me to Mention the Act Passed the 1st of May 1760 for Issuing £7410. Sterling, which Recites the several former Emissions, & Directs the time & manner of Calling in & Sinking the aforesaid £4422.16.0-1/2. This Act my Lords now Lyes at Home for his Majesties Royal Approbation, and altho' Possibly your Lordships may have Objections to it, yet my Lords unless it is Confirmed, we shall be Reduced to the Utmost Dilemma, for the former Law Expires the 17th of February next, and on this, tho' it never received his Majesties Approbation, does the above Sume depend & circulate, and unless I receive your Lordships directions on this head, and what I may assent to, in case his Majesty shall not be Pleased to Approve of the former Act, we shall really be involved in very great difficulties. Inclosed your Lordships have a Copy of an address I lately received on this Subject, and which I beg Leave to say seems a Matter of great Concern to this Province, and I very Sincerely Wish your Lordships would be Pleased to think Favourably of it.

By the most Exact Account I can get the whole Number of white

Persons Men Women & Children, now in the Province Amounts
to about 6100 & not more, and the Blacks to about 3600, this
latter is Agreeable to the Return of the Tax for the year 1760.
And with this I send your Lordships the Journal of the Proceedings
of the Governor in Council from the 2nd of October 1759 to the
8th of November 1760. The Journal of the Assembly I now send
down to the 12th of January last, and the next will begin with
the Proceedings of the new assembly, which only met on the
24th of March, & the Council Journals 22 October 1759 to 15th
July 1760.

The Indian Affairs Continue much as when I had the Honour
to write last, but it is really a most difficult Task to keep things
quiet with them. I believe my Prevailing on the Wolfe King to
go to Charles Town had a very good Effect, for at his return, he
Seemed greatly Struck at Meeting with some Mohawks & their
Conversation, also with seeing the Troops from New York. I Received a Talk from all the Kings Head Men and Warriours in the
upper Creek Nation the 29th Ultimate with Fresh assurances of
their Peaceable disposition, and that no Mischief shall be done,
at least not with the knowledge or Approbation of the Head Men,
who are all determined to keep Peace with us, and for that End
had sent down some of their Chiefs to desire it might be renewed
Strengthened & Continued. These People make 371 that have
been with me Since Mr. Ellis went away. I have for Some time
Past been Considering of the State of the Indian Trade, and see
many inconveniencies that are like to Attend the Present Method,
as there are too Many Licences granted by which Means several
indiscreet and improper Persons go amongst the Indians and Many
abuses and Irregularities are Committed, but I think very Soon
to lessen the Number of Licences which will Confine the Trade
in fewer hands, and by whom under proper restrictions I hope it
will be Conducted with more discretion and Safety to the Public.

We had a very forward Spring with fine Moderate weather
Which brought on the Mulberry Trees Surprizingly early, and the
Silk Worms were in general hatched and in all Appearance a very
great Prospect, but on the 5th & 6th Instant there was Excessive
Cold, Blasting Winds, and hard black Frost, which I'm Informed
and am much afraid has done great damage to the Worms & destroyed abundance, also hurt the Food for Some time, which may
have a further bad Effect.

The Handfull of Troops we have, I mean our two Troops of
Rangers, I find to be very usefull People, and indeed such as
will always be necessary in this Province, even on a Peace as

the kind of duty they do, and Services they are often Employed on, Cannot be done either by Regimented Soldiers, or independant Companys.

I do not Recollect any thing further Material to Trouble your Lordships with just now, I wrote on the 23rd of October, 23rd of December, 20th February & 9th March, of all which I sent duplicates.

The Journals, etc., Mentioned are in a Box and directed to be put on Board His Majesties Ship Dolphin, Capt. Marlowe.

Copy of the Assembly's Address to Governor Wright, April 13, 1761, Savannah, received July 23, 1761, read Sept. 3, 1761, C.O. 5/648, E. 28, concerning the act passed May 1, 1760, for issuing £7410. sterling, enclosed with Wright's letter of April 15, 1761.[66]

An Abstract of Grants Registered in Georgia from Jan. 27, 1760, to July 27, 1760, read Sept. 3, 1761, C.O. 5/648, E. 29.

Grant Dated 4th December 1759.
To Matthias Kugell for 100 Acres of Land in Christ Church Parish. Registred 1st February 1760.

Grant Dated 2nd October 1759.
To George Knapp for 150 Acres of Land in the Parish of Christ Church. Registred 1st February 1760.

Grant Dated 4th December 1759.
To Richard Cooper for a Lot in Hardwicke. No. 14, Registred 1st February 1760.

Grant Dated 2nd October 1759.
To Peter Tondee for 200 Acres of Land in the Parish of Saint Matthew. Registred 4th February 1760.

Grant Dated 2nd October 1759.
To Peter Tondee for 300 Acres of Land in the Parish of Saint Matthew. Registred 4th February 1760.

---

66. The address is not given here. It may be found in the Journal of the Upper House of the Assembly, April 13, 1761, CRG, XVI, 550.

Colonial Records 311

Grant Dated 2nd October 1759.
To John Goldwire for 300 Acres of Land in the District of Ogeche. Registred 4th February 1760.

Grant Dated 2nd October 1759.
To Benjamin Goldwire for 350 Acres of Land in the District of Ogeche. Registred 5th February 1760.

Grant Dated 2nd October 1759.
To Benjamin Goldwire for 200 Acres of Land in the Parish of Saint Matthew. Registred 5th February 1760.

Grant Dated 4th December 1759.
To Benjamin Goldwire for a Lot in the Town of Savannah No. 1 in the Third tything Anson Ward and 50 Acres of Land in said Tything and Ward. Registred 5th February 1760.

Grant Dated 2nd October 1759.
To Sir Patrick Houstoun for 200 Acres of Land in Christ Church Parish. Registred 6th February 1760.

Grant Dated 2nd October 1759.
To Sir Patrick Houstoun for 481 Acres of Land in Christ Church Parish. Registred 6th February 1760.

Grant Dated 2nd October 1759.
To George Dunbar for 500 Acres of Land in Christ Church Parish. Registred 6th February 1760.

Grant Dated 2nd October 1759.
To Michael Switzer for 250 Acres of Land in the Parish of St. Matthew. Registred 18th February 1760.

Grant Dated 4th December 1759.
To John Long for 250 Acres of Land in Christ Church Parish. Registred 20th February 1760.

Grant Dated 2nd October 1759.
To John Joakim Zubly & other Trustees for 102 Acres of Land at Vernonburgh in the Parish of Christ Church. Registred 22nd February 1760.

Grant Dated 2nd October 1759.
To John Joakim Zubly for 120 Acres of Land in Christ Church Parish. Registred 22nd February 1760.

Grant Dated 2nd October 1759.
To John Joakim Zubly for a Lot in the Town of Savannah No. 1 in the second tything Anson Ward and 50 Acres of Land in said tything & Ward. Registred 22nd February 1760.

Grant Dated 5th February 1760.
To Alexander Brown for 245 Acres of Land in Christ Church Parish. Registred 26th February 1760.

Grant Dated 5th February 1760.
To Alexander Brown for 500 Acres of Land in Christ Church Parish. Registred 26th February 1760.

Grant Dated 5th February 1760.
To John Holmes for 400 Acres of Land in the Parish of Saint Andrew. Registred 26th February 1760.

Grant Dated 5th February 1760.
To Thomas Hooper for a Wharff Lot in the Town of Savannah No.3. Registred 26th February 1760.

Grant Dated 2nd October 1759.
To John Gasper Wertch for 100 Acres of Land in the Parish of Saint Matthew. Registred 8th March 1760.

Grant Dated 2nd October 1759.
To John Gasper Wertch for a Town Lot & Garden Lot in Ebenezer And 50 Acres of Land in the Parish of St. Matthew. Registred 8th March 1760.

Grant Dated 4th December 1759.
To Roderick McIntosh for 500 Acres of Land in the Parish of Saint John. Registred 8th March 1760.

Grant Dated 2nd October 1759.
To John George Powlinger for 50 Acres of Land in the Parish of St. Matthew. Registred 12th March 1760.

Colonial Records 313

Grant Dated 2nd October 1759.
To John Michler for 200 Acres of Land in the Parish of Saint Matthew. Registred 12th March 1760.

Grant Dated 2nd October 1759.
To John Ulrick Fitzer for 50 Acres of Land in the Parish of Saint Matthew. Registred 18th March 1760.

Grant Dated 2nd October 1759.
To John George Buntz for 50 Acres of Land in the Parish of Saint Matthew. Registred 18th March 1760.

Grant Dated 2nd October 1759.
To Christian Bidenback for 50 Acres of Land in the Parish of St. Matthew. Registred 18th March 1760.

Grant Dated 2nd October 1759.
To Frederick Schremp for a Town Lot & Garden Lot in the Town & Township of Ebenezer & 50 Acres of Land in the Parish of Saint Matthew. Registred 19th March 1760.

Grant Dated 2nd October 1759.
To John Kiln for 50 Acres of Land in the Parish of Saint Matthew. Registred 19th March 1760.

Grant Dated 2nd October 1759.
To John Martin Bolzius & other Trustees for a Publick Lot in Ebenezer. Registred 19th March 1760.

Grant Dated 2nd October 1759.
To Jacob Cronenberger for a town Lot in Ebenezer and Parish of St. Matthew. Registred 20th March 1760.

Grant Dated 2nd October 1759.
To John Paul Miller for 2 Lots in Ebenezer & 50 Acres of Land in the Parish of St. Matthew. Registred 20th March 1760.

Grant Dated 2nd October 1759.
To George Miller for 200 Acres of Land in the Parish of Saint Matthew. Registred 20th March 1760.

Grant Dated 2nd October 1759.
To Samuel Lyon for 50 Acres of Land at Skidoway & Parish of Christ Church. Registred 20th March 1760.

Grant Dated 2nd October 1759.
To Adrian Loyer for 50 Acres of Land at Skidoway & Parish of Christ Church. Registred 20th March 1760.

Grant Dated 4th December 1759.
To William Rigden for a Lot in Savannah No. 6 in Belitha tything Heathcote Ward & 50 Acres of Land in said tything & Ward. Registred 21st March 1760.

Grant Dated 4th December 1759.
To Isaac Martin for a Lot in Savannah No. 8 in Digby tything Deckers Ward & 50 Acres of Land in said tything and Ward. Registred 21st March 1760.

Grant Dated 5th February 1760.
To James Jansack for 50 Acres of Land in Christ Church Parish. Registred 21st March 1760.

Grant Dated 5th February 1760.
To James Jansack for 100 Acres of Land in the Parish of Christ Church. Registred 21st March 1760.

Grant Dated 2nd October 1759.
To John Graham for 100 Acres of Land in Christ Church Parish. Registred 21st March 1760.

Grant Dated 2nd October 1759.
To David Cunningham for a Wharff Lot in the Town of Savannah No. 2. Registred 21st March 1760.

Grant Dated 2nd October 1759.
To Joseph Butler in trust for Sarah Boddie for 500 Acres of Land in Christ Church Parish. Registred 28th March 1760.

Grant Dated 2nd October 1759.
To George Sigfirst for 150 Acres of Land in Christ Church Parish. Registred 28th March 1760.

Grant Dated 2nd October 1759.
To Richard Milledge for a Lot No. 6 in the Town of Savannah in Tyrconnel tything Derby Ward & 50 Acres of Land in said tything & Ward. Registred 28th March 1760.

Colonial Records 315

Grant Dated 2nd October 1759.
To Richard Milledge for a Lot No. 7 in the Town of Savannah in Tyrconnel tything Derby Ward And 50 Acres of Land in said tything & Ward. Registred 28th March 1760.

Grant Dated 5th February 1760.
To Charles Pryce for 700 Acres of Land in the Parish of Saint Matthew. Registred 29th March 1760.

Grant Dated 5th February 1760.
To Hannah Ash for 100 Acres of Land in the Parish of Saint Matthew. Registred 29th March 1760.

Grant Dated 5th February 1760.
To Joseph Camuse for a Lot No. 4 in the Town of Savannah in Tyrconnel tything Derby Ward & 50 Acres of Land in said tything & Ward. Registred 1st April 1760.

Grant Dated 5th February 1760.
To Richard Milledge for 500 Acres of Land in the Parish of St. Matthew. Registred 1st April 1760.

Grant Dated 5th February 1760.
To Richard Milledge for 270 Acres of Land in the Parish of Christ Church. Registred 1st April 1760.

Grant Dated 4th December 1759.
To William Mills for 100 Acres of Land in the Parish of St. John. Registred 1st April 1760.

Grant Dated 5th February 1760.
To John Gordon for a Lot No. 2 in the Town of Savannah in the second tything Reynolds Ward & 50 Acres of Land in said tything & Ward. Registred 1st April 1760.

Grant Dated 5th February 1760.
To James Brown for 396 Acres of Land in the Parish of St. Paul. Registred 1st April 1760.

Grant Dated 5th February 1760.
To James Brown for a Lot in the town of Augusta No. 1 in the first Row. Registred 1st April 1760.

Grant Dated 2nd October 1759.
To John Graham for 500 Acres of Land in the Parish of Saint Matthew. Registred 1st April 1760.

Grant Dated 2nd October 1759.
To John Graham for 100 Acres of Land in the Parish of Saint Matthew. Registred 1st April 1760.

Grant Dated 4th December 1759.
To Christian Camphert for a Lot No. 7 in the town of Savannah in the Third Tything Anson Ward & 50 Acres of Land in said tything & Ward. Registred 14th April 1760.

Grant Dated 4th December 1759.
To Francis Lee for 200 Acres of Land in the Parish Saint Andrew. Registred 14th April 1760.

Grant Dated 4th December 1759.
To John Jagger for a Wharff Lot in the town of Savannah. Registred 15th April 1760.

Grant Dated 4th December 1759.
To Matthew Roch in trust for his Sons a Wharff Lot in the Town of Savannah. Registered 15th April 1760.

Grant Dated 4th December 1759.
To Thomas Clancey for 116 Acres of Land in the Parish of Saint John. Registred 15th April 1760.

Grant Dated 4th December 1759.
To Jonas Mick for 50 Acres of Land in the Parish of Saint Matthew. Registred 18th April 1760.

Grant Dated 4th December 1759.
To Gasper Garbet & Frederick Herb for a Lot in the town of Savannah No. 7 in the fourth tything Anson Ward & 50 Acres of Land in said Tything and Ward. Registred 18th April 1760.

Grant Dated 4th December 1759.
To Abigail Minis for a Lot in the Town of Savanah No. 5 in Hucks tything Percival Ward & 50 Acres of Land in said Tything & Ward. Registred 18th April 1760.

Grant Dated 4th December 1759.
To Abigail Minis for a Lot No. 3 in the Town of Savannah in Hucks

tything Percival Ward & Garden Lot of 5 Acres. Registred 18th April 1760.

Grant Dated 4th December 1759.
To Peter Dowle for a Lot at Vernonburgh together 50 Acres of Land. Registred 19th April 1760.

Grant Dated 4th December 1759.
To David Fisher for a Lot and 50 Acres of Land at Vernonburgh. Registred 19th April 1760.

Grant Dated 4th December 1759.
To Joseph Oakes for 300 Acres of Land in the Parish of Saint Paul. Registred 22nd April 1760.

Grant Dated 4th December 1759.
To Sarah Wisely for 50 Acres of Land in the Parish of Saint Paul. Registred 22nd April 1760.

Grant Dated 4th December 1759.
To Henry Tristee for 50 Acres of Land in the Parish of Saint Matthew. Registred 22nd April 1760.

Grant Dated 4th December 1759.
To Elizabeth Hendrick for a Lot in the Town of Savannah No. 3 In Sloper tything Percival Ward and 50 Acres of Land in said tything & Ward. Registred 22nd April 1760.

Grant Dated 4th December 1759.
To Thomas Millichamp for a Lot in the Town of Savannah No. 10 in Tower tything Deckers Ward And 50 Acres of Land in said tything and Ward. Registred 22nd April 1760.

Grant Dated 4th December 1759.
To Richard Dowdy for 50 Acres of Land in the Parish of Christ Church. Registred 22nd April 1760.

Grant Dated 4th December 1759.
To Thomas Frazer for 2 Lots and 50 Acres of Land at Vernonburgh. Registred 23rd April 1760.

Grant Dated 4th December 1759.
To Sigismund Beltz for a Lot and 50 Acres of Land at Vernonburgh. Registred 23rd April 1760.

Grant Dated 5th February 1760.
To Richard Dowdy for 50 Acres of Land in the Parish of St. Matthew. Registred 23rd April 1760.

Grant Dated 4th December 1759.
To Edward Hammond for 100 Acres of Land in the Parish of St. Andrew. Registred 28th April 1760.

Grant Dated 4th December 1759.
To John Elliott for 250 Acres of Land in the Parish of Saint John. Registred 1st May 1760.

Grant Dated 4th December 1759.
To Ann McIntosh for 450 Acres of Land in the Parish of St. Andrew. Registred 1st May 1760.

Grant Dated 4th December 1759.
To John Barnaby for 250 Acres of Land in the Parish of Saint John. Registred 2nd May 1760.

Grant Dated 4th December 1759.
To George Denninger for 50 Acres of Land in the Parish of Saint Matthew. Registred 2nd May 1760.

Grant Dated 4th December 1759.
To Jacob Nongazer for 2 Lots And 100 Acres of Land at Vernonburgh. Registred 2nd May 1760.

Grant Dated 4th December 1759.
To Adam Ordner for a Lot And 100 Acres of Land at Vernonburgh. Registred 2nd May 1760.

Grant Dated 4th December 1759.
To John Smyth for 200 Acres of Land in the Parish of Saint Matthew. Registred 2nd May 1760.

Grant Dated 4th December 1759.
To Urban Buntz for 150 Acres of Land in the Parish of Saint Matthew. Registred 2nd May 1760.

Grant Dated 4th December 1759.
To Jacob Mohr for 50 Acres of Land in the Parish of Saint Matthew. Registred 2nd May 1760.

Colonial Records 319

Grant Dated 5th February 1760.
To Benjamin Sheftal for 200 Acres of Land in the Parish of St. Andrew. Registred 6th May 1760.

Grant Dated 5th February 1760.
To Benjamin Irwin for 200 Acres of Land in the Parish of St. Andrew. Registred 6th May 1760.

Grant Dated 5th February 1760.
To Theobald Keifer for a town Lot and Garden Lot in the town and Township of Ebenezer. Registred 6th May 1760.

Grant Dated 18th April 1760.
To Joseph Barker for 200 Acres of Land in the Parish of St. Phillip. Registred 6th May 1760.

Grant Dated 5th February 1760.
To Sarah Rigby for a Lot No. 2 in the town of Savannah And Garden Lot of 5 Acres in Jekyl tything Derby Ward. Registred 10th May 1760.

Grant Dated 5th February 1760.
To Stephen Cater for 415 Acres of Land in the Parish of St. John. Registred 12th May 1760.

Grant Dated 5th February 1760.
To Martin Dasher for 100 Acres of Land in the Parish of St. Matthew. Registred 12th May 1760.

Grant Dated 5th February 1760.
To George Zeighler for 100 Acres of Land in the Parish of Saint Matthew. Registred 12th May 1760.

Grant Dated 5th February 1760.
To John Adam Treutlen for 50 Acres of Land in the Parish of St. Matthew. Registred 12th May 1760.

Grant Dated 4th December 1759.
To Joseph Gibbons for 150 Acres of Land in the Parish of Christ Church. Registred 16th May 1760.

Grant Dated 4th December 1759.
To Joseph Gibbons for a Lot No. 7 in the Town of Savannah in

Vernon tything Heathcote Ward And 50 Acres of Land in said tything & Ward. Registred 16th May 1760.

Grant Dated 4th December 1759.
To Joseph Gibbons for a Wharff Lot No. 6 in the town of Savannah. Registred 16th May 1760.

Grant Dated 4th December 1759.
To Joseph Gibbons for 1000 Acres of Land in the Parish of Christ Church. Registred 16th May 1760.

Grant Dated 6th December 1757.
To Thomas White for 100 Acres of Land in the District of Newport. Registred 3rd June 1760.

Grant Dated 4th December 1759.
To James Monroe for 150 Acres of Land in the Parish of Saint Andrew. Registred 9th June 1760.

Grant Dated 4th December 1759.
To Benjamin Farley for 62 Acres of Land in the Parish of Christ Church. Registred 9th June 1760.

Grant Dated 13th April 1760.
To John Gordon for 3 Lots No. 4, 5 & 10 West of the town of Savannah. Registred 10th June 1760.

Grant Dated 4th December 1759.
To George Threadcroft for 200 Acres of Land in the Parish of Saint Andrew. Registred 11th June 1760.

Grant Dated 4th December 1759.
To James Westly for 200 Acres of Land in the Parish of Saint Andrew. Registred 11th June 1760.

Grant Dated 5th February 1760.
To George Senior for 300 Acres of Land in the Parish of Saint Andrew. Registred 12th June 1760.

Grant Dated 5th February 1760.
To Margaret Grounidge for 100 Acres of Land in the Parish of St. Andrew. Registred 12th June 1760.

Colonial Records 321

Grant Dated 13th June 1760.
To Mary Bosomworth for 6200 Acres of Land in the Parish of St. John. Registred 14th June 1760.

Grant Dated 4th December 1759.
To John Ulrick Niedlinger for 150 Acres of Land in the Parish of St. Matthew. Registred 21st June 1760.

Grant Dated 18th April 1760.
To John Joakim Zubly for 500 Acres of Land in Christ Church Parish. Registred 21st June 1760.

Grant Dated 7th August 1759.
To Jonathan Bryan Esquire for 83 Acres of Land in the Parish of St. Andrew. Registred 1st July 1760.

Grant Dated 5th February 1760.
To Nicholas Cronenberger for 200 Acres of Land in the Parish of St. Matthew. Registred 2nd July 1760.

Grant Dated 5th February 1760.
To Benjamin Williamson for 250 Acres of Land in the Parish of St. George. Registred 3rd July 1760.

Grant Dated 5th February 1760.
To Thomas Sisson for 150 Acres of Land in the Parish of St. George. Registred 3rd July 1760.

Grant Dated 30th April 1760.
To Joseph Gibbons for a Lot No. 11 West of the Town of Savannah. Registred 4th July 1760.

Grant Dated 4th December 1759.
To Samuel Hammer for a Lot And 50 Acres of Land at Vernonburgh. Registred 9th July 1760.

Grant Dated 4th December 1759.
To Joseph Gibbons for a Lot No. 10 in the town of Savannah in Carpenter tything Deckers Ward And 50 Acres of Land in said tything & Ward. Registred 22nd July 1760.

The aforesaid abstract of the grants Registered from the 27 of January 1760 To the 27th of July 1760 compared with the Register

Book at Savannah this 26th day of July 1760.

Pat Houstoun, Register

An Abstract of Grants Registered in Georgia from July 27, 1760, to Jan. 27, 1761, read Sept. 3, 1761, C.O. 5/648, E. 30.

Grant dated 5th February 1760.
To Jacob Tiess for 2 Lots and 100 acres of land at Vernonburgh. Registred 5th August 1760.

Grant Dated 4th December 1759.
To Belthazer Reizer for 200 acres of land in the parish of St. Matthew. Registred 25th August 1760.

Grant dated 4th december 1759.
To Belthazer Reizer for 2 Lots in Ebenezer and 50 acres of land in the parish of St. Matthew. Registred 25th August 1760.

Grant dated 4th December 1759.
To Jacob & Elizabeath Maurer for 50 acres of Land in the parish of St. Matthew. Registred 26th August 1760.

Grant dated 5th February 1760.
To Jacob Dusseign for 150 acres of land in the parish of St. Matthew. Registred 26th August 1760.

Grant dated 1st July 1760.
To William Handley for a Wharff lot No. 4 in Savannah. Registred 27th day of August 1760.

Grant dated 1st July 1760.
To John Shave for 150 acres of land in the parish of St. John. Registred 1st day of September 1760.

Grant dated 1st July 1760.
To Isaac Lines for 300 acres of Land in the parish of St. Andrew. Registred 1st day of September 1760.

Grant dated 1st July 1760.
To John Steuart for a town Lot &c in Savannah together 50 acres of Land. Registred 2nd September 1760.

Grant dated 1st July 1760.
To James McHenry for 150 acres of Land in the parish of St. George. Registred 2nd day of September 1760.

Grant dated 1st July 1760.
To William Johnson for 50 acres of Land in the parish of St. John. Registred 3rd day of September 1760.

Grant Dated 1st July 1760.
To Matthias West for 250 acres of Land in Christ Church Parish. Registred 3rd September 1760.

Grant Dated 1st July 1760.
To George Bellet for 100 acres of Land in Christ Church Parish. Registred 4th September 1760.

Grant Dated 1st July 1760.
To John Gallash for 100 acres of Land in Christ Church Parish. Registred 5th September 1760.

Grant Dated 1st July 1760.
To Adrian Loyer for 300 acres of Land in Christ Church Parish. Registred 5th September 1760.

Grant Dated 1st July 1760.
To John Wereat for a Wharff Lot in Savannah. Registred 10th day of September 1760.

Grant dated 25th August 1760.
To Thomas Lloyd for a town Lot No. 8 in Savannah. Registred 11th day of September 1760.

Grant dated 1st May 1759.
To William Butler for 500 acres of Land at Ogechee. Registred 11th September 1760.

Grant dated 1st May 1759.
To William Butler for 200 acres of Land in the district of Great Ogechee. Registred 12th September 1760.

Grant dated 1st May 1759.
To William Butler for 100 acres of Land in the parish of St. Phillip. Registred 12th September 1760.

Grant Dated 5th February 1760.
To David Unseld for 200 acres of Land in the parish of St. Matthew. Registred 15th September 1760.

Grant Dated 4th December 1759.
To Andrew Sneider for 150 acres of Land in the parish of St. Matthew. Registred 15th day of September 1760.

Grant dated 4th December 1759.
To Andrew Sneider for 100 acres of Land in the parish of St. Matthew. Registred 16th September 1760.

Grant dated 1st July 1760.
To William Grover for 600 acres of Land in the parish of St. Matthew. Registred 28th September 1760.

Grant dated 4th december 1759.
To James Tebeau for a town Lot in Savannah No. 9. Registred 29th day of September 1760.

Grant dated 1st July 1760.
To Elizabeath Anderson in trust for 500 acres of land in Christ Church Parish. Registred 29th September 1760.

Grant dated 1st July 1760.
To Elizabeath Anderson in trust for her son for a town Lot & in Savannah together 50 acres of Land. Registred 30th September 1760.

Grant dated 1st July 1760.
To William Knox Esquire for 600 acres of Land in the parish of St. Matthew. Registred 1st October 1760.

Grant Dated 1st July 1760.
To William Knox Esquire for 50 acres of Land in the parish of St. Matthew. Registred 1st day of October 1760.

Grant dated 1st July 1760.
To William Baker for 100 acres of Land in the parish of St. John. Registred 2nd day of October 1760.

Grant dated 1st July 1760.
To William Baker for 100 acres of Land in the parish of St. John. Registred 2nd day of October 1760.

Grant dated 1st July 1760.
To John Stewart for 300 acres of land in the parish of St. John. Registred 3rd October 1760.

Grant dated 1st July 1760.
To Michael Downer for 50 acres of Land in the Village of Goshen & parish of St. Matthew. Registred 5th October 1760.

Grant Dated 1st July 1760.
To Jacob Ports for 100 acres of Land in the parish of St. Matthew. Registred 5th October 1760.

Grant Dated 7th November 1758.
To Alexander McDonald for 50 acres of Land in the parish of St. Andrew. Registred 9th October 1760.

Grant dated 1st July 1760.
To George Phillip Ports for 50 acres of land in the parish of St. Matthew. Registred 10th October 1760.

Grant dated 1st July 1760.
To Grey Elliott Esquire for 300 acres of Land in the parish of St. John. Registed 13th October 1760.

Grant dated 5th September 1758.
To Jacob Maurier for 200 acres of Land in the parish of St. Matthew. Registred 15th October 1760.

Grant dated 25th September 1760.
To Richard Hubbard for 200 acres of Land in the parish of St. George. Registred 16th October 1760.

Grant Dated 25th September 1760.
To Richard Hubbard for 100 acres of Land in the parish of St. George. Registred 16th October 1760.

Grant dated 1st May 1759.
To John Winn for 350 acres of Land in the parish of St. John. Registred 17th October 1760.

Grant Dated 1st July 1760.
To John McLeod for 100 acres of land in the parish of St. Phillip. Registred 18th October 1760.

Grant Dated 7th August 1759.
To Edward MacGuire for 250 acres of Land in the parish of St. John. Registred 20th October 1760.

Grant dated 5th February 1760.
To Richard Ratten for 300 acres of Land in the parish of St. Matthew. Registred 21st October 1760.

Grant dated 1st July 1760.
To John Quarterman for 150 acres of Land in the parish of St. John. Registred 22nd October 1760.

Grant Dated 7th August 1759.
To Palmer Goulding for 500 acres of land in the parish of St. Andrew. Registred 23rd October 1760.

Grant Dated 1st July 1760.
To John Lawson for 100 acres of Land in the parish of St. John. Registred 24th day of October 1760.

Grant dated 1st July 1760.
To John Reimshart for 100 acres of Land in the parish St. Matthew. Registred 25th October 1760.

Grant dated 7th February 1758.
To Thomas Red for 200 acres of land in the parish of St. Paul. Registred 25th October 1760.

Grant dated 2nd October 1759.
To Thomas Red for 300 acres of Land in the parish of St. George. Registred 27th October 1760.

Grant dated 27th October 1760.
To Joseph Ottolenghe for 300 acres of land in Christ Church Parish. Registred 29th October 1760.

Grant dated 27th October 1760.
To James Edward Powell for 20 acres of Land in the parish of St. Phillip. Registred 29th October 1760.

Grant dated 5th February 1760.
To William Wilson for 100 acres of Land in the parish of St. John. Registred 30th day of October 1760.

Colonial Records 327

Grant dated 4th december 1759.
To James Grant for 50 acres of land in the parish of St. Matthew. Registred 30th October 1760.

Grant dated 7th February 1758.
To Norman McDonald for 100 acres of Land in the district of Darian. Registred 31st day of October 1760.

Grant dated 7th February 1758.
To Joseph MacGuire for 200 acres of Land in the district of Newport. Registred 1st day of November 1760.

Grant dated 25th September 1760.
To John Simpson for a Public Lot in the town of Savannah Letter B. Registred 3rd day of November 1760.

Grant Dated 7th February 1758.
To Frederick Helvenstine for 200 acres of Land in the District of Goshen. Registred 5th November 1760.

Grant Dated 7th August 1759.
To William Johnson for 100 acres of Land in the parish of St. John. Registred 5th November 1760.

Grant Dated 5th September 1758.
To Minis Minis for a town Lot in Hardwicke No. 123. Registred 6th November 1760.

Grant Dated 1st May 1759.
To John Hopkins for 100 acres of Land in the District of Ebenezer. Registred 7th November 1760.

Grant Dated 7th February 1758.
To George Sheraus for 50 acres of Land in the District of Goshen. Registred 8th November 1760.

Grant Dated 7th November 1758.
To John Cornberger for 50 acres of land in the parish of St. Matthew. Registred 8th November 1760.

Grant Dated 1st July 1760.
To Benjamin Farley for 150 acres of land in the parish of St. Andrew. Registred 11th November 1760.

Grant Dated 28th March 1758.
To Ralph Kilgore for 100 acres of Land in the District of Augusta. Registred 12th November 1760.

Grant Dated 25th September 1760.
To Stephen Millen for 100 acres of Land in the parish of St. Matthew. Registred 12th November 1760.

Grant Dated 28th March 1758.
To Christian Dasher for 100 acres of Land in the district of Goshen. Registred 13th day of November 1760.

Grant Dated 5th September 1758.
To Simon Rouviere for 150 acres of Land in the district of Hampstead & Highgate. Registred 13th November 1760.

Grant dated 5th September 1758.
To John Rouviere for 300 acres of land in the district of Savannah. Registred 14th November 1760.

Grant Dated 4th July 1758.
To Hugh Morrison for 250 acres of Land in the parish of St. Andrew. Registred 13th day of November 1760.

Grant dated 2nd October 1759.
To Elizabeath Young for a town Lot &c in Savannah together 50 acres of Land. Registred 15th November 1760.

Grant Dated 2nd October 1759.
To Isaac Younge for 380 acres of land in Christ Church Parish. Registred 17th November 1760.

Grant Dated 2nd October 1759.
To Isaac Younge for 550 acres of land in Christ Church Parish. Registred 17th November 1760.

Grant Dated 4th July 1758.
To James Germany for 500 acres of Land in the parish of St. George. Registred 18th November 1760.

Grant Dated 1st July 1760.
To Christian Gamphert for 50 acres of land in Vernonburgh. Registred 18th November 1760.

Colonial Records 329

Grant dated 15th May 1756.
To David Dicks for 500 acres of land on the South side of Great Ogechee. Registred 19th November 1760.

Grant dated 4th december 1759.
To James Deveaux for 380 acres of Land in the parish of St. Matthew. Registred 2nd December 1760.

Grant dated 8th September 1756.
To James Deveaux for 500 acres of land at Little Ogechee. Registred 3rd day of December 1760.

Grant dated 1st July 1760.
To Parmenus Way for 100 acres of Land in the parish of St. John. Registred 4th December 1760.

Grant dated 25th September 1760.
To John Flerl for 100 acres of Land in the parish of St. Matthew. Registred 4th December 1760.

Grant dated 25th September 1760.
To John Flerl for 100 acres of Land in the parish of St. Matthew. Registred 5th December 1760.

Grant Dated 25th September 1760.
To David Stiner for 100 acres of Land in the parish of St. Matthew. Registred 5th December 1760.

Grant dated 4th December 1759.
To James Deveaux for 100 acres of land at Skidoway. Registred 5th December 1760.

Grant dated 25th September 1760.
To James Deveaux for a town lot Letter M in Savannah. Registred 6th december 1760.

Grant dated 25th September 1760.
To James Deveaux for a Wharff lot No. 3 in Savannah. Registred 6th day of December 1760.

Grant dated 1st July 1760.
To John Gordon for a Wharf lot No. 2 in Savannah. Registred 30th September 1760 which was omitted.

Grant dated 4th december 1759.
To William Deveaux for a Lot No. 130 in Hardwicke. Registred 9th December 1760.

Grant dated 4th december 1759.
To Thomas Schweighoffer for a town lot No. 10 &c in Ebenezer Together 50 acres of land. Registred 9th december 1760.

Grant dated 4th december 1759.
To Gilbert Grant for 100 acres of Land in the parish of St. Andrew. Registred 10th December 1760.

Grant dated 1st July 1760.
To John Monroe for 155 acres of land in the parish of St. Andrew. Registred 10th december 1760.

Grant dated 1st July 1760.
To Conrade Rahn for 100 acres of Land in the parish of St. Matthew. Registred 11th December 1760.

Grant dated 1st July 1760.
To John Kugell for 200 acres of land in the parish of St. Matthew. Registred 11th December 1760.

Grant Dated 1st July 1760.
To Christian Rottenberger for 200 acres of Land in the parish of St. Matthew. Registred 12th December 1760.

Grant dated 25th September 1760.
To Jacob Metzgar for 250 acres of Land in the parish of St. Matthew. Registred 12th December 1760.

Grant Dated 1st July 1760.
To Jacob Miers for 100 acres of Land in the parish of St. Matthew. Registred 12th December 1760.

Grant Dated 1st July 1760.
To John Brady for 100 acres of Land in the parish of St. Matthew. Registred 13th December 1760.

Grand Dated 25th September 1760.
To Pickering Robinson for 150 acres of Land in Christ Church Parish. Registred 8th January 1761.

Grant Dated 25th September 1760.
To Pickering Robinson for 1000 acres of land in Christ Church Parish. Registred 9th January 1761.

Grant dated 25th September 1760.
To Pickering Robinson for a Lot No. 95 in Hardwicke. Registred 9th January 1761.

Grant dated 25th September 1760.
To William Knox Esquire for a Lot No. 3 west of the town of Savannah. Registred 10th January 1761.

Grant dated 1st July 1760.
To John Joakim Zubly for 127 acres of land in the parish of St. Matthew. Registred 10th January 1761.

Grant dated 31st October 1760.
To Grey Elliott Esquire for the Island of Sapelo containing 9520 acres in the parish of St. John. Registred 12th January 1761.

Grant Dated 31st October 1760.
To Grey Elliott Esquire for the Island of Ossabaw containing 7600 acres in the parish of St. Phillip. Registred 12th January 1761.

Grant Dated 3rd december 1760.
To James Baillou for 200 acres of land in the parish of St. John. Registred 13th January 1761.

Grant Dated 3rd December 1760.
To Samuel Pelton for 50 acres of land in the Parish of St. Matthew. Registred 14th January 1761.

Grant Dated 3rd december 1760.
To George Crowber for 150 acres of land in the parish of St. Matthew. Registred 15th January 1761.

Grant Dated 3rd December 1760.
To John Martin Bolzius in trust for a glebe of 300 acres of Land in the district of Goshen & parish of St. Matthew. Registred 16th January 1761.

Grant Dated 1st July 1760.
To Robert Burton for 100 acres of Land in the parish of St. John. Registred 19th January 1761.

Grant Dated 1st July 1760.
To Elizabeath Burton for 150 acres of land in the parish of St. Andrew. Registred 19th January 1761.

Grant Dated 1st July 1760.
To John Fleger for 50 acres of Land in the parish of St. Matthew. Registred 20th January 1761.

Grant Dated 3rd December 1760.
To George Crowber for 50 acres of Land in the District of Bethany & parish of St. Matthew. Registred 21st January 1761.

Grant Dated 3rd December 1760.
To John Clayton for 100 acres of Land in the parish of St. George. Registred 21st January 1761.

Grant Dated 5th June 1759.
To John Pettygrew for 100 acres of Land in the township of Augusta. Registred 22nd January 1761.

Grant Dated 1st May 1759.
To Robert Hudson for 150 acres of Land in the parish of St. George. Registred 22nd January 1761.

Grant Dated 25th September 1760.
To Richard Germain for a town Lot No. 4 & Garden lot of 5 acres in Savannah. Registred 23rd January 1761.

The aforesaid abstract of the grants Registred from the 27th of July 1760 To The 27th January 1761 Compared with the Register Book at Savannah This 27th day of January 1761.

Pat Houstoun, Register

James Wright to the Board of Trade, May 16, 1761, Savannah, received July 23, read Sept. 3, 1761, C.O. 5/648, E. 31, answering the Board's Feb. 27, 1761 letter relating the colony's present state of defense and the current situation concerning the Indians.

My Lords

I did myself the Honour of writing to your Lordships on the 15th of last Month, to which I beg leave to refer, and should not have Troubled your Lordships again so soon, had I not yesterday been Honoured with yours of the 27th of February, and which I think it my Duty to Acknowledge by the very first Opportunity. The Account I gave your Lordships of the State & Condition of the Province, altho' not so Favourable as I Could have wished, is nevertheless a True State, as it then did, & yet does appear to me, with respect to the Number of Inhabitants, etc.

Doubtless my Lords the Common Interest of the Provinces of Carolina and Georgia, are & ought to be Considered as one & the Same, I always was Clearly of this Opinion and declared it Some years ago, when I saw little Jealousies Creeping in. The Operations & Effect of His Majesties Troops sent to Carolina must certainly be felt by this Province, but by a letter I have received from Colonel Grant[67] who Commands them, this Province has not been so much as mentioned to him by General Amherst, and I find he has no Instructions relative to it, but Conceive they are all Confined to the Province of Carolina. Nevertheless if this Province should be reduced to the Necessity of Applying to Colonel Grant, and to Carolina for Support and Protection, I should Presume Some assistance would be given. But this my Lords I hope is now out of the Question and I think myself Extremely happy in being able to Acquaint your Lordships that I have lately received the Strongest Repetition of Assurances from the Creek Country of their Friendship, and I firmly believe we

---

67. On December 15, 1760, Lord Jeffrey Amherst, angered by the Fort Loudoun massacre, ordered Colonel James Grant, former commander of the Seventy-seventh Royal Scots battalion in Montgomery's expedition, "to chastise the Cherokees (and) reduce them to the absolute necessity of suing for pardon." Organizing a punitive expedition, Grant set out from Charleston with an army "2600 strong" for the Cherokee country on March 20, 1761. Backed by a war faction in Charleston which thought the expedition would "bring money into the province" and protect their frontier plantations, the campaign was popular in South Carolina. In all this, Georgia's interests seldom received consideration either from Amherst in New York or from officials in Charleston. Wright's letter is a reaction to that neglect.

shall have no disturbance from them this Season.

I have had with me 475 Since Governor Ellis went away. They are most Troublesome disagreeable & Expensive Guests, but My Lords its absolutely Necessary to Countenance & Encourage them, and to take every Method with our Friends to Counteract the designs & Endeavours of our Enemies, and which I have been able to do for the Present. I am truly Sensible my Lords what a vast Expence the Crown has been at, & still is at, in Supporting this Province, in every respect as well as for the Encouragement of the Silk Culture, and this I have frequently Mentioned to the People, & how much it is their duty to Exert their Utmost abilities for Purposes of their own defence & Protection. But my Lords many of the People in this Province from their Education and Manner of Life, are not easily wrought upon, & it is very difficult to bring Such Folks to a Right way of thinking.

The People my Lords that I mean, who would on an Alarm quit the Province are a Parcel of Runagates from Virginia & North Carolina, a kind of Vagrants who live like the Indians by Hunting, & Stealing other Men's Cattle & Horses, of this Sort of People there are many as Governor Ellis well knows. They Sit down and Build a Hut, make little or no Improvements and are always ready to remove without loss or damage to themselves, and from such kind of Inhabitants with great Submission my Lords, little can be Expected in time of Real danger, and such we have not a few. On the Other Hand my Lords there are a great Many very Honest Men, good settlers and who I doubt not would behave Properly, but 2000 Savages my Lords against a handfull would have been Terrible and might have Shocked even Some of those who are well inclined. We well know how much a few hundreds harass'd many Populous Settlements in Pensilvania but this danger seems to be over for the Present year.[68]

Your Lordships great Wisdom I shall always with the Utmost Pleasure Submit to, and therefore say no more with respect to our South Boundary. The Other Measure I'm afraid must not be taken

---

68. For years, Indians and Scotch-Irish settlers had clashed in western Pennsylvania, prompting Benjamin Franklin to call for a congress at Albany, New York, for June and July, 1754, to discuss Indian Affairs. Wright also believed that southern governors should agree on a common policy toward Indians. Thus "Congresses" between Indian and governor became a popular device for treating with Indians.

up just now, but your Lordships may rely on it that I shall constantly have it in view, and Lose no seasonable opportunity of using my Utmost Endeavours to Accomplish it if Practicable. I must return my best thanks to your Lordships for Recommending a Supply of Indian Presents, and of Swivel Guns. Whenever the Presents come, the Utmost Frugality shall be observed in the disposal of them, and in such Manner as may be most Productive of His Majesties Service. The Matter of the detachment of the Independant Companys doing duty in Georgia Governor Ellis told me he would Endeavour to set Right at Home, and as he saw general Amherst I hope soon to hear from the Secretary at War about it.

The Power your Lordships are Pleased to give me to draw on Mr. Martyn,[69] & every other you may be Pleased to invest me with, I hope will ever be Exercised in such manner as may meet with your Lordships approbation. It gives me much Concern to say that the Silk Culture has met with a great Stroke, by a most Severe & unexpected Frost the begining of last Month, which it now appears has done more damage than was at first Apprehended. The Proposition with respect to the Purchase of Negroes seemed to be such a Favourite Plan, that I did not know how to refuse their request in Transmitting it to your Lordships as I did, tho' at the Same time I told them I thought it would not be granted, and that Governor Ellis had Mentioned to me another Application he had in View for this sume of money. I Humbly thank your Lordships for Approving of my Conduct so far, and shall ever make it my Study to Endeavour to deserve a Continuance of it. I must entreat your Lordships goodness in Pardoning this Imperfect answer to your Lordships letter, having had but a very few hours, which if I had not made use of, I should have Missed the Conveyance.

Sir Matthew Lamb's Report to the Board of Trade, May 19, 1761, Lincoln's Inn, London, received May 21, read May 27, 1761, C.O 5/648, E. 25, giving his opinion of fourteen acts passed in Georgia in April, May, and June, 1760.

My Lords

In Pursuance of your Lordships Commands Signified to me by

---

69. Benjamin Martyn, former secretary to the Georgia Trustees, was currently Board of Trade agent for Georgia.

Mr. Pownall's Letter wherein you are pleased to Desire my Opinion in Point of Law upon the following Acts Passed in the Province of Georgia in April, May, and June, 1760, I have Perused and Considered the same (vizt.)

1. An Act for Impowring Trustees to purchase a House in the Town of Savannah for the Use of the present and future Governours of this Province.
2. An Act for the more effectual putting in Force the Militia Act of this Province.
3. An Act to prevent Frauds in the making of Lumber.
4. An Act to Amend An Act Intitled An Act for repairing and and Rebuilding the Forts heretofore Erected in the several Parishes of this Province and for the better Securing the Town of Savannah by Erecting a Fort round the Magazine and Block Houses within the Lines of the said Town.
5. An Act to Amend and Continue an Act Intitled An Act for Establishing and Regulating of Patroles.
6. An Act for the better Regulating the Town of Savannah and for Ascertaining the Common thereunto belonging.
7. An Act for Raising and Granting to his Majesty the Sum of One Thousand One Hundred Pounds Sterling for putting the Town of Savannah and the Out Forts in the several Parishes of this Province in a better State of Defence.
8. An Act to Amend An Act Intitled an Act to prevent Masters of Vessells from Carrying off Persons in Debt in this Province.
9. An Act to Enable Feme Coverts[70] to Convey their Estates And for Confirming and making valid All Conveyances and Acknowledgments hereto fore made by Feme Coverts.
10. An Act for Reparing and Rebuilding the Forts heretofore Erected in the several Parishes of this Province And for the better Securing the Town of Savannah by Erecting a Fort round the Magazine and Block Houses within the Lines of the said Town.
11. An Act for Stamping Imprinting Issuing and making Current the Sum of £7410 Sterling in Paper Bills of Credit and for applying and Sinking the same.
12. An Act for Raising and Granting to his Majesty the Sum of £1118.3.8 Sterling that is to say the Sum of £668.3.8 Sterling to Defray the Expences of holding the Courts of

---

70. In law, a *feme* *covert* was a married woman.

Oyer and Terminer and some other Expences of Government
And the Sum of £450 Sterling for Subsisting Two Hundred
of the Militia for the Defence of this Province.
13. An Act for Ascertaining the Qualification of Jurors and for
Establishing the Method of Ballotting and Summoning of
Jurors in the Province of Georgia.
14. An Act for the more easy and speedy Recovery of small
Debts and Damages.

Upon Perusal and Consideration of the before mentioned Acts I
have no Objections to the first Twelve. As to the two last, there
were two Acts partly for the same Purpose Passed in 1757 which
were Objected to and were not Confirmed, And I must again Submit these two Acts to your Lordships. As to one of them in regard to the Qualification of Jurors, and the Method of Ballotting
as is therein Incerted; and as to the other, the establishing a
Court for Trial of Actions of Eight Pounds Sterling which has been
before Objected to for the Sum of Ten Pounds, as being too great
a Sum in this Province to be Determined by such a Court.[71]

Samuel Martin, Secretary to the Lords of the Treasury, to the
Board of Trade, June 19, 1761, Treasury Chambers, received and
read June 23, 1761, C.O. 5/648, E. 26, asking the Board's opinion of a request by Henry Ellis to the Treasury praying that he
may be allowed to keep a sum of money belonging to the Crown
to defray some of his expenses.

My Lords

By Order of the Lords Commissioners of his Majesty's Treasury I transmit to Your Lordships the Inclosed Memorial of Henry
Ellis Esquire late Governor of the Province of Georgia praying
that he may be Allowed to retain in his hands a Sum of Money,
due from him to the Crown, in order to reimburse to him several
Expences which he has been at in the Publick Service. My Lords
desire you will be pleased to state to them such Facts relative
to this Matter, as are come to your Knowledge, and to favour
them with Your Opinion whether it will be proper to grant the
Memorialists Request.

---

71. All these acts except No. 13 are printed in CRG, XVIII,
372-464.

James Wright to the Board of Trade, July 13, 1761, Savannah, received Oct. 27, read Nov. 20, 1761, C.O. 5/648, E. 32, containing his observations on several laws whose passage he encouraged.

My Lords

On the 15th of last Month I acquainted your Lordships that I had on the 9th of that Month assented to the Tax Bill & six Others, and now do my Self the Honour to Transmit to your lordships Copys of those Laws with my observations thereon Agreeable to His Majesties 33rd Instruction.[72]

By the Tax Bill £1060.15.0 Sterling is Raised by a new Tax and granted to his Majesty, and £119.7.4-1/2 the Surplus of the last years Tax, and also £93.9.2-1/2 Arrears of the former Tax not then Paid into the Hands of the Treasurer, making in the whole £1373.11.11 Sterling is Appropriated to defray the charges of this Government for the Current year as in the Said Act is Particularly Mentioned.

On this Law I should have little to Observe or Trouble your Lordships with, were it not on account of some of the Officers of the Crown, which Matter stands thus. Soon after my Arrival here, on inquiring & Considering what Tax it might be Necessary to Raise for the Support of the current year, I found an Estimate of some standing Expences, Which had usually been made out by the Governor & sent down to the Assembly to Provide for. The Inclosed Paper Markt A. No. 1 is a Copy of the last that was made by Governor Ellis, and on Examining into the matter I found that those Articles without any Material Alteration had been Constantly Provided for, from the Meeting of the first assembly after Governor Reynold's Arrival, and that the several Officers had Always received & Enjoyed the Same as Emoluments of their Respective Officers. It is also Consistent with my own knowledge, that in South Carolina the same Services are Annually Provided for, and the Officers Paid. Wherefore on the 29th of March I

---

72. The reference is to the instructions issued to Wright when he became Georgia's royal governor. Wright's thirty-third instruction is the same as that given in Albert B. Saye, ed., "Commission and Instructions of Governor John Reynolds, Aug. 6, 1754," Georgia Historical Quarterly, XXX, 142.

made out the Inclosed Estimate Mark't B. No. 2, and sent it down to the Assembly that they might make Provision for the Same as usual. Sometime after which, I found that a Committee of the assembly had Reported against making Provision for Sundry of the Articles Contained in the Estimate I had sent down, Vizt., those in the Paper Mark't C. No. 3. On considering which matter fully, knowing it to be usual in other Colonys & finding it to have been Constantly done here from the 1st year the Government was Established, Vizt., from 1755 to 1760, inclusive, and from a Consideration of his Majesties 58th Instruction which says, "It is our further Will & Pleasure that you do Countenance and give all due Encouragement to all our Patent Officers in the Enjoyment of their <u>Legal & Accustomed Fees Rights Privileges and Emoluments</u>."

I Say my Lords from these Motives & a View of the whole Annual income of Each office, and the Expence of Living in this Part of the World, I thought it incumbent on me to Signify my Approbation of those Allowances, and that they ought rather to be continued. Your Lordships will see that near the whole are Accordingly Continued Except the Article of £30 to the Provost Marshall for a Goaler, and that of £6 to the Chief Justice, which at his own request was Struck out. It appeared my Lords that this matter had been taken up & Promoted by Mr. Grover the Chief Justice with what View or design I shall not say, or make any Observations on that gentleman's Conduct at Present but fear I shall be Obliged to Trouble your Lordships ere long.

The Inclosed Paper D. No. 4, is a Copy of an address from his Majesties Council for this Province to me, desiring me to Transmit to your Lordships a Copy of a Report of a Committee of Council as an upper House or in their Legislative Capacity and which I have accordingly done, being the Paper Mark't E. No. 5, and which may give your Lordships some further Light into the matter I have mentioned relative to the Public Officers, tho' intended by them for other Purposes likewise. I shall humbly hope to have your lordships Directions whether the Annual Allowances mentioned in the Estimate Mark't B. No. 2 Should, or Should not be Continued, that I may regulate my Conduct therein, & make out the next Estimate Accordingly.

The next is a Law for Subjecting the Real & Personal Estates of absent Debtors to an Attachment for Payment of debts. This Act, My Lords, seems to be a Necessary & good Law, the Plan & Method nearly similar to that of Foreign Attachments in London, and is (I believe) the use & Practice in all the other Colonys, the only Material difference, that I see between this & the

Practice in London is, that by this Law <u>Lands & Real Estates</u> are made Subject & Lyable to be Attached for Satisfaction of debts, and here I must beg leave to Observe that Altho' this is Contrary to the Law & Method used in England, yet it Appears Reasonable & necessary here in America, from a Consideration of Local Circumstances, & is Expressly Consonant to the Statutes of the 5th of his late Majesty Cap: 7, for the more Easy Recovery of debts in his Majesties Plantations & Colonies in America. By which Statute Lands are made Lyable to & Chargeable with all just debts & demands of what Nature or kind soever, and Subjected to the Same Process etc., as Personal Estates are in the Said Plantations. Wherefore I Conceive that this Law, altho' it go's further than the Practice in London, yet (being on the Plan of, & Expressly agreeable to the above Act of Parliament) was proper for me to assist to, and Humbly Submit the same to your Lordships better Judgment.

The Election Law My Lords seems exactly Agreeable to the mode Pointed out by His Majesties Commission & Instructions. The Bill came first in a very different dress, & Contained several Extraordinary & improper things, which at Length were Expunged. I am hopefull the passing this Law will Prevent any improper Attempts on this Head for the Future.

The Act for granting to His Majesty £180 to Repair the Light House on Tybee Island, I am next to Observe upon, and my Lords tho' this may at first View seem not to be agreeable to His Majesties 27 Instruction Yet my Lords I must beg leave to assure your Lordships that it is for a most Necessary Service, for the general good not only of this Province, but the Neighbouring Provinces, as it is the most certain and best Land Mark for all the South Part of the Coast of North America. This Structure is in great danger of being totally ruined & falling down if not speedily Repaired, and from the Expediency of the Object in View, & its great & general Utility, and from a Consideration of His Majesties 23 Instruction which Says "You are Authorised to "give your assent to any Temporary Laws, for making Provision "to defray the Expence of Temporary Services, Provided Such Laws "Expire, and have their full Effect, when the Services for which "they were Passed Shall Cease & be determined."

I say my Lords from these Considerations, and the matter seeming to be within the intent & meaning of this Instruction I assented to the Same without a Saving Clause as mentioned, in the 27 Instruction. For, my Lords, had there been a Suspending Clause, the Light House Which has really Cost a vast deal of money, & is of the Utmost Importance, would Probably have fallen down before I had received His Majesties Pleasure therein. I chearfully Submit my Conduct herein, and hope it will meet with your Lordships Approbation.

My Lords I humbly beg leave to Observe further on this Point that Instructions wisely Calculated for & adapted to His Majesties Other Populous & Opulent Colonys, may not always be so Practicable & Convenient to be Strictly Observed in an Infant Colony, where the generality of the People are Rather in Indigent Circumstances. I only Mention this my Lords as a Reason why 5 years time is allowed for sinking the Sume to be Raised by this Act, and as some other Contingent Services may require raising small Sumes on this Plan hereafter I would Humbly hope to have your Lordships directions, if you think I ought not to assent to any Other Bills of this Nature, when Public Services seem to require it & the Circumstances of the People will not admit of Raising an Immediate Supply, my Lords, my Predecessors have both done this, & Carried it far, and it is constantly done in the next Province. But as it is my full Resolution to Pay the greatest Obedience to his Majesties Instructions & to have them constantly in View, and as this matter altho agreeable to the 23d Instruction Seems to clash with the 27th Instruction, Therefore I have taken the Liberty to Trouble your Lordships with so full a State of this affair. The duty Laid & Penalty Inflicted on Persons Importing delinquent Slaves etc. from other Colonies is a very Salutary Measure, & I hope will be Approved by your Lordships.

The Bill for Establishing a Ferry over great Ogechee River, is a matter of Public Utility and Convenience for the whole Province & I think is Settled on a Reasonable & Proper Footing.

The Bill for Continuing the several Militia Laws is likewise a matter of Public Utility & Convenience, & as Such seemed necessary to be Passed.

The Law for amending the former Act for the better Regulating the Town of Savanah & for assertaining the Common I found to be very agreeable to the People and as I saw nothing in it that Appeared to me, to be unconstitutional or improper, I assented to it.

Thus I have given your Lordships an Account of the 7 Bills I have assented to and hope for your Approbation. But if I have Erred, or gone too far in any Particular, I beg your Lordships indulgence in letting me know it, as that will Effectually Regulate my future Conduct in such Cases.

Our Silk is now all Wound off & weighed and amounts only to I think 325 lbs. This my Lords is but a small matter, but the greatest Appearance that ever they had here, was destroyed in two nights time by Excessive, hard & unseasonable Frosts, and there is likewise a degeneracy in the Seed. As Mr. Ottolenghe tells me he writes fully to Mr. Martyn on the Subject I shall not Trouble your Lordships further.

Affairs in general with Respect to the Province my Lords are much as when I wrote last, an Appearance of Flourishing but check'd & cramp't on account of our Situation with the Indians, and for want of more Territory as mentioned in mine of the 23d of december last.

I see by the London Gazette of the 14th of April that His Majesty has been graciously Pleased to Appoint me Governor in Chief of this Province, on which Occasion I Beg leave to return my best thanks to your Lordships and hope my Conduct will be such as may merit the continuance of His Majesties Favour & your Lordships good Opinion and Protection.

An estimate of the charges of government in Georgia for one year beginning Sept. 29, 1759, to be provided for by the General Assembly, read Nov. 20, 1761, C.O. 5/648, E. 33, enclosure A, No. 1, in Governor Wright July 13, 1761, to Board of Trade.

To the Justices of the Bench for holding two Courts	£6.0.0	
Clerk of the Crown for ditto	4.0.0	
Attorney General for ditto	20.0.0	
Provost Marshall for the Jaylor	30.0.0	
Ditto for Jurys	20.0.0	
Ditto for Maintenance of Prisoners	10.0.0	
Cryer & keeper of the Court	10.0.0	
Executioner	15.0.0	
Coroner	10.0.0	
		£125.0.0
To the Clk of the Council & Upper House	30.0.0	
Messenger & doorkeeper to ditto	25.0.0	
Clerk of the Assembly his Salary	25.0.0	
Incidental business to ditto	40.0.0	
Printing of the Laws	20.0.0	
Messenger & doorkeeper of the Lower House	25.0.0	
Secretary for Copys & Sealing of Acts etc	40.0.0	
Register of Grants & sending Copys Home	10.0.0	
		215.0.0

To the Public Commissary		20.0.0
Armourer for keeping in order 700 Stand of Arms		21.0.0
Fire & Candles for both Houses		5.0.0
For Contingent Services, Vizt.		
Negroes that may be Apprehended or Executed	40.0.0	
Apprehending of Other Offenders	20.0.0	
Repairs of Public Buildings	10.0.0	
Expresses & Other Incidental Expenses at this Critical Conjuncture. Say -	60.0.0	
Arrear of 1759	31.5.3 1/2	

	161.5.3 1/2
	547.5.3 1/2

Treasurers Commission at 5 per Cent	27.7.3	
Tax Gatherers ditto at 2 1/2 per Cent	13.13.7 1/2	

	41.0.10 1/2
	£588.6.2

Savanah 14th November 1759.

      Henry Ellis.

An estimate of the necessary charges of government in Georgia beginning Sept. 29, 1760, and ending Sept. 29, 1761, read Nov. 20, 1761, C.O. 5/648, E. 34, enclosure B, No. 2, in Governor Wright July 13, 1761, to Board of Trade, in Wright's hand.

To the Justices of the Bench for holding two Courts	£6.0.0
Clerk of the Crown for Ditto	4.0.0
Attorney General for Ditto	20.0.0
Provost Marshall for the Jaylor	30.0.0

Ditto for Juries. Summoning. 30.0.0
Ditto for Maintenance of Prisoners . 10.0.0
Coroner. 10.0.0
Cryer of the Court 10.0.0

For defraying the Expence of holding
the Courts of Oyer & Terminer a
Sume not Exceeding £120.0.0

To the Clerk of the Council & Upper
  House 30.0.0
Messenger & doorkeeper to ditto . . 25.0.0
Clerk of the assembly his Salary . . 25.0.0
Incidental business to Ditto 40.0.0
Printing of the Laws 20.0.0
Messenger & doorkeeper of the
  Lower House 25.0.0
Secretary for Copys & Sealing of
  Acts etc 60.0.0
Register of Grants & Sending Copys
  Home 10.0.0

For defraying the Expence of holding
the general assembly a Sume not
Exceeding 235.0.0

To the Public Commissary 20.0.0
Armourer for keeping 700 Stand of arms 21.0.0
Fire & Candles for both Houses 5.0.0

    Contingencies   £401.0.0

Negro's that may be Apprehended or
  Executed £40.0.0
Apprehending of other Offenders . . 20.0.0
Repairs of Public Buildings 20.0.0
Expresses & Other incidental
  Charges 60.0.0

Colonial Records 345

For Contingent Services a Sume not Exceeding	140.0.0
	541.0.0
Treasurers Commissions at 5 per Cent	27.1.0
Tax Gatherers ditto at 2 1/2 per Cent	13.10.0
	£581.11.6

To the above may be added Money for Purposes of defence and such other Necessary Services as may be thought Proper.

James Wright

27 March 1761

Wright's deductions resolved to be made from the estimate, April 14, 1761, received Oct. 27, read Nov. 20, 1761, C.O. 5/648, E. 35, enclosure C, No. 3, in Governor Wright July 13, 1761, to Board of Trade, in Wright's hand.

	£ s d
Chief Justice	6.0.0
Attorney General	20.0.0
Provost Marshall for the Goaler	30.0.0
Secretary for Copys & Sealing Acts etc	60.0.0
Register of Grants	10.0.0
Provost Marshall for Summoning Juries	10.0.0
From the Messenger & doorkeeper of the Upper House	12.10.0
	£148.10.0

Deductions Proposed to be made by the assembly.

J. Wright.

Copy of June 9, 1761, address from the Upper House of the Assembly to Governor Wright, received Oct. 27, read Nov. 20, 1761, C.O. 5/648, E. 36, enclosure D, No. 4, in Governor Wright July 13, 1761, to Board of Trade.[73]

Copy of the Report of the Committee of the Whole House, appointed to consider the extracts from the Journals of the Commons House of Assembly in the present session, June 8, 1761, C. O. 5/648, E. 37, enclosure E, No. 5, in Governor Wright, July 13, 1761, to Board of Trade, with the affidavit of William Clifton annexed.[74]

Georgia

    William Clifton Attorney general of the Province of Georgia maketh Oath as follows That this Deponent having seen an Extract from the Journals of the Commons House of Assembly of the said Province wherein is contained a Deposition of William Grover Esquire chief Justice of the said Province before a Committee of the said Commons House setting forth among other Things "That he had been informed whilst in England that additional Salaries had been given to the Attorney general and Provost Marshal on Memorials presented by them to the Lords of Trade suggesting that the Province did not raise Money for public Buisness but that he could not positively swear Lord Halifax told him so; but either his Lordship, Mr. Pownell, Mr. Martin, or the Attorney General told him so."

    This Deponent therefore as he looks upon himself to be the Person meant, by the Attorney general, he being about that Time in England, thinks it incumbent on him to declare upon Oath that he never informed the said William Grover either here or in England that Additional Salaries had been given to this Deponent and the Provost Marshal upon a Suggestion that the Province did not riase Money for Public Buisness, nor did this Deponent understand such Augmentation to be an Exemption of the Province from the Charge of public Buisness, he having yearly been allowed his Fees (as settled by the Governour and Council) for Prosecutions

---

73. Given in CRG, XVI, 608-609.

74. The Report is in ibid., 599-607.

at the Courts of Oyer and Terminer for which the general Assembly of the said Province have always provided.

(Signed) William Clifton

annexed to the Report by Order of the Committee

William Knox, Chairman

James Wright to the Board of Trade, Sept. 15, 1761, Savannah, read Jan. 20, 1762, C.O. 5/648, E. 39, containing an account of the colony, of the artifices used by the French at Mobile to excite the Creek Indians to hostilities, and asking for further allowances to Joseph Ottolenghe to induce him to instruct someone in the silk culture.

My Lords

With this your Lordships will receive a Copy of Mine of the 13th of July with a duplicate of the Bills Assented to by me on the 9th of June & my Observations thereon, Since writing which the material affairs of the Province in general Continue much the same. I have frequent visits from Numbers of the Creek Indians, seldom a week without, and from whom I receive the strongest assurances of their good Disposition, and this also from the Nation in the way they Reckon most formal & Solemn. That is on a general Summons for a Meeting of all their Head Men in their Public Squares or Places of Harangue. At these Meetings my Lords the most Solemn Engagements which these People ever make, or enter into, are Agreed upon, And they Promise to Observe all former Treaties etc., and my Lords to keep this kind of Friendship with them, has cost me infinite Pains & Attention. At the Same time that I receive these assurances, Some of the Perfidious wretches Murder our People. A Man & 3 Children have been Murdered by some of them Since I wrote your lordships last, and even Since those Murders, I have received Talks in the usual Stile. I have sent up a Formal Talk to the Head men in both upper & Lower Country, in which I demand Satisfaction, and Remonstrate on this Execrable Villany, at a time they are Openly declaring & giving me the strongest Assurances Possible of their Friendly & good intentions. You will See my Lords that there is no kind of security against these Savages but being put into Such a Condition as to be able to Compel them to do Justice whenever they Transgress.

I have frequent Accounts from the Albama Fort, which is in one of the Creek Towns, and where every Artifice Possible is Practiced to make a Breach between us & the Indians, and while the French are Suffered to remain there & at Mobile, we shall never be Safe against the Indians without some Military Force, and which must Baffle all Attempts to make this Province any thing Considerable. But I shall not Presume to Trouble your lordships further on this head as I did it before I left England & have Since, and shall only add that the more I see, the more am I Convinced of the Necessity of the measures I hint at. I am in great hopes the demand I have made on Account of the Above murders, will be Attended to by the Nation, have not yet received a Public answer, but have Private hints that the manner in which I have stated this matter to them Appeared striking & that they say I shall be regarded. I hope it will Prove so, but cannot say till I receive a Public answer.

This my Lords does not seem to be a Favourable time to Talk to the Indians about a Surrender of any of their Lands to the Westward, or a Release from our Engagement not to Settle above the Flowing of the Tides, as mentioned in your lordships letter of the 27th February last which is a Measure I shall Constantly have in View & not omit at a Seasonable Opportunity, and which I hope may yet offer ere long, if not by the time the Presents arrive.

The Silk my Lords is all put up ready for shipping, and as no Vessel is now going from hence it must lye till there is an Opportunity, and shall be forwarded by the first that offers and altho' we have been Unfortunate this year in Seasons, yet hope they may Prove more Favourable next. I shall use every means I can think of to Encourage & Promote this Culture, but fear it will only be Pursued by the Poorer sort of People.

Mr. Ottolenge who has the Direction & Management of this Culture is I think Perfect Master of the whole Affair, and in Case of his Death, I believe no other Person here, is Capable of Conducting it. He is Advanced in years and will very readily instruct another, but seems to expect Some recompence, or a Small Annuity, he behaves well in every other respect, and is a very usefull Magistrate, the most Active Justice in the Town, and I am Informed takes Nothing for his Trouble. I thought it my duty to make Some mention of this matter, that your Lordships may in your great Wisdom give direction therein if Needfull.

James Wright to the Board of Trade, Oct. 17, 1761, Savannah, read Jan. 20, 1762, C.O. 5/648, E. 40, informing the Board that the persons who settled at New Hanover in 1758 and subsequently were removed once again have returned.

My Lords,

On the first Instant I had the Honor to Receive your Lordships Commands of the 28th of April requiring me from time to time to give your Lordships frequent & very full Information of the State & Condition of this Province, as well with respect to the administration of Government & Justice, as to the Trade & Commerce thereof, also Regularly & Punctually to Transmit the Several Papers required by His Majesties Instructions, all which I shall most Carefully & diligently observe. I found the Journals a little backward when I came here, but have given strict Orders that they be Immediately brought up, and shall take care that they are kept up for the Future. I have already sent Two Copys of the Bills Passed on the ninth of June last, also the Minutes of the Council as an upper House, & of the Assembly to that time.

Your Lordships were likewise Pleased to send me a set of Queries for my speedy answer thereto, which I have now under Consideration, and shall Transmit my Answer as speedily as the Nature of the enquiry will Admit of. I think it my duty to Acquaint your Lordships that it has very lately come to my knowledge that a Set of People, who some years ago settled themselves to the Southward of the River Alatamaha at a Place by them called New Hanover, and who were in February 1759, by His Majesties Command & in his Name Ordered to remove from thence, did only make a show or appearance of so doing, and Immediately returned back to their Settlements, where they have continued ever since, & yet are, by the best Information I can get. These People in the whole amount to between 70 or 80 Men and are a Mixture of Runagates from the Two Carolina's Virginia etc. They are not settled together, but scattered about the Country and on Lands at Present not within my Jurisdiction or Authority.

But I must beg leave to Observe that notwithstanding this Nominal Boundary by the Kings Charter to the Trustees of the Southermost Stream of the Alatamaha, yet General Oglethorpe extended his Settlements Southward without any Regard to that Boundary, and Many Plantations were settled far beyond the Alatamaha and marks of Possession held & the Lands claimed quite to St. Juan's River, and there has been & to this day is by his late Majesties Order a Sergeants Guard kept at Fort William near the South End of Cumberland Island by a detachment from his Majesties Independant Companys in So. Carolina, not under my direction or Authority, but of the Governor of So. Carolina. The Inlet from the Sea at the South End of this Island is Called Amelia, & is at the Mouth of the River St. Maries I believe 50 Miles further South than where the New Hanover People are Settled.

I have Acquainted Mr. Secretary Pitt with this Matter, and also wrote to the Governor of Carolina on the Subject, as I think it my duty to do to your Lordships.

P.S. I did my self the Honor of writing to your Lordships on the 16th of May, 15th of June, 13th of July, & 15th of September.

Samuel Martin, Secretary to the Lords of the Treasury, to the Board of Trade, Dec. 16, 1761, London, read Dec. 17, 1761, C.O. 5/648, E. 38, directing the Board to lay before the House of Commons an estimate of the expense of the civil establishment of Georgia between mid-summer 1761 and mid-summer 1762.

Sir

I desire You will acquaint the Lords Commissioners of Trade and Plantations That the Chancellor of the Exchequer, hath received his Majesty's Commands, That their Lordships should prepare and lay before the House of Commons, an Estimate of the Expence attending the Colony of Georgia, from the 24th day of June 1761 to Midsummer 1762.

James Wright to the Board of Trade, Dec. 28, 1761, Savannah, read April 1, 1762, C.O. 5/648, E. 42, asking directions for the disposition of a sum of money now in his hands from the sale of forfeited lots near the town of Savannah.

My Lords

On the 17th of October I did my Self the Honor to Write to your Lordships Acknowledging the receipt of your Commands of the 28th of April and now take Liberty to Acquaint your Lordships, that on the expiration of the Term Appointed by the Law of this Province for Limitting the time of claiming Lands under Grants &

Nominal Titles etc. which was on the 20th of March last. It Appeared that Several Lots in the Town of Savanah remained without any Claim or Pretence of Right being made or given in, and by the Express words of the Law, all such Lots are declared Forfeited to His Majesty, and to be deemed as Vacant Land. And the Governor and Council are Authorised to grant the Same, to any Persons whomsoever.

This matter my Lords was taken under Consideration on the 21st day of April last, and it was then unanimously Resolved, That the said several Lots should be disposed of at a Moderate Price, and Public Notice was given that on the 22nd day of May such Vacant Lots would be disposed of and which was then done Accordingly to Sundry Persons & at different Prices amounting to £323 Sterling as will at Large Appear by the Minutes of the Proceedings of the Governor & Council on that day. This my Lords was the Amount of the Town Lots, and there are some 45 acre Lots, and 5 acre Lots that Lye beyond the Town Common which will raise a further Sume. But the time when they may be all disposed of, and the amount is uncertain, but it is Judged cannot in the whole with the above Sume of £323, Exceed £400. The grants for the above Town Lots are made out, and the Receivers Commissioner being Confined to the Receipts of the quit rents only, this Sume of £323 Sterling is in my Hands, Subject to such Orders as His Majesty shall be Pleased to give Relative thereto, which when received will be Immediately Complied with.

I must now beg leave to mention to your Lordships that it would be a very Acceptable thing to the Province if His Majesty would be Pleased to Permit the monies arising by the Sale of the Forfeited Lots, to be applied to some Public Provincial Building, or other use, the whole of which when the Lots are all disposed of, its thought cannot Exceed £400.

I must also observe to your Lordships that in the above Law there is a Provisoe, that Nothing Contained therein shall Extend to vacate the Right or Prejudice any Person under age, Non Compos,[75] or Imprisoned, at the time of making the act, Provided they Claim within 3 years after they come of Age, are Compos, or out of Prison, and if the Money is suffered to be applied to a Provincial use, then if any such Claim should happen to come,

---

75. In law, non compos referred to a person not of sound mind, mentally incapable of handling his own affairs. It often is written non compos mentis.

it may be thought Equitable for the Province to reimburse the Purchaser. I have now my Lords stated every Circumstance and Fact to your Lordships and shall hope soon to receive His Majesties Commands to whom this money is to be Paid, or to what use Applied.

On my Arrival here I found that Mr. Grover the Chief Justice had not been at Council for Several Months, but as I understood there was a very great difference subsisting between Governor Ellis & him, I Imagined it might be owing to that, and expected to see him take his seat in Proper time. But he not Coming, in February, I ordered a letter to be wrote to him requiring his Attendance, on which he came to me and brought a resignation of his Seat in writing. This I desired him to take back & reconsider the matter, and if he continued in the same mind, I would sometime afterwards Accept of his resignation, and which I Accordingly did about two months Ago. A man in Mr. Grovers Station my Lords might be very usefull to the Province, but this man does no one thing whatever, but attend the Courts at the Stated times, where there is little or nothing to do, a Court seldom lasting above a day. In Short my Lords its not in my Power to say any good of him. I Presume I need not now Recommend any gentleman to fill up this Vacancy in the Council, having formerly mentioned six, of whom only one is as yet appointed, Vizt. Mr. Elliott, at least no other Appointment is as yet come to my Hand. By this Conveyance I transmit to your Lordships the Minutes of the Proceedings of the Governor in Council from the 6th of January 1761, to the 26th of June Inclusive, and those Since that time are Preparing with the Utmost Dispatch, and I hope very soon to send em down to the 1st of January 1762. My Answers to your Lordships Queries will also be finished and Transmitted as Soon as Possible.

Our affairs with the Creek Indians are quiet, but My Lords I don't like the kind of Peace Settled in Carolina with the Cherokees, and am somewhat doubtfull as to its Continuance & Effect on my Neighbours the Creeks. I Cannot Say it Appears to me altogether in the Light Represented.

Sir Mathew Lamb's report to the Board of Trade, Jan. 22, 1762, London, received Jan. 26, read Feb. 17, 1762, C.O. 5/648, E. 41, upon seven acts passed in Georgia in June, 1761.

My Lords

In Pursuance of Your Lordships Commands Signified to me by Mr. Pownall's Letter wherein you are pleased to Desire my Opinion in Point of Law upon the following Acts Passed in the Province of Georgia in June 1761 I have Perused and Considered the same (vizt.)

1. An Act for Establishing a Ferry over Great Ogechee River at a Place called Pine Bluff and for Vesting the same in John Deveaux the Elder his Executors and Administrators for the Space of Six Years.

2. An Act for Raising and Granting to his Majesty the Sum of One Hundred and Eighty Pounds to repair the Lighthouse on Tybee Island and for laying a Duty on Negroes that have been above Six Months in any of the Islands or Colonies in America and Imported for Sale into this Province.

3. An Act for Amending an Act Intitled an Act for the better Regulating the Town of Savannah And for Ascertaining the Common thereunto belonging.

4. An Act to Continue several Acts for Regulating the Militia in the Province of Georgia.

5. An Act for Raising and Granting to his Majesty the Sum of One Thousand and Sixty Pounds fifteen Shillings and applying the Sum of One Hundred and Nineteen Pounds Seven Shillings and four Pence half Penny being the Surplus of the last years Tax Remaining in the Hands of the Treasurer, And the further Sum of Ninety three Pounds Nine Shillings and two Pence half penny being Arrears due from the several Collectors to be paid in, to the said Treasuror Amounting together to the Sum of One Thousand three Hundred and Seventy three Pounds Eleven Shillings and Seven Pence Sterling to defray the Charges of holding the Courts of Oyer and Terminer and some other Expences of Government.

6. An Act to Ascertain the manner and form of Electing Members to Represent the Inhabitants of this Province in the Commons House of Assembly.

> This is a new Law in this Province for the Purposes mentioned in the Title. Other Provinces have Laws for the same Purpose, They differ in the several Provinces, and the Propriety of this Law, and its being Suitable to this Province, must be Submitted to your Lordships.

7. An Act for Subjecting and making liable to Attachments the Estates Real and Personal of Absent Debtors in the Custody or Power of any Person or Persons within this Province.

Upon Perusal and Consideration of these Acts I have no Objection thereto in Point of Law.[76]

James Wright to the Board of Trade, Feb. 20, 1762, Savannah, read April 28, 1762, C.O. 5/648, E. 43, giving the measures taken to improve the colony's defense, informing the Board of Sir Patrick Houstoun's death, of some Negroes and cattle escheated to the Crown by the death of a half-breed, and of the appointment of a person to be joint agent for the colony with Benjamin Martyn.

My Lords

With this your Lordships will Receive my Answers to the several Queries your Lordships were Pleased to send to me, which I have given with the greatest certainty and Exactitude in my Power, and hope they may Prove Satisfactory to your Lordships.

My last was of the 28th of december, and I have still the Pleasure to Acquaint your Lordships that we remain very quiet with the Creek Indians and I hope shall continue so, if the Cherokee disturbances in Carolina do not break out again. If they should, I fear the Effect on the Creeks would be very bad. Your Lordships will also receive Copys of two Bills assented to by me on the 19th of December last. The one Intitled an Act for Erecting a Fort & Battery on the Island of Cockspur in the River Savanah, and a Lookout or Battery on Medway River, and the other Intitled an Act for Raising & Granting to His Majesty £440 for Erecting a Fort & Battery at Cockspur, and £100 for Erecting a Lookout or Battery on Medway, and for Sinking the same by a Tax on deer skins etc.

The Building of a Fort upon Cockspur Island I thought to be a very Necessary & Expedient Service, for the Protection of the Province & its Commerce in time of War, and for Enforcing a due Observance of the Laws in time of Peace.

Tybee Bar my Lords at the Entrance from the sea into this River, Lyes 15 Miles from the Town of Savanah, & Cockspur is about 12 Miles from Savanah, on the hither Side of the Sound, where the River begins to Narrow. This Island makes 2 Channels up the River, one on each Side of it, and the Fort & Battery

---

76. Acts No. 3 and 6 are in CRG, XVIII, 464-472, 479-481.

Proposed to be built, it is thought will Command both Channels into Savanah River, and by that means Protect the Town from being annoyed by any small Privateer, which might do a great deal of Mischief, even in the Night, unknown or discovered, for my Lords in July last, a small French Schooner came in & Lay very near this Island, and decoyed several Boats on Board, & Carried away Slaves to the Value of £1000 Sterling. The Vessel stayed there, from Early on Sunday Morning, till Monday at Noon, and in the Night time, sent up their Boat well Manned & Armed, with a design to cut out a Vessel & Carry off. But finding none fit for their Purpose, they returned. This Account I had from the Pilot & Other White People they had decoyed on Board, & who they afterwards let come away, keeping only the Slaves, and in the last War there was a Vessel Loaded with goods, taken & Carried away from this Island, by a Spanish Privateer.

My Lords there is Water enough there for any 20 Gun Ship, or I believe 40 Gun Ship in the Navy to Lye, and most of the large Vessels that come here take in only a Part of their Cargo at Savanah & then go down to Cockspur & take in the Remainder. This is found Necessary on Account of sand banks & shoals in the River between that & the Town, and therefore My Lords in every View, and on every Consideration, I Judged it a very Proper Measure for His Majesties Service & the benefit & advantage of the Province. The Measure was unanimously Approved, but the difficulty was to find money for it, and at length the Tax laid on Deer & Beaver Skins, as done by the Law now sent, was resolved on. This my Lords Appeared to me to be a very Just & Moderate Imposition on that Trade, for on taking a thorough View of it, I found the Persons Concern'd in it, Carried out of this Province to the amount of £26,000 Sterling per annum which all went to Charles Town for want of shipping to Carry it from hence. And which tho' in Fact a Trade carried on in this Province, yet Appears as the Product of S. Carolina, and altho' this is a most Profitable Trade to the Parties Concerned, and they are benefitted at least £6 per Cent by their Connection with this Province, that is my Lords they Carry on their Trade at so much less Expence than they used to do, or could do from Carolina, yet these People Paid little or nothing towards the Expence & Support of this Government, by which they were so much benefitted, and therefore my Lords a Tax was laid on all Skins Exported from this Province Except to Great Britain, and I hope my Conduct in this Particular will meet with your Lordships Approbation.

I also send by this Conveyance the Minutes of the Proceedings of the Governor in Council from the 3rd of July to the 15 of September inclusive, the last I sent was down to the 26th of June inclusive, I also send the duplicate of the Minutes of the Assembly from the 24th of March to the 9th of June 1761, also the Custom House Accounts from the 10th of October 1761, to the 5th of January 1762.

Sir Pat Houstoun one of the Council here, and Register of Grants & Receiver of the quit rents dyed the 5th Instant and I have appointed his Son, now Sir P. Houstoun (I believe a very deserving young Gentleman) for those offices, and for his Seat in Council. I would take Liberty to recommend Lewis Johnson, the Speaker, & John Graham, who with the four Names remaining of those returned by me formerly, make the Number directed to be returned for your Lordships Consideration to fill up the two Present Vacancies. But my Lords these are all Assembly Men & very usefull there and I fear I should want them greatly, and as the Council is Pretty full, I must Submit it to your Lordships whether you may Judge it necessary to fill up these Vacant Seats in Council Immediately or not. Or your Lordships may think Proper only to fill up one at present, for my Lords if I was to Lose 2 or 3 good Men of the assembly, I really don't know how their Places would be filled, and I might be put to some difficulty.

In the list of Offices your Lordships will See one of a very Trifling income to Mr. Charles Pryce, or rather several together, this Man is very deserving, and I Could wish him recommended for his Majesties Appointment, also Mr. Talley who is Naval Officer is a very deserving young Gentleman.

I have received a Letter from the Right Honorable the Earl of Egremont desiring me for the future to address my letters to him as Secretary of State for the Southern Department and have therefore by this Opportunity Acquainted his Lordship of the Vacancy Occasioned by the death of Sir P. Houstoun. This I have done in Consequence of the above Letter, and of a Copy of His Majesties Order in Council of the 15th of May last, sent out to me by Mr. Secretary Pitt. If I have err'd in this, I beg your Lordships Pardon, & shall hope to be informed, whether I am for the future to give an Account of all Vacancies to your Lordships only, or to the Secretary of State only, or to both at the same time, as I have not the Additional Instruction mentioned in the above Order, relative to the Mode of Correspondence.

I am to Acquaint your Lordships that by the Death of a half breed Indian Boy, some Negroes & a Stock of Cattle became vested in His Majesty for want of kin. This Boy was the Son of one

Spencer an Indian Trader, by an Indian Woman. The Relations of Spencer applied for Letters of Administration & a grant of His Majesties Right, but this I refused & Committed the Administration to Mr. Clifton the Attorney General in behalf of his Majesty. The Value is supposed to be £385 Sterling as by an Inventory returned to me, of which I now take Liberty to Inform your Lordships, agreeable to His Majesties 72nd Instruction to me that His Majesties Pleasure may be known therein. Mr. Clifton tells me the Relations of Spencer intend to Petition His Majesty on this Subject, in hopes to Obtain a Grant of the Premises from His Majesty.

I am also to acquaint your Lordships that Mr. Knox one of the Council here, & Provost Marshall, has Obtained His Majesties Leave to return to Great Britain, and that the Council & Assembly Prepared an ordinance appointing him Agent for this Province for one year, to Join with or assist Mr. Martyn and to which Ordinance I have given my assent.

James Wright to the Board of Trade, April 26, 1762, Savannah, received July, read Nov. 29, 1762, C.O. 5/648, E. 45, transmitting Journals of the Council and Assembly and several acts lately passed together with his observations upon them.

My Lords

On the 20th of February I did my Self the Honor to Write to your Lordships fully, and to Transmit my Answers to the Several Queries your Lordships were Pleased to send to me and which I did with the greatest certainty and exactitude in my Power. These my Lords, with Copys of Two Bills I assented to on the 19 of december last, one for building a Fort & Battery on Cockspur Island etc., and the Other for Raising & Granting to his Majesty £540 for that Purpose with my Observations thereon, & Reasons for Passing the same, and also some Minutes of the Proceedings of the Governor in Council, & some other Minutes, & the Custom House Accounts to the 5th of January last, were all put up into a Box and delivered on Board His Majesties Ship Dolphin at Charles Town, which Ship sailed from thence on the 9th of March, and I hope those Papers are all ere now got safe to Hand, and as they Contain the fullest & clearest Account of the State and Condition of everything here to that time, to them therefore I beg leave to refer your Lordships.

Since which my Lords all my Accounts from the Indian Country have been Favourable & I hope will continue so.

On the 4th of March I assented to Eleven Bills Vizt., The Tax Bill for Raising & Granting to His Majesty £1421.5.0 Sterling for defraying the necessary Expences of Government from the 29th of September 1761, to the 29th September 1762, a Bill for the Preventing & Punishing Vice etc. & for keeping holy the Lords day, a Bill for Building a Church at Augusta & Repairing the Parsonage House and Continuing the Tax on Tavern Licences and Appropriating the same, a Bill to Explain & amend the Act for the Recovery of small debts, Two additional Road Bills, a Bill for Making Provision for Printing the Laws of this Province, & Encouraging a Printer, a Bill for Obliging Masters of Vessels & other Transient Persons Importing goods to Pay a Tax for the Same, a Bill for Regulating the Pilotage, a Bill for Raising & Granting to His Majesty £193.10.0 for the better Support of Pilots, and a Bill for Exchanging a Part of the Town Common. This last Bill my lords I am interested in, but it was brought in without my knowledge or hearing that it was intended. It is Certainly Convenient for me, as it joins some Lands I have Purchased and am Improving, and its an advantage to the People, as they will gain about Seven Acres of Commonage Equally good. The Lands I have since Purchased to make the exchange, Containing so much more than the Part of the Common Exchanged with me. All the other Bills my Lords appear to me to be of Public Utility & Convenience, and nothing in them that I saw Contrary to His Majesties Instructions to me, or Repugnant to the Laws of Great Britain.

I found it necessary my Lords for the more Easy & better Collecting of His Majesties Quit rents to have the draught of a Bill Prepared, which was laid before the assembly & has been Passed by them. And by this opportunity I Transmit the same to your Lordships, Pursuant to His Majesties 68th Instruction, and think if Such a Law is Passed, it will be greatly for His Majesties Service, and May Prove Effectual for the Recovery of the Quit rents. I shall hope to have your Lordships directions thereon, & if Approved of, the sooner it takes Place the better.[77]

With the above Bills I also now have the Honor to Transmit to

---

77. Despite Wright's statement about the necessity of the quitrent law, it seems to have become lost in the bureaucratic mill at Whitehall and never to have been approved by the Privy Council.

your Lordships the Minutes of the Proceedings of the Council as an upper House to the fourth of March when I Adjourned them till October on Account of the quit rent Bill. Also two Copys of the abstracts of the grants Enter'd from 27 July 1761 to 27 January 1762, for your Lordships & the Lords of Treasury, and the Minutes of the Proceedings of the Governor in Council to this Month, and of the assembly to the 4th of March, will be all ready to send in ten days and if this Vessel does not Sail before, Shall 'em by her.

We have had a Favourable Spring for the Silk Culture, and it gives me the greatest Satisfaction to see a Prospect of a good Crop. Mr. Ottolenghe found an inconvenience in baking the Cocoons, and recommended the Building of a Stove Room to answer the end of Baking and which its thought will be of great Utility, and the Quality of the Silk much better. This I have agreed to, and it is now near Finished, the whole Expence of Materials & everything, will be from £50 to £60 Sterling. I beg leave to refer your Lordships to mine of the 17th of October and to my Report in answer to your Lordships Queries, Relative to the new Hanover Settlement, the very bad Effects of which are daily felt and growing, & they Seem at Present out of my reach & Authority.

An abstract of land grants registered in Georgia from the 27th of July, 1761, to the 27th of Jan., 1762, C.O. 5/648, E. 46, enclosed with Wright's letter to the Board of Trade, April 26, 1762.

Grant dated 7th July 1761.
To Henry Harramond for a town Lot etc. in Savannah together 50 acres of Land. Registered 30th July 1761.

Grant dated 13th April 1761.
To William Colson for 250 acres of Land in the Parish of St. George. Registered 30th July 1761.

Grant dated 13th April 1761.
To Abraham Lunday for 400 acres of Land in the parish of St. George. Registered 30th July 1761.

Grant dated 13th April 1761.
To Jacob Beale for 300 acres of Land in the Parish of St. Paul. Registered 30th July 1761.

Grant dated 7th July 1761.
To John Reitter for 100 acres of Land in the parish of St. Matthew. Registered 31st July 1761.

Grant dated 7th July 1761.
To James Cornock for a town Lot etc. in Savannah together 50 acres of Land. Registered 5th August 1761.

Grant dated 7th July 1761.
To Lewis Turner for 129 acres of Land being an Island and 2 Hammocks in Christ Church parish. Registered 5th August 1761.

Grant dated 13th April 1761.
To Jacob Mock for 200 acres of Land in the parish of St. Matthew. Registered 5th August 1761.

Grant dated 13th April 1761.
To Benjamin Stirk for 150 acres of Land in Christ Church Parish. Registered 6th August 1761.

Grant dated 7th July 1761.
To Joseph Wood for 450 acres of Land in Christ Church Parish. Registered 6th August 1761.

Grant dated 7th July 1761.
To Joseph Wood for a Wharf Lot in Savannah No. 1. Registered 6th August 1761.

Grant dated 7th July 1761.
To Lewis Johnson Esquire for a Town Lot & Garden lot in Savannah. Registered 7th August 1761.

Grant dated 7th July 1761.
To Moses Way for 150 acres of Land in the parish of St. Andrew. Registered 14th August 1761.

Grant dated 7th July 1761.
To Hugh Clark for 200 acres of Land in the parish of St. Andrew. Registered 14th August 1761.

Grant dated 13th April 1761.
To John Baker for 300 acres of Land in the parish of St. Andrew. Registered 14th August 1761.

Colonial Records   361

Grant dated 13th April 1761.
To John Gasper Hershman for 250 acres of Land in the parish of
St. George. Registered 18th August 1761.

Grant dated 13th April 1761.
To Phillip Jacob Greiner for 300 acres of Land in the Parish of St.
George. Registered 18th August 1761.

Grant dated 13th April 1761.
To Catherine Magdalen Greiner for 300 acres of Land in the Parish
of St. George. Registered 18th August 1761.

Grant dated 13th April 1761.
To William Knox Esquire for 500 acres of Land in the parish of St.
Matthew. Registered 28th August 1761.

Grant dated 23nd April 1761.
To Sir James Stirling Bart for 550 acres of Land in the Parish of
St. Phillip. Registered 2nd September 1761.

Grant dated 23rd April 1761.
To Sir James Stirling Bart for 550 acres of Land in the Parish of
St. Phillip. Registered 3rd September 1761.

Grant dated 7th July 1761.
To David Douglass for 500 acres of Land in the Parish of St.
George. Registered 24th September 1761.

Grant dated 7th July 1761.
To Lachlan McGillivray Esquire for 1000 acres of Land in the
Parish of St. George. Registered 26th September 1761.

Grant dated 7th July 1761.
To Peter Blyth for 300 acres of Land in the Parish of St. George.
Registered 24th September 1761.

Grant dated 7th July 1761.
To William Gerrard De Brahm for 300 acres of land in the Parish
of St. Matthew. Registered 25th September 1761.

Grant dated 13th April 1761.
To John Mackay for 50 acres of Land in the parish of St. Andrew.
Registered 25th September 1761.

Grant dated 13th April 1761.
To Andrew Way for 150 acres of Land in the Parish of St. John. Registered 25th September 1761.

Grant dated 13th April 1761.
To Thomas Lee for 200 acres of Land in the Parish of St. John. Registered 29th September 1761.

Grant dated 13th April 1761.
To Jacob Heinly for 100 acres of Land in the parish of St. Matthew. Registered 29th September 1761.

Grant dated 7th July 1761.
To Lucas Zeagler for 100 acres of land in the Parish of St. Matthew. Registered 29th September 1761.

Grant dated 13th April 1761.
To Andrew McCurrie for 100 acres of land in the Parish of St. George. Registered 30th September 1761.

Grant dated 7th July 1761.
To John Snook for a town lot etc. in Savannah together 50 acres of Land. Registered 30th September 1761.

Grant dated 7th July 1761.
To Mary Vanderplank widow for a town Lot etc. in Savannah together 50 acres of Land. Registered 6th October 1761.

Grant dated 1st July 1760.
To Josiah Powell for 460 acres of Land in the parish of St. John. Registered 7th October 1761.

Grant dated 1st July 1760.
To John Stailey for 200 acres of Land in the Parish of St. Matthew. Registered 7th October 1761.

Grant dated 5th February 1760.
To John Kill for 350 acres of land in the Parish of St. George. Registered 7th October 1761.

Grant dated 3rd December 1760.
To John Quarterman Junior for 300 acres of Land in the Parish of St. John. Registered 7th October 1761.

Grant dated 3rd December 1760.
To Arthur Carney for 150 acres of land in the Parish of St. John. Registered 7th October 1761.

Grant dated 3rd December 1760.
To Anthony Le Bon for 50 acres of land in Christ Church Parish. Registered 8th October 1761.

Grant dated 3rd December 1760.
To John Davis for 100 acres of Land in the Parish of St. John. Registered 8th October 1761.

Grant dated 3rd December 1760.
To John Davis for 200 acres of land in the Parish of St. John. Registered 8th October 1761.

Grant dated 3rd December 1760.
To Samuel Augspourger for 500 acres of Land in the Parish of St. James. Registered 8th October 1761.

Grant dated 3rd December 1760.
To Edward Somerville for 100 acres of Land in Christ Church Parish. Registered 14th October 1761.

Grant dated 3rd December 1760.
To Edward Somerville for a Wharf lot in Savannah No. 13. Registered 14th October 1761.

Grant dated 3rd December 1760.
To Edward Somerville for a Wharf lot in Savannah No. 1. Registered 13th October 1761.

Grant dated 25th April 1760.
To James Box for a Lot west of the town of Savannah No. 1. Registered 15th October 1761.

Grant dated 25th September 1760.
To Thomas Cross for a town Lot & Garden Lot in Savannah. Registered 15th October 1761.

Grant dated 2nd October 1759.
To Fredrick Fain for 120 acres of Land in Christ Church Parish. Registered 16th October 1761.

Grant dated 6th december 1759.

To Anne Margaret Finck for 50 acres of Land in the Parish of St. Matthew. Registered 16th October 1761.

Grant dated 7th November 1758.

To Jonas Mick for 100 acres of Land in the district of Goshen. Registered 16th October 1761.

Grant dated 7th August 1759.

To Francis Arthur for 600 acres of Land in the Parish of St. John. Registered 17th October 1761.

Grant dated 7th August 1759.

To Francis Arthur for 344 acres of Land in the parish of St. John. Registered 17th October 1761.

Grant dated 7th August 1759.

To Francis Arthur for 100 acres of land in the Parish of St. John. Registered 17th October 1761.

Grant dated 1st July 1760.

To Clement Martin Esquire for 400 acres of land in the parish of St. Matthew. Registered 19th October 1761.

Grant dated 1st July 1760.

To Clement Martin Esquire for 200 acres of land in the parish of St. Matthew. Registered 19th October 1761.

Grant dated 25th September 1760.

To Clement Martin Esquire for a Lot of 50 acres of land at Abercorn. Registered 19th October 1761.

Grant dated 30th April 1760.

To James Edward Powell Esquire for a Lot of 20 acres of land West of Savannah. Registered 19th October 1761.

Grant dated 5th June 1759.

To Grey Elliott Esquire for 100 acres of Land in the Parish of St. John. Registered 20th October 1761.

Grant dated 7th July 1761.

To Grey Elliott Esquire for a Wharf lot No. 10 in Savannah. Registered 20th October 1761.

Grant dated 13th April 1761.
To Lewis Johnson, Alexander Wylly & Thomas Bruce for a Wharf lot in Savannah. Registered 20th October 1761.

Grant dated 25th September 1760.
To Levi Marks for a town lot etc. in Savannah together 50 acres of land. Registered 20th October 1761.

Grant dated 1st May 1759.
To Levi Sheftall for 100 acres of Land in the Parish of St. Andrew. Registered 21st October 1761.

Grant dated 1st July 1760.
To Mordecai Sheftall for a Wharf Lot in Savannah No. 5. Registered 21st October 1761.

Grant dated 1st July 1760.
To James Graham for a Wharf Lot in Savannah No. 6. Registered 21st October 1761.

Grant dated 1st July 1760.
To James Parker for 135 acres of land in Christ Church parish & town lot & Garden lot in Savannah. Registered 21st October 1761.

Grant dated 6th December 1757.
To James Rutherford for 250 acres of land in the district of Ogechee. Registered 22d October 1761.

Grant dated 2nd October 1759.
To Donald Monroe for 100 acres of land in the parish of St. Andrew. Registered 22nd October 1761.

Grant dated 2nd October 1759.
To Conrade Etchard for 200 acres of land in the parish of St. Matthew. Registered 22nd October 1761.

Grant dated 4th December 1759.
To John Matthews for 100 acres of land in the parish of St. Phillip. Registered 23rd October 1761.

Grant dated 5th September 1758.
To Thomas Parker for 300 acres of Land being an Island between Vernon and Little Ogechee Rivers. Registered 23rd October 1761.

Grant dated 4th December 1759.
To Mary Bowling, Spinster, for a town Lot & Garden Lot in Savannah. Registered 23rd October 1761.

Grant dated 13th April 1761.
To Hannah Unseld & Elizabeth Meyers for 100 acres of Land in the Parish of St. Matthew. Registered 23rd October 1761.

Grant dated 13th April 1761.
To David Unseld for a town lot etc. in Savannah together 50 acres of Land. Registered 24th October 1761.

Grant dated 3rd December 1760.
To John Stacy for 50 acres of Land in the Parish of St. Andrew. Registered 3rd November 1761.

Grant dated 7th November 1758.
To Thomas Willson for 240 acres of land in Christ Church Parish. Registered 4th November 1761.

Grant dated 1st July 1760.
To Joseph Summers for 200 acres of Land in Christ Church Parish. Registered 4th November 1761.

Grant dated 1st July 1760.
To Alexander Wylly for 400 acres of Land in the parish of St. Phillip. Registered 4th November 1761.

Grant dated 3rd November 1761.
To William Mills for 250 acres of land in St. Johns Parish on Purchase from the Crown. Registered 6th November 1761.

Grant dated 3rd November 1761.
To his Honour James Wright Esquire for 2075 acres of Land in St. Andrews Parish. Registered 9th November 1761.

Grant dated 3rd November 1761.
To his Honour James Wright Esquire for 16 five acre Lots in Christ Church Parish. Registered 9th November 1761.

Grant dated 3rd November 1761.
To Pickering Robinson Esquire for a town Lot in Savannah No. 10. Registered 9th November 1761.

Colonial Records 367

Grant dated 3rd November 1761.
To Charles Watson Esquire for a Town Lot in Savannah. Registered 10th November 1761.

Grant dated 3rd November 1761.
To Charles Watson Esquire for a farm Lot No. 10 in the township of Savannah. Registered 10th November 1761.

Grant dated 3d November 1761.
To Grey Elliott Esquire for 500 acres of land in the Parish of St. Andrew. Registered 11th November 1761.

Grant dated 3d November 1761.
To Grey Elliott Esquire for 300 acres of land in the Parish of St. John. Registered 11th November 1761.

Grant dated 3d November 1761.
To James Read Esquire for 500 acres of Land in Christ Church Parish on purchase from the Crown. Registered 11th November 1761.

Grant dated 3rd November 1761.
To [Robert] Bolton for a town Lot No. 4 in Savannah. Registered 11th November 1761.

Grant dated 3rd November 1761.
To James Houstoun for 285 acres of land in Christ Church Parish. Registered 12th November 1761.

Grant dated 3rd November 1761.
To Joseph Gibbons Esquire for 300 acres of Land in Christ Church Parish. Registered 12th November 1761.

Grant dated 3rd November 1761.
To William Ewen for 500 acres of land in the Parish of St. George. Registered 12th November 1761.

Grant dated 3rd November 1761.
To James Box for 338 acres of Land in the Parish of St. Matthew. Registered 13th November 1761.

Grant dated 3rd November 1761.
To Thomas Kelly for 200 acres of land in the parish of St. Andrew. Registered 13th November 1761.

Grant dated 3rd November 1761.
To James Bratcher for 100 acres of Land in the Parish of St. Phillip. Registered 13th November 1761.

Grant dated 3rd November 1761.
To Mary Bowling for a town Lot & Garden lot in Savannah. Registered 13th November 1761.

Grant dated 3rd November 1761.
To Joachim Hartstone for 400 acres of land in the Parish of St. Matthew. Registered 14th November 1761.

Grant dated 5th February 1760.
To Daniel Donham for 250 acres of land in the Parish of St. Andrew. Registered 14th November 1761.

Grant dated 3rd November 1761.
To Peter Berger for 200 acres of land in the Parish of St. Matthew. Registered 14th November 1761.

Grant dated 3rd November 1761.
To John Eppinger for 300 acres of land in the parish of St. Matthew. Registered 16th November 1761.

Grant dated 3rd November 1761.
To Matthias Kugle for 350 acres of land in the Parish of St. Matthew. Registered 16th November 1761.

Grant dated 3rd November 1761.
To James Willson for a town lot etc. in Savannah together 50 acres of Land. Registered 17th November 1761.

Grant dated 3rd November 1761.
To George Bollinger for a town lot in Savannah in the third tything Reynolds ward. Registered 17th November 1761.

Grant dated 7th July 1761.
To James Baillou for 200 acres of land in Christ Church Parish. Registered 17th November 1761.

Grant dated 7th July 1761.
To James Baillou for a town Lot etc. in Savannah together 50 acres of land. Registered 17th November 1761.

Colonial Records 369

Grant dated 7th November 1758.
To Ann Green wife of Thomas Greene for a town lot etc. in Savannah together 50 acres of land. Registered 19th November 1761.

Grant dated 1st July 1760.
To William Camp for 300 acres of land in the Parish of St. George. Registered 19th November 1761.

Grant dated 9th December 1756.
To Lydia Dean, Widow, for a town Lot etc. in Savannah together 50 acres of land. Registered 19th November 1761.

Grant dated 3rd December 1760.
To Andrew Greiner for 200 acres of land in the Parish of St. George. Registered 20th November 1761.

Grant dated 25th September 1760.
To Michael Burghalter for 483 acres of Land in Christ Church Parish. Registered 20th November 1761.

Grant dated 13th April 1761.
To Benjamin William Borneman for 500 acres of Land in the Parish of St. George. Registered 21st November 1761.

Grant dated 25th September 1760.
To John Burnet for 150 acres of land in the Parish of St. John. Registered 24th November 1761.

Grant dated 25th September 1760.
To John Burnet for 57 acres of Land in the Parish of St. John. Registered 24th November 1761.

Grant dated 3rd December 1760.
To Benjamin Baker for 200 acres of land in the parish of St. John. Registered 24th November 1761.

Grant dated 7th July 1761.
To George Galphin for 499 acres of land in the Parish of St. Paul. Registered 27th November 1761.

Grant dated 7th July 1761.
To George Galphin for 499 acres of land in the parish of St. Paul. Registered 27th November 1761.

370   Colonial Records

Grant dated 7th July 1761.
To George Galphin for a town Lot in Augusta No. 4. Registered 27th November 1761.

Grant dated 7th July 1761.
To George Galphin for a town Lot in Augusta No. 10. Registered 27th November 1761.

Grant dated 7th July 1761.
To John Williams for 500 acres of land in the parish of St. Andrew. Registered 27th November 1761.

Grant dated 1st July 1760.
To Richard Baker for 250 acres of Land in the Parish of St. John. Registered 30th November 1761.

Grant dated 1st July 1760.
To Richard Baker for 100 acres of Land in the Parish of St. John. Registered 30th November 1761.

Grant dated 13th April 1761.
To Paul Dubors for 100 acres of Land in Christ Church Parish. Registered 1st December 1761.

Grant dated 7th July 1761.
To Audley Maxwell for 350 acres of Land in the Parish of St. John. Registered 1st December 1761.

Grant dated 27th November 1761.
To James Read Esquire for 238 acres of Land in Christ Church Parish. Registered 3d December 1761.

Grant dated 27th November 1761.
To George Glamer for 100 acres of land in the Parish of St. Matthew. Registered 3rd December 1761.

Grant dated 27th November 1761.
To Thomas Mills for 100 acres of Land in the Parish of St. Andrew. Registered 3rd December 1761.

Grant dated 27th November 1761.
To Stephen Millen for 150 acres of Land in the Parish of St. Matthew. Registered 4th December 1761.

Grant dated 27th November 1761.
To John Heinley for 100 acres of Land in the Parish of St. Matthew. Registered 4th December 1761.

Grant dated 27th November 1761.
To Christopher Cramer for 100 acres of land in the Parish of St. Matthew. Registered 5th December 1761.

Grant dated 27th November 1761.
To Andrew Greiner for 50 acres of Land in the Parish of St. George. Registered 5th December 1761.

Grant dated 27th November 1761.
To Peter Zipperer for 47 acres of Land in the Parish of St. Matthew. Registered 5th December 1761.

Grant dated 27th November 1761.
To Lachlan McGillivray Esquire for a Town Lot No. 2 in Savannah. Registered 7th December 1761.

Grant dated 27th November 1761.
To William Clifton Esquire for a town Lot in Savannah No. 8. Registered 7th December 1761.

Grant dated 27th November 1761.
To Thomas Eatton for a Town Lot in Savannah No. 4. Registered 7th December 1761.

Grant dated 27th November 1761.
To Mary Bryan, Widow, for a Town Lot in Savannah No. 8. Registered 7th December 1761.

Grant dated 27th November 1761.
To Benjamin Goldwire for a town Lot in Savannah No. 2. Registered 7th December 1761.

Grant dated 27th November 1761.
To Thomas Tripp for a town Lot in Savannah No. 6. Registered 7th December 1761.

Grant dated 27th November 1761.
To James Mutter for 200 acres of Land in Christ Church Parish. Registered 8th December 1761.

Grant dated 4th December 1759.
To Walter Denny for a town Lot & 50 acres of Land at Vernonburgh & parish of Christ Church. Registered 9th December 1761.

Grant dated 13th April 1761.
To Timothy Barnard for 500 acres of Land on Wilmington Island. Registered 10th December 1761.

Grant dated 3rd December 1760.
To John Gasper Betz for 200 acres of Land on Wilmington Island. Registered 11th December 1761.

Grant dated 3rd December 1760.
To John Michael Betz for 100 acres of land on Wilmington Island. Registered 11th December 1761.

Grant dated 7th July 1761.
To John Germany for 200 acres of Land in the Parish of St. Paul. Registered 12th December 1761.

Grant dated 7th July 1761.
To Robert Germany for 200 acres of land in the parish of St. Paul. Registered 12th December 1761.

Grant dated 7th July 1761.
To Samuel Chew for 50 acres of Land in the parish of St. Paul. Registered 12th December 1761.

Grant dated 27th November 1761.
To Thomas Goldsmith Esquire for a town Lot & farm Lot in Savannah. Registered 14th December 1761.

Grant dated 27th November 1761.
To Edmund Tannatt Esquire for a town Lot in Savannah No. 6. Registered 15th December 1761.

Grant dated 27 November 1761.
To Isaac LaRoche for a town Lot in Savannah No. 6. Registered 15th December 1761.

Grant dated 27th November 1761.
To Thomas Hamilton for a town Lot in Savannah No. 3. Registered 15th December 1761.

Grant dated 15th December 1761.
To John Milledge Esquire for 500 acres of land in the Parish of St. Phillip on Purchase from the Crown. Registered 19th December 1761.

Grant dated 15th December 1761.
To Michael Burghaulder for 50 acres of Land in Christ Church Parish. Registered 19th December 1761.

Grant dated 15th December 1761.
To Michael Burghaulder Junior for 50 acres of land in Christ Church Parish. Registered 19th December 1761.

Grant dated 15th December 1761.
To Michael Weinkauff for 43 acres of land in the Parish of St. Matthew. Registered 21st December 1761.

Grant dated 15th December 1761.
To Peter Tondee for a town Lot etc. in Savannah together 50 acres of land. Registered 21st December 1761.

Grant dated 15th December 1761.
To Joseph Wood for a town Lot in Savannah No. 6. Registered 21st December 1761.

Grant dated 7th July 1761.
To Jonas Mick for 150 acres of Land in the Parish of St. Matthew. Registered 22nd December 1761.

Grant dated 4th December 1759.
To James Sunier for 100 acres of Land in Christ Church Parish. Registered 23rd December 1761.

Grant dated 4th December 1759.
To Gasper Sneider for a town lot & fifty acres of Land at Vernonburgh. Registered 29th December 1761.

Grant dated 1st July 1760.
To William Dodds for 100 acres of Land in the parish of St. Matthew. Registered 31st December 1761.

Grant dated 25th September 1760.
To William Butler for 500 acres of Land in the parish of St. Phillip. Registered 31st December 1761.

Grant dated 3rd December 1760.
To William Butler for 350 acres of Land in the parish of St. Phillip. Registered 31st December 1761.

Grant dated 13th April 1761.
To Benjamin Andrew for 200 acres of Land in the parish of St. John. Registered 5th January 1762.

Grant dated 25th September 1760.
To Samuel Lewis for 100 acres of Land in the parish of St. Andrew. Registered 5th January 1762.

Grant dated 7th June 1759.
To Morgan Tabb for 500 acres of Land on great Ogechee. Registered 6th January 1762.

Grant dated 7th August 1759.
To His Excellency Henry Ellis Esquire for 500 acres of land in Christ Church Parish. Registered 6th January 1762.

Grant dated 1st July 1760.
To Thomas Peacock for 150 acres of land in the Parish of St. Andrew. Registered 13th January 1762.

Grant dated 7th July 1761.
To Thomas Christie for 350 acres of land in the parish of St. Andrew. Registered 20th January 1762.

Grant dated 5th January 1762.
To William Knox Esquire for 315 acres of land in the parish of St. Phillip. Registered 20th January 1762.

Grant dated 5th January 1762.
To Josiah Osgood Junior for 250 acres of Land in the parish of St. Andrew. Registered 20th January 1762.

Grant dated 5th January 1762.
To John Mullryne Esquire for 50 acres of Land in the parish of St. Phillip. Registered 20th January 1762.

Grant dated 5th January 1762.
To Catherine Mullryne for 500 acres of Land in the parish of St. Phillip. Registered 21st January 1762.

Grant dated 5th January 1762.
To Thomas Irwin for 250 acres of Land in the Parish of St. George.
Registered 21st January 1762.

Grant dated 5th January 1762.
To Thomas Irwin for 100 acres of Land in the parish of St. George.
Registered 21st January 1762.

Grant dated 5th January 1762.
To Mary Tatnall for 500 acres of land in the Parish of St. Phillip.
Registered 22nd January 1762.

Grant dated 5th January 1762.
To Samuel Lewis for 50 acres of Land in the Parish of St. Andrew.
Registered 22nd January 1762.

Grant dated 5th January 1762.
To Hugh Kennedy for 50 acres of land in the parish of St. Matthew.
Registered 22nd January 1762.

Grant dated 5th January 1762.
To John Gionovoli for a town Lot in Savannah No. 1. Registered 22nd January 1762.

Grant dated 7th July 1761.
To Thomas Carter for 150 acres of Land in the parish of St. John.
Registered 22nd January 1762.

The aforesaid Abstract of the Grants Registered from the 27th of July 1761 To the 27th of January 1762 Compared With the Registers Books at Savannah this 4th day of February 1762.

Pat Houstoun, Register

James Wright to the Board of Trade, June 10, 1762, Savannah, received Aug. 26, read Nov. 29, 1762, C.O. 5/648, E. 47, giving an account of the state of affairs in Georgia with respect to the silk culture and Indian affairs, and including a plan of the fort on Cockspur Island.

My Lords

With this your lordships will receive a Copy of my last of the 26th of April, & Mine of the 20th of February with my Report, to which I beg leave to refer your lordships.

I must now Acquaint your lordships that within a Short time after I had wrote my last, I received Accounts from the Creek Country not so Favourable as formerly. I found that the French had been very Active, and that some Indians in their Interest had been Raising Jealousies amongst the others, and Endeavouring to Influence the Nation, & Embroil us with them. And things wore but a gloomy aspect, but I have very lately had some of them down with me, and if they are to be credited, matters will yet Continue quiet. But these Wretches are such a kind of People, that its Impossible my Lords to Answer for their Conduct for a Month together.

The Reasons my Lords given for the Commotion amongst them, According to my Information, were, the French told them that an English Army was Coming against Mobile, and if they Succeeded, that they would be just in the Neighbourhood of the Creeks, & intended to Extirpate their Nation next. This alarmed 'em much & some Spys were sent down to see if any Preparations were making here, who were soon Convinced there was Nothing unusual, but on hearing that there was War with Spain, they were again alarmed, and had many Meetings & Consultations, at which some of them Harangued to the Following Effect, that the English said they were Victorious everywhere, had taken all the French Settlements at the Northward, and that they intended to take Mobile etc. and were now going to make War with the Spaniards, and would certainly take St. Augustine, and then what would become of them, that we should not forget the Murders they had Committed, and when Possessed of all those Places, would undoubtedly demand ample Satisfaction, & if every thing we thought Proper to direct, was not Complied with, would set the Numerous Nation of the Chactaws on them (these People join the French Settlements at Mobile & are mostly in their Interest).

These & many other matters were debated Amongst them & there was many divisions & Partys, and upon the whole I learn & believe the Resolution was to keep quiet till they saw further how things go on, but my Lords Certainly our Situation is very Critical with them, and this Circumstance I'm afraid has Produced an accommodation of the differences between the Spaniards & them. A great Part of the upper Creeks I believe have or Will agree to it, and am informed several have been at Pensacola to receive Presents on that Occasion, & Some few of the Lower

Creeks, who favour the French & Spanish Interest talk of going to St. Marks on the same Errand. But a Party that was down here last week tell me the Lower Towns have Suffered most from the Spaniards, and by far the greatest Part of them are determined not to make up the Breach. If this should Prove so, it will certainly be a Favourable Circumstance for this Province. But the French have taken infinite Pains to bring this about, and I have great reason to believe that some Villains to the Southward of the Alatamaha have received rewards from the Spaniards at St. Augustine to Endeavour likewise to Accommodate matters between them and the dangerous & bad Effects of that Settlement appear more & more every day.

It is with great Pleasure I can now assure your lordships that this has been a very Favourable Season for the Silk Culture, and that there has been delivered into the Filature 15101 lb. Weight of Cocoons, & Mr. Ottolenghe tells me that they are the best he has yet received, and Exceed the greatest Quantity ever made here by about 5100 Pounds. The Quality of the Silk is Extremely good & fine. The Premium My Lords on this Quantity of Silk & Other Expences attending the Management of that Article will Amount to about £2350 Sterling which Sume my lords I shall find myself under the Necessity of Drawing, and giving Certificates for, or that Valuable Commodity which your Lordships have had so long at Heart to Encourage & Establish as a Staple in this Province, will be lost, for were it not for the Parliamentary Encouragement I am very Apprehensive few would go upon it. But by the Continuance of that for a while longer, so many will be Established in it, that when it is Withdrawn, yet, being well acquainted with the Culture and having their Plantations of Trees & every thing in order, they will still go on, tho' at a very Considerably less Profit.

By your Lordships letter of the 27 February 1761, it appears that there was then a Balance in the Agents Hands on Account of the Silk Culture, tho' your lordships are not Pleased to Mention to what amount, and besides which my lords there was a Saving in the last years grant of £140.14.0 only £859.6.0 being drawn for, and 332 lb. of Silk was shipt from hence in February last, Suppose [it] may sell for £300, to which add the grant by Parliament for this year Say £1000, & at least 900 lb. of Exceeding fine Silk that is now almost ready to Ship, which I suppose may neat [net] £900. Therefore my Lords on the Strength of all these Sumes & to prevent the bad Consequences that must attend the Culture by a refusal to pay the Premium, and to Support the Credit

Interest & Advantage of the Province, I have declared that I will pay the Premium on the whole Quantity of Cocoons, and draw on, & give Certificates to the Agent for the amount of that, & the Other usual and Necessary Expences attending that Culture. Your Lordships see the Strength and Foundation I Propose to draw upon, and my reasons for so doing, and which I humbly hope you will approve of, I have my Lords in every respect acted with the greatest Frugality & Caution Possible, as Mr. Martyn can Clearly inform your Lordships, but I must beg your speedy directions with respect to this matter another year, and whether only so many Cocoons are to be received into the Public Filature as the £1000 (which I Presume will at least be Continued by Parliament) will answer the Bounty for, or whether none is to be received but the Produce of this Province, or whether any quantity that is brought is to be received, & that my drafts will be answered or in what manner am I to Conduct myself relative to this affair. I shall hope for your Lordships Commands on this Point which appears to me very essential to the Province.

I have now my Lords had the Honor to be in the Administration of this Government 19 Months, in which time I have stated many matters to your Lordships, Some of which I hoped for your Lordships commands & directions upon, being at a loss & under some difficulty without but have not been happy enough to receive any from your Lordships but of the 31 October 1760, 27 February 1761 & 28 April 1761. If others have been wrote, they did not come to hand.

By this Opportunity I send your lordships a Copy of the Minutes of the Proceedings of the Governor in Council from the 5th of January 1762 to the 26th of March inclusive, also the Minutes of the Assembly from the 10th of November to the 4th of March inclusive, also the Custom House Accounts from the 5th of January 1762 to the 5th of April, & the Abstract of Grants from the 27th July 1761 to 27th January 1762.

The Indian Presents being taken last Summer Proved very unfortunate, they are now arrived at Charles Town, & I hope I shall get 'em safe from thence, as they were never more wanted. I doubt not but Mr. Martyn will apply for more, for these being greatly reduced by the double Expence of Insurance etc., it will be impossible to attempt any thing with respect to the Lands claimed by the Indians, nor is this by any means a Proper time to touch on a Subject of that kind.

I am very Sorry my Lords to be under the Necessity of saying I have the greatest reason to Complain of the Conduct & behaviour of Mr. Grover the Chief Justice. He is Certainly a man of the most malevolent disposition, forward in thwarting & Opposing measures of Government and instead of giving the least assistance, or being of any use or service (Save only attending the Courts, which is next to Nothing) he is in Example & every other way injurious. I shall very soon take a view of his Conduct since my arrival, which I think will appear exceptionable & bad in almost every Particular, & what it was before I came, I doubt not but your lordships have heard from Governor Ellis.

P.S. 21 June

I have just received my Lords Pretty good information the Governor of Louisiana from New Orleans has sent a strong invitation to both the Cherokees & Creeks to come & see him, and that he is enabled to make them very Handsome Presents, two Vessels being lately arrived from old France with goods & Troops, and four more being daily Expected, all with Troops & Goods for his Friends the Indians, that will come & see him.

Inclosed, your Lordships have a Plan of the Fort now Erecting at Cockspur Island.

James Wright to the Board of Trade, July 26, 1762, Savannah, received Sept., read Nov. 29, 1762, C.O. 5/648, E. 49, explaining and enclosing a copy of a bill for better collecting quit rents in Georgia.

My Lords

Having wrote your Lordships fully on the 10 of last Month, by the Ships Vigilant & Violet, both which sailed from this Place, I have nothing now to Trouble your Lordships with, but to send a duplicate of the Bill which I found it necessary to Promote for the more easy & better Collecting of His Majesties quit rents, which Bill has been Passed by the assembly, and I now Transmit the Same to your Lordships, Pursuant to His Majesties 68th Instruction. I think if such a Law is Passed, it will be greatly for his Majesties Service, and may prove Effectual for the recovery of the Quitrents. I shall hope to have your lordships speedy directions thereon, as if approved of, the sooner it takes place the better. The 1st Copy of this Bill I sent in the Box with my letter 26th April, and the Copys of the Bills Passed the 4th of March last, all which I hope your lordships have received.

Scale to the Map of 100 Chains @ 40 p. Inch

144

Part of Tybe Island

Light house

Sound of
Sand Banck

Savannah River

South Channal

flat

North Channal

A
Cockspoor Island
B

Sand Banck

Sand Banck

Above is the Map of Cockspoor Island in the Embushure
of Savannah River, fortified with a redoubted Fayssoniere
Lt A. aible to mount Eleven great Guns & four Mortars or Hau-
bizers & a Batterie Lt B: mounting Three Guns of 18 pounders
the latter to Comand the North Channal being Closs under
the Batterus Shore & the former to Comand to Comand the
South Channal, the River being there under 20 Chains
Consequantly within point blanck in Width

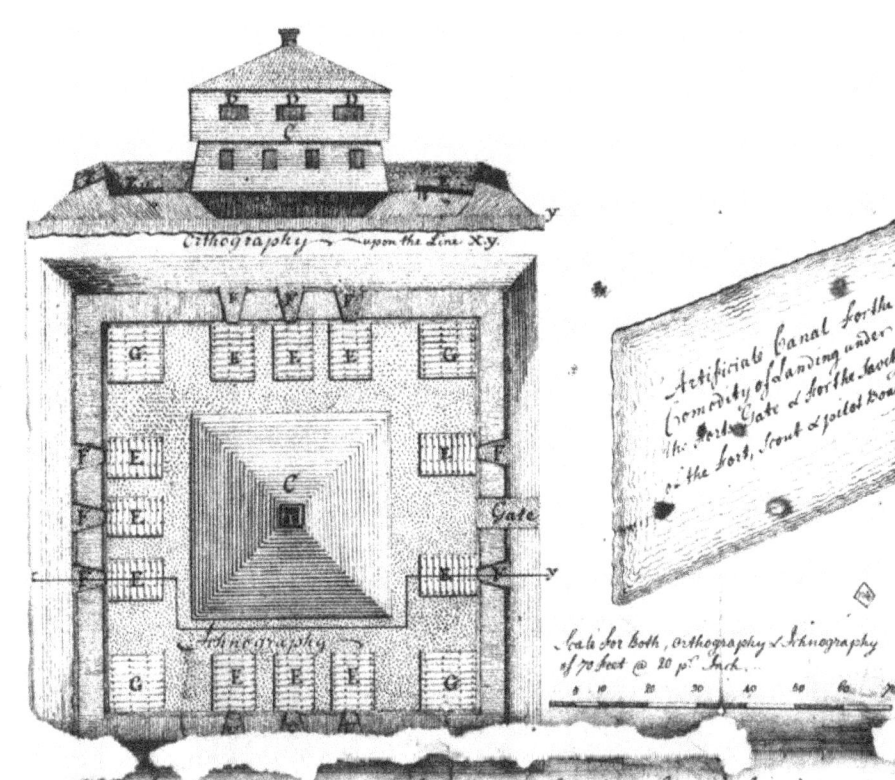

James Wright to the Board of Trade, Oct. 1, 1762, Savannah, read Dec. 7, 1762, C.O. 5/648, E. 51, relating to the state of silk culture and other affairs within the province.

My Lords

On the 2d of August I had the Honor to receive your Lordships letters of the 4th & 25th February and the 8th of April. And on the 20th anothers of the 3d of June. The 1st intirely relative to the Appointment of some proper Person to be instructed by Mr. Ottolenghe in the Silk Culture on which Subject I have had some Conversation with him, and find his apprehension is that after he has Instructed another sufficiently to conduct the business Possibly he may be laid aside in his old age unable to help himself or turn his Hands to any thing else, be reduced to distress. He is very inclinable to give the best assistance & Instruction in writing & otherwise to qualify another, provided he is assured of being allowed his Salary for Life or being continued in the Employment, as it is the only dependance he has for his Support, and Submits his Case to your lordships equitable Consideration, whose further orders on this Point I believe he will readily obey.

I wrote your Lordships pretty fully on the Silk Culture in mine of the 10th of June last, to which I beg leave to refer, & hope to receive your lordships speedy directions thereon, least that Culture should Suffer. I have not yet had the satisfaction to be Informed that the £1000 usually granted by Parliament has been Voted for that Service for 1762. Possibly Mr. Martyn may have wrote me of it, but if he did his letter miscarried, and I have been under some difficulty in getting the money to Pay the Respective Persons who delivered Cocoons into the Filature, and for the other necessary Expences attending that Commodity, the whole Expence of which amount to £2376.6.6 and for which I have given Certificates. The Fund for Payment of which I Presume to be as follows, Vitz., Granted by Parliament £1000. 1048 Pounds weight of the finest & best Silk ever produced in Georgia Suppose to neat [net] £1050, the Savings in the £1000 granted for 1761, £140.14.0 and the Ballance of £185.12.6 to come out of such other Savings as may be in Mr. Martyns hands. [I] am Extremely sorry to find that the 332 lb. of Silk shipt on Board the Elizabeth in February last was not insured, as the Proceeds of that would have answered all Ends fully, & left an overplus. I hope to be Honored with your Lordships answer to mine in June relative to the Silk Culture, least any Prejudice should happen, from an

Opinion that the Bounty will not be Continued, and that I may know how to Conduct my Self, and to Avoid the difficulties mentioned in that letter.

It gives me the greatest Satisfaction to have your Lordships Approbation of my Conduct, and Reasons for assenting to the several Bills on the 9th of June 1761. These Laws my Lords, as far as I have had any Opportunity of seeing, or judging of their operation & effect, seem salutary & usefull. A defect was discovered in that part of the Law laying a Tax on Transient Trade & on deliquent negroes Imported from other Colonies, which is Rectified by a Subsequent Bill Passed the 4th of March last, and I think it a very Proper Regulation.

My Lords in order to prevent all clandestine Trade & his Majesties Enemies from being supplied with Provisions & other Considerations, I judged it for His Majesties Service that Sunbury, a very well settled Town 25 Miles South in a direct line, but as the Road is made at least 40 Miles from hence, & having an exceeding good Harbour & inlet from the sea, should be made a Port of Entry. Therefore Pursuant to the Powers given me by his Majesties Royal Commission I have with the advice of the Council accordingly declared & Established the same to be a Port of Entry, and have appointed Mr. Thomas Carr Collector, John Martin Naval Officer and Francis Lee Searcher, of all which I have acquainted the Commissioners of His Majesties Customs & hope your Lordships will approve of my Conduct herein.

Immediately on the Receipt of your Lordships of the 8th of April relative to the Sale of the Forfeited Lots of Land in & near the Town of Savanah, I gave directions that all the grants that were ordered & had not passed through the Offices, should be immediately finished, and the whole of those Lots that were found to remain unclaimed & Forfeited, are now disposed of and amount to £663.12.7-1/2 Sterling the Reason of this difference my Lords is chiefly by one Lot, that is Built on and Improved, and which had been claimed by one Beneworth but has since appeared to be one of the Forfeited Lots & sold for £105 Sterling. This & some few other Lots since discovered to be Vacant, which were not known to be so till lately has raised the Sume from £400, as mentioned in Mine of the 28th of december last, to £663.12.7-1/2 which now the whole is settled & finished appears to be the Sume in my hands, and ready to be applied or paid as His Majesty shall be Pleased to direct, if towards Building our Church, it would be very acceptable.

Your Lordships approbation of the measure taken for the security of the Province & its Trade, by Erecting a Fort upon

Cockspur Island, and of the Provision made for Effecting that service gives me great Pleasure, and I hope whenever your Lordships are pleased to fill up the Vacancies in the Council that some tolerable good men may be found to fill their seats in the Assembly. The additional Instruction & order of his Majesty in Council of the 15th of May 1761, I shall take due care to Observe.

Memorial of the agent for Georgia, William Knox, to the Board of Trade, Dec. 7, 1762, London, C.O. 5/648, E. 52, setting forth the advantages of the silk culture there and praying that the encouragement given it by the public may be continued.

Humbly Sheweth

That your Lordships Memorialist has been made accquainted by Governor Wright in his Letters dated in Georgia 21 June last, That the Season had proved as favourable to the Silk Culture in that Province, that more than 15,000 pounds weight of Coccoons had been brought to the Filature in Savannah and the Silk reeled from them is of the very best quality. So large a quantity produced in one Season, is a Proof that the climate and soil of Georgia are well adapted to the culture of Silk and that the Bounty granted by Parliament through your Lordships recommendation, for the encouragement of that Culture has had a very good Effect.

Your Memorialist on behalf of his Constituents, with all thankfulness acknowledges your Lordships Goodness in obtaining for them the continuance of the Parliamentary Bounty for so many years past, and for the prudent manner in which your Lordships have always directed it to be applied. To this bounty and your Lordships application of it is owing not only the increase of the Silk Culture in Georgia, but its existence there. And when your Lordships perceive, upon reviewing the Lists of the Families employed in that culture, that near half the white Inhabitants of that Province are engaged in it, Few of whom could have supported themselves in so warm a climate by severer Labour, Your Memorialist hopes your Lordships will be of opinion, that the Colony of Georgia has not only been greatly benefited, but that the Frontier to his Majestys Southern Provinces has been greatly strengthened by the encouragement given to the Silk Culture.

Your Memorialist laments that the Progress of the Silk Culture has not been greater and more rapid since the first transportation of Settlers to Georgia in the year 1732. But your Memorialist beseeches your Lordships to consider, that it was not untill the year

1752 that Georgia became a Kings Government, and that it was only a short time before that year that the Inhabitants could have an absolute Property in their Lands, could have Slaves to assist them in cultivating them, or could have a free trade with the West India Islands. And as these restrictions prevented the Settlement of the Province and the production of other Commodities notwithstanding the large Sums annualy granted by Parliament for the Settlement of Georgia, so did they likewise obstruct the progress of the Silk Culture. Since the Colony came under the Jurisdiction of your Lordships Board, It has began to flourish. Its Inhabitants have increased. Its Trade and Products have become of National Importance, and the culture of Silk has made a proportionable Progress.

Your Lordships Memorialist begs leave to represent to your Lordships that the culture of Silk in Georgia has still obstructions to struggle with, which prevent its Progress. The Principal of these is the narrow limits to which the Colony is confined by His Majestys Commission to his Governor, and by the Treatys subsisting with the Creek Indians. The number of white Inhabitants at present in that Province do not amount to Six thousand[78] and yet by an account deliverd your Memorialist by the Surveyor General of Georgia in February last, it appears that there are not Lands in the power of the Governor and Council to Grant, sufficient for the accommodation of Fifty Families more. And where there is and can be no greater number of Inhabitants it is impossible for any culture to thrive greatly. What adds to the difficultys occasioned by the small number of Inhabitants, is, that their Settlements are confined to the Sea Coast. For in that situation the climate depends upon the sitting of the wind and is therefore always variable. A Southerly Wind blows immediately from the West Indian Seas and is therefore always warm, whereas a North Westerly wind by passing over the vast Continent of America which is coverd with Snow untill April, is in the Winter and Spring Months, always cold. Hence it often happens that when by the continuance of a Southerly wind for some days in February or March, The Mulberry Trees have put out their Leaves and the Silkworms have hatched. The wind has Shifted to the Northwest and brought with it so keen a Frost as to destroy the Leaves and perish the Worms. This could never be the case if the Settlements were carryed higher up in the Country, for the

---

78. Wright fixed the white population at 6,100 in his letter of April 15, 1761, p. 306, above.

Southerly Winds in the Spring would be cooled in their passage over the Land and consequently the Trees would not put forth, nor the Worms hatch so early in the Season, and therefore would not be liable to be destroyed by Frosts when the Wind shifted to the North.

Your Memorialist flatters himself that these obstructions to the Progress of the Silk Culture in Georgia as well as to the Settlement of that Colony will now be intirely removed by the accquisition of the important Countrys of Mobile and Florida. He hopes that through your Lordships Interposition the boundarys of Georgia will be greatly extended as well along the Sea Coast as up in the Country, and that so many Inhabitants will thereby be admitted and settled in such situations that with other valuable Articles of Commerce. The culture of Silk will be greatly increased and less subject to failure. The Large Proffits the people employed in it this Season have made will excite every other Inhabitant to attend to that culture, and with more hands and closer attention a large increase may reasonably be expected. With so fair a prospect of Success your Memorialist humbly entreats your Lordships to continue your care of this valuable culture, and as you have attended it in its Infancy, to cherish it untill it arrives at maturity. The continuance of your Lordships care may now soon raise it to a state that will manifest its Importance to the Nation. Without your Lordships regard it must droop and in a little time altogether fail. The People of Great Britain will then be deprived of one great benifit of the accquisitions made by the Peace. Your Lordships will not have the Honor of having added Silk to the other valuable productions of the Colonys, and half the present number of White Inhabitants in Georgia must quit that Province, to their own ruin, the weakning the Southern Frontier and preventing new Inhabitants from settling in the Countrys ceded to Great Britain in that Quarter.

Your Memorialist therefore humbly Prays your Lordships to take the Premisses into consideration and that your Lordships will recommend to Parliament this Session the further continuance of the Bounty on Silk raised in Georgia, and that your Lordships will not make any alteration in the manner of applying the said Bounty.

The Petition of William Gray to the Board of Trade, London, received and read Dec. 8, 1762, C.O. 5/648, E. 53, asking for a copy of the Board's representation upon which Reynolds was removed from the government of Georgia.

Humbly Sheweth

That your Lordships Petitioner in the year 1756 did arive in the Collony of Georgia on board an English vessel loaded with Deerskins which was entered at the Custom house in form and the Cargo intended to be disposed of there. But not finding the market to his mind he Cleard out for Charlestown in South Carolina when before his departure the Ship was Seized by order of Mr. Reynolds (who was then Governour of Georgia) and your Petitioner was made prisoner under the most absurd & groundless pretences. The Ship & Cargo being sold at the same time without any account ever being given of the application of the money arising from that sale for which unjust proceedings Your Petitioner has brought an Action against Mr. Reynolds in the Court of King's Bench for false imprisonment and Damages. As in all disputes between persons in a private station and those in power the prejudices are naturally on the side of Authority. Your Petitioner begs leave to Corroborate the justice of his Cause by demanding a Copy of the Representation this Right Honourable board made to the King showing the reasons why his Majesty should be graciously pleased to remove the said Governour.

Samuel Martin, Treasury Chambers, to the Board of Trade, Feb. 14, 1763, London, read Feb. 17, 1763, C.O. 5/648, E. 54, asking that the Board lay before the House of Commons an estimate of the expense for Georgia from June 24, 1762, to June 24, 1763.

Sir

I desire you will acquaint the Lords Commissioners of Trade and Plantations that the Chancellor of the Exchequer hath Received his Majesty's Commands, That their Lordships should prepare and lay before the House of Commons an Estimate of the Expence attending the Colony of Georgia from 24th of June 1762 to 24th of June 1763.

Copy of Order in Council of March 16, 1763, Court at St. James, read April 26, 1763, C.O. 5/648, E. 55, directing the removal of William Grover from the office of Chief Justice and one of the Council of Georgia.

Upon reading at the Board, a Report from the Right Honourable the Lords of the Committee of Council for Plantation Affairs, dated the 3d of this Instant in the Words following, Vizt.

"In Obedience to Your Majestys Orders referring to this Com-
"mittee an Address from the Council of Georgia, in their Legisla-
"tive Capacity to the Governor of that Colony (laid before Your
"Majesty by the Lords Commissioners of Trade and Plantations)
"together with a Report of a Committee of the said Council ap-
"pointed to consider the Journals of the Proceedings of the Lower
"House of Assembly, upon preparing the Tax Bill for the Year 1761,
"in which Report some Matters are stated relative to the Conduct
"of William Grover Esquire Chief Justice of the said Colony. The
"Lords of the Committee of Council this day took all the said Pa-
"pers into their Consideration, whereby it appeared, that a Com-
"mittee of the said Lower House of Assembly had come to a Reso-
"lution not to make any Provision for the Publick Officers of the
"Colony in their Tax Bill for the said Year, declaring that the
"Estimate allotted for those Officers ought not to be paid by the
"Publick of the Colony, in regard His Majesty had allowed each
"of them a competent Salary, That the said Resolution being of
"an unusual and extraordinary Nature, The Council of the Colony
"judged it proper to direct a Committee of their own Body to make
"Enquiry into the Cause thereof, and to Report whether there were
"any, and what Grounds for their coming to the said Resolution;
"That the Committee had thereupon reported, that it appeared to
"them to have been founded upon an Information the said Com-
"mittee of the Lower House had received from the aforenamed Mr.
"Grover, the Chief Justice of the Colony, and likewise a Member
"of Your Majestys Council there, who had not only voluntarily
"offered himself to appear before the said Committee of the Lower
"House, but had actually deposed upon Oath before them to the
"following Effect Vizt. That in a Conversation which he had three
"Years before in London with a Noble Lord, who was at that time
"the first acting Commissioner in Your Majestys Board of Trade
"and Plantations, he had been told by his Lordship (amongst other
"things) That he must expect no Fees for his Office of Chief Jus-
"tice from the Publick of Georgia, as the Province provided none
"in their Tax Bill for the Publick Officers for Publick Services.
"But the said Committee further reported, that notwithstanding
"this Information of Mr. Grovers and the Resolution taken by the
"Committee of the Lower House thereupon, that it appeared by
"the Estimate annexed to the Tax Bill passed for the said Year,
"that the usual Provisions were made therein for most of the said
"Officers, And the Committee then concluded their Report with

"the following Observations upon this proceeding of Mr. Grover
"Vizt., That a Chief Justice in submitting himself to be examined
"upon Oath before a Committee of the Lower House of Assembly,
"or to attend that House without Leave first obtained for that pur-
"pose, from Your Majestys Governor of the Colony, is a precedent
"which they apprehend to be of dangerous Consequence, and en-
"tirely subversive of the Constitution of the General Assembly of
"the Province, as established by Your Majestys Commission and
"Instructions to Your Governor, And likewise that the said Chief
"Justice had taken upon himself to report as the Words of that no-
"ble Lord Expressions that do not consist with the Knowledge his
"Lordship must be presumed to have of the Fact, by the Office his
"Lordships held at that time.

"The Lords of the Committee having thus laid before Your Maj-
"esty the State of the Case with respect to the Conduct and Be-
"haviour of the said Mr. Grover, together with the Sense of Your
"Majestys Council of that Province thereupon, take leave to make
"only this One Observation of their own, That in Case any Credit
"had been given to Mr. Grovers Information, the Publick Officers
"of the Province must have been left destitute of their Allowance
"for a whole Year, it not appearing that Your Majesty had made
"any such Provision in lieu thereof.

"Their Lordships do therefore humbly offer it as their Opinion,
"that the said Mr. Grover ought to be removed from his Post of
"Chief Justice of the Colony of Georgia, and likewise from his
"Seat in the Council of that Colony."

His Majesty this day took the said Report into Consideration, and was pleased, with the Advice of His Privy Council, to approve thereof, and accordingly to declare His Royal Pleasure, that the said William Grover be removed from his Post of Chief Justice of the Province of Georgia, and also from his Seat in the Council of that Province. And the Right Honourable the Earl of Egremont, One of His Majestys Principal Secretarys of State, is to receive His Majestys Commands for appointing some other Person to be Chief Justice of Georgia in the room of Mr. Grover. And the Lords Commissioners for Trade and Plantations are to recommend to His Majesty at this Board a proper Person to supply his Seat in the Council of that Province.

James Wright to the Board of Trade, Nov. 8, 1762, Savannah, read May 3, 1763, C.O. 5/648, E. 56, respecting the behavior of Chief Justice William Grover and giving his reasons for suspending him.

My Lords

The Extraordinary Conduct of Mr. Grover the Chief Justice appearing on all Occasions, and his whole behaviour being so excessively bad, and receiving Complaints against him, I found myself under a necessity of reviewing and Considering it and which I did from the time of my Arrival. The Result of which was, the Gentlemen of the Council Present declared "That it appeared to "them, and they were unanimous and clear in Opinion that Mr. "Grover's Conduct & Behaviour as Chief Justice has been & is, "dishonorable, partial, arbitrary, illegal, indecent, & not con- "sistent with the Character, duty & dignity of his Office, and "were also unanimous in Opinion that he is unworthy of, & not "fit to be Continued in the Office of Chief Justice of this Province, "and that it would be for the Honour & Service of his Majesty & "of this Province that he should be Suspended untill his Majesties "Pleasure be known thereon: and advised me to Suspend him Ac- "cordingly." And which I have done, and agreeable to His Majesties Instructions, am now to give your Lordships my Reasons for so doing, and which I conceive will most evidently appear to your Lordships from the following Narrative of Fact, and Observations upon them.

Governor Ellis left the Province on the 2nd of November 1760 and Mr. Grover tho' one of the Council did not attend for upwards of 3 Months, when I ordered a letter to be wrote summoning him, and requiring his Attendance, on which he came to me with a Resignation of his seat in writing under Hand & Seal. I desired him to reconsider the matter, & if he continued in the same Mind, I would sometime after Accept of it. And he continuing to absent himself, in October 1761, I received his Resignation, and Acquainted your lordships therewith. Here I would Observe that I Conceive it to be the duty of all Officers of the Crown to be assisting to Government in all things within their Respective Departments, and as Mr. Grover was one of the Principal Officers here, and received a Salary of £500 per annum for doing very little, it was more particularly his duty to have assisted in Council, but this he declined, & on the Contrary, has Constantly shewn a spirit & disposition to Thwart & Oppose proper Measures of Government.

With Respect to his improper Conduct in interesting himself with the Assembly about the Allowances to the Officers of the Crown, it would be Presumption in me to take any Notice of that, your Lordships having submitted it to his Majesties Consideration. On the 13th of July 1761, I received a Petition from George Leonard

& six other Soldiers belonging to the detachment of His Majesties
Independent Companies doing duty in this Province, complaining
of being Imprisoned by Order of the Chief Justice, on Supposition
of being concerned in an assault, and that altho' the Principal
Partys had settled the matter, yet they were detained in Prison,
to their own great grievance, & the detriment of His Majesties
Service, and therefore Praying Relief. On examining into the
cause of the Imprisonment of these People, it appeared by Mr.
Swetenhams deposition on oath, That on a Quarrel between him
& Mesrs. McKeithen and Willson at Frederica, he & several
Soldiers had been brought from thence to Savanah by a Warrant
from Mr. Grover to answer the Complaint of the said McKeithen
& Willson, and on his attending the Chief Justice he demanded
Bail of him with 2 Sureties to swear themselves worth £2000 Sterling Clear of Debt. This my Lords was £2000 each, tho' I observe
it is not so clearly expressed in the Minutes. That sometime
afterwards the Chief Justice told Swetenham that the Parties had
left the affair to him to make up, and gave Swetenham the following Proposal in his, Grovers, own hand writing, Vizt: "That
"all the Soldiers against whom warrants had been granted, shall
"be exchanged, & the same Number from Savanah sent to replace
"them, and shall not return to Frederica for 3 years, this to be
"stipulated by Captains Demeré & Goldsmith. The Prisoners to
"remain in Goal till the exchange is made. That Swetenham shall
"acknowledge his misbehaviour & sign a proper Acknowledgement.
"That Swetenham & the Soldiers shall continue on their recog-
"nizances, not to be prosecuted, unless any of the Parties shall
"be guilty of future Misbehaviour, or any of the Stipulations bro-
"ken. That Swetenham shall on his Acknowledgement of his Mis-
"behaviour give McKeithen a weapon of the same kind that he used
"on McKeithen (this tis said was a stick) to be used at McKeithens
"Pleasure, and that Swetenham shall pay McKeithen all Expences."

On which Mr. Swetenham (who is a Lieutenant in the Army)
told him it was Impossible for him to Comply with those Terms,
that he might as well give up his Commission, but that he could
procure one Person to swear himself worth £1000 Sterling and desired Grover to accept of him for Bail, who then said he would
take him & another, which other should not be obliged to swear,
and gave him time to procure the said Bail.

Notwithstanding which the said Swetenham was very soon after,
and within the time allowed him to procure Bail, taken into Custody by the Provost Marshall on a Warrant from the Chief Justice
ordering him to be kept <u>in close Imprisonment</u>, untill he should
be discharged by due Course of Law, and the next day the 26th

of June the said Swetenham compromised & made up the matter with McKeithen & Willson, as he understood for the Soldiers as well as himself, and then applied to Mr. Grover to discharge the Soldiers, and at the same time offered Bail for them to appear and answer the complaint of McKeithen etc. if required, which the said Chief Justice refused, & declared they should be kept in Prison till the Terms abovementioned were complied with by the Captains Demeré & Goldsmith and then again repeated them as before.

Thus the matter rested till the 11th of July when Swetenham applied again to the Chief Justice for their discharge, and received the same answer as before. Notwithstanding the abuse given by the soldiers (if any) was understood by all Parties to be made up & satisfied by the Terms agreed on the 26th of June which is supported by the depositions of Mesrs. Roche & Simpson, as well as by the discharge in writing given Swetenham, on which the Soldiers finding they could get no relief Petitioned as above. On Reading their Petition the Clerk of the Crown was sent for & directed to attend with the depositions that had been taken on the above Complaint, but the Chief Justice refused to send them alledging he kept them for his own Justification etc. He was then ordered to attend with them himself, which he accordingly did, & left them with the Clerk of the Council. On fully hearing and Examining into the whole affair, the Council were unanimously of Opinion that a Noli Prosequi[79] should be granted to the Petitioners, and which was immediately done.

This is the material substance of the Proceedings on the Representation of Leonard & others as appeared on Oath, & is enter'd in the Minutes of the Governor & Council on the 13 of July 1761, and from which I Conceive the Chief Justices Conduct appears to have been very illegal, arbitrary & Oppressive, in demanding Bail of Mr. Swetenham with 2 Sureties to swear themselves Worth £2000, Sterling clear of debt, which is the case of such an assault etc. as this appears to have been, in effect amounted to a denyal of Bail, a Grievance to the Party, & an offence against the Liberty of the

---

79. The Governor and the Council constituted the highest count in the colony, reviewing decisions made by provincial courts. In the case of the petition of George Leonard and others, the Governor and Council determined to notify the prosecution by a nole prosequi that prosecution in the case would be ended. This and other material on the suspension of Chief Justice Grover is in CRG, VIII.

Subject. Also in detaining the soldiers in Prison, & depriving them of their Liberty from the 23rd of June to the 13 of July, 21 days, tho' Bail was offered for their Appearance, and this even after the matter was Compromised between the Parties. But he refused Bail, & declared they should lye in gaol, till the arbitrary & unjustifyable Terms aforementioned which he demanded, were complied with, and which it was not Possible for either the Soldiers or their Officers to comply with. His behaviour was unbecoming the character & dignity of his Office, inasmuch as after he had allowed Swetenham a time to procure Bail, he immediately issued a Warrant against him ordering him to be kept <u>in close Confinement</u> a thing never done but in Capital or very extraordinary Cases. Also the Terms proposed by him in his own Hand writing to Mr. Swetenham (a Lieutenant in the army) were unbecoming the Station of a Chief Justice of a Province.

Neglect of duty in not reporting to me the Proceedings of the Court of Sessions with respect to Judgments Sentences or Fines set on any Person for offences or misdemeanours, that I might know what was done by the Court, and consider whether any Person proceded against might be a fit object of His Majesties Clemency and extend the same agreeable to His Majesties beneficent intention, & the Powers vested in me for that Purpose, no Report was ever made to me after December Sessions 1760.

Neglect of duty in not attending the Special Court of Oyer & Terminer held the 14th of April 1762. On a special Commission issued with the advice of His Majesties Council in Consequence of an address to me from the assembly for the Tryal of two vagabond Spaniards who had murdered a whole Family at or near Darien, Vizt, one Mackay & his Wife & 2 Negroes. The Chief Justice was very well and abroad the day before, and also the day after. This from many Circumstances appeared to me to have proceeded from a very bad improper and contumacious spirit and disposition.

Neglect of duty contempt & misbehaviour in not taking due Notice of, or shewing any regard to the order of the Governor in Council of the 27th of May 1762, Relative to one Pyles's giving security for his good behaviour etc. but on the contrary declaring to the Attorney General (as he the Attorney General affirmed in Council) and to others, that he would discharge the said Pyles at the Court of Sessions to be held on the 8th of June. At which time the Attorney General agreeable to my order & a Minute of Council of the 7th of June moved the said Chief Justice then in Court, to know what had been done with Pyles in Obedience to the above order of the Governor in Council of the 27 of May.

Finding that no one step whatever had been taken by the Chief Justice relative thereto, but that the said Pyles was in Custody of the Provost Marshall on Civil Process for debt, he then Moved that the said Pyles might be obliged to find Security for his good behaviour, & to appear at the next Court of Sessions, or that in default thereof he might be committed four days after which & not before the said Chief Justice Issued the Warrant of Committment, a Copy whereof is here inclosed.

From which Conduct appears a very great unwillingness to do his duty, and a disposition to thwart & oppose the Measures that were by me & the Council thought Expedient for His Majesties Service & the Safety of this Province (having positively declared that he would discharge Pyles) and which Warrant is of an unusual & extraordinary nature, Contains a false assertion as to my <u>Command</u> & shews very plainly the Malevolency of the Man.

I must here mention to your Lordships that Pyles is one of the New Hanover People or Settlers, and who had carried on a Provision Trade with the Spaniards at St. Augustine, and was certainly a very dangerous Person, his connection with them will more clearly appear from the Minutes of Council of the 27th of May last, which your lordships will receive by this Conveyance, and from the inclosed Copy of a letter from the Governor of St. Augustine to him, Mark't A, which was intercepted by Captain Demeré, then Commanding Officer at Frederica, & sent down to me. In Obedience to His Majesties 93rd Instruction and his Orders signified to me by Lord Egremont with the declaration of war, I judged it expedient that Pyles should find security for his good Behaviour.

In the Case of Tuke my Lords there seems to be the strongest Tincture of Partiality throughout from first to last, and the suffering a new matter to be set up & proved at the Tryal, which was foreign to the Action, & not made a Part of the Plaintiffs Case by the declaration & proceedings, I humbly Conceive was illegal. I shall not presume to say whether it proceeded from mere error & mistake or otherwise, but only to mention that there was a very great intimacy between Mr. Grover & Wood & Rivers, and that the moment Rivers's Tryal was over Mr. Grover left the Court, and did not go near it again, tho' it sat the next day, and have barely transmitted the Case to your Lordships, to whose Superior judgment the whole matter is Submitted.

With Respect to orders & references from the Governor in Council to the Chief Justices, I must observe to your Lordships That it is very usual, and the Common Practice for the Chief

Justices in the Colonies to sign warrants & take Conusance as a Magistrate, of Misdemeanours & Offences, and to Commit or bind the Parties over as the Case may require. This I know was constantly done by four Chief Justices in South Carolina During 21 years that I acted as Attorney General of that Province. In short my Lords this Man's Conduct in every respect is exceptionable & I think bad, and there are many other Matters of gross Partiality & Misbehaviour in Office besides these mentioned. And he has never once shewed the least respect, or even decency by meeting at the Council Chamber as is usual on the Kings Birthday etc. nor did he so much as attend on proclaiming his present Majesty, tho' in perfect health. Your Lordships will see I have not been hasty in taking up this matter. I was hopefull Mr. Grover might have seen his error & alter'd his behaviour, and it was rather with reluctance that I found myself under an absolute Necessity of taking notice of him. But my duty and Reputation would not suffer me to delay it any longer, and hope your Lordships will not impute my Tenderness to a Fault.

 I shall not trouble your Lordships with a longer detail of this man's general Misconduct, and altho' I could furnish many more Particulars that were not before the Council, I shall only mention one or two, for which be pleased to see the Paper Mark't B, which with other matters may easily be more Authentically transmitted if necessary. And I do very clearly agree in opinion with the Council, that he is unworthy, and not fit to be continued in the Office of Chief Justice, and that it will be greatly for the Honor & Service of the Province that he be removed. I have done what I thought to be an honest discharge of my duty to His Majesty and the Province, as well as to my own Character, and have not exaggerated or aggravated that matter against him. There are many things and Circumstances that it's next to Impossible to Represent on such an occasion, and which tho' consistent with ones own knowledge and striking to those on the spot, yet might not be so Proper to take Notice of, but if your Lordships would be Pleased to make any inquiry of Mr. Knox, I'm certain he can give an account of many instances of Misbehaviour etc. etc. in Mr. Grover. I shall not suppose my Lords that this man will be reinstated & return hither, sure I am if it should prove so, the whole Province will be in a Flame, for I can pronounce with the greatest Truth, that there is not 5 Men of any sort of Character that don't think it a happiness that he is like to be out of the Province. I can't help mentioning my Lords the great Contrast between Mr. Grover & Mr. Clifton, the Attorney General's, Conduct. The latter is diligent in his office and attentive to a proper discharge of his duty, assisting constantly in Council, and in all matters of Government that comes within his department, either as one of the Council or Attorney General, a well disposed man, and one who I really think very deserving.

I wrote your Lordships Twice lately relative to the Lot Money amounting to £663.12.7-1/2 and if it might be applied towards Building a Church and Court House it would be very pleasing to the Province.

P.S. 10th December. On the 17 of November the Inclosed Libel was published, which the Council & assembly thought it necessary to take Notice of, and appointed a Committee of both Houses for that Purpose, but were not able to fix it sufficiently, as your Lordships will see by the Copy of their Address now sent. Altho' the matter could not be fully proved to them, yet it is the general received Opinion that it came from Mr. G____r & his 2 or 3 adherents, and it seems to be a True Emblem of his inside.

The judgment paper of Wood and Sheftal vs. Samuel Pyles, June 11, 1761, Savannah, read May 3, 1763, C.O. 5/648, E. 57, enclosed with Wright to the Board of Trade, Nov. 8, 1762.

The Case of Wood & Sheftal against Ephraim Alexander, Samuel Pyles, and Joseph Pruniere.

On the 28th of August 1759, Wood & Sheftal Petitioned for a writ of attachment against the Goods & Chattels of Ephraim Alexander, for the Ballance of an Account due to them, and an attachment was accordingly Issued tested the 5th of June 1759 & returnable the 1st Tuesday in September following, a Copy of which was served on Samuel Pyles, who on the 17th of April 1760, Appeared & Acknowledged that he was indebted to the said Alexander in £77.8.11 & upwards, which sume Pyles was ordered to Pay over to the Plaintiffs Wood & Sheftal. And nothing further was done till the 20th of November 1760, when the Plaintiff Wood swore to a Balance of £77.8.11 Sterling due to himself & Sheftal, and then & not before the Plaintiffs gave Bond to prosecute their Suit, and filed their declaration.

On the 12 of March 1761 an affidavit was made that on or about the 5th of December Pyles was served with the above order of Court to pay the money acknowledged by him to be due to Alexander, over unto the Plaintiffs Wood & Sheftal, and that he had not paid the same on which the Court ordered an Attachment of Contempt to Issue against Pyles for not Paying the money.

NB The Attachment Law on which the above writ & Proceedings were Founded, Expired on the fourth of June 1760, and a new attachment Law whereby Lands were subjected as well as goods & Chattels was Passed on the 21 of June 1761 & not before.

And on the 11th of June 1761, Joseph Pruniere Petitioned the Chief Justice for a Writ of Attachment against the Effects & Estate Real and Personal of the said Pyles under the new Attachment Law, and Swore to a debt of £420.7.4 Sterling due on Bond, and also £152.5.6 Sterling for goods sold etc. which Attachment the Chief Justice ordered to Issue, and was accordingly done.

And on the Said 11th of June 1761, the Chief Justice made an ex parte order at his Chambers out of Court for Judgment against Pyles at the Suit of Wood & Sheftal for the Sume aforesaid Acknowledged to be due from him to Alexander, and the same day a Judgment was drawn up reciting all the Proceedings, which Mr. Pryce the Clerk of the Court was ordered by the Chief Justice at his Chambers to Sign, but he declined signing it as irregular, and then the said Chief Justice signed it himself, a Copy whereof is hereunto annexed. And an Execution was granted & delivered to the Provost Marshall the same day, and a House & Lot of Land seized by Virtue thereof the next day, as appears by the Provost Marshalls Indorsement thereon. And all this tho' the Attachment Law on which the writ was founded had Expired, and no Provision made by the new Law for reviving or continuing Suits commenced & depending under the former Law, and before any damages Legally assessed for the Plaintiffs against Alexander the Original defendant.

And on the 12 of June Pruniere applied by his attorney to the Chief Justice to have the said Judgment and Proceedings against Pyles Set aside for irregularity, and an order was made by the Chief Justice for the Plaintiffs Wood & Sheftal to attend at his House the next day to shew Cause why the said Judgment should not be set aside for irregularity. At which time Mr. Watson the Attorney for Pruniere gave the following Reasons to the Chief Justice for setting aside the Judgment & Execution. Vizt. 1st. That the Proceedings in behalf of Wood & Sheftal were had under an act which is since expired, & whereon no Judgment was obtained, or further Proceedings had, than barely Issuing the Writ of Attachment, filing the declaration, and Obtaining an attachment against Pyles for a Contempt in not complying with the order of Court made as aforesaid and that nothing more being done when the first act expired, the Suit abated, and the former Proceedings against Pyles and Alexander dyed, or drop't with the Act, when it expired, unless barely for the Contempt. 2nd. And if so, then there is no Law in being, nor anything whereon to ground or Warrant the Judgment & Execution now obtained, and Issued against Pyles's Estate Real & Personal.

3d. No Execution can vary from the Original Action, therefore if the Proceedings could stand under the former Expired Law, yet that only gave a remedy against the Goods & Chattels of absent debtors, and the Judgment enter'd up in this Case, and Signed by the Chief Justice, and the Execution Issued is as well against the Lands and Tenements as the Goods & Chattels, and therefore Irregular and not Warranted by Law.

4th. If the Proceedings under the former act could Survive & be Supported, yet no man can make use of two remedies at the same time, for the Same thing, as is plainly done in this Case, an Attachment of Contempt for not Paying the money, & an Execution to levy it, being both out & Existing at the same time.

5th. The Execution in this Cause Expresses to be for a Sume of money Recovered in our Court, before our Justices, whereas the Attachment (whereon the Judgment is obtained, and Execution Issued, are said to be grounded) was for a debt on Simple Contract, an Account sworn to & filed, yet no writ of inquiry has ever been Executed in the Cause to ascertain the Real damages or Sume due to the Plaintiffs, & to Support the Judgment, and authorise the Execution, so that in the most Extensive Sense, the aforesaid Judgment can only be said Interlocutory, and the Sume of money ordered to be levied by the Execution is merely Suppositious, and as such illegal, oppressive & in itself void.

6th. That the Judgment was moved for & obtained out of Court, which was irregular & Clandestine, and a Proceeding in itself sufficient to set aside every subsequent Act. These were the arguments urged & Reasons given by Prunieres Attorney for setting aside the Proceedings, and yet after several hearings on different days the Chief Justice at length Confirmed the Proceedings & Established the Judgment and Execution against Pyles.

On the 19th of March 1762 & not before an interlocutory Judgment was ordered & Signed for Wood & Sheftal against Alexander the Original defendent That a writ of inquiry might be Executed at April Court 1762 in order to Settle the true debt or damages due by Alexander to them, but no writ of inquiry has as yet been executed. Notwithstanding Judgment & Execution was had a year & half ago against Pyles as aforesaid.

NB all these matters are Fact, the Records in the Clerks Office I have Seen & Examined myself, and I have Mr. Watsons Brief by me containing the Reasons offered as aforesaid and which were given in writing, and Mr. Pryce the Clerk of the Court, declares the whole to be Fact & Truth.

The Attachment Act declares that Writs of Attachment shall Issue against the goods etc. of absent debtors, and that goods etc. being the Property of such absent debtor, in the Possession or Power of any Person, may be attached, and that attaching Part in the Name of the whole, shall make the whole Subject & lyable to any Judgment that shall be Recovered by Virtue of Such writ of Attachment. And that the Person Possessed of such goods etc. shall be Summoned to Appear at the return to shew Cause why the goods etc. attached should not be adjudged to belong to the absent debtor, and the Person is to appear Accordingly. If the Person neglects to appear, or does appear & refuses to discover upon oath what goods etc. he has belonging to the absent debtor, then such Person shall be Condemned for default of appearing, or discovering as the Case shall happen, and Judgment shall be given against his Proper goods & Chattels etc. The Plaintiffs debt or damage being first legally Proved, in like manner as in other Cases where Judgment is given by default. And if the Person appearing & discovering what goods etc. he has belonging to the absent debtor, shall refuse or Neglect to Pay or deliver the Same, over to the order of the Court, then Judgment shall be given against him so refusing or Neglecting, and Execution shall accordingly be awarded against his own Proper goods etc. These are the Words of the Law, but certainly no Execution could, or ought to Issue, untill the Plaintiffs debt or damages be first legally Proved, as directed just before in the very Same Clause, and also in the next following Clause.

And on this Law, and the Case as Stated, I should suppose that the Proceedings on the 1st act abated & were discontinued by the Expiration of the Law on which they were Founded, and the 2d or new Law Enacts That from & after the Passing of that act. Persons who shall not do as thereby required, shall be Lyable as thereby Enacted, Consequently could not Extend to Cases or matters done & transacted before the Law Passed, which only gives remedies in Cases etc. happening, or that may be done Subsequent, to the Law, & not Prior, and they ought to have Proceeded de novo under the new Act.

2nd. Proceeding against the Party on the Contempt (which is still depending to this very day, and the Man now actually in

Custody on it) and Obtaining a Judgment & Execution against him at the Same time, it is conceived was improper, and illegal, as Punishing a Man two ways at once, or twice for the same offence.

3d. As the Clerk here signs all Judgments, I conceive it was Irregular for the Chief Justice to sign the Judgment in this Case, being the only instance of his ever signing one. The whole Transaction appears to have been out of Court, & ex parte, which ought to have been in Court.

4th. It is Presumed that no Execution ought to have Issued against Pyles untill the Plaintiffs had first ascertained their debt against the Original Defendent Alexander, by Executing a Writ of inquiry, and that the Writ being only to Attach the Personal Estate, the Judgment & Execution could not Legally be against both the Real & Personal Estate as they are.

But the Fact & Truth is, that there was a very Extraordinary intimacy and connection between Mr. Grover & the Plaintiff Wood, and it is Probable that all these irregular & Extraordinary Proceedings were to favour Wood, & prevent the operation & effect of the attachment Issued for Pruniere, all which is humbly submitted. This is a Case that was not before the Council, but being one that Appears on Record, and on which an application of Complaint was prepared to be made to me, I have therefore stated it, altho' the Party stop't the Complaint, and it never came before me in a Public way, but is one of several that have come to my knowledge.

Another flagrant instance of attempting to prevent Justice, and basely departing from the honor & dignity of his office, was in the Case of a negro, the point being whether he was a Slave or Free, Vizt. one John Kenedy purchased a Negro and gave a Valuable Consideration for him. John Kenedy dyed & administration of his Effects was granted to Daniel Kenedy. The Fellow afterwards pretended to be free, and applied to the Chief Justice, who Appointed a Guardian to the Negro, in order to commence an action to try whether he was a Slave or not, agreeable to the negro Law of this Province, and the Chief Justice told the negro he would make him free, and sent for Mr. Burrington who was Kennedys Attorney and told him that the Negro was Free, and that he Burrington knew him to be so, and wanted to prevail on Burrington to advise his Client to set him Free, but Burrington told him he Could not do it, being clearly of Opinion that the Negro was a Slave, upon which the Chief Justice again said he was free, and should be so, and that at the next Court he would make him so.

That soon after Kennedy the Person who claimed the Negro,

came to Savanah, and the Chief Justice sent for him, and made
the Man drunk, and told him the Negro was free, and that he would
make him so, and advised him to Consent to his Freedom, which
Kennedy not being willing to do, Grover offered him ten Pounds
Sterling to free the Negro, but Kennedy refused it, and said he
would be advised by his Lawyer. On the 13 of October 1761 there
was a Tryal by a Special Jury, when they by their Verdict found the
Negro to be a Slave & not free. This Matter was also Notorious.

A judgment against Samuel Pyles, June 11, 1761, Savannah,
signed by W. Grover, Chief Justice, enclosed with Wright to the
Board of Trade, Nov. 8, 1762.

By Virtue of the said Writ of Attachment against the said Ephraim Alexander a certain sume of money due & owing from Samuel Pyles of Frederica in the Province aforesaid Storekeeper to the said Ephraim Alexander was attached in the hands of the said Samuel Pyles, and the said Samuel Pyles was Summoned to appear before the Justices of the General Court at Savanah on the first Tuesday in September in the year of our Lord one thousand Seven hundred & fifty Nine, to shew Cause why the said money should not be adjudged to belong to the said Ephraim by serving the said Samuel Pyles with a True Copy of the said writ, with a notice thereon Indorsed requiring him to appear & shew cause as aforesaid.

And whereas the said Samuel Pyles did appear before the Justices of the said Court and did allow & acknowledge that ho had of the Monies of the said Ephraim in his hands to the amount of Seventy Seven Pounds eight Shillings & Eleven pence money of Great Britain and whereas the said Samuel Pyles was ordered by the Justices of the said Court to pay over & deliver to the said Joseph Wood and Mordecai Sheftal the same sume of Seventy Seven Pounds eight Shillings & Eleven pence Sterling Pursuant to the Act of the General Assembly of the said Province in such Case made, the said Joseph Wood & Mordecai Sheftal first giving security as by the said act was required.

And whereas the said Joseph Wood & Mordecai Sheftal did give security as by the said Act was required, and the said Samuel Pyles was duly served with a copy of the said Order of Court. But the said Samuel Pyles hath refused or neglected, and doth yet refuse or neglect to pay over the said Money to the said Joseph Wood & Mordecai Sheftal in Obedience to the said order, whereby & by Virtue of a certain Act of the General Assembly of the said

Province in such Case made, the said Samuel Pyles is become lyable to pay & satisfy to the said Joseph Wood & Mordecai Sheftal the said Sume of Seventy Seven Pounds eight shillings & Eleven pence Sterling so acknowledged by him as aforesaid to be in his hands of the Monies of the said Ephraim out of his own proper Monies Goods Chattels & Effects, and Lands & Tenements & Real Estate of the said Samuel Pyles stand also Chargeable therewith. Therefore it is Considered.

Copy of a letter from the Governor of St. Augustine to Samuel Pyles, March 1, 1762, Frederica, read May 3, 1763, C.O. 5/648, E. 58, authorizing Pyles to transmit provisions and supplies to the Spanish in Florida. Enclosed A in Wright to the Board of Trade, Nov. 8, 1762.

Extract of a transmittal letter from Captain Demeré dated at Frederica the 1st of March 1762.

Sir

Some days ago Samuel Pyles received a letter from the new Governor of St. Augustine, & he sent it to me in order to get it translated into English, to know the meaning of it, before he should <u>Sail for that Place</u>, and desiring me to send him back the Governors letter with its Translation, which I refused, and have kept the Governors letter, and he is gone without either. His Cargo consists of Sixty large Hoggs, Corn & Pease, & a vast deal of other Trumpery.
Signed Raymond Demeré and directed to me as Governor of Georgia.

James Wright

NB His Majesties declaration of War against Spain did not come to my Hands till the 24th of May 1762.
The Contents of the Governor of St. Augustines letter is thus.

Sir

Having the Charge of this Government by the death of Don Lucas de Palacio late Governor of this Place. I herewith give you Notice of it, and to Proceed to this Place, with the Provisions and other Utensils, which are wanted for the Maintenance of this Government, at the Same time I shall acquaint you, that the <u>two hundred Head</u>

of Cows and Steers that you have Negotiated, must be ordered on their March hither, and to procure as many more as you can, to Come with great care, & let us want no fresh Meat, and in so doing, I shall have the greatest Attention, and take Pleasure in serving you.

       Signed Alonso de Cardones
       & directed to Mr. Samuel Pyles

Copy of affidavit of Capt. Thomas Goldsmith, Nov. 22, 1762, Charleston, read May 3, 1763, C.O. 5/648, E. 59, respecting the confinement of several soldiers by Chief Justice Grover's order, enclosed with Wright to the Board of Trade, Nov. 8, 1762.

Captain Thomas Goldsmith being duely sworn declared that he never consented to the Soldiers being sent to Gaol on Account of the Action brought against Lieutenant Swetenham by Mr. McKeithen, on the Contrary he applied to Mr. Grover to know by what Authority he had confined them Men, and desired he would release them, as it was very detrimental to His Majesties Service. Mr. Grover proposed (at the request of Mr. McKeithen) to Release them if Captain Goldsmith would keep them in the Town of Savanah, and send other men to Frederica to do duty, but that was what he could not Consent to, and was afterwards obliged to Apply to the Governor by Petition to have the Soldiers set at Liberty, in order to do duty at Frederica.
      Signed Thomas Goldsmith

So. Carolina Charles Town
Sworn before me 22nd of November 1762.

    John Hume J.P., Berkley County
       Copied from the original
       James Wright.

Mr. Knox was present when this affair was before me in Council and must recollect how the matter appeared in every respect.

Poem entitled "A Libel," Savannah, received May 3, 1763, C.O. 5/648, E. 60, enclosed with Wright to the Board of Trade, Nov. 8, 1762.

From Britains gay Island where Liberty reigns,
Where Flora and Ceres enliven the Plains.
Where George still with wisdom and glory defends
The Blessing which Nature profusely extends.
Whence comes it dear W____ that again thou explores,
from Regions so happy, American Shores?
Carolina her Agent must surely bemoan,
and each Votry of Hermes* re-acho the groan,
Thy Fortune aspiring, she no more can Raise;
His Sons shall no longer thy Eloquence Praise.
Is it ambition Courts thee with Soft soothing air,
or Power or Riches that make thee Repair,
To Climates so Sultry!
It is not ambition alone does invite,
but Power & Riches both equal delight;
For what makes all Doctrines most Plainly appear,
it cannot be less____ than a thousand a year.
When lordly I stalk a Phantom of State,
Though mean my appearance, my Heart is elate;
Plans of Castles I draw, make Speeches to F_ _ ls,
Who like____ and____ are my very good Tools,
a Council Submissive attend on my Nod,
or if Fractious they Prove, I'll suspend them by G_d.
Hoc voles my Motto, sic Voles my Rule,
Now damn you W_ll G___r who says I'm a Fool.

H. K. [?]

*The God of Lawyers and of Thieves

Address of the House of Assembly to the Governor, Dec. 10, 1762, Savannah, read May 3, 1762, C.O. 5/648, E. 61, desiring him to offer a reward for the discovery of the author of "A Libel," enclosed with Wright to the board of Trade, Nov. 8, 1762.[80]

Minutes of a Council held Sept. 21, 1762, Savannah, read May 3, 1763, C.O. 5/648, E. 62, respecting Mr. Grover's conduct

---

80. This address is printed in CRG, XIII, 753-754.

enclosed with Wright to the Board of Trade, Nov. 8, 1762.[81]

James Wright to the Board of Trade, Feb. 22, 1763, Savannah, read May 3, 1763, C.O. 5/648, E. 63, giving an account of the flourishing state of the province and other affairs of government.

My Lords

    I wrote to your Lordships on the 1st of October last, and sent a duplicate, I also had the Honor of writing to your lordships on the 8th of November, which lay for want of Opportunity till the 10th of December, in this letter of which I also sent a duplicate is contained my reasons for Suspending Mr. Grover from the Office of Chief Justice of this Province, and have not the least doubt but your Lordships will be Pleased to Approve of my Conduct therein, and Represent the same to His Majesty Accordingly. At the same time I forwarded to your lordships a Box with the duplicates of the Laws Passed the 4th of March last, and several Copys of the Journals & Minutes, which I hope will get safe.
    The affairs of the Province my Lords are at Present all quiet & easy. I have lately had a Visit from many of the Creek Indians, amongst whom was one Called the Gun Merchant, a Man of by far the greatest interest & influence of any Indian in the Nation, and who has not been either at Charles Town or Savanah for a great Many years past. He was coming down to Augusta in the year 1755 to meet Governor Reynolds, but was disgusted & returned back without seeing Mr. Reynolds. With this Man & Some others I had several Private Conversations & gave them also a Publick Talk, I see no Appearance of any Uneasiness amongst them, unless it is Occasioned by the Province of South Carolina having given the Cherokees a Trade on a Cheaper footing Since the war than they had before, which Such of the Creeks as are in the French interest, & I suppose set on by the French, Say is a Consequence of the war with the White People, and that if they (the Creeks) were to make war against us, they would get their Goods on better Terms too. Unless any uneasiness should Proceed from this Motive, I am not Apprehensive of any from them.
    The Province in general my Lords is in a very thriving Condition, our Trade considerably encreased, and our Produce this year will

---

81. These minutes are printed in CRG, VIII, 735-751.

be one third more, if not double what it was in the year 1760 when I came to the Government, and whenever His Majesty shall be graciously Pleased to extend my Authority & Jurisdiction, I doubt not but we shall soon have a great Number of Inhabitants, the only thing now wanting to make this in a few years a Province of as much Consequence to Great Britain as some others in our Neighbourhood. The Climate & Soil is at least equal, the Spirit of Industry very Great, and the People beginning to have Property & Foundation Sufficient to Enable them to make Considerable Progress.

I formerly mentioned to your Lordships Messrs. James Read, Lewis Johnson & John Graham as proper Persons to fill the Vacant Seats in Council, and now think their Places in the assembly may be filled when your Lordships shall be Pleased to approve of them as Members of the Council. I have long hoped for a return of the Quitrent Bill and your Lordships directions thereon, but have not yet received them.

Memorial of William Knox to the Board of Trade on behalf of Joseph Ottolenghe, read May 3, 1763, London, C.O. 5/648, E. 64, asking a gratuity for his past and present services as Superintendent of the Silk Culture in Georgia.

Humbly Sheweth

That your Memorialist having been informed by Governor Wright, that your Lordships have directed His Excellency to put a Person under your Memorialist to be by him Instructed in the Art of the Silk Manufacture, and that your Lordships are further pleased to say in your Letter to the said Governor Wright, that your Memorialist ought to Instruct such Person because of the generous Rewards heretofore bestowed on him. Your Memorialist therefore humbly apprehends it consistent with his Duty to your Lordships to lay before you a just state of his Services as Superintendant of the Silk Culture in Georgia, and of the Rewards which have hitherto been conferd on him.

For this purpose your Memorialist thinks it proper to recur to the time of the late Honourable Trustees for establishing the Colony of Georgia under whose authority the Culture of Silk was first attempted in that Province. The Person first employd by the said Trustees was Mrs. Camuse who continued to superintend the said Culture for the term of Six years for each of the two first of which she was allowed the sum of Sixty pounds and for each of the Four last One hundred pounds, besides the Rent of a dwelling House in the Town of Savannah. That in none of these years were there more Cocoons brought to the Filature that were sufficient to occupy One Bason & one Reel.

That Mr. Pickering Robinson, who had been sent to France at the expence of the said Trustees in order to get some knowledge of the Silk Culture was then sent over to Georgia to Superintend the said Culture at the time of whose going over the said Trustees were pleased to order a Tract of Land to be allotted him in the neighbourhood of Savannah, which Tract he has since sold for £1300, and assigned him a Sallary of One hundred pounds together with an allowance of Twenty five pounds for a Clerk. That shortly after Mr. Robinson arrived in Georgia he declared to the then President and Council, that he was not sufficiently accquainted with the Silk business to undertake the management of it and therefore desired the said President and Council to apply to your Memorialist to assist him therein.

That your Memorialist was accordingly desired by the President and Council to manage the said Culture, and for two years did conduct it, without any agreement for Salary, and that as Mr. Robinson had during that term the Title of Superintendant the Trustee allowed your memorialist only the sum of Fifty pounds for each of those years, but when the Colony came under the Inspection of your Lordships Board, it having been represented to their Lordships that your Memorialist had realy performed the Service Mr. Robinson was appointed to, their Lordships were pleased to order your memorialist the sum of One hundred pounds in consideration of his services in the two preceding years which made up his Salary One hundred pounds for each.

That your Memorialist has ever since continued to Superintend the said Culture and has the satisfaction of seeing it thrive under his management insomuch that there have been last Season brought to the Filature a sufficient quantity of Cocoons to employ Ten Basons and Ten Reels. That notwithstanding the increase of his labour consequent to so great an increase of the culture, your Memorialist has taken upon himself the additional burden of raising Seed for each successive year which business was, in the times of Mrs. Camuse & Mr. Robinson managed by other Persons to whom a gratuity was annualy paid on that account.

That your Memorialist has never had any augmentation of his stipend of One hundred pounds since he has been Superintendant of the Silk Culture. He has had no House provided for him, nor has he had any Salary for a Clerk as was granted to his Predecessors, neither has he ever made any charge for raising Seed.

Your Memorialist therefore submits it to your Lordships equitable & humane consideration, whether as his labour has been so much greater than that of either of his Predecessors and his allowances considerably smaller that he ought to be required without any compensation to communicate to another Person all that knowledge of the Silk Culture, which his study and experience has furnished him with, and thereby put it in the power of such Person to undermine your Memorialist in his employment, at a time of Life when it is too late to apply himself to another Profession and when his constitution is so much decay'd as to be unable to support Fatigues and anxieties.

Your Memorialist therefore humbly hopes your Lordships will be pleased to order him a gratuity in consideration of his Instructing all such persons as the Governor of Georgia shall think proper to put under him for that purpose and that your Lordships will be pleased to intercede with His Majesty that he may be appointed by His Majestys Royal Warrant Superintendant of the Silk Culture in Georgia with a Salary thereunto adequate to the labour now incident to that employment.

James Wright to the Board of Trade, April 20, 1763, Savannah, received June 27, read July 6, 1763, C.O. 5/648, E. 66, acquainting the Board that he had received information that South Carolina had resolved to grant all the land south of the Altamaha River.

My Lords

A Matter which I conceive to be a very Extraordinary Procedure of the Governor of South Carolina, is the Occasion of my troubling your Lordships at this time. I was informed that Mr. Boone[82] had come to a Resolution to give Grants for all the Lands to the Southward of the River Alatamaha, towards St. Augustine without Limits. And altho my Lords I received this Account in such a manner as to Admit of little or no doubt of the truth of it, yet as Mr. Boone had not thought Proper to take any the least Notice of it to me, and Considering His Majesties Commands Signified to the Governors of Georgia and Carolina on the 10th June 1758 relative to these

---

82. Thomas Boone was governor of South Carolina 1761-1764.

very Lands,[83] and for a Number of other Obvious Reasons, I could not think it Possible for Mr. Boone to take such a Step, and therefore desired Mr. Grey Elliott one of His Majesties Council for this Province to go to Charles Town to Mr. Boone on the Occasion, and in case it should prove true; I furnished him with a Protest and Caveat to enter against their Proceedings, a Copy whereof your Lordships have here inclosed. And on Mr. Elliotts return, it appeared that such a resolution was come to, and that on Tuesday the 5th instant Warrants were actually Issued for upwards of 343,000 Acres of Land to several Persons Inhabitants of So. Carolina in the whole not exceeding the number of 200 Persons.

The reception my Protest & Caveat met with from Governor Boone will appear to your Lordships from Mr. Elliotts attestation underneath it, and he could not get Copy's of the several Orders for Warrants, by which the Particular quantities of Land and Persons Names would appear, but if the Officers from whom these are to be had are not forbid to give them, (as the Secretary was to receive the Protest) I shall very speedily Transmit an exact Account to your Lordships. But Mr. Elliott came to the knowledge of part, Vizt. that 35,000 Acres of Land was ordered to 4 Persons, 16,000 Acres to one Howarth on Account of the Estate of James Michie deceased, 8000 to Mr. Thomas Smith Senior, 7500 Acres to Stephen Bull, and 3500 Acres to Mr. James Parsons, and that several other very large Tracts had been ordered for other Persons.

Your Lordships will very well Remember the frequent application from this Province for an extention of our South Boundary, a thing my Lords absolutely necessary for making this Colony Opulent and considerable, and your Lordships also well Remember the reasons that I conceive prevented it's being done, and which now by the happy Peace do not subsist. And my Lords when I was in daily expectation of receiving such Orders from His Majesty as would Effectually make the Province considerable, and put it in a Condition of being usefull to the Mother Country, to receive almost it's death wound or destruction by (what with great submission I conceive to be) an Extraordinary Stretch of Power by the Governor of Carolina, has occasioned a General discontent and dejection amongst the People. The Pretence my Lords for this Measure is the Charter to the Proprietors of Carolina, which extends to the Latitude of 29 inclusive, and which my Lords takes in St. Augustine,

---

83. Referred to as the "Rule of 1758," in which William Pitt forbade any settlements south of the Altamaha without crown approval.

Pensacola, and Mobile, and therefore Mr. Boone may just as well pretend a right to Grant those Places, as any Spot of Land to the Southward of the River Alatamaha. Indeed the Persons who have Warrants may Actually run out St. Augustine, for Mr. Elliott who saw and read some of the Warrants says they are in General Words without Limitation or restriction, but to take up and survey <u>Lands to the Southward of the River Alatamaha</u>, and it is humbly conceived that this Charter being Purchased by the Crown from the Lords Proprietors could no longer continue to Operate with respect to His Majesty, and who alone from the time of that Purchase had and still has the right of declaring what shall, or shall not be his Province of Carolina, without any regard to the Limits mentioned in the Charter to the Proprietors.[84]

I say my Lords this Procedure has struck a General damp and dispirited the whole Province. I have called this my Lords the death wound or destruction of the Province, for an Extention of Limits to the Southward if the Lands were properly parcelled out and Granted to People who would really Cultivate and improve them, would draw some thousand Inhabitants here. Whereas by this Step taken in Carolina, great Part of the Lands my Lords are ordered in very large Tracts to some wealthy Settlers in Carolina, who Probably will never see it themselves, and some of whom it's said have already more Lands in that Province, than they can Cultivate or improve. This My Lords is pretty well known on this side of the Water, and who having a great number of Slaves, claim

---

84. With the cession of Florida to Britain by the Treaty of Paris on February 10, 1763, the question of which colony owned the territory south of the Altamaha became an important one. This area had been used sparingly by Spanish from Florida, South Carolinians, and Georgians throughout the eighteenth century. Now it would be eagerly sought by British colonials for the first time. Technically the land belonged to South Carolina, having been included in her Charters of 1663 and 1665. Georgia had been given the land between the Savannah and Altamaha Rivers but no more, but with the exit of the Spanish from Florida it made sense to give this land to Georgia or to include it within a new colony. Boone was undoubtedly swayed by such a consideration in his rush to grant these lands to South Carolinians before that colony lost them. Wright was just as logical in wanting the grants stopped for he hoped that Georgia would secure additional lands here, as she did by the royal proclamation of Oct. 7, 1763.

what they call their Family Right, that is 50 Acres of Land for each Slave, altho' it's highly Probable that their Ancestors have already had Lands for those very Slaves, And it is well understood here that many of those Persons, Especially those who have the largest Tracts, have no intention to remove there or Settle them, but Probably some years hence when it begins to be valuable will Sell it, and in the mean time those vast Tracts of Land, are to lye waste and Unimproved, as very great Bodys yet do in Carolina and if they should do any thing at all with these Lands, it is expected it will only be by sending an overseer and a few Negroes just to make a trifling Settlement seemingly to comply with the terms of the Grant, or by way of taking Possession.

What I mention here My Lords is not barely Imaginary, but proceeds from a number of instances of the like kind in Carolina, and Facts which are well known to every body in these Parts, and what my Lords it is pretty certain will be the Consequence of these Proceedings in Carolina if they are suffered to take Effect.[85] I Speak with respect to the large Tracts, for Possibly some of those who have small Tracts may remove and settle them. Your Lordships will be pleased to observe that no less than 35,000 Acres is Ordered to 4 Persons, so that your Lordships see that if this Procedure

---

85. For almost a quarter century, James Wright had served South Carolina as attorney general and as provincial agent in London; now as Georgia's governor he used his knowledge of South Carolina's land policies against his former employer. Wright chose not to argue Georgia's case based upon Oglethorpe's settlements and military activity in the area from 1735 to 1742, but, rather, upon Carolina's well-known abuses of its land granting system. In this way Wright avoided the legal tangle inherent in Charleston's case while he played upon the Board's bias against land engrossment. Legally Wright appealed to the Crown's authority in the matter while he ignored Charleston's historical case. Briefly Wright argued that the 1758 ruling had not been withdrawn, and that without consulting its neighbor or its sovereign South Carolina prematurely granted lands in the area. Besides, Wright reasoned, these all were Crown lands now, especially since London had taken over the South Carolina charter in 1728. Moreover, he pointed out, Charleston had issued warrants in general terms, without definite boundaries, in large acreage to only a few families, thus violating the Board of Trade's land granting procedures worked out since 1730.

is not set aside by his Majesty, it will be the ruin of this Province, for my Lords 35,000 Acres of Land at 400 Acres to each Family, would Accomodate 87 good Substantial Settlers, who would each of them bring a Family of White People into the Province, besides Perhaps each as many, if not more Negroes than the Person in Carolina who holds 8000 Acres, and as many of the Grants to new Settlers would not exceed 200 & 250 Acres, your Lordships see it might very Probably accomadate 120 or 130 good settlers instead of being held uncultivated and waste by 4 Carolina Planters.

And my Lords this Quantity of Land was all ordered in One Day, the first Day, on about 200 Petitions, and I am Informed that the Surveyor General of Carolina, who is one of the Council has said that it is expected double that number will apply the next Land Day, or in a short time. And My Lords give me Leave to mention another Reason. Your Lordships will Remember an intention some time agoe, to remove the Seat of Government from Savannah, further South, and altho there might not be Occasion for that, whilst the Province remained confined to the River Alatamaha, yet with Submission my Lords, it may be a very proper Measure, when His Majesty shall be pleased to extend the Province, and the best Navigation, and most convenient Place in every respect for Trade and the Seat of Government is just where these great Tracts of Land are Surveying for the People of Carolina. How then my Lords is this Land to be come at? And what Town can ever be settled with advantage in this part of the World? Or supported when 343,000 Acres of Land all round is held by so few Persons, and it's highly Probable waste and unimproved, and 35,000 Acres of it by only 4 Persons. And this as I have Observed is only the quantity already ordered, and as much more will be, very speedily Possibly by the time this Reaches your Lordships a Million of Acres may be Granted to Persons now Settled in Carolina and the greatest part of which it's expected will continue to live there.

Your Lordships will also be pleased to consider how greatly this will affect his Majesties Service in the Settlement of this Frontier Province, and how much it must be weakened and impeded by these vast Tracts being held by such an handfull of People, who live in another Province. And this further Ill Effect it will have, for nobody will think of coming this way when they hear that the Carolinians have Ingrossed all the Lands, and how contrary My Lords does this Step seem to be to his Majesties Royal intention. And your Lordships will be pleased to Observe that those who have these very great Tracts, or any of the Persons who are to have these Lands have not one Negroe, or one Shilling Property on this Side of Savannah River.

I have had accounts my Lords of many hundred Families, I may
say some thousand People, who were ready to come into this Province (Chiefly from North Carolina) as soon as it was extended,
and I should be Authorised to Grant these very Lands, all which
will be prevented if these Proceedings are suffered to take Effect.
I must beg leave my Lords to mention another Objection against
these Grants, which seems an equitable one, on the side of this
Province. Mr. Elliott informs me, that one Mr. Young who has
some Negroes in Carolina, and also some in Georgia, Petitioned
for a Tract of Land for all his Negroes, and on his saying that
part of those Negroes were in Georgia, he was refused Lands for
them, and told he should only have Lands for such Negroes, as
he had in Carolina, so that your Lordships see the Inhabitants of
this Province are totally excluded. This my Lords seems to us
here, to be very unequitable that the People of this Province who
have Borne the Brunt and Fatigue of settling a new Colony and
who have encounter'd and Struggled with inumerable difficulties
and hardships, besides dangers from the Savages, and during
the War from the Neighbouring French and Spaniards, and who
by great Industry and Labour have Acquired a few Negroes, and
are in a Capacity of Settling out their Children, or making other
Settlements for themselves.

I say my Lords it seems to them hard & Unequitable, that they
are not to have an inch of these Lands, but that the whole or
most of the best, is to be swallowed Up by strangers who never
contributed One farthing, or one hours Fatigue or hardship towards
the Support of the Province. And for these Reasons and many
more that must occur, your Lordships will see why I call it the
death wound or destruction of Georgia. I have never yet my Lords
Granted any Lands but to People who Actually undertook to settle
and improve them forthwith, and only in moderate Quantities.
For my Lords it's the number of Inhabitants we Want here, and
altho' these Lands may be annexed to Georgia, Yet if they are
Ingrossed and held by the Carolinians, in the manner I have mentioned, it will nevertheless Ruin the Province. For my Lords as
I have already said altho' some of those who have small Tracts
may Probably remove there, and settle them, yet those who have
large Tracts, it is pretty certain have no such intention, and
never will. And your Lordships will Observe that no less than
343,000 Acres are ordered to less than 200 Persons, and which
quantity alone, would Accomodate a thousand very good Families
and Settlers, and such as are the Sinews, Wealth and Strength
of an Infant Colony.

It might be Impertinent in me to trouble your Lordships any further on this Subject, the consequence of which your Lordships will see with so much more Perspicuity and Extension than I can. On the one hand my Lords with great deference, it seems to be a considerable Step towards the Ruin of a very flourishing Province. On the other, the advantage rather of a private Nature, and this done (it is humbly conceived) contrary to His Majesties Royal intention, and at a time when even in Charlestown it is the General Opinion, and they daily expect to hear that those Lands are annexed to this Province, all which is Submitted to your Lordships Consideration.

As His Majesties Commands relative to the Settlers on these Lands was signified in June 1758 by the Secretary of State, therefore I have now wrote to the Secretary of State to the same purpose as I have done to your Lordships, in which I hope I have not Acted Improperly as my Instructions are to correspond with the Secretary of State on all matters that come from that Office, and as I conceive their proceedings in Carolina are in some measure contrary to those Orders.

On the 7th Instant I assented to 12 Bills and An Ordinance, which I have Ordered to be Copyed and as soon as they are ready, shall transmit 'em to your Lordships, with my Observations on them.

I have the pleasure to acquaint your Lordships that there is a very good Prospect of a fine Crop of Silk this Season.

P.S. My Lords I hope Nothing has Slip't my Pen but what is Consistent & Proper, if any thing should, I humbly entreat your Lordships will be Pleased to impute it to my Zeal for the Service of the Province I have the Honor to Preside over.

Protest and caveat of Governor Wright against the Governor of South Carolina's surveying lands to the southward of the river Altamaha, March 30, 1763, Savannah, received June 27, read July 6, 1763, C.O. 5/648, E. 67, received with Wright's April 20, 1763, letter to the Board of Trade.[86]

An abstract of grants registered in Georgia from Jan. 27, 1762, to July 27, 1762, received June 27, read July 6, 1763, C.O. 5/648, E. 68.

---

86. This protest and caveat is printed in CRG, IX, 40-44.

Grant dated 4th December 1759
To Theobald Keifer for a town Lot & 50 acres of Land at Vernonburgh. Registered 10th February 1762

Grant dated 4th December 1759
To George Uland for 150 acres of Land in Christ Church Parish. Registered 10th February 1762

Grant dated 25th September 1760
To George Uland for 50 acres of Land in Christ Church Parish. Registered 10th February 1762

Grant dated 13th April 1761
To John Mitchell for 146 acres of Land in the parish of St. John. Registered 10th February 1762

Grant dated 2d October 1759
To Christian Lurnburgh for 50 acres of Land in Christ Church parish. Registered 10th February 1762

Grant dated 2d February 1762
To Pickering Robinson for 1000 acres of Land in Christ Church parish. Registered 11th February 1762

Grant dated 2d February 1762
To Pickering Robinson for 500 acres of Land in Christ Church parish. Registered 11th February 1762

Grant dated 1st July 1760
To John Happacker for 50 acres of Land in the parish of St. Matthew. Registered 4th February 1762

Grant dated 5th September 1758
To James Whitefield for 400 acres of Land in Christ Church parish. Registered 4th February 1762

Grant dated 1st July 1760
To Edmund Tannatt Esquire for 900 acres of Land in Christ Church parish. Registered 11th February 1762

Grant dated 1st July 1760
To Edmund Tannatt Esquire for 100 acres of Land in Christ Church parish. Registered 11th February 1762

Grant dated 3d February 1762
To Samuel Fulton for 500 acres of Land in Saint Andrews parish.
Registered 16th February 1762

Grant dated 3d February 1762
To Samuel Fulton for 400 acres of Land in Saint Andrews parish.
Registered 16th February 1762

Grant dated 3d February 1762
To John Jones for 500 acres of Land in St. Andrews Parish. Registered 16th February 1762

Grant dated 3d February 1762
To John Jones for 500 acres of Land in St. Andrews Parish. Registered 16th February 1762

Grant dated 3d February 1762
To John Graves for 300 acres of Land in St. Johns Parish. Registered 17th February 1762

Grant dated 3d February 1762
To Lewis Smith for 400 acres of Land in St. Phillip Parish.
Registered 17th February 1762

Grant dated 3d February 1762
To James Fisher for 250 acres of Land in St. Johns parish.
Registered 17th February 1762

Grant dated 3d February 1762
To Burgon Bord for 400 acres of Land in Saint Andrews parish.
Registered 17th February 1762

Grant dated 25th September 1760
To Thomas Davis for 200 acres of Land in St. Matthews Parish.
Registered 17th February 1762

Grant 3d February 1762
To Thomas Morgan for 400 acres of Land in Christ Church Parish.
Registered 18th February 1762

Grant dated 3d February 1762
To Simon Frazer for 150 acres of Land in St. Andrews Parish.
Registered 18th February 1762

Colonial Records 417

Grant dated 3d February 1762
To Gasper Garbet for 200 acres of Land in St. Matthews Parish. Registered 18th February 1762

Grant dated 3d February 1762
To Martin Dasher for 200 acres of Land in Saint Matthews parish. Registered 19th February 1762

Grant dated 3rd February 1762
To Michael Weinkauff for 150 acres of Land in Saint Matthews parish. Registered 19th February 1762

Grant dated 3d February 1762
To Simon Rouviere for 150 acres of Land in Christ Church Parish. Registered 19th February 1762

Grant dated 3d February 1762
To Jonathan Fox for 100 acres of Land in Christ Church Parish. Registered 19th February 1762

Grant dated 3d February 1762
To Anthony Pagie for 150 acres of Land in Christ Church parish. Registered 20th February 1762

Grant dated 3d February 1762
To Joseph Shubdrein for 145 acres of Land in Saint Matthews parish. Registered 20th February 1762

Grant dated 3d February 1762
To Nicholas Shubdrein for 40 acres of Land in Saint Matthews parish. Registered 20th February 1762

Grant dated 3d February 1762
To Alexander McGillivray for 100 acres of Land in Saint Georges parish. Registered 20th February 1762

Grant dated 3d February 1762
To William Gibbons for 73 acres of Land in Christ Church parish. Registered 20th February 1762

Grant dated 3rd February 1762
To William Gibbons for a Wharf Lot in Savannah No. 14. Registered 22d February 1762

Grant dated 3d February 1762
To Lachlan McGillivray for a town Lot in Augusta No. 4. Registered 22d February 1762

Grant dated 4th December 1759
To [Matthias] Salfner for 100 acres of Land in Christ Church parish. Registered 22d February 1762

Grant dated 3d December 1760
To Robert Houstoun for 100 acres of Land in Saint Phillips parish. Registered 22d February 1762

Grant dated 2d October 1759
To George Motte for 50 acres of Land in Christ Church parish. Registered 22d February 1762

Grant dated 1st July 1760
To Baruch Norman for 150 acres of Land in Saint Andrews parish. Registered 22d February 1762

Grant dated 3d February 1762
To Lieutenant Robert Baillie for 500 acres of Land in St. Andrews parish. Registered 23d February 1762

Grant dated 3d February 1762
To John Lewis for 50 acres of Land in the parish of Saint Andrew. Registered 23d February 1762

Grant dated 7th July 1761
To Charles Story for 200 acres of Land in Christ Church parish. Registered 23d February 1762

Grant dated 5th September 1758
To William Sarcer for 65 acres of Land in Christ Church Parish. Registered 2d March 1762

Grant dated 5th February 1760
To David Keifer for 2 Lots & 100 acres of Land at Vernonburgh. Registered 4th March 1762

Grant dated 1st May 1759
To Francis Pary for 150 acres of Land in Christ Church Parish. Registered 5th March 1762

Colonial Records 419

Grant dated 4th December 1759
To Nicholas Hanner for 150 acres of Land in Christ Church parish. Registered 6th March 1762

Grant dated 7th August 1759
To John Hanner for 100 acres of Land in Christ Church Parish. Registered 6th March 1762

Grant dated 7th July 1761
To John Hopkins for 150 acres of Land in St. George's Parish. Registered 9th March 1762

Grant dated 13th April 1761
To George Whitefield Clerk for 500 acres of Land in Christ Church parish. Registered 15th March 1762

Grant dated 13th April 1761
To George Whitefield for 500 acres of land in Christ Church parish in trust for the Orphan House. Registered 16th March 1762

Grant dated 13th April 1761
To George Whitefield for 419 acres of Land in Christ Church parish in trust etc. Registered 16th March 1762

Grant dated 13th April 1761
To George Whitefield for 400 acres of Land in Christ Church Parish. Registered 16th March 1762

Grant dated 1st July 1760
To William Grover Esquire for 125 acres of Land in St. Matthews parish. Registered 17th March 1762

Grant dated 5th June 1759
To James Gray for a town Lot in Augusta No. 17. Registered 19th March 1762

Grant dated 7th July 1761
To John Wereat for 360 acres of Land in the parish of St. Andrew. Registered 26th March 1762

Grant dated 3d December 1760
To John McIntosh B for 500 acres of Land in the parish of St. Andrew. Registered 27th March 1762

Grant dated 3d December 1760
To Martin Fenton for 150 acres of Land in Christ Church parish. Registered 29th March 1762

Grant dated 4th December 1759
To David Ranstatler for a town Lot & 100 acres of Land at Vernonburgh. Registered 29th March 1762

Grant dated 3d December 1760
To Martin Fenton for 50 acres of Land in Christ Church parish. Registered 29th March 1762

Grant dated 3d December 1760
To Martin Fenton for 50 acres of Land in Christ Church parish. Registered 29th March 1762

Grant dated 4th December 1759
To Peter Young for a town Lot & 50 acres of Land at Vernonburgh. Registered 30th March 1762

Grant dated 3d December 1760
To David Dicks for 200 acres of Land in the parish of Saint Phillip. Registered 30th March 1762

Grant dated 7th August 1759
To Alexander Wylly for a Lot in Hardwicke No. 80. Registered 1st April 1762

Grant dated 5th February 1760
To Henry Miers for 200 acres of Land in Christ Church Parish. Registered 5th April 1762

Grant dated 13th April 1761
To Samuel Tomlinson for 250 acres of Land in St. Andrews Parish. Registered 6th April 1762

Grant dated 7th July 1761
To Murdock McLeod for 150 acres of Land in St. Andrews Parish. Registered 6th April 1762

Grant dated 2d October 1759
To George Noble for 100 acres of Land in the parish of St. John. Registered 6th April 1762

Grant dated 2d October 1759
To Robert Noble for 100 acres of Land in the parish of St. John.
Registered 6th April 1762

Grant dated 21st May 1762
To Thomas Camber for 450 acres of Land in the parish of St. Andrew.
Registered 1st June 1762

Grant dated 21st May 1762
To Thomas Camber for 450 acres of Land in the parish of St. Andrew.
Registered 1st June 1762

Grant dated 21st May 1762
To Samuel Fulton for 500 acres of Land in St. Andrews Parish.
Registered 1st June 1762

Grant dated 21st May 1762
To Francis Harris Esquire for 1300 acres of Land in Christ Church parish. Registered 2d June 1762

Grant dated 21st May 1762
To Mary McClelland Widow for 500 acres of Land in St. Andrews parish. Registered 2d June 1762

Grant dated 21st May 1762
To James McClelland for 350 acres of Land in St. Andrews parish.
Registered 2d June 1762

Grant dated 21st May 1762
To Mark Carr Esquire for 220 acres of Land in Saint Andrews parish. Registered 2d June 1762

Grant dated 21st May 1762
To Joseph Wood for 300 acres of Land partly in Christ Church parish & St. Matthews. Registered 3d June 1762

Grant dated 21st May 1762
To Robert Bevill for 550 acres of Land in Saint George's parish.
Registered 3d June 1762

Grant dated 21st May 1762
To Francis Goffe for 470 acres of Land in Saint Andrews parish.
Registered 3d June 1762

Grant dated 21st May 1762
To Henry Kennan for 400 acres of Land in Saint Matthews parish. Registered 3d June 1762

Grant dated 21st May 1762
To Henry Kennan for a Wharf Lot in Savannah. Registered 3d June 1762

Grant dated 21st May 1762
To Francis Goffe for a Wharf Lot in Savannah. Registered 5th June 1762

Grant dated 21st May 1762
To John Talley Esquire for a town Lot in Savannah No. 5. Registered 5th June 1762

Grant dated 21st May 1762
To Agnes Parker for a town Lot in Savannah No.2. Registered 5th June 1762

Grant dated 21st May 1762
To Deborah Houstoun for a town Lot in Savannah together 50 acres of Land. Registered 5th June 1762

Grant dated 21st May 1762
To William Glen for a town Lot in Savannah together 50 acres of Land. Registered 7th June 1762

Grant dated 21st May 1762
To Hugh Ross for 300 acres of Land in Saint George's Parish. Registered 7th June 1762

Grant dated 21st May 1762
To Hugh Ross for 50 acres of Land in St. Andrews parish. Registered 7th June 1762

Grant dated 21st May 1762
To Thomas Bassett for 500 acres of Land in St. Pauls Parish. Registered 7th June 1762

Grant dated 21st May 1762
To Phillip Howell for 400 acres of Land in St. Matthews Parish. Registered 8th June 1762

Colonial Records 423

Grant dated 21st May 1762
To Caleb Howell for 200 acres of Land in St. Matthews Parish.
Registered 8th June 1762

Grant dated 21st May 1762
To William Howell for 150 acres of Land in Saint Matthews parish.
Registered 8th June 1762

Grant dated 21st May 1762
To James Anderson for 500 acres of Land in St. George's parish.
Registered 8th June 1762

Grant dated 21st May 1762
To James McKay for 300 acres of Land in St. George's parish.
Registered 10th June 1762

Grant dated 21st May 1762
To John Lawson for 500 acres of Land in Saint Andrews parish.
Registered 10th June 1762

Grant dated 21st May 1762
To Griffith Williams for 500 acres of Land in St. Phillips parish.
Registered 10th June 1762

Grant dated 21st May 1762
To Thomas Marriott for 500 acres of Land in Saint Phillips parish.
Registered 10th June 1762

Grant dated 21st May 1762
To Joseph Gibbons for 50 acres of Land in Christ Church parish.
Registered 10th June 1762

Grant dated 21st May 1762
To Thomas Carter for 400 acres of Land in Saint Andrews parish.
Registered 11th June 1762

Grant dated 21st May 1762
To Joseph Raymond for 300 acres of Land in Christ Church parish.
Registered 11th June 1762

Grant dated 21st May 1762
To Gasper Starkey for 250 acres of Land in Saint Andrews parish.
Registered 11th June 1762

Grant dated 21st May 1762
To Joseph Andrew for 300 acres of Land in Saint Andrews parish.
Registered 11th June 1762

Grant dated 21st May 1762
To Silvanus Robinson for 250 acres of Land in Saint Johns parish.
Registered 11th June 1762

Grant dated 21st May 1762
To James Jarvis for 300 acres of Land in the parish of St. Paul.
Registered 12th June 1762

Grant dated 21st May 1762
To Richard Spencer for 176 1/2 acres of Land in Saint Andrews
parish. Registered 12th June 1762

Grant dated 21st May 1762
To John Gasper Greiner for 200 acres of Land in Saint Georges
parish. Registered 12th June 1762

Grant dated 21st May 1762
To Robert Houstoun for 100 acres of Land in St. Phillips Parish.
Registered 12th June 1762

Grant dated 21st May 1762
To Bryan Kelly for 400 acres of Land in St. Matthews parish.
Registered 14th June 1762

Grant dated 21st May 1762
To Bryan Kelly for 100 acres of Land in the parish of St. Matthew.
Registered 14th June 1762

Grant dated 21st May 1762
To David Dicks for 200 acres of Land in the parish of St. John.
Registered 14th June 1762

Grant dated 21st May 1762
To David Dicks Junior for 50 acres of Land in St. Johns parish.
Registered 14th June 1762

Grant dated 21st May 1762
To David Wetherspoon for 400 acres of Land in St. Andrews
parish. Registered 14th June 1762

Colonial Records 425

Grant dated 21st May 1762
To Richard Warren for 200 acres of Land in Christ Church parish. Registered 15th June 1762

Grant dated 21st May 1762
To John Shute for 200 acres of Land in St. Andrews parish. Registered 15th June 1762

Grant dated 21st May 1762
To John Shute for 200 acres of Land in Saint Andrews parish. Registered 15th June 1762

Grant dated 21st May 1762
To David Huguenin for 450 acres of Land in St. Phillip's parish. Registered 15th June 1762

Grant dated 21st May 1762
To George Delegal for 200 acres of Land in Christ Church parish. Registered 15th June 1762

Grant dated 21st May 1762
To John Francis Troiboudet for 400 acres of Land in Christ Church parish. Registered 16th June 1762

Grant dated 21st May 1762
To William Johnson for 150 acres of Land in Saint Andrews parish. Registered 16th June 1762

Grant dated 21st May 1762
To Simon Rouviere for 50 acres of Land in Christ Church parish. Registered 16th June 1762

Grant dated 21st May 1762
To John Rouviere for 50 acres of Land in Christ Church parish. Registered 16th June 1762

Grant dated 21st May 1762
To Peter Randon for 350 acres of Land in Saint George's parish. Registered 16th June 1762

Grant dated 21st May 1762
To John Hopkins for 200 acres of Land in Saint George's parish. Registered 17th June 1762

Grant dated 21st May 1762
To Bartholomew Farrer for 200 acres of Land in Saint Andrews parish. Registered 17th June 1762

Grant dated 21st May 1762
To Christian Dasher for 150 acres of Land in Saint Matthews parish. Registered 17th June 1762

Grant dated 21st May 1762
To William Alther for 150 acres of Land in Christ Church parish. Registered 17th June 1762

Grant dated 21st May 1762
To Arthur Carney for 100 acres of Land in St. Phillips parish. Registered 17th June 1762

Grant dated 21st May 1762
To Arthur Gibbons for 100 acres of Land in Saint Andrews parish. Registered 18th June 1762

Grant dated 21st May 1762
To Daniel Ryan for 100 acres of Land in St. Johns parish. Registered 18th June 1762

Grant dated 21st May 1762
To Benjamin Lewis for 100 acres of Land in the parish of St. Andrew. Registered 18th June 1762

Grant dated 21st May 1762
To Donald McIntosh for 100 acres of Land in St. Andrews Parish. Registered 18th June 1762

Grant dated 21st May 1762
To Isaac Baillou for 100 acres of Land in Christ Church parish. Registered 18th June 1762

Grant dated 21st May 1762
To Samuel Burnley for 100 acres of Land in Saint Johns parish. Registered 19th June 1762

Grant dated 21st May 1762
To Gasper Hack for 100 acres of Land in Saint Matthews parish. Registered 19th June 1762

Grant dated 21st May 1762
To Gasper Hack for 50 acres of Land in Saint Matthews parish.
Registered 19th June 1762

Grant dated 21st May 1762
To Bartholomew Nibling for 55 acres of Land in Christ Church
parish. Registered 19th June 1762

Grant dated 21st May 1762
To David Tubear for a town Lot & 50 acres of Land at Vernonburgh.
Registered 19th June 1762

Grant dated 21st May 1762
To Henry Nongazer for 50 acres of Land in Christ Church parish.
Registered 21st June 1762

Grant dated 21st May 1762
To William Russell for 50 acres of Land in Christ Church parish.
Registered 21st June 1762

Grant dated 21st May 1762
To Clement Martin Esquire for 200 acres of Land in St. Matthews
parish. Registered 21st June 1762

The above Abstract of the Grants Register'd from the 27th January
to the 27th July 1762 compared with the Register Book at Savannah
this 2d day of August 1762.

Pat. Houstoun Register

James Wright to the Board of Trade, May 6, 1763, Savannah, read
Aug. 4, 1763, C.O. 5/648, E. 69, respecting Governor Boone's
granting of lands southward of the Altamaha together with the
names of several persons given land and the number of acres
granted.

My Lords

On the 20th of April I did my self the Honor of writing to your
Lordships on the Subject of Governor Boone's granting warrants
to Survey the Lands to the Southward of the River Alatamaha, in
which letter my Lords I mentioned on the Information of Mr. Grey

Elliott several large Quantities of Lands that had been ordered to some particular Persons, amongst others that 16,000 Acres had been ordered to one Howarth on Account of the Estate of James Michie Deceased, but that I should transmit to your Lordships a particular Account, if I could Procure it from the Offices. And by a letter I have just received from Charles Town, I find that the Person I directed to apply has not yet been able to get an Authentic Account of the Lands ordered, and to what Persons. I am Informed that 27250 Acres were Ordered to Eleven Persons Vizt. to one Donnour on Account of Colonel Bees Estate 5000 acres, to Lord William Campbell 2000, to Charles Ogilvie, now in England, 2000, to Henry Middleton 3000, to one Stephens 3000, to Henry Laurens 3000, to William Hopton 2000, To William Guering 2000, and to David & John Deas and one Vanderhorst together 5250 acres.

But my Lords untill I can get proper Certificates from the Officers, it will be Impossible for me to come at the exact Truth and knowledge in this Case. The same Information that I received of these Tracts being ordered mentions that Mr. Grey Elliott was mistaken in the Accounts he gave me that 16,000 Acres was ordered to Mr. Howarth Who its said had only 1,600 acres, but all the other Parcels mentioned, I believe will appear to be right, at least they are so, from the best Information I am as yet able to come at. What I wrote your Lordships Relative to the Lands ordered to Mr. Howarth, was on Mr. Elliotts Information, who I sent to Charles Town on the Occasion, and who still Says that it was asserted to be so, when he was there. But as I have heard from other Hands that he is mistaken, and that Howarth has only 1600 acres, and as my duty & sole intention is only to state Facts according to the best Information I can get, and it would give me the greatest uneasiness to Misrepresent any one circumstance. Therefore I take this Opportunity to rectify that matter, which does not now appear to be as Mr. Elliott was Informed, and Represented it to me.

On Tuesday last a great many more Warrants were ordered to other Persons, for Lands to the Southward of the River Alatamaha, to the amount of about 160,000 acres as appears by their Gazette, but its not in my Power to give your Lordships any further Particulars. I shall only add that those large Grants will soon reach St. Augustine. Some its said have already gone far up St. Juans Lake or River, and the Creek Indians are greatly alarmed at seeing a number of armed men Surveying these Lands & marking Trees. They have sent Runners all over the Nation to assemble them together, and what the Consequence may be I cant yet say but am apprehensive it may Involve us in difficulties, for my Lords there

is a great difference between Extending our Settlements gradually
& easily, and an Appearance as tho' the whole country was to be
Swallowed up at once, and that by armed People. And this the
Indians say is a Confirmation of what the French have told 'em
"that we should take all their Lands from 'em, and drive 'em back
& Extirpate them in time."

James Wright, to the Board of Trade, June 3, 1763, Savannah, read
Aug. 4, 1763, C.O. 5/648, E. 70, informing the Board of the uneasiness of the Creek Indians over the rapid granting of lands south
of the Altamaha and of several acts recently passed in Georgia.

My Lords

On the 20th of April I wrote to your Lordships very fully with
respect to the Procedure of the Governor of South Carolina Relative
to the Lands lying to the Southward of the River Alatamaha, the
Consequences of which appear every day in a Stronger & more Injurious light. One thing which occurred to me at first, I did not
mention to your Lordships in that letter but have since in mine of
the 6th of May, that is the great Hazzard of bringing the Creek
Indians upon us, and imbroiling us with them. When I first arrived here my Lords I found the Province in very great danger of
a War with these People. It is Impossible for affairs to be more
Critical than ours were with the Indians at that time, and not
being in a Condition to Oppose or Repel them (a Nation of above
2000 Gun Men & reckoned the bravest & most warlike of the Indian Tribes) it has been my constant care & attention to Prevent
a Rupture & keep things quiet with them, and this was a most difficult Task I assure your Lordships.

And now seeing a great Number of armed Men riding all over
the Southern Part of the Country, has alarmed them very much,
and as I lately wrote your Lordships, they have had several Consultations upon it, and I have received a very strong talk from
them on the Subject of the Cession of the Lands by France & Spain
to His Majesty, and our Extending our Settlements, in which
amongst other things they Say, "That formerly the Lands that the
"White People Live upon was theirs, but now they believe the
"White People have forgot it, or think the Indians have no Lands
"belonging to them. That they hear we are going to take all the
"Lands which they lent to the French & Spaniards, and they are
"Surprized how People can give away Lands that do not belong

"to them. That formerly the White People were to drink on one "Side of the River Savanah, & the red People on the Other, and "this is what they Still want. But instead of that the White People "Settle a great way up the River, and back from it, on lands which "were never granted to them by the Indians on Sittilly [?] to the "Southward of Georgia (NB The Lands lately run out by the People "of Carolina to the Southward of the Alatamaha) and therefore de-"sire that all these straggling People may be ordered off, to Pre-"vent any Misunderstanding that may happen hereafter. That now "they think the White People intend to take all their Lands & throw "away the old talks, and that it makes their hearts Cross to see "their Lands taken without their Liberty," and more to the same Afect, so that your Lordships see how much they are alarmed at, & dislike the Cession by France & Spain to his Majesty, and also our Extending our Settlements nearer towards them, and that their Present disposition does not seem the most Cordial & Friendly towards us. But I am in great hopes that at the intended Congress so wisely judged & ordered by his Majesty all these Points may be better Cleared up & Settled.

 On the 7th of April my Lords I assented to the following Bills, Copys whereof your Lordships will receive by this Conveyance, and agreeable to my Instructions I now give my observations thereon, and Reasons for Passing them Vizt. An Act for Raising & Granting to His Majesty the Sume of £1934.9.0 Sterling for the use and Support of the Government of Georgia. An Act to Prevent damages which may arise from dam's or banks for Reserving or Stopping water. This my Lords seemed a very usefull & necessary Law, as the Planters in general make Reservoirs of water for their Rice Fields, and many inconveniencies happened for want of Proper Regulations in that Respect. An ordinance Appointing Mr. Knox Agent for the affairs of this Province in Great Britain. An Act Empowering the General Court of Pleas to grant Writs of Partition of Lands & Tenements held in Coparcenary, Jointenancy, & Tenancy in Common, in this Province, & appointing the Method of Proceeding therein. The Laws of Great Britain my Lords relative to these matters do not Extend here, and if they did Could not be Easily Executed. This Law my Lords is on the Plan of one in the Neighbouring Province, which has been found to answer the Ends proposed without any Objection or inconvenience for several years. It only differs in this Particular, that I have inserted a larger Number of Persons to make the Partition than are mentioned in the Carolina Law. An Act for Continuing an Act for Regulating the Assize of Bread, An Act for amending an Act for Constituting &

dividing the Several Districts & Divisions of this Province into Parishes etc., An Act to Amend an Act to Prevent the Building Wooden Chimneys etc., An Act to Prevent Persons throwing Ballast or Rubbish or Falling Trees into the Rivers & Navigable Creeks within this Province, and for keeping clear the Channels of the Same. This my Lords seemed to be a very necessary Law for Preserving the Navigation free & open, & is upon the Plan of the Statute of the 19 Geo. 2, only the Convictions on that Act are Final, and this Law allows of an Appeal to the General Court.

An Act to Prevent the bringing into and spreading of Contagious distempers in this Province; and to Oblige Vessels going out of any Port within the same, first to Produce for that Purpose, a Pass Port from the Governor or Commander in Chief for the time being, and to Prevent the harbouring of sick sailors & others. In this Act my Lords are several very necessary & usefull Regulations, adapted to the Local Circumstances & Situation of Affairs here, & such as Appeared to me unexceptionable & not inconsistent with the Laws of Great Britain. An Act to Empower the Commissioners Appointed in & by an Act of the General Assembly for the Repairing of Christ Church in Savanah, to Lay out a spot of ground for Erecting a Parish Church thereon. An Act for Regulating a Work house for the Custody & Punishment of Negroes, An Act for holding special or Extraordinary Courts of Common Pleas etc. A Law for this Purpose my Lords seemed very Reasonable for the Encouragement of Trade, that Transient Persons might not be Compelled to wait the sometimes tedious Proceedings at Law is such an one as I believe subsists in all or most of the Colonies, and I hope may appear without exception. An Act for Preventing Fraudulent Mortgages & Conveyances, and for making Valid all deeds & Conveyances heretofore made, in respect to any defect in the form and Manner of making thereof. This my Lords appeared to me to be a Just & Necessary Law, the first part is on the Plan of the British Acts of Parliament, and the latter Part calculated to Prevent Vexatious Suits, and Persons from being disturbed in their Possessions & Property, on account of any omission or trifling informality in the form of their Deeds or Conveyances. There formerly being very few Persons here Acquainted with the manner & form of drawing Deeds or Conveyances of Lands etc. upon the whole my Lords the several Bills I last assented to, Seemed to me to be of general utility & not repugnant to the Laws of Great Britain and hope they will also appear unexceptionable to your Lordships.

An abstract of grants registered in Georgia from July 27, 1762, to March 25, 1763, Savannah, C.O. 5/648, E. 71.

Grant Dated August 3rd 1762
To His Excellency James Wright Esquire for 177 Acres of Land in Christ Church Parish. Registered August 18th 1762

Grant Dated August 3rd 1762
To Jonathan Bryan Esquire for 600 Acres of Land in Christ Church Parish. Registered August 18th 1762

Grant Dated August 3rd 1762
To Jonathan Bryan Esquire for 300 Acres of Land in Saint Phillips Parish. Registered August 18th 1762

Grant Dated August 3rd 1762
To Jonathan Bryan Esquire for 300 Acres of Land in Saint Phillips Parish. Registered August 18th 1762

Grant Dated August 3rd 1762
To Jonathan Bryan Esquire for 150 Acres of Land in Saint Johns Parish. Registered August 19th 1762

Grant Dated August 3rd 1762
To Jonathan Bryan Esquire for 45 Acres of Land in Savannah township. Registered August 19th 1762

Grant Dated August 3rd 1762
To Jonathan Bryan Esquire for 8 Lots Containing 44 Acres of Land in Savannah township. Registered August 19th 1762

Grant Dated August 3rd 1762
To Mary Bryan Widow for 300 Acres of Land in Saint Phillips Parish. Registered August 19th 1762

Grant Dated August 3rd 1762
To Mary Bryan Widow for 200 Acres of Land in Saint Phillips Parish. Registered August 19th 1762

Grant Dated August 3rd 1762
To Thomas Maxwell for 850 Acres of Land in Saint John's Parish. Registered August 20th 1762

Colonial Records 433

Grant Dated August 3rd 1762
To James Woodland for 500 Acres of Land in Christ Church Parish. Registered August 20th 1762

Grant Dated August 3rd 1762
To Christiana Margaretha Barbara Von Munch, Spinster, for 647 1/2 Acres of Land in St. George's Parish. Registered August 20th 1762

Grant Dated August 3rd 1762
To Evan Lewis for 350 Acres of Land in Saint George's Parish. Registered August 20th 1762

Grant Dated August 3d 1762
To Mordecai Sheftal for 100 Acres of Land in Christ Church Parish. Registered August 20th 1762

Grant Dated August 3rd 1762
To John Young for 250 Acres of Land in Christ Church Parish. Registered August 21st 1762

Grant Dated August 3rd 1762
To Isaac Young for 100 Acres of Land in Christ Church Parish. Registered August 21st 1762

Grant Dated August 3rd 1762
To Isaac Young for a town Lot and 50 acres of Land in Savannah township. Registered August 21st 1762

Grant Dated August 3rd 1762
To Margaret the Wife of Thomas Young for a Lot of 50 Acres of Land at Abercorn in the Parish of St. Matthew. Registered August 21st 1762

Grant Dated August 3rd 1762
To Samuel Moore for 300 Acres of Land in Saint George's Parish. Registered August 21st 1762

Grant Dated August 3rd 1762
To William McDonnald for 200 Acres of Land in Saint George's Parish. Registered August 21st 1762

Colonial Records

Grant Dated August 3rd 1762
To William Bradley for 500 Acres of Land in Christ Church Parish.
Registered August 23rd 1762

Grant Dated August 3rd 1762
To William Bradley Junior for a town Lot & 50 Acres of Land in
Savannah township. Registered August 23rd 1762

Grant Dated August 3rd 1762
To James Bradley for a town Lot & farm Lot containing forty five
Acres in Savannah township. Registered August 23rd 1762

Grant Dated August 3rd 1762
To William Liddle for 200 Acres of Land in Saint John's Parish.
Registered August 23rd 1762

Grant Dated August 3rd 1762
To William Case for 200 Acres of Land in Saint George's Parish.
Registered August 23rd 1762

Grant Dated August 3rd 1762
To John Sheraus for 150 Acres of Land in Saint Matthew's Parish.
Registered August 23rd 1762

Grant Dated August 3rd 1762
To Christian Gieger for 100 Acres of Land in Saint Matthews
Parish. Registered August 24th 1762

Grant Dated August 3rd 1762
To Charles Watson Esquire for 100 Acres of Land in Christ Church
Parish. Registered August 24th 1762

Grant Dated August 3rd 1762
To Charles Watson Esquire for a town Lot & 50 Acres of Land in
Savannah township. Registered August 24th 1762

Grant Dated August 3rd 1762
To William Ewen for 53 Acres of Land in Christ Church Parish.
Registered August 24th 1762

Grant Dated August 3rd 1761
To Peter Gandy for a town Lot in Savannah. Registered August
24th 1762

Colonial Records 435

Grant Dated September 7th 1762
To Messrs. Harris & Habersham for 300 Acres of Land in Christ Church Parish. Registered September 27th 1762

Grant Dated September 7th 1762
To Messrs. Harris & Habersham for a Lot & 50 Acres of Land in Savannah township. Registered September 27th 1762

Grant Dated September 7th 1762
To Messrs. Harris & Habersham for a Lot & 50 Acres of Land in Savannah township. Registered September 27th 1762

Grant Dated September 7th 1762
To James Habersham Esquire for 300 Acres of Land in Christ Church Parish. Registered September 28th 1762

Grant Dated September 7th 1762
To James Habersham Esquire for 4 farm Lots containing 180 Acres in Savannah township. Registered September 28th 1762

Grant Dated September 7th 1762
To James Habersham Esquire for 2 farm Lots containing 90 Acres in the township of Savannah. Registered September 28th 1762

Grant Dated September 7th 1762
To George Austin for a Garden Lot containing 5 Acres & farm Lot containing 45 Acres in Savannah township. Registered September 28th 1762

Grant Dated September 7th 1762
To John Morell for 3 farm Lots containing 135 Acres in Savannah township. Registered September 28th 1762

Grant Dated September 7th 1762
To James McKay Esquire for a town Lot in Savannah. Registered September 28th 1762

Grant Dated September 7th 1762
To John Tuckwell for a town Lot & farm Lot containing 45 Acres in Savannah township. Registered September 29th 1762

Grant Dated September 7th 1762
To Lachlan McGillivray Esquire for 100 Acres of Land in Savannah township. Registered September 29th 1762

Grant Dated September 7th 1762
To Lachlan McGillivray Esquire for a town Lot in Savannah. Registered September 29th 1762

Grant Dated September 7th 1762
To Noble Jones Esquire for a Garden Lot containing 7 1/2 Acres in Savannah township. Registered September 29th 1762

Grant Dated September 7th 1762
To Michael Switzer for a Wharf Lot in Savannah. Registered September 30th 1762

Grant Dated September 7th 1762
To David Guinter for 400 Acres of Land in Christ Church Parish. Registered September 30th 1762

Grant Dated September 7th 1762
To John Stuart for 178 Acres of Land in Saint John's Parish. Registered September 30th 1762

Grant Dated September 7th 1762
To John Phillips for 150 Acres of Land in Saint Paul's Parish. Registered September 30th 1762

Grant Dated September 7th 1762
To James Edward Powell Esquire for a town Lot in Savannah. Registered October 1st 1762

Grant Dated September 7th 1762
To Edmund Tannatt Esquire for a town Lot in Savannah. Registered October 1st 1762

Grant Dated September 7th 1762
To James McHenry for a town Lot in Savannah. Registered October 1st 1762

Grant Dated September 7th 1762
To William Patterson for a town Lot in Savannah. Registered October 1st 1762

Grant Dated September 7th 1762
To Samuel Munday for a town Lot in Savannah. Registered October 2nd 1762

Colonial Records 437

Grant Dated September 7th 1762
To William Norton for a town Lot in Savannah. Registered October 2nd 1762

Grant Dated September 7th 1762
To John Joachim Zubly for a farm Lot containing 45 Acres in Savannah township. Registered October 2nd 1762

Grant Dated September 7th 1762
To Grey Elliott Esquire for 3 farm Lots containing 135 Acres in Savannah township. Registered October 2nd 1762

Grant Dated September 7th 1762
To James Harley for 100 Acres of Land in Saint John's Parish. Registered October 6th 1762

Grant Dated September 7th 1762
To William Ewen for a Garden Lot containing 5 Acres in Savannah township. Registered October 6th 1762

Grant Dated September 7th 1762
To Mordecai Sheftal for 2 Garden Lots containing 10 Acres & a farm Lot containing 45 Acres in Savannah township. Registered October 6th 1762

Grant Dated September 7th 1762
To William Smith for a Garden Lot containing 5 Acres in Savannah township. Registered October 6th 1762

Grant Dated September 7th 1762
To Thomas Bailey for 5 Garden Lots containing 25 Acres in Savannah township. Registered October 6th 1762

Grant Dated September 7th 1762
To Paul Dubois for 53 Acres of Land in Christ Church Parish. Registered October 7th 1762

Grant Dated September 7th 1762
To Frederick Helvenstine for 100 Acres of Land in Saint Matthew's Parish. Registered October 7th 1762

Grant Dated September 7th 1762
To David Nitchman for a town Lot & farm Lot containing 45 Acres in Savannah township. Registered October 7th 1762

Grant Dated September 7th 1762
To Joseph, Alias, Augustus Godlieb Spangenberg for a town Lot
& farm Lot containing 45 Acres in Savannah township. Registered October 7th 1762

Grant Dated September 7th 1762
To Charles Watson Esquire for 2 farm Lots containing 90 Acres in
Savannah township. Registered October 7th 1762

Grant Dated September 21st 1762
To Charles Watson Esquire for 100 Acres of Land in Christ Church
Parish. Registered October 8th 1762

Grant Dated September 21st 1762
To William Handley for 315 Acres of Land in Saint Matthew's
Parish. Registered October 8th 1762

Grant Dated September 21st 1762
To William Handley for 285 Acres of Land in Saint Matthew's
Parish. Registered October 8th 1762

Grant Dated August 3rd 1762
To William Bradley Senior for a town Lot & 50 Acres of Land in
Savannah township. Registered October 8th 1762

Grant Dated September 7th 1762
To Frederick Closman for a town Lot in Augusta. Registered
October 8th 1762

Grant Dated October 19th 1762
To William Grover Esquire for 100 Acres of Land in Christ Church
Parish. Registered October 20th 1762

Grant Dated November 2nd 1762
To Adam Croady for 150 Acres of Land in Christ Church Parish.
Registered November 13th 1762

Grant Dated November 2nd 1762
To John Willson for 300 Acres of Land in Christ Church Parish.
Registered November 13th 1762

Grant Dated November 2nd 1762
To Lewis Mitchell for 50 Acres of Land in Christ Church Parish.
Registered November 17th 1762

Colonial Records 439

Grant Dated November 2nd 1762
To John Rae for 450 Acres of Land in Christ Church Parish. Registered November 18th 1762

Grant Dated November 2nd 1762
To William Ewen for a Lot of 20 Acres of Land at Yamacraw in Christ Church Parish. Registered November 18th 1762

Grant Dated November 2nd 1762
To Ann Green for a town Lot in Savannah with the Garden & farm Lots thereunto belonging. Registered November 19th 1762

Grant Dated November 2nd 1762
To Henry Yonge Esquire for Six Garden Lots containing 30 Acres in Savannah township. Registered November 19th 1762

Grant Dated November 2nd 1762
To Henry Yonge Esquire for 100 Acres of Land in Christ Church Parish. Registered November 20th 1762

Grant Dated November 2nd 1762
To Thomas Cater for 300 Acres of Land in the Parish of Saint John. Registered November 20th 1762

Grant Dated November 2nd 1762
To John McCullock for 426 Acres of Land in the Parish of Saint Andrew. Registered November 23rd 1762

Grant Dated November 2nd 1762
To John McCullock for 500 Acres of Land in the Parish of Saint Andrew. Registered November 24th 1762

Grant Dated November 2nd 1762
To Frederick Holzendorff for 50 acres of Land in the Parish of Saint John. Registered November 24th 1762

Grant Dated November 2nd 1762
To Frederick Holzendorff for 200 Acres of Land in the Parish of Saint John. Registered November 24th 1762

Grant Dated November 2nd 1762
To Alexander Shephard for 150 Acres of Land in the Parish of Saint John. Registered November 24th 1762

Grant Dated November 2nd 1762
To Ann the Wife of Michael Mason for 500 Acres of Land in the Parish of Saint Paul. Registered November 25th 1762

Grant Dated November 2nd 1762
To Francis Mitchell for 550 Acres of Land in the Parish of Saint John. Registered November 25th 1762

Grant Dated November 2nd 1762
To George Moore for 200 Acres of Land in the Parish of Saint George. Registered November 26th 1762

Grant Dated November 2nd 1762
To John Milledge Esquire for 650 Acres of Land in the Parish of Saint George. Registered November 26th 1762

Grant Dated November 2nd 1762
To John Milledge Esquire for 100 Acres of Land in the Parish of Saint George. Registered November 26th 1762

Grant Dated November 2nd 1762
To John Willson for 200 Acres of Land in Christ Church Parish. Registered November 26th 1762

Grant Dated November 2nd 1762
To William Baker for 350 Acres of Land in the Parish of Saint John. Registered November 2nd 1762

Grant Dated November 2nd 1762
To Frederick Herb for 250 acres of Land in the Parish of Saint Matthew. Registered November 26th 1762

Grant Dated November 2nd 1762
To James Ogleby for 200 Acres of land in the Parish of Saint George. Registered November 27th 1762

Grant Dated November 2nd 1762
To James Taylor for 150 Acres of land in the Parish of Saint John. Registered November 29th 1762

Grant Dated November 2nd 1762
To John Thomas for 50 Acres of Land in the Parish of Saint George. Registered November 29th 1762

Grant Dated November 2nd 1762
To Jacob Hensler for 50 Acres of land in Christ Church Parish. Registered November 29th 1762

Grant Dated December 7th 1762
To Abraham Hood for a town Lot in Augusta. Registered December 14th 1762

Grant Dated December 7th 1762
To Richard Pace for 22 Acres of Land in Christ Church Parish. Registered December 14th 1762

Grant Dated December 7th 1762
To John Van Junior for 100 Acres of Land in the Parish of Saint Paul. Registered December 14th 1762

Grant Dated December 7th 1762
To Charles Weatherfoot for 150 Acres of Land in the Parish of Saint Paul. Registered December 14th 1762

Grant Dated December 7th 1762
To William Lindall for 100 Acres of Land in the Parish of Saint George. Registered December 15th 1762

Grant Dated December 7th 1762
To William Struthers for 500 Acres of Land in the Parish of Saint Paul. Registered December 15th 1762

Grant Dated December 7th 1762
To Ezekiel Harlan for 100 Acres of land in the Parish of Saint Paul. Registered December 15th 1762

Grant Dated December 7th 1762
To Thomas Hickenbottom for 100 Acres of Land in the Parish of Saint Paul. Registered December 15th 1762

Grant Dated December 7th 1762
To Isaac Wood for 100 Acres of Land in the Parish of Saint Paul. Registered December 16th 1762

Grant Dated December 7th 1762
To Bryan Ward for 100 Acres of Land in the Parish of Saint Paul. Registered December 16th 1762

Grant Dated December 7th 1762
To Grey Elliott Esquire for a farm Lot containing 45 Acres in Savannah township. Registered January 22nd 1763

Grant Dated December 7th 1762
To James Read & Grey Elliott Esquire for 250 Acres of Land in the Parish of Saint Phillip. Registered January 26th 1763

Grant Dated December 7th 1762
To Alexander Mackenzie for 150 Acres of Land in the Parish of Saint Andrew. Registered January 27th 1763

Grant Dated December 7th 1762
To Raymond Demeré Esquire for 425 Acres of Land in the Parish of Saint John. Registered January 27th 1763

Grant Dated December 7th 1762
To Raymond Demeré Esquire for 50 Acres of Land in the Parish of Saint James. Registered January 28th 1763

Grant Dated December 7th 1762
To Nicholas Lawrence for 400 Acres of Land in Christ Church Parish. Registered January 28th 1763

Grant Dated December 7th 1762
To Charles Reitter for 150 Acres of Land in the Parish of Saint Matthew. Registered January 29th 1763

Grant Dated December 7th 1762
To John Milledge Esquire for 50 Acres of Land in Christ Church Parish. Registered January 31st 1763

Grant Dated December 7th 1762
To John Milledge Esquire in trust for a town Lot & Garden Lot containing 5 Acres in Savannah township. Registered January 31st 1763

Grant Dated December 7th 1762
To Richard Baker for 150 Acres of Land in Saint John's Parish. Registered February 1st 1763

Grant Dated December 7th 1762
To Richard Baker in trust for 300 acres of Land in the Parish of Saint Andrew. Registered February 1st 1763

Grant Dated December 7th 1762
To Joseph Gibbons Esquire for 262 Acres of Land in the Parish of Saint John. Registered February 3rd 1763

Grant Dated December 7th 1762
To David Emanuel for 200 Acres of Land in the Parish of Saint George. Registered February 3rd 1763

Grant Dated December 7th 1762
To James Gray for 100 Acres of Land in the Parish of Saint George. Registered February 4th 1763

Grant Dated December 7th 1762
To Matthias Bidenback for 100 Acres of Land in the Parish of Saint Matthew. Registered February 4th 1763

Grant Dated December 7th 1762
To Frederick Helvinstine for 100 Acres of Land in the Parish of Saint Matthew. Registered February 5th 1763

Grant Dated January 4th 1763
To John Francis Triboudet for 150 Acres of Land in Christ Church Parish. Registered February 5th 1763

Grant Dated January 4th 1763
To George Cuthbert for 600 Acres of Land in Christ Church Parish. Registered February 7th 1763

Grant Dated January 4th 1763
To Joseph Ottolenghe Esquire for 4 Garden Lots containing 20 Acres in Savannah township. Registered February 7th 1763

Grant Dated January 4th 1763
To Francis Butterfield for 500 Acres of Land in the Parish of Saint John. Registered February 7th 1763

Grant Dated January 4th 1763
To Francis Butterfield for 500 Acres of Land in the Parish of Saint John. Registered February 7th 1763

Grant Dated January 4th 1763
To Joseph & Sarah Day for 500 Acres of Land in the Parish of Saint Paul. Registered February 8th 1763

Grant Dated January 4th 1763
To Henry Bell for 150 Acres of Land in the Parish of Saint Paul.
Registered February 8th 1763

Grant Dated January 4th 1763
To Thomas Cox for 300 Acres of Land in the Parish of Saint Andrew.
Registered February 8th 1763

Grant Dated January 4th 1763
To John Martin for 250 Acres of Land in the Parish of Saint Andrew.
Registered February 8th 1763

Grant Dated February 1st 1763
To James Edward Powell Esquire for 500 Acres of Land in Christ
Church Parish. Registered February 12th 1763

Grant Dated February 1st 1763
To Elizabeth Butler, Widow, for 500 Acres of Land in the Parish
of Saint Phillip. Registered February 14th 1763

Grant Dated February 1st 1763
To Elizabeth Butler, Widow, for 900 Acres of Land in the Parish
of Saint Phillip. Registered February 14th 1763

Grant Dated February 1st 1763
To Francis Arthur for 300 Acres of Land in the Parish of Saint
Andrew. Registered February 18th 1763

Grant Dated February 1st 1763
To Francis Arthur for 150 Acres of Land in the Parish of Saint
Andrew. Registered February 18th 1763

Grant Dated February 1st 1763
To Francis Arthur for 100 Acres of Land in the Parish of Saint
Andrew. Registered February 19th 1763

Grant Dated February 1st 1763
To Joseph Ottolenghe, James Deveaux, David Montaigut & William
Russell Esquires for 16 Acres of Land in Christ Church Parish
in trust for public Uses. Registered February 21st 1763

Grant Dated February 1st 1763
To Peter Randon for 200 Acres of Land in the Parish of Saint George.
Registered February 21st 1763

Grant Dated February 1st 1763
To John Walsar for a town Lot, 5 Acre Lot & 45 Acre Lot in Frederica township. Registered February 23rd 1763

Grant Dated February 1st 1763
To James Jarvis for a town Lot in Augusta. Registered February 23rd 1763

Grant Dated March 1st 1763
To Joseph Andrew for 150 Acres of Land in the Parish of Saint Andrew. Registered March 16th 1763

Grant Dated March 1st 1763
To Joseph Andrew for 262 Acres of Land in the Parish of Saint John. Registered March 16th 1763

The aforesaid Abstracts of the Grants, Registered from the 27th of July 1762 to the 25th of March 1763 compared with the Register Book at Savannah this 4th of April 1763.

Pat. Houstoun Register

James Wright to the Board of Trade, June 10, 1763, Savannah, Read Sept. 28, 1763, C.O. 5/648, E. 72, reciting the advantages from the continuation of the bounty on cocoons and congratulating the Board on the recent cession of Louisiana and Florida.

My Lords

I have had the Honor & very great Pleasure to receive your Lordships of the 20th of December last acknowledging the receipt of mine of the 26th April, 10th of June, 26th of July, and the 1st of October and it gives me infinite satisfaction to hear from your lordships that there is sufficient to answer the Bounties on the Cocoons without any restriction either to Number or Place. I am very clear my Lords that this is an article that may be brought not only to great Perfection, but extended to a considerable amount & value in a few years. But if the Bounty had ceased, I firmly believe it would have Decreased, & certainly been injurious to the Colony.

I had the greatest reason my Lords to expect that the Produce of this year would have very considerably exceeded that of the last, but an unfortunate Season of Cold Rains set in the latter end of April, which hurt the Food & did considerable damage. This happened my Lords when we thought every thing safe & secure, so that your Lordships see it depends greatly on the Weather as well as care and our Seasons here are very fluctuating, and a fine Prospect may in a few days be greatly reduced. However my Lords I have the pleasure to Inform you that 15472 lbs. weight of Cocoons have been this Season delivered in at the Filature, not at all inferior to last years in quality, and there is a few more yet to come, the Amount of last years was 15100 lbs.

I have communicated a Part of your lordships letter to me, to Mr. Ottolenghe & desired to know his Resolution that I may acquaint your Lordships therewith, and hope he will make no further difficulties. If he agrees to instruct another, I think he should be young, & bound by Articles to Serve the Province for a Number of years, and in the mean while to Qualify one or more. But as this need not be settled till towards next Spring, I hope your lordships will be pleased to Honor me with your Sentiments thereon, and what Allowance may be Proper to make the Person Mr. Ottolenghe may instruct. The Money received on Account of the Forfeited Lots will always be ready & Subject to His Majesties future directions. It is with Pleasure I find that your Lordships think the quitrent Bill is properly framed, and when I receive your directions thereon, I shall take the first Opportunity of getting it Passed into a Law. I observe what your lordships Mention relative to the Port of Sunbury, the 11th Section of the Statute of the 7th & 8th W. 3 Cap 22, really did not occur to me. I only on that Occasion consulted my Commission and Instructions, am glad your Lordships are pleased to Approve of the Measure, and as I acquainted the Commissioners of His Majesties Customs with what I had done. If they judge I have exceeded my Authority, I Presume I shall hear from them on the Subject. I can only say that I did not intend either to exceed my own Authority, or to encroach on that of others.

I most sincerely & heartily Congratulate your Lordships on the Peace which his Majesties Wisdom and equity has so happily concluded, so much to the Honor & advantage of Great Britain and of America in general. Pardon me my Lords for just mentioning that the immense advantage that will accrew to his Majesty by the Acquisition of Louisiana & fixing the French to their Natural Boundary of the River Mississipi, are not to be expressed, as well as those by the Cession of Florida, not only of the Settlements of St. Augustine & Pensacola; but the as yet almost unknown and invaluable Harbours in the Bay of Apalachee & along the Gulph of Mexico, almost the key of the Spanish Treasure. And now that your lordships are pleased to inform me that this Province will be freed from every obstacle that has obstructed its growth & Prosperity, and be no longer check't & cramp't, I have no doubt of its making great strides, & very soon becoming usefull to the Mother Country. Nothing I think can prevent this, unless the late Proceedings by the Governor of So. Carolina should be confirmed, and in that event, Georgia I concieve will receive such a Check as will still Obstruct its growth & Prosperity.

James Wright to the Board of Trade, June 22, 1763, Savannah, read Sept. 28, 1763, C.O. 5/648, E. 73, acknowledging receipt of the Board's instructions regarding the cession of Indian lands. The French and Spanish infuse bad notions among the Indians.

Sir

Yesterday and not before I received your letter of the 12 of December 1761, Inclosing His Majesties Royal Instructions of the 9th of December 1761 Relative to the Indian Lands etc. etc. and the Judges Commissions, all which I shall most punctually & duely attend to, and forthwith issue a Proclamation accordingly. I must observe that there is not one Person in this Province (that I know of) who claims a Foot of Land under any Indian Title or Purchase except Bosomworth, which affair was settled 3 or 4 years ago, and His Majesties grants given for the same. Nor has any Application ever been made to me for a Licence to Purchase of any Indian or Indians. I fear the late Carolina Proceedings may be attended with some of the very Consequences or inconveniencies intended to be remedied, and mentioned, or mean't in their Lordships Representation to His Majesty whereon the above Instructions are Founded. Where these dispatches have been so long detained I can't Conceive, they were forwarded to me by Governor Boone, and this shews the impropriety of sending dispatches for the Southern Provinces by way of New York. They seldom come to hand in less than 6, 8 & 10 Months, whereas were they given to the Agents to be sent by the first Merchant Ship that offers, they would Probably come to Hand in 2 or 3 Months at furthest.

The French & Spaniards are still infusing bad notions amongst the Indians, & telling them his Majesties intention is to destroy them. I have had many down with me lately on that Head, and notwithstanding all I tell 'em & my Endeavours to the Contrary, affairs seem just now very critical with them.

The memorial of Denys Rolle, M. P. and others, London, read Nov. 24, 1763, C.O. 5/648, E. 74, relative to their design of settling a colony between the Apalachee and Altamaha Rivers and enclosing a copy of a memorial presented to Lord Shelburne on the subject.

Whereas a Memorial (of which the inclosed is an exact Copy) was some Months ago presented to Lord Shelburn in Order to be laid before this Right Honorable Board, but by some Accident or Oversight (they are informed) his Lordship has not yet done it. Your Petitioners therefore beg Leave to offer to the Wisdom & Candour of your Lordships the Consideration of this Publick & (as they apprehend) most useful Undertaking: And as they have Reason to believe that had your Lordships been earlier acquainted with it they would have received all due Encouragement from the Board, it is therefore referred to the Consideration of your Lordships how far the Request of your Petitioners is capable of being received without Prejudice to the Steps that have been already taken by the Right Honorable Board.

ENCLOSURE

Humbly Sheweth that

Whereas the Settlement of Colonies in that part of the British Empire called North America has been attended with the most beneficial Consequences to these Kingdoms, has added much to the Honour of the Crown, has been a Source of the most profitable Commerce, & has also provided the means of Subsistence for very many persons otherwise destitute.

Under these Considerations the Petitioner with several other Gentlemen whose Names are inserted at the foot of this Memorial beg Leave to offer to your Lordships their Designs of settling a Colony in the Southern part of the N. American Continent; which they purpose to do in such a Manner as may do Honour to the Government, & effectually to answer the Good Ends of such an Undertaking.

The Plot which they ask for this purpose they would propose to extend from the Georgian Line on the North to another Line Southward, to be drawn Parallel to the Equator from 2 Miles below the Forks of the River Apalachicola to the River Alatamaha; to be bounded on the West by the First & on the East by the last of those Rivers.

On the South Side of the last mentioned River a Town will be immediately laid out & settled as fast as may be, & from thence a larger Town which is intended for the Capital is purposed to be extended on the Apalachicola; & such other Measures will be taken as may be most likely to insure the Success of this Undertaking.

And Whereas the Establishment of a Regular & Just Administration of Government is of the greatest Consequence to the Success of this Design, as by this Inducement Industrious Persons of various Countries & Employments may be encouraged to come & settle under the agreeable Prospect of being secured in their Rights & Possessions & the ready Administration of Justice.

And whereas our Natural & Near Connexion with the Indians of those Parts is unavoidable in itself so Natural, Justice & indeed Humanity require from us a Treatment suited to the Equity of their Pretensions as the true & Original Owners of the Soil. And as in this unavoidable Connexion with them many Disputes & Causes of Complaint will arise (in which our People will not seldom be the Aggressors) which by being speedily redress'd would prevent greater & heavier Inconveniencies & sometimes the most pressing Calamities.

For these & other Reasons which might be offered to the Wisdom of your Lordships the Petitioner & the Gentlemen concerned with him beg Leave to request that Considerations which appear to them so Important may be effectually provided for, either by the Appointment of a Governour at the Expence of the Crown, at least during the Infancy of this Expensive Undertaking; or by vesting the Powers of Government in Your Petitioner (in the same Manner as in Pennsylvania & Maryland) who are willing to establish a Government at their own Expence; in which they will endeavour to honour their Mother County, by diffusing & as much as possible extending that Liberty which is so great a Blessing to all Countries.

The Articles which are chiefly proposed for Commodities are; Silk in particular, which it is proposed to make a Staple, & which will be of the greatest Service to this Kingdom, where that Article is much wanted. Besides this Indigo & several other Commodities; & they have some Hopes of Wine & Oil which will be attempted.

William Reynolds of London, Merchant & and Elder Brother of the Trinity house.
George Buck Esquire Colonel of the Devonshire Militia.
John Buck Esquire his Brother a Captain in Ditto
This Family have been the most considerable Traders to America from the W. of England & are willing to exert

that Spirit again on the Obtaining such a Grant as is propos'd.
Robert Willan of London Dr. of Physick a Gentleman of good Character & Family & the Acting Person in this Affair.[87]

James Wright to the Board of Trade, Sept. 7, 1763, Savannah, read Dec. 1, 1763, C.O. 5/648, E. 75, informing the Board of the receipt of papers relative to governor's correspondence, to the peace proclamation, to Mr. Grover's removal, and containing an account of the present state of affairs in the province.

My Lords

Last week I had the Honor to receive your Lordships letter of the 29th of April Notifying to me that His Majesty had appointed your Lordships His Commissioners for Promoting the Trade of Great Britain and for inspecting & improving His Majesties Foreign Colonies and Plantations, and inclosing me a Copy of His late Majesties Order in Council, by which the Correspondence between your lordships Board and the Governors of the Colonies is regulated & ascertained, together with Copys of the Secretary of State's letters to the Board, and to the said Governors, explaining the said Order, and the additional Instruction given to the Governors in Consequence thereof. Which several Orders & Matters your Lordships may depend shall be very carefully Observed & Complied with by me.

I also received your Lordships' other letter of the same date, and agreeable to His Majesties Commands signified to me by your Lordships, I did immediately on the receipt thereof appoint an Early day of Thanksgiving to be observed by all His Majesties Subjects in this Province, in such manner & with such Forms of Prayer as have been usual on like Occasions.

I also had the honor to receive your Lordships letter of the 10th of May, with a Copy of an order of His Majesty in Council signifying His Majesties Pleasure for the Removal of Mr. Grover, which had Anticipated and Prevented your Lordships Consideration of my Reasons for suspending Mr. Grover from the Office of Chief Justice of this Province.

---

87. This memorial was refused by the Board of Trade.

I can with great Pleasure confirm & assure your Lordships of the Prosperous state of this Province, altho' the Running out of the Southern Lands, and the Cessions made by France & Spain, Occasioned great discontent amongst the Indians. I have lately received an Account that three men have been killed in the Upper Creeks, by a Party who have always been in the French interest & have Continually Laboured to involve us in a War with the Indians. This Account my Lords I believe may be True, tho' not absolutely Confirmed yet. But if it should prove true, I have great Reason to Expect that no further mischief will be done, and am very hopefull that at the Congress which is Proposed to be held the 15th of next Month, all Matters will be Explained, Cleared up, & settled amongst us.

It affords great Satisfaction & happiness to the People to be informed of your Lordships disposition to contribute to the benefit & advantage of this Colony in particular, and for which assurance I beg leave to return your Lordships my most hearty Thanks.

I find my Lord by the Receiver Generals Accounts that there will be great Occasion for a quit rent Law to enforce the Payment of His Majesties Rents, and whenever I have the honor to receive the Bill with your Lordships directions upon it, I shall take the first Opportunity of Endeavouring to get it passed into a Law. I observe what your Lordships are Pleased to Mention with respect to the Money arising by the Sale of the Forfeited Lots, which Sume will always be ready to be applied in such manner as His Majesty shall be graciously pleased to direct.

I have also received the Copy of Mr. Ottolenghes Memorial and your Lordships directions thereupon, and shall maturely weigh all the Circumstances attending that affair, and put it on such a Footing, as I think may most Conduce to the support & good management of that Valuable Article. The Produce of this years Silk is now ready to ship and will be put on Board a Vessel that will sail for London by the End of this Month. The whole Quantity of Pure Silk is 953 lb. weight so that your Lordships will see that altho' we received 298 lb. more Cocoons than the year before yet they have produced 87 lb. weight of Silk less than last year. Mr. Ottolenghe tells me that altho' the Cocoons first brought to the Filature were equally good with last years, yet the late Cocoons were not near so good, Occasioned by some very cold rains the latter end of April, which made the Worms turn Sickly, and the Cocoons were weak & did not yield so much Silk as those before that weather happened.

Memorial of Denys Rolle to the Board of Trade, London, read Jan. 23, 1764, C.O. 5/648, E. 76, praying that Cumberland Island may be granted to a group he represents.

Humbly Sheweth that

Whereas the Settlement of Colonies in North America has been attended with the most beneficial Consequences to these Kingdoms; Your Petitioner with several other Gentlemen whose Names are inserted at the foot of this Memorial beg Leave to offer to your Lordships their Design of making a Settlement in that Part of the World; which they purpose to do in such a Manner as may do Honour to the Government & effectually to answer the Good Ends of such an Undertaking.

The Plot which they would ask of your Lordships for this Purpose is a small Isle on the Coast of Georgia which they are informed is undisposed of & is known by the Name of Cumberland Isle.

And Whereas the Cultivation of Silk & Cotton would be of great Advantage to this Nation, as being at present extremely wanted; & Large Sums are Annually paid for them to other Countries: Your Petitioners have determined to direct their Attention in a particular Manner to the Growth & Propagation of those Valuable Materials of Commerce. Nor will their Attention be confined only to the above Articles. Several others will be attempted, particularly Wine, Oil & such Commodities as may be hoped for in a Warm Climate.

And as your Lordships have been pleased to honour us with Your Commands on this Occasion we beg Leave to refer entirely to Your Lordships the Manner of disposing or laying down the Terms of the Grant in a Way the Most agreeable to the Welfare of your Petitioners:

    William Reynolds of London Merchant, & an Elder Brother
      of the Trinity house.
    George Buck Esquire Colonel of the Devonshire Militia.
    John Buck Esquire a Captain in Ditto
      This Family have been the most Considerable Traders
      to America from the West of England & are ready to exert the like Spirit again upon obtaining such a Grant as is propos'd.
    Robert Willan of London Doctor of Physick, a Gentleman

of Good Character & Family: & the Acting Person in this Affair.[88]

James Wright to the Board of Trade, Nov. 23, 1763, Savannah, received Feb., 1764, C.O. 5/648, E. 82, informing the Board that the Creeks at the Augusta congress ceded a large westward tract to the province.

My Lords

I did myself the Honour of writing to your lordships on the 7th of September the Contents of which I beg leave to confirm & refer your Lordships to.

By a letter which I had the Honor to receive from your lordships Board, Dated the 27th of February 1761, the then Lords of Trade were Pleased to <u>Recommend it to me to Endeavour in all my Negotiations with the Indians to Obtain a Release from the Condition or Engagement in the Original Compact with them, by which we are bound not to Settle further up into the Country than the Flowing of the Tides</u>. Since which my Lords things have been so critically Circumstanced, between us, and the Indians, that no Favourable Opportunity has offered for even Mentioning that Affair to them, till the late Congress at Augusta, from whence I returned hither on the 15 instant, and have the Pleasure to Acquaint your Lordships that the Creek Indians then made a Voluntary Cession to His Majesty, of a Considerable Tract of Land to the Westward, which I believe Includes all our Settlements, and other Contiguous Lands claimed by the Indians, and gives Room for a great Number of new Settlements. This my Lords the Indians declared they did as a gratefull Acknowledgement of His Majesties great Clemency and beneficence towards them, in the general Forgiveness of all their Past Crimes & Offences. This Point my Lords I look on as a very Favourable Circumstance for the Province, and a Considerable Acquisition, and fully answers the Purposes intended by their Lordships in February 1761. No man can answer for the Fidelity of Indians, but my Lords they give the strongest assurances of their good intentions and every Appearance seems Favourable. In short if they behave amiss after this nothing will do but force. The

---

88. This memorial was refused by the Board of Trade.

Treaty settled at the Congress, and all Proceedings relative thereto, will be Transmitted to the Secretary of States Office as soon as they are fairly transcribed, from whence I Presume your Lordships will be Apprized of the Whole. I forbear to say more lest I should Transgress the mode prescribed for my Correspondence.[89]

The Silk is ship't on board this Vessel for the Amount of which I have drawn on Mr. Martyn agreeable to your Lordships directions & his request.

James Wright to the Board of Trade, Dec. 23, 1763, Savannah, received in March, read July 9, 1764, C.O. 5/648, E. 83, recounting the advantages from the Creek land cession, explaining the best methods of peopling the colony, and acknowledging receipt of four of the Board's letters.

My Lords

My last was of the 23d of November Informing your Lordships of the Cession of Lands made by the Creek Indians, and now do myself the Honor to Transmit to your Lordships a Copy of the Treaty, and a Map of Part of the Province of Georgia, shewing what Lands were formerly Ceded by the Indians to the Trustees, and what Part was Ceded at the late Congress. I have been much indebted to the Surveyors General for their assistance in Furnishing me with this Map which was in a great Measure taken from Private draughts & Materials Collected by Mr. De Brahm. This Cession my Lords cost me some Pains as I saw it was absolutely necessary to Obtain it, which will Appear from a View of the Map shewing our confined Limits and Part of the Lands having been granted & actually Settled before my Arrival here, tho' never Ceded by the Indians, which Acquisition my Lords together with the Extension of our South Boundary gives Room for a great Number of Inhabitants. If our Indian affairs Continue quiet I doubt not but

---

89. Additional information on the Congress of Augusta may be found in John Richard Alden, John Stuart and the Southern Colonial Frontier (Ann Arbor, Mich., 1944), 176-191. The minutes of the Congress are in CRG, XXXIX, and in the Colonial Records of North Carolina, 10 vols. (Raleigh, 1886-1890), X, 156-207.

I shall soon see the Province in a most flourishing Condition, Especially if due care is taken in the granting & disposal of the Lands.

Those my Lords that I humbly conceive will most effectually People, enrich & strengthen the Province at Present, are the Middling Sort of People, such as have Families, & a few negroes. According to the inclosed Specimen of an Application just made to me one Drury Dunn in behalf of himself and several of his Relations & others, for some of the Lands lately ceded by the Indians. Dunn himself at Present lives in So. Carolina, and all the rest are Settled in Virginia, and by this Method your Lordships see that 8550 acres of Land will Accommodate 16 Men, who with their Wives & Children make up 67 white Persons, and bring along with them 125 negroes. This my Lords will really be an Acquisition to the Province, and very different from granting 7500 acres to one Person, as was done last Summer to Mr. Stepehn Bull of So. Carolina whose grant was signed the 21st of May, a Man who has not a Shilling of Property in this Province, is settled in So. Carolina, and I may with the greatest Certainty say never will Remove to Georgia, but Possibly if forced to it, or afraid of losing his Lands for not complying with the Terms of his grant, may send an overseer & a few Negroes to make a show of Cultivation. But my Lords this I conceive is not Settling or Peopling a Colony. On the Contrary is Rather a Real Injury to it, and in this View and on this Consideration I grounded my assertions in my letter to your Lordships in April last Relative to the Carolina Proceedings to the Southward of the Alatamaha, and hope those Grants will yet be Set aside.

At the same time my Lords if Men of Substance such as Mr. Bull would remove into the Province and bring with them a Negro for every 50 Acres of Land, which I Presume is agreeable to the Royal intention undoubtedly such Inhabitants would be a great benefit to the Province, but I know, & see, so much of those things, that I am very Clear it will never be the Case of Mr. Bull, and many other of the Carolina Grantees who have large Tracts, unless a Law was to be made Obliging them to send a Negro into the Province for every 50 acres of Land granted them, or their grants to be Forfeited & Void. Something to this Purpose make them usefull to the Province, and I am Pretty Certain they will not Otherwise. My objections to those Grants my Lords are made with a True Zeal for His Majesties Service and the good of the Province over which I have the Honor to Preside.

P.S. 30 December. I have this day had the Honor to receive your Lordships letters of the 30th September & the 7th, 10th, & 11th of

October which I shall Pay the greatest Attention to, and answer by the next Opportunity.

Copy of the Nov. 9, 1763, Augusta treaty of peace with the Creeks, Savannah, read July 9, 1764, C.O. 5/648, E. 84, enclosed with Wright's Dec. 23, 1763, letter to the Board of Trade.

At a Congress held at Augusta in the Province of Georgia on the tenth day of November in the year of Our Lord One thousand seven hundred and Sixty three, By their Excellencies

> James Wright Esquire Governor of Georgia.
> Arthur Dobbs Esquire Governor of North Carolina.
> Thomas Boone Esquire Governor of South Carolina.
> The Honorable Francis Fauquier Esquire Lieut. Governor of Virginia.
> And John Stuart Esquire Agent and Superintendant of Southern Indian Affairs.

A Treaty for the preservation and continuance of a firm and perfect peace and friendship Between His most Sacred Majesty George the Third by the grace of God of Great Britain, France and Ireland King defender of the faith and so forth, And the several Indian Chiefs herein named who are authorized by the Kings, Head Men, and Warriors of the Chickesaws, Upper and Lower Creeks, Chactaws, Cherokees, and Catawbas, for and in behalf of themselves and their several Nations and Tribes.

Article the 1st

That a perfect and perpetual Peace and sincere Friendship shall be continued Between His Majesty King George the Third and all his Subjects and the several Nations and Tribes of Indians herein mentioned, That is to say the Chickesaws, Upper and lower Creeks, Chactaws, Cherokees, and Catawbas, and each Nation of Indians hereby respectively engage to give the utmost attention to preserve and maintain Peace and Friendship between their People and the King of Great Britain and his Subjects, and shall not commit or permit any kind of Hostilities, injury or damage whatever against them from henceforth and for any Cause or under any pretence whatsoever.

And for laying the strongest and purest foundation for a perfect and perpetual Peace and Friendship, His Most Sacred Majesty has been graciously pleased to pardon and forgive all past Offences and Injuries And hereby declares there shall be a general Oblivion of all Crimes, Offences and Injuries that may have been heretofore committed or done by any of the said Indian Parties.

Article the 2d

The Subjects of the Great King George and the aforesaid Nations of Indians shall for ever hereafter be looked upon as one People and the several Governors and Superintendent engage that they will encourage persons to furnish and Supply the several nations and Tribes of Indians aforesaid with all sorts of Goods usually carried amongst them in the manner in which they now are and which will be sufficient to answer all their wants.

In consideration whereof the Indian Parties on their part severally engage in the most solemn manner that the Traders and others who may go amongst them shall be perfectly safe and secure in their several persons and effects and shall not on any account or pretence whatever be molested or disturbed whilst in any of the Indian Towns or Nations or on their Journey to or from the Nations.

Article the 3d

The English Governors and Superintendent engage for themselves and their Successors as far as they can that they will always give due attention to the Interest of the Indians, and will be ready on all occasions to do them full and ample Justice. And the several Indian parties do expressly promise and engage for themselves severally and for their several Nations and Tribes pursuant to the full right and power, which they have so to do, That they will in all cases and upon all Occasions do full and ample Justice to the English, and will use their utmost endeavours to prevent any of their People from giving any disturbance or doing any damage to them in their settlements or elsewhere as aforesaid either by stealing their Horses, killing their Cattle, or otherwise, or by doing them any Personal hurt or Injury. And that if any damage be done as aforesaid, satisfaction shall be made for the same, to the party injured, and that if any Indian or Indians whatever, shall hereafter murder or kill a white Man, the Offender or Offenders shall without any delay, excuse or pretence whatever be immediately put to Death in a public manner in the presence of at least Two of the English who may be in the Neighbourhood where the Offence is committed.

And if any white Man shall kill or Murder an Indian, such white Man shall be tried for the Offence in the same manner as if he had murdered a White Man and if found guilty shall be executed accordingly in the presence of some of the Relations of the Indians who may be murdered if they choose to be present.

Article the 4th

Whereas doubt and disputes have frequently happen'd on account of Encroachments or supposed Encroachments committed by the English Inhabitants of Georgia on the Lands or Hunting Grounds reserved and claimed by the Creek Indians for their own use. Wherefore to prevent any mistakes, doubts or disputes for the future and in consideration of the great Marks of Clemency and Friendship extended to Us the said Creek Indians, We the Kings Head Men and Warriors of the several Nations and Towns of both upper and lower Creeks by Virtue and in Pursuance of the full right and powers which We now have and are possessed of Have consented and agreed that for the future the Boundary between the English settlement and Our Lands and Hunting Grounds shall be known and settled by a Line extending up Savannah River to Little River and back to the Fork of little River and from the fork of Little River to the ends of the South Branch of Bryar Creek and down that Branch to the lower Creek Path and along the lower Creek Path to the main Stream of Ogechee River, and down the main stream of that River just below the Path leading from Mount Pleasant and from thence in a straight Line cross to santa Sevilla on the Alatamaha River and from thence to the Southward as far as Georgia extends or may be extended to remain to be regulated agreeable to former Treaties and His Majesties Royal Instructions a Copy of which was lately sent to Us.

And We the Catawba Head Men and Warriors in Confirmation of an agreement heretofore entered into with the White people declare that We will remain satisfied with the Tract of Land Fifteen Miles Square a survey of which by our Consent and at our request has been already begun and the respective Governors and Superintendent on their parts promises and engage that the aforesaid Survey shall be compleated and that the Catawbas shall not in any respect be molested by any of the Kings Subjects, within the said Lines, but shall be indulged in the Usual manner of Hunting elsewhere.

And We do by these presents give grant and Confirm unto His Most Sacred Majesty King George the Third all such Lands whatsoever as we the said Creek Indians have at any time heretofore been possessed of, or Claimed as our hunting Grounds, which lye between the Sea, the River Savannah and the Lines hereinbefore mentioned and described. To hold the same unto the Great King George and his Successors for ever. And we do fully and Absolutely agree that from Henceforth the above Lines and boundary shall be the mark of division of Lands between the English and Us the Creek Indians notwithstanding any former agreement or Boundary to the Contrary. And that We will not disturb the English in their settlements or otherwise within the Lines aforesaid.

In Consideration whereof it is agreed on the part of his Majesty King George that none of his Subjects shall settle upon or disturb the Indians in the Grounds or Lands to the Westward of the Lines herein before described, and that if any shall presume to do so then on Complaint made by the Indians the party shall be proceeded against for the same and punished according to the Laws of the English.

In Testimony whereof We the underwritten have signed this present Treaty and put to it the Seals of Our Arms the day and Year above written and the several Kings and Chiefs of the several Nations and Tribes of Indians have also set their Hands and Seals to the same at the time and place aforesaid.

Pia Mattaw his ϕ mark	Attakullakulla's Mark
Captain Alleck his A mark	Kettagunsta Chote's Mark
Sampiafi his mark	Skyagunsta Ousteneka's Mark
Hootlipoahatchi F his Mark	Coll^o Ayres Mark
Nealuquesiapquo his Mark	Tuckaykungs Mark
Chiha Mico's Mark	Sarrui his Mark X
Shurashumastoby's Mark X	Eccoui's Mark

Tiftoy's Mark ⌣ ☉   James Wright Governor
                              of Georgia
The Wolf's Mark a   Arthur Dobbs Governor
                              of North Carolina
Willanawaw's mark ⌡   Thomas Boone Governor
                              of South Carolina
Amoyloy's Mark ⌠   Francis Fauquier
                              Lieut. Governor of Virginia
Chisco Talone's Mark ⌣   John Stuart Superintendent
                              South District
Clokoctas's Mark ∾

Fort Augusta, 10th November 1763.

This is to certifie that the above written is an exact and faithfull Copy of the Treaty of Peace and Friendship concluded with the several Governors Assembled and Chief Indians for that purpose.

        Fenwicke Bull, Secretary.

Names of persons applying to settle on lands lately ceded by the Creek Indians, received with Wright's Dec. 23, 1763, letter to the Board of Trade, read July 9, 1764, C.O. 5/648, E. 89.

	Acres
Drury Dunn himself & 18 Negroes	1000
Henry Dunn, the Same	1000
William Dunn, a Wife 8 Children & 16 Negroes	1000
John Dunn, a Wife 5 Children & 7 Negroes	500
Thomas Dunn, a Wife 7 Children & 8 Negroes	600
David Dunn, a Wife 5 Children & 3 Negroes	400
Lewis Dunn, 12 Negroes	500
Nathaniel Beddingfield a Wife 3 Children & 4 Negroes	400
Drury Burge a Wife & 3 Negroes	300
John Webb, a Wife 1 Child & 1 Negro	250
John Giles Thomas a Wife 6 Children & 5 Negroes	500
Francis Jones a Wife 3 Children & 6 Negroes	500
William Bellamy a Wife 1 Child & 6 Negroes	400
William Averis a Wife & 11 Negroes	500
William Baines a Wife & 3 Negroes	300

In all 16 Men, 51 Women & children & 125 Negroes . . 8550 acres
Stephen Bull a Carolina Planter, a grant Actually
    Signed for. . . . . 7500 acres
Thomas Smith Senior a Warrant for 8000
Rawlins Lowndes a Warrant for 7300

                                                              22800 acres

To 3 Carolina Planters not having a Shilling
    Property in Georgia

of Thomas Carr, Collector of the Customs for the Port of Sunbury, Georgia, for
uarters ending 5 January 1763 through 5 January 1764, received with Wright's
Dec. 23, 1763, to the Board of Trade, read July 9, 1764, C.O. 5/648, E.85,
d E. 87. These tables have been made from the quarterly reports, all signed
s Carr, Collector, and sworn to for their correctness before Governor James
All amounts of money are given in Sterling.

f Species of Goods exported to or imported from other Plantations in America
umerated Dutys received from the same

Quarter ending 5 January 1763	None
Quarter ending 5 April 1763	None
Quarter ending 10 July 1763	None
Quarter ending 10 October 1763	None
Quarter ending 5 January 1764	None

Account of Dutys arising on Foreign Rum, Spirits, Molasses, Sugar, &c entered inwards

Month day	In what Ship or Vessell imported	Frome Whence	By whom imported	Quantity & Quality of Goods	Duty
Quarter ending 5 January 1763					
1762					
Dec. 3	Schooner Jolly Robin	St. Croix	William Towers	Eight hhds. containing 500 gals of foreign molasses, (6 pr. Gal.)	£
Dec. 6	Sloop Haranger	St. Croix	John Weggery	Three Tearces containing 140 gals. of foreign molasses, (6 pr. Gal.)	£
Quarter Ending 5 April 1763					
	None				
Quarter ending 10 July 1763					
	None				
Quarter ending 10 October 1763					
1763					
Sept. 12	Brig Experiment	St. Croix	John Mules	Two hhds. Rum. 160 gals, (9 d)	£
				Two bbls Sugar, Wt. 750, (5 s)	£
Quarter ending 5 January 1764					
	Brig Olive Branch	St. Croix	Hugh Block	One hhd Rum, 98 Gals, (9 pr gal)	£
				Three bbls Sugar, Wt. 1860	£

Account of His Majestys Share of Fines and Forfeitures Received

m	Ship goods & ship forfeited or subject to Penalty	Cause of Seisure or Penalty	When process issued	Value by Appraisment or sale. In Sterling	Money Received	Charges	How the Charges Arise	Net proceeds	Kings 1/3
ing ne	5 January 1763								
ing s r, - tor	5 April 1763 Sloop Harranger, John Wiggery, Master from St. Croix	Having no Register	At a Court of Vice Adminralty held before the Honbl. Grey Elliott, Esqr. Judge Serrogate of the said Court on the 16 Jany 1763 Thomas Carr, Collector of His Majesties Customs in the Port of Sunbury in	Sold at Public Auction, Ship guns for the Sum of £161	£161.	Sundry Charges Amounting £52.0.3½	To Seamens Wages £22.19.8 The Judges fees £ 7.15.11 The Registers £ 3.12.2 The Marshal £10.5.0 The Advocate General £ 7.7.6 £52.0.3½	Net proceeds after deducting the Commission £156.19.6	Kings Moie after Expe Ded £3.

e of Georgia as well for the King and Governor of the said Province as himself, exhibited his Libell & Inf ertain sloop called the Harranger with the takle & furniture & all the goods, & merchandize on board the as forfeited the said Sloop not having a register or Certificate of her being registered according to the St rovided, to which a Claim was put in by John Wiggery on behalf of himself & John Willet as owners of sa ing of the merits the court at the ... day of ... decreed said Vessel & goods as forfeited one third part t ird part to the Governor aforesaid and one third part to the said Thos. Carr

ing 10 July 1763
ne
ing 10 October 1763
ne
ing 5 January 1764
ne

Account Current of Thomas Carr

er ending 5 January 1763

received on Molasses this quarter   £16.0.0

er ending 5 April 1763

ce due to His Majesty last quarter   £16.0.0   By Incidentals paid this Quarter

Balance due this Quarter

£

er ending 10 July 1763

Balance due his Majesty this Quarter

er ending 10 October 1763

Balance due his Majesty last Quarter   £

Dutys received this Quarter

£1

er ending 5 January 1764

Balance due his Majesty last Quarter   £1

Dutys received this Quarter

Account of Incidentals paid by Collector

Particular Payments	By what charge	Paid	Payment re

g 5 January 1763

None

g 5 April 1763

Half a years Rent of the Custom House £5.0.0

Sundrys for the use of the Revenue 2.0.0

£7.0.0

g 10 July 1763

None

g 10 October 1763

None

ng 5 January 1764

None

INDEX

Abercromby, Gen. James, career, 157n; corresponds with Ellis, 166, 168; plea for troops, 157
Abraham (Creek Chieftain), 80-84
Acadians, arrival, 137, 138, 142-143; history in Ga., 7, 7n
Acouthala (Indian chieftain), given presents by Ellis, 9
Alexander, William, land grant,* 116
Altamaha River, settlers expelled, 186, 187; settlements south of, 129, 175
Alther, Joseph, grant, 117
Alther, William, grant, 426
Amherst, Lord Jeffrey (Maj. Gen.), appointment, 185; sends expedition against Cherokees, 281, 282, 333, 334; to support troops in Ga., 335
Anderson, Elizabeth, grant, 324
Andrew, Joseph, grant, 424, 445
Andrews, Benjamin, grant, 235, 374
Arnsdorff, Peter, grant, 121
Arthur, Francis, grant, 364, 444
Ash, Hannah, grant, 315
Ashperger, David, grant, 114
Assembly, acts of, 33, 34, 38, 123, 124, 131, 132, 194, 215, 216, 226-228, 358, 359, 379, 383; acts approved by Privy Council, 279, 280; acts disallowed, 190-192; acts forwarded to England, 357; acts by Sir Matthew Lamb, 291, 292, 352-354, 335-337; by Wright, 430, 431; address to Board of Trade, 85; discontent of, 177, 178; dominated by Little faction, 31, 32; Ellis defends acts of, 284, 285; Ga. Society opposes, 36; resolutions, 202, 203; and Reynolds, 143-147; taxes, 202, 203; troubles with executive, 192, 193; Wright's opinion on acts of, 338-341
Atkin, Edmund, arrives in Charleston, 26; in Ga., 167; conduct, 212, 213, 225-227; powers not understood, 70; sketch, 26n
Atkinson, Joseph, grant, 61
Augspourger, Samuel, grant, 363
Augusta, Indian Congress at, 103; presents distributed, 136-138; site of fort, 40
Aurora (ship), captured, 128
Austin, George, grant, 435
Averis, William, land application, 460

Backer, Balthaser, grant, 110
Backler, Ezekiel, grant, 110
Bailey, John, grant, 49
Bailey, Kenneth, grant, 59, 61
Bailey, Thomas, grant, 49, 437
Baillie, Robert, grant, 113, 418
Baillou, Issac, grant, 117, 118, 426
Baillou, James, grant, 117, 331, 368
Baines, William, land application, 460
Baker, Alderman, alarms Ellis, 226
Baker, Benjamin, grant, 369
Baker, John, grant, 360
Baker, Richard, grant, 370, 442
Baker, William, grant, 324, 440
Barker, Joseph, grant, 319
Barnaby, John, grant, 318
Barnard, Capt. John, orders Indian presents, 76
Barnard, Edward, certifies Indian presents, 78, 139; justice of peace at Augusta, 78; grant, 109
Barnard, Timothy, grant, 372
Barns, John, grant, 118
Bassett, Thomas, grant, 422
Bateman, Mary, grant, 55
Beale, Jacob, grant, 359
Beddingfield, Nathaniel, land application, 460

---

*Hereafter land grant will be shortened to grant.

Bell & Harrison, London merchants, 151
Bell, Henry, grant, 444
Bell, William, grant, 236
Bellamy, William, land application, 460
Bellet, George, grant, 323
Beltz, Sigismund, grant, 317
Berger, Peter, grant, 368
Betz, John Gasper, grant, 372
Betz, John Michael, grant, 372
Bevill, Robert, grant, 421
Bidenback, Christian, grant, 313
Bidenback, Matthias, grant, 443
Birk, Christian, grant, 34
Blyth, Peter, grant, 361
Board of Trade, 91
Boarman, Michael, grant, 119
Boddie, Sarah, grant, 236
Bollinger, George, grant, 368
Bolton, Robert, 53, 244, 367
Bolzius, John Martin, grant, 62, 313, 331; and silk culture, 12
Boone, Gov. Thomas, grants land south of Altamaha, 408-414, 427-429
Booth, William, grant, 244
Bord, Burgon, grant, 416
Borneman, Benjamin William, grant, 369
Bortz, George Philip, grant, 240, 243
Bosomworth, Mary, claims against Ga., 5, 75, 90, 92-94, 102, 177, 256-263; and Levy, 94-98; compromise offered, 158-160; deed of settlement, 268-276; disturbs land values, 237; grant, 321; and Levy, 219, 220; and Patrick MacKay, 32; proposed settlement, 210-212; and Reynolds, 140, 141; and sale of Sapelo & Ossabaw, 253-256, 277; statement of account, 264, 265
Bosomworth, Thomas, agreement with Levy, 94-98; claims, 89, 90; encourages Indians against Ga., 22; misleads Indians, 23; plots against Ga., 89, 90; proposal, 91-94; Reynolds' opinion of, 140, 141

Bouquet, Col. Henry, 69
Bourquin, Benedict, grant, 241
Bourquin, Henry, grant, 115
Bowling, Mary, grant, 366, 368
Box, James, grant, 363, 367
Box, Philip, grant, 118
Bradley, James, grant, 434
Bradley, William, grant, 434
Bradley, William, Jr., grant 434
Brady, John, grant, 330
Brandner, Mathias, grant 49
Bratcher, James, grant, 368
Brims (Creek Chieftain), and Mary Bosomworth, 257n
Brooks, James, grant, 113
Brown, Alexander, grant, 312
Brown, James, grant, 315
Brown, John, Indian trader, 77
Brownjohn, Benjamin, grant, 47
Bruce, Thomas, grant, 236
Bruckner, Frederick, grant, 58
Bryan, Jonathan, Councillor, 210; grant, 238, 243, 321, 432
Bryan, Mary, grant, 371, 432
Buck, George, to settle colony south of Ga., 449, 452
Bull, Stephen, engrosses Ga. land, 455; land application, 460; land granted south of Altamaha, 409
Buntz, John George, grant, 313
Buntz, Urban, grant, 318
Burge, Drury, land application, 460
Burghalter, Michael, grant, 369, 373
Burghalter, Michael, Jr., grant, 373
Burgstainer, Daniel, grant, 61
Burnet, John, grant, 369
Burnley, Samuel, grant, 56, 426
Burnsides, James, grant, 237
Burrington, Thomas, Clerk of the Assembly, 26, 199; grant, 235
Burton, Elizabeth, grant, 332
Burton, John, grant, 53
Burton, Robert, grant, 331
Burton, William, grant, 53, 54
Butler, Elisha, grant, 122; recommended for Council, 303
Butler, Elizabeth, grant, 444
Butler, Joseph, Jr., grant, 60, 61
Butler, Joseph, Sr., grant, 60, 120, 314
Butler, Shem, grant, 61
Butler, William, candidate for Council,

Colonial Records 471

184; as Councillor, 210, 231;
death reported, 303; grant, 323,
373, 374
Butterfield, Francis, grant, 443

Cain, John, grant, 241
Camber, Thomas, grant, 421
Camp, William, grant, 369
Campbell, Martin, bond for Indian
presents, 76, 77
Campbell, Lord William, granted
land south of Altamaha, 428
Camphert, Christian, grant, 316
Camuse, Joseph, grant, 315
Camuse, Mary, in silk culture,
406, 407; sketch, 103n, 104n
Cardones, Gov. Alonso de, permits
Pyle to trade with St. Augustine,
403
Carney, Arthur, grant, 363, 426
Carr, Mark, grant, 110, 421
Carr, Thomas, Collector at Sunbury, 383; customs records of,
461-465; grant, 110
Carter, John, grant, 57
Carter, Thomas, grant, 375, 423
Case, William, grant, 434
Cater, Stephen, grant, 319
Cater, Thomas, grant, 439
Chapman, Edward, grant, 52
Charleston, Naval men of war
stationed at, 45, 163, 164
Charming Martha (ship), 27, 133
Cherokees, and back settlements,
245; capture Ft. Loudoun, 286;
chiefs invited to New Orleans,
379; and Creeks, 171, 246, 247;
desert Forbes's army, 167; effects of war with, 287; and
French, 30, 252; Grant's expedition against, 333, 334; invaded by Montgomery, 281, 286;
letter from trader to, 171; and
peace, 352; plots, 216, 217;
presents to, 80-84; raids, 214,
226-231, 250; trade with S. C.,
405; and Virginians, 171;
Wright's appraisal of, 293
Chew, Samuel, grant, 372
Chickasaws, as allies, 246, 248;
and Cherokees, 250; and English, 230, 231, 245; and French,

19; presents to, 77, 78, 80-84;
traders to, 76, 77
Chief Justice, 5, 21, 75
Choctaws, and French, 248, 285-288,
376, 377; trade with English, 91,
212
Christie, Thomas, grant, 374
Clancey, Thomas, grant, 316
Clark, Hugh, grant, 49, 50, 360
Clark, Nathaniel, grant, 242
Clark, William, grant, 50
Clarke, Donald, grant, 237
Clayton, John, grant, 332
Cleland, Surveyor General of Customs,
151
Clement, William, grant, 243
Clifton, William, Attorney General,
305, 346, 347; Councillor, 183,
184, 210; grant, 235, 371
Closman, Frederick, grant, 438
Cockspur Island, fort erected, 384
Collins, Thomas, grant, 243
Colson, William, grant, 339
Communications, by convoy, 177;
letters, 165; through S. C., 131
Cooper, Richard, grant, 310
Cornberger, John, grant, 54, 55, 327
Cornock, James, grant, 360
Council, inferior to Assembly, 182;
members of, 181-184; opposes
Ellis, 213
Courtone, Jerome, Indian trader, 77
Cox, Thomas, grant, 444
Cramer, Christopher, grant, 58, 371
Cranwetter, Maria Catherine, grant,
122
Creeks, attack Spanish settlements,
74; cede islands to Ga., 266; and
Cherokees, 216, 217, 246, 247,
250, 280-282; chiefs invited to New
Orleans, 379; and Choctaws, 212;
discontent of, 451; and Ellis, 45,
99, 103, 158; and English, 68, 163,
230, 231, 245; and French, 247,
286, 287, 348, 376, 377; gun men
in, 88, 89; insolence of, 73, 74;
and land cessions, 140, 453, 454-
456; murder traders, 251, 286; murder whites, 347; Ogeechee incident,
7, 42, 42n; peaceful relations with,
352, 354; and Savannah, 70; and
S. C. grants, 429, 430; and trade,

156, 405; treaty with, 100, 456-460; Wright's appraisal of, 293
Croady, Adam, grant, 438
Crooke, Harriotte, grant, 239
Cronenberger, Jacob, grant, 313
Cronenberger, Nicholas, grant, 113, 321
Cross, Thomas, grant, 363
Cross, William, grant, 48
Crowber, George, grant, 331, 332
Cubbage, John, 188
Cumberland Island, Fort William on, 156; settled by Gray's adherents, 17; settlements abandoned, 192
Cunningham, David, grant, 113, 314
Currency, act disallowed, 200-203; bill to issue, 12, 39, 40; necessity of, 20, 21; paper bills, 152, 153; state of, 306-308
Curtis, Henry, grant, 242
Cusmal, Jacob, grant, 236
Cussitusco (Cherokee Chieftain), 80-84
Customs, Sunbury records, 383, 461-465
Cuthbert, George, grant, 59, 443

D'Aranda, Don Illario, captured, 128
Darien, fort site, 40
Dasher, Christian, grant, 328, 426
Dasher, Martin, grant, 319, 417
Davis, John, Jr., grant, 62
Davis, John, Sr., grant, 62, 363
Davis, Thomas, grant, 416
Davis, William, grant, 62
Day, Joseph, grant, 443
Day, Sarah, grant, 443
Dean, Lydia, grant, 369
Deas, David, granted land south of Altamaha, 428
DeBrahm, William John Gerar, grant, 361; maps used for Indian cession, 454; plan to fortify Ga., 10; sketch, 10n
Debtors, asylum in Ga. for, 22, 33, 38; flee from northward, 184
Defense, against Cherokee raids, 229; fort act passed, 33, 40; guns and shot available, 298, 299; measures to improve, 285, 354, 355; Negroes to maintain fortifications, 297, 298; summary of troops in Ga., 293, 294; weaknesses of, 43-45, 165-167, 251, 283, 290; Wright endorses plan of, 291
de Heredia, Gov. Alonso Fernandez, 19
Delegal, George, grant, 425
Delegal, Philip, grant, 238
Demere, Capt. Raymond, commander of Fort Loudoun, 286n, grant, 442
Demetre, Daniel, grant, 242
Denninger, George, grant, 318
Denny, Walter, grant, 372
Depp, Valentine, grant, 111
Deveaux, James, grant, 46, 47, 329, 444; recommended for Council, 303
Deveaux, John, grant, 110
Deveaux, William, grant, 330
Dicks, David, grant, 329, 420, 424
Dicks, David, Jr., grant, 424
Dickinson, Paynter, grant, 119
Dickinson, Stephen, grant, 119
Dobbs, Gov. Arthur, 184
Dodds, William, grant, 373
Dolphin (ship), carries official papers, 310
Donnam, Daniel, grant, 110, 368
Douglass, David, and Indian presents, 75, 76, 77, 78; 139; Justice of peace at Augusta, 78; grant, 361
Dowdes, Richard, grant, 243
Dowdy, Richard, grant, 317, 318
Dowle, Peter, grant, 317
Downer, Michael, grant, 325
Downing, John, warns settlers, 228n
Dressler, George, grant, 116
Dubois, Paul, grant, 437
Dubors, Paul, grant, 370
Dullea, Maurice, grant, 58
Dunbar, George, grant, 311
Dunham, Daniel, grant, 235
Dunham, William, grant, 111, 235
Dunn, David, land application, 460
Dunn, Drury, land application, 460
Dunn, Henry, land application, 460
Dunn, John, land application, 460
Dunn, Lewis, land application, 460
Dunn, Thomas, land application, 460

Dunn, William, land application, 460
Dusseign, Jacob, grant, 322

Eatton, Thomas, grant, 371
Ebenezer, German settlers, 205; needs filature, 127, 128; raises silk, 126, 127
Elliott, Grey, buys Sapelo, Ossabaw Islands, 276; and Council, 303, 306; grant, 55, 325, 331, 364, 367, 437, 442; opposes S. C. lands south of Altamaha, 428; presents caveat to S. C., 409
Elliott, John, grant, 233, 318
Elliott, Peter, grant, 237
Elliott, William, grant, 51, 112
Ellis, Henry, arrives in Ga., 2; and Georgia Society, 36; and disallowed acts, 200-204; commission, 155, 157, 158; and Abercromby, 166, 168; and Bosomworths, 5n, 265, 266, 269-276; and Ga. acts, 283, 284, 285; health, 172, 218, 219, 249, 250; and Indians, 194, 245-246, 251, 252; instructions approved, 160; grant, 233, 244, 374; petition to keep public money, 337; succeeds Reynolds, 133; thwarts Creek plot, 280, 281; to commission privateer, 164; to dispose of Indian lands, 180; troubles with Assembly, 192, 193; troubles with Council, 212, 213; visited by Indians, 194
Emanuel, David, grant, 443
Emanuel, John, grant, 114
Eppinger, John, grant, 368
Ernst, Ludwig, grant, 112
Ershberger, Reysrick, grant, 112
Etchard, Conrade, grant, 365
Evans, Elizabeth, grant, 48
Evans, Middleton, grant, 113
Ewen, William, grant, 237, 367, 434, 437, 439
Expenses, of government, 179, 342-345; preparation of estimate, 350; 1759-1760, 219
Exports, to England, 178; to West Indies, 178

Fain, Frederick, grant, 363
Fairweather, Capt., dispatches miscarry, 165
Farley, Benjamin, grant, 49, 320, 327
Farley, John, grant, 115
Farrer, Bartholomew, grant, 426
Feaster, John, grant, 240
Fenny, Philip, grant, 59
Fenton, Martin, grant, 420
Filature, at Ebenezer, 205, 206; description, 162; proposed 213, 217
Finck, Anne Margaret, grant, 364
Fish, Jesse, agent at St. Augustine, 18; factor at St. Augustine, 107, 108
Fisher, David, grant, 317
Fisher, James, grant, 416
Fitch, John, grant, 234
Fitzer, John Ulrick, grant, 313
Fleger, John, grant, 332
Flerl, John, grant, 329
Forbes, General, and Cherokees, 214
Fort Argyle, needs repair, 10
Fort Augusta, needs repair, 10
Fort Barrington, southern boundary of province, 294
Fort Duquesne, and Cherokees, 229
Fort Frederica, needs repair, 10; watches Altamaha settlements, 186, 187
Fort Loudoun, attracts dissident Creeks, 73, 74; surrenders to Cherokees, 286
Fort Mobile, proposed expedition against, 248
Fort Tombigbee, center of French influence, 289, 289n
Fort William, 18; garrisoned, 185; threatened by privateers, 163
Fortifications, plan to construct, 22
Fowl, George, grant, 113
Fox, Jonathan, grant, 417
Frazer, Simon, grant, 416
Frazer, Thomas, grant, 317
Frederica, independent company at, 169; ruinous condition, 155, 156; threatened by privateers, 163
Friendship (ship), carries public papers to London, 283
French, at Fort Tombigbee, 289; capture Reynolds, 130; corrupt Indians, 131, 293; Creeks & Cherokees

invited to New Orleans, 379; encourage raids by Creeks, 251; influence Creeks, 86, 87, 216, 217, 247, 248, 285-287, 405; influence Creeks from Mobile, 347, 348; influence Indians, 139; influence must be reduced, 295, 296; influence on Mississippi, 99, 100; no new alarms, 42; plot with Creeks against Ga., 376, 377; privateer seizes Ga. dispatches, 31; privateers, 156, 157; privateers off Ga. coast, 44; schooner near Tybee, 355; set Choctaws against Englishmen, 288; treaty with Cherokees, 30; vessels sighted, 29
Fuick, Paul, grant, 120
Fulton, Samuel, grant, 416, 421

Gallache, James, grant, 55
Gallash, John, grant, 323
Galphin, George, grant, 46, 369, 370; oath on Indian presents, 79
Gamphert, Christian, grant, 328
Gandy, Peter, grant, 434
Gandy, Samuel, grant, 243
Garbet, Gasper, grant, 316, 417
Garralon, M., captures Reynolds, 133
George II, death mourned, 301, 302
Georgia Society, competes with Assembly, 36
Germain, Richard, grant, 332
Germany, James, grant, 328; oath on Indian presents, 79
Germany, John, grant, 372
Germany, Robert, grant, 372
Gibbons, Arthur, grant, 426
Gibbons, Joseph, grant, 53, 319-321, 367, 423, 443
Gibbons, William, grant, 239, 417
Gieger, Christian, grant, 434
Gionovoli, John, grant, 375
Glamer, George, grant, 370
Glen, William, grant, 422
Goffe, Francis, grant, 421, 422
Goldsmith, Capt. Thomas, affidavit against Grover, 403; grant, 372; report, 192
Goldwire, Benjamin, grant, 311, 371

Goldwire, John, grant, 311
Goodale, Edward, grant, 117
Gordon, John, buys land near Pipemakers Creek, 277; grant, 315, 320, 329
Goswandel, Thomas, grant, 54
Goulding, Palmer, grant, 326
Government, estimate of expenses, 342-345, 350, 387
Graves, John, grant, 48, 416
Graves, William, grant, 113
Gray (Grey), Edmund, Spanish Colony, 204; and Indians, 75; moves to Cumberland, 156, 187, 188; New Hanover settlement, 174n, 175; offers asylum for debtors, 38; relations with Spanish and Indians, 17-19; settlement resented by Spanish governor, 74; sketch of, 17n
Gray, James, grant, 419, 443
Gray, William, petition for information on Reynolds' removal, 386, 387
Graham, Anne, grant, 57
Graham, James, grant, 365
Graham, John, appointed Clerk of Accounts and Indian Commissioner, 26; grant, 238, 314, 316; recommended for Council, 356, 406
Graham, Mungo, grant, 233
Graham, Patrick, Indian agent, 141
Grant, Gilbert, grant, 330
Grant, Col. James, expedition against Cherokees, 333
Grant, James, grant, 327
Green, Ann, grant, 369, 439
Greiner, Andrew, grant, 369, 371
Greiner, Catherine Magdalen, grant, 361
Greiner, John Gasper, grant, 424
Greiner, Phillip Jacob, grant, 361
Gronau, Hannah Elizabeth, grant, 54
Gronau, Mary Frederica, grant, 54
Grounidge, Margaret, grant, 320
Grover, William, appointed Chief Justice, 169, 170; Councillor, 210; disliked by Wright, 352; grant, 324, 419, 438; needed as Chief Justice, 208; proposal, 213-215; removed from office, 387-389, 450; representation as Chief Justice approved, 305; sets slave free, 400, 401; suspended by Wright, 392-395; Wright

complains of conduct of, 379; Wright describes behavior of, 389-396
Gugell, John, grant, 120
Guering, William, granted land south of Altamaha, 428
Guinter, David, grant, 436
Gun Merchant, Creek chieftain presents to, 80-84; visits Wright, 405

Habersham, James, Councillor, 210; grant, 49, 435; representation as Secretary approved, 305
Hack, Gasper, grant, 426, 427
Hamilton, Thomas, grant, 372
Hammer, Samuel, grant, 321
Hammond, Edward, grant, 318
Handley, William, grant, 322, 438
Handsome Fellow (Creek chieftain), murders traders, 251n; presents to, 81-84; treaty with Ellis, 42
Hangleter, John, grant, 112
Hanner, John, grant, 419
Hanner, Nicholas, grant, 419
Hardwick, location of, 16; Wright opposes move to Ogeechee River, 297; sketch of, 11n
Harlan, Ezekiel, grant, 441
Harley, James, grant, 437
Harramond, Henry, grant, 359
Harris & Habersham (merchants), grant, 435; paper notes, 152
Harris, Francis, Councillor, 210; grant, 49, 421
Harris, William Thomas, grant, 242, 243
Hartley, James, grant, 109
Hartstone, Joachim, grant, 368
Hastings, Samuel, grant, 119
Heckall, George, grant, 56
Heinly, Jacob, grant, 362
Heinly, John, grant, 371
Helvenstine, Frederick, grant, 327, 437, 443
Hendrick, Elizabeth, grant, 317
Henry, John George, grant, 116
Henshaw, Joseph, loses dispatches from Ga., 31
Hensler, Jacob, grant, 441
Herb, Frederick, grant, 316, 440
Heron, Col. Alexander, and Bosomworth claims, 260-263
Herse, John Michael, grant, 56
Hershman, John Gasper, grant, 361
Hickenbottom, Thomas, grant, 441
Holderness, Earl of, instructions to Ellis, 67, 68
The Holland King (Indian chieftain), presents to, 80-84
Holmes, John, grant, 312
Holzendorff, Frederick, Grant, 439
Hood, Abraham, grant, 441
Hooper, Thomas, grant, 312
Hopkins, Anne, grant, 60
Hopkins, John, grant, 327, 419, 425
Hoppacker, John, grant, 415
Hopton, William, granted land south of Altamaha, 428
Houstoun, Deborah, grant, 422
Houstoun, James, grant, 367
Houstoun, Sir Patrick, Councillor, 183, 210; death reported, 356; grant, 114, 311; Indian presents, 136; qualifications, 218
Houstoun, Robert, grant, 418, 424
Hover, Conrade, grant, 230
Howart, land granted south of Altamaha, 409, 428
Howell, Caleb, grant, 423
Howell, Phillip, grant, 422
Howell, William, grant, 423
Hubbard, Richard, grant, 325
Hudson, Robert, grant, 332
Hughes, Bernard, warns settlers, 228n
Humphrys, John, grant, 235
Humphrys, Robert, grant, 242
Hunold, Elizabeth, grant, 62
Huquenin, David, grant, 425
Hyme, Maj. Henry, S. C. commissioner, 190

Imports, from Great Britain, 73
Indian lands, cession, 124; instructions for ceding, 447
Indian presents, arrival, 28; arrive in Charleston, 378; delivered by Little, 138; distribution, 29; expectation of, 130, 131; expenses of, 296; freight charges, 253; helps relations with Creeks, 287; Indians expect, 296; insured, 173; list, 75, 76; necessity of, 128, 129, 245-247; number given out, 131; and Reynolds,

135; to Chickasaws, 76, 77; to
  Creeks, 231
Indian trade, benefits go to Charleston, 355; licensing problems,
  309; regulations, 123, 124
Indians, disorders of, 17; expect
  presents, 26; raid families, 166;
  treaties with, 17
Irwin, Benjamin, grant, 319
Irwin, Thomas, grant, 375

Jagger, John, grant, 316, 242
Jansack, James, grant, 314
Jarvis, James, grant, 424, 445
Johnson, Lewis, grant, 360, 365;
  recommended for Council, 356,
  406
Johnson, William, grant, 323, 327,
  425
Johnston, George, oath, 79
Jones, Francis, land application,
  460
Jones, John, grant, 416
Jones, Mary, grant, 240
Jones, Noble, and Acadians, 142;
  Councillor, 210; grant, 240, 436;
  removed from Council, 181
Jones, Noble Wimberly, grant, 240
Juno (ship), arrives with Indian
  presents, 28, 29, 99

Keibler, Jacob, grant, 118
Keifer, David, grant, 418
Keifer, Theobald, grant, 319, 415
Kellett, Alexander, at Council, 143;
  complaint, 153; memorial, 133;
  petition for land, 152; Provost
  Marshal, 150; trip to London,
  132n
Kelly, Bryan, grant, 424
Kelly, Thomas, grant, 367
Kennan, Henry, grant, 422
Kennedy, Donald, grant, 115
Kennedy, Hugh, grant, 114, 375
Kennedy, William, grant, 115, 237
Kilgore, Ralph, grant, 46, 328
Kill, John, grant, 362
Kiln, John, grant, 313
Knapp, George, grant, 310
Knox, William, Councillor, 183,
  210; grant, 324, 331, 361, 374;
  memorial for Ottolenghe, 406-408;

memorial on silk culture, 384-386;
  to return to England, 357
Kougle, Matthias, grant, 244
Kraft, David, heirs' land grant, 46
Kubler, Jacob, grant, 234
Kugell, John, grant, 330
Kugell, Matthias, grant, 310, 368

Lackner, Martin, Sr., grant, 120
Lackner, Martin, Jr., grant, 120, 121
Lamb, Sir Matthew, objects to Ga.
  acts, 284; opinion on Ga. laws,
  291, 292, 335-337, 352-354; sketch
  of, 284n
Land, absentee grants vacated, 207;
  account of money from sales, 276-
  278; cession of Ossabaw, St.
  Catherine's, and Sapelo to Ga., 265,
  266; Creek cession, 453-456; deeded
  by Bosomworths to Ga., 266-276;
  fertility of, 16; forfeited lots sold,
  350, 351; forms for granting, 63-67;
  granted to South Carolinians south
  of Altamaha, 428-430; grants disturb Creeks, 429, 430; grants issued
  for sale of Bosomworth land, 300,
  301; grants need to be limited, 23;
  headright system attacked, 15; and
  Negro slaves, 208; poor time to
  negotiate Indian cession, 348; purchase law, 215; restricted by treaty
  with Creeks, 294, 295; 1763 treaty,
  456-460; south of Altamaha granted
  by S. C., 408-414
Land, Indian, instructions for ceding,
  447
Land titles, confused state, 6, 6n
Landferder, Veit, grant, 58
LaRoche, Issac, grant, 372
Laurence, Lt-Gov. (Nova Scotia), sends
  Acadians, 137
Laurens, Henry, granted land south of
  Altamaha, 428
Lawrence, Nicholas, grant, 244, 442
Lawson, John, grant, 326, 423
LeBon, Anthony, grant, 363
LeBreton, Thomas, agent for Levy, 220
Leckner, Veit, grant, 57
Lee, Francis, appointed Searcher at
  Sunbury, 383; grant, 316
Lee, Thomas, grant, 233, 234, 362
Leimberger, Christian, grant, 55

Leonard, George, petitions Council, 390-392
Leslie, Capt., of *Juno*, 28, 29
Levy, Issac, agreement with Bosomworth, 93-98; claim, 221; gives Bosomworth money, 23; petition, 219, 220-225
Levi, Nathan, grant, 55
Lewis, Benjamin, grant, 426
Lewis, David, grant, 235
Lewis, Evan, grant, 433
Lewis, John, grant, 418
Lewis, Samuel, grant, 374, 375
"A Libel", poem against Wright, 404
Liddle, William, grant, 434
Lindale, William, grant, 441
Lines, Issac, grant, 322
Little Warrior (Creek chieftain), treats with Ellis, 42
Little, William, acts for Reynolds, 139; agent to Board of Trade, 85 and Assembly, 147; and Bosomworth claims, 5; and Council, 181, 182; at Augusta, 137, 138; bond for Indian traders, 76, 77; charges against, 149-151; collects affidavits, 15; commissions presents, 141, 142; conduct, 20; defies Ellis, 13; explains actions, 34, 35; grant, 241; list of Indian presents, 75, 76; memorial, 125-128; neglects Minutes, 41; offices of, 149; omitted copying Minutes of Assembly, 38; replaced as Clerk of the Accounts and Indian Commission, 26; Reynolds' Secretary, 149; schemes in Assembly, 32; sketch of, 13n; as Speaker, 3, 4
Lloyd, Thomas, grant, 323
Lockerman, Jacob, grant, 244
Long, John, grant, 311
Loudoun, Earl of, asked to fund Rangers in Ga., 27; authorizes Rangers, 69; bills drawn on 157; designs of, 19; keeps Rangers, 168; notified of French alarms, 30; raises Rangers, 166, 169; supports Ga. Rangers, 8, 103
Love, George, grant, 58

Lowndes, Rawlins, grant, 460
Loyer, Adrian, Grant, 233, 314, 323
Lunday, Abraham, grant, 359
Lurnburgh, Christian, grant, 415
Lyon, Samuel, grant, 313
Lyttleton, Gov. Henry, and Cherokees, 217; Cherokee treaty with, 226, 227; conference at Port Royal with Ellis, 69; consulted on defense of Ga., 20; friendship with Ellis, 75; greets Ellis, 2; insulted by Creeks, 42; marches against Cherokees, 229; and New Hanover, 174, 184, 189, 190; Port Royal meeting, 85; sends Indians to Charleston, 34; to see Creeks, 29

MacBean, John, grant, 57
MacDonald, John, grant, 234
MacFrary, James, grant, 109
MacGuire, Edward, grant, 326
MacGuire, Joseph, grant, 327
MacKay, Daniel, grant, 234
MacKay, Donald, grant, 50
MacKay, Hugh, grant, 51
MacKay, James, Councillor, 210; grant, 50, 51, 58, 59, 423, 435
MacKay, John, grant, 361
MacKay, Patrick, appointed to Council, 180; Ellis opposes, 181-183; in Ga. affairs, 32n; grant, 48; rejected as Councillor, 2; removed from Council, 32
MacKenzie, Alexander, Council candidate, 184; grant, 442
Mackintosh, George, grant, 50
Mackintosh, John D., grant, 50
Mackintosh, John M., grant, 50, 56
Mackintosh, William, grant, 50
MacLoud, Murdock, grant, 234
Malatchi, Mico (Creek chieftain), 7; allied with Bosomworths, 140; presents to, 80-84
Manley, Peter, grant, 235
Marks, Levi, grant, 365
Marlowe, Capt., of *Dolphin*, 310
Marriott, Thomas, grant, 423
Martin, Clement, grant, 364, 427; council member, 183, 210, 303, 304
Martin, Issac, grant, 314
Martin, John, appointed Naval Officer at Sunbury, 383; grant, 444

Martyn, Benjamin, fails to send silkworm eggs, 30; forwards mail, 165; memorial, 172, 173, 217, 218; memorial on Trustees' funds, 1; opposes Reynolds, 37; plan to remove, 37; secretary to Trustees, 335n; sends silkworm eggs, 30; silk demands, 213; writes to Ellis, 103
Masey, Joseph, grant, 59
Mason, Ann, grant, 440
Matthews, Capt. Jacob, dies, 259; married to Mary Musgrove, 259
Matthews, John, grant, 365
Maurer, Elizabeth, grant, 332
Maurer, Gabriel, grant, 112
Maurer (Maurier), Jacob, grant, 322, 325
Maurer, John, grant, 112
Mauve, Mathew, grant, 52, 53, 240
Maxwell, Audley, grant, 112, 370
Maxwell, Thomas, grant, 432
McClellan, John, grant, 53
McClelland, James, grant, 421
McClelland, Mary, grant, 421
McCletaby (Cherokee chieftain), presents to, 80-84
McCollum, John, grant, 116
McCullock, John, grant, 439
McCurrie, Andrew, grant, 362
McDonald, Alexander, grant, 325
McDonald, Donald, grant, 111
McDonald, Norman, grant, 327
McDonnald, William, grant, 433
McGillivray, Alexander, grant, 417
McGillivray, Lachlan, grant, 234, 361, 371, 418, 435, 436; oath, 79
McHenry, James, grant, 323, 436
McIntosh, Ann, grant, 318
McIntosh, Donald, grant, 115, 426
McIntosh, John B., grant, 419
McIntosh, Lachlan, grant, 50, 243
McIntosh, Roderick, grant, 312
McKay, Angus, grant, 118
McLeod, John, grant, 325
McLeod, Murdock, grant, 420
Mercer, Elizabeth, grant, 47
Mercer (Marcer), Samuel, grant, 47, 48
Merchants, depressed state, 11

Mettear, Louis, grant, 120
Metzgar, Jacob, grant, 330
Metzger, John Jacob, grant, 114
Meyer, Ludwig, grant, 54
Meyers, Elizabeth, grant, 366
Michler, John, grant, 313
Mick, Jonas, grant, 316, 364, 373
Middleton, Henry, granted land south of Altamaha, 428
Midway (River), aid to commerce, 16; fort at, 155; fort site, 40
Miers, Henry, grant, 420
Miers, Jacob, grant, 330
Militia, Bill for, 33; reorganized, 25, 26
Milledge, John, grant, 373, 440, 442
Milledge, Richard, grant, 314, 315
Millen, Stephen, grant, 370
Miller, George, grant, 313
Miller, James, grant, 236
Miller, John Paul, grant, 234, 313
Millichamp, Thomas, grant, 317
Mills, Thomas, grant, 370
Mills, William, grant, 315, 366
Minga Mastobey (Chickasaw chieftain), presents to, 80-84
Mingo, Push Cush (Creek chieftain), presents to, 80-84
Minis, Abigail, grant, 235, 316, 317
Minis, Joseph, grant, 53
Minis, Minis, grant, 327
Mitchell, Francis, grant, 440
Mitchell, John, grant, 415
Mitchell, Lewis, grant, 438
Mock, Jacob, grant, 360
Mohawks, allies of English against Cherokees, 302, 303
Mohr, Jacob, grant, 318
Monroe, Donald, grant, 365
Monroe, James, grant, 320
Monroe, John, grant, 330
Montaigut, David, grant, 116
Montaiguts (merchants), trade with Georgians, 32n
Montgomery, Col. Archibald, army retreats, 286; raids Cherokees, 281; sketch, 281n
Moor[e], to lead expedition against French, 19
Moore, George, grant, 440
Moore, Samuel, grant, 433
Moore, William, grant, 113

Morell, John, grant, 435
Morgan, Thomas, grant, 416
Morrison, Hugh, grant, 328
Morton, John, witness, 98
Motte, George, grant, 418
Mount Venture, founded by Mary Musgrove, 258
Mullryne, Catherine, grant, 374
Mullryne, John, grant, 374
Munday, Samuel, grant, 436
Mutter, James, grant, 371

Naval Vessel, British, stationed at Charleston, 45
Negroes (See also Slavery), case to decide status, 400, 401; efficiency of labor, 208; law to tax defective, 383; to be purchased for provincial service, 297, 299, 335
Newberry, William, grant, 62
New Hanover, abandoned, 192; account of, 184, 185; bad effects of, 359; broken up, 188-190; commissioner sent, 178, 179; inhabitants return, 349; in Spanish interest, 176; list of families in, 188, 189; location, 187; settlement, 174, 175
Newport (River), aid to navigation and commerce, 16
Nibling, Bartholomew, grant, 427
Niedlinger, John Ulrick, grant, 321
Nitchman, David, grant, 437
Noble, George, grant, 420
Noble, Robert, grant, 421
Nongazer, Henry, grant, 427
Nongazer, Jacob, grant, 318
Norman, Baruch, grant, 418
Norton, William, grant, 118, 437

Oakes, Joseph, grant, 317
Oakfuskee (Creek town), incident in, 171
Ogeechee (River), fort on, 155; fort site, 40; Rangers stationed at, 69; strategic importance, 16
Ogilvie, Charles, granted land south of Altamaha, 428
Ogleby, James, grant, 440
Oglethorpe, James Edward, Crown debts, 102, 102n; fort on St. John's River, 175, 185; selected fortifications, 156, 349; treatment of Mary Bosomworth, 256-263; treaty with Creeks, 221, 223
Old Braket (Indian chieftain), presents to, 80-84
Old Oakley (Indian chieftain), presents to, 80-84
Opiya, Mico (Creek chieftain), and Bosomworth claims, 220
Ordner, Adam, grant, 318
Osgood, John, grant, 52, 233
Osgood, Josiah, Jr., grant, 374
Ossabaw (Island), claimed by Bosomworths, 90, 92-98; fine land on, 23
Ottolenghe, Joseph, baking cocoons, 359; fire loss, 162; grant, 326, 443, 444; gratuity needs to be settled, 446; indifferent health, 103; Little attacks character, 206; manages silk culture, 348; memorial for gratuity, 406-408; needs successor, 30, 31; sketch, 12n; to instruct others in silk culture, 382
Outerbridge, White, grant, 59

Pace, Richard, grant, 441
Pagie, Anthony, grant, 417
Paifamingo (Chickasaw chieftain), presents to, 80-84
Parker, Agnes, grant, 422
Parker, Anne, grant, 117
Parker, Henry William, grant, 117
Parker, James, grant, 365
Parker, Thomas, grant, 365
Parsons, James, land granted south of Altamaha, 409
Pary, Francis, grant, 418
Patterson, William, grant, 436
Paultisch, John Martin, grant, 236
Peacock, Thomas, grant, 374
Pelton, Samuel, grant, 331
Pepper, Dan, S. C. agent, 85, 86n
Perkins, John, grant, 117
Peters, Christopher, grant, 121
Peters, George, grant, 111
Pettygrew (Petitcrew), John, grant, 62, 332
Pettigrove, John, Indian trader, 77
Phillips, John, grant, 436
Pitt, William, approves Ellis' commission and instructions, 158, 161; asks

about Reynolds' conduct, 71;
congratulated by Ellis, 28; instructions to Ellis, 99; orders
troops raised, 41; settlements
south of Altamaha, 129; Warrant
for William Grover, 169
Pletter, John, grant, 112
Population (See also Settlers),
1757, 1758, and 1760 estimates,
44, 178, 309; descriptions of
settlers, 334; whites, 385
Ports, George Phillip, grant, 325
Ports, Jacob, grant, 112, 325
Pot ash, methods demonstrated, 26
Powell, James Edward, and Reynolds,
136; commissioner to New Hanover, 178, 179; Councillor, 210;
grant, 52, 326, 364, 436, 444;
report on New Hanover settlement,
187-190
Powell, Josiah, grant, 362
Powlinger, John George, grant, 312
Prethew, John, grant, 114
The Priest (Indian chieftain), presents to, 80-84
Pritchard, James, grant, 118
Privateers, at Savannah, 128;
French cruise coast, 164; French
threaten Fort William and Frederica, 163; from Bristol, 165; infest coast, 168
Pruniere, Joseph, attachment against
by Wood & Shefall, 396-401
Pryce, Charles, absent from Council,
231; Council candidate, 184;
Councillor, 210; declines Council appointment, 303; income for
office recommended, 356; land
granted, 315; to be judicial
clerk, 213
Public buildings, in ruinous condition, 25; money needed to construct, 27
Purrysburg, silk center, 126
Pyles, Samuel, authorized to send
supplies to St. Augustine, 402,
403; discharged by Grover, 393,
394; judgment against, 401, 402;
New Hanover settler, 394; storekeeper at Frederica, 401; writ
of attachment against, 396-401

Quarterman, John, grant, 326
Quarterman, John, Jr., grant, 362
Quit rents, act not returned from England, 406; act to collect, 358, 379;
law to collect needed, 451; unpaid,
124

Rabenhorst, Christian, grant, 46, 54,
61
Rae, John, grant, 439
Rahn, Conrade, grant, 120, 330
Rahn, Jasper, grant, 120
Randon, Peter, grant, 425, 444
Rangers, patrol southward to Altamaha,
176; raised, 166; unestablished,
177
Ranstatler, David, grant, 420
Ratten, Richard, grant, 326
Raymond, Joseph, grant, 423
Read [Reid], James, grant, 49, 232,
367, 370; Council membership, 2,
180-183, 303, 304, 406
Red-Coat King (Creek chieftain), murders traders, 251
Red, Thomas, grant, 233, 326
Reid, James (See Read, James)
Reidelsperger, Christian, grant, 52
Reimshart, John, grant, 326
Reitler, John, grant, 360
Reitter, Simon, grant, 115
Reizer, Belthazar, grant, 322
Reutter, John, grant, 110
Reutter, Simon, grant, 54
Reynolds, Gov. John, alters silk bounty, 206; answer to charges, 132-154;
articles against, 129, 130; Assembly
plots to restore position of, 32; authorizes paper currency, 200, 201;
Bosomworth affair, 14; expenses for
Indian congress, 103; fails to transmit minutes of Assembly, 38; in
French prison, 27, 28; land holdings,
151, 152; late appointees, 29; petition of William Gray against, 386,
387; proceeds from sale of condemned
vessel, 27; proposal to let Assembly
appoint militia officers, 26; raises
Rangers, 102; reasons for remaining
in Ga., 15; recalled, 202; relations
with Council, 181; relieved, 219;
speech to Assembly, 34; suspended
Councillors, 39; tax policy assailed

25
Reynolds, William, to settle colony south of Ga., 449, 452
Rigby, Sarah, grant, 319
Rigden, William, grant, 314
Rivers, Daniel Nunez, grant, 114
Robinson, Pickering, Councillor, 183; grant, 330, 331, 366, 415; memorial, 278, 279; in silk culture, 407; sketch, 278n
Robinson, Silvanus, grant, 424
Roch, Matthew, grant, 316
Rolle, Denys, memorial to settle colony south of Altamaha, 448-450, 452
Rose, Alexander, grant, 237, 244
Ross, Hugh, grant, 239, 422
Ross, John, murdered by Creeks, 251n
Rottenberger, Christian, grant, 330
Rouviere, John, grant, 328, 425
Rouviere, Simon, grant, 328, 417, 425
Russell, William, Commissary, 143; Councillor, 183; grant, 237, 427, 444
Rutherford, James, grant, 365
Ryan, Daniel, grant, 426

St. Augustine, center for Spanish expansion westward, 71; encourages runaways, 38; port for privateers, 176; problems at, 72; settlers drawn around, 19; supplied by S. C. & Ga., 176; trade with forbidden, 33
St. Catherine's (Island), claimed by Bosomworths, 90, 92-98; fine land on, 23; to be granted Bosomworths, 211
St. Croix (Island), debtors flee from, 22
St. Johns (River), boundary with Spanish, 18; divides debatable land, 175; Spanish fortify, 156
St. Mark's, Creeks raid, 108
Salfner, Matthias, grant, 418
Sallenare, Monsieur Dominique, French negotiator at Bayonne, 28
Sapelo (Island), claimed by Bosomworths, 90, 92-98; fine land on,

23
Sarcer, William, grant, 418
Sarzedas, Abraham, grant, 114
Savage, John, grant, 51
Savannah, fort site, 40; proposed distribution site for Indian presents, 29
Schremp, Frederick, grant, 313
Schweighoffer, Thomas, grant, 330
Scots, Highland, Dairen fort, 40n
Settlers (See also Population), from Carolina, 16, 17; gentleman from Bay of Honduras arrives, 29; poverty of, 20, 34, 44; under Trustees, 41, 42
Shad, Solomon, grant, 111
Shave, John, grant, 322
Sheftal, Benjamin, grant, 319
Sheftall, Levi, grant, 365
Sheftall, Mordecai, grant, 365, 433, 437
Shephard, Alexander, grant, 439
Sheraus, George, grant, 327
Sheraus, John, grant, 114, 434
Shipping, convoy system, 161; embargo on, 161
Shubdrien, Daniel, grant, 58
Shubdrien, Joseph, grant, 121, 417
Shubdrien, Nicholas, grant, 121, 417
Shute, John, grant, 425
Sigfirst, George, grant, 314
Silk, advantages of bounty on cocoons, 445, 446; bills of exchange drawn for, 21; bounty in doubt, 382; early frost damage, 309, 335, 341, 342; Ellis answers Little's memorial against, 204-207; employs many people, 12; expenses for, 1; favorable spring, 359, 377; filature burns, 162; good crop expected, 157, 382, 414; history in Ga., 406-408; memorial to rebuild filature, 217; money saved to be used for, 14; petition of Knox supports, 384-386; proposed filature, 213; ready for shipment, 348; observations on, 125-128; state of, 30, 103, 104, 213, 214; weather adversely affected, 451
Simpson, John, grant, 327
Sisson, Thomas, grant, 321
Slaves (See also Negroes), efficiency of labor, 208; held jointly in S. C.

& Ga., 413
Sliterman, Jeremiah, grant, 237
Smith, John, grant, 53, 11, 318
Smith, Lewis, grant, 416
Smith, Thomas, Sr., land application, 460; grant, 116; land granted south of Altamaha, 409
Smith, William, grant, 437
Sneider, Andrew, grant, 324
Sneider, Gasper, grant, 373
Snider, Henry, grant, 111
Snook, John, grant, 362
Snyder, John George, grant, 57
Snyder, Michael, grant, 56
Sola bills, history of, 262n; paid to Bosomworths, 262
Somerville, Edward, grant, 363
South Carolina, Cherokees raid, 230; currency abuses, 202; debtors flee from, 22; drains away Ga. trade, 11; influences Ga. Assembly, 101; rebellious government, 212, 213
S.C. (Charleston) Gazette, advertisement of land sale, 222, 225; Ga. treaty in, 226n
Spangenberg, Joseph, grant, 438
Spanish, encounters with Creeks, 211, 212; fortify St. Augustine, 156; to settle new colony in Fla., 100, 184, 185; vessel captured, 128
Spencer, John, grant, 58, 114, 234
Spencer, Richard, grant, 424
Spencer, William, grant, 121
Stacy, John, grant, 366
Stailey, John, grant, 119, 362
Stailey, John, Jr., grant, 119
Stainer, Christian, grant, 55
Stanley, Joseph, grant, 240
Starkey, Gasper, grant, 423
Stayley, Gotleb, grant, 111
Steadman, William, grant, 241
Stephens, _____, gives method of making pot ash, 26
Stephens, David, grant, 51
Stevens, John, grant, 52
Stewart, John, grant, 242, 322, 325
Stewart, John, Jr., grant, 109
Stewart, Robert, grant, 118
Stiner, David, grant, 329

Stirk, Benjamin, grant, 360
Stirling, Sir James, grant, 361
Story, Charles, grant, 418
Stroub, Peda Clara, grant, 119, 120
Struthers, William, grant, 441
Stuart, John, grant, 436
Stutz, Michael, grant, 109
Suckabatchy (Cherokee chieftain), presents to, 80-84
Summers, Joseph, grant, 232, 366
Sunbury, center for southern trade, 73; customs records, 461-465; fortifications, 155; recommended as port of entry, 383
Sunier, James, grant, 373
Swan, Richard, death sentence reprieved, 304
Switzer, Michael, grant, 109, 311, 436
Swyger, George, grant, 61

Tabb, Morgan, grant, 374
Talley, _____, Naval officer, 356
Talley, John, grant, 422
Tannatt, Edmund, recommended for Council, 303; grant, 232, 372, 415, 436
Tarquintz, Peter, grant, 118
Tatnall, Mary, grant, 375
Taxes (See also Assembly, quit rents), none imposed, 20; to sink paper currency, 21
Taylor, James, grant, 440
Taylor, Nathan, grant, 111
Teasdale, John, grant, 47
Tebeau, James, grant, 324
Thomas, John, grant, 440
Thomas, John Giles, land application, 460
Thomson, William (Master), captured, 133
Threadcroft, George, grant, 320
Tiess, Jacob, grant, 322
Todd, John, Jr., grant, 62
Todd, John, Sr., grant, 240
Tomlinson, Samuel, grant, 420
Tondee, Peter, grant, 310, 373
Trade, balance against Ga., 203; Sunbury to prevent clandestine, 383
Tradling, Frederick, grant, 115
Treaty of Aix-la-Chapelle, settles Ga. boundary, 175

Treutlen, John Adam, grant, 109, 319
Triboudet, John Francis, grant, 443
Tripp, Isaac, grant, 239
Tripp, Thomas, grant, 371
Tristee, Henry, grant, 317
Troiboudet, John, grant, 425
Truan, David, grant, 52
Tubear, David, grant, 427
Tuckwell, John, grant, 435
Turner, Lewis, grant, 360

Uland, George, grant, 415
Unseld, David, grant, 324, 366
Unseld, Hannah, grant, 366

Van, John, Jr., grant, 441
Vann, John, Cherokees raid, 228n
Vanderplank, Mary, grant, 362
Vanmunch, Charles, grant, 56
Vanmunch, Christian, grant, 55, 56, 433
Vanmunch, Thomas, grant, 56
Vincent, Thomas, grant, 241
Virginians, quarrel with Cherokees, 167

Walsar, John, grant, 445
Walthour, Jacob, grant, 122
Walthour, John Gaspar, grant, 116
Waltons (merchants of N. Y.), supply St. Augustine, 107
War King (Indian chieftain), presents to, 80-84
Ward, Aaron, grant, 113
Ward, Bryan, grant, 441
Warren, Richard, grant, 425
Watson, Charles, grant, 367, 434, 438
Way, Andrew, grant, 53, 362
Way, Edward, grant, 232
Way, Moses, grant, 360
Way, Nathaniel, grant, 52
Way, Parmenus, grant, 52, 329
Weatherfoot, Charles, grant, 441
Webb, John, land application, 460
Weber, Michael, grant, 54
Weidman, Ludwig, grant, 54
Weinkauff, Michael, grant, 373, 417
Wereat, John, grant, 323, 419
Wertch, John Gasper, grant, 312

West, Mattias, grant, 119, 323
Weste, Charles, grant, 59
Westly, James, grant, 320
Weston, James, grant, 122
Wetherspoon, David, grant, 424
White, Thomas, grant, 320
Whitefield, George, grant, 419
Whitefield, James, grant, 57, 415
Whiteside, John, agent for Levy, 220
Willan, Robert, petition to settle colony south of Ga., 450, 452
Williams, Griffith, grant, 423
Williams, John, grant, 370
Williamson, Benjamin, grant, 233, 321
Willson, James, grant, 368
Willson, John, grant, 438, 440
Willson, Thomas, grant, 366
Wilson, William, grant, 326
Winn, John, grant, 325
Winn, Joseph, grant, 118
Wisely, Sarah, grant, 317
Wolf King (Creek chieftain), expedition against French, 163; peaceable disposition toward English, 309; sketch of, 302n; visits Savannah, 302, 303
Wood, Issac, grant, 441
Wood, Joseph, grant, 239, 360, 373, 421
Wood, Joseph, and Mordecai Sheftall (merchants), judgment against Pyles, 401, 402; writ of attachment against Alexander, Pyles, & Pruniere, 396-401
Woodland, James, grant, 433
Wright, Gov. James, arrives at Charleston, 289; complains of Grover's behavior, 379, 389-396; explains Ga. laws, 338-342; grant, 366, 432; no communication from London, 378; poem against, 404; proposed as Lt.-Gov., 249; protests S. C. land grants south of Altamaha, 408-414; representation as Gov. approved, 305; sketch of, 411n; suspends Grover, 392-395
Wylly, Alexander, grant, 59, 366, 420

Yonge, Henry, grant, 56, 236, 439
Young, Elizabeth, grant, 328
Young, Issac, grant, 328, 433
Young, John, grant, 433

Young, Margaret, grant, 433
Young, Peter, grant, 420
Young, Thomas, grant, 245

Zeagler, Lucas, grant, 362
Zeighler, George, grant, 319
Ziegler, John George, grant, 239
Zipperer, Peter, grant, 371
Zettler, Mattias, grant, 121
Zouberbuhler, Bartholomew, grant, 55
Zubly, John J., grant, 311, 313, 331, 437

CPSIA information can be obtained
at www.ICGtesting.com
Printed in the USA
LVHW042152161021
700652LV00005B/106